Note: This is a revised monograph of my first edition, but includes minor changes such as a glossary of terms, notes on pronunciation, clarification of certain events, etc.

Note on pronunciation: words in Romanian with the letter *ş, ç,* or *ţ* are pronounced *sh, ch,* or *tz,* respectively. V in words of Slavic origin are generally pronounced *W*.

I dedicate this novel to my mother, my family, and to all the extinct Britons of Romania, who won't be here to read this epitaph.

Os gwelwch 'n dda, darllen ai mawr!

Architectural and glossary terminology of the Middle Ages:

- *Donjon,* central tower of a castle. Keep.
- *Arquebes,* primitive handgun of the 15th-century.
- *Oolite,* type of limestone.
- *Escutcheon,* heraldry embossed on stone, usually a hearth's mantelpiece.
- *Bawn,* castle enclosure.
- *Cnéaz, ruler,* or *governor* in O.Slavic/Romanian.
- *Mormaer,* ruler (c.f Gaelic>German>Slav>Daco-Romanian).
- *Ducats,* Italian currency.
- *Ungro,* relating to Hungary.
- *Hookah,* glass pipe for inhaling opium, as a vapour.
- *Barmkin,* low walled enclosure of a towerhouse, or fort.
- *Doamnă,* lady, adult woman in Romanian.
- *Domnişoară,* young lady, girl.
- *Villein,* French, a peasant.
- *Dynes,* archaic Brittonic, unmarried adult woman.
- *Geneth,* archaic Brittonic, young lady of child-bearing age.
- *Cariad,* archaic Brittonic, term of endearment.
- *Corbel,* stone structural support for an upper storey.
- *Condittiére,* Spanish for mercenary leader, an outlaw.
- *doxy,* woman of ill-repute, a lady of the evening.

- *teulu*, family, in archaic Brittonic.
- *Armașii*, police, bodyguards, in Romanian.
- *leman*, a consort, or mistress.
- *Vermiculated*, a type of artificial decoration, resembling wormholes in stone.
- *Malmsey*, type of wine popular in the Middle Ages.
- *Culverin*, a small cannon.
- *Cordial*, type of liqueur used in the Middle Ages.
- *Cantred*, archaic Brittonic, a county.
- *Oblast*, Russian, a province.
- *Ghazi*, Arabic, Muslim fighter against non-Muslims.
- *Sipahi*, Persian, a cavalryman.
- *Azab*, Persian, light infantryman.
- *Yaya*, Ottoman infantry.
- *Satrap*, Ottoman governor.
- *Greaves,* polished steel leg armour.
- *Gauntlet,* gloves of steel, with hinged fingers.

Chapter One.   P.5
Chapter Two.   p.24
Chapter Three.   p.32
Chapter Four.   P.48
Chapter Five.   P.55
Chapter Six.   P.63
Chapter Seven.   P.69
Chapter Eight.   P.97
Chapter Nine.   p.148
Chapter Ten.   p.155
Chapter Eleven.   p.167
Chapter Twelve.   P.299
Chapter Thirteen.   p.309
Chapter Fourteen.   p.322
Chapter Fifteen.   p.330
Chapter Sixteen.   p.331
Chapter Seventeen.   p.351
Chapter Eighteen.   P.373
Epilogue.   P.377
Afterword.   P.381

Albert Ernst

VLAD DRACULA: THE IMPALER

A Novel of Historical Horror

Copyright © Albert Ernst 2025

The right of Albert Ernst to be identified as author of this work has been asserted by the author in accordance with sections 77 and 78 of the Copyright, Designs and Patents Act 1988.

All rights reserved. No part of this publication may be reproduced, stored in a retrieval system, or transmitted in any form or by any means, electronic, mechanical, photocopying, recording, or otherwise, without the prior permission of the publishers.

Any person who commits any unauthorised act in relation to this publication may be liable to criminal prosecution and civil claims for damages.

This is a work of fiction. Names, characters, businesses, places, events, locales, and incidents are either the products of the author's imagination or used in a fictitious manner. Any resemblance to actual persons, living or dead, or actual events is purely coincidental.

Published by Cymmrodorion Publishing Group, 119 2nd St. W., Glaslyn, SK., S0M 0Y0.

2

Acknowledgements:

T.F. O'Rahilly's *'Early History and Myths of Ireland'*, without whose breakthrough and controversial discovery of the Picts of Ireland (and elsewhere), this story would never have originated; and Radu Florescu and Raymond T. McNally's *'Dracula, Prince of Many Faces: His Life and His Times'*, on which much of this novel is based.

Prologue

11 July, 1998 AD
Romania

The old friar shambled along the corridor of Snagov monastery, sweeping aside the garbage left behind by tourists. *We've sunk low*, thought Matei to himself, carefully sweeping the wrappers into a dustpan before depositing them in turn into one of the dust bins. The monastery was old. Nine hundred years old. Its brick/sandstone walls had witnessed Teutonic invaders, Turks, Hungarians and Mongol hordes ride by over the centuries, looking for loot and slaves for their distant Kingdoms. Orthodox and Roman Catholics alike fought for control of the fortified monastery like dogs over a bone. It sat hunched on an island, protected by huge Lác Snagov. Now, it was one of the country's finest historic monuments, under protection of the State. The Orthodox monks needed their tourist dollars to stay solvent. The brothers made a living by making wine and selling it to Western tourists.

Matei Antoneşcu walked slowly down the musty reredorter's hall, forcing his corpulent body to go the long way around toward his sleeping quarters in a vain attempt to lose weight. Too much cheese and buttermilk. However, halfway to his dormitory, he changed course at a whim, exiting the stuffy, ill-lit building and heading across the grassy environs of one of Romania's oldest, intact monastic edifices whose very walls seemed to echo with the past's momentous glories as well as the nation's infamies. He passed the ancient chapterhouse once outside, his shadow advancing before him like a sinister giant in the ages' redolent flickerings on the walls of derelict cloisters, then scurried past a ruined sacristy, finally entering the candlelit Byzantine chapel after hurriedly crossing a funereal, torchlit yard shrouded in darkness; pausing to say a few prayers at the altar. Unknowingly, he stood on *Ordog's* (Satan's) defaced tomb slab.

The monastery had once been huge, although much was in ruins now. Parts of it even Matei had not explored. All that was left habitable aboveground were the modern dormitory, the ancient chapel frescoed with gilded murals of piety, bell tower, chapterhouse, chantry, clerestory, a hospice, stables (all under reconstruction), some of the walls, and three weirdly fluted, Orthodox towers atop the chapel.

Naughtily Matei crept down the crypt's dusty, mildewed stairs, unable to resist a few spare minutes of exploring the old monastery. The crypt's nail-studded door was surprisingly unlocked. (He wondered at that; worried one of the lay brothers may be down here, clearly against the prefect's orders.) Matei carried a wildly guttering pine torch which he'd snatched from the stairwell.

The crypt's barrel-vaulted chamber echoed with Matei's ragged breathing, his torch casting eerie dancing shadows on clammy stone walls.

A low, man-made tunnel branched off to his right; dark, drafty. Lingering cobweb strands streamed from the ceiling as the old man pursued his objective. The aged friar laboriously stepped over a cordoned-off area prohibited to the tourists, hitching his brown cassock to his knees to do so while ignoring a sign in Romanian script forbidding entrance to the unsafe, crumbling sector. Matei was seventy-eight years old, but even at this age he still felt a delicious, childish thrill while exploring the monastery's underground precincts. When his superiors allowed him time off, that is. His was a steady daily chore of milking the goats or minding the cheese presses.

The tunnel was mortared. As he lifted up his torch a dark, ancient door with bars for a window beckoned from the end of the corridor.

Matei wondered uneasily if it wasn't one of the many torture chambers supposedly utilised (none of his acquaintances had found one though) during the monastic cell's heyday.

The room was dark; even Matei's torch failed to illumine its uncompromising gloom. To his knowledge, none of the brothers had ever explored the chapel's crypt and catacombs beneath, for it was forbidden to the monks. Only Matei was allowed here, and that only to clean up after the uncaring tourists. The reason was simple; the Devil's Spawn rested here. Vlad Dracula's tomb occupied a chamber nearby. A nondescript, shameful, hidden tomb which archaeologists in the 1930s had discovered during excavations (with Vlad's original tombstone above having been trampled on by centuries of deliberately disrespectful monks beside the altar). Not the vampire the foolish Westerners were acquainted with either. The real Vlad Dracula, known to Wallachians as *Vlad Ţepeş*, the Impaler. A man more terrifying than any vampire. Matei wasn't afraid of ghosts or demons. But Vlad had executed thousands of devout Roman Catholics and Orthodox adherents.

Matei crossed himself, shuddering uncontrollably.

He fumbled among the large assortment of rusty keys tied to his waist. He tried each in the padlock. None seemed to fit. He licked his lips, sweating with the tense anticipation of a child dipping his hand into a cookie jar. The abbot would scold him roundly if ever Matei were caught here.

At last, on the 39th key, the lock opened.

The door was heavy, thick, hinges so rusted it could barely move. The room was musty; smelling of unwholesome decay. Dust spores flew up as he tread cautiously into the chamber. *'Was this a prison?'* Matei wondered. *'Or an archive room?'*

No. It was not a prison. Nor an archive room.

A great, iron-bound chest sat alone in a corner, rusted and smothered with cobwebs. It, too, was locked. Once more Matei fumbled through his keys, fitting each large skeleton key into the padlock's slot.

It wouldn't open.

Matei cursed in Romanian, clamping his hand over his mouth, recanting. He was a devout monk, pious, not accustomed to the slang of the country peasants. He stood up slowly, turning to go. The lock continued to beckon, though no key could turn its corroded inner mechanism. *'Perhaps I'll speak to the bishop about this chamber,'* Matei mused. *'He may know of its origin.'*

A crack in the wall caught Matei's attention as he turned to leave, anxious to get back to his dormitory before someone missed him. He halted, peering short-sighted at the suspicious crevice.

It was a hinged door, small, 1 ft. by 1' across, dark oak to camouflage with the stone wall. A hasty affair. Curious, Matei swung the little door back, its rusted hinges complaining with a squeal.

He held up his smoking torch, squinting in its glare.

A book lay inside. Thick, heavy, leather-bound. Metal clasps still held the manuscript together, so corroded it seemed the bulky relic would fall apart in Matei's shaking hands. He blew the dust off, careful not to damage the cover as he opened the book.

The pages were not paper—they were parchment; goat or pigskin, tanned for writing purposes in days past. Very ancient. Yellowed. Brittle. It was a diary, handwritten long before the invention of the printing press by Gutenberg in 1440 possibly.

At first, it seemed the writing was nothing but chicken scratches. But as Matei looked closer, it suddenly dawned on him with a shock that this was written in shorthand Daco-Romanian; an ancient language comprised of Vulgar Latin and Dacian, the speech of the early Celts of eastern Europe—a dead language.

Matei had studied the old Latinized manuscripts of the bishop's library at Cozia monastery as a young man. He read the first line, struggling to interpret the odd Dacian dialect, a grammatical style familiar, yet eluding his tongue. Irish?? The writing was spidery, shaky, splotched with water at one time.

My father's name was Dracul.

The Devil. Or conversely, the Dragon, after the Order of the Dragon, an order of knights dedicated to fighting the Turks in eastern Europe, a Holy order. I was the second-eldest of eight sons and four daughters, future co-heir to the Princedom of Wallachia and claimant to Moldavia. I leave this diary as a testimony to my life and my countrymen who have been evicted from their lands and forced to become Gypsies! *Mine enemies have succeeded absolutely in bringing down my Principality, spreading lies and ludicrous tall-tales which I, alas, was too proud to refute. I watch from my window—a prisoner of King Matthias of Hungary in mine own castle of Hunedŏara—watching as a helpless line of declared heretics are being prodded toward the burning-stakes in the castle courtyard. The Catholic authorities had declared all Protestant and Orthodox followers excommunicated on Whitsun, torturing and defiling all those who refused to adhere to the Catechism.*

To the reader of this diary and the words contained herein, I challenge—I demand!—he who holds this account of my last days and the plight of our people to tell the world of what has been done. Turks rape and defile our women, enslaving them in harems, forcing our sons to fight for them in Sultan Mekhmed II's imperial army. The Catholic powers of Europe tacitly aid the Turks. The Turks! While we fight alone, where only the brave men prepare to die.

I, Prince Wladislaus Dracula—the Devil's spawn—dared to defy Mekhmed and Pope Pius II, while they divided up my lands and enslaved my people. I await now for the trial which will ultimately damn me and my countrymen.

Chapter One

6 July, 1447 AD
Southern Wallachia, Romania

A hot sun scorched the billowing oat fields of the southern ungro-Transylvanian plains, the looming mountains to the west snow-capped and hazy. The mountains formed a concentric wall of solid limestone/granite across northern Wallachia, a natural fortress protecting Hungarian Transylvania from invaders. A wagon train of nobles and servants rolled along at a brisk pace on a dusty trail through golden fields, headed for Roumeli Hissar, and ultimately, Turkish Bulgaria. At Roumeli, the imperial vizier of Byzantium would fill his new post, foremost the defence of the Bosporus Straits. The boyar, or Count, of Ploeşti had been ordered by his liege-lord Sultan Mured II to convey the bridal guests and prisoners of the Holy Roman Emperor John VIII Palaeologus to Sofia. Among the guests were the Emperor's daughter, Janina, and a bevy of concubines for the Sultan's pleasure. These were the dues owed Sultan Mured II plus the Byzantine emperor's oath of allegiance. In return, the Holy Roman Emperor based at Constantinople would receive a hefty year's supply of corn for his oath of fealty.

Among the prisoners were the intransigent Prince of Wallachia's seventeen-year-old son, his younger brother and a select group of high-born sons and relatives of local boyars, promised as ransom dues for the disobedient Prince's continued good behaviour. Vladislaus Dracul was a constant thorn in the sides of both the Byzantine emperor and Turkish Caliph. Lately he had intrigued with a mighty Hungarian voivode (warlord), Janós Hunyádi, the 'White Knight of Hungary' and Protestant Hussite agitator Jan Jiškra of Poland to wage a holy war once more on the invincible infidels. As if the debacle of Varna four years ago hadn't damaged eastern Europe enough. The Pope had excommunicated Vlad Dracul in May.

His son, Vlad Dracula, prisoner of the Sultan for the past five years, sat in a crowded wagon with six other hostages and concubines. They sweated in the heat, wiping their foreheads from time to time with handkerchiefs. Vlad and his brother Radu were returning from a brief, unexpected mercy visit to their father's modest Teutonic castle at Braşov, the first visit in almost six years. Vlad had been a prisoner at Egrigöz, western Anatolia, Turkey, since the age of twelve, his most recent prison at Adrianople for seven months. His father barely recognised him.

At Vlad's side, the three concubines wept, unable to bear the thought of being forced into a heathen Sultan's harem. They were virgins, only twelve/thirteen years old. The Sultan liked his girls young—very young. Vlad stared ahead, deeply annoyed, wondering how many years longer he would have to be the Sultan's prisoner. Maybe forever? The girls were no acquaintances of his. Still he felt sorry for them, for they were Dacians, like himself. Not the half-breed Romanised Saxons who had settled his country, dubbing the natives *Waelas*—foreigners. Wallachians. They had taken the best land for themselves, expelling the Wallachs and colonising Dacia Felix with loyal Magyars and Avars. The peaceful peasants had been almost overnight turned into wandering nomads living in caravans, thieving for sustenance, and a new, ignoble name grafted onto them.

Gypsies.

The old laws had been abandoned. The merchants of the Saxons' enclaves followed different, alien customs. Thracians, immigrants from Albania, and ever accommodating to the dictates of Rome, had claimed these troubled lands with the tacit blessing of Theodosius' consuls, bringing new meaning to the word 'genocide'. The later Saxon *Burgermeisters* now exercised a virtual stranglehold on all forms of mercantile trade. Like the Turks, they were free to molest a Wallachian woman (or child) if she had no chaperone. Girls no longer had rights to resist forced marriages. Brothels sprang up overnight in Saxon towns like poisonous toadstools. And the Saxon counts brought one more alien institution.

Castles.

They soared to the skies, great, mortared pillars of rectangular, square, or cylindrical stone donjons perched on inaccessible mountain peaks, the favourite eyrie of German adventurers. The Teutonic knights, or *ritters*, brought a code of feudal conduct which spread fear into the hearts of simple peasants. Unlike the crumbling legionary fortresses, these were not mere, military outposts forced on an intransigent, aloofly hostile alien populace. The Teutonic castles were offensive weapons, used to sally forth and conquer, pillaging and raping for miles around. The foreign ritters had no intention of fighting Turks. They were Saxons. They wanted land. They set up alien burghs, which quickly mushroomed into large, cosmopolitan towns. Churches and monasteries soon had to be fortified.

Vlad shook himself out of his reverie with an effort. Times like this he knew he must harden his heart to the little girls' sobs. Those laws were gone forever. It was a new country, one which Vlad had been away from for far too long. He had no idea how long till he would be home again. He must adapt now, like the Serbs and Bulgarians. He might someday be the heir-apparent should his elder brother Mirçea perish untimely—he couldn't turn the clock back.

A Gypsy caravan sat in a corner of a field, roasting a wild buck on an open fire. They were sad-eyed, emaciated, probably lost; on the run from some local slave-gang. Some laughed heartily, however. The local boyars would not tolerate them on their demesnes for long, would send out cavalry from their mountaintop citadels to scatter these loiterers. These particular wanderers were Dacians, highlanders by the looks of them; they spoke a tongue utterly unlike that of the Latin, Romany, or Slav dialects. They were also well-armed, self-confessed heretics, following a creed only similar to Rome's.

Chances were good that they were bandits, roaming the woods at will.

Several of Vlad's companions riding in the coach ahead of his shouted a hearty salute to the 'Gypsies' (who were not Gypsies), they too being half Dacian, albeit high-born. They waved their arms exuberantly as the ebony stagecoaches rolled past, mounted escorts behind the royal menagerie loading their crossbows in case of attack. Dacians were anything but predictable. They may escort a convoy through dangerous territory; they may rob a convoy. For a moment, Vlad could believe that he, too, was a Gypsy in a caravan. But alas, he was a royal prisoner, being rushed under high security to his new prison. He cried a salute, waving his hand out of the coach's passenger window. His voice was deep, guttural, utterly unlike his handsome face. (It would become a voice to inspire awe and, sometimes, *fear*.) The 'Gypsies' loitering before him were beautiful people, dark-haired with sun-bronzed, olive skin, clothes tattered but amazingly colourful. Some wore the ubiquitous, full-length tartan. Many were Jews.

The sparkling river Lóm meandered ahead, only seven miles from the boulder-marked Bulgarian border; rippling, unpolluted by the iron works and sewage effluent of German towns. The royal caravan halted at the river's mossy riverbank, soldiers dismounting to fill their emptied wineskins. Their horses strayed to its banks, dipping their muzzles into the chilly, midsummer stream. The convoy's guests were not prisoners—yet. The escorts were Vlad Dracul's men. Forests cloaked the deep, swift-flowing river's west bank; wonderfully cool and dark. Prince Dracul's unwilling entourage exited their stifling coaches, stripping down to their underwear, splashing into the cool, clean, invigorating waters. The girls wisely dangled their feet in the Lóm's current, lest the soldiers mistakenly take them for fair game.

The soldiers would not do that though. Prince Vladislaus Dracul would hang each and every one of them if the Sultan's concubines were sullied. Vlad knew that. His father told him so.

Vlad was a loner. He had one friend—Matei—who now sat beside him on a big, lichened rock near the bucolic, forested riverbank. The young wenches ran past in a game of hide 'n' seek, temporarily enjoying their freedom and forgetting the horrors that awaited them.

Matei turned to Vlad, winking in assumed collusion, calling to one of the older girls.

"Madelina! Come here, Vlad wishes to speak to you!" Matei shouted, ignoring his friend's punch to the shoulder.

A tall, doe-eyed brunette, Vlad's age, came forward timidly.

"Yes, milord? You wish to speak with me?" She simpered shyly, liquid, uneasy eyes darting to each youth's face.

Vlad shook his head, pointing to his friend who sat laughing on the colossal rock. Vlad was not accustomed to female company. Not at all. He'd just spent three months in solitary confinement prior to his short-lived return. Matei tossed a slimy stick at the girl, laughing as she ran away with a volley of curses; holding her frilly, colourful, Romanian folk-skirts high along the riverbank.

Matei was a year older than Vlad, with straight, dark, pageboy-style hair and big, pale blue, expressive eyes, his nose rather small and constantly red, as if he had a permanent cold. Vlad's shoulder-length hair was unruly, black as night, curly—like his father's—his narrow, high-bridged nose long and prominent. A typical, Slav nose. His eyes were deepest green, reflective, turbulent pools of mystery. Gypsy eyes. But not dark. Bushy black eyebrows nearly converged together on his high forehead, like the werewolf of antiquity, his gaunt face wide, handsome. He had a nice smile. He wore long, black leather jackboots, horseman's boots, terminating just below the knee, purple silk tights, and a black satin, red-silk-lined, ground-draping cape signifying nobility. A ruby Dragon brooch pinned the scion's high-necked, starch collared cape at his throat. Vlad was somewhat short for his age, shorter than Matei. But strong as a bull.

With a personality to match.

A bone hunting-horn brought the group of youngsters to their feet, heading back to the wagons with a morose, collective sigh. They lounged along the wooded riverbank, fully dressed now. Some of them would be returning, like Matei. Others such as Vlad would not. Not soon. Unless his father died or buckled to the Emir's demands. Vlad half-wanted his father to wage war on Mured, but feared for his own life. The Sultan had hinted at Egrigöz that Vlad would have his eyes blinded with a red-hot poker should his father rebel. As for the girls, Vlad prayed they hadn't heard the nasty rumours of what Arabs did to slave girls. At the age of twelve, they may be spared the pain and humiliation of female circumcision, unless rejected from Sultan Mured's overstocked harem. But then again, they may not. The Byzantine emperor's daughter was to be wed to the Sultan's son, as part of the treaty agreement of Constantinople.

The girls would be turned into *houris*—harem girls. In Europe, the Sultan's concubines were being dubbed whores, prostitutes, willing or otherwise. They would be taught the Oriental arts of love, the secrets of the harem—the Kama Sutra—or in the Turks' case, the Kama Houri. Those who weren't discarded and circumcised, that is.

The royal baggage-train left Transylvania's distant, lofty Carpathians behind, crossing into Bulgaria by noon. They traversed the mighty, muddy Danube at nightfall across a decrepit wooden bridge at the delta's narrowest point, the swollen river winding its way through eastern Europe, eventually draining into the Black Sea near the small garrison-town of Varna. The enormous river was much too deep, and wide, even to ford on horseback. At dusk, the wagon train halted in a prairie field well inside Ottoman-held Bulgaria. Night fires soon lit the camp, protecting the royal hostages from wolves or marauders. Cormorants and geese flocked over the Danube's estuary marshes; muddy, treacherous meadows the abode of smugglers.

Days passed as if in a dream. Hot, sultry days without a cloud in sight. Vlad slept most of the time, only waking once to study the swampy delta's bulrushes for pink flamingos, his favourite wildfowl. His father owned a dozen or so tamed flamingos at his palace-gardens of Tirgovişte, which Vlad used to pet and cuddle before his imprisonment years.

Gradually, the caravan left the Black Sea district of Dobrúja behind, travelling slowly southward towards the Bosporus where, with a bit of luck, the sweat-stained, fidgety retinue might find a warm, soft bed at the great fortress of Roumeli-Hissar, the mighty Byzantine castle on the Bosporus downstream from bustling Constantinople, built for collecting tolls. The Byzantine vizier had an urgent haste to rendezvous with one of his field marshals concerning fresh Turkish battalion-movements near Ismaitz, on the Sea of Marmara. An outbreak of skirmishes might delay the Romanian party's entry into the protection of the citadel's precincts. It was this reason which carried Lord Dracul's entourage the long circuit around Sofia, first to parley with imperial field commanders at Roumeli, then to deliver the hostages and guests to the Islamic city of Sofia. The Sultan, his mind benumbed by opium, was in no great hurry to receive them.

Gradually, as the scorching, Adriatic days flew past, the tiny blue Sea of Marmara came into view as Prince Dracul's caravan raced southwards. (In the midst of a daydream, what seemed a blink of an eye, it was gone.) The Black Sea once more floated into Vlad's sleepy eyes as he squinted into the pristine, pure blue glory of Mediterranean skies. Greek-Renaissance domes loomed on the horizon, as well as magnificent mock-Roman villas, palaces, artillery forts. Dunes strewn with marram grass sloped down to fantastic white beaches where distant, bronzed aristocrats sunbathed brazenly in the nude. The great city of Constantinople, Jewel of the Bosporus, reared hazily in the distance; Vlad could just barely make out the stupendous, awe-inspiring, stone-banded square towers and encroaching, power-lunging minarets (one of the concessions the back-stabbing Mohammedans had wheedled out of the brow-beaten Byzantine emperor). Yet amazingly, the faster the caravan's horses' hooves churned, the further away the Bosporus seemed to be. Almost reluctantly, Vlad dozed off again in the sweltering, Mediterranean sun.

A hand shook Vlad's shoulder. He slowly opened his tired eyes, squinting up at the sun crowning the Byzantine donjon's shoulder high up on its mound. The fortress was huge. Vlad had never seen anything like it. Massive, grey, crow-stepped ramparts soared above the glittering Bosporus, protecting the mighty round donjon on its mound. Great, round cannon bastions were being constructed to ward off the Turks of northern Bulgaria and from across the Straits, impressive, battlemented towers lacking machicolation. (Murder holes.) Masons and carpenters scurried around beneath the scaffolding, stopping to gape as the five royal carriages and attendant baggage-train rumbled up the grassy incline, nearing the portcullis gate. Battlemented walls and towers ascended to an azure, Mediterranean sky (soon to be rebuilt by the Turks during their investing of Constantinople, 1456; the massive fortress would become infamous as 'The Throat Cutter' as it blockaded the Straits from Byzantine aid). It would be a long climb up the castle's steep, stepped, barbican wall-walk, or wingwall, leading to the donjon.

The exhausted party stayed the night in the humongous round donjon, echoing with the tramp of boots on its spiralling stairs. Thunder roared overhead, threatening to bring down the walls. Yellow lightning flashed across the Black Sea. The castle garrison's boots kept the Romanian guests awake. The slam and rattle of portcullis and chains made sleep virtually impossible. The garrison was on the lookout. Again. Turkish regiments had been sighted two days ago on the Turkish side of the Sea of Marmara, preparing to besiege this life-link of the Byzantine Empire's waning influence. Should Roumeli-Hissar fall, Constantinople would be wide open for an all-out waterborne assault across the Bosporus Straits. The eastern Holy Roman Empire now shared Bulgaria with Turkey; the south-west half under Byzantine rule, the north under Ottoman suzerainty. The Turks were now preparing for the much-awaited attack on Wallachia—with Byzantium's begrudged support.

The garrison manned the battlements throughout the night, crossbows primed. Most were mercenaries; Normans, Teutons, Venetians, Bulgarian expatriates. The Kingdom of Bulgaria had long ceased to exist. As had Serbia. A settlement of Turks in Herzegovina had conquered that territory in the name of Allah, giving thanks to their God for their new Serbo-Croat lands. Soon the conversion of Europe to Islam could begin.

Vlad had no love for the mercenaries who manned this castle nor for the Byzantine Empire who struggled to maintain possession of it. *Traitors!* Allowing the Turks to cross the Straits unmolested, marching unimpeded through Byzantine territory to strike at Wallachia and Serbia, attacking Moldavia and threatening Greece, which only staved off invasion through enormous *baksheesh* payments. Disgraceful. Vlad lay awake in his cot, wondering what tortures to expect once he arrived in Sofia. The Muslims' harems sounded intriguing but Westerners were forbidden entrance on pain of death. Vlad knew most of the houris were Caucasians. Slave girls, captured in eastern Europe. The Sultans seemed to prefer the beautiful, pale girls.

Vlad listened to loud thunderclaps in the distance, pondering his future. If Mirçea were to die somehow…

Vlad swore to wreak vengeance on the traitorous, bigamous boyars for refusing to fight the Turks. They would rather wage war on his father or on the peasants. He vowed to shackle them together by the neck, forcing them to build him a colossal new castle with their bare hands. When it was finished, Vlad would execute each and every one of them, including their families. Yes.

He awoke to birdsong. His servants were busy packing what meagre belongings Vlad owned into burlap sacks for the long, return journey ahead. Vlad would've liked to stay and explore this cyclopean Byzantine castle, but he was under high-security guard at all times, and besides, there was no time. His party had been on the trail for over two weeks, stopping only to pitch their tents at night or refill their canteens. Guards patrolled the tents to make sure none of the guests, prisoners or concubines of Sultan Mured II were assassinated or were to escape. That would bring all-out war.

Blackbirds perched on the castle's unshuttered, Romanesque windows and battlements, squawking under a deep-blue Mediterranean sky, their beady black eyes flashing as Vlad Dracula stuck his head out the window. He inhaled the tangy salt-spray ocean air deep into his lungs, dropping his head in defeat. A hundred feet below and more, levies were shovelling grain into one of the fortress's numerous cylindrical wooden silos. *Croats,* by the look of them; they were dressed poorly, their drab clothes tattered and moth-eaten. Some looked as if they hadn't had a decent bath in months.

The boyar of Ploeşti's senior guardsman called from a nearby antechamber for Vlad to hurry-up. The escort was awaiting him below. Vlad was momentarily tempted to escape, but knew the castle garrison would find him soon enough. He had tried many times before. Sighing in resignation, he followed the liveried soldier-at-arms down the dim lit, turnpike stairs. Bracketed pine torches flickered in the youth's face as he passed, acrid smoke burning his eyes.

Kettle-helmeted soldiers gathered around the wagons and luxurious, velvet-upholstered stagecoaches. They were Dracul's men, dressed spartanly in leather jerkins and padded *gambesons* should outlaws attack. Their weapons consisted of great, round shields, broadswords, maces, crossbows and rare Carpathian longbows which were feared weapons to their enemies. Others held billhooks, tasselled halberds, spears, or pikes. They had the look of polished professionals but Vlad knew most were peasants. They earned little or no pay save for their meals and lodgings. The men-at-arms were loyal, decent, trustworthy to a fault. Not like the Saxon scum who manned this castle over the Bosporus.

Vlad's mother had been raped at sixteen by Magyars—Hungarians. She had been of royal birth, of Dacian descent, rescued by Vlad's Romano-Hungarian father in the ensuing battle for the Wallachian throne. The contending boyar factions had been defeated, but continued to be a serious threat. Thus, the Basarab-Dracul family had regained the ancestral throne of Wallachia. Vlad knew their enemies plotted even now at the fortified capital of Tirgovişte to overthrow his father and replace him with a Turkish puppet. True, the peasants might find some peace and time to reap the fields, but they would not be free. They would be forced to offer prayers to Allah, their women to wear veils.

The wagon train crawled out of the castle, picking up speed as the multitude of ebony carriages plunged downhill, the horses hitting level ground at a dead run upon an open trail northwards now toward Sofia, where the Turkish Sultan's son waited to marry his Christian bride. One of many brides. The Mohammedans were polygynous, their men free to take as many as four wives under Koran law—the wealthy even more. (Women, needless to say, might be stoned to death for such adulterous conflagrations.)

Sultan Mured had as many as eighteen at last count, not including the hundreds of concubines and slave girls scattered throughout his palaces. Arab women had few rights, though they did have the right to divorce. But that was a ruse. Only if her husband was willing to give up his wife and her marriage dowry was the divorce valid. Arab women could not choose their husbands. (Nominally, they were Turkish, or Bulgarians, etc., but under *Sharia* law, Arabic was the written and legal standard.) The Romanised, Christianized citizens of Romania and elsewhere were beginning to show the same tendencies, adopting Islamic customs wherever they went. Christianity, too, had done much over the centuries to destroy the pagan legal code, thereby turning sex and the female sex in particular into something shameful. To Vlad, such thoughts were not heresy, they were unchallengeable truth. The Bible was no European invention, but a Judeo-Christian corruption of Akkadian mythology. Fortunately, the Jews had adopted pagan, Galatian attitudes towards women upon their expulsion from Israel. Vlad had no love for Christians; to him, they were sissy, monkish men who avoided the honour of war. Woman haters. The Saxon counts especially, as well as the Norman adventurers from France. The Holy Roman Emperor of Byzantium was reputed to have an Arab-style harem at Constantinople.

Vlad hated them all. He wished his tiny country had the resources and willpower to crush them all; Teutonic knights, Norman adventurers, Turkish ghazis (Warriors of God), all of them. Next he would expel the Catholic bishops who turned a blind eye to so many evils, exorcising the Black Death rats as if they were demons. Anyone with half a brain could see that the unsanitary cities and towns and their mounds of excrement were the cause of the plague. The rats were not to blame; they only harboured the fleas which carried the contagious disease. (Of course the Dominicans' widespread burnings of cats as 'witches familiars' didn't help one iota!) The Saxon cities had no plumbing; they dumped their wastes into the gutters, never cleaning them. Like filthy Greeks.

Vlad was a heretic. Secretly, of course.

He thought God was a distant, alien ruler who looked down at the earth in resignation, shaking His head at the mindless, foolish humans. In the name of Jehovah they persecuted droves of perfectly harmless Jews, burning the wretches alive at the stake. Vlad had heard recently that at Toulouse, France, four hundred had been burnt in *one day*. The Church authorities also persecuted 'witches' by the thousands, burning them alive in their newly-proclaimed Inquisition. Witches! All they were, were harmless country peasants who dabbled in herbal medicines to aid minor problems of the health. Amateur alchemists, you might say. It was the unholy league of physicians and monks who framed these poor wretches, therefore eliminating competition. By the methods some of the professional surgeons and alchemists used, Vlad believed they should be persecuted. And by God, if he were in power he would! What in Christ's name did they think bloodletting would do? A man would sooner bleed to death than be cured. Royal surgeons believed that drilling a hole in a retard's head would let out their demons!

Joan of Arc had been burnt to death as a witch. The real reason was that she was a Gaulish woman who donned men's armour and beat the incompetent Anglo-Normans on the field while French kings and their knights cowered in fortresses like Chinon or Angers. The Pope had sanctioned her burning.

Vlad dozed, alone inside his thoughts as the stiflingly hot coaches rolled past tall prairie fields, stubble plains, the occasional winding, inland river or lethargic, Bulgarian stream. When the red sun began to sink below the western alps of distant Albania, the wagon-train halted on the open verge of a barley field, soldiers speedily re-erecting the rawhide tents while others built a large bonfire for the pampered, royal guests and prisoners.

Come morning, they were back on the dusty trail by daybreak, riding hell-bent-for-leather towards central Bulgaria and the looming Balkan mountains encircling the Islamicized city of Sofia. Vlad awoke once to vaguely recognise the great Meriç river flowing sluggishly northwards. Phlegmatic, longhorn cattle at its muddy, reedy riverbanks eyed the trundling convoy curiously through tall, obscuring bulrushes. The parched, seemingly endless, plains of Bulgaria gradually gave way to thin stretches of oak forest along deliciously-wet riverbanks. By twilight of the next day, the prairies had vanished. Vlad opened his eyes, surprised.

Thick, boreal forests loomed ahead. It was part of the mighty *Forêt Negrĕ*, the Black Forest, which once stretched across eastern Europe all the way from Bulgaria to the Germanies. Up ahead, foresters were busy sawing or chopping a considerable wedge of the sacred mixed forest to make way for agricultural use. It was this way in which the foreign interlopers endeavoured to break the natives' spirit. And how successful it was! Vlad looked away, literally choking on his rage. The doomed souls of his ancestors were being felled. Already, a good half of the ancient old-growth forest of Romania, Bulgaria, Bohemia, Serbia and Slovakia had been felled. Some woodsmen, such as these, were so callous as to slash and burn huge areas, depleting the vicinities of wild game and fowl so desperately needed by the scattered human population.

The coaches skirted the blazing area of forest, taking a wide trail through a dark, smoky section of canopied wilderness, hurrying lest the forest-fire engulf them on its westward rampage. The sawyers had not bothered to place sentinels along the boundaries to douse the inferno (as if they could), preferring to let it burn until heavy rains halted the abomination. (!) Smoke wafted about the royal wagons, stinging the eyes and clogging the nostrils and lungs of their uncomfortable passengers and the labouring teams of horses. The coaches had cushions, but as often as not the passengers found themselves sitting on raw mahogany, because their lilac bolsters had fallen to the floor. Or else the passengers would bang their heads and shoulders on the doors as the carriages bounced and jounced along.

Vlad's carriage swayed and veered on its iron axles, its huge, wooden-spoked rear wagon wheels wobbling, ready to fall off any day now. It banged and rattled with bone-numbing regularity, climbing one mossy incline then racing downhill with sickening irregularity throughout the hilly forest. A westerly sun barely peeped through the treetops, making the mixed, boreal forest this grim, green, superstitious stronghold that it obviously was. Werewolves were rumoured to dwell here, terrorising the Saxon frontier towns and villages on the forest's perimeter. Terrifying, grotesque monsters they were, half man, half-wolf. Vampires were feared even more, the undead *moroi* who returned from their graves to drink human blood. Occasionally the wagon-train would pass a woodsman's house deep within the darkening forest, straddling the trail like some fairytale witch's abode hung with garlic and talismans at its door. These were the newly established Bulgars and Saxons; usurpers, in Vlad's eyes. Since the Roman conquest *(through treachery)* and its hasty evacuation of Dacia a thousand years ago and more, the inhabitants had begun to adopt Vulgar Latin, Hungarian, and Bulgarian into the majority tongue. Here in south-central Bulgaria, a mixed Bulgar-Romanian ethnic strain (along with the intrusive, damned progeny from Saxony) predominated over the arid plains, and, further north, farmed the rich, agricultural expanses abutting the craggy, Balkan massifs. The Turks had brought yet another facet to the dialects, adding to the already established Bulgar language (almost identical to Russian). Except for the misplaced Vlachs and some heathen peasants, the sweet-sounding Celtic Dacian and later Galatian were virtually extinct.

Nevermore to be heard in the mouths of babes.

Vlad's *mamŭ* had been fluent in Dacian. She'd died when he was four, buried at Calimaneşti monastery in the Carpathian mountains of Transylvania, having given birth to Vlad's younger brother Radu.

Radu was also a ransom prisoner destined for Sofia. He rode in the wagon directly ahead, concealed by the carriage's heavy rawhide canopy. Like Vlad and his elder brother Mirçea, Radu was dark and heart-stoppingly handsome, except that his hair was straight as crow's feathers. His features were finer, almost girlish, and he was slender for his age—fourteen. The girls called him Radu the Handsome. Some of Vlad's older cousins, Matei included, called him Radu the Weak. Radu was stand-offish, aloof, preferring Scripture studies over his weapon drills. He was no fighter. Vlad would contest Radu's rule if by some strange chance he were ever picked to be his father's heir to the Wallachian throne. It wasn't that he disliked Radu. On the contrary; Vlad often had to fight Radu's battles for him. Radu had no stomach for wrestling or fisticuffs, would rather play meek than Dragon. It was just that Radu would not have the cunning nor the belly to fight the Turks. As prospective Prince of Wallachia he would be expected to be at the front-lines to prove his military worth. Vlad's father had rose to become Prince almost overnight in one bloody stroke, one severed head. Dracul had been a mere, adopted orphan of a Transylvanian boyar. He was of Romano-Hungarian descent—thus the name. And a new House of Wallachia.

A large contingent of soldiers now blocked the forest ahead. At first, Vlad thought they were Bulgarian guerrillas, freedom-fighters, *chetniks*, collecting their dues from unsuspecting royal travellers.

But no. They were not Bulgarians. Turks. They wore the characteristic turbans, white linen or gaudy, expensive silk wrapped in amazingly coiling shapes about their heads and pinned with exquisite jewels. White-robed ghazis, mostly (many wore the strangely-spired, turbaned helm so distinct to the Turkish Menace). The Ottomans' purebred, Arabian horses stamped and snorted impatiently beneath their spectacular masters. The ghazis' favourite weapons were mighty maces or war hammers, short Asian bows (composite bow, the deadliest weapon in all of Eurasia), sabres, tulwars, scimitars, metal-studded round shields, lances, poleaxes, padded leather armour with steel plates of Mongol design, all represented here. They were magnificent to behold; huge, dark-skinned men, foot soldiers as well, muscles bulging, their faces bearded, or with proud, tusk-like, drooping moustaches. Padded, dark-red tunics bared their bronzed, barrel chests to the dying sun. Some wore earrings.

Their leader shouted a command at the approaching convoy, seated on a fine white, Arabian stallion, forcing the coaches to halt. He spoke in Turkish, a slender man, young. The Turkish interpreter inside the leading stagecoach popped his head out of the carriage, giving a cry of greeting, praising the Sultan's son in the name of Allah, ensuring the nervous Muslims that the entourage were guests of Sultan Mured's, the Magnificent, King of kings, Allah's Chosen Warrior. The Turk smiled, bowing on his fine white warhorse, then dismounted.

He stalked toward the wagon train, lips compressed. The Turk screamed at the girls, peering through the windows, admonishing them to cover their faces in a male's presence. They did so. Hurriedly.

The Turk eyed the male prisoners with either disdain or pleasure. Some of them would make fine warriors. The interpreter joined him, discussing the guests and prisoners. He opened the passenger door to Vlad's coach, asking the name of one of the girls then rebuking her for sharing a carriage with a boy. Laetitia, she said. The Turk nodded, satisfied. He spoke again, eyeing Vlad with curiosity.

The interpreter stuck his head over the dividing board of the front seat. "His Highness would like to know your name, son."

Vlad hesitated, crafty eyes studying the Turks. Was this popinjay the Sultan's son? The Magnificent?! Ha, ha!

"Count Dracula be my name; Lord of Transylvania, Count of Bucovina; heir-apparent to the throne of Wallachia and claimant to Moldavia." Vlad bowed majestically; still seated.

The Turks exchanged words. The Sultan's son did not look pleased. "I said, what is your name, boy," the interpreter repeated.

"Vladislaus Dracula," Vlad reiterated, "son of Vlad Dracul, sovereign Prince of Wallachia." Vlad smirked smugly. He knew their tactics, all their forms of torture, physical or otherwise. Had withstood them all. The Turks at Egrigöz when he'd left had begun to fear HIM.

The Turks exchanged words of humour. The interpreter popped his head through the window, his garlic breath wafting in Vlad's face.

"His Highness says he shall remember you, dickface." The Sultan's son scowled menacingly.

The white-robed ghazis began to move out, shuffling their Arab steeds into formation, another contingent bringing up the rear; grim-faced, muscular arms folded. These were their servile, bare-chested escorts, on foot.

The Sultan's son lacked beard or moustache. He was youngish, Vlad's age. Precious, glittering stones adorned his immaculate, pure-white, stockinged uniform, high black boots reaching to his thighs. He mounted now, proud as a rooster. His turban sported a large, blue, peacock's feather on top. He wore no cape. Vlad hated him on sight, had this irresistible urge to jump out, wrap his fingers around the tall youth's throat and throttle him. Perhaps it was the slanting Mongol eyes, the way his eyebrows moved up and down, suggesting something more than homely. Or the way he fingered his cleft chin, looking down his nose at the guests as if they were slugs.

There was still another fifty miles or so until Sofia's fantastic minaret spires filled the skyline. A great mosque had been built there recently, a wonderful, domed structure with colourful, glazed roof tiles. Vlad had never seen it. Had never seen a mosque. Neither had any of his unwilling companions. Egrigöz had been a former Crusader fortress, not a Turkish religious mecca. Vlad had spent seven months in solitary confinement at Adrianople after his incarceration at Egrigöz for beating a sentry to within an inch of his life, and had departed from that glorious Hellenic city's imperial fortress at night, so he'd not seen the great mosque there either. Rumours of the Muslims' brilliant, onion-domed palaces and mosques were known throughout Christendom, however. In Spain, the Moors resided in an awesome, kaleidoscopic, colourful palace/fortress called the Granada Alhambra, defying the encroaching Spanish *Reconquista*. 'Twas said the palace's magnificent fountain was like a great, arched panorama of Moorish gold mosaics, with a mighty fountain base of stone lions at its apex. The grand palace was sprinkled with audience halls, baths, courts, a royal mausoleum, sumptuous gardens, and a harem the envy of the world.

Vlad was almost foolish enough to consider seeking entrance into the Sultan's infamous, forbidden harem once he reached Sofia. He was the kind of reckless youth who would risk his neck for such glories. He had never had a woman in his bed. Vlad was ashamed to admit it even to himself. His gaolers had kept him on a tight leash, restricting Vlad's pursuits to sword-drills and poleaxe-juggling to prepare for the day when he would, if not fill his father's formidable boots, then fight at his illustrious elder brother Mirçea's side. He was a skilled rider, familiar with the quintain, jousting equipment and the most sophisticated weapons. He had already won three jousting tournaments at Egrigöz. Vlad was especially intrigued with cannon and pikes. He would have to be, for the Turks were masters with cannon, having whole regiments dedicated to the new, roaring, iron guns.

Vlad dozed, snapping from his reverie when a voice shouted in awe. It was dawn; he had slept all yesterday and last night, a bad habit which lately had grown on him. So close to Sofia and their Arabesque comforts, the Turks had insisted the Romanian 'guests' sleep in their coaches rather than pitch their tents. The Romanians were sore and grumpy, unable to stretch their legs in the cramped, twin-bench carriages. Early morning blackbirds hopped away from the rolling coaches now, flapping about in the air only partially airborne, landing every ten feet like some monstrous flying machine of the future. The turfed green grass sparkled brilliantly beneath morning dew, burning Vlad's eyes. A red fireball sun balanced on the slender, multiple minarets of Sofia, glittering with coloured mosaic tiles. An unbelievable, checkered dome rose to a matching azure-blue sky, awesome in its glittering magnificence. The forests had retreated; only the grim, black, Balkan mountains surrounding the city and rich corn fields irradiating the pastoral landscape now, ripe with delicious, tasselled cobs of yellow corn (having its genesis beyond the frozen wastes of Asia).

Vlad's mouth gaped as his wagon neared a rectangular, arcade-machicolated, Balkan-style gatehouse tower. The great mosque towered above the city of Sofia, reaching its peacock-blue dome gracefully to a mirroring sky. *'Precisely like a huge, dark blue, tapered onion,'* he thought. Square corners lent the mosque an exotic look, massive doors recessed in a shady, square niche. It was wholly unlike any Western architecture Vlad had ever seen. It was simply magnificent.

The long-awaited convoy entered the dirty streets with a fanfare of horns and trumpets, alerting the Sultan's palace guard of his guests' arrival. The muezzin cries from lofty minarets were alien to Vlad Dracula's ears; high-pitched, wailing, keening, often cracking with emotion. The exotic scent of eastern spices filled the air.

And suddenly there it was. The royal palace. Fortified. Well-fortified. Stout walls with round, cone-peaked towers protected the Sultan and his massive army of guests, prisoners, concubines, slaves and extensive royal family.

The humiliation of it all seared into Dracul's son like a hot iron, watching grim-faced as Sultan Mured's loyal horse-guard got down to their knees and touched their pure white turbans to the ground in thanks, praising Allah for the delivery of their enemies' ransom dues. Vlad couldn't believe that John VIII (Byzantine emperor) had promised his military service to the heathens. The Sultan's soldiers genuflected in front of the ornate, iron palace gates, raising their eyes to God before rising to their feet.

The cobbled streets were packed with robed spectators. Most of the menfolk wore turbans. The veiled women wore white, shapeless garments, wrists tinkling with bangles and bracelets. Or conversely, a goodly number in black, their womanly shape obscured by the linen folds. They were offensive to Vlad's eyes. Women were meant to be seen, enjoyed. Not coddled and covered like fragile, obscene idols.

The coaches and attendant baggage-train banged their way through the city's second, fortified, machicolated gatehouse, passing beneath a looming portcullis between round towers. Here stood a complex barbican, a pair of long, stout walls parallel to the gatehouse at right angles to trap attackers. Its purpose was to squeeze enemy besiegers into a compact mass so defenders up on the wall-walks could fire their crossbows into the enemies' clustered columns. It hadn't worked. The fortress had been built by Bulgarians but taken by Turks. Since then, the Ottoman satraps had built additional defences and Arabesque living apartments, adding sumptuous ornamental gardens and marble fountains, quickly adopting the Occident's castellar building techniques. The royal city's ancient, outer walls and bulwarks had been allowed to deteriorate. The Crusaders had introduced true castellar architecture to the Middle East—borrowing from Romans, Greeks, and Arabs and adding their own unique twist. The new Renaissance palaces and colossal castles of Europe were every bit as sumptuous in their own, barbaric way as any Turkish fortress or Roman villa. Their lofty, machicolated, stone towers were far more difficult to besiege than any Roman fort (whose very size rendered it impossible to defend), utilising arrowslits, catapults, and *chemin de rondes;* machicolated, murder-hole passageways where defenders fired their deadly crossbows behind the security of stone walls, *twenty-foot-thick* walls in some cases; launching rocks from catapults and utilising iron yetts or towering portcullises of iron and wood to bar entry. Rarely could a professionally engineered, Late Medieval castle be burnt, for most now were built of stone, with slate or lead roof tiles. Tunnelling was even more hazardous, involving mining underneath towers to bring them crashing down, often on top of the sappers. Using picks to dismantle a castle wall might only succeed if besiegers were protected by wooden cats, or roofs, and only then if they could survive lightning sallies from a postern gate. Some of the finest castles were in the Middle East, built by Crusaders; Crac de Chevaliers, Syria, a monstrous concentric fortalice; Acre, likewise; or in Europe, Windsor, the premier castle of England; Hohensalzburg, Austria; the Alcazar of Segovia, Spain, to name a few. Vlad had seen none of them, but their notoriety was legendary. He wished his father had a few, though.

Now separated from the baggage-train, the five black coaches came to a rocking, shuddering halt outside the Sultan's palace quarters. Dust hung in the air, clogging Vlad's lungs and causing him to cough. The enormous, blue-domed mosque loomed in the distance above Mured II's lavish palace.

The passengers climbed out, stiff, sore, stretching their aching limbs. Some were vague acquaintances of Vlad's, though he hardly recognised them. Others were bitter enemies whom he vowed to destroy once he succeeded to the family throne of Wallachia.

Like Kai Crawdövich. A tall, boisterous, cinnamon-haired buffoon who had once thrashed young Dracula. A nineteen-year-old bully who thought nothing of murdering a peasant if he stood in his steed's path. Like his father, Kai was a lecherous Hungarian scum who hauled in hefty sums of silver each year for precious white slaves sold to the Turkish Emir. Half the population of Transylvania had been depleted because of their brisk trade. Another enemy of Vlad's, Dorgoi Bathóry, a short, muscular, Szekely noble's son, eighteen, stood by Crawdövich's side; companions of lechery and wine, and, secretly, homosexuals to boot. Only Vlad knew, having caught them in the act one night at Count Bathóry's castle of Crawdö, western Transylvania; so consumed with their homosexual rutting that they hadn't even detected his presence. It had been many years ago, before Vlad's imprisonment. He'd been only twelve at the time. Vlad would have snatched a sword from the wall and slaughtered them both had it not been Lord Bathóry's castle. But someday…

No. Not with a sword. Impalement. Y-e-e-s. Vlad had learned much as a prisoner at Egrigöz castle. For days, his Turkish gaolers would force him to watch the mass impalements taking place in the sandy courtyard, fellow comrades taken while sabotaging the Turkish supply lines.

The ghazis prodded the prisoners away, marching in opposite directions of the guests. Vlad wasn't sure whether the concubines were prisoners or guests, for they wouldn't be returning to Romania. Not ever.

Bathóry and Crawdövich were not prisoners. Vlad could hear their laughter as he was ushered away, talking behind his back, just loud enough to hear.

"Try not to become lost in Mured's harem, eh Vlad!" Bathóry cried.

"Don't let the buggers get you down!"

Vlad was old enough and strong enough to pummel them both. If only he had the chance. His elder brother Mirçea had been well-nigh astonished to see Vlad was no longer the little brother he remembered, but a powerfully built young man. Mirçea no longer laughed at Vlad. His father would punish him severely however if he laid a hand on these boyars' sons. The Bathóry clan were one of Dracul's few allies, and very, very powerful. Their castles and estates straddled the border of Hungary and Wallachia, with estates in Czechoslovakia as well. Another distant branch of the Bathóry family actually ruled Moldavia. Not all of the Bathórys were Vlad Dracula's enemies. Far from it. Matei was a Bathóry, a cousin to Dorgoi, twice removed. Matei and Vlad shared a common hatred of Dorgoi.

Vlad stalked down a bustling, crowded market-street, pushed every once in a while by his guards to establish their authority. Grim-faced, his eyes lowered menacingly, expression almost demented. *It is true,* Vlad thought to himself, with pride, *I am the Devil's son. The Dragon of Wallachia. Thine enemies best knoweth it now, and beware.* At times, his eyes could be soft, reflective, joyful. Others they could be pools of darkness, portals to Hell.

Mirçea was the eldest, granted. His prowess on the battlefield (i.e., the battle of Varna, 1444) was renowned across Wallachia. But Vlad had the cunning of a wolf, and he was *ruthless*. He would make a fine co-ruler. Even though Mirçea would have the lion's share, Vlad would have real power. Unknown to both his father and his brother, Vlad's stay at Egrigöz had turned him into a formidable warrior.

A street market was in progress. Unveiled Bulgarian women mixed with Arabs, eyeing silk, spices, gold ornaments, lingerie, their voices raised while heckling with the honest Arab stallholders, exchanging silver and gold for precious items. Turkish haberdashers thronged the sidewalks. Distracted farmhands wandered the aisles of the bazaar, getting their ears boxed should they bump into *sipahis* (Indian soldiers-of-fortune) who happened to be in a hurry. Some of the merchants were Jews, wearing their distinctive, round skullcaps and black linen clothing. Their women, save for a kerchief, were unveiled, freer than Christian women.

The ghazis stopped to haggle with a fellow Arab over some priceless Oriental heirloom. Vlad stood alone, watching, the rest of his fellow captives taken to different prison cells within the immense, colonnaded palace. A tall, graceful, veiled woman wandered about the bazaar stalls, eyeing the goods with a noblewoman's fussiness, never stopping for long. She said nothing, ignoring the stallholders' pleas, an astute business woman. She moved with a fluid, graceful manner, wide hips swaying seductively. The wench seemed important for the stallholders sought her attention above all others.

She noticed Vlad staring at her. His eyes had lost their insanity. He stuck out in the crowd, a Daco-Romanian of noble birth, wearing the gold/ruby Dragon brooch of the House of Dracul at his throat. Long, black whiskers protruded from his lip.

Their eyes met like a collision.

The girl was Caucasian. Piercing, dark eyes studied Vlad with interest, flickering down his cape-swathed stature. She stood provocatively with one hand on her hip, as if enticing. (He at first mistook her for a common strumpet.) She wore a black linen veil hiding her face except for the eyes. *Oh, her eyes!* Head tilted, she slowly drew back her veil, revealing her forbidden features.

Vlad gasped, mouth compressed.

She was stunning. Her luscious hair was dark, incredibly long and wavy; eyebrows somewhat thick, patrician nose extremely long, straight, and prominent. Eye-catching dimples and a false beauty mark on her left cheek elevated a handsome, well-formed face to one of classic beauty, eyes soft with the confidence of a siren. Her eyebrows arched aristocratically over large, bold, almond eyes, hair rich as gossamer silk with a slight tint of henna, washed in Turkish steam baths daily. A face of arresting beauty and sinful knowledge. Lips like full, sensuous fruit from the Garden of Eden. A forbidden cherry, waiting for Vlad to bite into them. He knew she was a *houri* at first sight. It was also a little-known custom among slave girls to lower their veils for fellow countrymen, for Arab rules were not binding on Westerners. Her hair was clean, shiny, shoulder-length. Lustrous.

A moment of recognition flashed between them before Vlad's guards prodded him onward. He smiled, winking rashly.

She covered her face and moved on, surprisingly not attracting the abuses of offended Muslims. Vlad's brutal guardsmen installed him in a prison belowground, corridors lit with flickering rushes. Barred prison cages held scores of Romanian, Bulgarian, Slovenian and even Russian prisoners. Some had been tortured or beaten black and blue. Others possessed firebrand markings on their foreheads or hands.

Vlad was placed in solitary confinement, as a sign of humiliation to new arrivals, away from the established inmates' pitiful cries. His was an earth cell, with bars making escape impossible. A fluttering pine-torch stood bracketed outside his cell, out of Vlad's reach.

He sat down on his cot, waiting. Praying. Hoping to *Annwfyn* (Samháin) the Turks wouldn't torture him again, this time.

Chapter Two

The ghazis prodded Vlad toward the Sultan's sumptuous audience chamber. They passed two muscle-bound, turbaned Arabs dressed in baggy, dull-black pantaloons and vests, arms and chests bare. Beyond, Vlad's astonished eyes sighted women in the colourfully tapestried hallway, half-naked, eyeing him with curiosity. Like his brother Radu, Vlad was handsome, but lacked Radu's girlish figure and expression and sweet temperament. Vlad was muscular, very, very muscular for his age, almost as powerful as the Turkish bodyguards. Soon, at the height of his virility, he would eclipse even them. He held his head high, arrogant, proud.

An enormous gilded chamber branched off to his right, and he was there.

And there she was.

Vlad could scarcely believe his eyes. His guards prodded him once, twice, forcing him to his knees, no easy chore.

The Sultan was magnificent. Somewhat overweight, grandiose, dressed in a flowing, scarlet velvet robe, jewels twinkling in sunlight reflected through a stained-glass, Renaissance skylight overhead. Mured wore dozens of splendid jewels; gold rings, silver bangles, sapphires, topaz, emeralds, rubies, amethyst, jade. White, swirl-patterned, marble pillars supported an antiquated cruck-framed timber ceiling—the remnant of a previous Bulgar palace. A huge, square ruby graced Sultan Mured's pure white turban, sparkling red brilliance. But the girl…

She was half-naked. No veil. A web-like headdress of pearls and black onyx strings embellished her locks. Her breasts were wonderful to behold, bound by a flimsy, maroon, lace bralette. Her deep cleavage made Vlad's mouth water. She studied him, head tilted with intense scrutiny, unsmiling. Other, nubile women also lounged about on scarlet cushions or yellow beanbags beside their illustrious Master, waiting on Mured hand and foot; all Caucasians, scantily clad in blue, pinkish, yellow or violet sheer-silk skirts, indescribably beautiful. They fawned on him like obscene smiling harlots, their faces raised for Mured's smiles of pleasure.

"You have seen the pleasures of my court, my harem, my beautiful women," Mured said at last. "You are a lucky man, Vlad Dracula. Not many Europeans get to glimpse my harem in full splendour. Look around, feast your eyes."

Vlad gazed about him. There were dozens of them, lounging on ivory elbows propped on red velvet cushions, playing coquettishly with their hair, gorgeous beyond belief. They smiled invitingly, as if goading Vlad with the knowledge of their untouchability. All save for one. Vlad's eyes strayed back to her, like a puppy begging for a bone. He glanced away, eyes straying back as if entranced. She licked her lips seductively, teasing.

The Sultan continued to speak. He addressed his interpreter, for Vlad had not learned his Turkish well (or so they assumed!) during his six years' imprisonment. Indeed, he'd received lashings for resisting it.

"You are here as your father's pledge of loyalty," Mured continued. "If he continues to show good faith, your stay may perhaps be terminated shortly. You need not fear for your life or limb—as long as Dracul toes the line. If not, well…"

Vlad had heard this before. He knew all Mured's threats, his promises of riches, of power.

Mured poured Vlad a crystal glass of red French wine, handing him the glass with a smile. His teeth were rotting badly. Mured had both beard and moustache, neither long. Vlad guessed his age to be in the mid-forties.

Vlad accepted the glass.

"I hope that in time we shall be allies, if not friends," Mured remarked with a wink.

Vlad kept silent. *Only in Hell, my friend, only in Hell,* he thought to himself. "Take him away," Mured ordered, allowing Dracula to drain his glass.

His guards dragged him to his feet, pushing Vlad back the direction he'd come. Once again in his earthen cage, the bars slammed shut, locking Vlad in the tepid darkness beneath Mured's palace. The torch had gone out.

He sat huddled on cold ground for hours, pondering his predicament. He had no way of knowing what time it was, whether it be day or night. Vlad knew as a second-eldest his future was bleak. With Mirçea on the throne, Vlad could rot in here forever. His father was ageing, but not ready for death. Not by any means.

His father had long-ago installed a bizarre, new invention in his castle tower near Braşov, a wonderful machine with moving parts and pointers which showed the time of day with Roman numerals. Full of swinging pendulums and cogs and springs, it was; once wound the machine would stay running without anyone's presence, a truly remarkable invention. The Germans called it a clock. It was installed in a crude, iron frame. Before the Turks demanded him as a hostage, Vlad would sit in front of the contraption for hours balanced on a beam as the great, iron bells tolled above him as the pendulums and gears slipped another cog.

Vlad loved trinkets. Whether they be weapons, toys, brooches or farm implements, few things in life could make his eyes shine as the new inventions flooding western and eastern Europe. Especially those gadgets with moving parts. His father had shown him once a fascinating and deadly new weapon; half-pike, half pole-axe, it also concealed a handy, razor-sharp clamp on its axehead, convenient for gouging and slicing through jointed armour, cutting to the bone. It was especially handy for clamping around the necks, arms, and legs of armoured knights. Vlad couldn't wait to try one out. Perhaps, with Mirçea's permission, he'd wage war on Hungary someday when his brother succeeded the father as Prince of Wallachia.

If Mirçea were to refrain from blinding Vlad and Radu, that is. And their five other brothers. Or fail to petition Sultan Mured for their release. Though Mirçea bore them no grudge, a crown was often more important than blood kinship.

Vlad's goal, however, was to unite all of Romania into one powerful, Orthodox state. With him as king, of course. Not a mere Prince. The Principality of Moldavia was being contested right now (the latest sovereign of that sorry country, Prince Bogdan, having been murdered in his bed) between Vlad's father and the as-yet unanointed King of Hungary, Ladislas Posthumous—a mere teenager. As underling, Lord Dracul owed the young King of Hungary allegiance as well as Ladislas' sworn enemy, Sultan Mured II. (The king's father, Ladislas [Jagiello] III, had died in battle against Mured II at Varna, 1444.)

Caught in his daydreams, Vlad dozed off.

He woke to the rattle of keys on iron bars. There were no windows, but somehow he knew it was daylight. Two ghazis (warriors of God) dragged Vlad from his cell, holding up a guttering torch to his face, ordering him in a strange language he didn't understand to follow. They cuffed him around the ears, impatient.

They led him to a great, barrel-vaulted, smoky hall, full of toiling, sweating Westerners who hammered away at iron forges, making weapons for their cruel Turkish captors. Ghazis armed with leather thongs strapped the backs of those who tired or lagged. All were men, prisoners of Sultan Mured's. Royal or otherwise.

The guards stripped Vlad of his black satin cape and red silk blouse, tossing him a leather jerkin—confiscating his precious, royal Dragon brooch of the House of Dracul. He was too shrewd to protest, knowing full well they'd beat him senseless, outnumbered as he was. One of them placed a heavy iron hammer in his hand, pointing to an anvil. Gave him a shove, kicking Vlad's ass.

"Fucking Turk," grumbled Vlad in Romanian, stumbling towards the anvil.

"What did you call me, boy?"

The Turk grabbed Vlad's arm, pushing his face to Vlad's nose. So they weren't ignorant monoglots after all.

"Nothing—term of endearment."

"Get to work, gook, or I'll kick your fucking face in, b-o-y!"

The Turk pushed him again, kicking Vlad's ass one more time with his leather sandal before moving on to his next victim. It was all Vlad could do not to strangle the turbaned little bastard.

He toiled in front of the anvil all day long and all night, wiping tears and sweat from his eyes. No one noticed. Vlad kept his bare back to the others, impotent rage filling his eyes with scalding tears. The sweltering chamber was like a hot, roasting oven, acrid smoke of wall braziers and half-molten metals' fumes stinging his eyes like sliced onions. He quickly discarded the sticky leather jerkin—showing his disdain to his abrasive Turkish gaolers, as if saying, "Is this the worst you can do?" (He soon regretted it.) The ghazis, taking up Dracula's challenge, lashed his bleeding back mercilessly to keep him toiling. (It was a test of theirs; a way of driving the hated pale-faced scions to distraction without attracting the Sultan's ire.) His new 'friend' strolled over every once in a while, poking his ugly, brown, pock-marked face into Vlad's, taunting. The strokes from his thong were especially painful (of course, to attempt retrieval of his heavy leather jerkin would bring a beating, which Vlad knew from experience). Occasionally he would kick Vlad in the ass, laughing with screeching glee. Vlad knew, KNEW he would someday kill this arrogant Turkish scum with his bare hands—slowly, painfully. Enjoying every minute of it. He couldn't live with himself if he didn't.

****

That day was not long in coming.

The Turk lashed Vlad's back hard. He spit in his face, laughing at the Devil's impotence. Occasionally he would place his hand on Vlad's derrière, suggesting lewd practices which the Turk insisted all Westerners took part of, surely. Were they not weak, sissy Christians who 'loved' the son of God? They who preached brotherly love instead of war and domination? And the women! They were whores, surely! The Turk explained his penchant for raping and torturing little white girls in Vlad's ear. Day after day, for one agonising month. Kicking his ass. Touching him. Strapping.

Finally Vlad went off the deep end.

Turned his smouldering red hammer on the offensive Turk one day, smashing his skull, hammering the Turk's head into a bloody, steaming pulp while straddling his chest on the flagstone floor before the guards could pry Vlad off the murdered ghazi. His eyes glowed with unholy vengeance, face contorted into a wicked caricature of a smile. (He jabbered veritably like a man in dementia!) The other prisoners watched in horror, at once delighted yet aghast at the Devil's son's bloodlust. Surely the boy was possessed. Vlad's guards immediately rushed him away to the beating room, holding him down, beating Vlad unconscious. When he came to, they dragged him, on his knees, toward the Sultan's audience chambers.

She was there again. Alone. The Sultan was absent, having gone to the lavatory. Vlad faced her, wild-eyed and bloody, long black hair in a tangled mess, his guards the only other persons in the marble-checkered hall. His face was puffy, bruised. Sore. He didn't regret what he'd done. A glowing warmth burned in his heart.

The girl lounged on a wide blue cushion sipping a crystal glass of cordial, serious, glancing at Vlad with dark, seductive eyes. He would have taken her there and then had his guards not been present, so alive with aggression was he.

The Sultan entered, surprised.

"Well, well, well. What have we here? What has he done to deserve this punishment?!" Mured cried, "You mongrel Iranian whoresons."

One of the three quaking guardsmen cleared his throat, speaking shakily. "He killed Abn-ze Dula-Mubarek, head forge guardsman, your royal Immaculate Majesty. Beat his head in with a red-hot hammer your Excellency, Allah's Chosen One, Our Leader."

The three guards knelt to their knees, paying obeisance, touching their turbans to the sparkling, black-and-white, checkered marble floor in hopes of forgiveness. Mured smiled, placated, seating his corpulent body into a bouncy blue beanbag chair. "Very well, then. You have done good. Allah is pleased. You shall be rewarded, I assure you. You may go now."

Vlad, fearful, turned to the Sultan when they'd left. The girl was smiling, looking up at her Master like a fawning strumpet. Was she smiling at Vlad's expense? Or amused by his bravery and violence?

The Sultan shook his head, puckering his lips.

"You have been here only thirty-eight days, Vlad Dracula, and already you've gotten yourself into trouble. Serena here is impressed. I, am not. You, Vlad Dracula, have committed sacrilege. Yes. In

Islam, the penalty for murder is death. Did you know that, Vlad Dracula?" The Sultan leaned forward, anxious.

"*Oes, fy gŵybod.*" (Yes, I know.) It took Vlad a long moment before realising he had spoken in Dacian. An alien tongue. Vlad often spoke in Dacian when he was flustered. Mured's interpreter frowned, puzzled, mouthing the words to himself.

"Yes, I know, Your Highness."

The houri sat up, ears perked. She studied Vlad with piercing, sharp, renewed interest, her arched brows furrowed.

"But as you are Lord Dracul's son and possible future heir," Mured continued, "I shall let you off with a mere flogging. I could not let you go unpunished, as it would demoralise my people and make them think I am weak. You do understand, don't you? You do understand, don't you?"

Vlad nodded, believing the Sultan to be totally mad, often repeating his phrases on a regular basis with a honeyed tongue. Mured exuded rude health; a permanent leer on his dark face, fat jowls, dressed in ruby, flowing robes edged with grey rabbit's fur. His eyebrows were almost non-existent. Vlad was sure Mured plucked them every week.

The girl ceased to attract Vlad's attention. And respect. She was not just another slave-girl in Sultan Mured's harem. She was his favourite, his concubine. She wore only a purple, lap-length robe crisscrossed over her breasts, sinfully tight, covering her bosom, thighs, and nothing more. Her perfect belly was bare, revealing a flat, well-muscled abdomen trained for belly dancing. The Sultan's belly dancers were infamous; gorgeous girls who frequently entertained scores of Arab men in smoky taverns, shaking their delectable derrières in front of their admirers, arms held high to reveal scantily-clad, globular breasts and soft, ivory-smooth skin. Vlad had never seen one, but adventurers returning from Arabia detailed the belly dancers' glories. Strips of lace and precious stones were said to hang from the girls' midriffs and breasts (where their patrons tucked their shekels of gold), the belly dancers wearing short, tantalising, gauzy white skirts of Damask silk. Yet their faces were always veiled (some decorum for modesty!). Vlad would have enjoyed watching this girl dance.

Sultan Mured seemed to read Dracula's mind, smiling slyly; beckoning for Serena to perform for her privileged guest.

Obeying her master's whim, Serena rose to her feet, stretching her arms high then relaxing, preparing for the sultry Arabian dance. It was an ancient exercise of body and spirit, similar to yoga. A quintet of Arab flute players entered the audience chamber at a clap of Mured's hands, always ready, beginning their exotic music.

The girl never smiled. Not once. Yet she twirled in and out of

Vlad's reach, wrists tinkling with bangles and bracelets, draping her slender, bare arms about his neck, his shoulders, coquettish as a doxy. It was this sexy reserve she bore that attracted Vlad. His eyes darted away from her bare belly and upper thighs, unable to resist returning. (Her washboard stomach caused Vlad's eyes to bulge!) Her legs were smooth, shapely; deliciously long. She looked down at him, a thin, gauzy-grey veil hanging over her eyes from a headband. Showing no inhibition, she shook her derrière in Vlad's face; arms raised, her upper and lower back bare. Vlad felt sure he would suffer a heart attack soon. His heart felt as if it were about to explode! A galloping race horse was thumping along in his chest cavity as he watched bells jangle around the *houri's* waist.

At last, the dance ended. The girl sank down onto her cushions, bowing, eyes hooded as the flutes trailed off in a discordant note. Sultan Mured clapped, applauding. Vlad was too stunned to do anything but stare. He'd forgotten completely about his bruises, his fat, bloodied lip. The music was alien to Vlad's ears. Mystical, Arabesque, reminding him of scorching deserts and Sahara sandstorms, hooded, veiled nomads, palm trees. Suddenly he felt incredibly thirsty.

"Ah, I see by the tent in your tunic that you are impressed and that you've never had a woman," Mured chuckled. "Perhaps I shall send her to you someday, if you behave and do my bidding." Mured would never do that. She was HIS love slave. So obedient and submissive, submitting to his every whim. Pain, pleasure. The Oriental arts of love. He had taught them to her as a virgin slave girl of thirteen, eleven years ago, breaking her in himself and sharing her with his soldiers upon her capture. Since then she had known no other.

Or so Mured assumed.

The houri's dark brown eyes grew wide, unbelieving. She had no idea the young rogue's age, but had no wish to be mated with him against her will. She'd heard of Vlad's reputation at Egrizöz, how he'd beaten and then tortured a Persian sentry who'd made the mistake of attempting to initiate unnatural relations with the youth one night in a holding cell. He was a crude barbarian; God only knew what he might do to her. It wasn't that she was afraid of becoming pregnant. That was impossible. She had been taught the ancient secrets of preventing conception (from one amongst the Sultan's seraglio). But she had known after Mured had taken her so roughly eleven years ago that she was barren now.

The Sultan grew weary of Vlad's moody silence, ringing a little silver bell summoning his guards. They dragged Dracula to his feet, taking him from the great audience chamber.

Chapter Three

The lashings began at dawn. Vlad's cries filled the courtyard, echoing among the pillars and cloisters of the former Dominican monastery of St Mary the Virgin in the middle of Sofia, surrounded by Sultan Mured's lavishly-sculpted palace walls. No monks resided here now (a decided minority, amongst an Orthodox populace), not since the fall of Bulgaria in 1371. Vlad Dracula's back was bare, bloodied; a whipping far worse than the short thongs the forge-masters had wielded. A powerful, muscular Indian Muslim lashed Vlad's back with a maniac's devotion, wielding a six-foot-long horsewhip. The rebellious Romanian was tied to a whipping post, his arms held high; bound at the wrists to the pole's iron ring.

His younger brother Radu was forced to watch, as were all the Western prisoners for the first hour as a warning against mischief. After a while, the dirt courtyard emptied, leaving Vlad alone with the whipmaster. The flogging lasted for three hours. Blood flowed from his lacerated back in a steady stream. This was not the first time Vlad had been subjected to the whip. Nor would it be the last.

At last, the Indian whipmaster finished his assigned number of lashings, rolling up his brutal implement with a professional's care. A strap more or less would mean his immediate execution at the Sultan's order. Pity. He would have loved whipping this white boy to death. The Sultan's chancellor stood by, watching and counting. Rajah was not to be trusted, had more than once killed men with the force of his whip. He had earned an unsavoury reputation lately as a killer of helpless men, driven beyond his allotted number of lashings. His last victim had been a slave girl convicted of stealing. (Usually thieves had their hand cut off.) Sultan Mured was already considering liquidating Rajah; his usefulness had passed.

Vlad hung to the post, gasping, sucking in burning lungfuls of air. He sagged to his knees, sweat pouring down his forehead, stinging his eyes. The Indian whipmaster seized Vlad's unruly hair, berating him loudly.

"You not murder again, hm? You not allowed to kill men, you hear me? You learn toe line, hm? You keep nose clean, or next time I lash you with bullwhip till you die. Hm? You regret killing Muslim? Hm?" The Indian jerked Vlad's head with each sporadic sentence. His Turkish was poor, stilted. Vlad nodded, utterly broken, scalding tears squeezing from his eyelids.

"Oh it okay, you need not cry, little bawl baby," the whipmaster taunted.

Vlad blinked back tears, leaning forward with a fearsome scowl. "When I am *Cnéaz* (Prince), whipmaster, I shall impale you alive; no matter where you are, I will hunt you down, shall impale you and a thousand other Turks as if on a forest of stakes."

The whipmaster laughed, cuffing Vlad across the head. "You dreaming boy, you not find me, I travel well."

"But you shall die horribly."

The whipmaster laughed again, strolling away.

A sudden movement from the cloisters caught Vlad's attention. A bevy of veiled Muslim women draped in black came from the pillared cloister area, toting pails of warm water, soap, and sponges. They had been ordered by Sultan Mured's palace guard to clean and dress Vlad's wounds, lest he die of infection or gangrene. Prince Dracul would not be pleased if that happened. For sure, his allegiance would be lost and war assured. Mured would prefer gaining Europe through peaceful means. That fool Pope Nicholas V even hinted to him last autumn that he might be willing to crown Mured as Holy Roman Emperor if he converted to Christianity. Mured was seriously considering feigning conversion as a means to world power. Not that he would convert to Christianity. It was a weakling's religion, and hypocritical. They preached peace and brotherly love, yet did they not take the Crusades to Islam, putting Allah on the defensive? Did they not torture and burn Jews? Mured despised Jews as much as they did, but he did not abuse them. He was shrewd enough to realise that it was their brisk trade which kept Islam afloat. Nor were his people allowed to drink alcoholic beverages; one of the main reasons why Christians hated and murdered Jews was because Christians were driven wild with idle rumours and superstition in their sinful taverns. The Jews, Mured realised, were better merchants because they did not spend all their money on whiskey and whores.

The women untied Vlad's wrists, letting him slip to the ground; gently washing the gouts of congealed blood from his back. He began to doze. A surprising, casual caress touched his cheek; soft, sensual. Vlad opened his eyes, blurred with fatigue. He could have sworn that this heavily veiled woman cradling his head in her lap whilst she washed his upper shoulders was the Sultan's premier concubine. Her eyes were large, dark, full of compassion, very much like 'hers'. Vlad raised his left arm in brazen curiosity, brushing her breast lightly with the tips of his fingers. She slapped his hand away, snapping a command. Vlad had forgotten her name already. The pain had made him delirious.

They hauled him up now, carrying him back to his isolated, subterranean prison cell. At least half a dozen women, taking him unescorted down into the labyrinthian prisons below the Caliph's palace. Fluttering, flickering torches failed to reveal their faces beneath their linen veils. *'Were they Turks?'* Vlad wondered. *Saudis? Moors? Iraqis? Iranians? Hindus?* Or possibly white women: Magyar, Armenian, Vlach, Russian, Serbian, Bulgar, Serbian, Moldavian, Slovak?

He wondered if they were good lovers. Or perhaps they were harem girls? Vlad could tell by the shape of clothes that they were young, comely. Maybe even beautiful. He began to despair of his ever having a woman, left down here to languish in Turkish dungeons, to starve to death perhaps.

The houris installed Vlad in his cell, leaving him on his side atop his straw-filled pallet, never a word from their mouths. They would not have spoken Romanian anyway; certainly not Dacian. Damned if he would speak Turkish, lest they inform the Sultan. Vlad had already broken his rule twice today; first in hated, feared Dacian; then in Turkish (which he wasn't supposed to be able to speak!). His back ached, though the linen bandages helped some to curb the excruciating pain. At peace, he closed his eyes, slipping off into a peaceful, erotic dream.

****

The ghazis put him to work in the palace courtyard, pushing a long, heavy wooden beam which operated the grindstones of the portable mill used to grind cornflour. The Romans had first invented (supposedly) the method for grinding flour in deep stone basins with cogs and gears almost two thousand years ago in Pompeii. Every day, day after day, Vlad would push the beam like a donkey, a slave, getting immense pleasure from watching the cogs, shafts and gears below going about their daily business, grinding, hammering, pulverising the corn kernels into delicious cornmeal. Every day while the ghazis weren't looking he would slip his hand into the basin with the cogs stationary, plunging a handful of sweet cornmeal into his mouth. All the more exciting and dangerous since he knew the penalty for doing so was decapitation of the hand for dipping into Sultan Mured's jealously hoarded larders.

Vlad no longer cared. Life ceased to have meaning. He'd been here almost four months now and snowfall was surely just days away, days which seemed to whiz by without slowing for mere, imprisoned mortals like him to catch up. Life had been like that for the last six, lonely years. He knew not what day it was. Or what month. Or what year for that matter. He'd long ago lost track. The Muslims, save for Ramadan, celebrated no holy days that he was familiar with. He missed the giving of presents at Christmas, had missed them these past six years, missed the smouldering Yule logs, holly, mistletoe, lovespoons *(llwycar)* given to a sweetheart.

Nor had he seen the girl he desired so. Not for many weeks. He was sure she had been sent to him as a sign, that *Arianhad* had given him Her divine favour. Vlad guessed the girl was entertaining Sultan Mured in his boudoir. That fat, lewd, bearded, brainless Muslim. Debauching her. Nor was Vlad pleased with the news that his stupid younger brother was learning to speak Turkish and was developing a brisk, and if rumour would have it, none too natural relationship with the Sultan's seventeen-year-old son and heir. Nasty rumours were circulating about the palace of the heir-apparent's 'liking' for boys. Some even whispered Mehmed was a homosexual.

Suddenly Vlad halted, head turning along with the lounging ghazis as the Sultan entered the courtyard. A faithful following of veiled women trailed into the cobbled precincts. *'These must be Mured's harem,'* Vlad thought to himself excitedly. One particular, winsome beauty caught his eye; her face only partially veiled. Was it her??

She laughed, closest to Mured's side. Her throaty, pealing laughter thrilled Vlad the Devil. He wanted her. Wanted her badly. Wanted to debauch many of Mured's promiscuous harem girls. Belly dancers. Oh, yes! Belly dancers. She was a belly dancer. A Greek goddess held captive by the Emir. Vlad twirled an unlikely scenario around in his mind of rescuing her, like the ancient bards of old, sweeping her away to his Transylvania mountain fastness-

But he was dreaming.

As the procession neared, the bodacious, laughing *houri* looked Vlad's way as he prudently began pushing the heavy, oaken beam lest he incur another lashing. His broad back was already crisscrossed with nasty white scars, completely naked except for a loincloth.

Their eyes met, held. She looked away, shame flooding her eyes. She was ashamed of being the Sultan's whore! Perhaps she was a slave girl? Not a willing *houri*?

The Sultan and his extensive harem moved on, dozens of them, pointing out various intricate details etched on corbels and cornices of the former Dominican monastery. They paused as they gaped, astonished, at the refectory's malevolently crouching, leering gargoyles; oriel windows upheld with pitch-blackened, wood brattices; or the quatrefoil, tri-lobed, arched, gothic windows of the despoiled chapel. The brass bells had been removed from the bell-tower. Shapely caryatids of wimpled nuns had been carved into suggestive, limestone cloister pillars. Original stained-glass was still intact inside the clerestory's traceried, rose, east window, a colourful feast for sore eyes. High above, on sorry-looking ramparts, rounded Slavic battlements guarded the old city, presenting an ominous vista to visitors approaching from the north. The monastery had been fortified eighty-seven years ago against marauding Bulgars upset with the monks' tyranny—and to hold off invading Turks under Orkhan the Glorious. The imperial city's derelict, Byzantine walls showed signs of crumbling, insidious decay. Lengthy, widely spaced, rectangular murder holes menaced the Sultan and his zenana, set into the monastery's roof line for pouring molten lead or boiling water onto unarmoured Bulgarians enraged about the high taxes and tithes (crop dues) the Dominicans demanded for their Holy services.

Vlad's younger brother Radu entered the expansive courtyard with his new friend Mehmed Çelebi—the Sultan's son. They chatted, discussing various Scriptural similarities between the Bible and the Koran. Mehmed Çelebi insisted the Koran was the Book of Truth. Radu was too easy-going to disagree, nodding his head at Mehmed's insistence. Vlad watched, gritting his teeth, hate and jealousy growing in his heart like a cancer, helpless as his naïve brother was being taught the Koran for what Mehmed Çelebi insisted was for the good of the Wallachian people. They would, after all, be converted Muslims soon, wouldn't they?

Over my dead body, the young princeling rankled.

Vlad watched in disbelief as, surreptitiously, the Sultan's handsome, eldest son's hand strayed to Radu's buttocks. At first Radu recoiled, but he had no constitution to resist. "Stop it!" Radu snapped aloud, fearing Mehmed's wrath. But no one else was watching, their eyes glued to a hectic dice-game in the sandpit.

The Sultan's son steered Radu toward the cloisters, his intent obvious now. The holy men raised their eyes to Allah, sickened, calling a hundred feet above from the towering minarets.

Vlad cried out.

"Radu!! Do not go with him! I order you, as your elder brother, resist! In the name of our father, Radu! Remember Wladislaus Ddraig, Radu!"

To no avail. Radu glanced back from the cloisters, afraid, given a shove by Mehmed Çelebi as he stumbled into the shadows, fearing Vlad's implacable wrath, his father's wrath. No one else understood, for the exchange had been shouted in Dacian dialect. They stared at Vlad with bewilderment, however.

The ghazis began to flog Vlad's back with leather thongs, ordering him back to work. There was nothing he could do. Disgusted, he pushed on the capstan beam once more.

While the surprised *houri* looked on, puzzled; her expression thoughtful.

Come nightfall, they shoved Vlad back toward his cell, first taking him to the mess-hall—allowing him to change back into his regular clothes beforehand. One thing at least: the prisoners were well fed. Each night they assembled in a great barrel-vaulted hall, preparing for their once-a-day meal. By sundown, they were drooling in anticipation of the generous rations of sweet corn (a newly discovered, and jealously hoarded, food staple from beyond the oceans), jellied beef, mutton, and pork, which the cooks piled into deep iron bowls. The Mohammedans had no use for the multitudes of hogs the Bulgarian populace raised, putting it to use to feed the silly Western prisoners; like Jews, Muslims were forbidden to eat pork. 'Twas often joked in Wallachia that the Sultan's captives were better fed than Romanians. Perhaps they should offer Mured the Wallachian crown? Vlad Dracul wasn't exactly delighted with these half-baked suggestion/jokes (tending to impale his detractors). Like his namesake son, it was the Magyar and Saxon settlers of Transylvania Dracul hated most. They detested him equally in turn. Their taxes were double those of full-blood Romanian peasants, though to be fair, many Saxons were wealthy burghers.

The hall was stuffy. Sweaty. Exhausted men wiped sweat from their brows, discussing the day's gossip or the next unmeant escape-attempt strategy. They had no intention of attempting to escape. Death would be the immediate result if captured. Vlad knew not one of them had the guts.

The guards had at least allowed Dracula to dress in his original raiments; sparing Vlad the humiliation of entering the mess hall in a mere loincloth.

Radu sat across the table from him, pale-faced, avoiding his brother's cold stare. Vlad tapped on Radu's metal bowl with his spoon, drawing his attention.

"Radu. Radu!" he hissed aloud. "Remember what father said?"

Radu nodded, his eyes aloof. The hall was crowded, noisy. The massive table greasy. Torch smoke burned the diners' eyes. Everyone was talking at once.

"Radu. Radu!" Vlad leaned forward. "Keep away from Mehmed Çelebi, you hear me? What were you two doing today?"

Vlad dared not speak in Dacian, not here, lest he attract the others' bewildered frowns.

Radu blanched, then blushed deep-red. He began to cry. Tears squeezed from his eyelids, rolling down his cheeks. He wiped them away angrily. "Nothing," he blurted, too fast.

Vlad shook his head, seizing Radu's hand. "What happened, man?"

Radu balked, pulling in vain. Shame filled his brown eyes, unable to meet Vlad's scorching green gaze.

"I see in your eyes what has happened," Vlad said in disgust. He dipped his spoon into his own steaming bowl, taking a mouthful of hot, delicious creamed corn and pork. "Mehmed Çelebi will die."

Radu shook his head vehemently, seizing Vlad's linen sleeve. "Do not touch Mehmed Çelebi, Vladislaus. Sultan Mured will kill us both if you lay a hand on him!"

Vlad shrugged, eyeing Radu with uncertainty. "Keep away from Mehmed. Do what you must. To die is better than to be sullied. You are not a woman, you are a man. Are you not?"

Radu nodded, defeated. He had no belly for conflict. He wished he could study his Scriptures and be left alone. He wanted to be a monk, but hadn't the courage to ask his father. Or his stepmother. She would scorn him for sure. A monk was not a manly profession.

Also their father had strictly forbid either Vlad or Radu to strike up friendships with Turks. No need to worry about that, Radu thought bitterly to himself. His relationship with Mehmed had gone irreversibly beyond friendship. His buttocks still hurt. He could taste the Muslim's semen in his mouth. Radu would never tell Vlad he was raped. Vlad would kill him. Plain and simple. He had no sympathy for cowards. Death before dishonour was Vlad's motto.

Vlad knew of Radu's desire to be a monk. He had told him so. He had insisted Radu ask his father for permission to become a monk. Radu had balked. Part of Vlad's concern was for Radu's own well-being (not all monks were monsters). Another was to assure his own succession to his father's throne should he and Mirçea come to blows—for there was often no love lost between brothers. Radu would be a mere puppet, dancing to Mured's wishes like a marionette on a string. Vlad pondered Radu's predicament. He had a vague sense Radu had been raped. But he didn't know for sure. Funny, the Muslims—like Christians—had a strict death penalty for homosexuality, but apparently it didn't apply to the wealthy. His fellow inmates had confided to Vlad that homosexuality was rampant amongst Muslims. It seemed the more puritanical they were, the more jaded their perversions. He'd heard the same of certain Christian sects who endorsed celibacy. Vlad knew one thing: if any of them approached him, he'd kill them. And if Mehmed had shamed Radu, Vlad would personally strangle the Muslim with his bare hands; slowly, painfully, delightfully. Vlad savoured his meal, enjoying the thought, replaying it over and over again in his mind like some exotic machine from the future.

The meal over, the prisoners were shuffled back to their individual cages. Vlad sat on his cot, listening to the steady drip of water from a nearby cistern. The earthen prison dripped water like an icy cavern. He wondered how cold it would be here in winter. Very cold. Prayed he might be set free by then. Not bloody likely. Vlad knew his father's heart like his own. Dracul hated Turks. It burned his soul to have to be the Sultan's sworn man. Dracul had kissed the Caliph's hem like most other east European princes. He and Vlad thought alike, the same ambition beating in their hearts. He had often said Vlad might make a better ruler than Mirçea, for, though Mirçea was a fine warrior, he often lacked resolve. Lacked ruthlessness. Vlad also knew his father would not hesitate to war against the Turks if he felt they threatened his borders, his Principality, even with Vlad and Radu their prisoners. They were expendable, he knew that. There were two younger brothers, Mihail and Andru, 10 and 12 respectively. Vlad's four sisters he'd barely recognised when he had visited Castle Brân this spring: Irena (4), Stephani (6), Anna (12) and Elizabeth (15). Vlad's stepmother, Caltuna, was only twenty-five, would bear more sons. Mihail and Andru were hers (three others had died recently, two in battle).

Exhausted, Vlad lay back on his cot, slipping off into dreamland.

****

9 December, 1447 AD

A new slave was put to work on the cornmill's beam. Vlad was hustled off to the royal training grounds to prepare for his induction into the Sultan's imperial Army of God (the much vaunted Janissaries). Sultan Mured had no intention of surrendering Vlad to the Prince of Wallachia. He would rather have him fight against Dracul! Shocking news had just reached Vlad from one of his fellow prisoners conscripted into the Janissary corps. His father had, half-heartedly, declared war on Islam two weeks ago, ignoring the Papal Legate's admonishments and threats of renewed excommunication, attacking the Sultan's troops inside Romania's borders with a large force of allied Moldavian, Hungarian, Wallachian, Albanian and expatriate Bulgarian regular infantry, along with a mixed cavalry of Norman adventurers and German *ritters*. Dracul's son Mirçea and the Hungarian viceroy of Transylvania, Ion de Hunedŏara, had led the attack; well-armed, mounted, with Italian bascinet-armour and Transylvanian mountain ponies. The Sultan's ghazis had been taken unawares, fleeing in disarray before the victorious coalition. The Turks fled across the border, crossing the swollen Danube, forced to abandon a goodly sum of gold and artillery.

Actually, Prince Dracul had been reluctant to assault the Turks, being egged on by his own son and allies. Dracul had refused to join battle himself until seeing the results of the mêlée.

But the Ottomans had soon returned; crossing the Danube once more with a formidable host and plenty of reinforcements and new, terrifying artillery. Monster cannon. Dracul's pikemen, caught alone in a skirmish near the Iălomita river in early November, and utterly routed, were later knocked out in a single barrage of cannon at the second Battle of Kosovo. An entire regiment of kernsmen had been destroyed on those windy Albanian plains. The Prince of Wallachia had artillery of his own, but it paled in comparison with Mured's gigantic, roaring, iron cannon. The moneylenders, armourers and gunmakers of Italy, Austria, and France refused to lend additional artillery, armour, or gold until existing arrears were put to right. Dracul had neither the resources nor time to hire either foreign armourers or to beg Swiss moneylenders for gold or silver. Indeed, Dracul had run out of time. His mercenaries soon deserted in lieu of payment. King Ladislas of Hungary, having lost most of his own mercenary army in battle to the Turks in Hunedŏara's brave but foolhardy assault, refused to declare (official) war on Turkey. The Western Holy Roman Emperor, Sigismund, was busy burning heretics in Austria and Poland. The Russians stayed neutral. They had their hands full with the Tartars. Should Dracul's outnumbered Romanians make headway against the Turks, they might throw in their lot. Should Wallachian resistance crumble the Muscovites would close up like clams, their only worries to defend their own distant borders around the fiefdom of Kiev.

Prince Dracul's army had been utterly decimated at the Battle of Kosovo, having rashly taken the offensive against Islam far to the south but greatly misjudging the size and strength of Mured's forces in occupied Serbia. His only remaining ally was fellow Prince Stephen (acting on behalf of his ailing father, Bogdan II) of Moldavia. (Of course this loss only reawakened old memories of another disastrous, and more famous, defeat on those same hotly contested plains almost one hundred years earlier.) Together, they watched their peasant foot soldiers slaughtered like pigs in a corral, run down on the vast plains of southern Wallachia upon the haggard remnants' return. Many deserted. More fled to the Transylvanian Alps to fight another day. In the lofty, misty Dinŭ Pass, eastern Transylvania, Vlad Dracul's dreams were dashed forever, his remaining forces destroyed by Sultan Mured's warriors of God; the ghazis, Azabs, sipahis and Janissaries feared nothing, least of all death, for they were promised immediate Salvation at death in their holy Jihad against the infidel.

Prince Stephen offered terms in early December.

With only an elite band of retainers and his immediate family, Prince Vlad Dracul took refuge in his modest Teutonic castle at Braşov, high up in the Carpathian Alps. It was not much of a fortress; a mere, rectangular watchtower (attached to an annex) with thin walls within an older, Norman-style shell keep on a low motte. (Mound.) Its only real defence was the great spur of rock it rested on. More commonly known as Castle Brân, former Teutonic fortress built in 1231 by the Order of Königsberg, site of Dracul's demise and illustrious, half-mad son's historic debut.

Vlad Dracul had wanted to build a larger, stronger castle, but it seemed his time had ran out.

Indeed, it had.

****

Young Vlad was handed a mighty Dalmatian pole-axe for his first lesson, its crescent steel gleaming. It had a monstrous curve to its axehead; sharp, spiked, deadly. 'Twas a lengthy weapon, at least four feet long. The seasoned ghazis juggled it as if it were a stick, laughing at Vlad's awe. They showed him how to hold it, how to handle it as they did. They were glad to show a Westerner their considerable military techniques. At least on this, Vlad could find a common interest with the Turks, for he shared an equal desire to conquer and a strong fascination with weaponry of all kinds. Only his intentions were somewhat different from what they had in mind.

Vlad was lucky to be alive. When he had first heard the news of his father's rebellion, Sultan Mured 'The Destroyer' had summoned Vlad to his marble audience hall, explaining the conditions on which Vlad were held. One of those, Mured explained, was Vlad's immediate execution should the Prince of Wallachia disobey. However, he explained, he'd become fond of young Vlad Dracula, allowing Vlad to have the honour of joining his imperial army to fight his own countrymen. A fate worse than death.

The ghazis of Sofia sat cross-legged now as they watched Vlad show off his formidable prowess with the staff and pike, defeating some of the finest pikemen in the city. Vlad was merciless; pummelling his opponents till they were on their knees and bloodied.

None could match his mastery of the awesome Iron Age-style, Dacian broadsword (a birthday gift of his father's). The Turks preferred short, slender, cut-and-thrust sabres, cutlasses, scimitars, or rapiers. Vlad was an expert with his father's short Dacian pole-axe, a forgotten art.

Many of the ghazis present were sheiks; they wore white, Arab-style headcloths banded with a black strap. Others wore turbans. Western converts to Islam usually wore neither (though Albanians donned the ubiquitous *fez*). Many were present. Vlad hated them. Would that he could swing his handy pole-axe in an arc and dismember them all.

The warriors of God slowly drifted away to their harems or alcohol-less taverns to watch the belly dancers. A few stayed behind, watching the odd fisticuff or brawl.

One of those was Mehmed Çelebi.

Radu was also present, at Mehmed's side at his insistence. Vlad was not pleased. Today he had just turned eighteen, feeling manly. Proud. Dangerous. He sported a virulent, black moustache, drooping down his chin. Vlad wore a scarlet cloth tied around his forehead like a renegade. A knee-length, dark brown, sleeveless linen tunic and black leather jackboots. No frivolous Norman tights. They were for namby-pamby, spoilt foreign town-dwellers. Bearded foreign devils.

Truly, he wore the look of a brawny barbarian well, his iron biceps and calf muscles sun-bronzed and bulging.

Vlad tossed Radu a staff in jest. Radu had no wish to cross staffs with his elder brother in front of an audience, albeit small. Mehmed Çelebi however was not so shy. He took the staff from Radu's hands, giving Vlad a challenging look with dark brown, menacing eyes. He dearly wanted to bash this Romanian popinjay's head in. Was determined to do so.

Vlad saw his chance to wreak vengeance on this homosexual who hung around his little brother like flies to manure. He exchanged glances with Radu, ignoring his warning signal. Vlad's green eyes sparkled with unholy wrath, eager to bring this stinking, bearded Muslim to his knees. Only a few ghazis and servants lingered in the cobbled courtyard to watch the fight.

Mehmed and Vlad jockeyed for position, greedy for the best possible spot of earth to brace their legs. They circled each other ominously inside the hard-packed sandpit. The mismatched youths eyed each other with smiles of ill-will, each anticipating the drubbing of the other. Vlad swung first. Missed. Mehmed, clad in iridescent robes of magenta and mink's fur, his effeminate fingers sparkling with gaudy, precious stones, danced in a circle, egging him on, unwilling to commit himself.

Their staffs began to hammer in earnest.

The Sultan's son was good. Fast. Lightning fast. Dracula's equal. But he lacked Vlad's brute strength and cunning, surprised only to find himself put on the defensive once more. Vlad's intention was only to beat the Turk into a bloodied pulp.

A rare shot caught Mehmed on the chin. Then another. And another. He felt Vlad's blunt staff butt-end him in the lip and cheek, his head jerking back in pain, flicking off the heir-apparent's gold-silk turban in the process. Mehmed was exhausting fast. He'd received a nasty cut on the lip and a gash just below his left eye, both bleeding profusely. His legs failed to brace in the correct position, taking on the stance of an amateur. Suddenly Vlad pounced, catching the Turk by surprise, choking the surprised Mehmed from behind with his staff after he'd drummed a tattoo on the Muslim's head, back, and shoulders for a solid minute.

"You don't want Radu as your bum buddy now, do you, Mehmed?" Vlad hissed in Mehmed's ear. "Now do you? Do you?!"

The heir-apparent choked, gagged, coughing as tears rolled down his cheeks. Mehmed was as much surprised to hear Vlad speak in Turkish as he was to be defeated by him! Vlad jerked. Jerked again. He spoke in Turkish which his unknowing tutors had taught him well, advising the Turk of his immediate demise.

"Enough!" The court physician had witnessed the confrontation, was not impressed by this show of brute force. This was not a jovial grudge-match between honourable ghazis, this was a vendetta. And the Sultan would be most displeased to learn that his beloved, eldest son had been beaten like a dog by a Romanian prisoner. Mured's wrath would be directed toward Mehmed.

Two reluctant, muscle-bound ghazis broke up the one-sided match as Mehmed's red face began to turn to a sickly blue. They hustled Vlad back to his prison cell while Radu looked on, proud of his big brother, vindicated. He stalked away, avoiding Mehmed's company.

Vlad sat in his cold, dark, earthen prison cell, glowing with satisfaction. His only regret was that he hadn't been able to finish the job. Mehmed would know better next time than to cross his shadow. He waited now for the retribution.

****

The retribution was not long in coming.

The same mad whipmaster lashed Vlad's bare back, laughing, drawing blood with his bullwhip. Only nineteen lashes had Rajah been allotted. Any more and his victim would most likely die of heart failure or loss of blood. Finally, the whippings over, the servants carried Vlad back to his cell. Deep lacerations crisscrossed his broad back, scars for life. The mysterious women-servants had once more bandaged the Devil's back, leaving him alone, in pain. In misery. Vlad sucked at air as if he were standing on the moon.

He could not lie down on his cot.

Vlad stood gripping the chilly iron bars for hours. Day passed into night. Outside, cold winter winds began to howl, the first December blizzard. He could hear it raging to a tempest; temperature dropping alarmingly by the hour. Vlad hugged his single wool blanket around his shoulders, his fingers numb, body shivering. He began to doze, head drooping to his chest, vaguely aware of the sound of footsteps approaching stealthily down the dark corridor. Vlad opened his bleary eyes.

The footsteps were light, unlike the ghazis' noisy shuffle. Fascinated, Vlad perked his ears, eyes straining in the torchlit semi-darkness.

It was a woman.

She was unchaperoned. Vlad wondered at that, for Muslim women were to be considered prostitutes, fair game, if seen unchaperoned on the streets at night. But then perhaps she had taken the subterranean passage from the Sultan's audience hall. He wondered momentarily if she were a prostitute, come to ply her trade. Vlad wouldn't mind—though he had no money, if that's what she was after. Nor jewels. Alas, he was in no condition to bed a woman anyway. Unless standing up, propped against the bars.

The girl was tall, shapely, robed in starkest black. She was Vlad's height. Her face veiled. *'Why doesn't the vixen unveil herself?'* wondered Vlad, irritated. She set her fluttering torch in one of the empty wall sconces, turning to face him.

Slowly, she drew back her veil.

It was *her*.

Loose curls and tidal waves of satiny, brown tresses flowed from her restricting headcloth like rich lava. She tossed her hair, eyeing Vlad warily. He was still dangerous. Her large, dark eyes were moist, excited—afraid. She was Romanian, Vlad had known that from early on. She had that 'look'. She'd be literally skinned alive if she were caught alone down here with this dark, handsome, barbarian prisoner (and, reputedly, one of the Ottoman empire's deadliest incarcerates). She, a *houri* from Sultan Mured's jealously guarded imperial harem, Allah's Chosen Ones.

Vlad kept silent, unsmiling, lest the ghazis in the distant, outer guard chambers hear his distinctive, deep-throated voice. His parents and siblings had often teased him that he was a bullfrog. Vlad leaned his forehead against the freezing-cold iron bars, admiring this love goddess. Yet wary of her.

"You are Wallachian?" Foggy vapours emitted from the girl's lush, sensuous mouth.

She spoke in Dacian, a wonderful surprise to Vlad's ears. Very few of the Rom spoke the ancient tongue; Bulgarians, practically none at all. Vlad was proficient in Turkish, Latin, Romanian, Greek, German, and Hungarian (and was beginning to learn Russian as well), unknown to all except for his father's private tutor, Mihnea Drovösovich.

"Da."

"I, too, am Wallachian. Your name?"

Iesu (Jesus), Vlad thought to himself, *surely she hasn't forgotten my name already?* Everyone in Sofia must know his name, by now. The Devil—or the Devil's Spawn.

"Wlad Dragwla; Count of Bucovina and Trawsgylwanywr. My father is Prince Wlad Ddraigh of Wallachia—but surely you know that. And you?"

"I am Serena Wladöskövichesicördoba. I had heard," she ventured, glancing warily down the corridor, "that you were an imposter; needed to be certain, but your accent is unmistakable now, I can see that."

Vlad nodded, pleased. A Cimmerian *Szekler*—he could tell by her accent. She spoke a patois of some Moravian, highland dialect. He'd gone four months without knowing her name, trying in vain to recall what Mured had called her; tantalised now by this rare sight of her angelic face. She was so stunningly beautiful, Vlad could scarcely believe she was one of God's creations. Now that she was here in front of him, alone, he did not know what to say. Instead, he stared at his feet.

She was experienced in such matters, knowing just what to do. She was no virgin, as he was.

She placed her hand on Vlad's, gently stroking as he gripped the iron bars.

"I can see you are a wolf; need the freedom to run, to hunt. To mate." She leaned forward. "You want to escape, don't you? You want to reap Muslims like *Samháin* in a corn field. I can help you."

Vlad's lidded eyes popped open, snapping from her sensuous spell. "Da! But my father would be—"

"Your father has been dethroned, Wlad Ddragwla."

Vlad was stunned; he had not heard. This girl/woman must have access to some very privileged information. "When? Is he—"

"I know not. Know not where he is or whether he is alive or dead. As the Sultan's most prized *houri*, I naturally hear such things."

Vlad leaned closer, studying her. "You enjoy being a prostitute. Why?"

Serena's brown gaze turned to disbelief, reproaching. Her face remained emotionless.

"Enjoy??" She laughed aloud, hard, her brittle laughter echoing eerily in the dank dungeon. Vlad reached out quickly, covering her mouth lest the ghazis come storming from their chamber. The feel of her warm, soft lips felt good to his fingers.

"Shh!" Vlad hissed. "They will come." Serena glanced down the corridor, subdued.

"But you do enjoy being a whore, do you not?" Vlad persisted. "Or were you abducted, perhaps?"

"Oes," whispered Serena timidly. "I was abducted eleven years ago from *Yr Transylwanwr* Alps near Timişoara. My family was murdered in their hovel, then set alight. I watched them die." She looked away, tears forming in her eyes at that terrible memory, as if it were yesterday. She hadn't thought about them in years, had deleted the memory from her mind. As she had deleted the memory of thirteen ghazis brutally raping her, taking turns as she watched her parents' wattle-and-daub farmhouse burned to the ground.

"Are you a Muslim, then?"

Serena shook her head. "I am a Christian—privately, of course. One of Sultan Mured's favourite executions for Christians is crucifixion."

Vlad knew that too. "Why are you here? In the dungeons."

Serena paused, glancing down at her sandals then up again. "I have a proposal."

"And that is?"

"I would help you escape."

Vlad glanced down the passageway, unable to believe his ears.

"There is one condition."

"What condition?" Vlad asked.

"You must take me with you."

That hit Vlad like a ton of stones, jerking him back to reality.

"Out of the question," Vlad retorted, moving away from the steel bars.

Serena scowled, then covered her face with her veil. "Very well. Then you'll stay here, for you are not yet man enough." She headed toward the corridor, burning with helpless anger. Defeated.

She meant to take her life tonight.

"Wait." Vlad's voice stopped Serena in her tracks. "What do you suggest?" Smiling, Serena meandered back to the cage.

"A diversion. Can you climb walls?" she added with a conspiratorial whisper and smile, sweeping back her veil. "Are you willing to kill? I can provide you with dagger, rope, and tackle. We would both have to climb the city's fifty-foot walls, then run non-stop till daybreak."

Vlad pondered this for a moment, weighing their chances.

"You do understand, of course," Serena added, glancing down the hall, "that should we be caught our deaths shall be slow, horrible, Arabian torture?"

"I will fight to the last," Vlad boasted. "Will you do the same?"

Serena studied him carefully, impressed with this exclusively male camaraderie Vlad was offering. She nodded. "Yes. I have lived in this luxurious Turkish *Hades* long enough. I shall die for you."

"And I for you. That I swear by my father's Order of the Dragon oath."

With that, she gently kissed Vlad's frigid lips, surprising him. Serena glided away, disappearing down the corridor.

Chapter Four

Yuletide, 1447 AD

Serena slipped Vlad the dagger as she browsed among the crowded market-stalls of Sofia. His guards had been shuffling their prisoner toward the palace courtyard for his early morning weapon-drills, having to cross the hustle and bustle of Sofia's bazaars wedged between the former cloisters of the city's ransacked, abandoned monastery. Serena hid the oversized dagger in the folds of her black, flowing robes, clutching the hilt in her palm. She slid the sharp dirk down Vlad's tunic while shielding the sight with her robes, slender hand resting tantalizingly on Vlad's bare chest for a long moment, her breast to his shoulder.

Four days later, Serena hurled Vlad a heavy hook over the deserted nunnery walls of the separate nuns' dormitory, where the virgin nuns of Christ once offered up prayers to God and grew herbs for medicinal purposes. When the warriors of Allah sacked the great city, the nuns were raped and enslaved; those who'd fled in time escaped to Constantinople, safe for the time being behind the imperial Holy Roman city's stone-banded walls, that last bastion of Byzantium.

Vlad's guards had been dozing—Serena had been watching from afar, perched surreptitiously on the city's deserted inner wall, peering from behind one of the notched, Italianate merlons. He caught the heavy grapnel with one meaty hand, wincing, stuffing it in a crevice behind a large, snowbound rock shaded by larch and some dead, rust-brown, blackberry bushes.

Next came the rope itself. 'Twas a wintry Sunday night, Christmas Eve, when Serena, free from her duties at the Emir's private apartments, inched the rope down a wall of the trefoil castle keep of Sofia, nudging Vlad's hand as he celebrated Christmas half-heartedly in the bailey with numerous other prisoners, granted this one surprise wish at the last moment by Sultan Mured. Snow cloaked the cobbled courtyard, thick and hard as packed dirt. The night was bitterly cold. Well below ⁻20°C. (Measured by increments of ice, known to the ancients, but lost in antiquity.) The revellers blew warm air into their hands, rubbing them, holding their hands over a blazing Yuletide bonfire, the bailey crowded and noisy with drunken cheers. They conversed with slurred voices, exclaiming over the unusually warm, freakish weather experienced these past two months while muttering expletives about last week's sudden, heavy snowfall. Few understood each other, a multinational coalition of Serbo-Croat, Albanian, Slovak guerrillas. Chetniks.

Vlad felt the rough, hempen rope graze his hand, surprised and shocked to realise that Serena was inching the rope from an arched, third-storey window high above. He craned his neck, seeing no torchlight above—the girl was working in utter darkness. He stood against the rough, stone masonry of the massive keep, cloaked in shadows, his own cape, and darkness, rolling the thick rope up in his hands with his heart in his mouth, fearful one of the inebriated Slav prisoners or, God forbid, one of the bewildered ghazis who stood watching the celebrations in consternation might come and catch him red-handed.

They did not.

Vlad fumed from within, furious with Serena for taking such a daft risk. Tonight of all nights! He stashed the rope inside an arrow-loop's niche, praying none of the ghazis would notice it in the bright light of day.

Elated, Vlad neared the bonfire, unable to believe he'd not been caught. *'Not only was this belly-dancing harem girl beautiful, but she had brains and guts to match,'* he thought to himself. If she were of royal blood, and he not a prisoner, he would seriously consider marrying her. But she was a peasant. Pity.

The Christmas revellers retired late, finally herded back to their individual cells, thoroughly drunk, by the disgruntled ghazis.

"These Westerners must have shit for brains," Abn-Zadul Faud remarked to his fellow ghazi guarding the outer corridor.

"Yes. The demon alcohol has gone to their heads; makes these Caucasians either mischievous as billy goats, or submissive as sheep."

"Or women," Faud shot back with an uproarious laugh.

Vlad listened from his cell, gritting his teeth as the two Saudis exchanged rude jokes about Romanian, Bulgarian, Serb, Polish, Slovenian, Albanian, Lithuanian and Macedonian perverted sexual mores all night long. Vlad's jailbreak was slated for dawn. Not only was Serena beautiful, intelligent, and daring but she was also educated. At the Sultan's court, presumably. She'd tied a clever parchment scrap scribbled with instructions and crucial information about the city's layout, the Balkan mountains, and surrounding countryside onto the end of the rope which he'd prudently stuck down his tunic. Vlad's first task was to murder the two ghazis who now joked about Wallachian women. He looked forward to it. Immensely.

The plan was simple. Once he had been hustled out into the streets of Sofia early the next morning at first light, Vlad would tell the two guards he needed to piss. They would naturally push him into an alley so as not to offend the holy men and the women gathering in the bazaars. He had the dagger hidden in his boot, in a scabbard. Vlad would have to be quick, plunging his long blade into their hearts and stifling their screams. He had the speed and the strength to do it. And the element of surprise. But did he have the luck?

Serena would be awaiting him at the disused northern wall of the old, fortified citadel. They would have to climb the wall-walk undetected, shimmy down the other side and run for dear life. It was winter—the sun wouldn't rise for several hours. And it was also very cold. Most of the city would be asleep. Their only concern was to climb the rope quietly, lest the guards manning the watchtowers and minarets sound the alarm. Nobody would know of their escape for at least an hour or two. From there, it would just be a matter of how long Vlad and Serena could run before their lungs burst or hearts exploded. And how long till the Turks brought out the bloodhounds.

Or how long till they froze.

Vlad stayed awake in his cot, memorising the Bulgarian countryside he'd passed whilst in the wagon-train. There had been small peasant allotments and the odd horse farm. He cursed himself roundly for sleeping through much of the journey from Wallachia through northern Bulgaria. But all he remembered were miles of endless foothills and dry, barren steppes. He would have to steal a horse if he and Serena were to stay alive. Kill wild game for food and furs or die. And find a cave or an abandoned forest dwelling. Vlad wouldn't hesitate a moment to kill a Saxon forester, those scum who robbed his native land of trees, felling the sacred oak groves of his illustrious ancestors. (If Dracula, son of Dracul, had his way, they'd hang from the branches like offerings to the gods, those bloodthirsty and exacting Deities of old!)

For, once, all of these lands had been his people's domains; the mighty Cimmerians of antiquity, whose gigantic, earthen burial mounds, dolmens, quoits, henges, mazes, and hillforts had dotted the forested uplands of Macedôn, Alban, and Elyneeka (Greece) before their vandalism and destruction by the Newcomers, the free lands of *Y Môr Canol-Dir* (the Mediterranean) before the sons of Milós invaded Europa from the dreaded Russian steppe lands. Shattering the peace of the Ages.

Vlad woke before dawn. Reached down to feel the comforting blade hidden in his boot. Yes. It was still there. Not lost in a sandy courtyard somewhere, as he had dreamt. Vlad sat up quickly, hearing the tramp of ghazis come to haul him to the training grounds. He said a silent prayer for this hour of need: for strength, for luck, and for Serena who was at this moment climbing the steps to the poorly maintained bastion's outer wall-walk where she would wait behind one of the empty crates stacked beside the battlements, watching for Vlad's appearance.

The two Saudis strolled toward the end of the corridor where Vlad's prison cell was, their smoky torches flickering faintly in the inky darkness. A rattle of keys and sabres being drawn from their scabbards sounded nearby. The ghazis would take no chances. They never did. Vlad wondered uneasily how he was going to get close enough to kill them before one of them plunged a sabre into his back or cried out. They opened the cage door. Seized him by the arm and hurled Vlad into the hallway—no bother with protocol here. They were Saudi swine, known as such even by Turks and Iraqis, had no concept of civility. Probably nomads from the arid Sahara, paid to fight in Mured's army. Berbers, Bedouins.

Abn-Zadul Faud gave Vlad a vicious shove, pushing him down the corridor. Faud's partner guffawed, jabbing Vlad in the rear with his sabre. '*Just two more minutes,*' Dracula told himself, '*two more and I shall indeed reap these Saudis like Samháin reaping a cornfield.*'

Outside it was still dark. The rare torch flickered in Sofia's filthy, dung-splotched streets, the air calm, quiet. The two ghazis pushed Vlad toward the torchlit cloisters a thousand feet ahead, sabres at their sides. The three neared the empty horse-stalls and silent market tables adjacent a dark, forbidding alley. Clouds obscured the late December moon. Very little snow remained on the provincial capital's frozen, ploughed streets.

Serena stepped out from an alley.

She called out coyly to Vlad's guards as they passed, hoisting her black linen robes up her glorious leg, baring a tantalising, naked upper thigh, offering her favours. Taunting. She was only a cheap alley prostitute—but dearly exquisite! The two ghazis gaped.

She held a torch, revealing her charms.

'*So this is what she had in mind!*' Vlad mused feverishly, hand creeping down to his knee-high boot concealed beneath a black, silk cape in total darkness, unnoticed by the leering, nodding, awestruck ghazis.

One of them lurched towards her, spellbound in his lust. This would not take long—a quickie. Vlad had witnessed this before; the usual alley bump-and-grind. They knew not who she was, her face veiled in black, eyes drawn to Serena like zombies.

The first ghazi felt Vlad's blade thrust into his back like a red-hot poker. By the time Abn-Zadul Faud had his sabre raised, Dracula's bloodied dagger was buried in Faud's thumping heart, plunging to the hilt. "Die, you bastard," Vlad whispered menacingly, holding Faud's weakening right arm with a satisfied smile, denying the debauched Saudi the chance to strike back with his razor-sharp, curved sabre. Faud sank to his knees, mouth dropping in shocked disbelief. His dark brown eyes rolled once, then began to glaze. Blood trickled from the corner of his mouth, spreading into Faud's black beard. When Vlad withdrew his dagger from the dead man's heart with a jerk, a jet-spray of warm blood spurted toward his face, into his mouth.

The other ghazi lay groaning at the alley entrance, his left lung punctured. Slowly, Vlad picked up the man's sabre and leisurely plunged it through the Saudi's heart, his boot on his victim's throat while Serena looked on, mesmerised. She hadn't seen so much fun in years. Vlad's ruby-red lips stretched back from clenched, sharp eyeteeth in a vicious smile.

Serena grabbed one of the ghazi's arms, helping Vlad haul the dead man deeper into the dark alley, leaving him slumped against a wall behind a wooden crate.

She beckoned urgently, guiding Vlad down the unlit alley towards a wall-walk stair. He tucked the sabre (having taken the guard's sheath) through his waist belt. The murdered ghazis had been so entranced by the sight of her that they hadn't even shouted out or screamed as Dracula's dagger was pounded into them. Serena took Vlad's hand, dashing stealthily up the steep steps to a parapet thirty feet above, compelling him to silence.

There were no patrols up on the parapet. Vlad and Serena crouched in the shadows, out of sight of the holy men high above in the minarets and the guardsmen snoozing in the round, cone-capped Bulgarian towers. The Turks had no need to be on guard, for their nearest enemy of any significance was Byzantium, a hundred miles to the south. Ha! Enemy! The city of Constantinople's domains had been reduced from that of Empire to city-state, surrounded on all sides, from north to south, east and west, by the Ottoman Empire. Constantinople was now an unwilling vassal to the Sultan of Turkey, Emir of Egypt, and Caliph of Jerusalem, allowing the Turks to march unmolested across Roman territory to strike at the enemy. Marooned in a sea of infidels. The only thing protecting the Holy Roman citizens from plunder and enslavement were the mighty, stone-banded walls and square towers; impregnable, unbreakable. The only safe refuge for five hundred square miles. (And by far the strongest redoubt of its day.) Vlad had not always hated Byzantium; indeed, it had once been a model of freedom and tolerance to the Western world for centuries. Unlike the heretic-crazed, witch-haunted Germanies, France, Castile (Spain), and Scotland, the monks had no special control over the government; were not exempt from taxes and lacked both the central authority of a Pope and the freedom to excommunicate. But recently delegates had been making blasphemous overtures to Rome for reunification between Orthodox and Catholic. And had achieved a partial agreement in 1439, officially, if not actually, joining the two Mother Churches. So at last, the Roman citizens of Constantinople had refused to fight for Emperor Constantine Dragasus (the newly-crowned Emperor), to fight for Byzantium, the new—Christian—Rome of the East.

So now they paid their dues, and bided their time.

****

Vlad's lungs burned, aching. His powerful arms felt like they were carrying a 200-lb. sack of flour. Serena was not that heavy. Not nearly. But after carrying her exhausted body for over half an hour she felt like it. She'd collapsed from exhaustion after having ran at a break-neck pace through packed snow (following trails made by teams of horses) for four hours straight. The sun was just barely clearing the eastern horizon, ascending the distant Black Sea, and with it came surprising warmth. He and Serena had fled Sofia's red sandstone walls almost five hours ago, running non-stop, driven by fear and adrenaline. A heavy leather sack full of furs and flint slumped from Vlad's neck, hanging down his back. Tall wheatfields stretched across the Bulgarian prairies for as far as the eye could see, blinding in their golden glare. To the south, the Balkan mountains reared bluish-white crowns to a deep blue winter sky. The fields had not been harvested this year, the peasants massacred after the latest uprising put down by the Ottoman Empire/Islamic Caliphate. The Turks had not bothered to burn their crops. There was no need. The inhabitants were dead. The Ottoman satraps had a surplus of corn and grain in the south—the ghazis were not farmhands. Hard snow crunched beneath Vlad's boots. The air was cold this morning. Freezing. But he could tell it was warming quickly, for the crusted snow seemed to gleam in the distance. Frost still clung to the golden wheatstalks. With a little luck, the snow might melt today. So tall were the wheatfields that they came up to his chin, effectively camouflaging he and the slumbering Serena, slung over his shoulder like a sack of oats. He could not stop. Though he must. No sign of any shacks or hovels on the horizon (from what he could see overtop the billowing wheat stalks), just an endless sea of mouldy grain which did something mighty queer to Vlad's sinuses and lungs. Something he'd never experienced before. His nose refused to breathe. His lungs congested, as if with a cold. Vlad stumbled on, coughing, watery eyes itching as he ploughed through the cereal field.

Their escape had been very narrow indeed. The climb down the prickly rope on the other side of Sofia's walls had been extremely difficult. Vlad's arms had felt like they were going to pop out of their shoulder sockets. Serena had fallen the last ten feet, miraculously unhurt. Then they ran, under cover of darkness. Except for the odd morning star, they knew not which direction they were running. Were they heading south toward Turkey, straight into Islam's hands? Or west to Albania? Too dark to sight any forests. The Balkan mountains encircled Sofia like a shadowy amphitheatre. When the mists rose and the sun also, Vlad knew exactly which way to go. North. Romania. Home.

Chapter Five

Vlad's legs collapsed by nightfall. Serena was on her feet again, refreshed after nearly an hour's sleep. They dragged themselves to a sunken, overgrown pit near the edge of a field, shaded by two massive, hoary oaks growing on its perimeter. It was an ideal spot to hide out for the night, since they had crossed the shallow Iškur river twenty-four miles northwest of Sofia, the river-water temporarily disrupting their scent tracks should the tracking Turks' bloodhounds pick up their trail. The overgrown pit would provide excellent camouflage, full of ivy vines and brambles. Much of the snow had melted. Serena cleared a spot for them to lay, luckily avoiding the briar patches, poison ivy, stinging nettles. She had discarded her clumsy veil once they'd escaped Sofia's walls. It wouldn't matter if she were caught without it—she'd be put to death anyway. After her rape and torture. But Serena was used to that by now. She had no intention of being taken alive. She had a dagger hidden down her bodice.

Vlad collapsed into the pit, stumbling the last few feet down its steep, slippery, leafy incline. Serena slumped beside him, aching all over. Her sandaled feet hurt, felt like they'd been walking barefoot over hot burning coals. Blistered. She had wisely slit the length of her robes to facilitate easier running. Her knees ached.

Both she and Vlad felt they may die right there.

Vlad lay panting against Serena's shoulder, smiling languidly as the twenty-odd miles of gruelling Bulgarian prairie gradually eased off from his bones. He felt as if he were a hundred years old, running his last marathon. Vlad's feet had turned into benumbed pieces of Indian rubber. His eyes ached; dry, swollen. The congestion in his lungs had finally wore off once he and Serena had left the wheatfields behind in exchange for barley fields.

Cramps wracked his legs at midnight. Serena massaged Vlad's thigh muscles, then his calves. Had he any virility left in him he would have taken her ministrations as sexual advances. Which they were. But even Serena had no desire for anything but sleep. This was just a foretaste of what was to come once Vlad had recuperated. She owed him that much for her freedom, temporary though it may be. And she had plenty to teach the boy. Satisfied, Serena lay her head on Vlad's chest, drifting off into languid, erotic dreams.

****

Sunlight drifted through the leafless trees, down into the shadowy pit. It was daybreak. The scarlet sun had just cleared the horizon, squatting on the distant, unseen Black Sea like a fireball. Vlad woke with a start, feeling a heavy weight on his chest. *Succubi??* He moved his right arm tentatively, feeling Serena's sleeping form on top of him, huddled beneath a sable fur. Vlad gently caressed her clinging Muslim clothing, feeling her up, brazenly exploring Serena while she slept. Vlad touched her soft, fleshy buttocks, feeling his temperature rise. This was an unfamiliar, exhilarating, almost frightening experience for him. Yes, he was rejuvenated indeed. He groaned inwardly, bringing up his left hand to softly brush back stray tendrils of dark hair from Serena's face, tracing her cheekbone. He would not make the first move, wanted Serena to beg, to crave for him, not to offer Vlad her body as a whimsical favour as a master might throw a dog a bone.

Serena was stubborn. She would not wake up, though Vlad suspected she was already awake, could tell by the way Serena tensed when he brushed his fingers against her buttocks. Only the heavy black linen stood in the way of their ultimate consummation.

Serena was awake. She played dead, furtively smiling as Vlad's hand roamed her back. It was a new game to her, this playing hard-to-get. She liked it.

Vlad moaned, irritated. Frustrated. This was one game he didn't seem to be winning. Was she going to keep him waiting all day? Surely eighteen years was enough! Vlad certainly had no intention of waiting here all day just so the Turks could come and catch her and he in the act of lovemaking. He wrapped his arm around her neck, inhaling the pungent smell of Serena's wavy, silken hair. *'Was this bathed in rosewater?'* Vlad pondered to himself, marvelling. Yes. Rosewater. It smelt good.

Finally, Vlad sat up, disgusted. "Let's go," he muttered, jerking Serena's clothing. He glanced down in shock, realising he'd bared her naked, pink shoulder, tearing the hem. She sat up, sad-eyed and bewildered, placing her hand on Vlad's chest.

"Don't you want me?" Serena asked in a hurt voice; pouting.

"Yes, I do, but 'tis clear you want me not," retorted Vlad, his Devil's pride hurt.

"That is not true, young Wlad," Serena cooed with a husky,

voluptuous laugh, gazing into his eyes with scrutinising, rapturous longing. "I want you very much." She bit her lower lip seductively.

"You do?"

Serena nodded, smiling, pushing him back into the trampled, snowy ground with a coquettish grin.

"I know what you need," she whispered. "Are you a virgin or no."

Vlad balked, unwilling to betray such a confidence.

"Ah, yes." Serena removed her flowing garments with a flick of her wrist and a sudden twist of her body, baring her globular breasts and well-toned belly.

Vlad gasped, agape.

"Put your hand here," Serena instructed, "and here," guiding Vlad's uncertain hand as she whispered in his ear, cooing. "That's it." He watched in amazement as she slid his hand past her belly, down to her pubic hair. And then she kissed him.

Serena's body was like a goddess's. Her pale breasts were full, round. Her shoulders emaciated, but not overly so. Her alabaster cheeks were high, rosy; easily worth a knight's ransom. Any one of the Caliphates of India, Abyssinia, or Asia would pay an elephant's weight in gold for her, young Vlad posited—a fitting prize for a mogul's seraglio. Pouting, she leaned forward once more, giving him a tender kiss on the lips; sensuous, groaning with pleasure.

She took her time, working her way down to Vlad's belly; licking, kissing. She nipped at his navel. Serena unlaced Vlad's crimson tunic to the groin, taking his length between her breasts.

Vlad had not known such pleasures existed. Perhaps a kinky Turkish fashion? One thing for sure; these Turkish Delights were one of their best guarded secrets. The harem women must learn their trade well!

Next she straddled his waist, smiling with surprised pleasure as she rode Vlad like a horse. This was something forbidden by the Church! All the more reason to enjoy it. And enjoy it they did. Serena screamed shrilly, Vlad's hands gently wobbling her breasts, waking only the slumbering, grey jays flitting about in the dead, shrivelled grass above. She rolled her eyes in delirium, shuddering, quivering; licking her upper arm's soft flesh while sharing this mutually agreeable orgasm with Vlad the Devil. Holding this bodacious woman in place, his hands on her lower back in that most delicate of embraces, his breathing quickening, Vlad entertained the idea that he had died during the night and gone to Heaven. She placed her hands on his chest, rocking, smiling, laughing all at once. Consumed by a rapacious lust neither had ever known, they revelled in the glories of forbidden flesh; partaking of each other like fruit devoured in a bacchanalian feast. Vlad rolled her over, fully alive now, lips on breasts like cow's udders, aroused to boiling over like a geyser; taking her as Serena sought his mouth with a deep, passionate kiss, sucking the air from him.

The sun soon neared midday. They lay panting on furs upon the slushy, flattened, wintry grass, sweating, heedless of the danger. A multitude of sable furs, exotic Turkish rugs, and ermine undergarments protected their nude flesh from the cold, mushy ground. Vlad knew that if they didn't stay on the move he and Serena would soon lose their head-start over the Turks who were surely close behind now. But Serena was like an addictive love potion, ginseng or belladonna in human form; a succubus. A good succubus, though. Certainly not the type those crazy Germans imagined hung about in trees at night waiting for male love-slaves. Vlad chuckled. He had heard a story recently of a supposed succubus in the Germanies who allegedly had taken men's private parts during the night. When the town organised a posse, they had discovered the lascivious, local priest's privy member high up in a village tree inside a nest, guarding a clutch of eggs! His was the biggest in the village!

Vlad sat up, pulling his tunic over his head and slipping into his white, woollen breeches. He cautioned Serena to hurry, for they must depart soon. He and Serena had an agonizingly long trek before they reached Romania. Upon reaching Wallachia's border and its stork-inhabited delta swamps, they must cross the mighty Danube, a particularly wide, deep, and treacherous river—the biggest and longest in Europe after the Volga.

Serena was glowing. Beaming. She pinned her Arab clothes back in place, reluctant to leave this shady den of earthly pleasure. It was warm today, unusually balmy for December—*Christmas!*, of all days! The snow was melting. The Bulgarian steppes shimmered in an unnatural heatwave, hazy in the distance. It was a bad omen though—drought for summer. The Black Sea lay far beyond Vlad and Serena's vision, but each fancied they could smell it on the wind from over two hundred miles away (in fact, the nearby Iškur's riparian fauna), the tang of kelp, fish, oysters—a sensuous, shared illusion if nothing more.

Serena leaned forward, gave her man a tender kiss. In all her twenty-four years, she had never known a lover who respected her as he did, careful to excite her pleasures rather than heed his own in a selfish rut. Nor had she been subjected to the slaps and blows usual of her Muslim customers; or vile, degrading name calling and filthy language. Over the years she had come to enjoy it, had known nothing else. Until today. She knew not what love was. The Emir and his sheiks had insisted Serena learn the art of lesbian love, although she cared not at all for it. The sheiks (secretly forcing Serena to do their bidding, through blackmail) often entertained bevies of beautiful women, for six women were better than one. Serena did have to admit that the women were better lovers than the men, though she knew it was an unnatural vice.

Vlad and Serena crawled out of the overgrown pit, half-expecting a Turkish army to be rampaging in the fields. Not a living creature stirred amid the unreaped barley. A warm winter sun glared in their eyes, unusually bright and sunny after a day and a night in the shade. The cloudless sky was blindingly blue; a snow-blinding sensation which left one's eyes smarting.

"Come on, this way," Vlad murmured, taking Serena's hand as he started out. The day grew warmer. Humid. The fields had turned into quaking quagmires, with slush melting all around. No wind. Muggy as a day in tropical, West Africa. Sweat poured from Vlad and Serena's foreheads in salty streams as they ran, stinging their eyes. The fields of barley and millet seemed to grow taller with each mile.

Vlad wondered with unease how long till the Turks (on horseback, and with tracking dogs) would be heard far off in the distance; but, he supposed, it being a holy day, the Mohammedans may have declared it a day of rest.

By late afternoon, they'd discovered a great expanse of ripe corn, though half-ruined with frost. (Also known as *maize,* it was so recently introduced, that some of the rustics refused to grow it.) It was tasty to their palettes though, having not eaten in two days. Some of the corn was still sweet. *'This was December—shouldn't be this warm,'* Vlad thought to himself. Bad omen. True, he and Serena were dressed for frigid, Bulgarian winters, overdressed, perhaps, with long woollen cloaks and fox-fur gloves. But the considerable snowdrifts had melted overnight, as if a fireball meteorite had strayed into Bulgaria's atmosphere. This time of year it should be -20°C. There should've been a foot of snow on the ground and another compacted beneath, the stalks withered and spoiled, Vlad mused to himself. There had been very little cold weather this winter, however. Just as well. He and Serena would've frozen to death overnight in a steppe's blizzard. And real winter could still arrive, any day. The more he thought about it, the more Vlad was sure this escapade was doomed.

By nightfall, their thigh muscles ached. They couldn't go on. The Carpathian mountains loomed in the distance; cloud-cloaked, misty, looking deceptively near, though in reality over three hundred miles away across the nearby Danube, which Vlad and Serena hadn't even sighted yet. By rights, he shouldn't have been able to see them. Vlad's eyesight was keen as an eagle's, though; it seemed as if the Transylvanian Alps were beckoning, calling their lost son home. There were many rivers to ford, lakes to circumvent, grasslands to trudge across, mountain passes to climb and cities to avoid, like Amlăs and Tirgovişte, before Vlad and Serena reached his father's mountain stronghold near Braşov. IF his father was still alive.

An outcrop of rock loomed from the darkness, black against a moonlit winter sky. Neither Vlad nor Serena had any idea where they were. Cold stars twinkled high up in the heavens, millions upon millions of miles away. So cold. Yet so hot. Vlad had no idea what they were, other than God's guiding lights above the mountains. Had someone told him they were supernova suns, red/blue giants, bigger, hotter than earth's own gaseous Sun, Vlad would've laughed in his face. As would fifty million other Europeans.

He and Serena trudged up the slope, their legs screaming for rest. The outcrop of tufa stone grew steeper with each yard; rough, conglomerate, uneven rock ideal for breaking one's neck on while climbing. Studded with withered cypress and quack-grass clinging doggedly to odd patches of dirt, like the last flora of a dying planet. The mount was riddled with holes, fissures, scraggly, natural rock pillars. One wrong step and either one of them could have a broken ankle. They wished they'd brought a pine torch. It was getter colder. Clouds were beginning to move in.

A great, gaping maw near the outcrop's rocky, rounded summit spurred Vlad onwards. He was sure it was a cave. The way it swallowed darkness, black as space, horizontally shaped like a goose egg. (To him, it seemed like the forbidden womb of the world.) Serena clung to Vlad's hand tight, her energy flagging. He half-dragged her up the remaining slope. Together, they manoeuvred over the treacherous, narrow rock ledges, grasping tufts of dried, dead grass as they hauled themselves up to the waiting crevice.

Yes, *by Mohammed's bones!* it was, indeed, a cave. Not big, but room enough for the two of them. Tonight, they'd had great luck. They had passed a well-mulched field of beets and carrots some deceased peasant had improvised for the winter. Under normal circumstances it would've been a daft, laughable undertaking, for such vegetables couldn't possibly hold out through the winter. But who would have thought they'd have a winter like this. Over the last one hundred years the weather in eastern Europe had been fluctuating wildly, erratically. Drought one year, floods the next.

Exhausted, they flopped down onto the tiny cave's unforgivingly hard, cold, stone floor. They had no torches, nor rushlights. Not even flint, since Vlad had lost the precious stone chunks from his satchel somehow during he and Serena's mad trek. Serena dumped her own, makeshift gunnysack of carrots, cabbage, turnips and beets onto the rough, frigid floor, sprawling against Vlad's chest. She had cunningly improvised the sack by tearing a length of her over-long robes from her legs, bundling the vegetables in her arms. The cave was pitch dark. No moon nor stars above now. Vlad and Serena shivered in the cold, sweat chilling on their bodies as they held each other tight. They had run when they could. A brisk, north wind made the black night seem even colder than it was. He wrapped his arm around her, holding Serena close for warmth; nuzzling her ear. Enjoying this sudden, comforting intimacy. The heat from her body felt good. Vlad soon dozed. Surprisingly, neither felt any need to make love, their bodies and brains drained, exhausted. Neither was there a feeling of disappointment about this simple fact. They had all the time in the world. Or no time left. Serena lay back in Vlad's strong arms, pondering this strange, miraculous romance. *'Should she become his mistress if he demanded such?'* she wondered. Vlad would not—could not—marry her. He was royalty, she a peasant-girl from Timişoara. Serena wondered what she would do if ever she returned to Romania. She didn't think of her home in Transylvania as Romania, though it be what others called her homeland—i.e., the land of the Romans. She and all true Wallachs referred to it as *Tîr Dacw Coed*—Land Beyond the Forest. Serena was Dacian foremost, despised Latins. They were decadent: had not the ancient Romans and earlier Greeks imported slaves from Dacia and Galatia by the thousands? Young girls as unwilling prostitutes, brave strong men to be thrown to the lions during the Romans' gladiator games in coliseums brimming with 50,000 bloodthirsty spectators? No, Serena was no Romanian; she would consign all Frenchmen, Spaniards, Italians and those who proudly called themselves 'Romanians' into the pits of Hell if she could. And Turks. And Germans. She was Transylvanian. Pure and simple. Nor had she any love for the pompous Pontiff in Rome, that slime-brain Nicholas V who executed her people by the hundreds of thousands! Though a Christian, Serena owed her primary allegiance to Wicca and *Samháin*; gentle goddess of fertility and wise, mischievous God of the underworld, respectively. This decade had witnessed the persecution of so-called 'witches'—worshippers of Lucifer! All they were, were mere Celtic pagans whose only crimes were mixing pharmaceutical herbal remedies for ailments of the body and mind and offering the least-wanted parts of slaughtered animals to their gods. This, to Serena, was no great crime, for the lamb or goat would be eaten by the hill-community afterwards, what they would've done anyway. Their sacrifices were not humans, were not burnt alive, were not mere wasted, healthy young animals left to rot (as was fane in Semitic ritual). There were no 'orgies' like the Christians claimed. No mass burnings of cattle, as proclaimed by chauvinist, Roman propagandists (who, themselves, secretly sacrificed human babies in Mithraic temples). True, Dacians did worship *Samhain*, or *Annwyn*, Death-Lord, the wise, old wizard of the underworld in the form of a billy goat. But that was because goats were smart and mischievous, but also loving pets. Human sacrifices were only condoned in certain cases of enemies (Romans, Greeks, Scythians, Assyrians, Gauls, Persians, Ossetians) who had committed atrocities such as rape, mass-murder, and other nefarious crimes. These, would burn; long and painfully. (In a wicker-man!)

It began to snow. Gently, floating down from slate-black skies, featherlight. Serena crawled to the cavemouth, stretching out her hand, feeling the icy snowflakes collect in her palm. She realised with surprise that this was the first time in eleven years that she had been out at night, and that she was crying. Not tears of sorrow or pain. Joy. A hot, splendid rush of adrenaline whizzing through her veins. Had she any strength left she would've got up, danced in the snow collecting on the ledge outside the cavemouth. But Serena was mentally, physically drained. It was all she could do to crawl back to Vlad's sleeping form again. She nestled up to him, cheek to cheek, smiling with contentment. She hadn't been happy like this since she was a wee lass. Serena closed her eyes, dreaming of her martyred parents.

Chapter Six

The bustling town of Giurgiu stunk. Chickens and pigs, cattle and horses had been herded into town for today's livestock barter. There was no money here. The Romanians had no currency; their Prince did not even mint his own coins. Dracul had no need for coins other than to purchase weapons—those his tenants couldn't forge themselves—i.e., cannon, gunshot, and knights armour. Vlad and Serena wandered into town in a daze, sweat-stained and exhausted. They were still half-drenched after swimming the freezing cold Danube, negotiating its boggy deltas four miles southwest of the gigantic fortress of Giurgiu. 'Twas a miracle neither had drowned nor died of exposure. But it was not a cold day; the early March sun promised (lied) a premature spring in southern Wallachia. It was noon; a cavalcade of snorting, cackling, whinnying, whickering, neighing, mooing, b-a-a-aing, and barking animals horded the single street of Giurgiu. Ordinarily the smell of goat, sheep, cow, chicken, pig or horse dung bothered Vlad not at all: indeed, it was a wholesome, earthy smell destined for the fields. But crowded as they were into the muddy street, and the fact that neither he nor Serena had eaten for two days made them both nauseous. Their last meal had been a wild mallard, Tuesday morning, shot in the Danube delta with a crude, hand-fashioned longbow made from ashwood and some sinew smuggled from Sofia. They would have preferred to walk across the dilapidated, wooden bridge on struts spanning the swift-flowing Danube, but knew Turkish soldiers would be guarding it. They would prefer begging a peasant for food rather than starve, but it seemed as if the entire Bulgarian peasant population had become deceased. Serena and Vlad kept an eye out for Turkish customs officers on the crowded, dirt street.

Vlad elbowed his way through the crowd, dragging Serena along. No one minded; this was normal practice—no phony etiquette here. These were good, earthy, honest Daco-Romanians, bilingual, some trilingual, would offer anyone with an empty belly a meal, even if they had only enough for themselves. Except for Turks, of course. They would offer them only a dagger to the heart.

Hand in hand, they headed towards the nearest inn—the only inn—hoping they might learn the whereabouts of Vlad's father, who was in hiding. The Saxon settlers of upper Transylvania and Bucovina had rebelled. Last he'd heard, Prince Dracul had been ambushed in the Rosul pass. That was *eleven weeks ago*, whilst still a prisoner of Sultan Mured's palace at Sofia. Serena and Vlad had hidden in the cliffs of northern Bulgaria, not daring to venture forth while Mured's bloodhounds and Janissaries prowled the district, the two escapees only travelling at night. They had hunted sporadically on the plains, Serena occasionally sprinkling drops of fox musk to confuse the Turks' hounds. (From time to time, hitching a ride with a wagonload of rustics heading north from the local marketplace.) She and Vlad had often stopped at night to carouse beside a twinkling riverbank or lonely stream, abandoning themselves. Vlad had yet to inquire amongst the villagers straddling the marshy deltas of his father's whereabouts, whether he be living or dead, lest an informant from one of Dracul's many enemies betray the Prince's possibly only free, living son. Or perhaps inform the Turkish authorities encamped on the river's island-fortress who controlled the bridge. There were many pretenders to the throne of Wallachia: renegade Bathórys, Daneştis, Laiotas, Lugosis, Gheorghienis, not to mention the young ailing, King of Hungary, Ladislas IV, who claimed northern Transylvania from the Bihor mountains to Moldavia's Carpathians to the east. Should a new Prince of Wallachia be chosen, Vlad and his family would be put to death. That was the way it was done.

A time-honoured tradition for the traitors of this land.

Vlad spotted a narrow, overhanging, grossly leaning, half-timbered building with a sign swinging low over the door. A caricature of a roasted boar had been crudely painted on the sign with blue woad pigment. Illegible Romanian script had once been present underneath; now only sporadic, faded gothic letters. Here Vlad and Serena would need coins, for the innkeepers made a brisk business from the foreign travellers who often strayed into this God-forsaken prairie countryside. Vlad hoped he could wheedle the innkeeper's allegiance either for or against Prince Dracul. If the innkeeper proclaimed for Dracul, Vlad would reveal his identity. That alone would secure he and Serena a meal and lodging, for the consequences of anyone offending a future *voivod* would be tremendous. A future *hospidar* could reward his followers far more richly than any pretender might. Vlad would hint darkly of the offending innkeeper's death—impalement. (A new and grisly execution adopted by Vlad's father, the Devil.)

The inn was dark. Smoky. Walnut-beams supported the ground floor ceiling. A smell of garlic and basil permeated the old, rustic tavern, wafting from a potpourri of herbs in an earthen vase and the familiar garlic-wreath hung over the door to ward off vampires, those bloodsucking fiends of the night who would not stay dead. Vlad chuckled to himself, amused at these odd, peasant superstitions. He was *not* a believer.

The tavern was empty. The thick, aromatic smoke of seasoned applewood burned Vlad and Serena's eyes as they sat down at the long countertop. Half a dozen empty bar tables and stools stood behind them. The floor was but dirty sawdust. Four great casks of beer sat behind a warped, greasy countertop on their rounded sides. German beer. Or Pilsner—Czech. Vlad was tempted to reach across and help himself to a tankard of ale, but decided otherwise lest the innkeeper stroll in. It would not be an auspicious start for a future voivode to be literally branded a thief! Vlad had no way of proving he was the son of Prince Dracul, who by all accounts seemed to be a well-loved ruler throughout Romania. Except among the noblemen, the boyars. And the Germans. They HATED Vlad Dracul, ever since he raised their tithes and added new restrictions to their movements and trade. Now the shoe was on the other foot: now Wallachians held the powerful Teutonic castles, and the Saxons could feel the noose tightening around their necks. Had they asked the Dacian princes for land, they would've received. On fair payment, of course. But the Saxons had pillaged and conquered since the 900s AD, finally destroying what the Romans hadn't already decimated. Their burghs were still the richest in Transylvania/Romania; free of Jews, Gypsies, Protestant Hussites, and beggars.

Not for long, Vlad said to himself.

He would milk them like a milch cow.

A shambling, jolly St Nicholas clone entered the room dressed in stark brown, suddenly beaming at the two new guests. The only guests. His beard and moustache were pure white, beard extending down to his belly, handlebar moustache bushy and unkept. His chubby cheeks were rosy, as if he'd come in from a ¯30°C winter's day. Vlad expected him to chuckle and cry, *"Ho, ho, ho, Merry Christmas to all!"* Twinkling blue eyes seemed to laugh at some private joke. The old man was perhaps in his mid-fifties, moustache, sideburns and beard hiding much of his pink face. He had a paunch to his belly—from sampling too much beer, Vlad guessed.

"Well now, what have we here! Guests at my wonderful inn, come to sample the finest German beer this side of Austria—" he looked at Vlad closely, noticing his walrus moustache and long, dark, curly hair, continuing his sales speech, "or would it be Russian vodka for you, young lad? Wallachian plum brandy? Eh? Eh?" The old saint raised his shaggy eyebrows twice, cajoling.

"We have no money," Vlad responded, "we just come here for rest from cattle stampede."

"No money! Ha! I know Wallachian man who have no money for sixteen years!" the old bartender cried amiably. "I haven't seen a German *deutschemark* for over two weeks! Why, no one in Giurgiu has money! No need for it. You got livestock here? Hm? Hm? One chicken will buy you and the beautiful young missus here enough plum brandy for a week. Credit included. Or are you a teetotaller?" The old man shambled toward a large, wooden bucket at the end of the bar-top, scooping up a mugful of cold well-water, bringing it to their spot at the counter. Vlad was feeling thirsty, as was Serena. She grabbed the mug, downing it with a voracious gulp while the innkeeper looked on with a satisfied smile on his face, his eyes twinkling. Vlad took the cup, draining the last bit of water leisurely, as if it were the last water on earth.

"We'll have that Wallachian plum brandy now," Vlad said with a smile.

Vlad looked at Serena and shrugged while the innkeeper poured two tin cups full of brandy from a crystal decanter kept underneath the counter for such times. The old man did not doubt their sincerity—they did not exactly look like boyars. Or filthy, thieving Gypsies, for that matter. And they were Wallachian, spoke with a strong Daco-Romanian accent. From the Carpathians, most likely. They were a welcome respite from the pompous Saxon travellers who occasionally frequented Radu's inn. He was not worried about money—Radu had all the fruit, meat, cheese, wine and vegetables he and his wife could ever need, providing enough to stock even the inn's kitchen, which fed the guests spicy *mītītii* (meatballs), blood sausages, goulash and baked, carrot pie.

Vlad and Serena were soon giddy from brandy on an empty stomach. Radu (introducing himself as *Radu the Szekely*, Proprietor) passed them a plate of cheese sandwiches, noting their gauntness and unhealthy pallor. The bread was brown; whole-wheat mixed with rye and mustard seeds. Mmm. Delicious. Vlad almost had to fight Serena for the last, huge sandwich. Radu chuckled. *Ah, young love,* he thought to himself. *Takes me back a few decades to my Magda...*

"Married, are you?" Radu enquired, slicing thick chunks of cheese from a large, round wheel of white goats' cheese. "Or engaged?"

"Umm, married," Vlad replied quickly, avoiding Serena's astonished gaze.

She blinked rapidly, expressionless.

"Tell me, old man," Vlad asked, nonchalant. "What has happened to Prince Dracul, these days? We've been away in desolate, accursed Bulgaria, herding swine, for weeks."

Radu blanched, saddening instantly. Wiped tears from his eyes with a sleeve, calm. The stone hearth in a far corner of the tavern gave off a volley of sparks. The old man crossed himself, looking up to the ceiling.

"Pardon me, I am a bit sentimental," Radu choked. "You've not heard then?" Vlad shook his head, suddenly cold inside.

"He's in Heaven now, I'm afraid," said Radu. "He and his entire family. Those traitorous Saxons of Transylvania done him away."

"How?" Vlad demanded, his voice low. A sharp lance pierced through his heart; hot, bitter. Papa…

"Dug a hole, six feet deep, they did; interred both Dracul and his brave son Mirçea—in different locations. Buried them alive, they did."

"Jesus."

"They dragged Prince Dracul out of his castle at Braşov one night while on a rampage, the Saxons, carried our *hospidar* by torchlight toward the village church where they buried him alive. Lord Mirçea…Lord Mirçea was ambushed along with his tiny retinue at Tirgovişte. And that's where they buried him—alive, and struggling, by God! No one seems to know what happened to Dracul's family. Rumour has it they were walled up alive inside the castle tower at Braşov. *Dietrichstein*, aye, the old Teutonic keep, if I remember well. Dracul's two remaining boys are prisoners of Sultan Mured II—that scumbag—in Sofia. They'll not likely see freedom till doomsday. The boyars of Bucovina, Transylvania, and Banat led the rebels who brought down the House of Dracul while Janós Hunyádi did nothing." Radu wiped a stray tear from his eye. "It is said King Ladislas of Hungary plans to annex Wallachia, now we have no Prince."

Vlad downed his brandy, his blood boiling. "Not if I can help it."

"Pardon?" The innkeeper leaned forward, tapping his ear. "What did you say, lad? I fear my hearing is not so good anymore."

Vlad thought now was as good a time as any. He gave the empty tavern a furtive glance, then spoke up. "Can you keep a secret, old man?"

"Please, please, call me Radu. Radu Ceuceşcu. Aye, I can keep a secret lad. What's on your mind?" The old man cocked his head, waiting for this young swineherd's awesome secret. Vlad whispered in his ear.

"I am Dracula. Prince Dracul's son and heir."

The old man's bushy white eyebrows rose to the ceiling. *Peculiar young fellow, this one,* he thought to himself. Too much brandy? Radu chuckled a Ho, ho, ho. "Aye, and I'm Sultan Mured II of Turkey."

Vlad seized Radu's wrist, scowling. "I am whom I say I am! Button your lips, old man, and you'll be greatly rewarded. If not..." Vlad looked down, crumpling a piece of brittle parchment in his fist. Radu became suddenly serious. And afraid. Serena looked on, admiring this show of intimidation on Vlad's part. She watched the old man go pale, raising a tin of brandy to his lips with a shaking hand and downing it with a single gulp.

"Your secret is safe with me, Your Majesty," Radu said. "Cross my heart upon my mother's soul!"

"Cut the bullshit," Vlad murmured with a disarming smile, "call me Wlad Dracul. I don't go in for that aristocratic poppycock."

"A-As you wish, young sir. Another brandy?"

Vlad shook his head, holding up his hand. Serena, too, refused, though she secretly wanted more.

"Tell me...Vlad," Radu whispered dramatically. "How did you escape Sultan Mured's court?"

"I had help," Vlad murmured, casual, exchanging glances with Serena.

"Then...you're not betrothed?"

Vlad shook his head. "Serena was a belly-dancer in Mured's harem. She helped me escape."

Serena laughed, crinkling her crescent eyes, kissing Vlad on the cheek. Radu smiled. He couldn't believe his ears. But should he trust this fellow?

"We need a room for the night. Possibly more," Vlad hinted, his dark green eyes piercing into Radu's. They seemed to hypnotise, like a serpent's. "Can you arrange this for us?"

"Aye," Radu replied immediately. "You can have the best room in my inn, for as many nights as you like. As you can see, there are no visitors. You may have my wife's and mine, if you like. Soft bed, fireplace..."

"No, I'll not be putting you and your missus out of your bedroom," Vlad murmured with a chuckle. "A...window room would be preferred.

"As you wish."

Radu hurried off upstairs, preparing their chambers.

An enormous hourglass stood on the counter to Vlad's right, looking like a sweets-jar for dispensing honeyed candy. Shaped like a glass number-eight, it trickled red sand into its lower half. Vlad leaned over, guessing the time. Late afternoon. Almost suppertime. He looked forward to supper immensely. As did Serena.

Chapter Seven

Swirling mist invaded the Carpathians.

Vlad and Serena had entered the Moldoveǎnu pass on foot, alone, legs tiring rapidly as they climbed higher and higher into the lofty pass, having entered the sub-Carpathians six hours ago. Vlad was amazed at how far the mountains really were, thought he and Serena would be able to reach the dark green, fir-forested peaks within an hour, they looked that close.

But looks were deceiving.

The great, conical peak of Moldoveǎnu loomed beyond the snaking Dimbǒvita river winding its way through the misty pass like a gigantic serpent, glowing greenish in the diffused sunlight. Vlad shivered. Not because he was cold. Which he was. But the Carpathians were every bit as intimidating, forbidding, and spooky as the villagers of Cimpǔlung claimed. If they thought it looked eerie, he mused to himself, they should try sleeping here for two nights as he and Serena had. Then they would know what fear was. Vlad was not a superstitious man. But here, where the flecked, white barn-owl hooted at night and flitted about in the moonlight like ghosts, where grey wolves barked and howled at the moon, silhouetted on the highest peaks beneath a monstrous, bloated white moon, one's imagination could run wild. 'Twas here in the Carpathians near Lake Hermannstadt that the Devil's School for necromancy, the Scholomance, conducted their initiation rites, dancing naked in the hills around Neolithic standing stones and ancient burial mounds. Men who entered these mountains alone did not always come back. If you had keen eyesight, you just might see the creeping wolf-packs silhouetted atop the highest peaks under a moon which always seemed to be full. Here, *strigoi* held sway, roaming these benighted forests for all eternity while searching, chittering noisily, for human bodies to possess. Northwest of the Transylvanian Alps was Hungarian land, though rightfully Wallachian, where the Mongol/mongrel settlers possessed a unique, and if one were to believe such rumours, rabid fear—paranoia—of *moroi, nosferatu* (undead). The Huns (Magyars) believed men rose from their graves to suck human blood with razor-sharp fangs and turned themselves into bats, or wolves. Utter nonsense. Out here, though, in the dark, one could easily believe such scary tales.

It was not yet dark. Not yet. But it would be soon. A sinister red glow emanated from the western Carpathians. Vlad did not at all look forward to sleeping tonight here in the mist and howling of hungry wolves. Nor did Serena. Who knew what other prehistoric creatures of the night lived here? No one dwelt here except hermits, foresters, and lunatics. Superstition was rampant throughout this part of Romania. Great, scaly red dragons were rumoured to inhabit Moldovĕanu, swooping down from the mountain with leathery wings to breathe fire on passers-by, or snatching them up in their talons to take them as food to their monstrous nests. Two-headed gooney birds were said to nest in scraggly old trees. Here mighty *würms* were said to burrow underneath the black soil, claiming victims with their slimy coils. Witches were everywhere. And sorcerers. Here the Druids were said to still hold sway, using magic and incantations to keep meddlers away with unpredictable, alpine, thunderstorm spells. All the more frightening since the Druids were said to be *moroi*.

Bah! Vlad said to himself. Peasant superstitions. Those shit-brained Huns would believe any scary tale.

Serena halted, urging Vlad to do likewise. She slumped down onto a mossy, lichen-splotched rock, closing her eyes with exhaustion. For once, Vlad did not mind. Serena was strong, and surprisingly hardy. For a woman. He sat beside her on the rock; but, firstly, giving her an awkward bear-hug.

"What do you think of my father's mountain hideout?" Vlad asked with a chuckle. "We may end up spending the night with wolves, or *moroi.*" He laughed.

"Do you miss your father, Wlad?"

Vlad became serious, nodding with a frown.

"I miss papa. And my family. I wonder how Radu is doing?"

Probably not so well, Serena thought to herself. *Fending off Mured's homosexual son none too successfully, no doubt.*

"Wlad?"

"Hm?"

"Tell me of your father. Was he a good man? A good ruler? You see...I never heard news from Wallachia while imprisoned in Sofia. Except for this recent uprising, of course. Do you resent him for rebelling whilst you were still Mured's prisoner?"

Vlad pondered this awhile. "Yes, I did resent him. Very much. But I knew he needed a united Romania more than he needed me. My father was a good man. A just ruler. All the Wallachians loved him, except these Transylvanian Saxon scum. They'll die for their mischief, I assure you, each and every one of them. I'll impale each and all, turn Transylvania into a cemetery, burn their crops from Tîrgu Mureş to Hajdúböszörmeny."

Serena's face went pale in the darkness, becoming serious.

"Have mercy on them, Wlad. Many are only innocent pawns in an endless stalemate."

Vlad glanced at Serena hard, his dark green eyes cold as Siberia. Serena's angelic, heart-shaped face implored him with anxious fawn eyes beneath pale moonlight.

Vlad's eyes softened. "For you, I shall show them mercy. IF they accept my rulership—which will be a long slog from here, I assure you. First I must find allies, and men who are willing to fight. To die. The boyars of these districts know naught of law and peace, only gluttony and corruption. I intend to change that."

"How?"

Vlad laughed, slapping Serena's skirted knee. "Do you really want to know?"

"No, I don't really," said Serena, horrified.

Vlad smiled. "I...intend to shackle the boyars and their accomplices together by the neck, march them to Braşov from Cluj, and then, do you know what I am going to do?"

"No, what?" She really didn't want to hear of it.

"I am going to force those traitors to build me a mighty new castle, the biggest in Romania."

Serena's scarlet lips slowly curved up into a lopsided smile, amazed at Vlad's brilliant plan. And mercy, for the boyars deserved worse.

"And then I'm going to impale each and all."

"Oh God, Wlad." Serena slumped forward against his chest, suddenly realising with despair that Vlad Dracula was quite mad.

****

Wolves howled and prowled the moonlit campfire. The beasts kept their distance, wary of the bonfire, waiting for a chance to strike when it burnt out. *Like werewolves*, Vlad thought to himself. He had no intention of letting it go out. Or even diminishing. He held a smoking, flaming torch in his right hand. Serena lay across his lap, her head pillowed on a bearskin. Vlad kept his broadsword at his side, hand twitchy, nervous. *'These wolves should not be that hungry,'* he thought to himself. Perhaps they were werewolves. Possibly they were skulking about in the bushes on two legs. Vlad shuddered. He shivered. Crossed himself.

'In the name of our Father, who art in Heaven...'

Serena moaned uneasily in her sleep, mercifully blanketed by a wolfskin. *'At least, they were warm,'* Vlad thought to himself. And, surprisingly, happy. They'd made love tonight; tender, caring, passionate. He brushed a stray tendril of dark hair from Serena's face. She was a beauty. Sultan Mured must miss her terribly. Vlad laughed aloud in the darkness.

His laughter echoed back at him eerily from the mountainous crags, menacing woods. Bats fluttered under a full moon, swooping down into the firelight. Vlad wore a garlic wreath around his neck, as did Serena. Normally he would have laughed at such superstition...but not here. Not in the Carpathians. Not in Transylvania. Vlad and Serena had been here in the southern Carpathian range for over a week now. Hopelessly lost. And hungry. Their only food had been the odd hare shot with his stolen crossbow. Vlad had robbed a German knight travelling alone beneath the massive, Swiss-like peaks rearing over the pine-clothed, serpentine Dimbŏvita river valley. He'd ambushed the knight from a bluff, leaping onto the German's back and throwing the lightly armoured *ritter* from his horse. Serena watched from a boulder beside the river as the two wrestled on its bank. Finally, Vlad ended the contest with a sickening blow to the skull with a rock, leaving the hapless *Saison* (Saxon) for dead. The beautiful white warhorse had bolted, though. 'Twas this reason why Vlad and his woman had strayed here into the Rosul pass. To find the horse. They did not find it. They had roamed twelve miles into the abandoned ghost land of the extinct *Cŭmbræ*, an ancient tribe exterminated by the Romans, allies of Dacia and renowned for their wanderings across Europe and Asia Minor. Legend had it that a large expedition of Cŭmbric adventurers left Dacia thousands of years ago to settle a mystical isle to the west, where no man had been before save ape-men, calling their new home *Cymru*. But, like the Dacians of Wallachia and Goidels (proto-Scythians) of Ireland, the *Cymraeg*—Welsh—had been conquered by the Saxons. Last he'd heard they were still surviving—barely. The King of England—God rot his soul—Edward I, had conquered *Cymru* (Wales) in 1282 AD. The Britons had just emerged recently from a bloody, vicious civil war, subdued once again by their hated Anglo-Norman magnates. Another stalemate. Crops had been burnt, whole districts exterminated by one side or the other. Vlad tried to remember the Britons' bloodthirsty leader—*Glendŵr*. That was his name. A warlock who'd disappeared into the mists of history without a trace, after defeat. (1415.) Vlad liked to keep up to date on European events. Information was slow, however. Usually six months after the fact. Other than the traitorous Catholic/Orthodox Reunification treaty of 1439 or the disastrous battle of Varna (preceding the Ottomans' investing of Greece, 1442, and subsequent famines and plague), there had been very little of importance to report. There'd been Joan of Arc's burning in France. That was the year of Vlad's birth, however. He couldn't remember what else. Couldn't give a damn either.

Vlad and Serena had entered the ghost town of Sīmeria in shock yesterday. No one there. All dead after the Great Plague. Desolate, the medieval, deserted village stunk with the unwholesome taint of decay and something *else*. (They'd soon discovered the source.) Wolves roamed the ruins. The odd skeleton lounged about in tumbledown, caved-in shacks or stone hovels, as if waiting for Resurrection. Vlad and Serena had covered their mouths with cloths lest they inhale the malignant bubonic plague spores. They didn't stay long. Avoided rats.

The spoils of abandon they'd coveted had proved to be preciously little.

Vlad slept fitfully. Terrible monsters, saurian-like, arose from his noisome, cesspool of dreams; great, herbivorous monsters of unimaginable size; scaly, serpentine *würms*; huge, prehistoric, vermilion-bellied carnivorous reptiles walking about on massive, twin legs; fire-breathing dragons; vampires; water beasties; ghosts.

Morning came with fog. So thick, Vlad could've cut it with his stolen broadsword. He closed his eyes. Wished he were somewhere else. Home. Back in his father's ancestral castle at Brașov, tucked peacefully in his cot in the highest tower. Where his mother had taught him to speak Dacian. (The villagers had thought her a witch!) Where the chiming, wondrous mechanical clock lulled him asleep. His stepmother would come in at night with a flaming pine-torch to sing Vlad a lullaby after his mother died. She was a good woman. Most sons hated their stepmothers. And Arabs—well, they hated their mothers. And sisters. As the Pope hated women, as did all monks, and all devout Roman Catholics. And Christians it seemed. Indeed, it seemed to Vlad that he was alone in this world of woman haters. He thought only the ancient Celts (Hallstadt culture, proto-Celts), before their Indo-Europeanisation, had any sensibility. First the *Allemanni* of Italy and Austria. Then the *Belgae* of northwestern France, Belgium, and the British Isles. And then the Gaels, Sarmatians (neo-Scythians), and Cymry.

And now the Dacians.

The Saxons were here too.

****

The ruined, burnt-out towers of Braşov castle jutted up from the mountain like a decayed set of lower teeth. Three crooked, blasted stumps on a mountain which seemed almost alive with malice. Hostility. Hatred. Pain. Sorrow.

Suffering.

The sight appealed to Vlad's twisted, morbid sense of humour. He'd decided he would build a new castle there, though it was here, in the Transylvanian Alps that his father had been dragged from the great keep one stormy night and buried alive. Here where Vlad's entire family (except Mirçea and Radu) were rumoured to have been walled up alive inside the castle. He intended to find his father's body and those of his family, even if it meant digging up the entire village. And then Mirçea's in Tirgovişte. That royal burgh would burn, he promised himself. Saxon scum! Vlad would make sure the traitorous villagers and *Burgermeisters* did all the digging and dismantling.

First he had to become Prince, though.

That would not be easy. Vlad and Serena had heard at Curtea de Argeş that the King of Hungary had declared for the Daneşti faction for the new, ruling House of Wallachia. He must be careful here, only a few miles from his hometown of Braşov, where his father had kept a luxurious townhouse, the superseding burgh of lower Transylvania. He could expect few allies save for the odd Wallachian nobleman. Also Vlad must be cautious never to be recognised, lest he meet his father and brother's inglorious fate at the hands of the filthy Saxons. Once these parts had been honest, Wallachian territory…but the German settlers were embarking on a unique phase of 'ethnic cleansing'.

Vlad planned to do a bit of ethnic cleansing himself once he claimed power. IF he gained power.

First things first. He must now find an ally. A Wallachian boyar. He knew exactly who to contact now; Tudur Gheorghieni, lord of Sibiu and one of Dracul's staunchest supporters, and Ion Dragoşi, Castle Brân's former castellan. Vlad stared up at the blackened, stone castle under a harsh April afternoon sun, squinting in its glare. Serena stood at his side, clenching Vlad's hand, awed by the sight of this soot-plastered ruin looming above them on its 250-ft. rock (at an elevation of 2500 ft.) like a giant. (The outcrop sat on the side of a mountain.) Yet it was not a large castle, only magnified by the mountain slope and the rank grasses growing in profusion along the steep cliff's incline. Spring flowers were in full bloom; daisies, aster, yellow daffodil, bee orchid, dandelions, blue Carpathian harebell, geranium, pink roses, gorse, broom, cowslip, primrose, purple heather; the air redolent with the resin-scented buds of spring poplar. Thistle thrived already on the lower slopes of colourful, flower-starred mountains, as did nasty stinging nettle. The gorge seemed uncrossable; the wooden bridge had been burnt.

Crows hovered around the castle ruins, as if searching for bodies. Serena shivered, the unbidden thought of Vlad's murdered family interred within its masonry creeping into her mind. She hoped he did not intend to go up there. Not today. Knowing him, he would probably begin prying the blackened stones loose himself. Serena wanted nothing more than to collapse into the cushiony, spring grass and sleep. Now they had found the castle Serena felt a shiver of foreboding, for Vlad would soon start searching out allies and soldiers. Generals. Field marshals. Boyars. Knights. Mercenaries.

Vlad was determined to get to the summit before nightfall. Trees cloaked he and Serena's ascent from the bustling village below, shielding the outlaw and his woman from hostile German eyes. Eyes which would see him hang, raping his slut while he watched, swinging, from the church gallows. The very fact that Vlad and Serena were unmarried, committing adultery, would justify their actions (there had been no posting of the banns, proclaiming their marriage). Indeed, it was a miracle Vlad's father had held out as long as he had. His royal fortress, Castle Brân, perched defiantly in this, the heart of Saxon resistance.

It had been three months since Vlad and Serena had first coupled in that Bulgarian field-pit. She had not conceived. As she knew she would not, though she wanted to. Serena prayed each night, to herself, for conception. But it was not forthcoming. She had been abused too many times at Mured's court.

Vlad, too, was worried. And annoyed. He had not informed Serena yet, but he intended to marry her. With or without his as-yet unformed royal council's permission. He didn't give a damn what the Pope and His bishops thought or said about the engagement. Nor the Patriarch of Constantinople. Serena was HIS woman, his choice. Vlad no longer cared that she was a peasant girl from Timișoara.

Castle Brân reared suddenly above the trees, instantly coming into view through a thick, green curtain of spring leaves. A scarlet sun hovered on its summit, slowly slipping below the wild, Transylvanian horizon, shadows lengthening by the minute. The fortress was close now, only fifty yards away; up through a gully, and then a prickly thicket of red rosebushes.

Serena felt suddenly uneasy. The ruin emitted a sense of twilit gloom and desertion about it. And something else. Misery. Yes, that was it. Misery. The smell of charcoal wafted on the rose-scented air.

Vlad entered the ruined bailey. Alone. Serena stood on the threshold, having scrambled behind him up a steep slope and through prickly rose-thickets, unwilling to enter this soot-blackened shell. High, ashlar walls loomed above her, enclosing the lone inner bailey in an oblong half-circle. The crenelations had been knocked off the walls, much of the derelict, ex-Knights' Templar fortress already dismantled. Its twin-turreted gatehouse gaped ajar; double, arched doors bearing the marks of axes splintered through its thick oak. Castle Brân's tall, twin gatehouse towers were D-shaped, arrow-slits protecting the angles where castle wall met rounded gatehouse tower. Their slate roof caps were missing. Soot blackened the arrow loops' inner slits. Serena entered through the pointed arch reluctantly, noting the gatehouse had no floors, now just an empty, burnt out shell. Murder-holes threatened from above. Scorched elms leaned weakly against the bawn, grim and eerie abodes of crows in this melancholy twilight; surrounding the outer ramparts with a skeletal palisade of stark, charred, leafless, ancient trees. Serena sought Vlad among the jumbled ruins, leery of being left alone in this horrid, masonry shell.

Vlad wore a brooding expression, wandering about the ruined inner ward with his hands in his tunic's pockets. His massive, hand-and-a-half style German broadsword hung from his swordbelt, dragging lopsidedly on the ground, sheathed in a simple leathern scabbard. It left a trail in the dirt. At his right, dwarfing him, stood what remained of Castle Brân's horse stables and ramp and the large sward of cobbles where knights had once trotted their fine-blooded warhorses into Dracul's regal stables. Serena glanced around, on the lookout for villagers who might venture up the mountain-spur to inspect the castle. No doubt for their own chosen *voivod*, whom the Huns were sure to (officially) elect. Or else to loot whatever might have been missed by previous looters. Ravens cawed and cackled maddeningly in the nearby trees.

Shadows were claiming the castle. Monstrous, long, misshapen shadows resembling grotesque birds of prey. Or bats. Vampire bats. Serena shivered. She did not like this place.

Vlad strolled to her side, nodding with satisfaction.

"We'll sleep here," he said without preamble.

Serena gaped, eyes bulging. "Are you mad?! Here? Tonight?"

Vlad's face darkened almost imperceptibly, as if a thunder-cloud had shadowed his features. His right hand shot out like a viper, seizing Serena's arm.

"Do not *EVER* call me mad."

He hissed the words, eyes blazing with unholy fury. His fingers dug into Serena's flesh like iron.

"I-I'm sorry. S-Sorry, truly I am. F-Forgive me?" Serena squeaked. Then gasped, tears filling her frightened, brown eyes as Vlad's fingers clenched tighter. "*Oww.*"

Vlad released her suddenly, as if nothing had ever happened. This was a side of him she had not seen before. Brooding, brutal. As if entering this accursed castle had changed him. It was not a side Serena liked.

Vlad swivelled, stalking back to the keep.

"Sorry," Vlad murmured with an embarrassed tone as Serena joined his side. She nodded, hurt, matching his stride as they ambled toward the former Teutonic stronghold's roofless, rectangular great tower. Serena's left arm hurt, welts showing up red beneath her woollen fabric. She rubbed the area, tears rolling down her cheeks. Dared not cry, lest Vlad flare up again. Not even sob.

They entered the towering, rectangular keep merging with the rock hillside through a wide, arched, chevron-moulded portal which had once been the basement entrance, sitting down in the darkness. Vlad cleared a spot with his boot, motioning Serena to sit. Ash lay everywhere. And soot. Great swaths of clinging soot and ashes. Charcoal, half-burnt pieces of wood. The furniture and timbers no doubt. Floor joists, ceiling supports. A square hole of purple twilight stood out clearly fifty feet above them, where a leaden roof used to be. Serena wondered morosely how the Saxons could simply torch the keep without bearing in mind the loving care artisans had crafted into its rich, sumptuous furnishings. Vlad, exhausted, sat down beside her.

His bare knee touched hers, intimate in this quiet darkness. Cuckoos and crickets kept up a lulling nocturnal chorus beside the castle pond. Though it was dark inside the tower, Vlad could discern the tears glistening on Serena's cheek. Not a sound came from her. Not a sob.

He reached out, tenderly brushing a tear away with his finger. "What…"

Serena sat stiff as a stone. She held her stinging left arm, her breath, pain still coursing through her skin. She had forgotten what pain was like, these past few months. Deceived into believing the nights of abuse were over.

"Let me see," said Vlad, taking Serena's injured arm.

He peered down at the bruised, discoloured flesh, noting the red welts where his fingernails had dug in through the fabric. Vlad was mortified. Enough light filtered down from the collapsed roof to see the black and blue bruises. Serena's garb was rolled up at the shoulder now.

"Did I do that?" Vlad murmured, gently stroking the welts where his fingernails had dug in through the fabric. It had a soothing effect, not at all displeasing. "I am sorry. Did not mean to hurt you, only to warn."

He leaned forward, face close to hers now. "Are you going to hate me forever?" He smiled.

Serena shook her head, avoiding Vlad's gaze.

Vlad tilted her chin, kissing Serena gently on the lips. She responded. "There is something you should know about me," Vlad said candidly, pulling back. "I'm not…right in the head, you see." He frowned, ashamed of this guilty admission. "I am subject to these…spells. Brooding. Depression. Anger, violence. 'Tis nothing inherited, however."

Serena raised her eyes, shocked speechless.

"I promise never to hurt you again," said Vlad. "If I do, slap me. Hard." Serena smiled.

Vlad turned his head. "Go on. Slap me. While I'm still feeling generous."

Serena laughed huskily, shaking her head, resisting his invitation. Her hand shot out, as if of a will of its own, slapping him hard across the face.

Vlad was not laughing.

"*Aaaaaaarrgh!*" Vlad cried, shaking his head like a wild beast, furious. Serena cowered back, scrambling away with shrieks of terror as he burst into laughter and seized her ankle, dragging her back to his side.

"I am Count Dracula, I've come to suck your b-l-o-o-d!"

"Oh Wlad, stop, someone will hear you!" Serena wailed, laughing despite herself.

"I am a vampire!"

Serena laughed aloud as Vlad playfully bit her neck, then sensuously kissed her jugular with a long, squelching hickey. She groaned.

"Ummm, yes, do that again," Serena whispered.

He did. Again and again. All over her body. Her belly. Breasts. Thighs. Buttocks. Stripping off Serena's clothes. He sucked on her toes.

They made love till daybreak. Slowly, languidly. Or wild, almost violent. Vlad seized Serena's hair as she climaxed beneath him. She raked his back with fingernails like talons, drawing blood.

Now they were even.

No ghosts here. No memories. No more pain.

(And then the dawn.)

****

Serena's hometown of Timişoara shimmered under a summer heatwave. She sat in one of the shadowy, gothic antechambers below the third floor of the keep embracing her long-lost relatives.

Vlad watched impassively in the solar as the Hungarian voivode and viscount and former ally Ion de Hunedŏara prostrated himself before the uncrowned Prince, exclaiming his fealty to Vlad. And his role in the deposition of Prince Vlad Dracul. Oddly enough, Vlad believed him. Though he and Ion disliked each other immensely, they both shared an almost fanatical hatred for Turks which had often bound them together as drinking companions during Vlad's brief three months' freedom at his father's court—almost liking each other. Almost. To top it off, Hunedŏara was the finest soldier/statesman in eastern Europe, with the most brilliant, strategic mind. Unusual for Huns.

Hunyádi's forced conversion to Rome, however, had gained him many enemies here in Transylvania, regardless of his pagan sympathies and secret adherence to the Orthodox faith.

Hunedŏara exclaimed in deep, rising voice how he'd been unable to control the German peasants after Prince Dracul had lost command of the people. The Turks had occupied virtually all of southern Wallachia. When Dracul had offered terms for surrender, Hunedŏara, stubborn to the last, had roused the peasants to rise up and expel the heathen invaders. As Dracul was still, theoretically, Prince of Wallachia, Hunedŏara was technically rebelling against him. He had committed unpardonable treason. He had not, Hunedŏara exclaimed in his loudest voice, ordered the Saxon peasants of Transylvania to bury the Prince alive. Nor had he taken part. But nor had he the manpower left to punish the Saxons. He was dependent on the King of Hungary for arms and money, but Ladislas seemed surprisingly unwilling to help free Wallachia from Islam's yoke. Surprisingly enough, the Wallachian peasantry had responded, temporarily expelling the Turks from Wallachia, much to the Ottomans' shock.

Hunedŏara shook with suppressed anger, his ruddy face flushed, blue eyes aflame. He knelt on his green-stockinged knees, shaking his cropped reddish hair at Vlad's vituperative accusations. His moustache bristled. It was clear young Dracula would not be appeased so easily. Treason could cost Ion his head.

Huneŏara's few mercenaries though had captured Timişoara's ageing cruciform castle in Vlad's name, ousting Vladislav Daneşti's supporters and proclaiming Vlad Dracula *hospidar* (Prince) of Wallachia though without the military means to back it up. And so doing, Hunedŏara had damned himself, now having been declared a traitor by his liege-lord King Ladislas of Hungary, the youth who held Ion's son Matthias, next in line to the Hungarian throne, hostage at the young king's castle of Vác. Vlad could do one of two things: execute Hunedŏara immediately or put him on trial for high treason. Vlad chose to do neither. Hunedŏara was much too valuable to sacrifice. Vlad needed him for new campaigns against the Turks.

In Bulgaria. And Yugoslavia.

The peasant population of Timişoara and surrounding countryside were overwhelmingly Wallachian; bilingual. They could be counted on to back Dracula's bloody campaign of reprisals against the Saxons. It would be seen as Divine retribution for the countless number of witches, Jews and heretics burnt at the stake in Cluj and Sibiu, the families and men slaughtered in petty wars and the women, girls and aye, sometimes even little boys raped by Huns and Saxons. The fields of Transylvania would soon glow red, flowing with German blood.

Vlad stood at the quatrefoil window, looking out over the dozing late-afternoon village with a vulpine smile on his face, imagining the impaled bodies of his enemies rotting in the hot summer sun. His green eyes virtually glowed.

Vlad told the kneeling Hunedŏara in his vaguest possible words that he would ponder this traitorous Hungarian's fate, nodding to the kettle-helmeted guards as they hoisted his most trusted ally to his feet and led him out of the great hall towards the barracks. Vlad would let Hunedŏara languish a few days in the dungeons, just to remind him of who was overlord. Just a little darkness and time to ponder his mistake. Then Vlad would release him, restore his title and power as viceroy of Transylvania and pretend nothing had ever happened, as if they were the best of friends. Ha! Not bloody likely.

The musty, great hall was soon empty. Austere. Only a plain, hooded stone hearth with sloping mantel provided heat for the winter months, cold and silent now. Small it was. The entire fort was tiny. It would look out of place among the big boys of Czechoslovakia, Austria, Hungary, France, Spain, Italy. There weren't many fortresses in Romania. Most were mere, round or rectangular watchtowers in the brooding mountains, surrounded by simple enclosing walls, or barmkins. Others were not castles in the regular sense at all, but oval, fortified church enclosures built by the Saxons as protection during Vlad's great-grandfather's vicious reign, Mirçea the Old. Wallachian fortifications possessed a unique, regional distinctiveness all their own, however. Distinctively, brutishly, like Serb or Slovak castles.

Vlad had much to learn about building castles. He chuckled evilly to himself. So would the boyars of Transylvania, once he claimed power—real power—and put them to work on his new castle at old Braşov, Castle Brân, the site of their treachery. Most had probably never done a day's work in their lives, grown fat on Turkish gold.

Most all of them had concubines, if not harems. Vlad would soon change that. When he got through with them, their hands and fingers would be shredded. Then they would die.

Vlad even had crude plans drawn out of his castle-to-be on parchment, doodled beneath wax candles on nights when there was a lull of royal councils. Or when he wasn't bonking Serena in his private chambers on the top floor of this slender pencil-tower. He smiled wistfully to himself. It was dark now, the candles wavering under a draught in their gold candelabra. Vlad stood for a while, reminiscing of he and Serena's astounding good luck, first escaping Sultan Mured's previously escape-proof stronghold in Sofia, sojourning here in Transylvania without being captured or hanged, and finally vaulted into contendership of the much-coveted throne of Wallachia with the support of the famous Hungarian knight, Janós Hunyádi. *'What more could a man and his woman ask for?'* Serena would be his Princess, with a suitable new name and fake history…let's see…hmm, an exiled boyar's wealthy daughter from Moldavia. Excellent. If Serena's kin weren't here, he would probably be with her now. It would not be seemly to hustle Serena up the tower tonight while she was reminiscing with her family. She had no siblings who remained alive. Even the friends she'd known had grown up and gone, or been sold into slavery. Her only contacts were Vlad and her relatives. Had it not been for them, she would have had to sell herself on the streets. Was a time, once, when spinsters could go off to the mountains, own their own land, raise livestock.

No longer.

Vlad knew what his new castle was going to look like. Castle Brân would require only minor rebuilding and a new curtain wall/shell-keep (already had he second thoughts on that design). But Vlad's other project…a totally new fortress high up in the Făgăras foothills overlooking the Argeş river near Cimpŭlŭng, designed specifically for artillery. Massive. A polygonal bailey, with roundish towers on the outer walls and enormous, pepper pot turrets. A pastiche of turrets, Renaissance galleries, and gables. A huge, square, thick tower in the middle ward. Or perhaps D-shaped, apsidal. Over seventy feet high. No skinny round donjon for him. Round towers were much more advanced in military design, allowing bowmen to cover all angles and much less subject to mining or picking. But cramped. Christ, were they cramped! Like this one. Vlad looked around. Crude stone masonry, large blocks. Rough. Not whitewashed. Round solar chamber. No chintz tapestries, mahogany ceiling panels, minstrel galleries, wainscoting, nor chandeliers. Decrepit ceiling timbers, worm-rotted. Tiny hearth which wouldn't warm candlewax in these mountains during winter. Smoky. Drafty. Round, gouged-out chambers too small. Sparse furnishings. Spiral stairs meant for midgets.

Vlad slumped down at his desk, propping his chin with pointy fingers, pondering his next battle strategy. Flickering candlelight from silver candelabrum illuminated eyes like emeralds, the eyes of a man possessed with a mission. He could not stay here long. This old fortress was much too insecure (Vlad mulled over seizing the large, but stoutly held, citadel of Făgăras with its new and deadly ramparts of Italic design). Prince Vlad Danești II and his Turkish-backed army had last been reported eighty miles southeast of Timişoara. At this time, Vlad could not risk a battle with Danești's Hungarian factions. But he realised to flee would mean voluntary exile until future victory secured the throne. Vlad had no army to speak of, only Hunedŏara's few mercenaries here in Timişoara castle.

Vlad dozed, face-down on his oak desk, candles sputtering as they burned down to their last inch. Wax dripped onto his parchment plans, drying instantly. Grotesque shadows flapped their wings from distant, rounded corners like demons. Or bats. Vampire bats. *Moroi*. A slender door led downstairs to Vlad's right, open. Another narrow, closed portal to his left.

One of those shadows detached itself from the stone wall.

"Wlad, wake up. It's past midnight. Come. I shall tuck you in."

Serena shook his shoulder, startling him; waking Vlad from a brutal nightmare writhing with bloodsucking, reanimated corpses and other nefarious creatures of the night. He groaned, rubbing his eyes sleepily.

"Come, love. Time for bed."

She draped his shoulder with a slender arm (these same biceps once fettered with a harem dancer's bangles), petting Dracula's curly hair like his maternal mother used to do.

"Where are your kin?" Vlad asked with a yawn.

"Downstairs. In the guest chambers. This castle is well-nigh deserted, you know." Serena bent down, pouting her rouged lips as she kissed Vlad tenderly.

"No, not the safest place to be, is it?"

Serena shook her head, pulling Vlad by the arm from his throne-like chair. "Come on, lazybones. Off to bed with you."

Arm in arm, they headed toward the tricky, worn turnpike leading up into darkness, its walls barely lit. A death trap. They were newel stairs (spiral): steps winding round a central pillar with only a slender, wooden rail to hang onto. Serena held a silver, flickering candlestick in her left hand, leading the way. Vlad realised to his chagrin that he was quite drunk, tipsy from too much wine. He hadn't realised that he had drunk so much *slivŏvitz*. Wasn't accustomed to it. Serena held his hand tight, lest he tumble down the steep, narrow stair. He was not that drunk. But tired. Dead tired. Wasn't sure if he was fit for hot and heavy sex tonight. Serena would understand. She was the most compassionate creature he'd ever met. Like a mother deer; a pet and fawn Vlad had once owned. Like his deceased mother and stepmother. Serena was surely the only woman in the world who could comprehend Vlad's insane rages, his fanatical hatred of Turks, Huns, Germans. Every nationality in fact, except the *Keltoi*. Extinct as they were.

Serena understood.

After their intense lovemaking, they lay awhile in each other's arms inside their single cot, listening to the black night as thunder roared across the nearby Bihor mountains to the northeast. Like a lion, thunder bellowed throughout the wee hours of morning, sending stark white lightning-flashes down to the ground. The slender castle tower shook with each reverberating *boom!*, searing flashes of lightning blinding in their intensity. Ever so close. Serena cowered with each nerve-shattering boom against Vlad's chest, fearing electrocution high up here in this lethal castle tower; for she detested the Satanic crash of thunder, the choking sluice of rain. Vlad lived for it. He stroked her wavy hair absent-mindedly, not afraid of the lightning or the dark, nor what supernatural creatures dwelt within. Vlad quite enjoyed summer thunderstorms, they bringing him fond memories of his dark-haired mother singing him lullabies in Dacian as a boy when he was afraid of the dark. And vampires. And bats. The old castle tower of Brân had been packed with bats. As was this one. Vlad could vaguely hear their squeaks and fluttering of wings in the darkness, could even see them, flitting about when lightning lit up the gothic bedchamber. As it did now.

"Wlad?"

"Oes."

"Where do we go from here?"

"Nowhere. For now."

"I mean, what are our plans?"

Vlad lifted his head. "Our plans?"

"Da…I mean…you must marry soon. What shall I do? Where shall I go?"

"I am married."

"What?!" Serena sat up, angry, hurt. Betrayed. She felt like a houri again.

"I am married to you. You just haven't realised it till now." Vlad ran his finger lightly down Serena's bare back, down her exposed spine.

Serena furrowed her brows, uncomprehending.

"In the Old Times," Vlad continued, "bedding together and a vow of faithfulness among our *bobl* was considered a marriage contract, presided over by the Druidic priests."

"Wlad, you must be serious," Serena retorted. "You know we cannot marry; it…it would be like siblings marrying. I am a peasant. You are *voivode*. Your subjects would reject you if you chose me."

"To Hell with my subjects!" Vlad shouted, sitting bolt-upright. Serena jerked away. "Romans! When my reign is done in Romania, people will say that I, Wlad Draigh, eradicated Wallachia of all half-breeds. Call it 'ethnic cleansing'."

"For better or for worse, Wlad, they are your subjects, your countrymen," Serena murmured softly.

"No!"

Serena sighed. She was only beating her head against a brick wall when talking to Vlad about the Latins residing in Wallachia, planted here as settlers and spies during Trajan's reign in 106 AD. It was the one subject Vlad was totally unreasonable about.

Serena pondered this. Vlad was a baptized Christian. Of Daco-Romanian language, too. Why did he pine for the *Keltoi?* Yes, they were well-nigh extinct (technically, they were). Yes, their laws and customs were fair and honest. Yes, the Romans had exterminated them, committed genocide; turning them out of their torched homes (hunting them down like dogs; or exiling them to the mountains and certain starvation). Was he merely insane? His father had been half Hungarian, on his mother's side. Vlad hated Hungarians. Serena found it hard to sort out who Vlad meant: Magyar Christians, or Huns, as in Orientals or Mongols or whatever the hell those people happened to call themselves. They seemed to change their name every century. Tatars now, weren't they? Serena did not know. Serena did not care.

"A gentle shepherd has gentle sheep," Serena murmured playfully, remembering an old, obscure nursery rhyme. Was it Myrddyn?

"And mean dogs are well-respected dogs."

"That is true."

"Well then," Serena murmured, "can you not be a nasty, old sheep-dog; benevolent, but peevish too?"

"I shall try. As long as you are there to guide me," Vlad added, turning to her, holding Serena in the crook of his arm; her head nestled against his neck.

"I shall always be there."

Serena had no idea just how little time she had left to live.

****

14 August, 1449 AD
Tirgovişte, Transylvania

Greek fire flew over the walls.

Vlad's trebuchets and mangonels lobbed small boulders over the Renaissance city's ramparts, besieging this strategic burgh. The boyars of ungro-Wallachia returned fire, deadly Greek Fire. They were trapped here. They had to face it, they were trapped. Vlad Dracula had brilliantly isolated the royal city from the surrounding countryside, offering the foolish peasants riches and gold for their undying support. They'd come from the surrounding Carpathian mountains, besieging the mixed force of German, Hungarian, and God help them, Romanians. From the slender, round Chîndia watchtower built by Vlad's own grandfather within the palace walls, the boyars watched. The royal capital's inhabitants knew not what their fate would be. And the fate of their Hungarian boyars. From the magnificent, trellised, ornamental royal gardens of Tirgovişte's grand ducal palace, the urban folk watched Vlad the Bad's rocks raining down upon the city's cobbled streets. (Dracul—*Evil*; Cymric *Drwg.*) The smell of roses, urine, poppies, and putrefying death permeated the air. Burst cattle carcasses lay in the streets, their maggot-crawling intestines strewn about the cobbles. The Gypsy fortune-tellers had prophesied the merchants' demise. And the lawyers. Impalement. A sea of blood and intestines. For seven long weeks with drought and their bodies weak, the townsfolk had held out. But on this hot, sultry day it seemed their luck had run out. For the Dragon's massive, rag-tag army had encamped in the vicinity's withered rape fields at daybreak, preparing for the renewed siege of Tirgovişte. Amazingly, in less than five months the *'Impaler Prince'* had pushed the all-powerful boyars back from Transylvania, down into deepest, sub-Carpathian Wallachia.

Cruel, hostile Wallachia.

Repeated sieges of Tirgovişte had brought starvation and disease. Also the Great Plague—the Black Death. Vlad had the support of the people. Despite his atrocities. Often he seemed a bit confused over who were his enemy and whom were his allies. He did not understand the rules of chivalry. This terrified and puzzled the boyars. Instead of taking ransom prisoners on the battlefield he would slaughter all. His army was made up of outlaws and Gypsies. *Gypsies!* Godless wanderers. Nomads. Delirious nomads, with strange languages and even stranger customs. Vagrants of every nationality, wandering endlessly, displaced from homes in various countries. East Indians, Bedouins, Kelts, Egyptians, Cossacks, Armenians, Bohemians. The boyars soon learned to leave their camp followers well away from the battlefield, lest they be enslaved in Vlad Ţepeş' massive labour camps. Despite mountainous odds, Vlad Dracula's surprisingly disciplined horde would slug it out with the paid mercenary armies of Turkish and Hungarian-backed regiments. Leather-clad men in conical, Viking-style iron helmets would sweat it out with their opponents till sundown, swinging maces, pole-axes and shields at their much-better equipped mercenary foes who wore hauberks, iron scale armour, gambesons, full knight's armour and rode mighty, silk-draped, armoured warhorses. A volley of arrows and spears would reduce the odds dramatically in just one clash (including a skilfully orchestrated campaign using pit-stakes and bear traps).

And own the blood-soaked fields when the sun had fallen.

Bootless back the mercenaries would trudge, minus their armour, horses, and weapons. On the run.

The Devil and his armies seemed to fight with a fanatical zeal, not recognising defeat. Never blinking at the face of death in the form of robotic, metal-armoured knights and snorting, fiery-eyed warhorses. As if they had a cause to die for. As if reclaiming the land. Cleansing ethnic mistakes.

And now the royal citadel had fallen.

Vlad's troops rushed into the breach made in the city walls, surprising and overwhelming the gap's too-few defenders. From parapets, thrilled women watched Vlad the Devil dispatch scores of foes, hacking men to pieces with his broadsword with a maniacal fervour, eyes gleaming as he looked up from his cape-cloaked warhorse at the maidens thronging Tirgovişte's walls. Battle-frenzied Wallachs leapt down from the wallwalk now onto the backs of knights guarding the steps to the parapets. More surged forth from rectangular belfries onto the crenelated wallwalk, taking the Byzantine-inspired bulwarks within minutes. Their eyes glowed with unholy glee. They leapt from roofs, from grain silos, from church towers into the throng, heedless of the danger or distance. Some plummeted thirty feet into the embattled defenders' arms. And they were well armed. Not well clothed, perhaps, but very, very well-armed. Their spiked maces, tulwars, lances, broadswords, arrows, shields, spears, longbows and pole-axes homemade in rural forges.

The thirty-six remaining boyars of Banat watched with dismay and consternation as the townspeople, utterly defeated, surrendered, begging Dracula's mercy. They received. Vlad had ordered the residents and their chattel spared should they capitulate within a certain time limit. His own camp followers, too, stayed a wise six miles back. No need for his soldiers to go on a raping spree with their own women and children so near to return to. Unless a Turkish or Hungarian army should come up from behind with a *blitzkrieg* sneak attack. Vlad had also cautioned his unseasoned soldiers that should they break this rule they would be swiftly reprimanded. He stood at the market-cross now, attired in cavalryman's jodhpurs, bloodied silks, and Tyrolean armour, accepting the cowed aldeormen's oaths of fealty as they knelt on one knee.

Astride an ebon warhorse, Vlad Țepeș' smug, head-held-high smile, demonic moustache, incited the hatred of all who opposed him.

At sundown, there were six impaled bodies on tall stakes in the empty palace courtyard.

There were twenty-five the next morning. Thirty-seven by late afternoon under a blisteringly hot summer sun, gagging the entire Renaissance city. These were the traitorous merchants, whose finances fuelled the independent-minded Transylvanian boyars' mercenary armies. Vlad's Gypsies went about their grisly task with an almost fanatical zeal, impaling the guilty through the abdomen, stakes cross-beamed to keep the stiffening bodies from slipping down the slick, fifteen-ft. poles. The townspeople watched from their windows, both fascinated and horrified, defenceless. Their only weapon was propaganda.

Which they used well.

Foremost of which was that the Prince had impaled the city's entire population of 30,000 through the buttocks.

There were only 10,000 citizens in Tirgoviște.

****

The next town to fall was Craiova. No massacre here. The population was overwhelmingly Wallachian. There were many bilingual Daco-Romanians, who spoke both Vulgar Latin plus a smattering of Dacian. Few Saxons. Most fled after rumours of Vlad Dracula's atrocities in the north. In German towns. 20,000 in Tîrgu Jiu. Which was ludicrous, everyone knew, because Tîrgu Jiu only had 5000 residents—a mere, chartered enclave. Five rebellious boyars had successfully besieged the town of Craiova on Assumption Day (a holy day), August 15, taking the burgh by nightfall. These were the last of Bucovina's boyars to continue holding out (for that northern *oblast's* nobility had much to lose, not least their Hungarian-held estates). One hundred forty-six captured boyars and their sons awaited sentencing in dungeons scattered across Wallachia, unaware of the horrors which awaited them.

Not impalement.
Not beheading.
Not hanging.
Slavery.
Then execution.

****

Vlad paced the great hall of the ageing, ineffective limestone castle tower at Craiova, cursing his enemies. He was Prince in all but name. Vladislav Danești II still held the much-coveted ancient throne of Wallachia and the sacred *taliath*, or crown, taking cowardly refuge at Giurgiu under the Turks' protection. All of Danești's boyars (save those in absentia in Ottoman domains, Hungary, or Byzantium) had been captured. Awaited sentencing. Some below in the earth-dungeon (oubliette) beneath the rectangular donjon. Vlad's head hurt, aching, like a poison-barbed flower had been slipped inside his ear. He was furious for no reason. In just under one year, he had reconquered most of Wallachia and lower Transylvania, from the Căliman mountains to the Dobrujian steppes of Moldavia. True, Serena had not borne him an heir. But Vlad was young, had plenty of time. He needed a son, would settle for a daughter. Anything but a barren woman. Serena was edgy too, knowing she could not conceive but keeping the truth from him lest he discard her. As far as the general population was concerned, Serena was Vlad's mysterious, high-born mistress. They were unaware of their marriage vows pledged before the ageing bishop of Erlau at Tirgoviște only days before he expired.

Serena was worried for naught. Vlad had no intention of discarding her. If worst came to worst, he could always sire a child from one of the village wenches—unless it were he who was sterile—though Serena would not be pleased. The child would be hers to raise though, as if it were her own. It was unconventional, taboo perhaps, but then Vlad was an unconventional man. It would, of course, be expected of him to disavow her and marry a fruitful heiress. No annulment would be necessary, since it would, after all, only be a matter of discarding one's mistress (!). Vlad only wished Serena would stop pretending morning sickness and claiming pregnancy when she clearly wasn't. Vlad could see it in her eyes. The fear. He had tried to explain, once, much the worse for drink, but fell laughably short of his intended meaning. She clearly thought he meant to impale her or slice her belly open, silly wench. He had joked about doing this one night not long ago, much inebriated from too much *ţuica*. Serena had gone pale. The great hall of Tirgoviște's ducal palace had ceased its chatter, servants homing in with big ears. At least half a dozen servants and emissaries had overhead Vlad say to her, tongue-in-cheek, that if she were really pregnant he should cut her belly open and see.

It would be the greatest mistake of his life.

****

October 30th, 1450 AD

A mile-long black iron chain fettered the necks of 540 convicted Wallachian boyars. They stood sad-eyed along the flagstone main street of Timişoara which had once been a Roman military road. Vlad sat his mighty roan warhorse, triumphant as Trajan himself, parading at the head of his army surging into the streets. His long, walrus moustache hung down to his chin, hair past his shoulders. He wore leather war gear, his legs bare; a conical, red, feathered cap banded with gems sat atop his head. A terrifying sight to behold. A barbarian. Beardless. The twenty-year-old uncrowned Prince of Wallachia. Satan himself.

The boyars still knew not what their punishment would be.

Serena watched from the pencil-tower as the fettered boyars and their pampered progeny were prodded forward down the gravelly street. She leaned out of the gothic window, sighting Vlad far below some distance to her left on his prancing warhorse. The dizzying height of the great tower made her eyes swim, guts lurching as she glanced down the cylindrical wall's masonry terminating sixty feet below in the castle courtyard. Serena waved a handkerchief wildly, smiling gayly from the unglazed, unshuttered window.

The prisoners were disoriented. Hungry. Men, women, children. Only a week ago most had been celebrating Mass in St Peter's cathedral, Tirgovişte, dressed in their very best finery. Satin/lace brocades, velvets, furs. Sparkling jewels. They had gathered in the capital for All Hallow's Feast under safe conduct. Should have known better, with Vlad Dracula's guerrilla army only forty leagues away. Prince Daneşti had been conspicuously absent. But Vlad had treacherously broken the truce, riding into the royal city at the head of 5000 soldiers. Immediately, he ordered the boyar factions placed under house arrest after grilling them in the great state-hall of Tirgovişte's ducal palace for over two hours. Overnight, the knighthood of Daneşti's power base were reduced to zero.

Vlad put up his left hand in a vague gesture of acknowledgment, unaware of the two fingers sticking up signifying himself as a werewolf, an agent of Satan. He had his eyes on the crowd, searching their faces with forest-green, expressionless eyes. Yes, the townsfolk feared him. Too much it seemed. Puzzling, since he had been nothing but good to Timişoara's merchants, even issuing new statutes declaring their status as a special trading burgh.

To hell with them, he thought. Let them think what they will. If they wanted to see him as Old Nick himself, all the better to keep them in line.

He smiled.

****

Dirty black hands piled stone after stone upon stone onto the wet mortar. Other stooped men rammed down the rubble/mortar-core mixture into the castle's cavity walls. Heavy, squared quoins were being levered into position in the corners of the walls by block and tackle. Pulleys brought loads of large, dressed rocks up the side of the edifice toward the impressed workers standing on wooden hoardings near old Braşov castle's roofline.

The impressed workers were the boyars of Transylvania.

More scurried on the ground far, far below, digging ditches or levelling the sides of the motte. Bracken ferns grew in profusion, a mini forest having grown up among the ruins of Vlad Dracul's old castle (formerly *Dietrichstein*), recently dismantled except for the eastern curtain wall, donjon, and impressive, round-turreted barbican gatehouse. Castle Brân's remaining ramparts and state rooms were being rebuilt and whitewashed. The boyars were exhausted and emaciated, bare feet torn and bloodied from their two-hundred-mile trek from Timişoara.

If the boyars had one thing to be thankful for, it was the knowledge that it was here at Castle Brân that they were labouring, and not the behemoth, unholy fortification springing up at Poenari, Curtea de Argeş, ninety miles to the southwest. There Vlad Ţepeş, *the Impaler,* had begun a wholly new castle on a mountain spur above the Argeş river, where the bulk of the boyar faction and their families now slaved away for their terrible master. At this moment, soldiers wielding bullwhips at Castle Dracula lashed the bleeding backs of nobility high above the swift-flowing Argeş. Bricks were being baked to supplement the stone ramparts, the rebellious boyars given the unenviable chore of mixing the bricks, then kiln-baking and hauling them on their backs up the mountainside. At a rocky spur, spanning a deep, wide ravine, a pulley had been constructed in lieu of a bridge where, brick by brick, the pulley-line was manned by men, women, and children who passed the dangling bricks on to several waiting pairs of hands. And, yes, the castle was coming along nicely.

The boyars were quickly becoming expert bricklayers.

Dozens however had perished on the long, dusty trek from Timişoara to Arefū village, beaten to death by overzealous guards. Others had died of dehydration or sunstroke, their corpses left to decompose on the dusty dirt/gravel trails while the unlucky ones trudged on through the steep, winding, canyon-like mountain passes or treacherous, lowland bogs.

Vlad Dracula looked on from the barbican-way of Castle Brân now, supervising the refurbishing of this ancient Teutonic fortress, smiling with devilish glee as his enemies rebuilt the awesome great tower he had planned himself. (He was especially proud of its unique, bevelled roof.) His plans were somewhat restricted by the original layout of the castle, however. He must follow the rock formation of the mountain's spur. One could hardly destroy the entire castle to make way for new works. (Much of the residential block was still habitable.) Vlad turned and strolled away from the great gatehouse, his eye on the distant village graveyard far below, the scene of his father's live burial. He followed a faint trail down the outcrop toward the Saxon village, stopping to marvel at blue rhododendron, yellow lilies, his eye furtively on the lookout for chauvinist, alpine pasture-land, Romanian peasantry. His trailing Wallach bodyguard would think nothing of it—many a great poem had been composed to sweethearts by long-extinct bards describing such flowers' glories and comparing them with their own lovers' attributes. Their odd plaid tartans singled the men out as outcasts among Romanians. Hated. A hot sun overhead burned the men's hair from a pristine, deep blue, Wallachian summer sky.

The village of old Braşov lay down in the valley, as if cowering from the brutish castle being reconstructed on the cliff above which would someday become the largest fortress in Romania. Each day Vlad would come out here by the gatehouse, peering through its wide arch as his high-born slaves worked away. He liked to watch the square donjon grow day by day. Eventually he would connect the entire complex to the curtain wall and whitewash the exterior (his father's great clock still chimed the hours from its lofty watchtower). Serena seemed to see something morbid about this weird behaviour, cautioning Vlad not to become a tyrant. He had laughed at that. Vlad quite liked the idea of being a tyrant.

Other days he would wander about the village cemetery, searching for signs of new burial.

Searching for his father's grave.

Vlad had yet to have the cemetery dug up. He wanted the villagers to tremble a bit. He had posted an offer of 1000 *leu* for the person who would step forward and inform Vlad of Dracul's whereabouts. And surprisingly enough, he meant to keep his word should the informant prove correct.

The peasants of Transylvania had obviously not bargained on Vlad's escaping Sultan Mured's palace. Prince Daneşti II could not help them. They had expected a Prince Palatine from Germany to be ruling them now. Not a bloodthirsty Wallachian bent on their destruction. Least of all the most-loved younger son of the voivode whom they had just buried alive twenty-one months previous! Not to mention Vlad's elder brother Mirçea, tortured and buried alive at Tirgovişte. The brother, incidentally, whom Vlad had recently exhumed at the royal capital's cemetery—where brave Mirçea had been found face-down six feet under with both his arms and legs broken. Vlad had had Mirçea respectfully interred at Cozia monastery beside the Olt river.

There had been a spate of impalements at Tirgovişte's ducal palace afterwards, a grand total of 674 thieves, rapists, murderers and brothel owners.

Prudently, there had been little resistance from the Saxons when Vlad's army converged on the poorly fortified mountain-village of old Braşov sheltering below Castle Drear mountain. The fortress's real name was Brân (Braşova to Slavs), named after its legendary Celtic ruler in pre-Roman times. But the castle had earned its secondary nickname not because of atrocities committed in its dungeons or suicides, but because the old Knights Templar stronghold was notoriously ill-lit. Prince Dracul had not bothered to renovate the decrepit, Teutonic donjon, save for the fashionable Swiss clock installed. He was often visiting his subjects—had no time for court etiquette.

Fat lot of good it did him.

His Transylvanian tenants had overthrown him when his back was turned.

Prince Dracul had been walking the tightrope for far too long; when it finally snapped he was plunged into the ravine of death. His was a no-win situation from day one of his reign. Faced with Wallachian peasants, downtrodden serfs, who owned no land, Transylvanian Saxon merchants who held land and plenty of power, pro-Hungarian boyars, pro-Turkish boyars, dissident monks. Vlad could not win. And he had not. Now his was an unmarked grave.

His son Satan, Lucifer or *Ordog* to Romanians, roamed the ancient cemetery of old Braşov, stopping to read the nearly illegible inscriptions on hoary, lichen-splotched tombstones or wooden Maltese crosses, admiring the skull and crossbones, Latin inscriptions or rare, marvellously traceried, Celtic *La Tène* stone crosses. Vlad glanced around, noting if anyone were lurking about the nearby bushes (for his lax bodyguard now lounged about the cemetery with their backs against the mossy headstones of their ancestors, soaking up the June sunlight like snakes). Funereal wooden posts, carved as if by magic, showed where the substantial, Slavic populace's own dead lay, the bizarre markers contrasting weirdly, but aesthetically pleasingly, with the others. (No less than *seven* separate nationalities, including Szekeler, Russian, and immigrant Turk, were crowded within the rustic, alpine resting place.) Vlad studied the various flora growing in profusion inside the log-fenced cemetery, picking wildflowers for his beloved from thorny rosebushes. He carefully cut them, dropping the fragrant flowers into a burlap bag. Noting no new earth among the weeds, he glanced over his shoulder for signs of intruders before calling out in Old Vlachian for his comrades to follow.

Vlad returned to the castle now, frustrated once again in his search for his father's grave. He walked down a narrow lane from the village cemetery towards the mountain trail winding a brambly, treacherous path toward his yet-unfinished citadel. Serena would be awaiting him inside the recently renovated barbican-gatehouse. Its floors had been replaced; seasoned spruce-fir timbers from the abundant, sub-Carpathian forests of Transylvania, which surrounded the region. He inhaled deep, enjoying the sharp, piney musk-smell of fresh lumber drifting about on the midday mountain air. Several bodyguards stalked ahead of him, a few behind, protecting their lord from sneak attack. Not that any *villein* would be foolish enough to take him on in single combat with either sword, battle-axe, mace, nor dagger, all of which Vlad was proficient in usage. But a sniper bowman or crossbowman would be another matter…

His nine *Armașii* (personal bodyguard) were of mixed Goidelic/Brittonic ancestry, an uneasy alliance (to say the least!) of Wanted brigands on the run from Saxon and Orthodox Church posses sworn to eradicate these worshippers of Lucifer from the face of continental Europe; to extirpate these sinners' "non-Aryan," non-Roman tongues for the good of all. And woe betide those who stood in the Church's way. (Most were ex-highwaymen, offered pardons if they would join Vlad's heretical Crusade.) The majority remaining in this century 1450 were of Cambric descent: the remnants of an indigenous, peaceful, Neolithic race of swarthy *Keltoi* formerly ranging as far afield as Asia Minor, and, once, Egypt. Their later foes, the *Gelonae* (Scythians, or Scotti), had been utterly decimated by the ultra-efficient Romans for their sacrifices of concubines, horses, and slaves. It was their black magic which had set off Europe's newly-proclaimed Inquisition like gunpowder. These much-hated adversaries, the *Gaédheltschach*, had set up their blasphemous empire in Greece—the

Dorians—whom had enslaved their own Prydainic ancestors in Galatia. Now they were bitter allies, each staving off extinction, necessarily but grudgingly banding together. (They lived as bandits when they lived at all.) The Dorians had suffered the same ignominious fate of the Cimmerians whom they had overcome, themselves overwhelmed in 1000 BC by Phoenicians from Syria. Vlad guessed that if they didn't stop their constant bickering and internecine warfare (consisting of cattle raids, assassinations, and abductions) they would be extinct by century's end.

A small contingent of ambassadors stood in the barbican-way, dwarfed by Castle Brân's looming walls as Vlad trudged up the incline toward the outer gatehouse. They were Turks—come to feel out the terrain, the mood of the villagers of Transylvania. Also come to verify for themselves if the awesome rumour that Vlad Dracula—escapee—was now unofficial ruler of Wallachia.

They were indeed astonished.

As Vlad's personal bodyguard approached the gatehouse, three of the six Turkish ambassadors strode forward, demanding in impudent Turkish to see the pretender/Prince of Wallachia.

"I am Lord Dracula," Vlad retorted. "Vlad the Great; voivode of ungro- Wallachia." He shouldered aside two of his bodyguard, hand on his mighty, wooden sword-hilt lest one of the Turkish ambassadors turn out to be an assassin. He presented an awesome sight to behold; head held high, arrogant. Long, black, walrus moustache, plaited, drooping past his chin. Leather war gear: jerkin, laced tunic, polished steel greaves and breastplate, ebon, knee-high leather boots, pointed wood/leather cap upon his head. Huge, bloodshot, wide-open green eyes from last night's overflow of *ţuica*. (Plum brandy.) Beardless. All of the richly attired ambassadors of Islam standing before him wore trimmed beards and long, drooping moustaches. Their heads were pig-shaven, egg-shaped under enormous, elaborately coiled, white turbans.

One of the ambassadors very impudently and very, very unwisely ordered Vlad to return with them as a prisoner of Sultan Mured II on pain of invasion and great bloodshed. The imperious Turk also informed the unamused Prince that he was being demoted from *hospidar* of Wallachia to Count of Bucovina.

"You shall come with us underling, vassal Count of Bucovina, back to Sofia. Come. Come. Come, underling, you are no Prince. You are but a boy." The Turk laughed in Vlad's face.

Fatal mistake.

Vlad put his arm around the Turkish ambassador's shoulder, speaking in a very congenial tone that he MIGHT be willing to return, but that he would need a couple of hours with his council to discuss this, and that in the meantime why don't the six illustrious ambassadors join him as his guests, share a bottle of *ţuica* in the barbican tower. Luring the Turks—very friendly—toward the castle's gatehouse like a spider luring flies with its sticky web.

They entered the solar two floors up inside the barbican's gatehouse. The six nonplussed Turks had been ushered up a winding flight of worn, fire-blackened steps ascending into darkness. "You see, my council would be very bereft and alone if I left them," Vlad's booming voice echoing off the stone walls (sounding as if he were in a barrel), "they may not understand my leaving." All the while careful not to betray the terrible fate which awaited the ambassadors above. A bevy of soldiers brought up the rear.

A well-lit, rectangular, spacious hall, or solar, awaited their presence, its only furnishings a large, oaken desk and sapphire-blue, brightly polished, circa-1300 suit of Milanese knight's armour on one rough-hewn wall. A lone cresset fluttered mesmerizingly in its iron sconce, half-burnt. The six ambassadors spread out, uneasy now. Other than their small, armed contingent downstairs in the billet chambers sharing a flask of *ţuica* with the Romanian guardsmen, the Turkish emissaries had no forces nearby lest some mad voivode wish violence upon them.

That would be unlikely, unless he were insane. Large Turkish battalions lay crouched only a few miles from the Romanian border should a hostile boyar commit an act of violence against His Immaculate Superlative Majesty's faithful ambassadors of Islam. Of Allah.

Vlad seated himself at the great desk, removing his conical cap, looking supremely authoritarian now. He eyed the ambassadors with sudden disdain, eyes monstrously huge, loose plaits and black locks tumbling over his broad shoulders like some wild barbarian chieftain. Which he was. He poured himself a crystal glass of brandy, nonchalantly inching forward his left hand and caressing a small, curious, oblong knob upon his desktop. Vlad watched one particular ambassador with interest, smiling unholily as the offending Turk stepped over a certain invisible boundary…

Suddenly a yawning, five by five-ft. square chasm opened up beneath the Muslim's feet, plunging him into a waiting pit below. Vlad's fingers pressed upon the smooth, rectangular knob, face contorted in triumph. Vengeance.

"Oh, SO sorry, Your Highness," getting up from his chair, stalking over to the precipice.

The ambassador's single, bloodcurdling, strangled scream echoed throughout the barbican—suddenly cut off.

"Forgot about that little boobytrap," Vlad said aloud, peering down into the pit with a gruesome smile.

Fifteen feet below, dark brown eyes staring glassy, unseeing, the Turkish ambassador lay sprawled in a horrible parody of sleep. Twelve-inch spikes impaling his body like a bed of huge needles. Blood still spurted from his pierced heart. Punctured eyeballs and grey brain-matter topped the deliciously sharp iron spikes rivetted into the ceiling of the soldiers' quarters below. His head impaled like some gruesome Celtic treat on Walpurgis Night, sans the candied apple.

The other ambassadors stuttered aloud and begged for mercy now as Vlad turned his unholy eyes on them.

"It seems you gentlemen/Turkish fuckers haven't doffed your turbans to *Vlad Țepeș*," Vlad said aloud, grinning, "voivode, warlord, Prince of Wallachia and soon to be King of Romania. Let me strengthen your traditions for you."

Vlad nodded to his gloating soldiers, still smiling. A dozen or so came forward, suddenly wielding iron hammers.

"Tack their turbans to their heads."

Their screams could be heard till daybreak.

Until the last Turk in Castle Brân's gatehouse expired.

Serena waited up in her chambers above, covering her ears.

Chapter Eight

27 August, 1453 AD.
Argeş Valley, Little Poenari Mountain (Near Curtea de Argeş), Transylvania

The river Argeş shimmered below the Făgăras mountain range in a purple haze, winding through the valley at the foot of Castle Dracula's 1000-foot crag, sheer walls of granite on one side merging into the recently mortared stone-and-brick curtain walls built by slaving boyars. The valley echoed with the bleating of sheep and the shouts and whistles of shepherds, their vicious, spike-collared sheepdogs barking somewhere down the valley. The river was dark and sluggish; polluted with the effluent of upstream German towns.

Towns soon to be exterminated by Vlad.

Vlad stood at a gothic lancet-window of the great, slender, cylindrical watchtower, recently erected to supplement the huge, quadrangular donjon adjoining as a lookout tower and last refuge. Vlad smiled wryly, with the sure knowledge that his two newest strongholds would be well-nigh impregnable short of prolonged starvation-siege. And their legendary construction would be the stuff of legends for future generations. Two camps of humiliated boyars had been simultaneously building castles at old Braşov and Arăfu for almost five years. They had finished the castle overlooking the Argeş river two weeks ago, had known their time was nigh. A disorganised flock of terrified boyars had organised a shoddy, last-minute uprising in their camp below the misty, rolling, fir-dotted green valley across the river thirty days ago, but Vlad's Vlachian mercenaries had routed them on horseback, assembling the defeated boyars in the courtyard of Castle Dracula after their humiliating march up the mountain.

For thirteen days, the screams of the impaled shattered the peace of the Făgăras foothills.

Five hundred forty-six boyars in all—representing the flower of Transylvania/Hungary's nobility. Their distraught wives and daughters were allowed to flee to Hungary upon the condition of never returning. Their word would have no power; they were only women, which in Hungary would disallow them from royal claims; chances are their word would not be believed anyway. Who would believe the sheer extent of Vlad's crimes? Lest they return, they were warned of a similar fate as their kin's. Prince Danești could not help them. The throne of Hungary had been vacant for three years since the premature death by plague of the young king, Ladislas Jagiello V, whose heir-apparent—the son of Transylvania's viceroy—was not yet of age. The present regent, however, would be furious once he knew of Prince Vlad's unlawful impalements of Hungarian knights and boyars. John Hunyádi (János Hunyádi), viceroy of Transylvania, would not help them; it was his all-encompassing power as voivode of Transylvania which secured Vlad's rule in the northerly Bucégi mountains, protecting the Tyrant from Danești's long, Turkish arm of the law. The Gypsies went about their ghastly business in a manner unusually different from their predictable joviality and laid-back—some would say 'lazy'—ways. A multinational rabble of Romany, Szgany, Bohemians, Celts and war-happy *Combrŏgos* who'd all been the victims of Aryan discrimination perpetrated the impalements. (With honour.) They skewered the traitorous boyars gleefully, vengeance for the multitudes of Gypsy wives, daughters and—aye—even sons sold to the Turks and Arabs as sex slaves, filling the aristocrats' treasure chests with silver, gems, and gold, used in turn to keep the semi-nomadic Vlachs from farming soil which'd once rightfully been theirs, even luring nomadic, East Indian settlers to cultivate the land with promises of territory and gold. All in vain—the nomadic Romany had preferred their caravans.

The horrific stench of rotting corpses permeated the courtyard, ward, baileys, and towers of Castle Dracula now. Dried, almost mummified, impaled boyars' bodies crowded the cobbled courtyard on fifteen-foot stakes mortared into the fortress's paved precincts. Fine brocades of velvet, silk, satin and lace hung limply from the grisly cadavers in a motley, autumn-coloured display of wealth and power. Not a breath of wind on the mountaintop stirred to clear the twilit air of putrid flesh. Crows hovered cryptically over the castle towers. No man dared strip the raiments from the cadavers' bodies, for theirs were the clothes of blood-money. Visitors arrived daily from all over Transylvania to gape at this gruesome display in mad Vlad Dracula's courtyard high above the Argeș. Some, especially Saxons and Swabians, brought back ludicrous tales and exaggerations to their hometowns. Others such as foreign ambassadors, dukes, barons and diplomats, particularly from Catholic nations, reported amazing numbers to their courts who were at odds with the Orthodox-protecting *Našis* (Prince; O. Slavic 'father') of eastern Europe who refused to allow the Pontiff's Inquisitor-Generals to 'cleanse the Balkans of its heretics'—namely Protestant Hussites, Orthodox followers and pagan adherents of Wicca.

Vlad was saddened today.

Even the sight of his impaled arch-enemies failed to lift him from this eddying sea of gloom and Transylvanian mist within and without his mind. For he had just heard the news last evening. News to shock and sadden every man, woman, and child in Christendom. Something so unbelievable, so astounding that most had refused to believe it at first. But soon monastery bells, church bells, castle bells across eastern and western Europe, in every city, were tolling a wake for the Queen of Cities, the Jewel on the Bosporus.

Byzantium had fallen.

Constantinople, invincible they had believed, fell to Sultan Mehmed the Conqueror, August 1.

The eastern half of the Holy Roman Empire no longer existed. The balance of power had now shifted to Frederick III of Austria, the new Holy Roman Emperor. The Catholic powers of Europe seemed to have settled into a strange lethargy, almost alliance, with the victorious Turks. Surely if they could not subvert the eastern European Greek-Orthodox (whom had unanimously rejected the formalised accord joining their Church under the temporal authority of Rome before the fall of Constantinople) to the True Faith, perhaps Mehmed could reduce the rebellious *Našis* of the Baltics: Russia, the Ukraine, Lithuania, Estonia, Romania, Bulgaria, Albania, Serbia, Slovakia, Slovenia?

Vlad turned away from the narrow, unglazed window. Arched wooden shutters banged noisily as a fierce Transylvanian east wind whooshed through the Argeș valley, howling high up in the Făgăras mountains and foothills surrounding the vicinity in a precipitous, concentric circle.

It was dark now. Blackest night, no moon nor stars. A cannonading roar of overhead thunder pounded across the mountains. The slender tower shook. Vlad had stood here since mid-afternoon, pondering his alternatives, his mind elsewhere as dark cumulonimbus clouds rolled in sneakily over the wild mountains. Candles fluttered erratically in their gilt candelabrum scattered about the tiny, tapestried chamber on small tables or on top of giant, iron-bound treasure chests. The unbelievable, horrid stench of impaled, month-old corpses was carried aloft on the brisk wind like a tunnel from Hell. Vlad Dracula gagged on the noisome smell momentarily, righting himself. He would have to get used to this smell, learn to love it, even, he scolded himself in Romanian. There were more trials and tribulations ahead.

The stink brought back unsavoury memories; Vlad lying awake in his straw pallet inside Egrigöz fortress, western Anatolia, where the smell of impaled, rotting corpses had kept him awake and vomiting at night; in daylight he would crawl to the bars high above to peek out the lone window as the gory executions took place in the hot, arid, dusty courtyard.

Vlad shook himself out of his unbidden memory. He stood on the highest floor of the cylindrical/rhomboidal watchtower, seven storeys up. This was the sentries' lookout, part of their begrudged circuit throughout the grand castle. Or conversely, Vlad's mysterious study chamber, learning the secrets of the stars and Gypsies' tarot cards. (It was his hobby.) Black satin drapes fluttered mesmerizingly about the mysterious archive chamber's numerous 'fetishes', armoury, and sole window, or draped over the castle's 'Christian' altar. Few windows pierced either the watchtower or the machicolated great tower mortared onto it, nor arrow slits for that matter. The amalgamated structure would compensate with its bulky solidity, nonetheless. Above the keep's third storey, however, the rare, Renaissance windows on the mountain's cliff-side were as spacious as any in Europe, with delicate freestone engravings or mouldings on carved cornices and lintels. A steeply sloped, slate-roofed, conical witch's cap topped the cylinder of ten-foot-thick masonry. Vlad's redoubt was built of ironstone, limestone, and red brick, with generous amounts of soft, pliable sandstone for the lintels and corbels. Flower-sculpted mullions on windows lent the fortalice a Renaissance palace's aspect. White, ashlar quoins reinforced the corners of square towers. Jagged, crow-stepped battlements guarded the mountain pass on a steep incline; a stiff walk for the sentries. The macabre fort was constructed with the latest Austrian and Norman technology (though of Byzantine/Serb design), very much a Teutonic castle, if not in ownership. Vlad was very proud of it. Italianate loggias were being skilfully built in the courtyard beside the Orthodox chapel. Vlad was proud of both slave-labour castles built by toiling boyars—Brân and Castle Dracula (which was by far the bigger undertaking, requiring extensive Pipe Rolls of expenditures, since Brân only needed minor reconstruction)—mayhap he should organise another battalion of boyars someday, who were sure to cause trouble in the future?

Hmm. Yes. Vlad smiled to himself. Yes, that would be an excellent idea. Perhaps his capital at Tirgovişte? A bigger watchtower?

He pondered his situation. Vlad, to his dismay, wasn't the only man claiming himself Prince of Wallachian land. In fact, Vlad was the usurper, steadily nudging aside the official Prince of Wallachia, Vladislav Daneşti, who still held a dwindling loyalty of followers near Schassburg (Sighişoara, in Romanian). Dan II, of the Daneşti clan, was still, technically, voivode of Wallachia. He had no boyars left to implement his offensive strategies. Vlad had impaled them all. Almost all. A few had proven records of loyalty and unblemished honour who had served Vlad Dracul. These boyars (whose service had been exemplary), had given the distressed, disavowed Gypsy factions sanctuary on their lands, among the few in eastern Europe to do so. Yet a small handful of boyars had fled to Serbia, to seek Turkish help against Vlad Dracula.

Vlad's most amazing, controversial decree during his brief nine months' official reign as Prince of Wallachia had been to knight low-born peasants on the battlefield for feats of valour, automatically elevating some into positions of great power. A new, loyal regime of boyars had been audaciously created from the ranks of peasants; Vlad passing out certificates on rabbit skins to the common man—securing their tenure on lands in Transylvania for all eternity.

Menacing shadows flickered in the corners, ominous wings thrown by candles half-drowned in their own wax. Only yellow stubs remained in their brass candelabra. Some were mere wicks floating in melted beeswax in ornate silver saucers, with Dracula's heraldry etched inside. The pine torches in their sconces were unlit (for no servant dared to interrupt Vlad's 'rites').

A lone spider crawled along the rough, stone masonry. Vlad snatched it between his thumb and forefinger, popping it into his mouth. Mm. Tasty.

Well, actually, not so tasty.

Vlad grimaced, spitting out the arachnid, sour, acrid juices from its ruptured abdomen burning his tongue.

A shocked, horrified manservant crept away from the room's open, ogee-headed doorway, scurrying downstairs to spread the news.

Mad Dracula. Spider eater.

****

25 December, 1456 AD (Old Julien Calendar), Wallachia
Royal Palace, Tîrgovişte

The Christmas banquet was brimming with the finest wines, the choicest duck, boar, venison, poultry, rabbit, mutton, pheasant, capercaillie, goose, and quail, *sărmala* (stuffed cabbage leaves), dressing, *mititii*, the finest, freshest vegetables, the tastiest German ale, Slovak beers, French red wine, champagne and Wallachian plum brandy, the most scrumptious, fruit-filled sweet pastries. Vlad Dracula sat enthroned at the head of the banquet table, admiring the food on an empty stomach and the faces of the beautiful women dressed in silk, lace, glittering jewels, crinolines and furs present at his coronation feast. Temporarily ousted and expelled from Transylvania by Daneşti II in fall of 1449, his new-model army had never looked back. His initial defeat at the battle of Balteni, near Cetestăni-Bucharești, had led Vlad to an astounding series of victories over Daneşti's few remaining boyar-factions. Come 1456, only Sighişoara with its fourteen mighty round donjons had held out, until December 6, four months after Vladislav Daneşti II had been defeated in battle near Tîrgsor, had the great city surrendered. Dracula had bested Dan in single combat, unhorsing the traitorous pretender and disarming him with one blow from his morning-star-shaped, ball-and-chain mace. Daneşti had begged for mercy, for that which he would not receive. Vlad had had the Prince beheaded, after forcing Daneşti to dig his own grave amongst a meadow, afterwards named the Meadow of Sorrows. Sighişoara had bitterly capitulated in the midst of winter, during blizzards, without further reprisals.

Serena caught Vlad's glances at the beautiful women sprinkled about the banquet tables, gave his hand a jealous squeeze. She was Princess Cjnèatasha, an obscure heiress from Moldavia. He glanced at her, amused. They'd just celebrated their eighth, wonderful anniversary together four days ago. Serena had been with Vlad from the start, having followed him into two years' Moldavian exile. The other women and girls present tonight were boyars' daughters, prized fillies most likely destined for Saxon *margraves* or Hungarian chancellors. Or Venetian merchants.

Or Turks.

Another worry dogged Vlad's mind as he watched the colourful, stripe-clothed jugglers and court jesters, listened to the minstrels and minnesingers, some French, some German.

His half-brother, Vlad the Monk (an Orthodox monk), had proclaimed himself *voevode* two weeks ago at Timişoara, but with a puny following. The monk's followers were entrenched at Bistritz, a large city in northeastern Transylvania. Vlad hadn't even known of Vladislav's existence until a couple of years ago. He'd been the offspring of a high-born Transylvanian noblewoman; one of Dracul's many mistresses before his marriage to Caltuna—Vlad Dracula's stepmother. Indeed, there were so many hazy claimants to Dracul's brood that Vlad had no idea how many illegitimate brothers and sisters he actually had, for the Vlachs had a highly peculiar method of dividing up estates. Unlike the Normans and Saxons controlling all of Europe, the Wallachians had no stigma of illegitimacy—no disgraced, pregnant women carrying unwanted babes. Family possessions were divided amongst all at the death of the parents, fair enough for peasants, but disastrous for nobility. Once a boyar or voivode died, his entire clan would plunge into a state of permanent internecine warfare, burning crops, raping, pillaging, whole demesnes being massacred.

Vlad thought having a barren wife had some things to be commended, smiling cynically to himself as the banquet was in full swing.

He couldn't stuff another raspberry pastry, another turkey wing, mutton leg, pork haunch, chicken thigh, beef steak or *patisserie* into his bloated belly. Vlad had drunk enough French red wine to fill the castle garderobe (latrine) for a week. His hooded eyes watched double images float by in front of him, too hammered to protest at each refilled glass poured by the servants. Harp players, flute masters, lyre minstrels, troubadours, minnesingers all took their turns up on the high wooden dais, their glorious soprano/falsetto voices or the gentle Yuletide melody of musical instruments falling like rain on Vlad's ears, lulling him to sleep. His less-inebriated mistress/wife Serena (aka Cjnèatasha) sat at his side, fending off the occasional advance and hairy hands on her thigh by courtiers too drunk to realise that if the master of Wallachia should catch them they would most likely be impaled in the morning.

Neither, of course, realised they were being set up.

The Saxon minnesinger plucked at his small harp lackadaisically, watching the warrior-Prince with eager, bright blue eyes as Vlad Dracula held a slurred conversation with one of his more trusted boyars, equally inebriated. Michael Beheim, ex-soldier of fortune, former Teutonic knight and Crusader, disgruntled Roman Catholic slowly tuned his harp strings, nodding nonchalantly toward the Bosnian diplomat/Turkish assassin-spy standing aloof in a dark corner wearing a crimson satin cape and bright, aquamarine-blue silk blouse with matching tights and pointed red shoes.

The assassin was not here to kill Vlad Dracula.

Though he'd like to.

****

Brother Hans watched from a corner of one of the long, thick, heavy oaken trestle tables, cautious with his drinks, a holy Benedictine monk masquerading as a Venetian merchant and moneylender come to offer his services. His opaque, pale grey eyes, too, glowed with anticipation. Not with anticipation of an assassination. Not for personal gain. Not for money. Hans anticipated the chronicles he would write—with Michael Beheim's assistance—of the tyrant who denied Wallachia of the True Faith, and the just mercy of the Inquisition to cleanse the souls of the Unclean Ones—through fire, should they be unrepentant sinners or unfortunate backsliders. Brother Hans still seethed inside. Four months ago—a hot August day it was—Vlad Dracula had personally requisitioned the holy relics of St Luke and St Mark from Brother Hans, Jacob, and Blasius, devout Benedictines from St Gall monastery Switzerland, who had crossed into Wallachia from Hungary to preach the gospel of Christ. Instead of the welcome they had expected, good, hot food, warm bed, immunity, the insolent Prince had intercepted the monks at Craiova, a strategic frontier town. His heathen soldiers ransacked the Benedictine wagon full of holy relics and pamphlets for the poor, advising the monks of their trespassing into Romanian territory, confiscating their goods at the portcullis-gate into the town. The three monks and several lay brothers had been on foot, barefoot, heading eventually for Transylvania—wild, hostile, heathen wilderness.

The Prince himself had come out of his fortress, scolding the three devout monks for half an hour. He then audaciously ordered the trio up to his hilltop fortress, as they had had no 'passes' to enter Transylvania.

In the town below, a dozen or more Romanian, Magyar, Szekler or Saxon malcontents had been recently impaled in the town square. Their crime? Highway robbery and subversion for an independent German, Magyar, or Szekler state. Anathema to Vlad's eyes.

The three brothers were led up the spiral stairs of a lofty cylindrical tower, one of three great *'turris magnis'*, where they could view the grisly scene below. Vlad Dracula grilled them at length; of their mission, their thoughts on Wallachia, their opinion of the horrible sight below, their opinion of HIM. He questioned them at length of their own beliefs, of their faith, which he thought was a bit hazy and unclear, saying so himself. Saying he believed them to be madmen, sissies, fit for the black dresses they wore. Said he would impale them on the spot if they so much even hinted of Papist dogma while in Wallachia. And their holy relics? Bah! Garbage. The good friars watched in utter dismay as a mob of dirty Gypsies piled the relics in a heap below, lighting a bonfire in the courtyard. The monks dared not protest for fear of impalement, not failing to notice the (surely pagan?) gold stake/altar in the middle of the throne hall. A phallic symbol? Vlad then told them to get the Hell out before he boiled them and had them for supper.

Brother Hans knew not of the Turkish spy's presence or intentions. Beheim, a Saxon minstrel, knew of the Bosnian Muslim's presence but not directly of his plans. He hoped the assassin was here to murder the Prince; that was why Beheim had bribed the castle garrison into allowing the diplomat into the banquet—bribed with gold *leu* and homosexual favours. Enough gold coins for the four guards of the Princess's private chambers to escape into Yugoslavia. Two large bags each—courtesy of the Holy Roman Emperor, Frederick III of Austria.

Vassal of the Sultan of Turkey.

Vlad Dracula slumped forward suddenly into his half-eaten trencher (bread slab), too drunk to stay awake for the midnight Yuletide carols, his faithful Vlachs sober at his side, ever-vigilant. The banquet had degenerated into a drunken revel. Half of the men had drunk themselves under the tables already. The ladies flirted openly now with the courtiers, regardless of marital status. Serena, resigned, signalled for her chamberlain, Miháil Floreşcu, to take her away.

A shadowy figure along the tapestried wall followed.

Candles flickered out. Rushes burnt low, pages too preoccupied or inebriated to tend to them. A lone, clear hourglass on a table in a corner sprinkled its last few grains of sand into the bottom. The few sober castle attendants and guards ushered out the remaining revellers to their outbuilding's quarters.

****

Serena entered her bedchamber, exhausted and wobbly. Tipsy. Miháil had left, locking her door. Guilty. Knowing he'd be handing over the keys to the Turkish assassin who'd requested he have his way with her first. Miháil strode immediately toward his own gothic chambers, surreptitiously dropping the heavy keys into the assassin's hand as he passed. Miháil felt especially guilty of the five Romanian conspirators, for he'd been fond of Vlad Ţepeş' strong-willed, low-born 'wife'. Floreşcu had seen through Dracula and his peasant mistress's façade early on, for Serena had been too awkward and provincial to be of noble blood. Princess Cjnèatasha Moldítsa, indeed! He had been her chamberlain for three years now.

But the money…the amount was unbelievable. More than he would ever hope to make in ANY post in Dracula's Princedom. Sultan

Mehmed's resources were, after all, limitless.

Miháil paced quickly now. Bosnia, his new destination as Pasha. A few sumptuous clothes, sword, dagger, packed into leathern sacks. Quick. Quick! A faint scream echoed from above, reverberating through the strangely empty palace corridors. Another. More frenzied this time. Muffled now. Miháil ground his teeth, shutting out the awful sounds of luxurious bedsprings creaking. Steady now, hopeless screams, full of agony and humiliation.

Miháil swung the sack over his shoulder.

****

Serena never heard her attacker enter.

He grabbed her from behind, arm around her neck, struggling as she bit his hand with fang-like teeth as he tried to muzzle her. Drew blood. He forced her onto the silk curtained, blood-red, four poster bed, overpowering her, ripping open her sheer, orange shift. Serena screamed into the open palm of his hand, frustrated, horrified as he entered her, helpless as he raped her, slowly, brutally. She could see his unfamiliar features in the dim candlelight.

Béla Blásko had not had such fun in years, not since Sultan Mured II had allowed him to rape Mara, the Sultan's new Christian bride from Constantinople, the night of the wedding feast. She had been a virgin.

Clear though, that this dark wench had not enjoyed their coupling. Clawed, scratched, bit. Béla had punched her face in return, a dozen times or more; he'd lost count. *Too bad*, Béla thought to himself. He drew a long, slim dagger from his sheath. She spat in his face. Serena screamed, hysterical, muffled as the victorious Muslim, blood-brother of the notorious Order of Assassins, lowered his dagger lovingly to her belly. Furious, enraged at the mutilation between her legs to come.

But she had been spared once, many years ago. Circumcision was not her fate tonight. No. And she had been raped for the last time, would miss Vlad's tender ministrations for all eternity, knew that when the dagger slit open her belly.

Disembowelling her in her bed.

****

Vlad woke with a humongous headache. 'Twas like the time when he was five years old and ventured into his father's bell-tower at

Braşov where the tremendous, ten-foot, cast-iron bells had set his ears ringing for weeks.

The palace hall was dark, its marble hearth subdued, silent. Vlad lurched from the now-silent trestle table, collapsing onto the floor. Something was wrong. If he hadn't known better, he would've sworn he were poisoned.

Something quivered inside his belly, the way it did in battle when he sensed danger at his back. Call it intuition. He shouted out loud for his seneschal, Cirstian Mohács.

"Yes sire?" The seneschal strode into the great hall. As luck would have it, one of the few sober men in the castle. And one of the few men loyal to the Impaler.

"Order the gates drawn, drawbridges up. No man leaves this castle."

"But sire—"

"Do it!"

"But sire, some have already left."

"*CLOSE THE FUCKING GATES! NOW!*"

"Yes sire." Cirstian knew better than to disobey one of Vlad's orders. He rushed toward the main gatehouse, ploughing through knee-deep Christmas snow, waking the sleeping guards with the flat of his sword; watching as they raised the drawbridge and lowered the two, huge, iron/wood portcullises. The clank of rolling chains and slamming iron spikes on icy cobblestone must have awakened the entire palace. Cirstian reported back, saying nothing was amiss, the Princess's chambers (or so he was told) safely locked. Vlad nodded, relieved, slipping off into a fitful sleep, slumped on the cold, flagstone floor. Drunk. Unaware of the darkness and sorrow awaiting the morrow.

****

He woke slowly from a pleasant dream. Of paradise. Bright and indescribably colourful, full of wonderful, fresh-scented roses, lilacs and crocuses rather than impaled human innards. The glorious fragrance of cinnamon and lavender haunted the fay, surreal air. Serena had been in his dream, holding his hand, guiding Vlad toward the Corinthian portals of Heaven. The pearly gates stood open, untended, peaceful, the rush of a nearby waterfall tantalizingly close, but out of sight. Apple, cherry, and plum trees littered a wonderful, leaf-carpeted trail towards Heaven. Autumn leaves, spectacular in the multicoloured, Otherworldly brilliance. A vast, exotic orchard full of fruit trees laden with strange fruits the likes he'd never seen before led the way. Grassy hillocks, ferns, falling, fluttering, twirling leaves; mossy, lichened rocks, vegetation, wildflowers, trees all seemed to glow with a phosphorescent, radiant, yellowish hue. Leprechaun land. So peaceful. So...homey.

Vlad woke suddenly with the sun shining in his eyes from a stained-glass, traceried, oriel window illuminating the barrel-vaulted hall. The ground floor was silent. No servants about. He sat up groggily on the hard, cold, flagstone floor, the dream quickly receding from his mind. Like a poem of tragic love collected by his great-grandfather from the last bard. Dead now. Long since dead. Even the name not to be remembered.

Vlad stood up, wobbly, brushing the dust from his fine, silken raiments. He wore a crimson, ankle-length cape, black blouse, purple tights. Once dapper, crumpled now. Silently berated himself; an assassin could have entered the hall whilst he slept, plunged a dagger through his heart. Cirstian's few sober guardsmen still eyed the doors no doubt.

Feeling better now, he strode towards the turnpike leading up to his chambers within an octagonal, many-sided, lead-roof-capped tower with its distinctive, bell-shaped peak. And dearest Serena's down the hall. He realised with alacrity that, except for innumerable war campaigns, last night was the first night in eight, glorious, passionate years he'd been away from Serena's side. Never had he taken a mistress or peasant to his bed during his punitive expeditions. The throbbing of his head Vlad easily ignored now, carelessly dashing up the unlit, badly worn steps. A heavy layer of pristine, Yuletide snow lay on the ground this morning, visible from inside the stairwell, through one of the turret's loopholes.

Vlad halted at a silk-sashed, lime green entrance to the royal domicile's gold-tapestried, stone hallway. Black beads of jet danged from the pale green sash. Immediately Vlad's skin began to prickle as he took notice suddenly of the hall's awful, tomblike silence, the unnatural absence of the hustle and bustle of manservants, chambermaids, guardsmen and other staff members of Tirgovişte's ducal palace.

"What the...?"

No guards in sight. All four. Gone. Serena's door at the far end of the hall was closed. Dust motes danced through the early morning sunlight; refracted through an arched window at the end of the hallway rife with arcane occult tracery. No matter. The guards were obviously passed out in the next corridor. They would be swiftly reprimanded. A good dunking with their thumbs tied behind their backs in the city pond would serve them right.

Vlad fumbled with the keys at his leather belt, unlocking the door, entering with a smile, faltering...

"Are you awake yet, my laz..." Voice trailing off, bewildered, narrowed eyes unable to register the carnage on Serena's bed for the greenish, intestinal gore and bright, crimson blood, still liquid, cloaking and camouflaging the nubile, nude, female figure which had once been his wife, sprawled suggestively on the carmine, silk-draped bed.

Exposed innards still steamed in the princess's cold bedchamber like a butchered animal's offal; noisomely nauseating even to one such as he. Amorous thoughts instantly fled Țepeș' mind.

Vlad stumbled forward in slow motion, retching, eyes overflowing. As if he were wading through water. Unbelieving.

He knelt at Serena's side, taking her small, stiff, cold white hand into his own, sobbing, weeping. Sad. Angry. Furious. Tears of rage and revenge. Of bitter betrayal by his own castle guards.

Vlad raised his head, howling at the daylight-hidden full moon. Like a wolf.

"*N-O-O-O-O-O-O-O-O-O!*"

Out in the snowbound courtyard, servants halted from their chores, carrying buckets of water, armloads of rushes, straw, or hay, eyes darting toward the slender, cylindrical Chîndia watchtower of Tîrgoviște's hilltop fortress. No one rushed to the tortured man's aid, locked away in his earth-pit dungeon. No one questioned. Vlad's policy of terror had been too effective. Just another poor soul being pulled apart on the rack, murmured servants and soldiers amongst themselves.

Only one man went to his aid.

"*N-O-O-O-O-O-O!!!! N-O-O-O-O-O-O-O!!!!*"

Cirstian retched at the horror. His deep blue eyes bulged from his head. Vlad was truly insane, would never live this down. Killing his mistress with his own dagger. All because she was barren. Sad, because Cirstian knew Vlad really loved Serena. But sometimes Vlad went off his head, barely rational, wild with rage for the most minor discrepancies. Last evening Vlad really had went off the deep end, disembowelling his mistress/wife in a drunken fit of rage. Which was so unusual and ironic, even for him, not exactly known for his predictability. In essence Vlad had doomed himself, for so many courtiers had heard him boast of his intention of slicing open his woman's belly to produce the faked child. He and Serena had sat together last night, smiling, holding hands at the banquet table. Like newlyweds.

And now mad Vlad Dracula knelt at his murdered mistress's bedside, crying shamelessly, howling at himself with rage. And sorrow.

Pity.

Cirstian stood indecisively at Vlad's quaking shoulder, Cirstian slumped against the stone wall in a state of repulsed awe. Revulsion. His stomach turned. Never had he seen or heard the Dragon of Wallachia blubber before. The grisly sight atop of Serena's blood-spattered, chintz-draped, four poster bed was truly horrible. Cirstian's blood turned to ice with the sound of Țepeș' unearthly howling. The man was totally unhinged. In the impalement yards, Cirstian had learned to control his nausea, never for a moment daring to turn his nose up at the smell; taking some comfort in knowing the victims were worthy of their punishment. 'Twas a favourite of the Turks, who used it to keep their Serbian, Albanian, and Bulgarian populations in fear, docile. Vlad had brought the idea back from Turkey on a large scale, using it to force his unwilling countrymen to defy the Turks. But this...

This was *ghastly*. A beautiful, exotic, high-cheeked brunette in her prime: lovely, voluptuous, sexy; her intestines strewn about the four-poster bed's rich, red comforters and floorboards now, ruptured, horrible smelling, permanently ruining the bedsheets and floor rushes. No one would ever inhabit this memory-haunted room again. Might as well knock the entire tower down. And the stink. Gagging.

The wench's brown, glassy, lifeless eyes stared accusingly at Cirstian, her head lolled back on an ebon pillow. Clotted blood had dried beneath her nose. Her nose had been broken.

Even the Moorish tapestry on the wall was blood-spattered and torn, from some monumental struggle, presumably.

Vlad's caterwauling had diminished into pitiful sobs now. He muttered incoherently to himself. Cirstian wondered what to do. If he touched the deranged man, he would most likely take Cirstian's head off with a single smote of his broadsword, still strapped to his waist. Cirstian felt detached pity for this lunatic murderer, killing his mistress in a moment's unstoppable rage. His purest impulse was to flee the palace, flee Romania. Instead, Cirstian murmured soothingly from a safe distance, feeling ridiculously as if he were placating a retarded criminal.

Vlad's head snapped up, like a hunted animal. Revenge glowed in his uncanny, dark green eyes. Saliva trickled from his lips.

Suddenly Cirstian knew he'd got it all wrong. These were not the eyes of a repentant murderer. These were the eyes of a wolf, his mate murdered by hunters. Gleaming with fury, cunning, revenge, and the power to carry it out. A swift night ambush on helpless peasants for the death of his soul-mate. A lifetime's goal.

"V-V-V-Vlad, you did not…did you?"

Vlad had stopped his sobbing and weeping, deadly-calm now.

"If you believe I have, friend Cirstian, I shall impale you, on the spot…"

"N-n-no, you did not…could not," stuttered Cirstian, immediately aware of his own impending doom/mortality.

"*I swear!*" hissed Vlad, clutching his sword hilt to his chest with both hands, "I shall avenge her! Each man involved in this dastardly plot shall suffer ten times this *doamnă's* fate, ten times her pain for forty-eight hours. I swear thy shall be done. I swear, I swear! I did not kill…'her'."

For the next twenty years, Vlad never again mentioned Serena's name but once. Always referring to 'her'.

****

Fog obscured the Argeş.

They buried her quickly on the headland above, well away from Vlad Ţepeş' grim, ochre castle. No grave marker, only a pitiful, crude cross made of tied sticks. Vlad had constructed it before daybreak, tears in his eyes. It would disintegrate in a matter of months from the wind and rain. And after his demise no one would remember she had ever existed. Only four workers, three bodyguards, and one priest stood beside the empty, open grave. Vlad stood grim-faced, like a stone, as the Orthodox chaplain intoned the sacraments and Last Rites. He had not even told Serena he'd loved her, all these years. *What a fool.* By his cold, expressionless demeanour one could not help believing Vlad had murdered Serena. The chaplain believed so. As did the four unfortunate peasants from Arefũ chosen to dig the grave. Already tall-tales were circulating throughout the castle nearby concerning his mistress's demise, right down to the minutest, lurid details and the very words Vlad had spoken at the disembowelment ceremony.

To exasperate matters, rubbing salt into Vlad's wounds, guardsman Priboi Hlinäny had maliciously spread false rumours about the ducal palace at Tirgovişte concerning a certain 'paramour' of Cjnèatasha's, and Vlad's subsequent, enraged actions…

A brisk, cold, north wind from the Moldavian steppes blew on the headland, laden with moisture. Much of last week's snowfall had melted during the unseasonably warm Carpathian weather, temperatures rising to above freezing. The scent of larch pine lingered in the air. The sun had not quite risen yet. Neither was the sky dark, but a lurid mauve. Vlad remembered Prince Daneşti II digging his own grave in a marsh near Tîrgsor on another fog-smothered dawn, a day of triumph and retribution. But for every joy was a bigger sorrow. This, was Vlad's greatest sorrow. Walking about in a daze, always asking himself '*Why*'... A zombie. Walking the battlements of Castle Dracula at midnight. *Moroi*. Undead.

Vampire.

Henbane and garlic began to show up on every doorstep, over shuttered windows, doors, thresholds, throughout the accursed fort and the Magyar hamlet of Arefû below. And the rumours were spreading like uncontainable wildfires throughout Transylvania. For discretion's sake, Vlad had ordered Serena's body carted eighty miles upriver to his royal retreat above the Argeş—out of sight, out of mind. He also wanted to be near her, intending someday to reinter her in the castle mausoleum (which was still in the planning stages), afraid the citizens of Tirgovişte would exhume her body, mutilate it, or perhaps sell her body parts in dried form as Mummy medicine—a booming trade. Or use her wasted flesh for sick, necrophiliac ceremonies.

Serena's horribly mutilated body had lost plenty of blood in her death chamber. But one could never tell by the great, red stains spreading on her pure-white burial shroud. She was light now. Her innards had been burnt in the royal citadel's incinerator (Tirgovişte) last weekend after dark, her slashed intestines too much of a disgusting mess to load onto a cart. The manservants had balked at the gruesome chore of hauling her by-then dried stomach, kidneys, and intestines down the palace stairs. Finally a mad Gypsy had been found to do the job, sixty-eight-year-old Matei Cateşcu.

The stink now was unbearable. Even Vlad's cast-iron gut turned. Serena had always smelled so fresh and intoxicating whilst alive, having been taught the civilities of hot, Turkish steam baths. She had often smelled of perfumes—flowers soaked overnight in water. Her stiffened corpse was seven days old already. Vlad had ordered her bedchamber walled up, never to be seen again.

The shifty-eyed master of Făgăras stood fuming, riled that the local undertaker had shown such insolence and disrespect: many funerary details had been ignored or botched, a slight which Dracula, *Son of the Devil!*, vowed to right with tears and blood.

Serena's coffin was of the crudest, makeshift, sprucewood possible. Two burly men leaned down, preparing to ease the coffin onto their shoulders. Vlad spoke up.

"Wait. I would look at her one more time."

He dreaded looking at that angelic, peaceful, ashen face. But Vlad had something to say to her, knew she would be listening. Perhaps at his side, even now?

The men moved back, eyes downcast, wary of this monster who had eight days ago disembowelled his mistress just for fun. Cirstian remained immobile, stationary, bound to secrecy. Let the superstitious fools think what they will. It will soon be over.

One good thing: Serena's chamberlain, Miháil Floreşcu; captured when Vlad had ordered the drawbridges raised that fateful night. Trapped like a rat in a hat outside the castle walls, but unable to cross the man-made gorge spanned by a wooden bridge—abruptly dropping off into space when the drawbridge was raised on the opposite side, leaving the poor schmuck sprawled beside his horse in a moat made foul by the palace's latrine chutes. He was apprehended after a brief sword-duel, on horseback, with five of Vlad's unsuspecting mercenaries.

Vlad stepped forward now, removing the wooden slab and pulling back the white shroud covering Serena's pale face. She seemed to be almost smiling, so ironic considering the large cavity where her barren belly used to be. Her puffy, glassy eyes were mercifully closed. Vlad whispered, lest the peasants carry wild tales back to the castle.

"Forgive me, Serena, for you deserved a better burial than this. You were supposed to lie in a gilt coffin in a great marble tomb, half-conceived as yet in my mind, thirty years from now. Wait for me, please?"

The frail chaplain watched, convinced this tyrant was mad, Vlad's face expressionless, eyes dull. No remorse. No regret. Worse still, he spoke the Devil's secret language, whispering lest one of his three Gypsy henchmen carry lurid tales back to Castle Dracula.

It was a witch's charm, the chaplain believed, meant to pin the poor girl's soul to the earth in eternal limbo, powerless against Vlad Dracula's sorcery. Forever to do his bidding.

At last, Serena's rough wooden coffin was lowered into the promontory grave, the sound of dirt on wood as the shovels worked away echoing in Vlad's head for years to come. Empty, cold inside, he turned away, wandering aimlessly back to the castle. His only destination the dungeons where Miháil Floreşcu was being slowly, excruciatingly, pulled apart on the rack. Vlad would watch all day.

****

The old warhorse was dead.

A new stud had emerged from the blood-contest for the title of viceroy and/or voivode of Transylvania. Ion de Hunedŏara—Janós

Hunyádi to Hungarians (although Wallachian-born) had succumbed to the dreaded bubonic plague during a summer drought, 1456, at his townhouse in Buda-Pest. Hunyádi had been largely responsible for Dracula's enthronement at Tirgovişte, not only supplying Vlad money and arms but also refuge during the outlaw-Prince's intermittent sojourns in northern Moldavia—Transylvanian territory—where Vlad had struck up a friendship/alliance bond with Prince Stephen Cĕl Mare of the infamous House of Muşat; his own cousin. Dracula had stayed an enjoyable two years at Muşat's sumptuous royal palace at Suceava; hunting, hawking, discussing theological principles with fellow *voevod* Stephen over games of backgammon, speaking in their own, rare, Dacian language. Hunedŏara (Hunyádi), the White Knight, had been responsible for encouraging the soon-to-be King of Hungary—his own son, Matthias—to accept Vlad Dracula's claim as official Prince of Wallachia. Hunyádi, with Dracula at his side, had led a mildly successful joint Wallachian/Hungarian summer Crusade, 1455, into occupied Serbia. Hunyádi and Ţepeş had returned to Romania with vast chests of loot and many Turkish ransom-prisoners.

Hunyádi's to be ransomed for immense profit.

Dracula's to be impaled at his capital of Tirgovişte—mere entertainment.

The capital's residents plugged their noses for an extended two months while the four hundred Muslim corpses decomposed under a merciless autumn sun in the market-place. Townsfolk began to wear garlic wreaths, for the Dragon-spawn's reputation had preceded him to the ancestral throne. *Ţepeş*, the Impaler. (Romania's most terrible *cnéaz* in history.)

Vlad had drained his Muslim victims' blood into silver bowls, offering their blood as libations to Mother Earth. (Having partaken of it, first.)

"Her" chamberlain died predictably slow, painfully, at the *nosferatu's* eyrie, Dacian *eryri*, in Transylvania, Castle Dracula-on-the-Argeş.

Soon the legends had him sprouting wings and inhabiting coffins, unknown to unwise Vlad Dracula. A young pawn.

A legend in his own lifetime.

Mihály Szilágy, 'The Lion', had been finally elected as viceroy of Transylvania after a brief and bloody mini civil war. He shared with Vlad a hair-trigger temper and equal paranoia. It only took the subjects of northeastern Transylvania two months to get under his skin and provoke his foulest traits. Add to that a literally insane Vlad Dracula and what was a mere squabble turned into a full-scale undeclared war. The Saxons of Bistritz, good Germans, good Catholics all, prepared for the defence of their new Fatherland.

Vlad's small hand-picked mercenary army—mostly Hussite Poles or enticed Gypsies—marched on Satul Nou in June, 1458. They burnt the crops along the Transylvanian Alps and in the Swabian valleys, rousting the families out of their hovels before setting their wattle-and-daub huts alight. They besieged the glorified village—a well-fortified trading post—for two hot, sweltering weeks, firing flaming arrows over the limestone walls. The villagers had anticipated the Dragon's coming, burning the nearby fields, thereby denying Țepeș' troops sustenance as they besieged the fortified hilltop village. Rotting, maggot-infested carcasses—swine, cattle, chickens, sheep, humans it didn't matter—were lobbed over the thick, stone monastery walls with clumsy, ill-functioning trebuchets: huge wooden/rope/leather carriage-slings with wooden gears or pulleys. Men dangled on ropes as counterweights to the heavily loaded slings—not a few being catapulted into the air before remembering to let go, plummeting to the ground. When the village fell, Vlad's army utterly destroyed it, undermining walls, torching houses, sacking its monastery chapel and ransacking and looting the recent, burgeoning nunnery.

They raped the nuns hiding in the barricaded nunnery.

Vlad watched from a hill as the village burnt.

He sat his bay warhorse now, watching with grim satisfaction as the fortified fur-traders' post crackled and smouldered below. To him, divine Retribution for the *Saison* trappers and big-game hunters who'd depleted his beloved Transylvanian countryside of wildlife. Vlad's ears picked up the terrified screams of the villagers, neither knowing nor caring what his soldiers were doing below the bluff. They were Germans. Or Magyars or Szeklers. Scum. When his army had gone, they should thank their cruel, heartless God that he had not impaled the lot of them. As for the nuns, he did not care either; but would sorely regret his folly in the years to come.

When the flames had died and the gloating, sex-starved men had left, there were forty-six impaled defenders in the smouldering ruins. The nuns and villagers crawled out from the charred buildings, screaming abuse at the departed victors; some left fatherless, some pregnant, without husbands, for the Widowmaker had passed; others emotionally or physically abused. Or sullied. Some of the nuns were left pregnant.

The monks had been slaughtered like turkeys.

Mihály meted out the same rough justice to Bod and Hosman, minor fortified villages. Not strategic towns; they just were in the way. Like some great tornado, a living, breathing beast, Mihály's Hungarian recruit armies rolled over the villages like a vengeful God. And, like a tidal wave, absolute carnage and ruin was wrought in a matter of minutes. The gatekeepers of Bod had neglected to close the gates, not expecting their own viceroy to attack, without warning, from the feral, western Transylvanian forests. When the Hungarian army had passed, not a soul was left alive. At Hosman, Vlad Dracula massacred the town after fierce resistance and great loss, the few survivors fortunate to escape into the wilderness or the conifer-mantled, Carpathian mountains by torchlight. They had successfully resisted Szilágy's arson and pillage only two days previously. Bells tolled from German towns on Sunday after Mass, mourning the blood shed of fellow comrades.

Casolts surrendered without a fight when Dracula's crimson/black, tail-in-mouth Dragon standard billowed into view, cresting a mossy hill. The villagers had enough sense to realise that they were badly outmatched. Their puny wooden barricades wouldn't last a day. Vlad's army poured into the streets, uncharacteristically lenient as his cavalry clopped, two-by-two, through the gaping, log-built gatehouse. The humiliated villagers, burghers, and tradesmen—mostly Magyars or Szeklers—watched uneasily from the side-streets as Vlad made his customary, dramatic appearance. Silk-attired, stoutly armoured he rode: head held high with a crafty, hatefully smug look on his face and a feathered, satrap-style, pointed cap atop his head. After the last soldier (Cirstian) had entered the humbled burg, Vlad flew through the gates like a whirlwind on his bay warhorse. He galloped to the village square, leaping down from his horse, where he reminded the villagers of their impending taxes and restrictions to come for their insolence. They being Hungarians, perhaps the least hated of Vlad's foes, he let them off easy, dispossessing them, then looting and burning their village.

On the other hand, the well-protected city of Bistritz, upon hearing of Vlad's atrocities, held a quick council in the square great tower. They chose to fight, confident in their mighty fifteen-foot-thick red sandstone walls. And they were correct. Vlad's half-brother, Vlad the Monk, watched from the great Orthodox monastery's bell-tower as his arch-nemesis was repelled again and again. Vlad and Mihály's combined forces utilised scaling ladders, penthouse troop-transports; thwarted by wicked metal pails of boiling water. Time and time again Vlad's siege towers were set alight. The ballista and assorted siege-engines were bombarded from above, smashed even as his Gypsy conscripts were busy loading the slings or bolts. Men were tossed screaming from the battlements as quickly as they gained them. Women and children dumped loads of rocks onto their besiegers, or used crude, hand-fashioned bows and arrows against the Incarnate. After a three-month siege, after countless tirades and tantrums, his forces suffering horrendous casualties, Vlad withdrew, watching from a distant hill; eyes smouldering as Mihály Szilágy continued the siege in vain. Knowing his Turkish-loving half-brother, monk-kissing kin,

lover of Romans, was celebrating Bistritz's assured victory over the Tyrant. But he'd be back, Vlad said to himself. And they'd be sorry…
They'd be sorry.
They'd be sorry.

****

5 November, 1458 AD
Borgo Pass

Matei inched the red checker forward, tantalizingly slow, snatching Vlad's black victim with a greedy hand. Mihály Szilágy watched, wide-eyed and puzzled, leaning over the table. His long, tangled blonde hair dangled into his empty gold goblet. The three men sat on the fifth floor of Vlad's newest acquisition, Rodna castle, an old Hungarian fortress given to him by Szilágy for his help in suppressing the rebellious Germans of northeastern Transylvania. It boasted a fine, cylindrical tower, surrounded by a meagre, lozenge-shaped curtain wall, the tower connected to the covered wall-walks via a series of interconnecting, ragstone outbuildings. The castle was already four hundred years old, its Teutonic builder unknown. Its finest attribute no doubt was the secret passageway below the keep, down into the mountain and out near the head of the stark, craggy Borgo Pass a thousand terrifying feet below—a tunnel remarkably similar to the limestone dungeons of Castle Dracula. In springtime, mists invaded the pass, making navigation difficult. Another plus.

Vlad frowned. Matei Bathóry was one of the few opponents allowed to defeat him and live. Vlad saw a simple game of three-man checkers as another dimension of war, three-dimensional, using strategy rather than broadswords or crossbows as weapons. He didn't like losing. Abhorred it. Szilágy was no less affronted. His brain was too slow and confused to win even a game of checkers. The pieces were round ebony and ivory atop a marble checkerboard. Szilágy cursed. Cursed again. Matei knew better than to gloat in front of these two. He'd seen countless sieges and counter-sieges in either's army to know their wild unpredictability. Vlad continued to frown. Mihály bellowed for a jug of *ţuica*, preferring to drink himself silly rather than murder Vlad's companion and one of Mihály's few competent warlords.

A shy, shapely servant-girl of seventeen rushed forward with a fresh jug. She filled Mihály's goblet shakily, aware that she'd be filling his bed tonight too. There were worse fates. Josefa knew to her relief that

Szilágy, off the battlefield or absent from the great hall, was a puppy in his own chambers. She hated to admit it, but a nice man really, once away from his boisterous, drunken companions who were real louts. Josefa's best friend and fellow maidservant had often shown up at the castle blackened and bruised by her lover or by her promiscuous, shameless father. Josefa swore that if she had three wishes, one would be to hex Mari's old-goat-of-a-paedophile father.

The other to inform Vlad Țepeș of the old man's 'indiscrepancies'. And to watch the old bastard die on a stake.

She'd been molested by him too.

This Vlad Dracula character she didn't know about, though. He was ruggedly handsome in a primal way, masculine, but quiet and subdued. Debonair and refined, Vlad's etiquette was; exemplifying the finest of Old World traditions. Wolfine and disquietingly aloof, he studied the room's occupants as if they were to be his next meal. Any romantic thoughts Josefa may have entertained were instantly frozen by the misdeeds and mass cruelties he had inflicted on his own people, boasting of the prowess of his alien-sounding *Draigh-a-goch* standard (she had no idea what the three words meant). *Tsepesh*, they called him. The Impaler. Tonight was the first she'd laid eyes on her new master, and her blood ran cold. Green eyes. Jealousy. A monster on his back. This man didn't need a monster on his back. He was a monster. Such a beautiful, docile, schizophrenic murderer. Venomous snake. No. *Dragon. Ordog*—Lucifer. He wore a small, conical, green velvet cap (banded with precious jewels) atop his head with peacock feathers up the front, black locks flowing down his broad shoulder in handsome disarray. Josefa was sure he was not yet thirty. Pity.

Just thinking about his atrocities made her ill.

Dracula stood up from the table, announcing his farewells, bowing formally, stiffly, at the waist. Josefa's legs turned to instant jelly, knowing it would be her duty to accompany the Dragon Prince up the turnpike to his rooftop chambers, she to carry the candles and a full bucket of water. She was terrified. Normally, male servants tended to such chores inside the castle, especially above-kitchen, but the region was in short supply of able-bodied young men (courtesy of, yes, Vlad). So sixteen young girls had been summoned a year ago. Their wages? *Nil.* They'd been told by the local boyar that they were fortunate to have a bed inside the castle and a decent meal once a day.

Thankfully he hadn't noticed her yet. Josefa was a slim, pale, dark-shrouded ghost with straight, black, purple-sheened hair flitting about the shadows of the castle, doing her duties. All the local menfolk told her she was pretty. Even her doting peasant father, Yacob. Josefa was unaware of that obvious asset/curse.

Vlad hollered for a servant, uncharacteristically raising his voice.

Such a quiet, morose man. But a lion really. Josefa rushed forward, simpering, curtsying to her new master and liege-lord. She bent at the knee awkwardly, small even for her gender, and her age. She had a long, perky nose, though few noticed in the dark shadows. Josefa thought it too big. Her eyes were a deep, sea blue.

Vlad looked at her, sneering. (Or at least she interpreted the sardonic, curled lip as such.) Dracula's black, plaited moustache partially obscured his sensual, blood-red lips. Obviously he'd be expecting a squire, not a wench. Josefa felt suddenly much smaller than her five-foot height. She felt like a worm.

He swivelled away towards the stairwell, swirling his bulky, black, satiny cape dramatically about himself with his left arm, ascending the stairs.

Josefa followed with a short candle, quiet as a mouse. She preferred it that way. Around this tyrant she preferred to become invisible.

Their footsteps echoed eerily on the narrow, corkscrew stair. They clutched a frayed rope, for the stairs were too confined for any railing. Josefa tread carefully, while Vlad veritably rushed up the dark steps. He seemed to see in the dark, like a cat. He stopped at the top landing, waiting for the serving wench.

Josefa glanced up, terrified, expecting a tirade for being so womanly and slow. Instead, the master of Rodna eyed her impassively in the darkened stairwell. *'What, no rebuke? No oaths or shouts?'* Josefa thought to herself. This was surely a first.

When she turned to Vlad on the top step to apologise (almost simpering), Josefa noticed that his eyes were no longer on her. They were focused on a small, brightly-embroidered tapestry in the hallway. And they were full of tears. Something Vlad remembered, a long forgotten gift the night of his first wedding anniversary. When Serena's death chamber had been mortared up, it stayed inside. Vlad's eyes were glazed now. There'd be plenty of *ţuica* to drink tonight. Vlad never worried about nightmares. His every day was a nightmare.

Josefa followed, silent, her footsteps padding behind his like an obedient puppy. She found it oddly disturbing that this psychopathic monster experienced genuine human emotions. Somehow it jarred against everything she knew. Black was black; white, white. Mari Hzégy's father, for instance: crude, mean old man—a lecher, forcing himself on his sixteen-year-old, motherless daughter. Even Mihály Szilágy, civilised and gentle in his bedchambers, but obviously dim-witted and crass. (A stutterer!) In fact, objectively, Josefa couldn't remember meeting a man, young or old, whom she liked in a platonic, sibling sort of way.

Vlad swung open a heavy, narrow door; halting, disappointed, in the middle of his new, poorly-lit, master bedchamber. It was small.

For a Prince of Wallachia. Crude. Hexagonal. No whitewash, bright tapestries, Persian carpets, furs, nor candlesticks. A very cold, austere room. More like a prison than a lord's chamber, really. There were thick bars on the door. No hearth. Primitive, built before the invention of the small, inglenook chamber-hearth. Vlad grimaced, shook his head. His new castles, Brân and Castle Dracula, were much more up-to-date. He wouldn't be visiting *this* tower of gloom often.

The 'Impaler Prince' cursed aloud his displeasure; repeating himself in Magyar, then in Romanian, for his simpering, one-woman audience.

Josefa filled the wall-sconces with candles. She moved jerkily, with a glazed look in her eyes, like a frightened rabbit. Vlad wondered why the castle's former owner had to have girls doing men's chores on the dilapidated upper floors. At this rate, this skinny little wench would soon have arms like trunks carrying pails of water up seven stories. He felt suddenly inexplicably angry with the mores of these Hungarians. But then, they were Catholics.

"Are there no boys or men in these parts?" Vlad said suddenly.

Josefa froze; she lit the candles slowly, aware of her heart thumping wildly in her breast. Her master spoke in Magyar, albeit poorly. Her right hand shook. Obviously he had not bothered to hone his Hungarian. Josefa turned to face him, meeting Vlad's eyes. She'd long since learned that the best way to face psychopaths was to look them in the eye while speaking, for should they sense fear, they pounce like a Transylvanian wolf.

But this man's eyes were forbidding. Were they green? Brown? Or black? (She couldn't tell in the dim candlelight.) Luminous. Like lanterns, they bore into Josefa's skull. Hypnotising. She found to her terror that she could not speak. She seemed to have devolved into a monkey.

"Cat got your tongue, girl?"

Josefa shook out of her terror, replying shakily.

"Most of the men in these parts have been summoned to serve in the Holy Roman Emperor—Frederick III's—army in Siebenpfalzer. Others were ravaged by the dreaded *buboe* a few years back, Your Royal Highness."

"I see—your name."

"Josefa Szilägihäilägny."

"Very good." He paused. "You shall be my chambermaid from now on."

Josefa's mouth dropped open in shock, eyes widening in disbelief. "But sire…that is an honour reserved for older matrons who have worked their way up from the kitchens."

Vlad turned away, tossing his long cape over an antiquated, balsam-wood bureau. "So consider yourself promoted. Or do I need to knight you first with sword and Bible?" Vlad chuckled. Obviously he had no understanding of Hungarian ethics. *'Were Vlachs promoted this way?'* Josefa wondered.

"You can start by sweeping this floor," Vlad said, gesturing. The timber flooring was ancient, filthy. No one had occupied this bedchamber for many years. Come to think of it, no one had occupied this castle within living memory, a mere watchtower towering over the Borgo Pass. "When you've done that you can bring me a jug of *ţuica* so I may put myself under as I do every night. After that..." Vlad turned to her with a wry, cunning smile. "After that, the choice is yours."

Josefa could not believe it. Was he flirting with her? Or—even better—offering her a dismissal from her usual midnight duties? Including Mihály Szilágy, the Tamed Lion? A thorough good night's sleep would be a gift from Heaven.

Josefa immediately busied herself at sweeping the grimy, dirt-crusted floor, scurrying around the chamber like a mouse, darting around Vlad's feet as he sat at an old, worn table making notes with a faulty quill pen. The ink was old; drying up. Vlad cursed, snatching another, sharper goose feather from a clay cup.

"Sacrilege!" Vlad pounded his right fist hard on the small table. Josefa jerked away.

Vlad notched down details of the castle, the tiny village opposite, the craggy Borgo Pass far below. Planning spur-based towers, concentric, crenelated walls, barbicans, gatehouses, drawbridges, yetts, portcullises, machicolations. All of which would never be. He knew that. The best he could manage right now was a portcullis in the western gateway. Perhaps a sally-port someday. His father's once-massive treasury had vanished to a few gold *leu* because of his bloodthirsty son's never-ending feuds with local boyars. Upon Vlad's surprise capture of the boyars at Tîrgovişte, 1450, he had asked them, "How many princes have you known?" Many had answered, "Ten." Some fifteen. Others five, others twenty five. "It is because of your treacherous dealings. All of you must die!" Vlad had shouted angrily. Vlad hadn't even begun to amass the immense payment due to Sultan Mehmed Çelebi as his vassal. His only other option was to enlist Romanian peasants (the infamous *Dervshish* corps) to fight in Mehmed's armies overrunning Yugoslavia, threatening Hungary and even Austria, where the Hapsburg Emperor Frederick III quivered at his castle in Vienna.

"Sacrilege!"

Josefa started, returning once more to her dustpan and scraper; on her knees.

"Sacrilege!"

The mere thought of enlisting Wallachian boys to conquer Christian lands for a Muslim army sent Vlad into a rage. The world was unfair. Only three hundred years ago the Crusaders had been besieging Jerusalem, driving the Saracens back to Arabia. Now even Spain was occupied by Islam—the Moors of Morocco. (And one of the many defender-clients, contributor/progenitors of the mysterious Basques.) It was all the fault of the French and Germans, of course. The French King Louis VIII preferred to burn Albigensian heretics in Langue d'oc in 1223 rather than fight Moors or Saracens. Now the Turks were the ruling power of Mediterranean Europe. If only the French and Germans had half as much courage as Charles Martel who had expelled the Moors from France in 738, or Richard Couer de Lion, "The Lionheart," who pummelled Saladin at Jerusalem before being arrested and held ransom by the German Holy Roman Emperor in the 1100s.

Well, Vlad had had enough. Tonight, he decided he would not pay the 15,000 *lei* that fag Sultan Mehmed demanded. Nor would he enlist Wallachian youths in a Turkish army.

Vlad, was the new Couer de Lion.

Llywelyn.

Or more precisely, the *Ddraigh y Du.* (Black Dragon.) War time.

(Meaning, a blood-drenched free-for-all, killing for the sake, impaling with glee, and a gleam in one's eye…)

****

Vlad had written enough. His table candle was now a wick floating in its own wax. Josefa scrubbed the floor at his feet, lazily, in no hurry. Her master didn't seem to mind, did not threaten her with beatings or sexual assault, as so many Hungarian voivodes and boyars had. So far. Vlad pushed back his tall, traceried, throne-like chair.

"Enough. Bring me that jug now, girl, or there'll be no sleep for me tonight."

Josefa whizzed down the spiral stairs, sure-footed, guttering torch in hand; having done this for over a year now (one dare not tarry when contemplating a *boyar's* booted foot or gloved hand). She paused momentarily downstairs in the massive, barrel-vaulted kitchen, helping herself to a slice of goat's cheese from the pantry. She knew she'd be horse-whipped if ever she were caught. In the cellars was the liquor. THAT she would not touch, for her life be forfeit.

Fearfully, Josefa crept down the derelict, unrailed, wooden stair (a short section) to the ancient, subterranean cellars below. The air was dank and musty down here. *And cold as an alpine ice cavern.*

Snowflakes clung to the splayed sill of a midnight-black arrow loop. It was snowing heavily tonight. Outdoors, 'twould be a wintry, snowbound paradise come morning, Josefa thought nostalgically; especially in this hoar-frosted, fir-clothed, northern Transylvanian landscape. Chrismas scenery, unique to the beautiful, yet forbidding, heavily forested, high-altitude Borgo Pass. For days a silvery, icy sheen would coat the trees, mountains, streams and rivers. Star-shaped snowflakes would cling till spring. She concentrated hard on the image, girding herself for the frigid trek below.

Josefa crossed herself superstitiously in the inky, frigid darkness, for *moroi* were said to dwell down here in the clammy, limestone cellars. 'Twas rumoured the small toll-castle had been built by an unknown *voevod* long ago to entomb Satan below the keep. She wondered uneasily if HE was still here. Old Nick. Lucifer. The Devil. Dracula. She wondered if her new master were *nosferatu*—one of the undead. '*Could he appear down here without descending the turnpike from his chambers?*' wondered Josefa. She hoped not. Prayed not. He seemed…almost nice. Perhaps he only waited for her to doze, then sink his fangs into her milk-white neck. Or perhaps he had transformed himself into a bat, climbed the castle wall upside-down and entered the hidden cellars via a crevice at the base of the great, cylindrical keep on its outcrop of rock, waiting to spring at Josefa now?

She shivered. Her pine torch's flame wavered dangerously. Slime coated the spiral stair descending into the gruesome caverns' bowels, a terribly cold, horrifying abyss where one's imagination could run wild throughout these endless passages at will. Josefa's legs were turning to jelly. She hated this part of the keep, the castle. Abhorred it. Yet she dared not disobey her master's orders. Or any man's, for the Church stated clearly that woman must submit herself to man, that woman was not to teach a child even. Women had been burnt for far less. Joan of Arc, accused of witchcraft because she dared to don men's armour and fight her oppressors. And then was hypocritically 'reinstated' as St Joan for her martyrdom! Hungary was alight with witchcraft trials. As was Austria. It was said witches were tied with their arms behind their backs, then suspended in mid-air by the Inquisitor-Generals, arms popping out of their shoulder sockets.

Or roasted alive, slowly, over a bonfire while dangling upside-down from a rope, German style. Fingernails pulled out. Thumb screws were utilized to crush people's thumbs, excruciatingly painful. Spiked chairs, chests, cages…hot iron boots on the feet. Toes smashed with a mallet. Forced to sit on white-hot metal seats. Forced to walk on coals…dunking with hands tied behind the back. If she floats, guilty, if not…Paradise.

Secretly, Josefa didn't believe in witches. The old cronies she'd met in the village were amazing herbalists, better than the monks. Often they were senile however, talking like loose cannon, sometimes just one brick short of a load. Never would this secret flee her lips, lest she be betrayed by one of the Church's many informants skulking about Wallachian and Transylvanian land. Dead was the fool who confided in friends or spoke carelessly to strangers. Everyone knew the Pope was anxious to begin the Holy Inquisition in the Orthodox lands of the east. Everyone kept their mouths shut, if they knew what was good for them. Transylvania was just emerging from a second Dark Ages, since 1349. The buboe had already visited thrice.

Josefa, chiding herself for her squeamishness, tentatively descended the last, few, spiral steps into the caverns, shuddering with the cold, for her linen shawls, warm woollen clothing, were no match for this below-freezing mortuary. Grotesque stalagmites ahead leered uglily at her acrid-smoking torch like misshapen, lumpish gargoyles from the Netherworld. This was no place to be mulling such thoughts, scolded Josefa to herself as she wandered among the cellar's mouldy, wooden wine racks—the *daemons* might be listening.

She snatched a clay *ţuica* jug from a near-empty wine rack, quickly exiting the cavernous, earthen wine cellars—thankful the chore was nearly done. Now to climb the massive, spiral stairwell adjoining those wooden deathtraps above, provided her fluttering pine-torch stayed alight. She knew rats and other vermin inhabited this subterrene, limestone chamber, but fortunately her torch kept them at bay, while denying her eyes their gruesome, unwelcome sight. She knew they were watching, could feel it somehow. Watching for her torch to flicker out, so they could scurry all over her and devour her flesh until nothing remained save a picked-clean skeleton.

Josefa stifled a scream as shadows jerked about her, imagination imbuing them with sinuous movement.

Up the cellars' slippery, slimy, spiral stair. No *dracul* yet. No *nosferatu*. Bats darted at Josefa's torch, threatening to extinguish it or entangle in her uncombed, mousy hair. She screamed aloud, shrilly. Shrieked. Cried out at her leathery-winged assailants, condemning them to Hell. Nobody would hear her. The cylindrical, stone shaft encased her like an upright sarcophagus. This was only the fourth time she'd been down here. She knew she would never get used to it; not with her heart in her mouth. Wide though it be, the stair was still too narrow for her liking, stone walls coated with gooey slime. Darkness smothered Josefa like a damp, mouldy shroud.

When she entered Ţepeş' chamber on the fifth floor of the keep, her master stood staring out the open, arched, unglazed window toward the Transylvanian Alps to the southeast. The night was overcast, pitch black. A cool winter wind blew into the austere, frigid bedchamber, billowing the four-poster bed's sheer, yellow curtains, accompanied by a flurry of fine white snow. Vlad had removed his cloak and peaked, red velvet cap, wore only his long tunic and horsemen's boots now. He'd removed his silken pantaloons. He stood there, still as a stalagmite (pensive and brooding while fathoming more victims), his brown tunic cinched at the waist with a thick, coarse, hempen rope. The air was just below freezing—a modest, Transylvanian night by any standard. His bright, blue-dyed, rawhide boots were topped with grey rabbit's fur, leather clogs pointed at the toe. Knee-high cavalryman's boots. Vlad's great two-hand broadsword (one of several, of varying size and usage) he'd removed from his scabbard; swordbelt encircling his waist. Dracula's massive sword stood propped in a corner against a bureau, as tall as Josefa was. (She doubted she could even lift the thing, let alone swing it.) It boasted a long wooden hilt—an inverted cross—with bright, steel handguards laminated with gold gilt. Vlad wore no tights nor stockings now, his long tunic concealing his manhood from the flustered serving-maid, for he loved the cold, made him feel more a man. His tapering legs were long, thick, and hairy. Powerful. His black locks streamed out demonically as a frigid north wind entered the room.

 Josefa placed the jug of *țuica* on the table at Vlad's side, stepping back with a curtsy, awaiting new orders. Or hopefully a reprieve. Vlad grasped the earthen jug by its handle, uncorking it, taking a long, careless swig. Brandy trickled down his chin, his walrus moustache, plaited in the latest fashion. (Left unwaxed, it reverted to its normal growth instead of the rakish, demented style of the *condittiere*.) He no longer bothered with goblets, needing to get drunk in a hurry before Serena's mutilated image came to haunt him in his bedchambers. Vlad despised himself all the more for his drunken addiction, for it had been that which had allowed Serena's Turkish assassin into her boudoir that night. Yes, he knew his name. And where he lived. Béla Blásko, Basarab Laiota's foremost henchman, one of Vlad's most dangerous enemies along with his own half-brother Vlad the Monk; Basarab Laiota, father of twelve, devout Orthodox, with a healthy brood of heirs to snatch Vlad's kingdom. Laiota's henchman (sold-out to the Turks) was taking sanctuary in Srébrenița, Bosnia-Herzegovina.

 Vlad would find him. Had to. Could not live with himself it he did not. He would chase Laiota and his thugs across the northern steppes, across the frozen wasteland of Siberia, across the hostile Transylvanian Alps and Carpathian mountain ranges. Across the fiery lake of Hell. Never rest. Sell his soul for divine retribution.

 And he would torture young Blásko and old man Basarab slowly, painfully, gleefully at his new treasure-store/dungeons of Snagov monastery in southern Wallachia, sixty miles north of the newly-chartered burgh of Bucharest. He would force the swine to run around on their hands and knees in a circle, occasionally levering open the trapdoor at his leisure, where a bed of spikes awaited. Whether the Orthodox monks liked it or not. If they protested, Vlad would expel them from their strategic island-monastery/fortress.

Josefa waited patiently for dismissal. None was forthcoming. Her feet began to hurt. Vlad guzzled the plum brandy like a madman in a desert. The jug was empty within the hour, a whole gallon of potent, liquid fire. Țepeș' eyes blazed now. Immediately he set to work smashing the four, ornate mirrors hanging on the walls with a large bronze candelabra. He did so with a smile. Quite pleased with himself. Vampires were supposed to abhor mirror images, were they not? Well then, I'm a vampire! Vlad thought maniacally to himself. *Count Dracula, Lord of Hell!* The title had a certain, catchy ring. Josefa cowered near a suit of burnished knight's armour in a dark, cluttered corner, terrified, unnoticed. Suddenly Vlad turned on her, almost frothing at the mouth. He hurled the empty jug at a wall, smashing the vessel into a dozen pieces.

"Begone, wench!" snarled Vlad, "lest I forget I be a gentleman and take you on my bedsheets."

Josefa blanched. The deranged warlord spoke in such a hoarse, low, menacing tone, voice badly slurred; he seemed barely rational, incoherent, on the verge of drinking himself dead. She spun from the chamber, tripping, fleeing this insane *mormaer*.

****

She knelt over him, legs braced for flight. Sunlight shone through the lone window, the room still possessed by shadows. Or demons. Josefa cocked her head, listening for a breath. Dracula lay on his bed, dressed, but asleep. His puffy eyes were closed, his mouth open. Josefa waited, indecisive, wondering whether to summon the castellan. It was well past noon. Her dark brown, homespun skirts would hamper flight if Vlad suddenly pursued her down the gothic corridor.

Suddenly Vlad's eyes popped open, green lanterns eyeing her impassively. Josefa shrieked, slamming back against the stone wall, knocking her head.

Vlad already had his dirk raised, unsheathed and close at hand lest an assassin come in at night. Vlad was a light sleeper.

Like the dead, in fact.

Josefa sobbed, her head turned away; struggling to retain

composure as the Beast glared at her. A wolf in sheep's clothing. Vlad's head had tilted towards her. He sat up in one swift motion, like a vampire rising from his coffin. A scarlet, satin cloak covered his bare thighs immodestly.

"Have you come to kill me?"

She couldn't have been more shocked at Vlad's odd question.

"Or bury me?"

Vlad swung his legs to the floor, groaning, his head splitting, stomach churning. But he was getting used to this. Vlad stood up unsteadily, swaying.

"I feel like I died and went to Hell." He spoke in Dacian.

Josefa, appalled, tapped her ear, shook her head. For a moment, she thought she was the one with the hangover.

"Pardon? I-I did not understand what you said, sire."

"You heard right, girl. I spoke in Dacian—a Celtic language, which you would not understand. You're Hungarian." He spat.

"I am also half-Romanian, sire."

"Big celebration."

Josefa gasped. This man had no love for his fellow Romans! She spoke before she thought.

"Do you not love your own people, sire?"

Vlad glared at her. She felt herself shrivel before his withering gaze. And then he laughed. A maniac's deep, mocking laughter. Then serious again.

"Not my people. You're all Latins." Vlad spat. He watched the spittle cascading a hundred feet to the empty courtyard directly below the arched, chevron-moulded window. "It was not enough that you Romans had to exterminate us, but you steal our land, our language as well. Our heritage. While I am Prince of Wallachia, no Romanian may expect mercy from me."

The blood drained from the pretty wench's face.

"Fear not, *llances* (girl), I'll make a special exemption for you. If you will firstly fetch me a cup of soap and a razor. I wish to shave."

Josefa curtsied, her knees turning weak. "As you wish, My Lord."

****

5 June, 1459 AD
Bucharest, Wallachia

The wooden palisade of Bucharest glowed in the early morning sunlight. Stout logs and fresh lumber smelled of pine, pitch, and spruce-fir plus a smattering of seasoned oak, wafting across the waving prairies of southern Wallachia. The slender Dumbŏvitza river dissected the royal burgh like a bluish-purple ribbon. Vlad and his thirteen councillors had overseen the last, naked fir-log hammered into place along the palisaded ramparts of this newest burgh, recently completed. Within the earthworks and ditches loomed spectacular Renaissance, rambling, half-timbered merchants' dwellings alongside inns, taverns, stone hovels and wattle-and-daub shanties. White turkeys (recently imported from a mysterious Paradise to the west) gobbled pleasantly, some perched atop the enclave's thirty-foot walls and parapets while watching the royal procession below with cute, bald, wattle-skin heads. Black geese hissed threateningly at passersby. Chickens cackled incessantly, their squawks carried over the ramparts and across the dry ditch. Besiegers would have to surmount the seventeen-foot-deep ditches and banks. Vlad intended to rebuild the walls soon, in stone, whenever his state coffers were full (he planned to fill the ditches with water immediately, turning it into a moat, also planning to conceal stakes underwater to impale those foolish enough to swim across during a night attack). The diamonds, beryl, amethyst, crystal, gold, silver, sapphire, emeralds, moonstone, garnet, and turquoise only recently confiscated from his enemies' families—the former boyars of Transylvania—had greatly enhanced Vlad's treasury stored in vaults at Snagov monastery. The Turkish ambassadors were still demanding these jewels which they knew Vlad had, in lieu of vassalage payments he had gotten behind on. None dared to venture into Wallachia, however.

Not since he'd sent Sultan Mehmed his ambassadors' scalps.

Vlad had no intention of paying.

He had just finished signing a proclamation of Bucharesti's trading privileges inside his command tent when an emissary from one of his most hated enemies stepped into the tent, without warning. Vlad's mail-clad bodyguards stood at attention, stepping in front of the uninvited emissary.

Vintilă Florescu, that pompous, half-breed egomaniacal jewel collector/boyar who sold his tenants for a living to the Turks was, along with a handful of boyars, one of the few warlords to defy Vlad's armies, boosting Vlad's half-brother, Vlad the Monk's, power and prestige in northeastern Transylvania. His emissary, Gregori Cushăni, now unravelled a parchment scroll; a declaration of Vlad's excommunication by the Patriarch of Warsaw on behalf of the Greek-Orthodox church. Vlad scanned the Old Church Slavonic script, then slowly, methodically crumpled it up into a ball, setting it on fire with a burning ember. The emissary was mute, his tongue cut out years ago to prevent his betraying his master's strategy or whereabouts.

"This means nothing," Vlad murmured. "Toilet paper. The Patriarch of Warsaw has no authority over Romania. His attempt at reunification with the Romany Harlot will go unheeded in my country."

The mute emissary withdrew another scroll from his tunic, unravelling it for Vlad's eyes. The emissary's eyes gleamed, gloating. Oh, if only he could speak…

It was a Papal Excommunication, an obvious, but clever, forgery by some remote Venetian letter-forger. Vlad laughed, tossing the Anathema Bill to his *Tsigany* guards who juggled the scroll playfully, uproariously, tossing it amongst themselves. Vlad then shredded the parchment with his bare hands, eating the pieces before the unimpressed emissary.

The emissary then handed Vlad a small scrap of parchment in Vintilă's own handwriting, informing the Prince of Wallachia of his official discharge as *mormaer*, decided by Floreşcu's eleven hand-picked councillors. A mere, macabre joke. The signatures were of men whom Vlad had never even heard of; certainly none who made up his Privy Council. The joke had gone far enough.

"Very good," Vlad cried, tossing the scrap parchment into a roasting campfire. "Gentlemen, feed this emissary of Vintilă's well, for he is an important man. Feed him roast duck, rabbit, and plenty of wine—and then, impale him!"

The Gypsy thugs laughed, seizing the startled emissary and dragging him from the tent.

****

Vlad ate his scrumptious meal in front of the well-fed, richly clothed, impaled emissary, formerly of Vintilă Floreşcu, boyar. The dead man's satin clothing flapped in the wind, snapping high above. Vlad sat at a plain wooden table, savouring his meal. (Whilst dipping his slice of bread into a bowl of his enemies' blood, smiling.) The emissary and a score of others topped the stakes in the muddy marketplace of Bucharest. Dozens of spectators watched from the flagstone streets with awe, dirty-faced and unwashed. Vlad sat alone, alone with his thoughts, the stink of ruptured guts not even registering on his olfactory senses. He was thinking of a dark night, three years ago, a celebration, a woman who'd once called herself his wife…

Four…five…six, seven to go. Vintilă himself was too powerful to apprehend, so Vlad impaled his emissary on Serena's behalf. The four bedchamber guards assigned to her apartments had been caught trying to cross the Hungarian border at Oradia by Mihály Szilágy's troops, handed over to Vlad for a lump sum. They now languished on the rack or the torture-wheel in Snagov's vaults. By day and by night. Vlad had reneged on his promise of keeping them alive for a mere forty-eight hours, keeping them alive with smelling salts. Serena's chamberlain had finally expired after a three-week session of torture, over two years ago, hanging by his thumbs. The Orthodox monks dared not enter the torchlit vaults, or attend to the prisoners' pain. They steadfastly recorded Vlad's atrocities. Four hundred and six impaled in May, 1458. Tîrgsor razed. Crops along the Carpathians burnt. Starvation in Szekler land. Women and children disembowelled. Unfaithful wives and pregnant, unwed girls flayed alive. Mothers forced to eat their boiled sons as Vlad looked on, laughing. Whole villages boiled alive in gigantic cauldrons, their heads sticking out of holes.

All rubbish, of course.
If only Vlad knew.

****

The Borgo Pass shifted in and out of mist. Premature spring once again promised a lie; although most of the snow had melted, more was on its way to murder the first spring buttercups. A lazy stream gurgled alongside the rocky, rutted, potholed track as Vlad's tiny retinue rolled by in four, royal black carriages. The meltwater flowed from the northern Galician-Carpathian mountains; cold, clear, refreshing. Glacial water.

Vlad had inexplicably taken a liking to this hostile corner of northeastern Transylvania. For one, it was almost devoid of people. Few inhabitants braved this alpine pass amongst the spruce-forested Rodnei mountains. Only the odd lumberjack or eccentric spinster or perhaps a roaming caravan of misplaced Gypsies dwelt in this wonderfully eerie, fir and pine wilderness. 'Twas a mountainous purgatory composed of evergreen conifer, oak, Carpathian elm, maple, and birch. The midafternoon sun cowered behind the remote, cloudy, Apŭseni peaks. Perhaps it was this wildness and empty, echoing freedom which lured Vlad back to the ancient conical-peaked castle towering ahead on its craggy summit. (Of which, hundreds of years later, not a single stone would remain standing.) A not so comfortable castle, but peaceful nonetheless. At night, wolves howled eerily from the peaks of the nearby Rodnei mountains, a comforting, familiar sound to Vlad's ears. Eurasian eagle owls hooted, bats pricked the air with their high-pitched squeaks, ravens argued and cawed from their treetops nudging the old castle keep. A cool, refreshing wind often whistled through the valleys (whereas, by night, fluttering bat's wings strummed the air like an unholy Summoning from the Pit). He could sometimes even hear the rustle and swish of grass and leaves or larch boughs high up on the fifth floor of the conical watchtower. Or at least he fancied he could. The souls of his long-dead Wallach ancestors would whisper to him at night.

But, perhaps, the memory-haunted minstrel galleries of Castle Dracula, where 'she' and Vlad had often strolled hand-in-hand along the wainscoted upper galleries, admiring huge paintings by pre-eminent Hungarian artists in the dead of night, or discussing fluttering ancestral banners and coats-of-arms in the sophisticated 'Knights Hall' had soured Vlad's pleasure of his majestic, Princely fortress. Now it was primarily a garrison fort. There he would always remember the girl he had loved, the woman whom he would've sacrificed his own life for had he been given the chance. Or at least he had always told himself such. Here, in the tranquil midnight silences of the Carpathian mountains of northern Bucovina and the unfamiliar environs of the old castle, he could almost forget the Princess had ever lived.

It was daylight now, serene in its own furtive way. That word. Vlad scratched it from his mind. It reminded him too much of someone he used to know, was now believing himself slowly exorcising the memory from his mind. He was winning. He returned to this ancient castle high up in the Borgo Pass for that very reason, for it seemed to act as a balm, a sedative. The nightmares out here in this sepulchral 'Land Beyond the Forest' seemed to fade away. It had been almost three years now since the 'incident' which had changed Vlad's life irrevocably. Here he was calm. No longer at war with himself. Here 'she' rarely dragged her chains into his nightmares, dragged her mangled body, moaning, enticing.

Inviting.

Vlad's chaplain/confessor, Molasar Timeşcu, had informed him one Sunday morning that this image, this often sensuously alluring creature of the night was a succubus, come for his semen, and later his soul. The Orthodox priest believed devoutly, whole-heartedly in this preposterous suggestion. Molasar was a simpleton.

Alone, after Sunday worship at the island-monastery's chapel of Snagov two weeks previously, Vlad had laughed till tears filled his eyes. He'd always thought brother Molasar was such a level-headed, practical old man. Vlad had balked when the monk offered to exorcise the succubus haunting his dreams. (Or vampire?) Molasar was officially, of that moment, no longer Vlad's chaplain. And he'd stopped confessing.

Felt better for it too.

After all, how could he possibly atone for his atrocities? Vlad had a vague idea of the numbers impaled. But he had woke up one morning wondering (becoming cognizant of certain disquieting rumours) whether all of those impaled were guilty. A monster of his own creation, a dead, reanimated corpse struck by lightning which had shambled out of its watchtower to terrorise the innocent.

Perhaps not.

Certainly the Orthodox monks had tried to ease Vlad's conscience, suggesting he make endowments for new monasteries. Relieving him of his treasures, and making themselves rich.

After two years in power, a certain wiliness, a certain wisdom, opened Vlad's eyes to their endeavours.

He soon put a stop to it. Eight monks and three nuns were implicated in a scandal this winter to 'unburden' the poor, melancholy, foolish Prince of Wallachia of his treasure stored in vaults below Snagov monastery. Five of the monks were beheaded, three acquitted. The three elderly nuns had been defrocked, expelled from Wallachia on pain of death should ever they return. Happily, Vlad thought to himself, There were three times as many nuns (a safe refuge) in Romania than there were monks, or there would be serious scandals. Of homosexuality, sado-masochism, bigamy, over-powerful bishops like in the West. The Prince Palatines of Germany, for example. Wealthy, all-powerful, preaching celibacy, keeping concubines. Or the Papal Legates of France, where the Pope—one of many Popes—lived at his sumptuous Papal palace at Avignon. The same bishops who had burnt Joan of Arc for witchcraft, yet allowed that sacrilegious child-murderer Gilles de Rais to thrive at his castle of Tiffauges, burning his apprentice at the stake instead. Gilles de Rais, flower of nobility, sex-slayer of hundreds upon hundreds of innocent little boys and girls. Yet did HE get excommunicated? Did he get burnt alive at the stake? No. Vlad thought to himself: *Thank Duwes (Goddess), this is Orthodox Wallachia, not Catholic France, Castile, Aragon, Poland, Austria, Hungary. Here I can tax the monks dry.* He smiled.

The four regal, black carriages and their teams of white, blinkered horses lumbered over a narrow, humped, stone packhorse-bridge spanning a small stream, still gurgling and frothing with last week's meltwater flowing from the mountains. Vlad's accompanying retinue was not large; ladies-in-waiting, chamberlains, boyars, seneschals and foreign dukes. With Vlad was a rare specimen, an English duke inflamed with zeal to fight the Turks. Sir John Tiptoft, Earl of Worcester, captain during the Hundred Years' War with France see-sawing back and forth, was here on his own funds, booty from pillaged French towns. Also eager to learn Vlad's fascinating impalement techniques which he was considering implementing in England against Yorkists. *Țepeș* had liked him at first sight. A true knight, and inveterate Crusader, Lancaster also impressed him with his shrewd obeisance owed to a Wallachian Prince. For Vlad was gaining a name for himself, a certain notoriety and respect among the Renaissance Emperors, Princes, Kings, etc., etc., of Europe. The word was out. Vlad would be honouring his father's title as a knight of the Order of Dragons sworn to fight the Turks. Even though Vlad wasn't a Catholic. (His father had been a closet Orthodox follower.) Vlad's first act of defiance as a Turkish vassal was to refuse the new Sultan, Mehmed 'The Conqueror', the dues owed him. Vlad simply refused to travel to Constantinople to kiss the Sultan's silk robe-hem. With Mured's death, Mehmed had proved himself to be even more formidable than his father. It was Mehmed who had stormed Constantinople, capturing the Golden Horn (Bosporus Straits), a feat never permanently achieved before (although the Venetian Crusaders had done so once, through treachery). But Vlad took heart. The valiant Serbs of Belgrade had defied Mehmed's cannons and Janissary corps, much to the surprise and celebration of Western Europe in 1456, the year Dracula was crowned and three years after Mehmed's conquest over Byzantium. Even the Serbians had been surprised when Sultan Mehmed II's army had retreated from Belgrade's impregnable fortifications.

(The *'Impaler Prince'* had begun to admire, and appreciate, the pugnacious Slav nations for defying the Ottoman Menace with such obstinance.)

At last, Vlad's much anticipated castle tower loomed above the fog, its peaked cone poking a hole in the sky, ascending to heaven. Granted, it was a cold fortress. But peaceful. It lacked the multitudes of chain-squealing, iron-slamming portcullises present in much larger castles—such as Tîrgsor, Cluj, Făgăras, Tirgoviște, Sighișoara, Sibiu, or Hunedŏara. It was not a Norman, nor even Byzantine-inspired, fort—it had yetts—swinging, miniature portcullises made of rows of crisscross iron bars more familiar in Irish or Scottish towerhouses. The watchtower had been built by some paranoid, unknown Teutonic knight. Vlad had heard of one Edwardian Anglo-Norman stronghold— Caernarfon, North Wales, Great Britain, where King Edward I in 1294 had built a monstrous figure-of-eight citadel with eight massive, octagonal towers, where, 'twas said, five tremendous portcullises inside the stupendous King's Gate protected that fortress's so-called 'Eagle Tower' *donjon* and various other, multi-turreted towers. A crude joke was circulating currently in Europe: *'What do you call a wench with five vices: chastity, greed, lesbianism, wine, and haughtiness?'*

A Caernarfon nun.

Impregnable.

Impregnable this castle was not. A mere watchtower; peasants could storm this mountain toll-collector's bastion, except there weren't enough peasants in these parts to bother.

Forks of white lightning speared down from the midday sky, dashing behind the cylindrical great tower, its stone plagued with ivy and its mortar crumbling away. A green patina of age coated the masonry. Overcast purple-grey clouds glowered over the pass, as if challenging the approaching carriages to combat. All knew who would win. Up in these limestone mountains a thunderous, rain-soaked onslaught could be heard for days, crashing thunder the Hand of God, lightning forks Satan's hot-forged pitchfork.

A brisk west wind blew through the pass. No crops grew here; just endless tracts of larch, pine, and alpine fir; ageless in their monotonous verdure. Only a wide, logged slash through the wilderness allowed the carriages passage toward the disused, semi-abandoned fortress staffed by servants and one mad butler. Vlad had ordered the pathway widened only last spring; before that, the castle had been slowly mouldering away like an unburied skeleton up on its mountaintop. Clearly this relic of darker days had been no great loss for Mihály Szilágy. Indeed, he possibly was glad to be discharged from the burden of its upkeep. No more cartloads of fresh timber to replace its rotten floors for him. And because of the wet climate, the floors had to be replaced every fifty years. Owning a castle, even a small border watchtower such as this, was expensive business. A literal pain in the neck. An immense *chateâu-fort* like Angers, Chinon, Chateau de Gaillard in France, or Krac, Beuregard, or Marqab in the Middle East, or Hohensalzburgh, Rheinfels, Marksburg, Falkenstein, or Hochosterwitz in the Austrian Holy Roman Empire with their multitudes of gateways and portcullises would surely tax even the richest lords, Vlad mused.

Castle Brân, Tirgoviște, Castle Dracula, and Sighișoara citadels were worry enough.

Thunder rumbled over the tiny, squarish gatehouse as Vlad's entourage entered the castle's inner precincts, having traversed a decrepit wooden bridge spanning a slim, foggy gorge. Vlad sat motionless, alone inside the foremost coach, eyes impassively taking in the obsolete, cross-slit arrow-loops in solid stone walls, or the great Romanesque pillars and cruciform, rounded windows of the derelict chapel inside the redoubt's trapezoid-shaped bailey. A Renaissance portico had been belatedly built against the great hall outside the keep. The odd mullioned-and-transomed window or Italianate loggia graced the newer, two-storey great hall, a relatively recent attempt by some former voivode or boyar of Transylvania to transform the derelict castle into a liveable, Italianate palace.

A visitor to the keep would've noticed a short, gaunt, richly dressed lord of Transylvania, *boyar*, Prince of Wallachia, exit from the leading *calèche* with the grace of a cat. A long-haired, beardless, powerfully built voevode with straight, black, plaited moustache and tiger eyes, marvellous crimson or shiny, black, silk/fur raiments plus a long, heel-brushing cape, terrible to behold. (Vlad's head held high, smug as a Carpathian wildcat.) Satan himself, come round the bend to terrorise the gullible villagers of Transylvania, to initiate newcomers into his black Sabbath rituals. A man with cold, ruthless green eyes, sunken cheeks and sensuous, blood-red lips. But there were rarely any visitors to this castle, least of all in winter, even if it did promise (lie) premature spring. Only eccentric antiquarians or 'castellologists' would deem this mortared iceberg worthy of a winter visit, someone perhaps used to the long winters of Scandinavia, not the pampered Latins of southern France, Spain, Italy.

Josefa watched from a gothic third-storey window as the master of Rodna stalked toward the keep with long, confident strides, his cape streaming behind him, a green, feather-topped, conical velvet cap—encircled by a band of jewels—crowning his black locks. She was one of only eighteen permanently employed staff at the keep. But she was not looking forward to this unpredictable warlord's return to his desolate, private demesne. When Vlad had departed little less than two months ago, Josefa had offered thanks to the Virgin for sparing her blood. In the derelict, dusty chapel outside the keep she had spent much of her hours, praying for Salvation against the cloyingly-inviting dreams Josefa had been having of this Transylvanian devil. She had taken to wearing a large, silver cross around her neck plus her rosary beads, for vampires were supposed to fear the cross, were they not? Josefa's jugular had not been punctured. She had made sure, checking every morning with a tiny hand-held mirror. That too Vlad detested, shying away whenever a mirror was spotted.

The truth was more mundane. Vlad simply couldn't face himself in a mirror, for his guilt was too much to bear.

He strode into the dark basement chamber of the keep, jogging up a cramped, stone, spiral stair to the first floor where a miniature yett guarded the entrance, worked via pulleys and chains. Behind a partition were the tower's secret, forbidding cellar stairs and subterranean chambers where servants feared to tread. Prince Vlad paused at the yett, shouting a command, waiting impatiently as the iron grate rattled and clanked upward slowly. Beyond the bars lay the circular great hall; empty, dank, and disorderly. The large, herringbone-patterned, arched hearth in the rear wall was cold and silent, devoid even of ashes. The servants had been scurrying for a week to get the castle ship-shape and spic 'n' span clean. Not wishing to share a stake in the cobbled courtyard with a murderer or highway robber. Since Vlad's usurping of the castle from its former boyar (whom he'd had skewered), there had been a weekly spate of impalements, gruesome to behold but even more so to smell twenty-four hours a day.

Only that very hour had a manservant managed to clamber down the main hall's chimney, cleaning its clogged flue and in mortal fear of Vlad's response (due to delayed apprisal of the cantankerous *hospidar's* arrival).

"Bath! Get me a bath! Quick-like," Vlad hollered, watching in resignation as the wenches scrambled for pails, rushing towards a well in the kitchen to his left. "I would wash the horseshit from myself," he muttered, half to himself. Next thing, Vlad mused, the serving wenches would be offering to give him a sponge bath and rub-down, like a Turkish bath. A harem. Another time, another place, he would have smiled at the thought. But not now. Not here.

In fact, he felt nothing at all.

Certainly it was within Vlad's rights as *voivode* to own a harem. Within his law to demand each virgin wench ask for permission to marry a suitable bridegroom. Even within his law to demand first lay with her on her wedding night (as Father of the people). However, these were Aryan laws grafted onto earlier Prydainic, *Brittonic* oral custom—Slav/Teutonic laws which Vlad—the first Dacian in many generations—ignored. Judeo-Christian laws—Islamic—barbaric.

Josefa panicked when she heard the servants scurrying up the stairs to the lord's master bedchamber. A bellow chased them up the narrow, spiral stairwell. "Slow down, you're spilling the God-damned water on the stairs!" Josefa dashed into a tiny garderobe (bathroom) to the right of a massive four-poster bed, clearing out the dirty sponges and rags from the great washtub. She froze with a dread certainty: as Vlad's chambermaid she would be expected to help him bathe. Literally. And in the nude. Though he had never requested it of her, she knew this was also the first time Vlad had requested a bath at Rodna castle these brief, two years he'd owned it.

Josefa felt sick.

Here he could sink his retractable fangs into her neck at will, leisurely, unhurried. (He was rumoured to be an inveterate blood drinker!) He would roam her body with his hands...

'Stop it! Stop it! Stop it!' Josefa collected herself with difficulty, standing rigid, a nightmare statue smiling brittlely as Vlad strode into the bedchamber. She curtsied hurriedly, legs turning to Indian rubber.

Recalling the smell of impaled human cadavers as she looked into his eyes. And he smiled, vulpine, nodding a greeting.

"Good eve-ning." His strange, foreign accent put instant foreboding into Josefa's heart. A deep, oddly-lilting voice which set her nerves ajangle. Her gorge rose to her throat, needing to vomit, knowing she must not. A great ball of loathing sat in her stomach like lead, where this afternoon's lunch had been.

"G-Good evening, my lord," she croaked. Cleared her throat. "Good evening, my Lord."

Vlad looked at her queerly, mildly amused, eyes lingering. Yes, they feared him these wenches. Good. He liked that. Instant obedience. Their work left much to be desired, though. Must correct that.

"Good evening, Lord Dracula," said the six serving wenches in unison, curtsying as one, exiting the chamber at Vlad's stately nod of dismissal.

Josefa busied herself at unfolding the woollen towels, heart in her throat. She unpacked the soap bars from their elaborately carved wooden box as Vlad flung his black, silk cape onto an ornate, dilapidated, rosewood, early Renaissance bureau. He gave her puzzling, questioning glances as Josefa swirled the hot, soapy water inside the garderobe, noticing her shapely woman's rump so vainly clothed amid layers of dark, heavy linen. (Hungarian modesty!) Her hair bound with a pink kerchief, her teenage breasts tantalizingly, yet not quite, hidden. It was dark inside the latrine, and cramped, no windows. Not even an arrow-slit. And dreadfully cold. (She almost welcomed the bath water's warm embrace, despite the knowledge of who she'd be sharing it with.) Only a short, box-like, wooden structure with a hole in the middle for a toilet abutted against the washtub alongside a small stack of moss. The walls were like ice. Josefa half-expected Vlad to sidle up behind her and pat her bottom. Or pinch.

Vlad had removed his scarlet, silk blouse, laced at the front. He squeezed past her through the doorway, his hairy, barrel chest bare. Stuck his hand in the steaming-hot water, closing his eyes with relief, tossing his head as a horse would, indicating Josefa's dismissal. She did not understand. Their eyes met for a moment, hers bright and pleading, Vlad's emotionless.

"Get out. I'm not a baby, do not need your help."

Josefa's blue eyes lit up for a second, then she curtsied, exiting the steamy, tiny garderobe where she was sure Vlad Țepeș would be fondling her inside the washtub. And she was immensely grateful.

And yet...sad.

She contemplated the strange mentality of this diabolically harsh, but just, ruler, whose decrees against common, everyday customs and sudden impalements, often without trial, seemed at times arbitrary, others as wisdom of the gods (having glanced out a window early this morning, she'd been surprised to see old man Hzégy skewered on a stake, due, no doubt, to a certain little 'bird' who'd apprised Vlad's castellan of the incestuous iron-monger's assaults on various young girls): amongst others, his curious 'head tax' on non-Vlachian families comprised of eight or more children.

"Wench! Another towel."

Josefa jerked awake, slumbering near the doorway to Vlad's chamber. She scrambled to her feet, snatching a long, red towel from the bureau's drawer, ready to rush it to him.

But Vlad already stood in the garderobe doorway, dark green towel wrapped around his waist and nothing else. Josefa froze, shocked speechless.

He snatched the towel from her hand, annoyed with this dumb creature who stared at him as if he were a satyr. As if she'd never seen a man's half-naked body before. Vlad knew Josefa was Mihály Szilágy's main prostitute whenever Mihály visited the castle (once, the man had even recommended her to him!). Josefa wouldn't see it that way, merely gratefully accepting the gold coins for sex, after the fact.

Vlad would disagree.

He felt anger, staring at this simpering, coquettish servant wench. And... *lust.* Vlad tossed the proffered towel aside, seizing her narrow, bony shoulders. Kissing her mouth hard while she stood, wide-eyed, surprised, stiffening in his hands.

She neither struggled nor acquiesced. Merely froze, like a mouse caught red-handed in a pantry. When Vlad released her, Josefa was amazed, her pride mortally wounded. For she could see the disinterest in his eyes.

For he did not find her sexy.

She'd felt no bulging hardness beneath his towel.

For Vlad, nothing. Zippo. Zilch. No desire, no passion, not like...Serena.

"Beast!" Josefa spat in his face, her wits fled, terribly angered by this stupid man who dared not find her irresistible! The voivode blinked, as if caught in some past reverie.

Vlad cocked his head a moment, wiping spittle from his eye, suddenly realising what she had said—had done. His gaunt face reddened, grimacing, green eyes glittering. And then he slapped her. Hard.

Josefa's head rocked back, stunned by the smacking force of Vlad's vicious backhand. She slammed against the rough-hewn wall, knocking her head, slumping against a highly-polished, Carpathian elm, burlwood vanity mirror/bureau beside a 12th-century, burnished suit of German knight's armour. She sobbed, waiting for the next blow. She knew he had the right to beat her senseless, to take her again and again on his feather bed. To rape her. To bind her. Blood flowed from her nose, staunched now with her cloak's sleeve. Her body anticipated the next brutal blow. A punch?? A kick?? A dagger??

It did not come.

Vlad stared at her for what seemed an eternity. Green eyes emotionless. Fists clenched. Remembering a day at Braşov castle eleven years ago. Another time. Another woman. Tears of anger, hot, remorseful rage, trapped inside all these years, of unfulfilled vengeance, bravado vows never to be put to right. Quiet tears. Not tears to flow down one's cheek, causing wracking sobs. A man's tears. His face expressionless, no snot running down his nose. And all the while Josefa, timid serving wench, stared back, dumbstruck.

"I am still in bereavement," Vlad muttered at last. "I'll not see another woman until my beloved is avenged…if it takes forever, and ever, and ever."

"Y-Your beloved?" Josefa replied at last.

"Yes—my wife. Assassinated by Turkish dagger. I have sworn to swim the oceans of the world searching for him!"

"But…" Josefa was suddenly deeply confused. She dared not accuse Vlad of disembowelling his own mistress. Perhaps he was mad? Deluded.

She was flabbergasted. Everyone in Romania knew Vlad had disembowelled his high-born mistress. She was not his wife; there had been no marriage ceremony or feast recognised by the Church. And Vlad reputedly had many mistresses. An entire seraglio at Tirgovişte, like his Turkish contemporaries and overlords. He had made this bizarre story up, to expiate his sins. Surely he did not believe God would forgive him of such heinous sins?

"You do not believe me." Vlad spoke it as fact. "If you do not, I shall have you put to death immediately. Speak."

"I-I-I believe you, sire."

But did she?

"You lie!!!"

Josefa cowered in a corner, expecting the blow that was sure to come.

"You are a poor liar, girl. Look me in the eye and tell me you believe me. Now!"

Josefa sobbed, mortally afraid, tears streaming down her cheek. "I-I do not know what to think," she moaned.

"My Gypsies are below in the great hall, girl. Do you want me to bring them up here? Speak."

"O-O-Oh, please…" Josefa regained composure quickly, straightening up. "There are stories."

"Stories?" Vlad's blood ran cold.

"Atrocities. Whole villages boiled alive…"

Vlad's face turned ashen.

"What else?"

"That-that-that you disembowelled your mistress."

The room fell silent as a tomb.

"Lies!! All lies!! All must die for these fables! All must die! Whom did you hear this from?"

"S-Strangers, sire, mere strangers."

"What did they look like? How were they dressed?"

"They were…monks."

Vlad nodded suddenly, taking a deep breath, colour returning to his sunken cheeks. Now he knew what was happening. But never the full extent.

"Get out."

"Yes sire."

Vlad seized her arm as she rose to leave, drawing her brusquely towards him.

"See to that," nodding at her bloodied nose. "Consult my private physician; Ion Deschambers. And in the morning you will find four gold *lei* under your door as a token of my apology. Speak to no one of what we have just said, or you will most certainly die."

Josefa's blue eyes sparkled, for she had been expecting a blow, or worse. "Yes, Your Excellency."

And she exited the master bedchamber.

Still alive.

****

They gathered around the body at the foot of the stairwell like carrion crows. Still dark outside, with the sun just emerging in the east. The cylindrical, great tower echoed with the astonished voices of servants and ruff-collared courtiers as Vlad made his way down the steps of a narrow, spiral stairwell, unaware of the death by misadventure meted out to one of his serving wenches.

His smoking torch lit the gruesome, blood-smeared scene below. A young woman lay bloodied and stiff on the hall's flagstone floor, her body twisted and battered. No one touched the corpse or went too near in fear of the dreaded bubonic plague. That was not the dead wench's affliction, however. By the shape of her, she seemed to have been a curvaceous young woman. Dark-haired, her face turned toward the stone wall in a frozen gaze, features hidden. Streaks of blood made the stairwell's steps slippery. No one offered to come forward and reveal to Vlad the dead woman's identity, assuming that he already knew. A white linen strip of clothing streamed down the dark stairs for ten feet or more. Apparently the wench's dress hem or slip had caught on the uneven masonry, tripping the unfortunate girl to her death thirty feet below. She had been running too fast, a common fault of hers, either out of joy or fear.

Of course the reason no one came forward was that Vlad had murdered her. Vlad eyed the strangers suspiciously, asking one question.

"Who is she?" His voice echoed hollowly off the dark, shalestone walls. No one seemed to know. Or care.

Vlad turned her over with a pointed boot, expecting to see the plain face of some unknown wench.

What he saw struck grief and dismay into his heart, a bitter, almost alien emotion. Yet suddenly real again.

Josefa.

So foolish and carefree, like so many other girls her age. Having never been raised in a castle, she'd not realised the mortal danger of a steep, dim lit, spiral stairway. And now it was too late. Vlad glanced suspiciously at the courtiers and servants.

They were staring at him in a most peculiar way. As if he were a mad, rabies-infected dog frothing at the mouth. Rumour had it the girl was Vlad's mistress, herself the subject of wild innuendo and vicious jealousy amongst the older matrons of the castle. Why he had murdered this innocent wench they did not know. Nor did they want to know.

He was not amused. Vlad glowered at them, silent. *HOW DARE THEY!* he thought to himself. *ALL MUST DIE, ALL MUST DIE!*

"Do something with this…(could not bring himself to say it)…'thing'," watching as the servants brought forth a blanket and wrapped it around Josefa's cold, stiff body, feeling as if he'd just pounded a stake into his own heart.

****

20 August, 1461 AD Tirgovişte

The monks had suggested Dracula atone for his sins by summoning a great feast for the poor, the ageing, the crippled and the mentally handicapped. The beggars and Jews and Gypsies too were also to attend. A massive, wooden barn the shape of an upside-down ship's hull on the city's outskirts was to be the feast hall. Vlad had serious misgivings of this idea, abhorring the notion of feeding hundreds, possibly even thousands of underprivileged Wallachians and useless beggars. The boyars' lands had been freed, why did they not farm the fields rather than beg? The Gypsies he could understand, but Vlad suspected most of the beggars were merely lazy. St Bartholomew's Day was approaching, one of the holiest days of the year (and, soon to be, one of the blackest and most dreaded for Romanians). One thousand chickens, four hundred geese, three hundred duck and pheasant, fifty-eight ibex and chamois, two hundred hogs, thirty cattle and ten horses had been requisitioned across the countryside to feed the starving multitudes during the upcoming week-long celebrations. Tons of rutabaga and cabbage had been arriving since this morn via wagons and land-sledges. It was a hot, sultry, aquamarine-blue day. Not a cloud in the Wallachian prairie sky. A beautiful, midsummer's day. Great outdoor bakehouses had been constructed for the event. The Catholic monks of Tirgovişte followed Vlad around the barn's grassy precincts, pleased with their success in convincing this guilty, heinous *Cnéaz* of Wallachia of the righteousness of this gesture of goodwill towards those he had suppressed.

And pleased with what was to come.

The black Benedictines crowded the gravel causeway leading back to royal, heavily fortified Tirgovişte, walking leisurely behind their voivode two-by-two, back to the majestic monastery at the city's centre. Each tonsured monk felt sure they had lured the Dragon away from the evil, child-sacrificing Orthodox monks of Snagov monastery. Ready for his baptism perhaps? They looked supremely grotesque under a bright noonday sun now, sweat beading their bald, moon-shaved tonsures on top of their heads, skin turned brown as dried prunes from tending sheep in the countryside all day long. All were grossly overweight, practically tripping over the long, black linen habits reaching to their sandals.

And all the while, each was thinking of the Jews, Gypsies, and useless vagabonds who would be attending St Bartholomew's Feast. Several monks had run away from the monastery this last week, having found out its unholy plan of 'redemption and salvation for the sinners'. An *auto-de-fé*. (Act of faith.) No one would ever know. The few escapee-monks had already been captured and walled up alive at the Dominican monastery of Sighișoara. Vlad would make the perfect scapegoat, for had he not suggested once that the beggars be dealt with, if not enlisted in his peasant armies, then some other drastic solution? In public he had boasted this, at Sighișoara's great hall inside the gigantic, battlement-capped Jewellers' donjon, one of fourteen similar towers along that city's stout, stone, hilltop walls.

Vlad walked ahead, flanked behind and in front by his loyal bodyguards. Some were Gypsies, discontent with a life of wandering in caravans, a lawless life, unsure where or when their next arrest or eviction would come from. Through blatant discrimination they were barred from employment and farmwork. Forbidden to own property under Magyar, Szekler, or Saxon rule. A short, dark folk, descendants of the wandering hunter-gatherer/semi-nomadic Celts of eastern Europe. Dacians, Scythians, Parthians, Cimmerians, Gauls, Alemanni, Suevii, Corvinii, Belgae, Picts, Cornovii, Rus. Under the Romans they had had many names, none correct. Under the Romans they had often rose up in rebellion, massacring the Latinized inhabitants of the foreigners' towns, destroying entire legions, as Boudica had done, as Vercingetorïx had done. Now they were hybrid *Romany*, dispossessed caravans roaming across Europe, stealing clothes from clotheslines, livestock from farms, goods from town shops. A Gypsy could be hung on sight, without trial.

Many now received a scant meal twice a day in Vlad's homegrown army, their caravans tagging behind the main camp-followers with sad, expectant eyes. They were still strangers, but more welcome than before. Especially now, since Wallachia was up in arms. The Turks had issued their ultimatum, and it had come and past. Wartime was about the only emergency when Vlachs stood as one. Vlad Dracula had issued a call-to-arms as the church bells tolled on Whitsun in Tirgoviște. War, with no prisoners taken. A decree had been stated that cowards and traitors would instantly be put to death. And they knew what death.

Wallachia's prairies were ripe for harvesting. Oats and barley, rapeseed, wheat, einkorn, millet, lentils, turnips, and beets. The golden fields waved under a gentle breeze beyond the notch-merlon, ochre, Italianate city walls. These Cornucopian cereal fields would provide winter oatmeal and porridge (*mămăglia*, the staple diet), apple and rhubarb crumble pie, barley for horses, goats, pigs, and cattle. The beet greens would be stored in sand inside root cellars, the beets made into pickles and *borscht* (beet soup). Within the city walls, beyond the weird, notched merlons, each *Romaniĭ* family had its extensive plot of cabbage, corn, carrots and whatever other fruits or vegetables they could nurture in that rich, prairie soil. It would be a long Turkish campaign. The large Renaissance cities of Wallachia would likely be the first to fall, the villages and countryside pillaged for a fifty-mile radius. Crops would be burnt, either by the victorious invaders or by the retreating Romanians. The Wallachians expected defeat. Indeed, it seemed like a ritual enacted every decade. (They would of course be mauled, their Prince chastised and obliged to pay compensation for the Ottomans' troubles.) They were the front-line, protecting Moldavia, cannon fodder for the war-hardened, battle-crazed Janissary corps, sipahis, ghazis, and Azabs inflamed with the zeal for a holy war, or *Jihad*, which the Europeans alas did not share. To the marauding Turks, this was proof of the Christians' unwillingness to fight or die for Jehovah. It was commonly joked among Muslims that the sissy Christians feared to meet their Maker, lest He spit on them for not fighting for His name while applying at the pearly gates of Heaven.

But Vlad had changed all that this year by offering his countrymen two simple choices: they could die by Mehmed's sword, or they could die by his. The choice was not difficult to make. Especially with a sword at one's throat and a torch-wielding thug nearby ready to torch one's own family inside their thatched, wattle-and-daub prairie hovel.

That was Vlad's way. Bribery first, bullying when *ducats* proved useless. The Wallachian peasants weren't cowards, they were just sick of warfare, civil strife, private aggrandizements, wanted to stay at their crofts and eke out a rare, decent crop without having it burnt or reaped by Turkish ghazis or Romanian freedom-fighters. The boyars on the other hand MIGHT be willing to fight if the price was right. Or they might accept a bribe, a Turkish *baksheesh*, and then turn into traitors by joining a Turkish contingent during the last charge against their defeated countrymen. Others would merely stay away at their mountain fortresses, using their castle's bell-towers as fire beacons to warn of approaching Turkish regiments. The foraging *sipahis* were the worst of all, stealing livestock and grain and raping the women and girls, regardless of age. No royal chronicler dared mention these darker deeds when introducing their finished scroll to their masters, paid in fact for what they didn't write.

But in Vlad's case, the Pipe Rolls spared no detail. And elaborated on shamefully grey details.

****

23 August, 1461 AD

Tirgovişte, Northern Wallachia

Mehmed's forces struck with lightning-speed across the mighty, murky Danube, surprising Vlad's drunken contingent at Craiova. They took the walled town, massacring its inhabitants to a man, impaling the fortified citadel's defenders with wooden stakes arranged in a neat horseshoe around the ancient market-cross. (After raping the women and girls, the odd beauty carried off into Turkish slavery.) Across the district, the bloodied Crescent flag pounded home the message of Islam's harsh, imperialist, indomitable rule; skewering the obstinate and churning the borderlands' shareholders under their iron-shod hooves and their metal hammers of war. Vlad Dracula, that mucus-brained, weakling sycophant, as the Muslims called him, was away inspecting fresh-faced recruits from southwest Moldavia, a similar, semi-autonomous Principality of Romania. Stephen (future *Cĕl Mare*—the Great), Prince of Moldavia, resisted the temptation to retaliate against his cousin and fellow *voevod*, as Vlad Dracula would be Moldavia's front-line against the Turks, and possible future ally. Admittedly, Stephen thought Vlad was nuts to challenge the Ottomans, lords of Arabia, Persia, Egypt, Turkey, Abyssinia, and Mediterranean Europe; but Stephen liked Vlad. He had met the Wallachian Prince thrice already, entertaining Ţepeş at Stephen's royal palace of Suceava, a fellow *'Combrŏgos'*, Wallachia and Moldavia experiencing an almost unprecedented period of peace and mutual alliance.

Vlad sat now in a gloomy, candlelit chamber on the third floor of Tirgovişte's cylindrical, Chîndia watchtower. (Recently rebuilt by him.) He was drunk, and feeling sorry for himself. Beeswax candles in bronze candelabrum flickered under a cool summer draught, the palace watchtower echoing with the *whoosh* of drafts and booms of thunder as a midsummer thunderstorm raged outside its ten-foot-thick, lower spur-walls. White lightning flashed in the east, beyond the open, gothic, bubbled-glass window and Moldavian peaks. Vlad sat alone, for he had no true friends, only mutual alliances. He had celebrated (if you could call it that) his thirtieth birthday last Christmas, alone and unloved. Indeed, despised. He had no children, no heir nor heiress, no close relatives that he knew of, or cared to know of. Only enemies. Several half-brothers who were vying for his crown. Vlad the Monk, self-styled Prince of Wallachia and voivode of Transylvania foremost, and stubbornly resilient, difficult to root out. Tirgovişte had recently successfully resisted an assault by the Monk's supporters, among them Bogdan Dobăca, one of the most powerful warlords in upper Transylvania and a Szekler. Dobăca and Vintila Floreşcu had both sided for Dan II until the pretender's execution that black summer of '56. A new pretender, Dan III, had vied for Vlad's throne until this spring, when Dracula had beheaded the challenger after forcing Daneşti to recite his own burial rites, depriving Dobăca and Floreşcu of their nominee. Now they backed the Monk to the hilt, with four Hungarian mercenary armies at the behest of King Matthias of Hungary and the payroll of several wealthy European merchants, among them the German Count of Rosia, Peter Gareb de Waresmarth, and Venetian merchant Peterman de Longo Compo.

Bogdan Dobăca was safe and secure at his well-fortified village of Sercaia, having resisted Vlad in person as Ţepeş' army attempted to storm the triple-concentric earthworks and spur-based stone walls and battlemented, D-shaped bell towers. The powerful warlord rode out from the sally gate this spring with a cluster of picked knights. Bogdan slipped past Vlad's preoccupied retainers, engaging his rightful overlord in a mounted sword duel, finally unhorsing Vlad and preparing for the kill.

Vlad had only saved himself by thrusting his sword-point up between the boyar's legs as Dobăca stood over him, sword raised with both gauntleted hands over his head. The upthrust hit a tender area, disabling the challenger.

He thought of that now with acid bitterness, cursing loudly to no one in particular, the draft in the Chîndia watchtower threatening to extinguish the fluttering candles. Vlad swore to avenge himself on Dobăca, would cut off the boyar's head with Bogdan's own sword, and his testicles too. He would mount them in the palace courtyard for all to see. He would impale Bogdan's family en masse: men, women, and children. Vlad had learned from his mistakes. This latest confrontation had been the closest he had come to death on the battlefield in twelve years, since his initial usurpation of the Wallachian throne. He had held power for almost one year, before Daneşti II had regained the hallowed crown and ancestral throne in 1449. Hard to believe it had been five years since Vlad's official coronation here at Tirgovişte's ducal palace. The night Serena had been murdered. Vlad no longer felt such hot pain at her memory, just a cold, empty aching inside his heart for what might have been. A covetous desire for stolen years. They had shared almost eight, glorious years together.

Truly, those who said, *''Tis better to love in vain than never to love at all,'* didn't know their arse from a hole in the ground.

A tear trickled down Vlad's cheek, the brandy loosening up memories best left dead and buried. The cherished years snatched from him. Wracking sobs soon filled his very being, just a lonely old man, thirty already, greying at the temples and friendless. A Dacian Prince amongst Romanians, Magyars, Szeklers, Slavs, Albanians, Gypsies, and Germans. Strangers. A foreigner in his own country, his native tongue on the brink of extinction. A Vlach. To the newcomers, scum, unworthy of rights or respect. And tomorrow he would host a grand feast for the poor on the outskirts of Tirgovişte. To feed the vast multitudes of people whom he had for over a decade abused and neglected. Or as chroniclers unknown to him as yet would write, boiled alive, impaled up the anus, eaten alive, roasted alive then eaten.

Vlad Dracula, a very great and powerful FLY STUCK IN A WEB.

He slumped forward at his desk, at peace with himself, drunk unto oblivion, crystal brandy decanter slipping from his sleepy, sticky fingers.

While Vlad slept, the poor, the aged, crippled, beggarly, hungry, cold, the Gypsies of nearby districts burnt. He sat slumped at his desk, at peace with himself, sure he had been forgiven by his people at last. Vlad slept past midnight, through to dawn, unaware that some Higher Power had rearranged the Holy feast schedule. The starving, sad-eyed Gypsies, the old, the maimed, the destitute sat at great trestle tables in a huge, drafty wooden barn outside of Tirgovişte, enjoying their scrumptious meal, the first decent meal they'd had in weeks when the soldiers were ordered to bar the huge, double doors. It was sundown. The poor folk had been feasting on St Bartholomew's Eve, without royal supervision, only the large rabble of Franciscan and Benedictine monks attendant. Yet another of Vlad's most trusted councillors had defected to another contender—none other than Vlad's younger brother, Radu the Handsome, Mehmed's sycophant. Now there were four contenders: Radu the Handsome, Vlad the Monk, young Dan IV (Daneşti), and the latest, Basarab Laiota. The luckless, drunken Prince of Wallachia did not hear the screams of six hundred roasted peasants, did not see the sparks lighting up the night for miles around. His chamber door was locked by Priboi Hlinäny's order. Frantic messengers from miles around had been turned away at Vladislaus Dracula's door, the miserly *hospidar* safe inside with six guards at attention at his bedroom door. Outside his window, at nine o'clock p.m., an angry crowd of peasants and townsfolk bayed for Dracula's blood but were barred from entering the hilltop palace by two immense, stout portcullises. Instead, they rioted in Tirgovişte till dawn.

And when he awoke the next morning, Vlad had wished he could've closed his eyes forever.

Chapter Nine

He wandered about the ruined barn for hours. White bones still protruded from the charred remains. Soot everywhere. And vast, dune-like hills of smouldering ashes. Hot coals still fumed a thin, wispy miasma of pungent smoke. A thick layer of pale grey, ankle-deep ashes smothered the high grass, fine as dust, clogging his nostrils, making him cough as he poked among the still-glowing embers. A great, black, rectangular mound of smoking coals and former timber-beams signified where the old barn once stood. The ashen skyline seemed forlorn, alien, without the derelict building's familiar outline on the horizon. It was a dismally grey day; dreary, depressing, stamped with the imprint of unimaginable suffering, the grass scorched fifty feet in each direction. One flax field had nearly evolved into a foxfire. No one else except for Vlad's private regiment were in sight. Most of Tirgovişte's citizenry had drunken themselves into oblivion after the riot, chased out of the streets by Dracula's mounted troops after the rioters attempted to scale the palace walls by torchlight. Tirgovişte's church bells and monastery campaniles tolled mournfully now. Everyone else except for Vlad's soldiers were at Sunday Mass, praying for the souls of these poor sinners. Extra proof of Dracula's guilt; he was not at church. Rarely was these days. At least one thing was a relief, said a Dominican priest at Mass inside Tirgovişte cathedral this morning: *"Those sinners whom had unfortunately rejected God's Truth had, yes, achieved Redemption when purged by the soul-cleansing pyre. God is embracing them now. Yes, even the Jews. And the Gypsies, well, no great loss."*

Priboi Hlinäny had had the good sense and good fortune to escape to Hungary six nights ago, the night of the feast, where he was at this moment being welcomed at King Matthias' court in Vác castle on the Danube.

Only Vlad's private retainers believed he hadn't ordered these wretched destitutes burnt alive. They watched fidgetily as he paced about the sooty ruins, turning over a child's thighbone with his pointy black leather boot. He bent down, picking it up, stuffing it in a burlap sack as an heirloom and keepsake to these unjustly murdered peasants' memory. Face devoid of emotion. Knowing that a good proportion of the pyre victims were among the last Dacian speakers in all of Romania and mainland Europe. In the years to come, villagers and peasants across Romania would stubbornly hold to the belief that he was innocent, their secret creed fading with the years like a dying flame. At the end of Vlad's reign, extinguished. (Many Romanians would even applaud his extirpation of Wallachia's dross in the centuries to come.)

Someone had to pay for this.

But compared to this, the Turkish advance last week into Wallachia was of greater importance. The mighty Wallachian island-fortress of Giurgiu had been bombarded by Mehmed's one hundred field cannon, then stormed in force by his mounted ghazis and Janissaries' infantry corps. The first wave had been beaten back. And the second. But the third overwhelmed its defenders like a tidal wave. The defenders were impaled en masse, as at Craiova. This news was devastating to all Romanians, as Giurgiu was one of the newest, most sophisticated, powerful artillery fortresses in all of Europe. Vlad's father, Dracul, had built it over a ten-year span. Vlad Dracula and his ill-equipped, malnourished, poorly-clothed peasant army would be retreating today, toward the Alps, much too inexperienced and heavily outnumbered to dare challenge the Turks on the battlefield. Vlad's fourth division at Craiova had challenged Mehmed as the Turks jettied their low dhows (ships) across the Danube, only to be routed. Rumour had it that it was to be a winter campaign, unprecedented, a war to end wars. Mehmed Çelebi, 'The Conqueror', planned to complete the conquest of Wallachia this winter. And Moldavia come spring. And there was not much the inhabitants could do about it. (Prince Stephen, Vlad's Moldavian ally, had promised cannon and several battalions - but no *official* support.) Hungary had egged Wallachia into declaring war on Islam. Now King Matthias seemed surprisingly reluctant to help. Even though Hungary's own borders would lay within striking distance of the Ottoman empire. Rumour had it that Matthias, Wallachian-born no less, had struck a deal with Mehmed to share Romania between themselves; Wallachia and Moldavia to the Turks, Transylvania to Hungary. Much loot and spoils of war could be anticipated. Perhaps every Western nation should join in on it?

Four thousand troops stood, sat, loafed, lay or straddled their sagging mounts, ready to move out. Some had already decided to desert, would do so upon entering the sub-Carpathian Bucégi mountains. Some could not fight with a clear conscience for a monster like Prince Wladislaus Dragwla, a wampyr who'd burnt alive six hundred gullible, innocent poor folk last weekend without the least guilt. Only days later, he had begun a senseless, barbaric purge against the decent, honest, Holy brothers of Tirgovişte's community of Benedictines, Franciscans, Carthusians and Dominicans, an act no good Catholic could forgive. Exactly a year ago Vlad had ruined his reputation irrevocably after his mass-extermination, St Bartholomew's Day, of the corrupt citizens of Amlăs, reputedly impaling 20,000 in one day (in any case, technically impossible). (Five hundred had been burnt, two thousand impaled, seventy-five beheaded.) Surprisingly, few had actually witnessed this grisly event. (Even fewer had survived Ţepeş' savage suppression of such vindictive rumour mongers.) 'Twas said however that Prince Vlad the Horrible had impaled the entire Dominican monastery's brotherhood of monks and lay brothers. Vlad's fervent Wallach retainers seemed oddly tight-lipped, however. Others within Vlad's regiment knew the odds stacked against them surviving the first charge of Mehmed's holy-war-crazed, mounted ghazis were simply mountainous, as high as Tibet's Mt Gosaintan. Vlad would hold court in the mountains, like a Neolithic chieftain, minus hall, castle, or latrines (toilets). And he would enjoy it, Dacian barbarian that he was. The plan was simple: recruit, hit-and-run, and impale, impale, impale! Medieval circuitry. Catapult stones from above, from road verges, from bluffs, crags, trackway ridges. Ambush, sneak-attack. Take no prisoners. Those women and children willing to follow were welcome, though they knew full-well the hardships and dangers to come. The camp followers would arrive next week. If the war went badly and women and children across Wallachia were systematically raped or sold into slavery by Mehmed's roving Janissaries, the summons would arrive for Ţepeş' bondsmen to enter the majestic, brooding mountains, east, north, and west, where Vlad's peasant army was at this moment building stockades around marshes, bogs, and cold mountain tarns. Hempen ropes were being spun by old, professional cord-wainers which would be used to transport goods and the infirm onto the loftiest peaks, where folk would be safer. (Otherwise, neither man, woman, nor beast would be exempt from Mehmed's rapacious villains.) Every Wallachian knew (snicker,

snicker) that the plains-hopping Turks were no mountain climbers. Indeed, they hated these forbidding, fir-mantled, Carpathian Alps.

Vlad mounted his huge bay warhorse, dressed like a true barbarian. Leatherclad. Only his long, black cape betrayed his nobility. Biceps and thigh muscles bare, bulging, hardened by swinging sharp pole-axes, heavy maces, broadswords, war hammers, staffs, lances, and firing arrows (which he was proficient at) at his hapless, and (soon to be), headless, opponents. (Vlad's muscle-bound physique, atypical of Wallachia's ruling elite, rippled with raw, brute strength; more that of a brawny Caucasian wrestler than of an aristocrat.) He was a hardened veteran now, not the young stripling who had been toppled after nine months in power during 1448–1449. He would not fall so easily now. A mere, jewel-studded diadem bound his greasy black locks. At his side hung his trusty three and a half-foot, two-hander, Dacian broadsword (a gift of his uncle, Demitri), a broad, ferocious hacking weapon. At his hip was a hefty ball- and-chain spiked mace with wooden pole-grip. His enormous stallion, *Garmüch*, an anamita-yellow stable stud, had a stout longbow strapped to his flank—a quaint, rare sight.

Vlad's men, alas, were not so well equipped. They wore the customary padded, clumsy, sweaty leather gambesons, chainmail hauberk-skirts, wool vests, iron kettle helmets, gloves, steel gauntlets. Their weapons? Crossbows, composite bows, *arquebus* (primitive handgun), longbows, rapiers, falchions, scimitars, tulwars, sabres, Viking-style battle-axes, Dalmatian pole-axes, pikes, spears, halberds, round iron shields. Few broadswords, horses, lances, maces, war hammers dignified their now-assembling columns. Even fewer arrows to load their useless bows. (They were still in the manufacturing stage.) For now, every man must fend for himself. Vlad wondered with grim black humour if he should order these young striplings to beat the Turks back with their bows, a truly ridiculous thought. One volley from Mehmed's bronze cannon would have their bellies ripped open on the field more efficiently than Vlad's impalement techniques could ever be. The best he could hope for right now was a sudden, inexplicable surge of national pride. Or an earthquake. He knew most Romanians would prefer to make peace with the Turks, even be ruled by them. And, he deeply suspected, be converted to Islam by them. The new Latin half-breeds had no stomach for blood. Yes, Vlad's secret joke amongst his fellow *Combrŏgos* was correct: despite the Romanians' illusory resemblance to men, they were really women!

He gave the order to move out, flanked by thirteen trusted and not-so-trusted councillors and advisors—most of them loyal ex-peasants elevated to the status of boyar. (No less than four eminent astrologers rode at his side; soothsayers and diviners.) Vlad's pampered courtiers, alas, were also present, sweating and driven mad by sandflies and mosquitos. It was a mercilessly hot, sultry day. The way Vlad's court was swelling and becoming more untrustworthy day by day, perhaps it was time he organised another boyar march and a new castle built, Vlad mused. But where. Turnu Rosu? No, there was already a castle there, the 'Red Tower', named evermore after the Turks thrown from its blood-stained ramparts or cut down while attempting to storm it during one of Vlad's illustrious ancestors' reigns. Bistritz? Satul Nou? Yes, fitting. Four of Vlad's boyar companions had proven their worth over the years: the boyars Mihail Galeş, Matei Báthóry, Cirstian Mohács, and Tudur Mihály. They rode at his side now, proud, moustachioed warriors, middle-aged, married, with large families (Vlad was DEEPLY jealous). Of the five official years of his rule, Vlad had failed to sire even one child. Partly because of his hatred for Romanians; partly because Romanian women hated him even more. (For scarcely anyone in Transylvania/Wallachia was without his or her harrowing story of a loved one or relative having been murdered by the 'Impaler Prince'.) Rape was not his way, as with so many other men: a wench who loathed him did not turn him on. And they ALL loathed him. Why, he hadn't a clue. Of all these years, not one had come to his bedchambers offering her favours.

He glanced disconsolately at his wretched retinue, then gave the order to move out, louder this time. The clamour of his captains' shouts and bugles blaring reverberated among the milling horses, pack mules, donkeys, marching men, and rolling, rumbling supply wagons—Vlad's meagre baggage-train. His was only one of many divisions. Northwest toward Tîrgu Mureş they'd be heading, up the willow-draped Dimbovita river and beyond majestic Moldŏveanu, the highest peak in Wallachia, where his armies would encamp near the river Mică, ensconced between the Bihor and Făgăras foothills to the west and Harghita massifs to the east. Vlad's encampment of civilians and soldiers would be defended on three sides by Carpathia's steep, jagged highlands—a vista of forbidding, impenetrable limestone/granite mountains flanked by tall, evergreen, montane forests of pine, fir, and spruce.

A detachment would be sent via the Prahova valley to Cimpŭlung, Molduvenesc, and Satu Mare, villages in the central Alps where fortified palisades were being built for literally herds of terrified mothers, children, and grandparents too old to fight. All Wallachians had by now realised the dread seriousness of the Turkish advance, the Turks having sailed up the Olt in small troopships all the way to Drăgăsani, raping and pillaging like brown Vikings with impunity;

looting, impaling, destroying fortified enclaves. Monasteries were sacked, even the Saxons' ingenious, fortified church-enclosures. (A goodly number of forts had already been razed to the ground, among them Ungra, Rupea, and Homorod.) The Turks would not be satisfied, this time, however, to halt at the Carpathians' jagged ramparts. Instead, unbeknown to the hapless Romanians, they had come with ballista, cherry-wood-mounted bronze cannon, donkeys, packhorses, camels, royal elephants and mountaineers from Tibet. This was to be a war to annex, not a mere show of force like all the other times. Wallachian women and children were being taught by Vlad's recruits how to use crossbows and how to fashion their own longbows from yew (clumsy as these unfamiliar mass-murder weapons were, at a hefty two pounds '[and the devil to draw!]'—if nothing else, they could club their enemies to death!); how to wield swords and operate catapults and giant slings of war; at the very least, instructed to hail loads of rocks onto the besiegers' heads when all other weapons were in short supply. 'Twas to be a fully-armed nation, a nation of Amazons and proud warriors. Cowards, needless to say, were not to be tolerated. The choice, however, was between the organised tyranny of an imperialist regime or of a seemingly-mortal Wallachian madman bent on genocide. Dracula ordered his field commanders to put to death wounded Wallachian soldiers showing tell-tale wounds in the back.

And most horrible of all, impale each and every soldier of Islam captured. When the Turks and their Persian allies reached smouldering, abandoned Tirgovişte, they would see a sight never before witnessed by mortal eyes.

****

10 May, 1462 AD
Sighişoara, Harghita Mountains

They sighted the great, fortified city from miles away. Tremendous battlement-capped round donjons soared above the few wispy white clouds, black witch's hats topping the fourteen citadel towers like spires. It was a hot, hazy day. Spring was in full bloom, belying the fact that across southern Wallachia civilians were being slaughtered, looted, and literally carried off in a manner unprecedented in the history of Europe. Transylvania's blue mountains, emerald hills, purple heather and crystal clear, gurgling, bubbling, forest-cloaked rivers sung a happy tune, lying to the people, as if singing, *"It's all right, it's a warm day, come out and play. Come play with the Turks."* Vlad listened dejectedly as his soldiers buzzed with indignation, having witnessed a traumatic scene first-hand from a high bluff while fleeing the destroyed region around Bucharest. Vlad and a small reconnaissance mission had rode south to witness from afar the burning of his new capital. Bucharest's citizens had foolishly believed they could strike a deal with Mehmed to spare their new, stone-walled city. Mehmed had acquiesced. But once the portcullises were raised the ghazis rushed into the city, uncontrollable, so enraged with bloodlust and vengeance for Dracula's ghastly impalements, breaking their Sultan's promise while he watched—a replay of Constantinople.

As Vlad's retinue returned to the safety of the northerly mountains of ungro-Wallachia, they had watched, helpless, from a bluff in the Bucégi mountains as a twelve-year-old girl was brutally, savagely, senselessly gang-raped by a large contingent of Turkish Janissaries.

Dracula had ordered his bravest knights to follow him down the steep, snarly bluff, to ambush the foragers while they raped the poor girl in a glade. They would die if need be, making a knights' pact, hand-on-hand. But alas, Fate had shown a joker card, for the scraggly outcrop had proven too precipitous to traverse their horses down; a sheer, limestone crag eighty feet high, badly overgrown and deadly treacherous near its obscured, bramble-hidden edges. Vlad had ordered his knights to abandon the plan. To scramble down the incline, on foot, without the element of surprise would not only be slow and suicidal, but pointless. Finally, around sunset when the foragers moved on and crows circled in the red air, a brave young lad had volunteered to scramble down the bluff to rescue the still, bloodied child left for dead in the glade.

Young Matthias Turgus had returned fifteen minutes later, sad-eyed and shaken, voice cracking and tears in his eyes. The child was...mutilated...used and abused by over one hundred grown Turkish men, and then when finished her pubescent body tossed aside like so much trash.

Dead. Beaten to death.

All this while Vlad and seventeen knights watched, powerless, from above...each Turkish Janissary having his turn with her while she cried and screamed hopelessly.

And that, was when the tides of war changed.

And in the summer of '62, *50,000* Turkish soldiers were impaled alive.

Chapter Ten

24 May, 1462 AD
Harghita Mountains

They ambushed the Turks by day from the Carpathian mountains to the northeast. Vlad's vicious, victorious insurgents would return to the Moldavian Alps untouched. Sultan Mehmed's gargantuan, invincible army had retreated temporarily from the burnt capital of Bucharest after fierce resistance and countless casualties. Day by day, scouting expeditions returned with captured Turkish foragers, whose main job was to gather food from the scorched countryside any way they could when the fighting was slack. Hundreds of semi-independent militia groups throughout Wallachia and southern Transylvania, hiding-out in small caves, caverns, outcrop niches, oak, birch, sycamore and beech groves, in gullies, mountain passes, river gorges, ravines and underground souterrains or *fogous* (Iron Age passages) captured and herded their Turkish bounties under nightfall toward Ţepeş' forest enclave in Transylvania, paid in pilfered, Saxon gold, where the victims' screams would be unheard as they were gruesomely, sadistically, impaled. Vlad's own formidable renegades would strike at night, even worse, ambushing the sleepy Turks while they sat around their campfires. The Wallachs knew the country like mountain goats; some were shepherds, others former brigands. They struck in darkness without torches, like bats, depending solely on their ears. It was not enough to slaughter the vanquished. They had the survivors impaled on the spot, carrying long stakes specially-made for the purpose. Then they carried the stiff, impaled corpses in horse-drawn litters toward a field outside of Tîrgovişte, fifty miles south of the former royal capital still loyal to Vlad's Cause, usually by night.

Wooden palisades had been built around numerous marshes near Tîrgu Jiu, where women and children waited nervously for the main Turkish assault. Others were scattered east and west, even forbiddenly-so in the Hungarian hinterlands of Transylvania. Mihály Szilágy did nothing to hinder Vlad's brazen actions, though he was forbidden by King Matthias Corvinus/Hunyádi to engage the Turks in combat or even to resist. The best Szilágy could do was offer Vlad regiments from his own private recruits in Bucovina. Men were being sawn in half by Mehmed's torture-masters in Drăgăsani for resistance. Dracula sent hundreds of plague-victims incognito into the ditched Turkish camps with the promise of gold should they somehow survive the dreaded buboe virus. A Papal Legate from Rome had arrived in Buda-Pest, urging the Hungarian king to seek a peaceful resolution to this sordid war. (The depredations of the Muslim dogs falling, heh, heh, not surprisingly, on Hungary's deaf ears.) But while the Papal Nuncio was parleying with Matthias, another secret mission was urging mad Vlad Dracula to carry out his Order of Dragons' oath to the full.

Meanwhile Vlad found it slightly (only slightly) ironic and amusing, much to his chagrin, that the Papal Legate would flatter him by urging Vlad to fight for God. Vlad shocked the Italian Man-of-God by replying that he wasn't fighting for God, but for country.

And then he impaled the Papal Legate on a one-hundred-foot pine pole outside his wilderness court hall, for all to see.

****

2 June, 1462 AD

Tîrgovişte, Wallachia

A great, stinking semi-circle of impaled, decomposing cadavers met the Turks' shocked eyes as they prepared to encamp outside Tîrgovişte's 'No Go' zone. Some of the impaled were fresh, others still writhing and wriggling on their high stakes, impaled only hours ago. They moaned pitifully as their comrades neared, blood and greenish-blue intestinal fluids soaking their impalement stakes. Yet it was too late for help, even for Sultan Mehmed's internationally renowned, skilled doctors; the vanquished's internal organs were punctured and ruined. It was only a vainglorious testament to their will to live, dying twenty-five feet above their gaping, bug-eyed comrades.

These wretches were not merely the victims of hit-and-run raids as they were earlier. Now *Kaziglu Bey*, the Impaler Prince, had begun to openly challenge Sultan Mehmed's invincible army on the field. And to every Turk's dismay, he would own the battlefield at sundown while Mehmed's hardened, veteran Janissaries retreated in disarray. Mehmed had faced other spirited European leaders and been turned back, notably Vlad's own brother Mirçea while Mehmed was commander of his father's legions in Dracul's reign, and Skanderbeg of Albania, still a thorn in Mehmed's side; the Serbs had resisted Mehmed's imperial army through trickery and treachery, led by their own formidable despot, Vúc Brancovic; and John Hunyádi (aka Ion de Hunedŏara) had performed great feats on the battlefield against Mehmed's illustrious father, Mured. But none, none had went to this length. Vlad had ignored all rules of etiquette, of diplomatic mercy and immunity. He had ignored diplomatic channels altogether. This was supposed to be a holy *Jihad*, with some rules of decent conduct. And ghazis could not lose.

But the true enormity of this ghastly, macabre display of defiance had Sultan Mehmed's camp disintegrating into pandemonium as his army neared. From a distance, they'd had no idea of the sheer extent of Dracula's atrocities. They had begun to set up their tents the previous nightfall, almost cheerful as they unfolded their backgammon boards, stuffed their pipes with hashish, their hookahs with opium.

And then, suddenly materialising through the last, straggling stands of old-growth beech forest, Mehmed's army sighted Vlad's gruesome theatre of mockery looming above the younger saplings. No one could have imagined this sight in their wildest nightmares. In the history of the world, this was unprecedented. Not content to arrange his cruelly murdered, tortured victims on mere fifteen-foot poles, Vlad had gleefully constructed a truly staggering crescent of *twenty-five-foot* stakes (or higher) for a two-mile radius around and in front of distant Tirgovişte. Countless, rotting, richly-dressed skeletons now decayed beneath a blistering early summer sun, the hottest within living memory, some of the bones bleached white already. They seemed to bow formally at the waist in the early morning sunlight. Gigantic stakes protruded through ivory-white ribcages, great poles braced on either side by massive, V-shaped, upside-down wooden beams. Eyeless, black sockets stared vacantly across the scorched Transylvanian fields, jaws stretched wide in eternal agony; the last moments of their horrible deaths etched into their skeletal expressions. They grinned wide, smiled evilly down at their living fellow ghazis. Others were somewhat fresher, sticks of putrefying meat, gagging young and old alike. Magnificent silk turbans of varying colours topped the skulls balanced twenty-five/forty feet above.

Mehmed's troops shrieked and wailed at the sight, for this was not a mere, few impaled ghazis, or even hundreds. Thousands perhaps, tens of thousands, the horrible, crowded palisade stretching to either horizon, as far as the eye could see. The noon sun burned high in the southern sky, so hot, men were frying eggs on their iron shields in the back ranks. The ghazis tore at their hair, terrified. The promise of Paradise no longer seemed so appealing. The fate of Mehmed's army towered above them, as if predicting each ghazi's future should he be captured or ambushed. The holy fervour was gone. Each knew he could not go on. Unlike the siege of Belgrade, or the Albanian campaigns or those of Bosnia and Montenegro, the Ottoman soldiers of Allah had not merely been resisted, this time. Their massive army had evaporated to only a third of its former size, their field cannon captured. "Kaziglu Bey" had not taken the customary route of holding prisoners for ransom, as all honourable warlords did. The Impaler hadn't even bothered to spare Sultan Mehmed's high-ranking emissaries, ambassadors, Pashas or diplomats, having them impaled like all the rest but on higher stakes, befitting their status.

A lone, towering stake stood in the centre of the throng, awaiting its exalted intendée—*Mehmed Çelebi*. It had his name written on it in Cyrillic letters, towering twenty feet above the tallest stake.

Mehmed Çelebi knelt inside his party-coloured command tent, begging Allah to return His Chosen Son to favour, to smote this mad tyrant Vlad Dracula with lightning bolts, to clear the Wallachian prairie fields, dark forests, and haunted mountains of Romanian resistance like a hurricane. *"A man capable of such marvellous deeds is surely worthy and destined for greater things!"* cried Mehmed as his personal scribe feverishly jotted down his master's decree, before hurriedly leaving the tent. The young scribe halted in front of one of the highest poles, suddenly vomiting as he gazed up at the Emir's former chronicler, the Greek Catavolinos, still dressed in his best, Syrian-silk, brocaded, Damask flowing robes, colourful shiny fabric and brilliant jewels winking in the merciless sunshine. Grinning shamelessly. Mehmed sobbed shamelessly, alone inside his gold-fringed tent, weeping with anger and shame at his own cowardice, for, Allah forgive him, he could not go on. *Tsepeşh* had won, had stolen all of Mehmed's cannon, destroyed his army; even the Sultan's loyal, European Janissaries had fled in panic at the decisive battle of Bucharest one week ago today, attacked without warning (or even suspicion of the diabolical horde's presence!) near the voivode's accursed island/fortress of Snagov, fleeing the marshes as they watched their Ottoman comrades ambushed and horribly slain at sundown by *Kaziglu Bey's* own warband—Dracula's favourite war time.

Not one of Mehmed's trusted advisors and diplomats had returned alive. Not one had he now. All were with him, sixty miles south of Tirgovişte, in body; thirty-five feet above his command tent. Hamza Pasha, dearest friend, advisor and fine war-leader towered conspicuously above the other skeletons and cadavers in various stages of decay, gruesomely attired still in his fine, silk, colourful brocades, magnificent white silk turban and scarlet, satin cloak. Impaled. A mere, bleached skeleton. The Greek Catavolinos, Mehmed's ablest, finest European advisor, diplomat, and moneylender, skewered also. Mehmed's favourite homosexual consort, the Greek Catavolinos had recently supplanted Dracula's effete younger brother Radu of the Sultan's seemingly natural caresses. The Greek had had so much energy and much to teach Mehmed, for it had been a curiously venerated—and still was—trait of both the Greeks, and, later, Romans.

But Catavolinos grinned macabrely up on his stake of Lebanese cedar now, more permanently impaled than he could ever have been in life. (The stake rising through his palate.)

"Allah, Allah, why hast thou forsaken me?" begged Mehmed. His knees were sore from two hours of kneeling on the sacred, gold-embroidered rug inside his sumptuous command tent. Mehmed touched his forehead to the mat repeatedly, praying, chattering to his silent Lord and beseeching the Holy Prophet Mohammed to intervene with Allah on Mehmed's behalf. There was no response inside the sweet-smelling, incense-laced pavilion, only the mortified cries and Turkish mutterings of soldiers outside breathing putrid, rotten-egg-smelling human flesh, gaping up at their unfortunate comrades impaled on stakes twenty feet and more above.

Unfortunately, for the Oriental cooks trying to prepare dinner for the multitudes of soldiers plus their ever-fussy, articulate, overweight gluttonous Sultan, the awful stink wafting across the charred plains and rawhide tents on a capricious west wind upset the cooks' stomachs and finely-tuned chefs' olfactory senses (the stench was, in any case, *inescapable*). Surely no man would wish to eat today. And, unfortunately, not all the corpses on towering stakes were bleached eight-month-old skeletons long since stripped by ravens. Some were mere skin and bones. Others however were maggot-infested, far-from-fresh cadavers, their ruptured bellies slowly drying out and utterly horrible-smelling, brains still being eaten out of their broken craniums by crows and ravens craving the grey, salty, dried brains. Already devout Muslims were puking behind their tents. Indeed, no man had much stomach for food today.

Mehmed had some quick decisions to make. Should he forge on, push for the Carpathians, where he knew Mad Dracula and his macabre comrades were hiding away in nooks and crannies? Besiege Tirgoviște, their former capital? Or retreat into Yugoslavia and Bulgaria and wait for a better opportunity. Dracula may reign forever. Or he might be assassinated tomorrow. (Çelebi yearned to seize the twisted voivode's unreachable, private redoubt in southern Transylvania, which practically begged to be taken.) Mehmed knew the hearts of the Romanian people, knew it was Dracula and his mysterious Cymri/Gypsy brotherhood who controlled this war, hypnotising these gullible fools with his huge, demonic green eyes and fiery speeches and tirades. As soon as Dracula disappeared Mehmed knew the Romanians would surrender willingly, without a fight.

One other option Sultan Mehmed toyed with more and more recently was the shocking offer by Pope Pius II himself, that simpleton in Pope's mitre, an offer so tempting and disturbing that Mehmed—like his father before him—had brooded for days.

None other than the Holy Roman Emperor's crown if Mehmed would convert to the Christian faith, a faith for sissies and cowards. Jews. Deep inside, Mehmed knew he could become baptized and fake conversion, and then, with power in Western Europe consolidated, renege on his pledge to Christ. (Whom Mehmed and all devout Muslims knew was a mere charlatan and sleight-of-hand artist, not the son of God. Mohammed, they knew, was the Messiah.) But Mehmed's pride and sense of honour told him that was not right. These infidel Caucasians must recognise his military authority, Allah's true light, or else the Paradise of Islam would be toothless like the old, defunct, Byzantine Empire.

But to continue on would be madness. Retreat now, before the misery of defeat destroys his once-fine army. Winter would approach in under three months, miserable and cold in these hostile plains and Carpathian mountain ranges. Especially without sufficient weaponry and food supplies (which Vlad had sabotaged or stolen, through subterfuge). Mehmed could withdraw, reconnoitre in Yugoslavia for a surprise fall or spring attack. There was no other way. For the first time in holy Islam's history, its holy war, the army was threatening to disintegrate, desert, flee disorganised before the infidel enemy.

That, Mehmed couldn't allow to happen.

He stepped outside his tent to inform his faithful ghazis of the Good News.

****

4 June, 1462 AD
Sighişoara, Transylvania

Vlad had watched alongside his men, on horseback, wearing a knight's hauberk as the dispirited Turks retreated from the scorched stubble fields of Tirgovişte, his entire army hidden away in the overgrowth or on cliffs, bluffs, hills, or valleys, ready to attack. Dracula's disciplined army, 20,000 strong, looked to their mounted leader with anxious eyes as the Turkish bugles sounded from the smouldering, blackened fields. Vlad sat his horse motionless, watching sternly from a bluff as if challenging Mehmed to sight his midafternoon silhouette dwarfed beneath a faint, daylight obscured, three-quarter moon. Inexperienced foot soldiers holding spears or halberds trembled with the fear that Vlad Ţepeş might foolishly risk battle as the Turks prepared for an orderly retreat. Yet ready to attack should the Ottoman horde forge on. Dracula's guess had been uncannily correct: he had learned their fear tactics during his six years in captivity at Mured's court, knew the Turks' respect for gory theatrics. He had learned of their impalement techniques at the former Crusader fortress of Egrigöz in western Anatolia, how they had persecuted Orthodox Christians cunningly hiding-out in the tufa outcrop-caves of Gorëme, Turkey. Vlad had watched the crucifixions, mesmerised, during his brief seven months at Adrianople.

Now he smiled macabrely as his columns once more neared the great, fortified, Saxon city of Schassburg (*Sighişoara* to Romanians), an outpost of Hungarians, Szeklers, Saxons, and Swabians. Vlad hadn't washed for weeks, now felt deliciously barbaric as he rode (like a much-feared, Mongol steppe mogul) at a sedate pace at the head of his semi-loyal army. He had partaken in the fighting as they had, had fought hand-to-hand combat with professional Azabs and Janissaries, had literally slept in the saddle. All his soldiers were dirty, begrimed, sweat-stained. Some had spent considerable time digging trenches, up to their necks in clinging, black marsh soil or bog mud. Vlad's hair was greasy, lank, black moustache drooping over his chin and caked with dust, no longer fashionably plaited or sticking out straight from his rosy, sunken cheeks. (It was also much shorter than was his norm, and sensibly trimmed.) Some of his troops had bathed in lagoons or sloughs, only to come out muddier than before and covered with leeches. Like his Romanian soldiers, Vlad wore no stockings; only a grim, dark brown, thigh-length immodest tunic (with Dragon heraldry), woolskin vest, and black leather jackboots. (Overtop he wore, as a mantle, his dreadful ebon cape of Hell-spun silk.) He wore a simple coil of orange rope around his forehead, though studded with diamonds. Had any man in Wallachia been a fiercer combatant than he they might have taken Vlad's head for the mocking crown alone.

Vlad was 31 years old this summer, but felt jubilant, much younger, perhaps 24. His green monster-eyes were keen as an eagle's, still.

Up ahead, the great, arched, wooden gates and iron portcullises of Sighişoara were already open or raised, admitting their sacrilegious hero into the walled, fortified, northern city, the cowed residents burying their grudges for the moment.

Nonetheless, as Dracula's entourage victoriously entered the cobbled city streets, there were no parades, no banners waving nor bells tolling, no grand welcoming committee of Romanian mayors or ealdormen. Only silent, terrified,whispering folk who lined the dirty, dung-splotched streets, gathering in a market cross/square near the fetid city's communal well. The man who had impaled thousands, raped nuns, boiled peasants, drank blood, forced mothers to eat their own children was coming to visit THEM. Vlad was no St. Nicholaus.

The townsfolk gathered in morbid curiosity near the market-cross, in awe of this mad, wicked, brilliant warlord riding proudly at the head of his Wallachian soldiers. His head held high, craftily eyeing the cowed populace. Several churls backed away from the big, uncovered communal well, crossing themselves with the Evil Eye and fingering their cloaks nervously. One brave Hungarian lass and child however failed to realise who was riding into the square, merely expecting a God-like local boyar, continued to crank the well-pulley as Vlad's cohort halted fifty feet away, exhausted and thirsty.

The wench failed to heed her fellow townsfolks' pleas and dire warnings to come away from the well. She cranked hard on the pulley's handle, determined to collect her pail of ice-cold water. A small girl of five hid behind her big sister's black skirts shyly, intimidated by the knot of filthy, bloodied soldiers dismounting in Schassburg's market-square. Some lounged lazily now against the market-cross, as if sunning themselves. A sudden fanfare of trumpets and muted cheers blared: the soulful murmurings of a nation exhausted by a year and more of dreadful, death-to-the-last-man war against the Turkish Leviathan. The neighing of horses and cloppity-clop-clop of iron horseshoes on cobblestone, tongue-clicking, and snapping of whips filled the air. Some of the townsfolk stood aside on the cobbled street behind the two unsuspecting girls, curious of this morbidly gruesome *Naši* honouring their northern city of Sighişoara. They strained their necks, sighting Vladislaus Dracula among his more trusted *Armaşii*, boyars, and advisors. And what a sight to behold! Never was Vlad more at ease, exuding confidence, as when he was at war, sure that his mission was ordained by God, whether it be destroying rebel boyars or invading Turks. (His secret Gypsy name among his fellow Wallachs was *Catgi*, 'War Hound'.) Prince Vlad, enveloped in his majestic, fear-inspiring, ebony cape, the Devil himself come to visit the Saxons of Sighişoara. He marched towards the well, haughtily surveying the crowd; his tongue thick and parched, red lips chapped. His advisors and bodyguards followed, glad to be resting and home for a while in Sighişoara where, surprisingly, Vlad himself had been born in a grand townhouse now serving as an inn. Those few with money might find a brothel or a willing wench (even though Dracula had outlawed brothels and prostitutes, the punishment for requesting their services…death).

Too late, Voica Nyireghyáza cranked, panicked, on the lumbering, heavy water pail, suddenly realising by the awed bilingual whispers of *'Dracula!'* who this royal visitor was. A horrible little man. The dreaded, child-murderer Wladislaus Dragwla, a voivode of Transylvania and *Cnéaz* of Wallachia—wampyr. *Kaziglu Bey*. Vlad Ţsepeşh. The Dragon. Satan's Spawn. 'Twas rumoured Vlad responded enthusiastically, shamelessly, to all these names.

She had just raised her pail over the rim when Vlad put his hand on the uncovered, stone well-head extending three feet above the cobbles. He glanced about, unsmiling, noting the grim, terrified, mortified faces of Sighişoarians gathered at a safe distance in a tightly packed throng. Here were mothers, children, grandparents. Suspicious of Vlad's purpose in Sighişoara, almost as suspicious of him as he was of them. They wondered uneasily if he were here to conduct some awful Inquisition from the castle as they had heard had begun in Spain, France, Scotland, Portugal, Austria, Poland, Germany. Admittedly, not one citizen of Sighişoara had actually witnessed Vlad's atrocities other than the horrendous, infamous 'Forest of Stakes' south of Tirgovişte. As for his blackest, cruellest deed, St Bartholomew's Massacre (1461, Tirgovişte), there were uneasy rumours that somehow the not-so-pious Benedictine monks of Tirgovişte's priory had started that fateful fire which had charred more than six hundred Gypsies, beggars, and cripples. So disturbed were the Catholic populace of Sighişoara that they had said an extra Mass to resolve any doubt in their hearts.

Yes, Vlad had a sacrilegious predilection for Holy-day massacres: St Bartholomew's Day, his favourite holiday for sneak attacks; last year, St Bartholomew's Massacre, the six hundred-plus beggars, elderly, Jews and Gypsies of Tirgovişte; August 24, 1460, St Bartholomew's Day in Amlăs, where Vlad had impaled thousands of miscreants, burghers, and Dominican monks. Saxon Amlăs was Transylvania's version of Sodom or Gomorrah.

Charred and abandoned now, as a result of mass hysteria; its six hundred impaled citizens looking like nothing so much as a grisly display of barbequed shish-ka-bobs from a distance; the numerous monastic orders well represented, as was typical of Vlad's 'egalitarian' policies.

Voica snuck a sideways glance at this infamous murderer and was shocked. She had expected an ugly, leering, lecherous, smelly old goat. (Instead of the shrivelled, thrust-jawed caricature her fellow Magyar portrayed him as, the *hospidar's* robust physique was veritably enviable.) True, Vlad smelt strong from weeks of living in a saddle, but in a natural, masculine way, no different from Voica's own, absent brothers or her bedridden father. And he was…*handsome*. Young. Not a day over thirty, she'd wager. But most arresting were his eyes. Deep green as the Moldavian hills, sensitive to ridicule but dangerously intriguing, mantled with heavy, arched, black eyebrows almost meeting over the classical nose. The true sign of a werewolf or vampire.

When Vlad's impassive green eyes rested on Voica's face, flickering appreciatively down her heavily swathed body, he felt something he'd not felt in almost six years. For, God curse his soul, she was the very image of 'her'. Serena. There, he'd said her name, if only to himself. Absolution. A tiny, bonneted waif tugged at the curvaceous young *doamnă's* skirts, asking in Romanian who the weird stranger was. Had Vlad been anyone else he might have laughed at the child's tactlessness. He did not. Only stared sternly, at a loss to describe this feeling of emptiness, the past fourteen years seeming like a pointless series of obstacles and personal defeat. Not since that fateful day in Sofia, the Sultan's palace…

Voica felt sure he was going to impale her. Immediately. And her innocent sister, Maria. But then he spoke.

"I would drink from your water pail, *domnişoară*." It was not a request.

"C-Certainly, Your Highness." Her girlish, timorous voice shook. She tucked little Maria behind her, as if to protect the child from whatever tricks Dracula contemplated. When little Maria had rashly referred to Vlad, Prince of All Wallachia, as 'weird', Voica's mouth had dropped open, mortified. She had expected some sort of stern rebuke, perhaps even a lashing while stripped naked and tied to the square's whipping post reserved for the more-fortunate Gypsies, beggars, and thieves.

Vlad drank, aware of the girl's mystified, wide-eyed stare. He drained almost half the pail, thirsty as a camel whilst his soldiers brusquely lowered buckets by rope down the deep well. Then, sated, dunked his sweaty, dripping face into the refreshingly-cool water, withdrawing with a gasp.

The water would be ruined, Voica knew that. The haughty *voivode's* face dripped grime and sweat into the crystal-clear water, the true sun-bronzed tone of his skin showing through at last. To Voica's astonishment, Vlad rushed the pail down the well, filling it up, cranking the windlass's iron rotor hard as the brimming pail sloshed and lumbered its way up. He then grasped the bucket by its handle, setting it down on the stone well-shaft with a satisfied smile; bowing formally, gallantly, at the waist. (Such gentlemanly behaviour was entirely out of character for him, as everyone knew!) Voica was pleasantly surprised, curtsying elegantly. Then a horrible thought struck. Maybe he was enamoured of her, wanted Voica in his bed tonight! To become his mistress would tax Voica's soul. The thought of mating with a child-slayer such as he literally made her ill. She could feel her gorge rising, tasted the bile. Or—God help her— perhaps it was Maria he wanted. That wasn't unusual; many men preferred children over women. Many girls were already married and pregnant at twelve, forced marriages the norm rather than the exception throughout Romania nowadays.

Vlad continued to eye her warily, puzzled by the look of horror and disgust on this pretty wench's face. And baffled and enraged at the similar looks given him by the rest of the dishevelled, dirty onlookers. As if he had ransacked their city (one of the few he hadn't), pillaging and plundering for three statutory days as was customary with the Turks. As if he had raped their daughters and granddaughters, sodomised their boys. Indeed, he had horribly mutilated and executed such malefactors by the thousands, making himself puzzlingly unpopular by bringing back-by-decree the old *Celtaidd* laws—the *Cyfraith Wladwaladŵr*.

He turned back to his councillors as Voica let out a thankful sigh of relief, crossing herself fervently, thanking the Virgin for sparing her and Maria from this madman's bloodstained grip.

But halfway to his smoke-grey horse, *Smŵg*, Vlad turned, eying this lovely well wench speculatively, wondering who the lucky husband or lover might be. (Perhaps her suitor could have an accident of some kind, an unfortunate, but necessary accident? he rationalised.) The wench was well into her late teens he'd wager, a virgin perhaps, her untamed, chestnut hair bound chastely (upon his arrival) beneath a translucent grey headscarf. For sure, she was the diamond of Sighişoara, a dusky, dark-haired ruby with big, deep blue, expressive eyes like fathomless pools of passion. Long, upswept, black eyelashes on crescent-moon eyes. She had a large, perfect nose of grace and erotic sensibilities, lush, pouting lips shaped like a squat, blood-red heart. Her figure tall, lithe, buxom. (Had he not trusted his intuition better Vlad might've suspected this girl/woman to be a lady of the evening, for only harlots, freethinkers, and hussies wore the fashionable kohl and rouge with such practiced finesse.) Even her drab linen garments failed to obscure the girl's fabulous hourglass figure, her slender hands remarkably fine for a *villein*. Vlad mused sacrilegiously to himself that he'd love to have her as his bosom buddy. It was within his power, he knew; as Prince of Wallachia, he had the God-given right to take any woman, married or no, as his mistress, a totally unacceptable custom to Vlad, introduced by the hated Gaels, then the Romans, and then the Magyars and later Saxons. Vlad's father had tried to resist it, in vain. Dracula had never been tempted. After 'her', his sex drive had conveniently vanished; forever, he'd hoped.

Until now.

Vlad turned to one of his more trusted bodyguards, murmuring.

"Bring the wench to me, tonight, when all is dark."

The henchman looked at Vlad as if he had requested the guard journey to Morocco to bring back a white monkey. In all these years, Vlad had never requested a peasant wench. All of his soldiers had speculated why. Țepeș had gained another secret nickname, a joke amongst his retainers around the campfires late at night while he slept inside his guarded tent. Vlad, the *Icicle!*, they called him amidst roars of laughter. This was dangerous, for Vlad would deal harshly, decisively, with such traitors.

The guardsman wondered uneasily what Lord Dracula would do to this pretty wench. Rape her? Mutilate her? Impale her? Beat her senseless, probably, then force sex on her, sodomise her as she lay gagged and bound to Vlad's bed. Gwalchmai snapped out of his morbid mental wanderings, chiding himself, reminding himself in Brythonic that he'd never actually seen *Draighwl* do any of these things. But Gwalchmai heard stories. Strangest of all, because he as one of Wlad's bodyguards should have witnessed such crimes. But he'd not. If men went to Heaven on lack of sexual misdemeanours alone, then Wlad Draighwl was surely in the running. Gwalchmai had never heard cries of pain, especially female cries, from the warlord's bedchamber. He remembered Wlad's first consort, a sweet, gorgeous woman of extraordinary generosity who'd supposedly died at Draighwl's hands. Gwalchmai had been only fifteen when Cjnéatasha died, six years ago. He had not understood then.

He did not understand now.

Chapter Eleven

They led her up the hill toward the castle's main gatehouse, brusquely pushing the girl through a sinisterly-looming portcullis arch, first crossing a misty, wooden drawbridge and then beneath a massive, iron-studded portcullis slotted in the outer groove high above. Three arched machicolations, one above the other, guarded the rough-masonry barbican's gatehouse from attack. Wolves howled outside the citadel's steep, overgrown banks and extraordinarily thick walls, lurking anonymous somewhere in the Transylvania scrub-wilderness beneath a full moon and cloaking fog. From a distance, the town clock tolled deeply, forlornly from its square, Italianate clocktower with its heavy, forbidding machicolations. As soon as Voica and her two rude guards entered the twilit bailey the great portcullis began to rattle downwards with a sudden *slam* on cobblestone. Twin, D-shaped towers of knapped flint flanked the gothic gatehouse entrance, each topped with a shapely, tapering, multi-sided black spire. Compared to the other fourteen, humongous, battlemented round towers, the gatehouse was rather small. The great towers all boasted blue-slate witch's hats spaced equidistantly along the buttressed walls. These were not mere towers, but *donjons,* each with a nickname. Tailors', Barbers', Jewellers', Furriers', Butcherers', Goldsmiths', Council towers. Each named after a guild. Some of the towers no doubt held languishing prisoners in either *oubliettes* (pit-dungeons) or regular, barred cells. Voica wondered tearfully which dungeon would be hers.

Her escort had not bothered to ease her fears, having pounded hard on Voica's father's door, demanding the old man's daughter accompany them to see the *Naši*. She had had to feed her poor *tată* cold goulash, for the ghoulish soldiers would not wait. They joked amiably to each other now about how they would like to take her down a side alley for a threesome, or perhaps infamous Grope Lane where the illegal brothels perilously plied their trade; perhaps even hand the girl over to *dominatrix* lesbians. They laughed uproariously at the absurdity of the idea, treating the quaking spinster almost as if she were a fellow soldier, never for a moment realising that she was a well-raised, terrified, twenty-two-year-old virgin. Gwalchmai tried to assuage the girl's mounting terror, unsuccessfully, almost apologetic now (and not a little frightened himself), knowing full well Vlad's penchant for skewering soldiers even suspected of assaulting young maidens. He was not succeeding; the poor girl blubbered and sobbed, tears rolling down her cheeks. Gwalchmai's friend broke up with laughter, speaking to both.

"Vlad Dracula means to impale you, girl, with that mighty nine-inch icicle between his legs!"

The wench was hysterical now, would not budge, stubborn as a mule. The guards pulled on her arms, unable to move her as she cried out, wailing. They became suddenly frightened as they neared the looming, slate-grey Jewellers' Tower where Vlad Țepeș had his headquarters. Dracula would be wroth if he discovered they had upset the girl so, for his tempers were scarcely predictable at best, fatal at worst. But Vlad NEVER requested to see anyone in person, especially peasants, unless he was very angry. Killing angry. Like the two Genoese ambassadors, whom having failed to doff their skull-caps had the misfortune of having their caps tacked to their heads after Vlad had discovered they were Turkish spies in Mehmed's pay. That, Gwalchmai and Tuned agreed, had been a gruesome, bloody affair, one they had both witnessed. Indeed, had wielded the hammers.

They took Voica into a small antechamber on the second floor to calm her down, assuring her (Ha!) of Vlad's good intentions. They brought her sweet honey cakes, which she'd accepted like a little girl along with the Gypsies' solemn apologies. They pleaded for her to compose herself for Dracula's awesome presence, talking amongst themselves in ancient Daco-Wallachian.

And that, was when they discovered to their surprise and delight that Voica spoke Dacian also, one of the few *Cymraeg* in Sighișoara and all of Romania. A Vlach.

Dracula waited listlessly, seated at his desk writing memos for no one in particular. He was a lonely man; Vlad glanced up anxiously as the thick, leather-padded door to his chambers creaked open, two liveried guards ushering in their cowed prisoner. The girl hung her head, shoulders hunched as if expecting a blow, following the two sentries into Vlad Dracula's empty council chamber. Two wax candles flickered in their brass wall-sconces, harassed by a draught, another on Vlad's polished desk of Congolese mahogany. He drummed his fingers nervously, pleased she was here at last. He knew what he would do; he would ply the girl with drink, loosen her up, coax her into a conversation. If she desired him, fine. If not, well…

Voica sank to her knees on the bare, wooden floor like a ball of lead. Dracula realised with some discomfort that she was kneeling on the secret trapdoor where sharp spikes waited below like some Venus flytrap. He moved his hand away from the desk's lever with a jerk, not wishing to murder the girl.

She waited now, trembling, twisting her slender, pink hands. Vlad did not miss that, keen to notice every detail. Voica did not speak or even breathe, waiting for the *moroi's* tirade. (She swore her little sister would pay for this!…If she survived this night, that is.) The two caped guards discreetly obeised, then left, softly closing the door behind them.

Voica looked up, mortified. Vlad had slowly risen from his desk, eyeing her with aloof curiosity. Such a frightened, timid little fawn she was. (He could overwhelm her protests easily, Vlad thought; this woman's demure acquiescence virtually assured a satisfying tryst provided further struggles didn't force his hand: much as he enjoyed murdering those he despised, a lowly peasant's demise at his hands was not high on his priorities at the moment.) Two obedient, shiny-black alaunts crouched to his right, his only true friends; growling deep within their throats. They were Vlad's favourite hunting dogs, powerful, intelligent. And utterly merciless. He snapped at them, cowing the girl/woman instead.

"Quiet!" The two spike-collared bitches whimpered, settling down sad-eyed on their front paws.

Vlad moved slowly, purposefully, toward the girl, letting his terrifying reputation speak for itself. He set one foot down in front of the other, like a lion creeping up on its prey. He had no intention of frightening her, greatly underestimating his own awesome reputation. (The *'Devil's disciple's'* unnerving presence, however, sent chills up and down her spine; she quivered like a mouse.) Yet he was not a tall man, only 5' foot 9" inches, though stocky. To a Romano-Hungarian like Voica, he seemed rather short.

Dracula had the build, however, of a professional rabble-rouser.

Vlad's bearing was that of a potentate, whose fire-bearing sword induced legendry, obedience, and submission to all the land: a more feared man in all of Romania there had never been, nor ever would be again; even the maiden's eyes betrayed such.

"Your name," he demanded.

Voica's breath caught, then came out in a rush.

"Voica Nyireghyáza, Your Majesty."

"My name is *Vlad Ţepeş*," announced Vlad. "The Impaler. But you do know that."

She nodded, her head low. "Everyone knows that, Your Eminence."

"Indeed? And has my reputation preceded my arrival?"

"Yes, your Immaculate, Glorious Majesty."

Vlad bristled, saying nothing. Did she expect him to give her a royal title for this buttering-up, like so many other peasants Vlad had instantly knighted and promoted to boyar status for their valorous deeds and ingenuity on the battlefield?

"You are...Hungarian?" Vlad's Hun was stilted and insecure. But he instantly recognised Voica's Magyar accent.

"Yes, Your Royalty."

"Stop!" Vlad's voice turned deadly calm. "Do not butter me up, girl."

"Yes...sire."

Vlad relaxed, stepping back to his desk, pouring full two silver goblets with Wallachian plum brandy, beckoning her.

"Come here, lass. Sit down. Ease your mind. Here—in this chair."

Obediently, Voica rose, seating herself in a magnificent spare chair, whose tracery, realised she with alacrity, was that of a spider's web!

"I brought you here because I admired you," Vlad admitted without preamble. "But I shall not force myself upon you. I am Wallachian. First we talk. Then..." Vlad shrugged deeply, a slight, wry smile showing on his red lips. His green monster-eyes twinkled with humour. He was dressed differently now, Voica realised. Marvellously bedecked in a long, rippling, ebon cape with red-silk lining, matching black jodhpurs and scarlet, silk blouse. His cufflinks were of gold; silver chain-links holding a large sapphire bound Dracula's unruly, black hair. An exquisite, sapphire/ruby/emerald Dragon brooch cinched his stiff-collared cape at the neck. "At dawn, if you like, you may leave unsullied. But I shall require your formidable feats of conversation for as many nights as I care to tolerate your presence." Vlad chuckled.

He did not look like a man bent on murder. Voica realised that he had a certain charm, a certain black humour behind his bluff, mean exterior.

"What would you have me talk about, sire?" Voica asked, suspicious.

"The weather. Romanians. Wallachians. Gypsies, Catholics. Christ. Tell me, do you believe Christ walked on water?" Vlad waited expectantly, leaning forward, big eyes lit up in some private scheme.

"Of course. Don't you?"

Vlad hesitated. "I suppose so," admitting at last.

It was then that Voica realised to her horror that Vlad was a heretic! An atheist or—God forbid—agnostic. Fit for the pyre. The Papists would burn him alive if given the chance. Voica was Orthodox. She, too, was in constant danger, including her family.

"Do you love Muslims?" Dracula leaned forward, garlic breath wafting in Voica's face. Nonchalantly, he picked up a garlic clove from his desk and popped it into his mouth. This shocked Voica more than his question, for vampires abhorred garlic did they not?

"O-Of course not," Voica stammered, put off by Vlad's interrogations. "But I would prefer to be at peace with them," she offered.

"Never!! I'll not rest in my grave until Islam is laid low! Then you admit to being an Islamic Papist?" Vlad asked suddenly, mood changing.

Voica froze. The correct answer would determine whether she live or die. She had expected Vlad to be if not pro-Muslim, then indifferent to their aspirations, like his father and grandfather (Mirçea the Old). Indeed, Dracula was rumoured to be hand-in-hand with Mehmed until the momentous war last year. His atrocities against Turkish soldiers had been commended by all patriotic Romanians, though each secretly dreaded their ramifications.

"No—no, I do not love Turks. I abhor them."

She watched Vlad's gaunt face, reading his expression. Had she said the right thing? Or would he strangle her here and now with his hairy, bare hands.

Vlad's face muscles relaxed, eyes shining triumphantly. Voica had said the right thing. Satisfied, he poured himself another goblet of brandy.

"Most Wallachians would prefer to kiss Mehmed's ass, I deeply suspect," Vlad admitted, his deep voice rumbling. "You are indeed a rare woman, er…"

Vlad wriggled his fingers, trying to recall.

"Voica, sire."

"Er, yes." Vlad's memory was notoriously spotty, especially with names. Hungarian names. *W-oica.* Odd name.

Voica glanced pleadingly at the rosewood, pillar-handled hourglass on Vlad's desk, noting with despair that its yellow sand level had barely dropped. An entire night of this sadistic tyrant's tirades would be unbearable. Had he not disembowelled his mistress, forced mothers to eat their children whilst still alive?

"You are a very beautiful young lady," Vlad said suddenly, turning to her with murky, speculative eyes.

Voica's head jerked up, surprised 'T-t-thank you'. She had never thought of herself as particularly attractive. She envied the golden tresses of the Saxon.

"You remind me of a precious young woman I once loved," remarked Vlad. "Your eyes; they dart about so furtively, yet candid. But hers were dark." He sat down slowly at his desk, remembering...

Surely it was too much risk to lose one's heart to a woman, now. His enemies would deal with Vlad's mistresses as they had done with 'her'. He was not willing to risk that again. Belatedly, Vlad decided to send her away, never to return to his chambers on pain of punishment. But as he turned to expel her from the castle, he recognised that infuriating 'look'.

She was staring at him mighty queerly. A look Vlad had recorded all these years, but never understood. And then...suddenly...he understood. And he was not pleased. Slowly, he rose from his high-backed, crimson-cushioned, sparklingly polished, oakwood throne, ready to explode.

"You think I am mad, do you not?" Vlad's gravelly voice was low, deadly calm. He wondered whether to strangle this innocent-looking wench or plunge his dagger into her breast.

Voica sat stunned. Wide-eyed, tearful, she shook her head fearfully, realising too late that Vlad meant to destroy her immediately. He would impale her in the castle courtyard slowly, horribly; her poor *tată* would call out for her in the morning in vain, eventually discovering that his unwed, eldest daughter had been impaled Freya's Day morning at Sighişoara castle. It was that which broke her.

She sobbed unashamedly in her hands now, silently cursing God for allowing Vlad Ţepeş, this, this *monster!*, to impale her in her prime.

Vlad watched, bewildered, as Voica broke out in tears in front of his very eyes. She sat hunched in her web-traceried, gothic chair, covering her face; tears spilling down between her fingers. Her whole body shook. Voica's weeping temporarily melted Ţepeş' frozen heart, her sobs and heart-rending gasps that of an innocent little girl. He could not for the life of him comprehend why this young wench wept so suddenly now, as if he had declared his intention to impale her. Or as if he'd had his hand on his dirk handle, ready to destroy her.

Vlad shook her shoulders hard, trying to rattle some sense into her. "What is wrong with you!" he shouted.

"P-p-please, please do not impale me, I beg of you," Voica blubbered. Her royal-blue eyes were beseeching, misty; overflowing with tears.

Vlad laughed aloud then, his mad laughter filling the council chamber. Fists on his hips, he eyed this foolish girl with a mixture of disdain and amusement, shaking his head, wondering bemused about the scare stories told this impressionable little girl by gullible parents.

Tonight his wits must have fled for sure, for this tall, womanly, buxom child was surely twenty years his senior, pulling the wool over Vlad's eyes. He looked down at her sternly, head tilted back, waiting patiently for the girl to compose herself before expelling her from the castle for ensnaring him so. At last, Vlad tilted Voica's chin up, looking deep into her beautiful, cerulean-blue, watery eyes.

"Gather your wits, girl," he murmured. "My patience is waning. Dry your eyes, *llances*, then leave this castle."

"Y-y-you mean to let me go?" Voica stammered, suspicious. "To live?"

"Of course. What did you think?" Vlad chuckled grimly.

"I-I thought you meant to impale me, sire."

"Impale you?? Sweet lass, I reserve that cruel, infamous punishment for traitors, Turks, and spies, not fresh-faced young girls like you. You cannot be more than fifteen, innocent. A virgin perhaps?"

Voica sputtered. "Wha…? Fifteen? I am not, I'm…"

"Enough—"

"Twenty-two."

Vlad halted mid-sentence.

"TWENTY-TWO! You wish! You are but a rosy-faced child, a baby. Big girls don't cry," Vlad assured her.

Voica was angry now. She began to speak in Dacian, a common fault of hers when flustered, like her *Szgany* father. Her mother had often chastised her for speaking the foul language in public. Indeed, the two guards who'd escorted her into Vlad's chamber had warned her: "Say the wrong word, lass, and you die-" The barbaric, long-haired guard had grabbed her arm. "Speak Dacian, and thou shalt live." A warning she'd foolishly forgot to heed. Until now. And to her horror, she had just called Vlad, *the Impaler!*, a loathsome, green, wart-faced, scaly Dragon. Griffin. Winged würm.

Vlad's face grew red, eyes widening. Too shocked to speak. In all his travels, true Wallachs were rare; even the Vlachs had begun to adopt Romany, the old tongue dying within Vlad's lifetime like a withering blue flame.

"Ydych chi Gymraeg? Albanŵr? O Gwyddel?" Vlad asked tentatively, still unbelieving. (Are you Cimmerian? Albanian? Or Gael?)

"Oes. Mae I Cymraes. Tad 'fy Dacw o Sipsy." (Yes. I am Cymric. My father be Dacian Gypsy.)

Vlad smiled slowly, elated, unable to believe his luck. A Dacian (Roman name—*'Dacw'*: Cymric *'Beyond'*; *'Land beyond the Forest'*). Like Serena. He immediately knew he must protect this girl, her family, lest they fall prey to the Inquisition which roasted these poor, downtrodden, once-proud, defeated warrior folk on funeral pyres. A race which had once defied Rome, slaughtering whole legions like buffalo. They had sacked Athens for revenge, and, later, Rome (twice, as the Vandal/Goth vanguard); turned back and eventually overrun the armies of Hammurabi of Babylon, Ramses II of Egypt. They'd humiliated Xerxes' Persians on the Scythian plains of Russia. When the imperial Roman Empire (with Germanic and Gaulish backing) had finally overcome Dacia, had overrun the Prydeins' (brethrens) mighty, concentric raths (earthwork hillforts) and slaughtered, maimed, expelled or enslaved with Gallic support the native Neolithic strain, the Dacians had ceased to be. A people who'd painted themselves blue, and (according to Roman propaganda), went into battle naked (!), riding war chariots outfitted with scythes in their spokes (hence the Scythians). And during Rome's four hundred-year reign, had been assimilated as Romany.

Voica was as pleasantly surprised as Vlad was. In all her years, she had never met a true Wallachian, had never met a Cŭmbrian other than an old laundry woman/Gypsy who resided on the shabby outskirts of Sighișoara in a tumbledown, mud-brick hovel, where Voica had as a little girl spent many hours learning the tarot cards or astrology after her mother died (and still did, secretly). Voica's father had settled down in Sighișoara as a blacksmith, marrying a Hungarian seamstress who had died in Voica's youth. Irena, Voica's lifelong secret mentor, had also settled down with a husband, a Magyar who had despised her language and customs, who too had since died. The old crone was stoop-backed now, hobbling about with a cane, but still lucid and well over one hundred years old.

She had earned a dangerous reputation over the years as a witch and curse-lady; a soothsayer for the common folk (Irena hailed originally from the Caucasus mountains of Georgia).

"I am indeed pleased to meet a fellow Wallachian," Vlad said slowly. "Alas…I fear we may soon be no more. Not even I can turn back the tides of history."

Voica said nothing. Her elation had quickly subsided into melancholy, knowing with shame that Romania's worst, most bloodthirsty, psychopathic tyrant in history, Vlad Dracula, was of her own blood and dialect. His atrocities against the Rom (i.e., St Bartholomew's Massacre, 1461) were a disgrace. For years, since Vlad's premature usurping of power in 1449 whilst Voica was still a child, she had clung to the myth that Dracula's atrocities were due to his being of mixed Hungarian/Romanian ancestry, or his having been raised in a Turkish court. As had all other Romanies.

Vlad filled up her goblet again, still smiling, his mind wandering. Voica meanwhile sat hunched, dreading the hour when Dracula would take her to his private chambers. She wondered whether to resist, but knew she could not, preferring rape over death. Vlad could destroy her in so many ways: he could boil her alive; flay her flesh from her bones; throw her to the royal lions and hyenas; impale her through the vagina until the stake pierced her mouth; up the anus till the stake pierced her entrails; crucify her; quarter her; behead her.

"If you insist on sitting there like a deaf mute," Vlad remarked in Dacian, irritated, "I shall eject you from my castle—aye—my Kingdom. What say you to that?"

Voica thought long and hard on this. "You have the power to do as you will, my lord," replying at last.

"Indeed—I have," Vlad responded. "Complete loyalty I have. I could do what I want with you. But I am a reasonable man, and a fair and Just ruler who has harmed no one unjustly."

Voica could only stare. This tyrant before her truly was a master at deluding himself! A fair and just ruler! Yet he gleefully boiled children alive, drank their sacrificial blood from bowls!

She downed her *ţuica* quickly, determined to leave this madman. The worst he could do now was kill her. He had already mortally offended Voica's Gypsy heritage.

Voica stood up, surprising Vlad as she slowly set her goblet on his desk (glaring at him like some woman obscenely accosted on the street), gathered up her pleated, deep blue skirts, spun around, and rushed for the open door.

Vlad watched, stunned, as Voica dashed for the gaping doorway. As she neared the exit he shot forth from his bizarre throne, angered now.

A foot away from the pointed, ogee-arched exit, from the stairs and freedom, Voica was intercepted by Vlad's powerful, silk-caped frame blocking her path. He slammed the door, glaring at her like a vicious wolf. He drew his bejewelled dirk and held it to Voica's slender throat.

"Get back to your chair before I skin you alive—personally, with mine own hands," Vlad growled. "Get back there!!"

Voica jerked away, terrified by Vlad's booming voice, the utter insanity and evil of his black soul. She believed utterly then in the tales told around nighttime campfires and indoor, stone hearths. Vlad was a necromancer, a summoner of the dead, calling forth the Powers of Darkness to defeat his enemies (which were legion). He had drunk virgins' blood in black Sabbath rituals, ritually sodomising then cannibalising his victims, protecting his Transylvanian mountain eyrie with a magic spell.

"Sit!" Vlad shouted.

Voica sunk into her chair, drawing away as Vlad leaned forward threateningly, his black alaunts growling menacingly.

"No man walks away from me!! No one!! You impetuous wench! Would you have me slay you now or later? I shall torture you slowly, painfully!"

Voica began to weep again, turning away from his wine-scented breath. She deeply regretted having let her feelings rule her head.

"Don't you know what I could do to you?! Why do you run from me! Answer me!"

Voica merely blubbered, too horrified to respond.

"Sacrilege! You are a stupid, mindless woman!"

"I—I feared you would kill me," Voica sobbed at last.

"I shall kill you!"

Vlad breathed deep, exhaling with a loud hiss lest his wild temper take over. She was an innocent babe after all, knew not what she say. At once, he began to calm down. Vlad sat down at his polished throne, slowly, tiredly. He knew not of the Combrogo/Romany, even after all these years. He had believed foolishly that he was one of them, a nomadic warrior.

"I shall not kill you." Still no response.

"I—shall—not—kill you. Why would you think such blasphemy? Answer me, *dynes*."

Voica shrugged her shoulders despondently.

"Who am I to you? To yours. An ogre? What have I done to the Romany?"

Still Voica would not respond.

"Have I…drank blood? Boiled mothers? Hmm?"

"Yes."

Vlad blinked. "What?! Lies!! All lies!! Recant!" He jumped to his feet, wrenching a huge broadsword from the wall behind his desk. "Recant! Recant or die! I have warned you once!"

Voica held firm. "It's the truth!"

"Your truth!"

"You lie!! You are a tyrant!" Voica screamed. "*I hate you, everyone hates you!*"

Vlad flung the heavy sword against the stone wall to his right with a clamorous clatter, eyes blazing, lips stretched back in a maniacal grin. He breathed heavily, whirling on the startled girl. Clenched her throat with his hairy, powerful hands, squeezing tight…

Vlad shook her twice, then released her. Voica gasped, coughing as her murderer clutched her tenderly to his breast. After a while, Voica regained her breath, strangely calm now within this stranger's strong, cape-cloaked arms. Prince Vlad's manly odour filled her nostrils, oddly alluring. Terrifying, for this was a sacrilegious murderer embracing her. 'Twas like her father, gentle and harmless, nothing at all like the psychopath of legend. Voica wondered momentarily if Vlad intended to suck her blood now that he'd caught her trust. And…her lust.

She raised her head, breathing softly against his cheek. Vlad held her tight, temporarily squeezing the air from her.

"Hang onto me, Oh God, lest I lose what is left of my sanity," Vlad whispered.

"You could seek help," Voica ventured at last.

"What?"

"For your soul, I mean. It is never too late."

Vlad released her, puzzled. "It is never too late for what?"

"For forgiveness…even…even for St Bartholomew's Massacre…and for Amlăs," Voica whispered quietly.

"I do not understand."

Voica stared back. Vlad had duped himself totally.

"You should not have burnt those poor people…but, I suppose, God can forgive you."

Vlad furrowed his brows. "Yes. You are right. I should have guarded the barn closer."

It was Voica's turn to frown. Vlad was senile, it seemed, prematurely so. "You do not understand, my lord," speaking more forcefully now. "You should not have burnt those poor wretches. Gypsies, Jews, beggars, cripples. All were innocent in God's eyes."

Vlad stared in bewilderment. He laughed aloud then, heartily. The mocking laughter of a madman.

And then, slowly, he understood.

"Heh, heh, heh, er…huh? Wha…? Did you say 'I'?"

Voica nodded, bewildered.

Vlad's face turned ashen. He slumped down at his desk and macabre throne like a man informed of his family's death.

"Dear God. Say it is not so. Say the Romanians do not blame me as their scapegoat."

Voica breathed deep, angry now, impatient. Dealing with Vlad was like dealing with a spoilt five year old. She nodded, unable to meet this pitiful monster's eyes. "It is true. And many other things as well."

Vlad leaned forward, suddenly anxious. "What else?"

Again Voica inhaled deep, rolling her eyes. And then she began.

Vlad snatched a quill pen from his ink blotter, writing furiously, repeating Voica's blasphemous accusations as if he were counting turnips.

"Boiled mothers alive, sodomised boys and girls (?), raped nuns, monks and dwarfs, and?…ate human flesh, drank virgins' blood, practiced incest, bestiality, tortured babies, boiled entire villages, impaled thousands, formed a sorcerer's coven, cast spells, turned myself into *moroi* (vampire), next?…blasphemed the Bible, roasted heretics, Jews and Gypsies, robbed the poor, tortured and robbed monks, despoiled abbeys and nunneries, starved the Magyars, Szeklers, and Saxons, flayed children for fun…"

The list went on and on. By the time Voica had finished, the candles had burnt to within an inch of their sconces. Vlad sat back, mortified, horrified, staring down at the list of 'alleged' atrocities. Either he had been a murderous sleepwalker all these years or…

Vlad nodded. "Ex-cellent. Ex-cellent. Brilliant strategy. I could not have done better myself," Vlad lisped. He rubbed his chin. "I shall not rest in my grave until these lies are rectified," he murmured.

Voica was astounded. Still he did not believe?

"These are all lies, my child. All lies. You do believe me, don't you?"

Voica shook her head, wide-eyed, too astonished to do otherwise. She did not believe him. He did not sound sincere, even now. He sounded almost condescending: playing with her, like a cat with a mouse. His eyes stared into hers, hypnotising, boring into her skull, green portals to Hell…

"Look into my ey-es," Vlad whispered.

She looked, drawn as if to a magnet.

"You DO believe me, don't you?"

Against her will, Voica nodded her head, suddenly sleepy, afraid. Her eyelids closing like leaden shutters.

"I am a good and just man, Prince of Wallachian land, ruler of Transylvania. A Wise Man. Do you believe me now, *geneth* (girl)?"

Voica nodded.

"Go-od."

Horrified, Voica slipped off into sleep.

****

She awoke in Dracula's bed. Alone. Still clothed. The sun had risen hours ago. Dust motes danced in the filtered, muted sunlight shining through the lead-paned oriel window's crimson balcony drapes. Vlad's bedchamber emanated evil; drapes and curtains black or fiery red. Brilliant, gold-embroidered tapestries displayed scenes of war and bloodshed. An inverted gold cross (!) hung on a stone wall to her left, noticed Voica Nyireghyáza with horror. Moorish tapestries portrayed the betrayal of Mohammed. The great four-poster bed she lay on was of black oak surrounded by deep purple, silk, Damask drapes. A black satin canopy arched overhead in an opulent flourish of creases and frills, whilst Oriental hangings lent the stark walls a touch of civility, booty from Mehmed's gored armies or Ţepeş' savage local campaigns. Voica floated dreamily on Vlad's cushiony, down-filled mattress beneath a pile of purple velvets, cerulean silks, sable furs. A scarlet pillow held her soft, flowing, auburn tresses like a glove. She raised herself to her elbow. To her right, slightly behind her, a small, unglazed, quatrefoil (four-lobed) gothic window—reminiscent of Benedictine cloister windows sashed with a sheer, black silk *portiere* (curtain). The smell of frankincense and myrrh tickled her nostrils.

Voica had no idea how she'd got here. Her last memory of last night had been Vlad's deep, disturbing green gaze...his cunningly deep voice, soothing, enticing...

Her clothes felt warm beneath the mountain of blankets. Too warm. She felt mortally weak, as if all the blood had been drained from her body. Her neck hurt. Frightened, Voica slowly raised a hand to her neck, feeling...

Bruised. She felt for the tell-tale pinholes where Vlad's fangs had penetrated her jugular. Finding none.

Terrified, confused, she wondered what to do. Her poor father would be waiting for her in vain, worrying, realising that Voica hadn't returned last night to feed him this morning's *mamăglia* (gruel). Should she leave, sneak out of the Jewellers' Tower somehow and attempt to escape unnoticed from the enormous fortress? But how? The portcullises would be down, sentries patrolling the parapets. Could she summon the energy, even? Or should she await her fate, await Dracula's morbid intentions. He had obviously been fooling her all along, pretending innocence for those unspeakable crimes even as Voica's tongue felt swollen by reciting such horrid blasphemies. And then the *Cnéaz* had gazed into her eyes, utilising the Black Arts to weave a spell upon her. Voica wondered if Ţepeş had fondled her, copulated with her as she lay asleep in his bed, then fled the chamber as sunrise peeped over the easterly Moldavian-Carpathian mountains. If so, he must've either pushed up her skirts or dressed her once more after the unspeakable act. The abominable *nosferatu!*

Slowly, Voica sat up, still bone-weary from last night's terrifying emotional confrontation with one of the undead. *Moroi.* She set her stockinged foot down to the bare, teak floor just as Vlad Dracula opened the bedroom door. Voica froze.

Vlad softly shut the door, stepping forward.

"You fell asleep. As had I, ere I would have expelled you from my castle before dawn." He spoke with a slightly embarrassed tone, as if caught in a lie. His Wallach accent was somewhat rustic, Voica noticed. Vlad's was the dialect of the frozen northerly regions; a near-depopulated area of Bucovina's hinterlands, she presumed. "Worry not, I have sent a messenger to your father's house with a clever white lie, informing your sire of your required presence, along with other Sighişoarians, as nursemaids for the night."

Voica glanced at Vlad with a hostile, abused glare, pouting, not believing for a minute. He had ogled her body like a pervert while she slept, perhaps drugged or ensorcelled.

"I have not touched you," Vlad intoned, as if reading Voica's mind. "You may make the necessary private inspections once you return home if you like."

She had no reason to disbelieve him. And yet...

"Go now. My messenger shall escort you through the city."

Voica straightened her dark, peasant clothes, face expressionless as stone. She did not believe Vlad for a moment, knew he meant to impale her in the citadel's courtyard. After the things she had accused him of, how could he not? She had accepted that horrible fate last night, with much tears. All along, Vlad Ţepeş had misled her. Pretending kinship, good intentions, but waiting like a spider after mesmerising his prey into complacency.

Vlad followed her with his eyes, bewildered, before matching her pace and escorting the resigned girl down the shadowy, echoing, spiral stair. On the last step, he turned to her, clutching Voica's arm. A lone pine-torch sputtered uncertainly on the wall; the Jewellers' Tower's stairwell a dark, claustrophobic spiral towards her unknown destiny.

"Speak to no one of what has passed between us, you hear? If not, I destroy you now. And, er...I shall request your presence again tonight. Is that all right with you, *domnişoară?*" Vlad had once more lapsed into Romanian, pressed alluringly against Voica's well-rounded breast.

Voica stared in disbelief. For a brief, baffling moment, she believed he truly meant to spare her. But no. Vlad Dracula was renowned, indeed, infamous, for his sly deceptions and betrayals. He was an elaborate hoaxer. A professional sleight-of-hand artist (taught by his Romany soothsayers, crooks and thieves all, thinketh many).

She nodded anyhow.

Vlad led her out into the hazy, late morning light of day, handing Voica over to a single cloaked messenger with a stately nod. Then he turned and stalked back to the enormous, round keep. Voica's escort gently took her arm, leading her toward the inner gatehouse where the great, spiked portcullis mawed wide. He relaxed his grip.

Voica pulled away, walking bravely now toward the empty, stake-laden, cobbled courtyard. No cadavers topped the charcoal-hardened stakes today. Indeed, none had for many months, not since Prince Dracula's last grisly visit.

"*Domnişoară!* Not that way! This way," cried Vlad's startled messenger. Voica heeded him not. The courier strode forward, forcefully steering the surprised young woman back toward the gatehouse. '*If not here, then where would mine execution be?*' Voica wondered. The *hospidar* was a constant game-player, always confusing his victims. She sighed, resigned. Dispirited.

And then they were through the citadel's outer gatehouse, down the hill toward the dirty city streets and Voica's home four blocks away.

An amazing, buoyant feeling of euphoria swept over her like a tidal wave as she kept pace with her swift, teenaged escort. She began to truly believe that Lord Dracula meant to reprieve her, even after her bitter name-calling and accusations of his evil. Men had died for far less. She felt like skipping, though would feel foolishly childish doing so in front of Prince Dracula's royal messenger. As a young woman, she had quickly learned to keep her emotions in check and to cover her hair or clothing chastely with shawls lest an aggressive *machismo* take her as fair game. Certainly, she would never let herself be seen skipping like a little girl. (Nonetheless, she enjoyed, recently, the almost *risqué* habit of wearing cosmetics; a titillating fad, the fashionable thrill of seeing the looks of envy on the faces of maidens and the puppyish devotion of local boys.) Since puberty, Voica had learned to defend herself in the gloomy streets and narrow alleys of Sighișoara. Her four brothers were away in Italy serving as mercenaries for some wealthy Milanese merchant. Her father had been bedridden since she was sixteen, since her stepmother's death. Voica's three younger sisters depended on her as matron of the house. She knew not what ailed her father. She had no relatives to protect her; rather, she had found she needed to protect herself from them, including one lecherous old uncle. Voica had no time for courtships, spurning unwanted advances from various, disreputable *gaji*-boys.

She half-expected Vlad's retainers to block her path, Țepeș himself at the head of his warband mounted on his mighty grey warhorse; to gallop forth and smote Voica's head from her crouching shoulders with a great, double-headed, Dalmatian pole-axe.

It didn't happen. Astounded, Voica halted at her father's brick townhouse's door to thank Dracula's messenger.

****

5 June, 1462 AD
Sighișoara, Carpathian Mountains

Voica was led, nervous, into Vlad's master guest-chamber in the Jewellers' Tower, an austere, tapestried, heavily-draped, echoing hall. Her legs were shaky; her lungs ached. She gasped for breath, exhausted from the brisk climb up the steep, treacherous, spiral stair to Vlad's audience chamber on the fifth floor of the keep. A constant flow of royal visitors, diplomats and entertainers passed Voica and her two guards; boyars, ambassadors, ladies-in-waiting, foreign princes, couriers, monks. Some were mere children; others old men and stooped grandmothers. Some were nannies, wetnurses, chambermaids.

Vlad's royal seneschal strode forward, attired in brilliant yellow, flowing robes, ushering the three towards Dracula's private apartments. The girl was important now, held vital, damning information regarding Vlad's dubious reputation. Only Cirstian knew the girl's true mission. As far as the others were concerned, Voica was Vlad's mistress.

Vlad waited impatiently in his stark chamber, drumming his sleek, long-nailed fingers on a wooden windowsill loudly. Rain tapped noisily on the robust, round donjon's leaden roof tiles; a crashing boom of thunder rattled the windowpanes, and Voica's fraying nerves. *Would she survive this night?* Vlad stood looking out over the torch-lit, blazing courtyard where his latest impalement victims towered among the blood-stained cobbles. They were pimps, notorious thugs who worked the grimy alleys of Sighişoara on misty nights such as this, kidnapping girls and women alike, forcing the subdued victims into degrading prostitution while collecting their ill-earned coins. (Thus, Ţepeş mercifully spared the 'working girls'; impaling their accomplices instead—men, women, children—through buttocks, vaginas, mouths.) Last weekend the misled citizens of Schassburg, good Germans, good Catholics all, had captured a dozen young whores lured from local brothels, subsequently burying the poor waifs alive on the outskirts of Sighişoara, as was their custom, misinterpreting Vlad's motives. (He had impaled them alive for their stupidity, as was his wont.) Vlad's decree against brothels had proved ineffective so far. The Latin *machismos* and German *Krauts* were relatively undaunted. The child-stealers knew no fear, their good Christian lives expendable, as if they were fighting a holy war. As if theirs was a religious cause for the good of all. (Much inducing—*bribing*—had they attempted for the Impaler Prince's severe, unrelenting ear.) Vlad was more than willing to impale every man in Sighişoara to root the johns and Madams out. He was that far gone.

The labour camps he'd set up, for those who'd survived the brutal realities of forced prostitution (venereal disease, beatings, etc.) had greatly increased the State's production capacity, Vlad's greatest advantage in his Holy war against Islam.

Voica curtsied awkwardly, shyly, her crinolines feeling strange as she entered the fast-emptying great hall, her guts churning. Vlad eyed her impassively as her escorts exited the partitioned chamber with a respectful bow, then he strode forth, taking her hand. He raised Voica's slender hand to his lips, eyes upon her face, kissing deep her soft flesh, as if absorbing her salty essence. (She almost expected him to turn over her palm and bite her wrist!) "Enter freely,of your own will," Vlad intoned, drawing Voica into the hall. His eyes settled on her neck, glaring. "Remove that idolatrous symbol," Vlad grumbled, pointing a crooked finger at the silver crucifix hanging at Voica's throat. She started, frightfully removing the large Christ-on-the-Cross and her jade rosary beads. She had hoped they would protect her from Vlad's wizardry, his very essence of evil. Now she removed them for fear of reprisal, woefully jeopardising her mortal soul. Luckily, he hadn't noticed the coil of garlic slung around Voica's slender neck, hidden beneath her dark brown, camouflaging head shawl.

"If you fear I be a vampire, then you may inspect my teeth," grumbled Vlad in disgruntled Hungarian. He knew she would not, also knew that *moroi's* fangs were retractable in any case. "Or fear you that I am a werewolf? Wererat? Ah. A wampyr bat." He'd automatically switched back to Dacian, knowing the girl was fluent in the old language. And, he suspected, preferred speaking in the Old Tongue over her native, crude, barbaric Mongol/Slav Hungarian. Or lisping, slime-brain Romanian, for that matter. Voica, indeed, preferred Dacian, though her vocabulary was stilted after years of disuse. Only her father kept it alive at all. None of Voica's siblings spoke Vlachian.

"Do you not subscribe to Iesu's (Jesus') teachings?" Voica asked after a moment, settling herself in a tall, decrepit wooden chair which Vlad had graciously pulled out for her from an immense trestle table. She had stuffed her rosary and crucifix in her brassiere, hiding them from Dracula's hostile eyes.

"I subscribe to no man's teachings but mine own," Vlad answered haughtily. "They are: when slapped on one's cheek, destroy thine enemy; when betrayed, show no mercy."

Voica had nothing to say to that. Such were the tenets of barbarians, not civilised Romanians.

"And he who lives by the sword dies by the sword," Voica ventured bravely, immediately regretting it.

"Ie—but there are worse ways to die." Vlad paced, stopping to fill two bronze goblets full of *ţuica*.

"Ah. You have been studying the Ten Commandments. Have you come to excommunicate me too, girl?" Vlad suddenly leaned forward, his breath no longer smelling of garlic or wine. "Let me tell you something, *geneth*. I have learned in my years that priests are unworthy of the Kingdoms of earth, let alone Heaven. Of those I have met, all over time have proven themselves charlatans, speaking much, but saying nothing. Not one would I call friend. Not one. They speak of sin, *yet they don't even know what sin is.*"

Voica was left speechless.

"You are a very bitter man, sire," responding at last, her pride too hurt for caution.

Vlad eyed her warily for a moment. He liked that about the girl, her candid honesty even though she knew he might impale her. Others had been brutally honest with Vlad, and had been impaled for their honesty while others were spared. Two Dominican monks came to mind, two arrogant old crows whom Vlad had requested at his palace of Tirgovişte for interrogation. One old friar had cursed Vlad's name, the other lying to save his skin. They had stared at his sacred, gold, scimitar/broadsword. Vlad had impaled them both.

"You have a candid tongue. I like that in a woman. You worry not. I not impale you, *benyw* (woman)."

Voica was immediately, soul-wrenchingly grateful. "Thank you, sire."

"Call me Wlad. Or, *Wladislaus.*"

"Oes…Wlad."

Vlad downed his brandy, setting the empty goblet on the great trestle table.

"Come." He held out his hand, drawing Voica towards the open, unshuttered, gothic window. Beyond its lead-framed glass, the odd torch fluttered in the eerie, rain-sodden courtyard far below. Voica looked out the diamond-paned window, out into the cobbled, flickering courtyard eighty-four feet below, then screamed hysterically. She pulled away, leaning away from the window against the rough, cold, stone wall, hands covering her face. Sobbing.

Vlad gripped her shoulders impatiently, shaking her. "Do you cry for them?!" he hissed. "But for me, you would most likely be spending your nights in a bordello enduring great pain! Those are thugs out there. Pimps! I have shown no mercy and they can expect none. All Gypsies during my reign hail my name, for they are freer now than for many years. Would you pine for these wretches? Hmm?"

Voica shook her head, too horrified to speak. The image of sharp, pointed stakes protruding through chests, jaws, stomachs and buttocks seemed burnt inside her mind, behind her eyelids.

"You do understand what I mean." Vlad closed the shutters, leading her back to the trestle table. "Such sights were never meant for female eyes. But it is necessary, for who will stand for the old, the weak?"

"But-but why? Why…like that?"

"Fear. Power. And…respect. Above all, respect. I am Wallachian. I cannot watch my countrymen debased so. As my father's sole surviving heir, as a Dacian, I am honour-bound to destroy traitors and foreigners who have resided in my country since Attila's reign. Their traditions are not ours. You, as a Gypsy girl, do know that. Our women are not free. Our men are not free. That I shall change. And those who disagree, who interfere, well..." Vlad nodded grimly toward the wall, the hideously-impaled cadavers beyond. "They shall suffer, grovel horribly, before I watch with glee as they die."

Vlad's eyes lit up with an unholy fervour, the eyes of a madman at peace with himself.

Voica was suddenly, deeply confused. Dracula had rightfully earned his reputation as a woman-hater. Hadn't he? He had made legends in his own lifetime. Women were said to have been ripped open from throat to navel for not providing husbands with decent clothing, too lazy to sew their men's breeches or mend his cape. And yet this tyrant denies all!

"You think I am mad," Vlad commented, answering for her. Seeing it in her eyes.

"I-I do not understand what you are," Voica muttered. "I—the stories. Cannot forget..." She squinted her eyes, as if trying to remember half-forgotten fables. Fairy tales.

"Lies!! Tall-tales! I am a pawn. I have offered Wallachians freedom from Islam's yoke, and from Hungary's. These Germans are viruses, pestilent plagues choking the oakwood."

Voica turned away, tears forming in her eyes; confused, frightened, sympathetic. She wanted to believe. She wanted to believe Vlad Dracula was a man of honour, an uncommon man, Prince of Wallachian land. This morning, her *tată* had blessed the Virgin Mary for sparing his eldest daughter, so certain was he that Dracula—the *Dragon Prince*—had murdered Caltai's beloved and devoted daughter. Voica's younger sisters had rejoiced equally.

"I want to believe," Voica murmured with a deep, resounding sigh.

"Then believe. Follow thy heart. I am not your enemy, nor yours. Ask any Gypsy, any nomad you meet, Romany or no, those with sad eyes and hungry *plentyn* (children) the verdict about *Wladislaus Dragwla*. All will tell you they are freer now than in decades; better fed, protected, clothed. Ask them, *llances* (lass). Seek a caravan, seek the truth from those who are downtrodden; for the burghers and middlings hereabouts will tell you only lies and half-truths..."

Voica nodded, suddenly determined to do just that. A Gypsy caravan was loitering, temporarily, beyond Sighişoara's outskirts, a nomadic tribe originally from Simeria; outcasts: disaffected, persecuted. Hungry. She would seek them out. Seek the truth. Demolish Vlad Țepeș' delusions once and for all. And then...and then she would escape. Pack her belongings and flee to Moldavia's alps or the hoary, western highlands of northern Transylvania, marry a Gypsy like she should have done long ago. She had considered escaping Sighişoara this morning, to bundle her clothes, some food, and necessary survival items into a gunnysack and flee tonight, although terrified of being apprehended by Vlad's elite *Sarmataîi* cavalry or the dangerous kidnappers roaming these fetid, dung-splotched, cobbled streets. But who would care for Voica's sisters? Her father?

Dracula interrupted Voica's troubled thoughts. "This war is not yet won," he remarked casually, stubbing his finger on the enormous, scarred trestle table. "Or over." He sat down, eyeing Voica with candour. She stood up, paced nervously between the walls then sat down again, waiting for his tirade. Tonight, Vlad wore a stately ceremonial headdress, an emerald-green, velvet cone topped with colourful, azure peacock feathers above his forehead—banded with a luxurious array of precious jewels. He reminded her of an oversized gnome, a Scythian fairy-Prince—one of the Little People who were said to revel inside their sacred mounds. A rather nasty little gnome. "The Turks have temporarily withdrawn to Bucureşti, to await further orders," Vlad continued, tapping his nervous, hairy-knuckled fingers. "They will wait for a winter campaign, unprecedented, wait for us to become overconfident, spring upon us like black widows devouring their helpless, smaller prey."

"How do you know this?" Voica inquired, curious.

Vlad leaned forward, smiling macabrely. "I have studied their ways, spent six years in Anatolian prisons at Egrigöz, then Adrianople, a few months in Sofia, watched Turkish torture methods and countless executions of fellow Slavs. I have learnt their fear tactics and military thinking. The torture masters taught me well—unwittingly. This year, we have countered the Turks' every move, guessing their every motive. Unless my Principality should suddenly perish, we shall hound Islam back to the very gates of Mecca—IF Hungary and her Western, pampered neighbours join my holy Crusade."

Voica shook her head dejectedly. "Hungary will never march against Mehmed. I know—I, too, am Hungarian. I have heard them talk. They would prefer to pay ransom rather than fight while Romania stands to absorb Islam's transgressions. The Hun would never fight beside the Rom. Hungary has yet to recover from the last fiasco."

"Yes. You are right. You are a smart woman, I like you. Indeed, unless Romania is safe, we will fall soon, like Macedonia, Bulgaria, Albania, Greece, Serbia, Slovakia. I predict we shall fall come 1490 if King Matthias should ignore my pleas. And Hungary in…" Vlad grimaced. "1526. Near Mohács, I dare say. Austria shall be next."

Voica had never thought of that before. The idea of Islam knocking on the gates of Vienna chilled her blood to ice. What the ghazis would do to her, her children and grandchildren. Should Austria fall, it would be like a domino effect, leaving the whole of western Europe open to Islamic conquest. Spain and the British Isles would be virtually at Turkey's mercy, for the Ottomans could easily assemble an invasion fleet ten times the size of that which William the Conqueror had organised to pacify those sacred, emerald isles—the last of Voica's race. Muslim women had even fewer rights. They wore full face veils (the infamous *niqab*, or *burka*), not mere headscarves. And, if those horrendous rumours were true, suffered horrible, humiliating, painful circumcisions as Jewish boys did. Sutures, to ensure a maiden's chastity until marriage. Voica felt her bile rising. If those rumours were true…then all sympathisers must die.

"Soon I depart for Bucureşti, to rebuild my new capital," declared Vlad. "But first I must travel eastwards into Moldavia's alps, a territory I am not familiar with. Nor, to my knowledge, are any of my contingent based here in Sighişoara; I travel hence to recruit willing partisans who would fight against the yoke of Islam. Fearful, I tell you, is the death-toll on mine vassals: for every hero who parry's the Turk's sword, ten are trampled underfoot the heathen's steed! Diplomatic channels at this stage, you see, are useless, for *Princep* Stephan of Moldavia would demand payment and marriage alliances for conscription of his countrymen. Which I cannot afford right now, and anyhow such negotiations would prove too slow and spongiform."

Voica listened eagerly, her curiosity suddenly perked. It would've seemed to her that men's issues such as war and matters of statecraft would interest her not. But Vlad seemed to accept her as a semi-equal, speaking to her candidly of such momentous decisions as if she were a man, a seneschal or chamberlain. And, more importantly, the subject of Moldavia's Carpathians intrigued her, for her father had been Moldavian, born and bred in the Ciŭcŭlani mountains, amongst the *Alăni* clan. As a little girl she had accompanied her *tad* into those hostile, coniferous mountains, learning the lore and herbal remedies from the local Vlachs, Gypsies who still lived unbothered up in those craggy, eastern alps. Voica's father would seek out the semi-nomadic Vlachs, a people who chose their homes and chose when to leave, unlike the displaced, Christianized Romany who travelled all over Romania searching for a place to camp for the summer, setting up tinkers' camps, knowing not where tomorrow's food and clothing would come from or when the local voivode or boyar would chase them off. If they were allowed to own sheep and cattle, they would provide for themselves, but Romany were forbidden ownership of such chattel.

Voica wondered indecisively if she should volunteer Vlad information. He might sneer, despise her for offering information to a man, a *voevod* no less. The teachings of St Paul specifically forbid a woman from teaching men, or even a child. And yet Vlad was Dacian too, would remember that the Druids, or *Wid*, were women and men too who worshipped the goddess Wicca, or *Ma Gog*, an egalitarian religion later tainted by the hated Celto-Scythians (Goidels and Iranians), blonde newcomers who brought human sacrifice and internecine warfare to the Fairy Folk—the builders of tumulus.

"I..." Voica halted, aborting her suggestion of help. "I-I am familiar with those lands, Your Excellency," she hinted. "My *tată* took me there numerous times as a young *merch* (girl) while gathering herbs and greens for eating and medicine. If you wish, I could draw you a map of western Moldavia."

Vlad halted, his goblet suspended at his lips before the drinking. He set it down slowly, eyeing this brave girl with a shrewd, cautious stare.

"You are literate," he asked warily, refilling his goblet with a raise of his heavy brow.

Voica shook her head, mouth open, crestfallen. Eyes betraying her shame. She would have liked to be of service to her country. Vlad would wish to negotiate with the wary, distrustful Vlachs of Moldavia's alps bordering Sighişoara to the east. He would rely on their support most, for the Romanian, German, Magyar, Szekler populations of Wallachia were completely untrustworthy for a winter campaign against the Turks. They would prefer to pay ransom dues to hold off Turkish thugs.

Vlad rose to his feet, stalked toward an ornate, antiquated bureau, bringing back a stiff, brittle parchment roll for Voica to scribble on and a goose-feather quill pen in ink-well. "Can you draw?" he demanded.

Puzzled, Voica nodded; sitting prim and proper dressed in petticoats of rose taffeta (an heirloom of her deceased, seamstress stepmother's) on an ancient, throne-like chair with her hands folded together.

"Draw. I shall write."

She scribbled all over the parchment, describing familiar places to Vlad with bated breath. He wrote down names in Romanian shorthand, finally shaking his head in disgust.

"Ugh! This doesn't make sense, lass! I cannot understand the meaning of these chicken scratches. Are these mountains? Or foothills? And these?" He jabbed a finger at the parchment. "What are these? Trails? Or rivers?" Vlad rolled his eyes in disgust, mortally impatient. "This is too complicated for me. My scouts would get lost for sure!"

Voica cowered, unable to offer any useful suggestions. The layout WAS complicated, the mountainous heath country of western Moldavia littered with ancient dolmens, ravines, drumlins, meandering rivers, elk trails, springs, cataracts, benighted forest. All such things would be used as identification markers, but useless to those who had not familiarised themselves with the local landmarks. The Vlachs had done such, as had Voica and her father, and his fathers before him.

"I need a guide," Vlad murmured to himself. "Mayhap I should distribute reward posters? Hm." He paused, glancing craftily at his charming guest. "Know you any Moldavian *Tsigany* in or near Sighişoara?" Vlad queried suddenly.

Voica thought hard for a moment, remembering not a one. "There is only my father-…" She shut up.

"And?"

Voica hedged. "H-He is bedridden and…" Her eyes brimmed with tears, glancing down. "He is dying."

"I see."

Vlad sighed, glancing disconsolately at the messily-scribbled parchment. "Well then, I guess there is no alternative. *You*, shall join us."

Voica glanced up in astonishment. "That would be unseemly, my lord. No place for a young woman." She shook her head emphatically.

"Are you defying me?" Vlad shouted.

Once again, Voica grimaced, cowering low in her throne-like chair, expecting a savage blow or worse. "P-p-please…"

"You shall accompany me," Vlad insisted. "Do not worry, lass. You shalt be safe in my entourage. Is it your chastity you worry about? Or are you a virgin? Never mind. No soldier of mine would touch you or even lay eyes on you in a covetous way. I have trained my puppets well; all know to defy me would mean instant death—impalement."

Voica grimaced again.

"I shall arrange for a nursemaid for your ailing father. 'Tis the least I can do for a fellow *Waelas.*"

Suddenly he leaned towards her, wrapping a powerful arm around Voica's shoulders in an intimate way, squeezing, hugging. Rubbing her shawl-clad shoulder as if she were a sister, cousin, or familiar friend.

"You think I am a monster, still. What is it you fear?"

Voica tried to lean away, gasping as Vlad touched her face, her rosy, burning cheek, tilting her face towards him. She stared wide-eyed, deep blue eyes pierced with twin, black orbs of confusion and terror. Long, black eyelashes—heavily laden with kohl—surrounded her wet, bright eyes like bristles. Vlad gazed with longing into her innocent, girlish eyes, instantly desiring this peasant wench; so virtuous, curvaceous, yet maddeningly beautiful. And then he remembered that she was, indeed, a mature, young woman; ripe, buxom, and '*Oh, so pleasing to the eye!*' Less than ten years Vlad's junior, and mating age. Well over mating age. Not a child whom he might molest as a paedophile as so many others did. Not a Greek. Indeed, many a child-molester had felt Vlad's vengeful stake through their black hearts.

"Your men would think I am your mistress," Voica admitted sulkily, eyes swivelling away.

Vlad chuckled, his *bandito's* moustache brushing her cheek. "And would that be so bad? I desire you. As a stag desires a she-deer." Slowly, he brought his lips against hers, at first gentle, almost brotherly. Then demanding, aggressively parting Voica's soft, cushiony lips, tongue darting in wonder at this curiously familiar yet amazingly novel experience. The years had not dulled his senses. Voica responded with a mixture of curiosity and fear, leaning away yet seeking with her lips. Moaning. Squirming like a restless child. Her eyes shut involuntarily with ecstasy; when she opened them, misty and far-away. Vlad's left hand strayed absent-mindedly to her soft, protruding breast, gently squeezing, cupping, caressing; seeking warm female flesh while slipping into the folds of clothing to discover with delight her leather brassiere, a new and curious device meant to protect a woman's integrity somehow.

"Don't…please," insisted Voica huskily, shakily, when Vlad pulled away to gauge her reaction.

"You do not desire me." Vlad sounded bewildered, dejected, yet not at all angry. Indeed, he was elated, jubilant, still breathless from this growing semi-adolescent lust, a feeling he'd assigned to the dark, musty vaults of his youth. This tall, olive-skinned, Hungarian *belle* was absolutely scintillating, ravishing, a woman he was growing to respect for her bravery, honesty, and wisdom.

"I-I hardly know you, sire," Voica replied. "I—I do not know if I can trust you. But I want to. I want to like you, to…to love you."

"I will prove myself then. A duel, with your strongest contender. Name your foe, and I shall destroy him. What say you, *cariad?*"

Voica shook her head, blushing, neck flushed with excitement, her breath catching. Vlad was a monster. A psychotic murderer. Vlad was a Dacian, a good, wise ruler who spoke her tongue, valued her customs. The conflicts of information were tearing her apart. Her soul was in mortal jeopardy. Yet was it a sin to love one of your own kind, to choose your own mate? Or was it destiny that every young maiden have her mate chosen for her, regardless of her feelings. True, Vlad Dracula would take her as a concubine, not a wife.

"I see." Vlad released her slowly, straightening up, reorganising his injured, paranoid psyche. "Very well. You wish to retain your chastity a while longer—I understand, and commend your honesty. Therefore I'll not push my advances on a beautiful woman such as you, for you are a worthy." Vlad sat down once more, recomposing himself.

"I am a lonely man, er…"

"Voica, sire," forwarded she after a moment.

"W-Voica. As I say, I am a lonely man, have no true friends—"

"Why?"

Vlad raised a shaggy black eyebrow, nonplussed at this attractive woman's interruption.

"As I say," Vlad continued, slowly, "I have few friends, no truly likeable companions except for these fellow, boisterous Gypsies."

"But why have you no friends?" Voica persisted stubbornly.

"I…" Vlad frowned, hesitating. "I do not know."

"The people hate you, sire."

Vlad gave Voica a shrewd, glittering glare, downing his drink to hide the fury in his eyes. "They do not hate me."

"They do hate you, sire."

Vlad lowered at her with his most hostile stare, but felt his anger, his resolve dissipating like a storm spent. This sweet, charming young lady was much too guileless, too breathtakingly beautiful to hate for long.

"Alas, the truth has come at last," he responded finally. "For too many years I have lived apart from Romanians, have felt more at home with Gypsies than with the Rom. I did not hear nor see the rumours."

Voica had nothing to say to this. She did not pity Vlad, nor envy him. He had made his own bed of thorns, now he must lie in it. She also knew the chance of redemption was past.

"Enough. I wish to speak no more of this. We shall play chess, now. Know you how to play chess?" Vlad asked.

Voica nodded, smiling, pleased to drop this volatile subject. "I do, sire. My father taught me."

"I must warn you," Vlad remarked, standing up to fetch his favourite chess board, "I am a master chess-strategist, do not like defeat, so—let me win." He laughed aloud, his deep, gruff voice rumbling within his throat.

Voica was more than a match for him. She could have let him win. But there would have been no sport, no challenge. A victory would truly test Vlad's integrity, decide Voica's mind whether to guide his expedition or flee come dawn. If Dracula's reputation showed itself, Voica would die tonight for cuckolding him in a game of chess.

Yet she enjoyed the game, seeing it as a physical challenge against Vlad's monstrous forces of evil. She wondered uneasily if he would use his formidable Black Magic powers to influence the game, her mind, hypnotising Voica into seeing an illusion. Vlad Dracula was rumoured to be one of the last of the priest/magicians of Old Wallachia; a warlock, sorcerer. Wizard, conjurer of magick. Strangely enough, she felt no fear, no foreboding of imminent doom. In fact, she rather fancied (!) his morbid company, felt more at ease with Vlad *'The Impaler'* this moment than with any man she'd known, enjoyed the rare opportunity to speak her cherished Dacian with a fellow Wallachian. (Her mind boggled at the irony of it all.) Vlad's reputation had proven itself bigger than the man, a legend in his own time. Mythology seemed to have enveloped this 'Great and mighty, bloodthirsty berserker' with a mist-like mixture of fact and fable.

Vlad sat back at last, silently acknowledging defeat to his utter shock and dismay, having been defeated by a peasant wench no less (though a wicked, bewitching enchantress who concealed her guile).

He began to chuckle to himself. Then laugh. Soon Vlad was roaring with amusement, head tilted back; tears rolling down his rosy, emaciated cheeks.

"What is so funny, Your Majesty?" Voica asked in bewilderment.

"'Tis nothing of merit," responded Vlad, slowly becoming serious once more. "'Tis just that I was thinking: you believe me to be a monstrous warlock, a practitioner of the Black Arts, *moroi* no less. *Nosferatu.* One who shall return after death to continue his undead reign as voivode of Wallachia, with power to move roiling, black clouds over the sun near Castle Dracula as enemies draw nigh. And I think of you here, now, as an enchantress, a wily, white witch who snares men's souls and outsmarts with guile. A captivating witch—a *dewines*."

"I—I am not a witch," replied Voica with quavering voice.

"So you say. But you are an enchantress."

Voica blushed, glancing down at her hands and unable to respond. "Another game," Vlad insisted. "I shall win, or die in the attempt!"

Eventually, Vlad did win. But halfway through the match, he broke the concentrating silence.

"St Bartholomew's Feast was meant to atone for my transgressions in Transylvania—ydy—even for the Saxons."

Voica broke her gaze from the black/white ivory chess pieces, her hand froze on a white horse's head. She was puzzled. She would have preferred Vlad to at least abandon his delusions of innocence, would respect the man, the Prince, more as a cruel but just ruler. She could never love the man. Or, for that matter, even like him. Despite his dark, mysterious, handsome looks.

"You do not believe me."

Voica avoided comment.

"St Bartholomew's Massacre was an unfortunate accident. A

misunderstanding."

Voica cleared her throat timidly. "What do you mean, lord?"

"An elaborate hoax," Vlad continued, murmuring, his glazed eyes never leaving the jewel-inlaid, wooden chess board at the head of the immense trestle table. "Mind you, I have no reason to love vagrants and cripples. Or Jews. But burn them? No. I prefer slavery over such drastic measures. I have many castles yet to be built."

Voica glanced at Vlad in surprise, amazed at this unusual candour which she'd thought Țepeș incapable, her hand froze on a rook.

"I was duped," Vlad continued, deceiving himself and no other, Voica believed. "The Catholic monks of Tirgoviște snared me into inviting heretics and dross to the feast. Those Roman Papist priests have suffered ten-fold from me after I sacked and burnt their monastery, torturing these 'saints' at my fortified island-monastery of Snagov."

Voica gasped aloud. "God shall not forgive you for that," she whispered, aghast.

"Your God will not forgive these saints in hell for burning those Jews and Gypsies," Vlad countered hotly.

That stunned Voica. She stared at Vlad, catching his eye, her mouth agape.

"Expect no tears from me, *domnișoară*. I learnt many years ago whilst a prisoner of the Turks to harden my heart like stone. I," Vlad emphasised, jabbing his chest with a powerful thumb, his palms astoundingly hairy, "I endured horsewhipping at Adrianople and Sofia, watched Romanian girls and various other women raped in their cells, watched countless courtyard impalements at Egrigöz, patriots beheaded and mine own, faithless brother Radu the Handsome debauched by none other than Mehmed himself. I am a partisan, a freedom-fighter for all of Europe to follow. And a Wallachian. As you, are Wallachian. And I tell you now, *merch*, that I have better things to do than feed droves of useless people and then roast them. Aarrgh! What a waste of food, livestock, vegetables, wine, and grain! Food which could've fed my armies, relieved our populace from the drought. Remember! Vengeance is mine, saith the Lord. And By God, so it shall be! Mine, as well as His!"

Voica had no argument against that. More and more, she'd begun to understand Vlad's atrocities. And she agreed: traitors, pimps, Turks and religious fanatics—whether Orthodox, Catholic, Muslim, Protestant, Buddhist or Hindu—must die. All woman haters. The non-Cymry would never understand, their customs and religions more analogous with Indo-Afro-Oriental societies. Therefore, oriental Bulgars, Szeklers, Huns; Catholic Germans, French, Italian, Portuguese, Spanish, Scottish, Irish were veritable targets of Vlad's insane master-plan. The only thing protecting the Orthodox populace (a minority, in Transylvania, at least) from *The Stake's* implacable wrath were two things: (1) Christian congregations couldn't fully understand Old Church Slavonic; (2) the Church lacked central authority over government. Yet Voica shivered with horror, for she, too, was half-Hungarian, on her departed, blessed mother's side. It was Gnátasha's maiden name she had adopted. Voica's father, Caltai Mllöyneskvyxi (adopted name), was Dacian, born and raised in the Moldavian alps of northeastern Bristrita-land amongst the semi-nomadic Vlachs (Slavonic 'V' replacing 'Waelas'), an ancient land of dark mountains and forbidding forest which legend claimed had risen from volcanoes while the human inhabitants wandered amongst it. Even so, the very designation, the very blood of Dacians could now bring hanging or burning by fanatic Judeo-Christian Saxons now settled in Romania. Therefore, the natives preferred the adopted name 'Wallachian' with pride, content to identify themselves with a vague Romanian, Thracian, Slav, Saxon, Magyar, Szekler concept of nationality. A kind of flawed multilingualism, but with no peace.

"This weekend I intend to march eastwards, into northern Moldavia, to recruit willing partisans for the holy fight against Islam," remarked Vlad, reaching forward to snatch Voica's rook with a smile, "and then I shall return to Castle Dracula above the Argeş to plan my campaign." He shifted uneasily, glancing at Voica with a shrewd, hopeful glance. "If you wish, you may accompany me. I…could offer you a position amongst my servants at Castle Dracula; a chambermaid or chatelaine perhaps." Vlad cleared his throat while Voica looked crestfallen. "The pay would be good, though not exorbitant. My new state mint is just beginning. You in turn would receive a home among my court, a sizeable dowry, and a solid stone roof over your head." Vlad barked a sudden, macabre laugh, realising with black humour just how cold, drafty, how uncomfortable a mountain-top citadel could be in the dead of winter, even a grand ducal fortress such as his. "Or, you could be my mistress."

Voica stammered, utterly horrified. "I-I-I cannot, sire. My father—h-he needs me, cannot survive without somebody to feed him, change his sheets, his bedpan…"

Vlad frowned, nodding reluctantly; deeply disappointed. "I understand. Ah!," he cried suddenly, "but you could bring him along, could you not?"

"I-I do not think father would survive the shock of moving, of leaving his homeland."

Once again Vlad frowned, pursing his bright red lips, defeated once more. He'd won the chess game. But not what he'd wanted.

They gathered wearily in a tight formation amongst the jagged, rocky peaks of the Moldavian Alps bordering Wallachia to the northeast. Lakes in this area were scarce, and the foot soldiers were thirsty, as were their horses and pack mules. On the highest peaks, snow crusts still lingered on the ancient, hazy blue mountains. Purple bell-heather swept downwards from steep, intimidating, lower slopes. Above the carpet of heather, fireweed made its exotic appearance in scattered patches of purple, pink, or fiery red. Vlad took in this lofty, picturesque sight with an expansive, appreciative gaze as he dismounted his roan gelding, sweat-stained and grimy; sore and exhausted. They hadn't eaten since sunrise yesterday, their provisions of dried meat, nuts, vegetables, salmon, or pike having been exhausted. Dracula's infantry reserves had been busy these past few days fishing in local rivers and streams for trout, or, as a last resort, the giant, native, Carpathian sturgeon weighing up to 1800 lbs. The bozo in charge of food supplies at Sighişoara had stupidly neglected to pack soda and flour with the skinny, emaciated pack mules. (Vlad's men were, indeed, hard pressed to grind enough of the local roots in their mortars and pestles—a poor substitute for flour.) Ordinarily, he would've overseen the mules' baggage himself to ensure such travesties of wisdom did not occur. The miller in charge of Sighişoara's monastic flourmill Vlad deeply suspected was an imbecile all along, perhaps deliberately withholding the flour rations. He would spend a month doing public penance in the stocks for his tight-fisted ways. Nothing perishable could be afforded, so Vlad's armed escort had had to content themselves with dried or smoked goods. Their pigskin canteens were empty, hanging, almost useless, around the lost foot soldiers' necks. He called for his treasurer to bring forth the royal guide, watching impatiently as a massive, piebald warhorse trotted forward. Behind Cirstian's steed, an equally large, dappled grey destrier fought its way forward among the clustered, old, battle-axe-accustomed nags of Vlad Ţepeş' armed escort. The vicious mare raked her herbivorous enemies with tombstone teeth, jostling, bumping against solid, rounded bellies and flanks. She rolled her eyes, as if unwilling to endure its terrified rider's weight. But in reality the old mare was an excellent beast, having never thrown a rider nor kicked a farrier; her foals were prized for their intelligence and strength among Vlad's numerous, royal stables at Castle Dracula, or scattered in various royal fortresses across Wallachia/Transylvania. The horse had been broken-in by Vlad himself, many years ago. Her violence towards other steeds was part of her nature, indeed, her training. An almost spoilt nag.

Cirstian Mohács rode forward, moving his beast aside so the impatient mare at his rear could pass. Voica clung with white-knuckled hands to the steed's leather reins, lest she fall and be trampled underfoot. This weekend was the first she had ever ridden a horse. At once, upon sighting Vlad's familiar, cape-clad figure and sniffing his scent, the warhorse settled down, halting, snorting loudly and whickering as her master patted her muzzle. A sheepskin-clad henchman stepped forward, cupping his hands together whilst forming his burly, hairy, bare arms into a horseshoe as the girl-scout dismounted self-consciously amongst a chorus of catcalls and admiring male stares.

"Desist!" bawled Vlad, his ire rising. A feeling of insane jealousy and propriety swept over him. A kindred tenderness towards the lone female of his camp. "The next to whistle shall die horribly!" he cried. The troops ceased their whistling, slowly, many daring perhaps to take their voivode on in single combat. Many were Latinized Gypsies, not recognising a man's divine ancestral claim, only the power to claim leadership through martial prowess and to hold it against all comers. Some of those lacking sense in the past had challenged Vlad to a sword-duel and been defeated by him, only to be impaled for their impetuousness. Thus, even Gypsies had begun to hate the Dragon-Lord of Făgăras.

Fortunately for them and for Voica's squeamish nature, none stepped forward from their ranks.

She dismounted cautiously, straightening her red/yellow, pleated skirts, facing the *Cnéaz* at last while his kernsmen crowded around to eavesdrop, besotted all. Prince Vlad's gaunt, handsome face was flushed, angry, his plaited black/grey moustache sticking out across his face; curled up at the tips like a Spanish *bandito's*. Voica, too, was angry (not so much at him, but for the inconvenience of her being here).

Precipitous crags reared above Vlad's royal vanguard like cyclopean Greek giants observing the Argonauts' procession. Rockslides, violent and recent, were much in evidence. Great flocks of pigeons wheeled overhead, startled, roosting on verdant escarpments or decaying elm-trunks where woodpeckers hammered away tirelessly, relentless in their pursuit of grubs. Native saxifrage dotted the uplands.

Vlad Dracula (never known for his patience) had misunderstood Voica's directions, perhaps deliberately so, having led his troops northward, beyond the Rodnei mountains, beyond disputed Moldavia and into the grassy steppe lands of the *Rus*. Those Gypsy/Slav settlements wouldn't help, had no stake in fighting hostile Turks beyond their own jealously guarded domains. (They had their own problems to deal with, namely, the Crimean Khanates, Tatars, recent converts to Islam.) Vlad had hastily ordered his escort to retreat to mountainous, neutral Moldavia; now encamped amongst the northern-most fringes of western Transnistria, but utterly lost. He had crossed the shallow, placid river Prŭt two days ago, heading southwards into Prince Stephen's suzerainty. His cohort had sighted none of the ubiquitous Vlachs' caravans whilst returning from these disputed grasslands, nor, for that matter, had his expeditionary force encountered Cimbric-speaking 'Gypsies' in Russian lands (save for the unwanted, vagabond, East Indian Romany); only the endless, waterless steppe lands and pine-clad Cŭicŭlei mountains of north-central Moldavia. Now Vlad waited for Voica to verify her directions.

"Where are we?"

Voica had expected a more vehement response, and was ready to defend her fledgling scouting skills. She was, perhaps, more angry for having to accompany these boorish louts against her will and their ceaseless banter, catcalls, whistles, and jokes full of innuendo. Granted, she felt no fear amongst them (at least, not while in Vlad's company), nor were their jokes and banter lewd or lascivious. Nor were they insulting, though they made her feel unwelcome. (Unlike a Turkish or Hungarian army, which would have used her as an unwilling prostitute.) Yet Voica had been raised in her mother's firm belief that men and women should be segregated, for such armed company was no place for a woman. But Vlad had insisted she accompany him, sixteen days previous. And *no* man defied Vlad Dracula.

"In the Griglözes pass, we are (Vlachian geography), near *llyn* (lake) Demos, Your Highness," replied Voica wearily, sweeping back her dark, sweat-dampened hair from watery eyes; sick of travelling, hunger, thirst, discomfort. (Her butt hurt, saddle-sore.) Tired of these men's presence. And of Vlad's; his grisly anecdotes and disturbing tales of treachery and iniquity and harsh, swift punishment meted out to his 'enemies'. "That is, to the west of the Fair Forest of Drubils beyond Moldavian Carpăti and east of Durwen. Seek, we must, the Crooked Needle mountain—that one-" pointing north towards the Cŭicŭlei range as she spoke, her big, penetrating, ocean-blue eyes never leaving Vlad's face, "on the eastern fringe of the mount, below the summit. To identify their niche we must locate the granite flat side of Mount Crugnitzöv and travel parallel to it for half a mile or so, where the *Szgany* reside. But," cautioned Voica, Vlad nodding tentatively all the while, "we must approach with caution, for, unless Prince Stephen of Moldavia has left them unharmed, the Gypsies will flee at the sight of you and your small escort party, Your Majesty."

"How?" Vlad asked, incredulous.

Voica cocked her head, pursed her lips; frowning. "They shall pack their belongings, my lord," she continued, "their children, clothing, tools, foodstuffs and load their wagons, flee north, west, east, or south—possibly with their goats and sheep follow a trail higher up into the mountains. They have no reason to trust a *woiwod* of Wallachia, alas, for your father did not treat them as well as he might…"

"He did—"

"I am sorry, Your Excellency, but his subjects did not," Voica retorted, surprised at her own brazen candour. "The German counts of Bistritz supported them not. The merchants, farmers, and townsfolk cheered the Catholic monks as they led our folk to the burning stakes for a Dominican *auto-de-fé*. You, sire, should know that."

Voica had spoken with a soft, righteous conviction, silencing Vlad's refutations, knowing because she had witnessed the mass-executions of Sighişoara, Tirgovişte, Cluj, Sibiu, Alba Iulia, Ungrea, and Tîrgu Mureş as a child. Her father had been an itinerant peddler selling trinkets before his crippling disease had afflicted his bones, his lungs. She had been only thirteen when Voica and her father watched, horrified, the first wave of burnings at Tîrgu Mureş. The Inquisition had meant to exterminate heretics, but the Saxon settlers had gotten out of hand that spring of '52, burning witches, Jews, but mostly beggarly, thieving Gypsies. She had witnessed the Germans' bloodlust, watched the dogs bay for more blood when the last human wretch had burnt to chars. The fires had not been hot enough, leaving the strangled victims scorched and leathery, crisp as fried bacon. Afterwards, the Franciscan diocese had proclaimed new rules and regulations for the burning of heretics, foremost was the use of hot-burning cedar beneath the stakes. Afterwards, there would be only ashes…

Voica returned from her horrid memories, realising that Vlad was staring at her in a highly peculiar way. A look of guilt, for he had been powerless to stop Daneşti II's madness during his Moldavian exile in Suceava. (And Prince Stephen, preoccupied with bringing to justice the murderer of his father, his own uncle, Petru Aron, had been unwilling to intervene, knowing the neighbouring Principality was under the Turks' control.) Tears had involuntarily formed at the corners of Voica's huge, half-moon eyes, causing stares and whispers as she sobbed once and angrily brushed them away with the sleeve of her blue linen blouse. Her best friend, Mair…had been among the first to succumb to the Germans' blasphemous, cleansing flames…only fourteen and, secretly, pregnant (by the local vicar, no less). Voica had imagined the helpless cries, long ago, those stormy nights when the Saxons raped Mair within the dungeons of Sighişoara castle before the execution...

For weeks, she had imagined Mair's cries, the scratching at her window at night.

The burning she had avoided.

"Very well," Vlad declared, turning to his restless, kettle-helmeted foot soldiers. "Set camp for the night. I want volunteers to mount now, to search out game for our feasting. *Volodomir*, escort these rambunctious knaves throughout the hunt," motioning his eighteen-year-old squire to lead the assembling rabble. "And eat none of the kill, or the consequences for all shall be enormous!" he warned, finger raised in all-wise, absolute authority. "Make haste, thou jelly-brained dogs!"

He took Voica's arm, gently leading her away from the milling horses. "Come, sit down while these good knaves dig a campfire. Warm ourselves soon, we will: our feet, hands, legs. Roasted game we shall eat tonight, or my name is not *Wlad Tsepeşh!*" Vlad cried. "Cirstian and his knights are fetching water; his group have located a stream not far away..." he chuckled mirthlessly, "or so his accursed messenger sayeth!"

Voica was in no mood for Vlad's discourse. Nor his company. The memories had soured her spirits. She wished she were a sorceress, able to wave a magic wand and have him disappear, or turn him into a warty toad. (Along with his clangorous, foul-mouthed cohort.) She sat down wearily, bone-tired, her eyelids heavy as lead and dry, sore. Drooping. Her thighs muscles ached, as if a rough, drunken rabble of coarse men had had their way with her. Twilight was approaching; stars soon twinkled high above in purple-grey skies, a bloated, Swiss-cheese full moon threatening to roll down from the twilit sky. An enormous, grey, Eurasian eagle owl hooted sepulchrally from a distant treetop. Primordial choruses of wolves' howling sounded from the distance, out on the grassy, Transylvanian plains or from the gloomy, green wilderness, or from hillocks crowned with lone, skeletal, dying wych-elms or perhaps a scraggly old oak where Druids once worshipped before the decadent Romans, Huns, and Saxons chopped all the trees down. Voica stared up at the crater-pocked moon, mesmerised, wistfully imagining planet caravans roaming its pale, rough surface. Vlad's armed escort sat cross-legged around the roaring, crackling, spitting campfire, dolefully singing ancient Gypsy fables of stolen land and crushed hopes, broken hearts and unrequited revenge, their spirits sodden with wine. A copper cooking pot, nearby, bubbled over an open fire. The occasional five-stringed lute or tambourine accompanied the melodious, exotic Gypsy tunes from the

Cimmerian Twilight Era with its unmistakable Celtic roots.

They sat for a long time; famished, eyes and ears alert for enemy scouts. The Turks wouldn't be straying this far north, however; at last report, their crippled, decimated army had withdrawn to Drăgăsani. Prince Stephen of Moldavia would not attack, even within his own borders, although he coveted Chilia and Galăti (Vlad Dracula was his cousin and only ally).

Finally, Vlad's triumphant retainers returned with a fine young stag, speedily quartering the buck in the firelight. Every man's mouth watered, anticipating the roast venison to come. Voica fingered her beads, her rosary, nervous; trusting also in the silver cross beneath her shawl. She still distrusted Vlad, sure he was a *wampyr* waiting to seduce her into immortality, the eternal undead.

He could seduce her easily tonight, she was certain.

Țepeș' troops rose suddenly with an impromptu salute, toasting their esteemed liege-lord with raised tankards and sombre expressions of *Victory at all costs!;* a clamorous din of metal on metal and hale, prideful shouts of near-deification.

"Have you sought out your Gypsy caravan in Sighișoara," Vlad inquired, handing Voica a piping-hot, steaming quarter-leg of venison. She burnt her fingers accepting the joint, grimacing, suppressing a cry for at least a distressed hiss of pain. Vlad held his own joint, grimacing also, before tearing into the hot, spicy, salted flesh. "Mmm, tasty venison," congratulated Vlad, beaming at his youthful camp cook, Rasalom. "I asked thee a question, *domnișoară*," remarking at last, "please answer me."

Voica hesitated. "I have, Your Excellency. And was much surprised. For among true Vlachs your name is as honey in their mouths, as your name is excrement in the mouths of Saxons, Szeklers, and Magyars. They have told me," Voica continued, eagerly, "of your decrees against Inquisitor Generals. That your pillage is their food, when blight destroys crops and their enemies force them to quit their domains. As you know, sire, we Gypsies are pacifists, as are Jews, and greatly resent forced conscription into Romanian armies and slave-camps. But you, Your Majesty, do offer the soldiers and their families safety and a full belly, a fate unknown to most Gypsies. Indeed, they sing great eulogies to you, lord Dracula, as a Great and Just ruler."

Vlad beamed, smiling with pleasure, seeking nothing more than universal praise. The very act changed his ruddy, emaciated features, transforming this macabre-looking, barbarous warlord into a sort of benevolent Prince with open-handed generosity. Then he frowned.

"I—I can ill-afford to feed vagrants," Vlad began haltingly. "Nor do I rob the rich to feed the poor. I do that to fill my own coffers. As long as my fellow Romanians uphold my laws, fight for their country, they shall live and prosper. But hear ye!" cried Vlad, his voice rising alarmingly, deep and bullish: "he who reckons with my House, the House of Dracula, must know his place and know his rights. Gypsies, too. None shall be spared my rod of justice or of vengeance, nor can I exclude Gypsies be they even of mine own blood. All those who defy my law will surely die…"

The men around the campfire perked their ears. Voices stopped; the implication was thus: Gypsies could expect no mercy; Vlad Țepeș had just issued a new proclamation: Hence, Gypsies would surely be expected to work the land as serfs, handing over their hard-earned produce to greedy, Renaissance-enlightened (Ha!) landlords. German landlords, no less. Serfs were slaves. Such had been drummed into Gypsy boys from the day of birth. An insidious murmur of discontent rose forth from the camp, unnoticed by Vlad. The *Tsigany* had not forgotten the dozens of families—Gypsies—which Vlad had allegedly burnt on St Bartholomew's Eve at Tirgoviște…innocent all, guilty only of destitution…

"Let me tell you of Castle Dracula," Vlad offered suddenly, "the biggest, most advanced Romanian fortress of its time. Impregnable." Voica tensed, not wishing to hear any more bloodcurdling tales of butchered bodies, impalements, beheadings, burnings…she already knew of that infamous stronghold's notorious, burgeoning reputation as torture-camp extraordinaire.

"Thy majestic fort is sited high up in the forbidding Argeș valley, Făgăras mountains; opposite the hill of Poenari and the nearby village of Curtea de Argeș, where golden eagle, curlew, red kite, nightingale, whooper swan," Vlad counting off on his fingers his beloved wildlife, "spoonbill, egret, stork, cormorant, wood cock, snipe, badger, Carpathian brown bear, hedgehog, wolverine and falcons roam free. Foxglove, gorse, broom, purple heather, alpine fir, larch and pine," continued Vlad, "bluebells, clover, caraway, Ladies' Mantle, red fescue, oak, elm, birch, beech, aspen, and alder thrive. Below thy mountain, downstream, is the sleepy, tiny village of Arefŭ. This is where I go when matters of state sit heavy on my shoulders, when life's sunlight is eclipsed by tragedy; for me, there is no more tranquil, calming, remote spot in all of Wallachia/Transylvania— *ydy*—Romania. You would like it, I am sure."

Vlad lapsed once again into a morose silence. "I am lonely," he murmured at last. He reached out, took Voica's hand. Kissed it. "Ever since…Serena died, I have been living undead, for there is no sunshine in my life, only night—"

"Who, milord," Voica interrupted, is "Serena?"

"I do not wish to speak of her."

Most of the men slept. Bright stars shone down from midnight-black skies, half-moon cloaked by encroaching clouds. Dark, rolling rainclouds moving in to dump their long-awaited rains on drought-parched Transylvania. Voica could hardly believe her ears. Was Vlad proposing to her in some vague, unclear way? She wanted to run away, to tear this burgeoning burden of sympathy from her breast, despising herself for pitying Vlad Dracula, "Scourge of God." If she did not exorcise this feeling from her heart, she would find herself loving him, adoring Vlad's oddly handsome face, forgetting his unforgiveable atrocities.

If only she could believe. Have faith in her ability to resist Vlad Dracula's fatal attraction. She was only a weak woman, however, too weak to fight his hypnotic stare which made her blood simmer, his uncanny ability to read her every thought and emotion, knowing her weaknesses by heart. A conjurer of dark deeds; never his face a book. He told her that he was innocent; Romanians, Saxons, Swabians, Slovenes, Magyars, Szeklers, Albanians, Russians, and Gypsies claimed Vlad was a monster, unworthy of the light of day. If they weren't such cowards, they would bury Dracula alive, as they'd done to his elder brother Mirçea at Tirgovişte, and (later) his father at Castle Brân. The Gypsies wavered between calling him a saint and a leper. The Romany dubbed Vlad the *'Tyrant of Wallachia'*, while the dwindling *Cymbräe* praised him as *Cad-Wladwaladr* (War Patriot), *Haûl*, The Shining One. The two rival Gypsy factions were bitter enemies, linguistic strangers (one speaking mostly Daco-Romanian, the other, Romany), often waging pitched battles for territory; the Romany always fleeing in disarray. Voica needed to know. She needed to know if Lord Dracula be good man or fiend. And yet she knew she could never know. She must love him or turn away, possibly forfeit her life and that of her family. And yet, she knew she teetered towards loving the Impaler—even enjoying his company. Would fall any moment now.

****

The *Szgany* clan chief greeted Vlad uncertainly inside the lavishly decorated, colourful caravan wagon. Two dusky grey Percherons stood placidly before the wagon, still hitched to the high, thatched vehicle while grazing the rich, green mountain grass. Various purple/red/pink *Digitalis* (foxglove) dotted the overgrown mountain trail, sweeping upwards into the impossibly steep, craggy, overshadowing peaks; twisted, heavily burled Carpathian elm clung teeteringly to a rock ledge. Other wagons with arched canvases crowded the verdant clearing, high grass overtaking the jumbled camp. Clotheslines slumped between withered ash trees, loaded with stolen clothes pirated from Bistritz or Sighişoara. The children were skinny, dirty-faced, and mortally curious as Prince Dracula strode toward their band leader's kaleidoscopic wagon. They followed like moths, ignoring their bewildered, unaware mothers' admonishments. For sure, this short, dark, curiously caped stranger was of noble bearing, his ebon cloak draping the ground at the heels of his latticed, black leather boots. His hairy, muscular legs bare. Beneath Vlad's crimson-lined, nobleman's cape, a red silk, brocade blouse of thigh's length revealed an emerald brooch at his throat, signifying the dreaded House of Dracula. The *bwgan* cometh. (Bogeyman.) Men turned their gaze from Vlad's imperious green stare, fearing his insane wrath. He who committed such atrocities among Saxons would not go unnoticed, even among Gypsies.

Mothers began to scurry after their children, panicked, dragging the curious tykes away as Lord Dracula entered the sumptuous, richly-adorned leading wagon, bracing his pointed boot on a wooden step to vault himself into the covered wagon's dark, cramped interior. Two bodyguards with tasselled halberds had already preceded him, preparing Vlad's arrival lest an enemy take their Prince unaware with dagger or mace. His oddly unnerving, straight, waxed, plaited, neo-Scythian moustache presented an awesome sight to the shaking Gypsy leader seated inside at a tiny, wildly painted table. The Great Prince bowed formally. Molatai knew not what Dracula's mission here in neutral Moldavia was, nor did he want to know. Was he sizing them up for his next purge? Other than that, Molatai had no idea what Ţepeş wanted, especially of him. Had the *woiwod* been dethroned? Molatai thought not. Even his *Szgany* clan was not that out of touch with their neighbours in nearby Transnistria, had heard of Dracula's extirpations, including rumours of Vlad the Bad's odd habit of 'speaking in tongues'! Here it was, early June, and Prince Vlad was honouring this impoverished, young, stalwart Gypsy leader (newly chosen) with his infamous presence. How flattering! Molatai would rather entertain a python.

"I am Dracula; son of the House of Dracul, Prince of Wallachia, voivode of Transylvania," reiterated Vlad as the young Gypsy buck stood up on shaky knees to offer this diabolical madman the ceremonial kiss of peace. Vlad spoke in fluent German, at once forgetting that this backwoods tinker-king would speak no *Deutsche*. He winced. German was the court language of eastern Europe, used to greet royal guests (most of whom issued from the Holy Roman Empire, that iniquitous den of serpents based in Nuremberg). Vlad spoke again, in Dacian, his dialect rusty from years of disuse, puzzled at once by the look of awe and surprise on Molatai's smooth-shaven face as the younger man stood clutching Vlad Ţepeş' bejewelled, war-hardened right hand. (Vlad kept one eye on his fingers, lest the Gypsy slip the rings from his hand.) The two men embraced, each giving the ceremonial kiss of peace on the other's cheek. Molatai was surprised at this Wallachian voivode's modest height, for Vlad's reputation had preceded him. He was not a tall man, but powerfully built, although no shorter than most. But Molatai had expected a magnificent, gigantic, cape-cloaked berserker. Certainly not a fellow Dacian, a Vlach, who, despite the slight, premature greying of his temples and bizarre moustache, looked not many years Molatai's senior. (He eyed the notorious *seignior's* crimson silk, dragon-embroidered tabard with undisguised envy.) This royal stranger dressed wondrously (though judging by his hairy legs and the breastplate Molatai felt beneath Vlad's tunic, the warring voivode meant to wage war on some unlucky foe); minus his leather chaps, chainmail leggings, greaves, iron gauntlets, and pointed, Viking-style helmet. (Vlad wore a silver breastplate beneath his tunic/blouse.) Molatai fervently prayed it was not his *Szgany* caravan Vlad meant to annihilate.

The two leaders and their cohorts sat down (ceremonial drinks passed around) inside Molatai's cluttered wagon. Four Gypsy companions flanked their leader around the little round table; indeed, they were *teulu,* family. Vlad wasted no time, speaking up.

"I am here to seek recruits. As you well know, my fellow *Szgany,* Turks threaten to annex the wonderful, clean, unsullied land of Wallachia, wish to rape our women and enlist our boys into their *dervshish* corps. Now I am sure, my faithful friend," Vlad continued, "that you may think *'What threat are Turks to Romany?',* but your Moldavian peaks are no barrier to Mehmed the Conqueror. You think you can hide behind these lofty, majestic, frozen peaks, to roam afar should Muslims overrun Wallachia, and eventually, Moldavia. But you are wrong, my friend…*Szgany* no escape Ottoman empire, any more than Bulgars and Albis and Serbs, because, this time, Mehmed has Christian allies."

Vlad let his words sink in a moment, watching pleased as the Gypsies exchanged frightened glances. They couldn't be sure whether Vlad was lying or telling the truth. He sat poker-faced, having spent many a night gambling around campfires with his fellow *Combrŏgos* (comrades-in-arms). In this case, surprisingly, Vlad was not lying. He had recently discovered damning documents condemning King Matthias of Hungary of signing a peace/alliance treaty with Turkey in a diabolical plot to divide Wallachia, and eventually, Moldavia as well. Vlad's extensive spy-network at Matthias' royal castle of Vác, Buda-Pest, had ferreted out the documents with much difficulty and great risk.

"No offence intended, Your Royal Majesty," Molatai began at last, "but I do not see how we *Szgany* can help, for we are few and my tribe even fewer. Nor are we war-hardened veterans who can handle the battle-axe nor pike or duel with the sword so expertly. Indeed, we are men of peace, Your Excellency, have been so since the legions of Rome scattered our clans, the Huns of Attila and your Teutonic, Saxon merchants after Rome. I must admit, we are perplexed as to why Your Royal Highness should seek us. Your great armies seem to be holding their own against the Turk."

Vlad pondered this a moment. "What you say is true, young *Szgany*, young *Cymro*. But think you that without my intervention you would be free to roam this great land unmolested? I share your hatred of Saxons and Huns. Under my rule, you shall be safe, as you have been safe. Have there been *pogroms* in Wallachia since I came to power? No. Not a one. While other countries burn heretics by the thousands, you, friend *Szgany*, have known peace since the House of Dracula regained the ancestral throne, your heritage as well as mine."

Molatai frowned, nodding. "What you do say is true, *Arglwydd* (Lord) Draighwla," Molatai admitted. "But there is one atrocity I fear my people could never forgive you, syr. St Bartholomew's Massacre, a feast in which you, yourself good syr, invited Tirgovişte's Gypsies, and subsequently locked the great barn doors and torched fourteen families. I am sorry, but I must be frank. We shall not help. Do what you will with us."

Vlad flushed with anger, averting his stormy eyes and staring at his black latticed boots. His moustache quivered. The Gypsy companions at Molatai's side fingered their long dirks nervously, fearful of this berserk *hospidar* of Wallachia, a land they'd once called home but recently dispossessed from. Now, the outlawed Gypsies resided—temporarily—in western Moldavia under Prince Stephen's benevolent rule—one of their kind. Wallachia's southern plains, Transylvania's heartlands, had proved off-limits to semi-nomadic *Cimbri*, the Saxon cities hostile to *Szgany* (a Hungarian term to confuse their enemies).

"Truly I say to you," murmured Vlad, hands outstretched imploringly, "that fateful, horrible day was not my doing, but the works of your enemies."

Molatai shifted uneasily, giving Vlad a queer, probing look. "What mean you?"

"The Catholic monks of Tirgovişte. I have elicited confessions from them through torture, have also heard first-hand accounts from willing ex-monks from Tirgovişte, and as you well know, Pope Pius—that shithead—has excommunicated me for evermore for such ghastly deeds. You and I are brothers in truth, for these pestilent douche-bags who dare subvert my country ride or walk unmolested because of the Church's influence and universal power. What choice have I but to toe the line? My fellow European neighbours side with the Church, could destroy my Principality if they had a mind to do so. The great powers—Poland, Hungary, Austria, Gaul, Ysbaenia—could destroy my commerce through diplomatic pressure alone. I need Transylvania's merchants to finance my impressive war host."

The five Gypsies exchanged glances, at once frightened and hopeful.

"Ask what you will of me," Vlad asked suddenly. "Name your price. For your freedom, your safety, what could induce you to fight again for your country as our glorious ancestors had. Gold? Jewels? Baubles?" Vlad raised his heavy eyebrows in a suggestive manner, goading the Gypsy council which seemed strangely devoid of elders. Perhaps a plague had taken the old and weak?

The five startled *Szgany* exchanged wild glances, answering in unison.

"Land!"

Vlad paused a moment. He had a vague feeling that he'd somehow overstepped his authority, though his word be law. This was certainly one wish he could never grant. He would soon be without a throne if he did. Vlad knew more than most that the Saxon settlers viewed their tenure as a divine right (his fellow Romanians would be even more difficult to dispossess). Hesitantly, Vlad shook his head.

"Land I cannot grant."

"Help we shall not give."

The Gypsy leader spoke with conviction. Molatai knew of Vlad's notorious rages, knew this powerfully built *mormaer* could unsheathe the heavy broadsword lying across his bare knees and, with one stroke, have Molatai's bloodied head in his hand. Or, for that matter, lop the caravan leader's head off with one of his henchman's pole-axes. Vlad's forces could utterly decimate this small, pastoral tribe of goatherders and mountain shepherds. The *Szgany* leader stared boldly, waiting for Dracula's insane ultimatum. He was sweating profusely now, salty beads trickling down Molatai's forehead, his patrician nose, broad jaw; dripping into his open mouth from a clean-shaven upper lip. His eyes were watery, glassy, dark brown orbs of uncertainty in an olive face. His long hair felt like a fur rug inside the sweltering, colourfully-painted, cluttered Gypsy wagon full of charms and talismans such as garlic and henbane to ward off evil spirits. (Another ruse.) The hot mid-June sunlight made Molatai and his mortified Gypsy comrades' skin prickle and itch beneath their colourful, thread-bare attire. Each knew their charms and crucifixes would not save them from the Impaler's wrath. Legend had it that Dracula's

House was a vampire's spawn. But Vlachs didn't believe in vampires.

Vlad's cold, hypnotic stare became less hostile, his resolve wavering. "We could make a deal."

Again the *Szgany* council exchanged glances, this time of triumphant disbelief.

"Ah, yes, but could we believe you? We are not sure we believe your version of St Bartholomew's," Molatai said testily.

Vlad's green eyes lit up, widening as he suddenly leaned forward, angry. "I swear by my father's grave, and on Mirçea's too!" he hissed, eyes blazing, "that what I have said is true. Why would I burn my fellow men? My reputation speaks for itself. All men know I am no friend of monks, especially Catholic monks! Dare you disagree? Defy me and you shall die now!" Vlad spoke through clenched teeth, his blood boiling.

Molatai leaned away from Dracula's wine-scented breath, suddenly, irrevocably convinced of Vlad's honesty. It was true. Ţepeş had earned the wrath of every European nation for his bloodcurdling, inhuman treatment of Transylvania's Catholic Saxon settlers over the years. Even the *Szgany* could not remain unmoved by Dracula's alleged cruelties, none more so than the numerous, hideous (bogus) tales of Ţepeş personally slicing open the bellies of Swabian women too lazy to sew or mend their husbands' breeches. Or flaying the wretches alive at Tirgovişte market-square, laughing as they died slowly, tied to a flaying post...

"What sort of 'deal'?" demanded Molatai at last, suspicious. He was getting anxious, palms sweating. He had no idea how he could mobilise the numerous Gypsy clans to volunteer in Vlad Ţepeş' army, even for land. They would never agree, seeking gold and jewellery for themselves, content to steal their clothes and food from lowland German towns or cities. Laziness was becoming inbred.

"Saxon land for you and yours," Vlad said honestly. "The peasants can be relocated—*in Hungary! Ha! Ha! Ha! Ha!*" He settled down again, becoming dead-serious. "Near Bucharesti. You are familiar? 'Tis mostly marshes and forest, but there are some good lands, rich, dark, fertile soil for growing cereal crops, carrots, cabbage, beets, or what have you. Eternal tenure be yours. Settle these lands, and you do me a great favour, for the Saxons cause me naught but restless nights and never-ending nightmares. I have still not forgiven them for burying my beloved, elder brother Mirçea alive at Tirgovişte, my *tad* at Braşov; nor for beheading my family and stuffing them in the cellars at Castle Brân. Settle these lands, good *Szgany*, and we—as Dacians—shall reverse the tides of Hunnish hordes and Teutonic intruders. This time, we shall *throw back!*, the Roman legions. And I will have avenged my House, and mortared the House of Dracula solid for a thousand-year reign. And you, my fellow *Cymry,* shall prosper with my House."

Vlad drew his dagger from its sheath, holding it to his outstretched arm and rolling up his silken, scarlet sleeve. "Have you the bravery for a blood-pact? Be you man or woman?"

Molatai shifted nervously in his seat, affronted, nodding as he watched Vlad slice the tanned skin of his own forearm, blood trickling down his elbow. He raised his eyes in triumph, handing Molatai the blade. "Know that you can trust my word, for my blood is now your blood, and my salvation *hangs* on this sacred act. Thine council and my warriors' oaths of fealty be thy witness."

Molatai imitated Vlad's actions, slicing with a grimace his own forearm while repeating the *hospidar's* oath.

The voivode stood up, sheathing his bejewelled, brown-handled dagger with a smug smile. "I commend you, brother, for your wisdom shall bless your tribe, your wives, your comrades, your children and grandchildren. Fare you well. And, I beg thee, remember—I need *archers;* men experienced with the hunt. I shall trust you to convince your fellow *Szgany* of my obvious righteousness. I shall come again, one week hence, to commence conscription."

With that, the mad voivode left Molatai's ceremonial wagon.

****

28 June, 1462 AD

Sighişoara, Harghita Mountains, Transylvania

Voica cried and cried.

The sound of dirt hitting her father's coffin swelled in her ears, drowning out the incantations of the Orthodox priest standing over Caltai's open grave. A smell of ozone prevailed over withered flowers and fresh dirt. The ancient cemetery was full, crowded; though almost totally devoid of mourners. Caltai was only an old Gypsy tinker, unloved, unwanted. His four unwed daughters wept alone without even relatives who cared. Destitute now, without a home, for the Saxon *burgermeisters* of Sighişoara would surely dispossess the helpless young girls from their papa's run-down, mudbrick townhouse. The black-cassocked, white-bearded priest chanted Caltai's Last Rites with a bored, uncaring drone, eager to return to his cell in the city's Orthodox monastery and continue his self-flagellation. He sprinkled holy water into the old Gypsy's open grave as two surly gravediggers shovelled black, earthworm-wriggling soil onto the oakwood coffin. Voica wore mourning garments, her tear-streaked face veiled. As were her three sisters; Gwenivor, Marya, Mahlia, younger look-alikes of their big sister—their protector now. A penniless, futureless damsel in distress—a part-time seamstress—whose only hope lay in selling her backside on the streets. Her sobbing siblings stood apart from her, near the simple, carved wooden cross serving as a headstone. Caltai's death had been long awaited. The derelict cemetery had no more room for tombstones, having extended to the very limits of the rusted, corroded, Gothic iron railings which veered and swayed drunkenly with each heavy gust of wind. Lowering, grey clouds pressed down upon the graveyard beyond the city limits, daemonic wind howling as the Reaper scythed another soul. Voica could almost hear the wailing of lost souls as the vicious east wind tugged at her garments, threatening to rip them from her back. A tornado of souls. She braced herself, lest the Satanically shrieking wind sweep her away as if she were a witch on a broom. Schassburg's cemetery railings creaked in protest at the assault. The chapel bell tolled nearby; sited just on the outskirts of cruel Sighişoara within the desolate, bone-mouldering graveyard. *B-o-n-g-g. B-o-n-g-g. T-o-n-g-g. D-o-n-g-g.* Each bell carrying aloft a different timbre on the wind. Once such familiar tolling of the enormous, brass bells would have been peaceful, lulling Voica asleep as she lay in her pallet. But times were a-changin', and with her father's departed shade flew her fondest memories into the whirlwind of Souls. The great, Romanesque spire of St Petr's cathedral loomed black against slate-grey clouds, dormers staring out over the city like black eyes, towards the grim Carpathians sprawling north and east or the dreaded Transylvanian Alps to the southwest, where the gruesome voivode ruled with an iron fist at his blood-soaked Castle Dracula-on-the-Argeş. Voica had never been there, had never seen Vlad Ţepeş' gigantic, brooding fortalice high up on its shadowy mountain spur. Never wanted to. The wind here on the outskirts of Sighişoara was cool, moist, with storms on the way. Summer thunderstorms with hail and lightning probably. The capricious weather had cooled dramatically, alarmingly, since last summer and this spring's terrible, parching droughts.

Voica covered her tear-streaked face with her kerchief, as if to hold back the wracking sobs threatening to break her apart. Overnight, an emotional levee had burst: Leaving her and her siblings bereaved and utterly devastated, like a village inundated under tidal floodwaters. Sighişoara's cemetery shifted in and out of the blurred vision between her fingers; Maltese crosses, Slavonic markers, skull-and-crossbone headstones, death angels; all had been graffitied with swastikas and lewd filth unworthy of a cemetery, a place of rest until the dead moved on to Resurrection. This particular corner of Schassburg's necropolis had long-since been singled out as the resting place of heretics, of Jews and Gypsies. It had once been excommunicated—in fact, many times. Nearby lurked the city's sinister crossroads, where the vicinity's Anathema were buried. Rumours persisted like cobwebs of tortured souls wandering this barren section of the huge, wrought-iron-bound cemetery, the engraved skull and crossbones or peacefully smiling angels providing fuel on dark nights for such lurid fantasies. Prostitutes had been found strangled here, buried where they fall in unhallowed ground. Sighişoara castle's fourteen, grim, cylindrical peaked donjons loomed in the storm-tossed blue/grey distance on its hill; built of red brick, limestone, German half-timbering up high in domestic state apartments designed exclusively for the nobility, triangles of black-and-white timbers overhanging numerous mural galleries and battlemented, machicolated *chemin de rondes.* (Fighting platforms—i.e., hoarding made of stone.) Details around her showed up in stark, colourful detail, as if this weed-infested, thorn-plagued, bone-scattered graveyard had been lit up by summer lightning. Mounds pushed upward toward the sky, the result of generations of unenlightened, constant, multiple burials. Others were larger, grim, overgrown relics of mass burial, the nameless, sad resting place of countless 1349 AD Black Death victims. So careless and callous had successive caretakers been, that the bones of tilting, headstoned graves literally poked through the earth as the result of numerous, stacked burials. Tombs reared in the hazy distance; the horrible abode of bats.

 Voica's tears were as much for herself as they were for her sisters or her long-suffering father. Now with Caltai gone, her own safety was in peril, for without her bedridden *tată* to keep her at home she would be expected by Sighişoara's citizens to marry and raise a family. She had no dowry, for her father had been unable to save enough lei, deutschemarks, dinar, or florins for her future, let alone his three remaining daughters. She could apply to the Church, but knew the council elders would choose Voica a husband most suitable to THEIR interests on condition of supplying her with a dowry, be they Orthodox or Catholic. Worse, the city Madams and child-kidnappers might attempt to abduct her or one of her underage sisters, forcing the girls into degrading prostitution.

 Voica glanced about the ancient, lichen-splotched cemetery, morbidly trying to detect fresh earth where the six, unfortunate young harlots had been buried alive by the city's unholy alliance of Saxon, Romanian, and Magyar zealots. Vlad's punitive impalements had cooled their ardour for hooker-baiting. For now.

She wiped her tears away, sweeping back her dark, silk, translucent veil. She had to concentrate now on making her way back to Schassburg safely, for dusk was approaching. This burial ground was anything but safe in such diffused daylight, for *nosferatu* and werewolves were said to roam its empty tombs at night, while putrefying ghouls were rumoured to unearth fresh corpses to devour their flesh. Voica whipped the black veil from her hair, swivelling to march back to Sighişoara's grimy, fetid streets where her father's desolate, empty townhouse awaited. (Her *familia's* dwelling occupied the broken-down, segregated district comprised mostly of Jews, Greeks, and Poles; a rat-crawling sewage conduit, odious and neglected, extant nearby.) She halted, calling over her shoulder peevishly to her three weeping sisters, then turned away. Then she screamed!

Vlad Death stood there, immobile as a gruesome, twilit statue, arms crossed. His shimmering, high-collared, ebon cape hid his features, his sharp, emaciated, pallid face with its big, heavy-lidded eyes; the narrow, high-bridged nose and full, sensuous, blood-red lips—the lips of a wampyr. Atop his head sat a pointed, red velvet cap—banded with jewels—with a large emerald at its centre and lone white feather on top. At first, Voica thought he was a thug, come to abduct her or steal her chastity.Or—God forbid—a demonic ghoul meaning to strip the meat from her bones, for legend said the undead cannibals preferred living human flesh even more.

"What do you do here, *domnişoară?*" Vlad demanded. He spoke in stilted Romanian. "Have you become one of the undead?" He snickered, becoming dead-serious once more. "Or have you sold yourself; become a bawd. Prostituting yourself behind the stones."

Quickly, Voica shook her head, wide-eyed, fearful, crumpling her veil tightly in her hand; dreadfully nervous of Ţepeş' hostile, unpredictable wrath.

"Do you lie?! Do you betray my trust, girl? Speak!"

"No," answered Voica shakily, her voice cracking. Her three siblings rushed to her side; gazing up in awe at this debonair, richly-attired stranger. "We are here to mourn." She raised her tearful, blue eyes, suddenly bold. "And why do you be here, sire? Do you search the graves."

Vlad smirked, raising his eyes to the darkening, rolling skies. "I do enjoy roaming the cemeteries, having become more accustomed to death than life itself; I am neither ghoul, werewolf, nor nosferatu. Nor do I search the graves for new bodies amidst the jumbled, stone, coffin slabs. And as you well know, *domnişoară*, they are all empty—the work of grave robbers stealing corpses for their fine clothes and inherited, ancestral jewels."

Vlad lowered his voice, suddenly menacing.

"You have not answered me, lass. Have you lost your senses?"

"We mourn for our *tată*!" cried Voica angrily. She gasped, raising a hand to her mouth, as if holding back years of torrential, pent-up anger. Her sisters clutched her garments, her second eldest, Mahlia, putting an arm around Voica's waist protectively. She sobbed aloud with fear and undisguised sorrow, knowing Vlad could kill her for such insolence as to raise her voice to a voivode.

Vlad merely raised a shaggy brow, searching each girl's bereft, tear-streaked face. "Indeed?" The youngest stared up at him quizzically, as if he were a giant, a Norse berserker.

"Indeed!"

He stepped forward suddenly, gripping Voica's arms with vice-like hands, shaking her thrice while her sisters berated him loudly. Amazingly, Vlad did not rebuke them. Then he surprised her, embracing her with more tenderness than she'd thought this madman capable, stroking her dark, coppery hair as if it were gossamer silk; assayed from the Orient's finest bazaars. Voica's three siblings stared in awe, recognising this sinister, handsome *mormaer* (Great Lord) as none other than Vlad Dracula, the Impaler, the Beast of Transylvania—666. The terrifying ogre who'd been driving their big sister to distraction these past two weeks.

Vlad nestled against her neck, hair in his mouth, her breasts pressed alluringly against his broad chest. He inhaled her tantalizingly familiar fragrance, Serena snatched from the Lost Days, as if resurrected from her Argeş' headland grave. *Perhaps reincarnated?* She stood perhaps an inch shorter than he, fit perfectly into the crook of his arm, just as Serena had.

Then Vlad's hand slid up to her neck, caressing the base of her skull, tenderly, softly stroking Voica's silky hair as she moaned with pleasure. Her father had often treated her thus, though in a perfectly innocent way. Vlad's right hand boldly moved between her shoulder-blades, lowering, lowering, until suddenly caressing Voica's heavily clothed rump. She squirmed in his grip, gasping for breath, her clothes stifling and damp. Her eyes opened momentarily, then closed in ecstasy; softly biting her lower lip. She half-feared, half prayed Vlad would strip the hot clothes from her lust-fevered body, to bare her ample breasts and suckle them like the babe she never had.

He released her suddenly, tilting her chin. Their eyes met searchingly, hers watery, ocean-blue in a bronzed face surrounded by wavy, dark hair with copper highlights, his deep, dark green as a Transylvanian spruce-fir forest and unusually sensitive. They kissed, tentatively, then urgently, as if swallowing each other, tongues darting and lusting snake-like; swirling, miniature wet serpents coiling in a sexual frenzy. Amorously embracing this temperamental warlord, her face locked into his, she could scarcely believe what was transpiring! Voica gripped his lower lip with her mouth, clamping onto him like a doxy, passion mounting in a crescendo of alien emotions. His enormous, iron-thewed arms encircled her waist, squeezing tight as Voica rubbed his upper back, clawing, her temperature rising to dangerous, unfathomed levels, moaning deep from within. Their lips smacked wetly as each fought for supremacy, twisting their heads in a passionate, orgasmic kiss which threatened to compromise their stolid dignity. Voica pulled back at last with an effort, her younger sisters agape; cheek pressed against Țepeș' bristly, contorted, waxed moustache. "Don't," she begged, her voice quavering, shaky. "Don't take me here, sire."

"I shan't," he whispered, dolefully catching the eyes of the three flabbergasted, younger bystanders standing huddled nearby. "Even I have my dignity. The tales you hear are surely untrue, for I've no reason to destroy adulterous folk or fornicating teenagers. Indeed, it really is none of my concern."

Vlad spoke again.

"Come away with me, *domnișoară*. Come to Castle Dracula. Bring your three beautiful sisters. You have no friends here, nothing left to tie you down now your father is gone. Tell me, lass," Vlad insisted, "your *tată*. Did he suffer long? How did he die?"

Voica sobbed, wiping a tear away. "We know not. He just never woke up one morning."

Vlad nodded, as if to appease his own soul.

"Come with me; I will provide for you. All of you. I shall provide dowries for your sisters. You will be safe at Castle Dracula, as all my courtiers and servants are safe, even though Turks overrun my country. Castle Dracula shall be our eyrie, to reign immortal. Come."

"I-I am honoured," sniffed Voica, "to be your paramour, a-a-as you command, milord. Yes. We will come with you—for better or for worse."

Vlad turned, sweeping his immense, bat-like cape around Voica's shoulders, enveloping her, whilst, unbeknown to him, the creepy, hunchbacked caretaker of Sighișoara cemetery hobbled off toward the Dominican monastery on the city's outskirts to report Dracula's latest, undead conquest as he passed a year old, tattered-clothed skeleton suspended on a gibbet opposite the rough, broken-rubble entrance gate. The skeleton leered gruesomely, a Renaissance reminder of such enlightened times.

****

Castle Dracula reared up on its shadowy, green mountain-spur like some jagged, primordial bastion of crazed giants, an unholy Alcazar, intimidating the wild ungro-Transylvanian scenery for miles around while brooding over the thatched, huddled village downstream below Lesser Poenari mountain. The compact, towering fort had recently replaced Hunedŏara and Rodna (also dubbed Castle Dracula) as Vlad's favourite abode. Castle Brân, superb as it now was, Vlad rarely visited except for state occasions inside its marvellously wainscoted *Rittersaal* or interrogations of prisoners inside its gloomy, barred cells, the dreadful scene of his family's demise. As a new residence of a Count, voivode, and Prince of Wallachia, Castle Dracula now boasted the finest, richest, most comfortable yet militarily formidable apartments in all of Transylvania, befitting an absolute ruler such as Vlad. Indeed, perched high up on its overgrown, grassy mountain-ridge like a brooding red/grey dragon, Castle Dracula was well-nigh impregnable, spreading its stone-brick wings across the mountaintop while eyeing the older castle ruins of Poenari across the valley suspiciously. On the side least steep, the fortifications presented an awesome array of gigantic red-grey, stone/brick, D-shaped artillery towers to ward off enemies who might consider clawing their way up the steep, slippery incline (too steep for a massed infantry charge). The blood of countless victims smeared the citadel's cobbled courtyards and thick, interior, polygonal walls, dried on as an ochre paste, a sight wholly unexpected by visitors approaching up the winding, hairpin mountain path. Local legend swore that Vlad had ordered the mortar mixed with the blood of Transylvanian peasants. The lofty Făgăras foothills resounded even now, in the fading dusk daylight, with the eerie howling of wolves. Falcons pierced the early evening sky with their airborne screams, soaring high above the squarish castle keep as if ready to swoop down into the bloodied courtyard. The enormous fort presented an impressive, two-faced profile to local Transylvanians; one side facing the verdant foothills and stony alpine meadows with an almost delicate array of battlements, gables, murder-hole galleries, gargoyle waterspouts or exquisitely foliated cornices, lintels and outbuildings' Late Gothic dormer windows more commonly found in French *châteaux* than seen in Romania. The tower's opposite profile loomed menacingly, brutishly over the Argeş river, a massive, flat wall of virtually windowless masonry (until the fourth floor) abutting an immense, cylindrical watchtower; an unwelcome sight indeed for weary travellers riding up the Argeş valley on storm-tossed blue/grey days. Dusk would be descending soon, and a full moon predicted by local soothsayers, Gypsy caravans who'd set camp on the mountainous crag beyond Little Poenari's walls in a thicket of recent clearings. The inner enceinte was utterly inaccessible, a one hundred fifty-foot plummet and thirty foot gap separating twin, split crests on the outcrop resembling two distinct ridges from a distance. Above the castle, the mountains divided, before merging once more. A retractable drawbridge and stone bridgehead supported by massive girders ensured the Renaissance citadel's impregnability, but also sealed its fate should besiegers burn the bridge, for cliff-side replenishment under siege would prove almost impossible except via rope and pulley (a large outer bailey protected the bridge). However, the castle was supplied with up to a year's worth of stored grains, dried produce, salted meats.

Yet it was not a new construction, for a previous fort had been on the site: built in 1206, but later destroyed by the Turks, much of the footings and some of the ancillary buildings still remained of the old fortress.

'Twas a wild, macabre environment for such a court, thought the new lady of the manor (and, soon to be, chatelaine), the landscape endowed with a terrible beauty of its own, fir-clad and brooding, the agrarian hand of man unknown and unwelcome; only the most doughty approached the fortress's walls without trepidation, no matter the triviality of his petition. A simple request could mean the gallows at Vlad's harsh court.

Voica's breath caught in her throat, heart beating wildly. She felt like fleeing, like leaping out the open coach window and plunging to the forested valley far, far below. Vlad sat at her side, grinning triumphantly, so pleased to see his Serb-built, Teutonic-Italianate palace/fortress towering to his right as the four-in-hand, ebon carriage rounded another cliff-shouldering, hairpin bend. A switchback trail, sandy and rough, wound its way up toward the monolithic fortress. Tall, notched, Italianate merlons and spooky, gothic lancet-windows in garderobe bartizans or rectangular buttresses loomed over the rutted, rocky, broom-festooned trail from ten-foot-thick walls. Vlad clutched Voica's slender, pink hand possessively, though he'd not yet bedded her. She was his lady now; it would be her duty from now on to please her master in any way he desired. She wore a brilliant, saffron/pink silk gown, pleated at short, elbow-length sleeves and daringly exposing her proud, buxom, heaving cleavage, as befitting Vlad's newest mistress. The coach rolled, jostled, squeaked, rattled unbearably up the ungodly steep, zig-zag mountain path, iron-shod wagon wheels practically dragging with loose debris as the four, pure white draft-horses laboured up the mist-laden trail toward grim Castle Dracula on the Argeş. Bracken ferns dotted the grassy, gravelly trail, as if the forbidding citadel above had been uninhabited for years. Thorny briar patches grew in profusion along the thistly mountain path. Vlad's redoubt bristled with the latest ogee-headed gunports, outdated (but usefully intimidating) longbow slits, cylindrical, elongated bartizan turrets ending as pointed as pepper pots, square, deadly, machicolated garderobes with rectangular murder-holes beneath in the latest German fashion, and stone hoarding, or *chemin-de-rondes* (way of the rounds), all along the upper curtain walls. Red brick reinforced the upper section of the outer walls against future artillery bombardments. The massive troop-fort boasted fine, Late Gothic, pale-grey, two-storey limestone dormer windows without compromising the palace's defensive properties. Ample, Austrian-style, domestic half-timbering graced the upper levels of square towers astonishingly devoid of windows, having only meagre arrow slits, while round towers ensured resistance to bombardment, battering rams, or picks via their deflecting, rounded surfaces. Vlad was indeed proud of his castle.

As well he might be, for it was the premier instrument of aggression in all of Wallachia/Transylvania; a notorious redoubt for the undisputed master of these lands. (Although nominally a vassal of Hungary, as Prince, Vlad flaunted his power over Transylvania's hinterlands. He knew full well, as did his regal overlord in Buda-Pest, that Dracula's armies could easily route Hungary's undisciplined host.) The underling had surpassed his overlord in nearly every facet of war: his tenants obeyed without question, willing to sacrifice their lives even in the face of the most hopeless of odds, and in not a few engagements, *dying to a man*. A Wallachian's life was, if nothing else, short.

A long ramp led up to the castle, steep and treacherous. The massive timbers giving no sign of the enormous weight of the entourage, so stoutly was it built.

The black *caléche* entered the citadel's outer ward, a lightly defended, walled enclosure opposite the castle, separated from it by a deep rock fissure and a long, timber bridge leading to the inner gatehouse. Voica peered out the window, down into the appalling, abysmal chasm as the coach approached. The outer ward's trackway was rough, overgrown, sandy, causing the conveyance's iron-shod wheels to spin. Littered with rocks and sticks. Golden eagles hovered above like vultures, as if waiting for the three coaches and their passengers to pitch over the shalestone ravine's dizzying precipice.

At last, Vlad's royal carriage rumbled across the lengthy girder bridge, halting at the end of it, blinkered horses neighing nervously and stomping as they waited for the arched drawbridge to slowly span the empty, horror-inducing chasm. The tremendous, terrifying distance to the basin's scraggly floor caused Voica vertigo as she peered out of her window. Behind Țepeș' coach of state, two identical black carriages awaited. Inside, Voica's young sisters gazed ahead with a mixture of trepidation and excitement, for they, too, were aware of Vlad Dracula's ominous reputation. (A reputation for *deceit* and *murder*.) They could easily understand their elder sister's fatal attraction to him, however; it wasn't often one met a Dacian, a Prince, *Domnei* no less, whose charms were renowned across Europe and Asia Minor. (The ancient Greeks had dubbed them *Illyrians*, for their melodious lyrics, enchanting harp stanzas.) Up ahead, Voica had her first glimpse of the behemoth castle's impressive Renaissance courtyard, eyes settling morbidly on the rough, ochre-pasted walls of the inner bailey, barely registering the horrid, red-stained torture stakes which stood mercifully unburdened by stinking, decomposing, human cadavers. Through a spacious, rough-keystone gatehouse arch she could discern some of the fortalice's fine corbelling, cornices (purely decorative roofline machicolations, in the neo-Roman fashion), colour-banded stone or various intricate sculptures in honey-coloured sandstone. An oddly terrifying, leering, winged *wyvern* (dragon) crest attracted her gaze above the massive, stone-checkered gatehouse's triple assemblage of arched murder holes over a cobbled entranceway. The fortress's forlorn parapets seemed to rise upward forever in a profusion of multi-level battlements. Rounded, German machicolations crowned the upper walls like blind arcading. To the keep's right, a Corinthian portico with colossal, swirled-marble pillars approached via an intimidatingly steep flight of dark, limestone steps seemingly arising from a shimmering, blue, square pool near the stables led up from a depression in the courtyard; twin, horn-like obelisks welcomed the visitor grimly inside a dwarfing, gothic courtyard with left-sided horse ramp. (All of this attached to a grandiose, great hall; venue of feasting, murder, and intrigue.) Vlad's castle was pure Late-Gothic Renaissance, sporting huge D-plan towers of mixed stone-and-brick along its east and west curtain walls—roofs partly conical, flat at the rear. Between baileys, numerous rectangular, peaked-roof outbuildings of mellow, pink sandstone built into the inner curtain wall showed off the latest, foliated, multangular oriel windows with bright, stained-glass, heraldic coats-of-arms; at the rear of the enceinte, Flamboyant Gothic terraces and ornamental, freestone corbels or cornices above Grecian-style funerary urns and bogus Roman statues inside the castle's surreal, herringbone-patterned courtyard. The inner ward's cobbles were coloured and diapered, saw Voica to her delight. Castle Dracula's unique, apsidal '*turrus magnus*' (dwarfed in height by its slender watchtower) stood towards the rear alongside a cluster of other buildings, flush with the mountainside; half square, half rounded; heavily battlemented, as were all of the stronghold's towers, parapets, and covered walkways. A tiny drawbridge and short, earthen ramp led to the keep. Twin, round towers, diagonally offset, protruded from each side of the imposing great tower, barely visible behind the donjon's bulk, their battlement-crowned roofs rising above the Byzantine fort's domicile of last defence. Its spur-based, rounded side (abutting a large, square forebuilding with stairs leading to the second floor), faced the castle's heraldry-engraved gatehouse entrance, capped with a *chemin-de-rondes*. Halfway up the great tower, a balustraded, crown-like conglomeration of battlements and ominous machicolated, Italianate balcony (similar to the one at Tîrgovişte's Chîndia watchtower) provided Vlad a grisly lookout over the hundred-metre-wide impalement yards below. Other towers flanking the irregular, polygonal curtain walls were also flat-roofed; D-shaped, tetrahedral, round, or square, whilst others were topped with slate, fish-scale, steeply attenuated witch's hats. Bizarre turrets and latrine chutes jutted imposingly from red-brick, Slav-battlemented, crow-stepped ramparts. Other towers were low, unbattlemented cannon bastions, artillery platforms designed specifically for gunfire.

Voica gaped, unable to believe the opulent magnificence and brutal authoritarian military capacity of Vlad's strongest, most infamous citadel. For it was here that Dracula had forced the cowed boyars to build him a mighty new castle, watching gleefully as the former tyrants slaved away, shredding their fingers to the bone, their once-fine silk brocades grimy and torn. Afterwards he had used their confiscated treasuries to pay the multitudes of artisans, stone masons, carpenters, brick-layers and engineers who would construct him a fabulous *Rittersaal*, or knight's hall, minstrel galleries, pitch-blackened, oversailing, Bohemian-style timber galleries, and cloister-like halls for the new Prince of Wallachia. Afterwards, Vlad had had the entire lot impaled in his finished fortress's outer courtyard, exiling their bereaved and impoverished families. Most had fled to Hungary, Czechoslovakia, or Poland, waiting to extract their vengeance.

Much sooner than Vlad believed.

The passenger door opened at Voica's side where the faithful Count Cirstian welcomed Vlad to his royal castle. "Welcome, Lord Dracula," Cirstian exclaimed, giving a stately bow, "may you bless this dutiful household with as much happiness as you had left before." Voica gazed about with glazed eyes, mesmerised, barely recalling her coach having lumbered across the sinister drawbridge into the marvellous fort's inner precincts, nor hearing the iron-shod wheels and cloppity-clop-clop of the four horses' iron horseshoes on metallically ringing cobblestone. Vlad nudged Voica's ribs, signalling her to debark from the royal carriage. She did so, graciously accepting lord

Cirstian's hand as she disembarked from the metal steps of the jet black *caléche*, her coiffed, awkward, clumsily coiled hair feeling unnaturally heavy atop her head and coming undone. The sun was setting now, crimson-red as it dipped below the hazy Bihor mountains to the west. The unsettling, primordial chorus of wolves' howling nearby snared Voica's fear, bearing it aloft on the wind like bats' wings. She stared around uneasily, uncertain whether it was the baying of wild, Transylvanian wolf-packs or of Vlad's own kennels. (He had an affinity for such things.) Majestic Vlad Dracula, Prince of ungro-Wallachia, disembarked next, then his faithful companion Matei Bathóry from the coach's front passenger compartment along with his elder brother Tudur, Vlad's secretary-treasurer, before Cirstian closed the doors. Behind Vlad's coach, Voica's three sisters exited clumsily from their ebony carriage, exclaiming in awe. Voica's eyes settled on the intimidating red/gold armorial crest of the House of Dracula on her carriage's door with a sense of detached wonder, the royal crest bearing a goat's head (!) and a vicious, fire-breathing, serpentine dragon. Dracula. Spawn of Satan. (Its glint-eyed he-goat seemed to watch her with cunning guile.) The Latin inscription merely reiterated Vlad's commitment to the Order of the Dragon, like his father before him.

Servants drifted from Vlad's mighty, gothic castle, at once eager and terrified at Vlad Dracula's return. It was here at Castle Dracula that Țepeș initiated his most gruesome horrors, systematically torturing then executing Turkish prisoners and 'sympathisers'. For these, he reserved the infamous boiling cauldron, scalding the skin of his screaming prisoners-of-war who'd dared to rape and pillage Lord Dracula's Wallachian countryside. He'd captured five thousand already since his deliciously-wicked 'Forest of Stakes' campaign, the Turks bumbling into Vlad's marsh and forest mantraps by the dozens like hapless insects, filling the castles of the land with Turkish wretches destined en masse for notorious Castle Dracula and its grim, dark, subterranian dungeons. The mass impalements near Tirgoviște, combined with Vlad's latest diabolical offensive had cut Mehmed's army to a third of its former size; all the more impressive since Mehmed had levied a call-to-arms to every able-bodied Turkish male and had renewed the *dervshish* conscription from occupied eastern Europe. At the height of summer the soldiers' barracks across Wallachia were already overcrowded with doomed ghazis. Those Mediterraneans forced to fight in Mehmed's infamous Janissary corps were welcome to join Vlad's unholy Crusade, upon capture.

Should they spit on the holy Crescent flag and denounce their Mohammedan faith, that is, a religion of sadists and sodomites, as everyone knew.

Voica wrinkled her delicate nose, noting the sour stench of urine wafting from the nearby barracks. Mercifully, she was spared the smell of decaying corpses, for in that Vlad was enlightened, having his murdered victims burnt in a massive, cylindrical incinerator of brick beyond the castle's precincts, thus eliminating the spread of disease. (Often the tramp of his henchmen's boots echoed throughout the fortress's dark, dank, clammy corridors late at night, keeping his noble, foreign guests awake as the grisly henchmen carted the bloodied remains about under cloak of darkness.) However, many a maimed, mutilated cadaver still waited below-ground for incineration, for Vlad's stooges could barely keep up with the bodies. Voica shuddered at the thought of Sultan Mehmed's implacable wrath, worrying for her country's future once Țepeș is gone. Which, considering the state of political upheaval in eastern Europe, especially after the Black Death, may be tomorrow. It was well known that Vlad's contenders were pro-Muslim, including his own brother Radu and half-brother Vlad the Monk. Dracula's latest arch-enemy to claim his throne was none other than the much-loathed Basarab Laiota 'The Elder'. Vlad still sought this traitorous fiend and his infamous Muslim-convert spy/henchman, desperate to exact unholy vengeance.

Vlad and his leman neared the immense, brick/stone, thimble-shaped donjon, arms linked together; she in trepidation, he anxious to relax at his favourite, familiar eyrie and plan his next offensive. Here he could hunt stag, watch his impressive, peregrine falcons soar high above the conical, slate-roofed castle towers, inspect his troops, tally up numbers of new Gypsy recruits from Moldavia flowing in day by day and wander the forests below searching for *boletus* mushrooms (and hallucinogenic ones too!), fragrant jasmine for his castle chambers, marsh leek for his larders and rabbits (not sacred hares, though) for the pot. Also he would oversee the drying of fruits, vegetables, fish, and meat, ensuring his monstrous fort's impregnability during siege and keeping the inhabitants of the nearby districts fed throughout winter while other feudal tenants watch their folk starve. The old lords—those few remaining—had lost contact with the peasants (and with nature), having abandoned the Old Country skills such as drying, smoke, and brine-curing. The absentee landlords spent much of their time in aristocratic, expensive townhouses in garden-haven Tirgoviște, Schassburg, or Albiu. Now they contented themselves with bad meat, decayed vegetables, and mouldy fruit throughout the long, cold, snowy, alpine winters. Vlad had more sense.

To his superstitious tenants, however, he was an accursed sorcerer. Warlock, conjurer of magick.

Together, Vlad and his mistress entered the oblong keep's ashlar, square forebuilding, hand in hand, climbing the steep, wide steps toward the second-storey entrance to Lord Dracula's anachronistic great tower. (Yet the edifice was virtually new; lacking the patina of age of more outdated seignorial dwellings.) As in the latest Byzantine/Norman technology, the castle had only one main access to the keep, ensuring the warlord and his immediate family's safety from fickle mercenaries. Below the *donjon* were extensive, subterranean, limestone dungeons. Sculpted figureheads and lifelike, grinning gargoyles on pliable freestone leered down on Vlad and his retinue as they ascended the forebuilding's dim lit, lime-washed stairs; decorative corbels holding orangish, wavering, smoking torches in their basins. Cirstian, Matei, and Tudur brought up the rear along with an escort of armed men. Grotesque shadows leapt out from smooth, ashlar walls, forcing Voica to stifle a shriek lest Dracula think her unworthy of his marriage bed. Bat wings hovered monstrously, as big as a man, though whether real or mere shadows she did not know.

The keep seemed to moan with the unearthly sound of draughts.

Finally, Vlad and his trailing retinue reached the second-floor entrance; their passage blocked by a heavy, spiked, iron/wood portcullis-like yett. Beyond the latticed bars, Voica could see a scurrying knot of white-clad servants forming into a neat, half circle. The tapestried, great hall was rounded at one end, like a Byzantine chapel's apse, and dismally dark (the keep would later be rebuilt, under Turkish rule, in no way resembling the original). Smoky. Voica could discern however the wonderful, balustraded, quatrefoil-arcaded minstrel gallery, polished and winking in the mellow glow of enormous, twin, partially-lit crystal chandeliers swaying gently, as if pushed by unseen hands, though really only buffeted by strong drafts inside the great tower. Majestic banners, pennants, and colourful coats-of-arms of the various baronies of Transylvania fluttered softly, high up in the shadows of a distant, groin-vaulted ceiling. Vlad's linen-clad servants wore a look of real fear. Their master was *voevod;* a blasphemous sorcerer and *moroi* too. He slept down in the family mausoleum beneath the cellars and only came out at night (never mind his numerous daylight sightings—vampires were tolerant of a certain amount of sunlight)! His servants had yet to discover Dracula's dirt-packed coffin hidden down in the castle's gloomy vaults. Voica could not help sneaking a frightened, sideways glance at Lord Dracula's sallow, handsome, face. (Vlad had a sorrowful, almost *boyish* expression which was ever a source of wonder to her.) She still half-believed much of the slanderous tall-tales told of him.

Rush mats covered most of the vaulted, stone/brick second floor. A hint of thyme and sage lingered in the air, strewn amongst the rushes. Smoke stung Voica's eyes, her nostrils. Vlad hollered impatiently for the gigantic yett to open. Beyond Voica's line of vision, someone rushed forward, unbolting the great yett and swinging it open with a tremendous effort and a grunt. A lanky, close-cropped, dim-witted giant of a man, clad all in black, stepped into view. Vlad strode forward, smiling triumphantly as he entered the apsidal, splayed-windowed, musty hall with his mistress/wife and accompanying entourage in tow. Voica clung fearfully to his hand, her dark, unveiled hair somewhat dishevelled, looking like a wild, subdued Hungarian warrioress captured in a punitive raid. Her blue eyes stared, starkly, untrustingly. Tonight she would fill Vlad's bed and take over the household's rule as matron. She would fill her master's goblet, count the larders and scold the jealous maidservants who had sought for so long without success to catch Vlad's eye. And they would despise her.

"Good evening, Lord Dracula," cried the servants in unison. Men and women, boys and girls, paid obeisance and curtsied as one; some awkwardly, others graceful, well-practiced. The blasphemous Prince bowed back, stately, bemused.

Vlad's ageing, overweight, matronly chambermaid strode forth, immediately tattling on her fellow under-servants and exposing their mistakes and 'indiscrepancies'. Some had stolen from the castle's larders; others had been caught upstairs in *flagranté delicto*, rollicking in the empty, chintz-draped, exquisite four-poster beds while their master and extensive court was away. Dulcena exposed their adulterous behaviour—shocking behaviour to her eyes. Vlad shifted his eyes away from her face, staring menacingly at the guilty, ashen, pleading men and women. He thought it all a joke. Many a time old Dulcena had brought these adulterers to his attention, obviously expecting Vlad to punish them for their 'sins'. And, horribly, sometimes he did, especially those aggressive males accused by maidservants of sexual assault. A quick, democratic council would usually, speedily, verify the accused's innocence—or guilt. (In case of deadlock, the old, time-honoured rite would suffice: the accused would be required to seize a *white-hot rod of iron* to prove his innocence!) A maidservant found guilty of wrongful, deliberate accusation would suffer the perilously-endangered man's punishment in his place. Impalement. However, the very fear of such punishment kept his lackeys and servants in check. Periodically Vlad saw fit to dispose of some tiresome, royal courtier, contemplating such even as they raised their silver goblets in his praise. A higher stake for them, befitting their elevated, royal status. Honesty, above all, was demanded at Vlad's court. He cared not where the manservants put their wangs, or with whom—as long as with consenting, heterosexual adults. Homosexuals would be reserved for a gruesome, and fitting, type of impalement.

Vlad pulled Voica along while her siblings followed meekly, like a father with a shy child, drawing her toward a massive, sprawling, oaken trestle table. He admonished her mildly, half-coaxing her to relax, to sit down and introduce herself to the servants. He noted her pale complexion, her haunted, staring eyes. Vlad was mildly amused yet exasperated too, slumping down beside her on a long wooden bench. He hugged her close, stroking Voica's pale, blushing skin with war-hardened fingers, straying boldly down to the embroidered hem of her neckline and onto her warm, heaving bust. He nestled amorously against her crazy nest of dishevelled, brown hair. Vlad sat beside her, one burly arm around Voica's shoulder like a benevolent, incestuous uncle. That, he was not. She was his mistress, his property now under Hungarian common law.

"Hear ye!" Vlad shouted, instantly silencing the murmuring hall brimming with courtiers and curious servants. "This is my new chatelaine, Voica Nyiregyháza, and she is to be respected and obeyed at ALL times. Any man who disobeys or offends her femininity in any way shall die instantly. And any woman. Have I made myself heard?"

"Yes, Your Majesty," the terrified Szeklers echoing in unison. Vlad spoke in German, even as he loathed the foul, crude tongue. A language of uncouth barbarians. But the court language of eastern—Teutonic—Europe.

"You need not fear these wretches," Vlad murmured in Voica's exposed ear, his breath tickling. "Most speak Hungarian, though not well. These we call *Szekely*. Their ancestors were Mongols, although their fathers are German. Do not fear to ask whatsoever you desire," reminded Vlad with a jab of his elbow, "they will obey unfailingly."

Voica winced, nodding grudgingly, her ribs suddenly smarting.

Vlad uncharacteristically lowered his hand, massaging Voica's hurt ribs. "Why, you are a soft filly," exclaiming in wonder, chuckling, "I am sorry; do remind me of my boorishness, *llances*, lest I break your bones. I am used to hard-drinking, rough-playing rogues. I shall remember to play softly. Hmm?" He whispered in her ear, brazenly brushing Voica's breast with his hand as she stiffened. Her yellow-silk-encased lower arm rose to move away Vlad's hand, her hand on his only tending to excite him more.

She gritted her teeth, smiling tolerantly of this shockingly-public show of affection. Voica wondered morosely if she could ever love this man. Yet she was immensely grateful for his having rescued her and her siblings from certain forced prostitution in far-away Sighişoara. Vlad offered her free room and board plus lifelong security and riches, while all he asked in return was her love, loyalty, and rearing of his children. Strange that. Vlad had made no mention of children, legitimate or no, and precious little of his family, only of his bereaved father and elder brother. Vlad had tearlessly confided in her of their deaths, and of his subsequent vow of revenge while he and Voica travelled by carriage through the beautiful, but lonely, Făgăras foothills of southern Transylvania. She had gained new insight on his atrocities and self-confessed insanity. Only weeks before, Vlad had visited his father's recently-completed tomb at the chapel of Balteni, near Bucharest. Before that, he had visited Mirçea's now vandalised tomb at Cozia monastery, near the Olt river.

Voica's trillium-blue eyes roamed about the great hall, aghast at being here within the notorious, dreaded, blood-stained walls of Castle Draculeşti. She dreaded tonight's initiation into womanhood even more. Wished she could get drunk. Belatedly, she caught the pitying eyes of her three sisters, putting on a brave, dimpled smile for their benefit.

The enormous '*Rittersaal*' was simply incredible. Its red-brick, vaulted ceiling receding into sinister shadows high above, pointed crests and heraldic coats-of-arms in white plaster moulded onto embossed groin vaults and gothic fan-vaulting. Several shadowy, dimly lit, cloister-like balconies high above led off into utter, space-void blackness on either side of her. Voica gazed about the great hall, awestruck, her heart beating wildly; all too aware of Vlad's hand resting proprietarily around her narrow waist. Flustered, she replayed in her mind all she had fantasised a man of her choice might do to her on her wedding night. She wondered if he was a good lover. (Considering the considerable difference in weight between the two, she resigned herself to his *spanking the monkey.*) At the hall's opposite end a gigantic, rectangular hearth on chevron-moulded pillars roasted the morrow's oxen on a spit, its tapering, stone hood rearing up towards a distant ceiling. A great fire roared, crackling, in the fireplace. Splendid minstrel-galleries overlooked the hazy, candlelit hall, bulbous balustrades made eerie by the fluttering of gaily-painted ancestral banners high up in the frightening shadows where ruff-collared courtiers flitted about like ghosts.

Vlad asked for no wine nor *ţuica*. He called for snacks, angel bread, dried salmon, beef jerky. Honeyed sweets for his new sweetheart, the shy, lovely, buxom Hungarian *Tsigany* who was the ache of his loins and of his stone-cold heart. Indeed, it seemed the great Iceberg-Prince had melted. Vlad's dangerous green eyes sparkled with merriment, temporarily forgetting his previous mistress's unforgettable demise. Soon the wine was flowing freely, however, his retainers and few remaining, loitering courtiers rejoicing at Vlad's unusually sunny disposition. (Usually he sat brooding at his lavish, purple-chintz-draped, black oak throne in the great audience hall outside the keep for days, glum, staring off into space as his courtiers danced, gossiped, schemed.) Voica sat unwillingly now on his lap, smiling brittlely, dreading midnight.

Soon macabre tales circulated around the enormous, heraldry-engraved hearth, roaring, crackling, and spitting as tomorrow's oxen was roasted on a spit (the unenviable toil of sweating manservants). The tantalising aroma of cooking fat, exotic eastern spices, and meat made the revellers' mouths water, anticipating the evening's scrumptious, celebratory feast; Hungarian *goulash*, dumplings, shashlik, *rushik* (mushrooms served in vodka), veal, pheasant, goose, partridge, turnips and plum pie. Old wives' tales of werewolves and vampires and unpredictable elk stags, of unprovoked Carpathian mother bears, wild boars and dangerous forest gangs: thugs who preyed on travellers for jewellery and women to sell to the Turks. Vlad (toasting his guests in merriment) joined in, spinning a fictional yarn of the House of Dracula, an immortal, ancestral bond dedicated to the conquest of the world and spawning Satan's undead plague. Voica wasn't laughing, neither were her three young sisters, although Vlad and his cronies laughed uproariously.

Everyone else believed.

****

Vlad shook her shoulder gently. He was not drunk, wanted to savour this evening. She had hoped he would be. Hoped he would be flat out on the floor. Voica's head lolled on his shoulder, dark shawl hiding her bare, heaving bustline. In a deep slumber, she reposed, innocent as a child, the *ţuica* having made her giddy, then sleepy. Now her great, blue, doe-like eyes popped open, realising with a start that the chamber was speedily emptying, guests and servants exiting the keep's banquet hall. It was dark now. The hall's crystal chandeliers were out, candles having long-since sputtered into nothingness. Only a smoky oil lamp and guttering, acrid pine torch lit Draculeşti's yawning, black, cavernous '*Rittersaal*'. Empty minstrel-galleries and polished mahogany panelling loomed above, where the court's minstrels had only a few, short hours ago sung their *Naši's* praises and expertly plucked their instruments to the best of their ability while the courtiers ate their lavish feast at Lord Dracula's benevolent table. Gothic hallways and shapely, ogee-arched passageways led off into abysmal darkness, glowing red eyes of rats piercing the gloom. Smoke fingers hovered near whitewashed walls, as if waiting to grab some unsuspecting victim. At the rear of the great hall, battle-axes, falchions, scimitars, pikes, poleaxes, lances, armour, swords, maces, hammers of war, metal gauntlets, round iron shields hung from wainscoted panels in various symmetrical patterns suiting a Prince of Wallachia, Lord of Transylvania, God's representative on earth.

At last, to Voica's dismay, Vlad rose from his stool by the fire, drawing her along as if in a dream toward his chambers.

He hoisted her up into his arms as if she were a sack of oats, walking confidently now down a long, vaulted passageway twisting wildly, a serpentine illusion inclining downward to some horrible subterranean destination. Guttering torches sputtered as he passed. Suddenly Vlad mounted a turnpike, carrying Voica, upwards now, towards his private, royal apartments. She gave a sigh of relief, watching superstitiously as the smoking wall-torches whisked by, as if themselves moving. She feared he might collapse backwards, down the wide, steep, spiral stairwell. Vlad's castle layout was indeed odd, following no rational pattern, as torturous and confusing as Dracula's mind.

Voica gave a startled shriek. A tiny bat fluttered away, up the dim-lit stairwell, leathery wings flapping as monstrous shadows on the mixed stone/brick wall. Firelight shone in the creature's eyes a moment, giving the furry, nocturnal rodent a red glow to its otherwise beady, black eyes.

"What is it?" Vlad asked, perplexed.

"A bat," Voica squeaked. She cringed, as if expecting some stupendous, winged monstrosity to swoop down the stairwell.

Vlad laughed haltingly. "A bat?? Do you fear that tiny little bat? Why, my love, that little bat is but a pipsqueak among giants! My castle is thronging with friendly bats. Indeed, they are my pets. You shall learn to love these furry, cuddly rodents."

Voica whimpered. (She had a paranoid fear of bats.)

Vlad halted, kissing Voica with a sudden, passionate embrace as she moaned in surprise, her arms coiled about his neck. She had not expected it, nor had she expected the intensity of her desire. He had not kissed her since that fateful, stormy day in Sighişoara, almost a fortnight ago. He stroked her burnished, silken hair, delighted, excited. He inhaled deeply of her fragrance, so wonderfully familiar in that gloomy stairwell. Jasmine. (It reminded him of Serena's hair.) Voica relaxed, cradled in Vlad's powerful arms, the back of her dun-stockinged legs pressed deliriously against his bulging, muscular forearms. The sound of her and Vlad's surging, open lips smacking wetly together turned her on. She felt unbearably heavy now in his arms.

With a triumphant cry, Vlad strode up the few remaining steps, his fluttery, black silk cape billowing out behind him like a long, outstretched, leathery pair of clawed bat's wings.

He set her down on her feet inside the wainscoted bedchamber, smiling tenderly, brushing Voica's blushing cheek with a feather-light finger. She ran her tongue along Vlad's index finger coquettishly, gripping and kissing his palm. She had never seen him look so natural, so at ease and carefree in another's company. She was scarcely an inch shorter than he, his face now buried in her bosom. He had always wore such a stern, merciless countenance, his unnatural moustache highlighting his odd, emaciated features, for Dracula torturously forced his *condittiére's* moustache to grow outwards across his sunken cheeks. He also plaited it with wax and hot tongs. Vlad's eyes were huge now, monstrous green crescents of compassion.

"You shall not regret this night, *breila* (primrose)," Vlad murmured, removing his scarlet-lined, black silk cape with a brisk, stately sweep of his arm, tossing it onto an enormous, canopied bed. Voica's arms encircled his neck, his hands meeting tantalizingly around her slender waist at the small of her back. "We shall reign forever, you and I, howling at the moon like wolves, for we own the night. I shall make love to you now."

Voica shuddered, her eyes closing involuntarily as he stripped the brown, woollen shawl from her shoulders. Next he unlaced her tight yellow bodice, softly squeezing her breasts together with both hands as she gasped with unbelievable pleasure. The thought ran through Voica's mind, *So he is a monster, but he treats me kindly...*

Vlad unlaced his blood-red silk blouse down to the navel, exposing his bare, hairy chest. Voica's heart thumped wildly, blood rushing in her ears, her breathing heavy. She raised her eyes questioningly, meeting Vlad's mesmerising stare. "You are mine now," he murmured. Voica nodded.

Next he unlaced his pantaloons, dropping the baggy, black silk trousers to his ankles, stepping out of the Turkish-style breeches like a stamping stallion. A solitary pine-torch flickered in its brass wall sconce, barely illuminating Vlad Dracula's nether regions. Voica glanced down, gasping in surprise, meeting Vlad's impassive eyes with unspoken, twinkling assent. He was, indeed, a stallion.

Vlad removed his blouse entirely, tossing it onto a maroon, velvet-upholstered chest. Next he softly kissed Voica's blushing, alabaster-smooth, yielding cheek. And then, surprising her, forced her lips toward his muscular chest while reassuringly stroking her coiled, plaited hair, coaxing soothingly. "Taste me," he whispered, "kiss my skin. Suck my salty flesh."

Voica moaned with delirious passion, obeying, softly sucking and kissing Vlad's breast. She felt something amazing growing inside her, threatening to explode, terrifying in its heady unfamiliarity. Her legs felt weak, trembling, as one might after a long, gruelling run in the countryside. The smell of Vlad's manly odour filled her very being. Her breasts ached to be held again, nipples erect, waiting...

Vlad released her. "On your knees."

"Sire?"

"Your knees."

Startled, Voica obeyed, eyes trustingly catching Vlad's own. Her gown hung limply from her shoulders, the cool, humid Transylvanian mountain air soothing her sweaty, fevered breasts. *"I love you,"* she mouthed silently, smiling sweetly yet still deeply disturbed, nervous. Voica waited patiently on her rump, compliant as a doxy; legs tucked beneath her. A horrible thought invaded her mind: perhaps Dracula meant to compromise her, then destroy her for her wantonness. He was rumoured to do so to unwitting maidens.

She'd begun to rise, uncertainty misting her eyes.

Gently, oh so gently, Vlad pushed her to her knees once more.

He made her do something with her willing, heart-shaped mouth she'd never imagined before. Voica moaned deep within, overcome with wanton lust, her head bobbing...

At last, half-ashamed, half exultant, Voica rose to her knees (having collapsed in a swoon), her lusty, blue eyes afire. She kissed her master's upper leg, running her tongue, her hand, up his hairy thigh. Dracula stood silent, a nightmare statue; an incubus sent to entice, subdue, the intent to *overwhelm her with mad love* momentarily alight in a mystic's eyes. His lady of convenience shuddered with carnal longing. Vlad breathed heavily, expended, softly clutching the base of Voica's skull to his midsection, eyes closed with vulpine satisfaction; lips curled up with an evil smile. Voica's sweating body quivered with primeval lust. *"Take me now, milord, I am yours,"* she whispered hotly, licking her lips seductively.

He pulled her up by the shoulders, drawing Voica's saffron/pink gown over her head, then her white shift, baring her pale, high, globular breasts; touching each with a warm, wet tongue. Groaning aloud, he laid her gently onto his dreamily floating, down-filled bed, exploring with experienced, patient hands as Voica ran her salivating tongue along his lips, his tongue; softly biting Vlad's lower lip. He kissed the length of her moon-washed body, concentrating on her stiffening, excited pelvic area, Voica's diaphragm childishly ticklish. Vlad ran his slick tongue over her skin as if it were some sweet, exotic, frozen treat of the future. Next he kissed and sucked on Voica's large, soft breasts, exploring the fleshy, tender mounds of pleasure as she gently stroked Vlad's unruly, shoulder-length, black hair. *"A-h-h, you're so lovely,"* he murmured, flicking a warm, wet tongue sweetly over Voica's erect, pink nipples. And then he mounted her, riding her like an ocean wave to crash onto a tropical, paradise beach into a million pieces. They locked together like a puzzle, moaning, groaning, crying out softly, wailing; their limbs possessing each other's body. Wisely, Voica resisted clawing Vlad's scarred back lest he bite in return. She cried out in amazed, delirious disbelief, grimacing and smiling all at once, parched mouth seeking Dracula's hungry, wet kiss, his crocodile-wrestler's neck, shoulders, chest. At last, she climaxed, her ruby lips forming a satisfied 'o'.

"I'm cumming, Vlad, I'm cumming," she whispered aloud in his ear.

She lay still a long while, too excited to be true. Vlad lay atop of her, still inside; breathing heavily, his black, sweat-dampened locks straying into Voica's open mouth. She sucked them. She couldn't believe the beating of her heart, the slick, sweaty fire of her skin. Her breasts heaved under his weight, goosebumps forming between her bosom. Vlad lowered his lips tenderly to her chest, kissing the sweat from his paramour's cooling neck, then her breast. Voica groaned aloud. She stroked his shoulder tenderly, at once knowing all her fears to be untrue, for a better lover she could not imagine! What had happened to the horrible tales old wives scolded into their impressionable, young female charges? The sex act was spoken of in hushed, embarrassed tones (if at all), too traumatic to be spoken of fondly. Many matrons had been twelve-year-old brides mated with men thrice their age, the girls not even in puberty yet. Slav, misogynist clan patriarchs of eastern Europe had long decreed it so, bigamists since the time of Attila the Hun whose hordes had swept into Russia from the Punjab of India (with untold scores of impressed Hindus), eventually merging with the already Indo-Europeanised Goidelic/Iranian Scythians, Thracians (Albanians), Slavs, Indo-Germanic Teutons, and Greco-Roman civilisations. Young girls had once been sacrificed as concubines in the Scythians' kurgan mounds to accompany their Aryan masters into the Afterlife, the *Tir na 'og*. (Land of Everlasting Youth.) Voica thought of this now with a chill, recalling grisly stories about Prydainic sacrifices of their enemies in huge wicker-men to combat their foes, who challenged the Picts' dominion on three fronts across Europe and Asia Minor, origin of steel: the Germans, High and Low dialects; intrusive, archaic *Euskara* (Greater Cimbria's oldest nemesis: invaders from the east, driven off and emasculated after millenniums of savage, tribal warfare; and, later, allied with Rome); the *Gwyddels* (Goidels), or Land Thieves, cattle reivers at heart; and the later Greeks, then Romans. Sex had long ceased to be a subject of thrill and innocence. Yet Voica had felt no pain, no humiliating bleeding nor beating for her inferiority. Afterwards it was not uncommon for menstruating girls to be locked up in earth closets for days on end, in the Judeo-Christian fashion.

Cautious, Vlad rolled over, out of breath. His lower back ached. Moonlit dust-spores frolicked above the canopied bed, a full moon glowing high in an Oriental sky. Voica's head lolled against his shoulder. She smiled coyly with sexual gratification, running her fingers through her wild hair ecstatically; purring like a vixen, her eyes aglow. She watched Vlad's face, watched his dark green eyes sparkle in the moonlight. She was *madly in love* with him, Voica suddenly realised. No stranger irony could her world encompass. The room was lit by neither candle, rush, nor torch now, the wind having snuffed the wall sconces.

Draughts moaned spookily in the sleeping great tower. Voica listened to the sounds of the night, her head resting on Vlad Dracula's hairy chest. He stroked her hair lazily, murmuring eccentrically to himself, counting obscure bats clinging upside-down from the corner of his massive, master bedchamber. Voica covered her mouth, suppressing a shriek of terror as she sighted the huge, furry, obnoxious, leathery-winged fruit bats, harmless rodents which preferred mice and fruit nectar over human blood. (!) The ceiling was of the finest, Italianate rococo plaster, moulded into cherubs pointing their arrows at Voica's bare breast; fur blankets barely covering her. Spikes of exquisite stucco hung from the darkened, ivory-white ceiling like stalactite. Vlad's own red and purple dragon-heraldry coiled and frolicked up in the receding darkness.

"There are ten bats in this room," Vlad murmured, "Josef, Tudur, Caltai, Eduordo, Aaron, Caltuna, Moses, Lucifer, Endina and Decibal. They are my pets, and are friendly. See how peaceful they sleep? Remember not to disturb them while they slumber, lest they bite, for the furry rodents are ill-disposed to petting at such short notice."

Voica giggled, unable to resist.

"Do not laugh, *domnişoară*. They are my pets; part of my royal menagerie. I have trained them over a seven year span."

"Really?" Voica raised her head, eyeing Vlad admiringly. "Indeed."

Voica gaped, unable to believe her ears. *'How could any man as powerful, wealthy, and handsome as he be so lonely as to befriend bats?'* she wondered. Wasn't he afraid of rabies?

She sank languidly into the dreamy, down-stuffed bed, half sprawled on Vlad's outstretched, war-scarred body, still smiling. Traced a line of deep, stern wrinkles on Dracula's face, wondering how this barbarous, long-haired Wallachian berserker could be such a fantastic lover between the sheets.

"Did you enjoy what we experienced tonight?" asked Vlad suddenly. He had switched back to Dacian, meandering in and out of the two, unrelated, Romanian languages at will.

"Ie, I did, sire; much to my surprise."

"You were a virgin."

"Ydy. I—"

"You've never had a lover?" Voica detected a note of scepticism in Vlad's query.

"*Nage*. Honest, sire, I have never. I did not bleed as much as I'd thought, but I was chaste. I have been faithful only to my father."

"Very well, then, I believe you." Vlad paused, then spoke again. "Woica?"

"Hm?"

"Call me *Wlad*. Or Wladislaus. Or better yet, call me *Cadwladwaladr*."

Voica laughed softly. "*O'r gorau.*" (Okay.)

It began to rain. Dark clouds had rolled in over the western Bihor mountains as they lay in each other's arms, in a daze. Vlad shifted his head, watching torrents of rain cascade down outside his single, bubble-glazed, gothic window to the four-poster's right. Streaks of glossy rain poured down the bubbled glass, occasionally lit by wild lightning flashes. Thunder grumbled overhead; a low, throaty growl building into a crescendo. Then a bark. A thunderclap of unusual ferocity directly above shook the great tower, booming throughout its echoing passages. Vlad momentarily raised his head until the explosion subsided, half-fearing the masonry might come crashing down, or perhaps a direct lightning hit. Translucent, Damask-silk drapes hung from the arched canopy, open where he peeped through the curtain towards the blustery night. Frills added a sumptuous grandeur to the purple bed drapes. A high, fluted tympanum (shell) acted as a headboard; fragrant, polished cedar of Lebanon (from the Greek island of Cyprus).

Voica reached out, softly tickling Vlad's chin with her small right hand, giggling girlishly, appealingly as she stroked his smooth, beardless under-chin. He responded with a throaty chuckle, snatching Voica's hand away, briskly rubbing her freckled, ivory smooth, rounded shoulder with his left hand.

Vlad sat up, whisking closed the mauve, diaphanous drapes to block the cool, moist, Transylvanian night air, pulling Voica up with him in a crouched, claustrophobic seated position beneath the four-poster bed's bright, orange canopy. He leaned forward slowly, tantalizingly, tilting his head; kissing her expectant lips as a youth might kiss a fellow virgin. Their lips met shyly, tentatively; squelching liquidly in the midnight silence; nipping. Voica tensed, excited, her slender arms going about Vlad's shoulders. Her lips parted ecstatically, moist, cushiony, forbidden fruit railed at by Christian monks for centuries. She groaned aloud, moaning, crooning as Vlad softly, wickedly squeezed her breasts. She withdrew from his kiss with borage-blue, crescent eyes of wonder, unfastened plaits straying between her bustline. Vlad kissed her again, softly sucking Voica's upper labia, tasting her wine-scented breath. Again she pulled back, tentatively darting out her tongue to meet his own, mammoth, thrusting tongue. She moaned aloud. Her whole body trembled, quaking, an earth-shattering climax threatening to prematurely end this heavenly intimacy. Vlad lowered his face, dipping his tongue between her fabulous cleavage. She licked her lips in rapture; cradling herself for his pleasure. *"I think I'm going to cum,"* Voica whispered in his ear, rubbing his nose with her own; tongue darting into his earlobe. Wisely, Vlad lifted her heaving buttocks up from his thigh, taking her even as she sat spread-eagled on his lap, facing him.

This time it was even more incredible. Voica smiled languidly, matching Vlad's rhythm, crooning softly as he sucked on her neck. She cried out softly, ecstatically, clamping her eyes tight. Her smile widened, a jester's smile, laughing giddily as she shook her head wildly and rode Vlad like a rocking horse. At last, he cupped her soft, glorious, fleshy derrière as Voica exploded with a scream welling from the top of her lungs.

Servants and guests stalked their lonely chambers, grumbling, cursing Dracula for torturing another innocent wench. Torches fluttered in the hands of worried manservants pacing the castle passageways. Up above, on the fourth floor, Vlad Ţepeş was skewering his gorgeous, jealousy-inspiring, favourite wench as she experienced multiple orgasm. She was his first woman in six years, so he had a lot of pent-up sexual frustration to vent on her willing, young, Daco-Romanian/Hungarian body.

Voica lay back, exhausted and drenched in oily sweat, exhaling loudly as Vlad collapsed upon her. She hoped she hadn't awakened the entire castle.

"Errrgh," Voica's throat rattling with hoarse satisfaction. Her lungs hurt. Her throat was parched and sore. Even Vlad's semen could not appease her thirst. As if reading her mind, the voivode raised a crystal goblet of water from a rosewood, rolltop bureau, coaxing his surprising mistress to swallow the blessed holy water from his chalice. Voica was immediately, deliciously aware of the sinful blasphemy of this act, swallowing the water even as she maintained a loving, twinkling gaze on Vlad's bemused green stare.

"You are a very hungry vixen," croaked Vlad at last. Like a satyr, he sought her lips once more, the years of enforced celibacy having suddenly given him the staying power of a stallion. Voica chuckled throatily, nodding as he possessed her body, her globular breasts nodding in time to Vlad's patient rhythm.

She cried out, twisting and turning; writhing in ecstasy as he pinned her to the dreamy, undulating, King-size bed. Voica reached out, clutching the shapely, balustrade-like bedposts with both hands as she arched her back, catching Vlad's shocked, gratified stare with a triumphant, passionate gaze of fire and watery-blue conquest as Vlad Țepeș ejaculated deep inside her now-impregnated womb. Afterwards, he descended between her soft thighs, penetrating her dreams for months to come with the fond memory of Vlad's dark head between her thighs, kissing her pubic hair.

It was a fleeting, doomed paradise.

They lay back in each other's arms, listening to the sound of rainwater dripping from the great *donjon's* overhanging, lead, griffin spouts.

****

Voica stared in bewilderment at the portcullis blocking the damp, dark, musty entrance to Castle Dracula's cellars. As of yet no one had told her the cellar/dungeons were off-limits to all—except for prisoners. Only Vlad and his gruesome henchmen were allowed into these rat-infested, subterranean cells. Turks and Romanians, Frenchmen, Italians, Venetians, Spaniards, Portuguese, Genoans, Greeks and Persians all languished within the ever-dark, diseased dungeons. It was the horrible price they paid for lending money and arms to Turks, or for their conversion to Islam. (Thus, the *bourgeois* merchants of eastern Europe fought back in the only way they knew how; false propaganda, blackballing Vlad's name.)

Suddenly a looming, cowled figure arose from the steps below, causing Voica to cry out and jerk back involuntarily.

Vlad stood there behind the rusted, crusted iron bars (remnants of an earlier, archaic fortalice), clothes fringed with fur; dressed splendidly as usual with a wide, green, alligator-leather band around his hair encrusted with brilliant gems, and a colourful plume of feathers sticking up from his high forehead. He was as surprised as Voica was. His eyes glowed with an unholy, triumphant fire. Lord Dracula's silk cape shimmered around him like an Ethereal presence. Clearing his throat, he unlocked the interior, swinging yett, his hand heart-pullingly close to Voica's as it rested on the corroded, iron bars. It was raining; a steady, monotonous drizzle beneath a glowering, blowing, charcoal-grey daylight sky. Vlad swung the inner yett towards him, barking a command as Voica started in fright. But he was not addressing her, directing his cantankerous wrath at his dim-witted servant, Igor. The lumbering, hunch-backed goon crept forward up the dark steps clutching a wavering torch, leering gruesomely, questioningly at Vlad with a horrible, pale-blue eye, the other permanently shut, puffy, and grotesque. His staring, watery eye was huge, big and round as a walnut, giving Voica the creeps as it settled on her face. Premature wrinkles marred the midget's brown, sweaty face. Vlad had a predilection for dwarfs and misfits of all kinds. Many were servants in high positions, highly irregular indeed. (Especially in a medieval, European society which used such outcasts as zoo displays, slave labour or—worse—framed as innocent, scapegoat criminals, executed on the spot without trial, or murdered at birth.) It was Dracula's fondness for misfits and keen understanding of wild beasts which enhanced his terrible reputation as a sorcerer, a warlock. Vlad owned large kennels of tamed wolfdogs at Castle Dracula, Hunedoara, Rodna, and Colteşti. Voica glanced at him in surprise as his henchman worked the portcullis-lever, grunting with effort as the chain bar rumbled, the small, secondary, iron/wood portcullis rising slowly with an infuriating squeal as Vlad stared impassively across the cross-hatched bars at Voica's timorous stare. Strangely enough, she still feared him, in a weak-kneed, primeval sort of way. She knew not why, for he'd never raised a hand to her.

Nary a word in anger, either; nor cold-cast eye. Voica couldn't even imagine disobeying Vlad, He Who Commands Obedience.

He stepped out into the muddied courtyard, only inches away from her as the grotesque, hunch-backed henchman scurried away down the cellar steps, the bobbing light receding with him.

"You are soaked," droned Vlad, not moving to touch her. He still had the memory of his latest victim's eyeballs in the palm of his hand bouncing about in his mind.

"I—I was lonely," stammered Voica, mesmerised by Vlad's gaze, tracking his eyes with her own. She pulled her cloak closer, her bones numb. "I came looking for you, and I enjoy a walk in the rain."

"Are you bored?" asked Vlad. "I can find something for you to do."

Voica shook her head, suddenly fearful, lest Dracula's personality change now that he'd bedded her. But his eyes showed no malice. Indeed, no emotion at all.

"Come," Vlad said at last, breaking the spell. "Ere we die of pneumonia out here," leading her by the arm back to the looming, gothic great keep. Rooks soared against the dark, blustery sky, flapping together as the ravenous flock perched on the tallest of Castle Dracula's many watchtowers. The 175-ft. conical watchtower straddled the spur, its splayed masonry plummeting down to meet the rough, natural granite of Little Poenari mountain. The slim, smooth tower vaguely resembled a cylindrical pencil, a monstrous, fluted, mechanical flying machine of the future ready to explode into the sky, topped with a bluish-grey, slate, fish-scale, conical witch's hat. Below the parapet, a characteristic, box-like, machicolated latrine chute over the precipice provided a convenient toilet. The keep's lofty, unassailable lookout-tower boasted only two, narrow windows in its entire height, one in the middle, one on top; thick, round walls staring out across the wild, picturesque Argeş valley, the spectacular Făgăras foothills of fir-forested southern Transylvania.

Arm in arm, they entered the donjon's twelve-foot-thick walls, climbing a steep flight of stairs inside the quadrangular, keystone-arched forebuilding. However, Vlad halted halfway up, opening a thick, metal-banded wooden door with a set of large skeleton keys tied to his tunic's belt, emerging onto the basement's vaulted first floor; drawing Voica by the hand into the dark, cavernous chamber.

"This is the intermediate, or above-ground, floor," echoed Vlad eerily, expertly lighting a pine torch with his flint. "Below is thy family mausoleum, two storeys down." He shut the massive door, the hollow keep echoing with its reverberating *slam,* turning to face her with a mischievous smile on his lips. "An ingenious storeroom, it is. Immediately below are the keep's grain stores, albeit on flagstone. This is the heart of thy castle; from here, all levels of the keep—and the castle proper—can be traversed via secret passages honeycombed into these thick walls which, except for my custodian, only I know about. Cleverly concealed, you see; they could elude a master engineer's inspection! Come. I shall show you the luggies—my spy closets! From these I can monitor my servants, detect which be traitors and which loyal. But I have brought you here into this empty, musty, man-made brick cavern for another reason, my love. For I have a burning secret, a vengeful joy inside my heart which yearns to be told!" Vlad leaned forward conspiratorially. "Also, words for your ears alone, concerning a certain fiend who dealt me wrongly, humiliatingly, many years ago," Vlad whispered. His voice echoed cryptically off the walls, still booming long after his tone had dropped to a concealing, cunning whisper. He took her hand once more, leading Voica towards a menacing, Perpendicular Gothic passage leading up into the bowels of the keep. Voica's heart lurched, reluctantly allowing him to lead her into the clammy, dank, stone corridor. Vlad held a flickering torch, treading cautiously up a narrow, ramp-like tunnel burrowing deep within the donjon.

The tunnel made a sharp right-angle turn, ending suddenly at a blank, stone wall. Vlad turned to her, winking, then reached up to light one of the twin torches in its bronze wall-bracket. Voica watched in disbelief as he levered the flaming torch sideways, listening, bewildered, as a loud grating noise, a rumble of stone on stone, filled the corridor. "Heat activated. Inside this wall-sconce is a socket connected to the torch; push the lever to the right, the secret passage opens," droned Vlad, watching pleased as the concealed door rumbled open, revealing a black maw as the huge, stone lintel swung inward. The smoke from his fluttering pine-torch wafted in her face as the musty, mildewy passageway's dead air rushed out of the tomb-like mezzanine.

"Beyond is the mausoleum, below us," Vlad murmured, "where I shall someday rest undead." He laughed cryptically, his deep, weird laughter echoing eerily down the length of the dark, musty corridor. He took her hand, leading her forward, stooping, finally halting at a steep, narrow, spiral stairwell inside one of the keep's thick, outer buttress's walls. He motioned her to follow, starting up a slick, treacherous, limestone stair.

Voica held out her left hand tentatively, recoiling with a shudder as she came into contact with the slimy, cobwebbed walls flanking her shoulders. She felt claustrophobic; never had she encountered such a miniscule, uncomfortable chamber, so cramped she could barely see what treacherous turns spiralled above. (It seemed to her like nothing more than a redundant crawlspace, a work crew's hasty effort to cover a botched job.) Vlad literally had to inch his broad form sideways up the spiral stair, his barrel chest, broad shoulders making the task almost comically ludicrous. He held onto a thick, hempen rope, hauling himself awkwardly up the black abyss whilst clutching a guttering torch in his left hand. The rough, scratchy hemp burnt his palm, prickly and dry from years of disuse; in fact, considerably older than the castle itself. Yet Vlad did not flinch, inching upward his immaculately attired, cape-cloaked frame despite gravity's downward pull.

The tower's slick steps were awkward, uneven, blackened with bat guano and knee-high; greasy deathtraps for the hasty or unaware. Four servants had died since Castle Dracula's inception, foolishly exploring this secret stairwell and its myriad of passages. (Their cause of death, nonetheless, unknown.) Vlad had admonished his staff furiously, hoping they'd eventually realise their peril. In any case, those who knew the secret would not be leaving the castle. Not ever. At last, Vlad halted, stepping inside a narrow, stone cubicle. He pressed his eye to a small, round, slanting peephole, peering gleefully down into Castle Dracula's busy great hall. Servants scurried back and forth, chattering hurriedly, attending to the morrow's oxen feast. The soldiers of the realm would be gathering belatedly at superlative Castle Dracula-on-the-Argeș, to submit their oaths of fealty to Vlad and his holy, blasphemous Cross. In the various courtyards and baileys, they would practice their drills under Dracula's stern eye, throwing javelins and whirling their hefty Dalcatian pole-axes about or honing their marksmanship with novel, mandatory longbows, composite bows, *arquebus* (risking having one explode in one's face!), or deadly, trigger-operated, windlass-loaded crossbows. Each had best pray their marksmanship was as accurate as Lord Dracula's. They were the partisans, unpaid, patriotic *villeins* who formed the very backbone of Prince Dracula's army during times of war.

"Look." Vlad propelled her toward the peephole, grinning with morbid satisfaction as she peeked through the tiny, circular, thick-walled peephole's chamber. It was also a ventilation shaft, widening toward the end of its chamber into a round, two-foot gap above the hall, unsuspected by the servants. Like a kaleidoscope, colours and shapes drifted dizzyingly in and out of Voica's view. Her palms were sweating, aghast at what the servants below were saying, listening uncertainly to the excited mixed German-Hungarian accents. Puzzled, she pulled back to catch Vlad's amused gaze.

"They gossip like shrews," Vlad murmured, his fervent Daco-Wallachian accent close to Voica's ear. "They gossip about us, about our wicked, nighttime bed games."

Voica still distrusted Vlad, somehow suspecting he might devise to do away with her here in this hidden chamber. Only Vlad and his butler had keys to this secret stairway (an escape route down into Poenari's mountain tunnel), themselves hanging on Vlad's coarse rope-belt cinching his silk pantaloons along with a multitude of large, heavy skeleton keys for the whole of the castle. They jangled ceaselessly against Țepeș' ceremonial sword of State (handy for decapitating wrongdoers on a whim) or against his swordbelt's buckle, the silvered falchion hanging from an old, leathern strap around his left thigh, where connecteth its brittle, rawhide scabbard. Vlad had yet to assign a castellan to the great castle, seriously considering Gheorghini Calova, count of Banat.

"Why—why do you bring me here?" Voica asked fearfully.

Vlad raised a shaggy eyebrow in amusement, noting the fear in her voice. "Why do you think? Do you believe I mean to harm you here, *doamnă?*" Voica looked away, her cheeks suddenly flushed.

Vlad tilted her chin, turning Voica's head to meet his level, piercing gaze. "I have a secret—one I would not wish my servants to hear—a secret I shall hold you, *dynes*, to secrecy. Within these underground dungeons, *benyw*, languishes a bloodthirsty Turkish whipmaster whom I'd had reason to hate once, ransomed to me by our 'Lord of the Universe', Sultan Mehmed Çelebi himself, can you believe it!" Vlad snickered cynically. "The whipmaster it was who caused these terrible scars on my back you so marvelled at, he who haunted my nightmares all these years. At last, I have exacted vengeance! Thy foe hails from Baghdad, ransomed to me by a famous Slovakian bounty hunter with Mehmed's consent, if you can believe it! He shall hang first by his thumbs, then languish on the breaking wheel, then, at my whim, he shall be impaled for horsewhipping a future Prince of Wallachia!"

Voica turned away, unable to bear Dracula's insane rantings. Vlad seized her chin, forcing her to face him.

"Still you pine for them?! Turkish infidels, defilers of your country, madmen who ride to spread their Crescent like plague! These ghazis who enter Prince Dracula's country will surely die, each and all! And you, my love, had best not hold your nose or turn away at the stench of their impalement. Do you understand?"

Voica nodded tearfully, fearful, stepping away.

Again Vlad seized her arm, propelling her towards him. Suddenly hugging her tight.

"Do not go away angry, *llances*," whispered Vlad in Voica's exposed ear. He stroked her hair, cheek to cheek, as she wrapped her trembling arms about his neck. "Your flux," Vlad murmured soothingly, "has it stopped? Has your morning sickness abated?"

Voica nodded, feeling Vlad's relief course through his body like a resounding sigh of redemption. "It has come at last, the son I crave." He offered a whispered prayer to the Old Gods, holding Voica's slim, buxom body tightly, possessively. Sated, the two lovers—unlawfully wedded, and pariahs to the Church—turned to creep back down Castle Dracula's abysmal, hellish stair.

****

Voica could not bear to look. Another Turkish ghazi was roughly hoisted up into the air on a winch, then brutally rammed down upon a sharpened, charcoal-hardened, wooden stake held expertly in a Romanian's calloused hands. Four burly men held the bound ghazi from a bier as a fifteen-foot stake pierced his ribs with a sudden gush of scarlet, glistening blood. An unearthly scream rent the midday air, rising above the din of cheering onlookers. A knot of sheepskin-clad men hoisted the top-heavy stake up vertical as the impaled wretch screamed incessantly, crying aloud to Allah even as the blood-smeared stake was secured at its base with A-frame, wooden braces. A horrible stench wafted across the cobbled courtyard, for some of the stakes had punctured ghazis' stomachs or intestines, sickening Voica as another victim's belly—a bearded Janissary's—was ruptured upon a skewer. Her guts lurched, threatening to spew out the gothic lancet-window and into the paved courtyard seventy feet below. Prince Vlad stood far below, directly in the line of Voica's vomit should she lose control of her wits. He glared up at his hapless victims, no remorse disturbing his psychotic, ordered brain. She hated him yet loved him, for Vlad was a paradox; stern and merciless in battle or rough justice, loving and tender towards his passionate paramour. She shuddered at the thought of herself languishing up on those stakes should Vlad turn against her. Voica swore that must never happen.

Dracula's mistress stood aghast, visibly shaken; the man whom she'd pledged herself, body and soul, stood below, *clapping and gloating like a shrouded, winged demon:* His eyes aglow with an unhealthy, sadistic pleasure. The malevolent look of madness and smug certainty, the jutting chin of a demigod, made Voica Nyireghází shudder.

She stood alone at the window, watching, horrified, as hundreds of Turkish ghazis, sipahis, Janissaries and Azabs garbed from head to foot in pristine white linen, their dark heads topped with matching, coiled white turbans, were skewered mercilessly, horribly, slowly by hordes of gleeful Wallachian thugs up to their elbows in Turkish blood. The Wallachians' sheepskin, cream-white vests turned crimson as Voica watched, blood spurting every direction from punctured arteries and hearts. Some of the impaled died immediately, others lingering, lingering, stakes penetrating neither vital organs nor major blood vessels. (Others, such as local Pashas once stationed along the Bulgarian border until captured by Vlad's *chetniks*, had the ignoble fate of having had stakes driven up their posteriors for ordering the extermination of entire Romanian border villages.) Mouths gaped in horrific, astonished, frozen pain as Vlad Death's prisoners of war were speedily dispatched. Vlad looked on with a vulpine, evil grin, eyes twinkling as his enemies paid the terrible price for raping HIS women, HIS children, HIS siblings, or looting HIS towns HIS cities and HIS villages. Dracula had no mercy. And no mercy for weak, caring fools. Voica clutched the four-foot-thick stone windowsill, her eyes streaming with pitying tears. No one else was in the bedchamber (although Cirstian had hinted he might drop by to make sure Voica witnessed the travesties). Vlad would never understand; she had not witnessed Romanian girls raped en masse, sawn in half, or carried off to Islamic harems as he had. She had never been horsewhipped, beaten senseless by infidels. Never experienced the infamous Chinese Water Torture, or had pins and needles stuck in her toes for fun (as he had). Vlad would despise her for sympathising with these human garbage. Voica's hands tightened against the masonry, her long fingernails pressing hard, finger joints vainly trying to gouge a piece out of the sill. She sobbed cravenly. Voica raised a hand, pressing her mouth in helpless terror. She wore neither veil nor wimple, as was customary with the Norman/Saxon masters of western and eastern Europe; her tresses plaited in archaic Dacian fashion.

The atrocities had started at daybreak this morning.

Dracula had been pacing up and down the antechamber's hall last night, anticipating the morrow's fête. He must have sumptuous food for his guests and courtiers while they watched (horrified) his Gypsy goons chop his victims' bodies to pieces, yeah, impaling, maiming, and scalding the vanquished Janissaries, foragers, and traitors. Then Lord Dracula had come to bed, ravishing his bewildered, passionate mistress as she lay unaware of the daylight scene to come.

Vlad had been gone when Voica awoke this morning. It was daybreak; the sun just creeping up in the mountainous east. She had whisked back the mauve, Damask bedcurtains, eyes smarting from the orange blaze illuminating the bedchamber. She felt weak, queasy, vomiting shamefully in a chamber-pot while standing shivering in a translucent pink shift. Her bust had been exposed, goosebumps growing below her swannish neck as the cool midsummer air assailed Vlad's master bedchamber, stark in the early morning sunlight. Dew coated the foliage rioting for space on the mountainside of the keep, dark green plants sprawling wildly before the first freak snowfalls of far-off September ended their cycle. Mist poured through the unshuttered, open, gothic window, cool and refreshing though bitterly cold on Voica's bare skin. She rubbed her arms, pacing, then headed toward the garderobe down the hall…

And that was when she saw the first, few, impaled cadavers as she glanced idly out of the corridor's south window. Voica screamed; prudently, quickly covering her mouth lest the castle attendants awaken. She stared, sickened, gaping at the grisly sight beneath Castle Dracula's window. Dark, sightless, uprolled eyes stared fiendishly up at her from forty-foot stakes (although most were lower), as if accusing, mouths contorted in twisted leers, their huge, yellowed teeth mawing wide.

No one else had stood down in the cobbled courtyard. Vlad Dracula was nowhere to be seen, nor his grim, ever-present henchmen. Voica searched the shifting tendrils of mist below the open gothic window for signs of movement, seeing none. A fireball sun hovered above one of the D-shaped eastern curtain towers, casting a long black shadow of death over the voivode's hideous, Renaissance castle.

She stood now beneath a hot noon summer sun, recalling this morning's nightmarish memory as if it had occurred only moments ago. But Vlad Țepeș' gory spectacle still towered below the lead-framed, bubbled glass window on forty- or fifty-foot stakes, increasing by the hour, assailing Voica's delicate sensibilities with the appalling stench of ruptured innards. (The lowly *ghazi* were on smaller stakes, denoting their status.) She looked away with disgust as one of Vlad's henchmen began chopping to pieces a dead body, lopping off its limbs with grim, lustreless eyes. Gypsy eyes. Deep within her thumping heart, Voica knew she could hardly blame this Gypsy miscreant for chopping off these once-living Turks' arms, heads, hands, and legs. Who was she to judge the *Szgany*? Certainly they had reason to treat life so casually, for had the Turks and Persians not paid Vikings then Venetians then Saxons solid gold for Slavic slaves. (Slav—Latin, Norse; "slave.") Before them, it was the Oriental Huns, Avars, Szeklers, Mongols, Greco-Romans, and Tatars whom had captured and sold Slavs throughout their Asiatic-Mediterranean empires.

Men scrambled below, loading dismembered body parts into wheelbarrows then hauling the blood-oozing limbs toward a great, thatch-covered wagon sitting beneath Castle Dracula's gaping gatehouse. A dozen ragged, motley-clothed *Szgany* stood idly beside the wagon, dwarfed by the massive, checkered-stone gatehouse's twin, polygonal-plan towers. Menacing, overhanging murder-galleries perpetually guarded both sides of the portcullis grooves, such machicolation unusual for existing on the bailey's interior as well—indicative of Vlad's paranoia. Above the loitering, swarthy, plaid-tartan-clothed Gypsies, notched Italianate merlons and rounded, Slavic battlements overlooked the thriving, Transylvanian hinterlands; a land of rocky pinnacles and heavy forest.

Voica's stomach threatened to heave overboard as men began chopping off the heads of Vlad's victims. Crimson blood gushed forth, pumping like artesian wells, splattering the faces and woolskin vests of misguided Romanian patriots. She covered her mouth with a shaky hand, watching spell-bound as another ghazi was hoisted into the air to a chorus of cheers and whistles. Much jeering accompanied the raucous revelry. The murdered, impaled bodies were being brought down for dismemberment even as live, kicking, shrieking men were being raised aloft on their poles. Blood streaked a miniscule forest of stakes crowding Castle Dracula's 100-ft.-diameter inner ward, dripping in globs down the impaling stakes crammed even against the spectacular, ashlar-cornered, balconied great hall betwixt keep and adjacent outbuildings. Topping the tallest stake, well over seventy-five feet above—on a massive, framework pedestal—Vlad's Indian nemesis (stake protruding through his mouth) who'd whipped him so many years ago bowed incongruously at his punctured buttocks, dead since early dawn—sold out by his own master, Mehmed Çelebi II. Which proved also that Vlad and the Sultan of Turkey, bitterest enemies, could still do business. Occasionally, a caped, sheepskin-clad troop of soldiers hauled a struggling Turk from the dungeons, preparing another sharpened stake. Across the river valley, hundreds more of the unfortunate Ottoman captives were at this moment being impaled on Poenari—Hill of Pain, or herded downriver toward the secret entrance to Vlad's citadel high above the Argeş river, marched unceremoniously up a steep, subterranean, limestone tunnel towards Castle Dracula. Voica was immediately, unbiddenly reminded of the gruesome funerary rites doled out to suspected, reanimated corpses rumoured to walk the night by superstitious Orthodox peasants who ought to have known better. She had witnessed such desecration, watched siblings and family of deceased loved ones shed pitiful tears, wailing, shredding their mourning veils in anguish as the Orthodox priest hammered a stake into the corpse's heart, stuffed the dead girl's mouth with garlic, then decapitated the undead *strigoi* with a sharp shovel. All this had taken place at night—Walpurgis Night—inside the gothic cemetery on the outskirts of Schassberg. A host of fascinated bystanders had gathered for the gruesome ceremony, morbidly whispering as the blasphemous 'Christian' rites were enacted. Voica had known the girl since childhood, though Alcuna had been several years her senior. She had perished in that dark year of '58, the year Vlad had brutally crushed the Bistrita faction. Yellow fever had taken many more such victims, as had small-pox and the dreaded buboe. (Not everyone witnessing the *strigoi's* dispatch had been certain of the girl's technical death.)

    Suddenly Vlad sat down to eat, seating himself at the head of a long, oaken trestle table sited in the middle of the cobbled courtyard, its coloured, diapered pavement chillingly incongruous. He reclined at his red-velvet-draped, royal throne: a tall, opulently polished, black oak monstrosity carved with rioting foliage and vulgar, writhing figures roasting in the fires of Hell. Blood spread out across the cobbles at his feet like glistening, red water. Ţepeş' unwilling companions joined him, grumbling quietly as they sat down to feast. Vlad clapped his hands majestically, summoning his royal chefs. A horde of white-robed Asians rushed into the courtyard, exiting the Renaissance outbuildings with silver trays laden with roast beef, whole suckling pig, veal, venison cutlets, pheasant, ptarmigan, mutton, goose, and duck. The major-domo raised a silver, rounded lid, lowering the jewel-inlaid platter for Dracula's fussy inspection. Vlad glanced up, pleased, addressing the Chinaman in his own Mandarin dialect (which he knew a smattering of). The Oriental bowed, bobbing, gushing with Pekinese gratitude. Vlad's austere companions grimaced, their appetites non-existent.

    One by one, the Oriental chefs filled the guests' golden plates. Vegetables, too, were introduced, hidden within sumptuous gravies as if an afterthought; Brussels sprouts, green wax beans, lentils, peas, maize, carrots, beets, and stuffed, glazed cabbage. Chow Mein, too, introduced, courtesy of the ancient Shang dynasty, full of delicious bamboo shoots (cultivated in Transylvania by Vlad's Chinese chefs, horticulturalists *extraordinaire)*, rice, and various other goodies not normally available in sub-alpine Transylvania. Stir-fries abounded, in a delicious, exotic glaze. Vlad nodded graciously at the four clean-shaven Mandarins and his seated retainers, boyars, courtiers, and councilmen. Well over fifty men lined either side of the tremendous oak trestle, their wives and children thankfully absent.

The midday sun beat down upon the gloomy revellers' heads, though unable to warm the men's hearts. A glaring, deep blue, cloudless sky vaulted the horizon; fringed by a motley assortment of orange/red-tinted, exotic Japanese maples intermixed with hardy Transylvanian spruce-fir. The thimble-shaped castle keep loomed behind Vlad's banquet table and slightly to its right; sinisterly battlemented, *chemin-de-rondes* covering all sides, including the slender, twin, mountainside buttresses and gloomy, protruding watchtower.

The men began to eat. They proceeded to stuff the exotic, sumptuous, Eastern foods into their dry mouths and down their throats, tasting bile as they stared up at the unavoidable human cadavers skewered before them and encircling their banquet table, eyes rolled up into their skulls. Lips were curled back from mawing teeth. Ebbing moans still floated down from the grisly stakes, chilling the blood of Vlad's mortified vassals. Blackbirds argued noisily with rooks or crows over the spoils, even now picking out the Turks' eyes, whether dead or not, before flapping back to their stark, treetop roosts to fight over their treats. Large blue butterflies fluttered past the horrified revellers' noses. The boyars, courtiers, ealdormen and knights ate hastily, eyes lowered; they could hardly wait to finish, to exit the behemoth table so Vlad's multitudinous, common soldiers—a dozen (all heroes) from every regiment of the Realm!—could have their turn at the feast. A billowing, blindingly white dragon against a violet, silk background spat crimson fire atop the great keep's flag mast. Servants leaned out from cloister-like, three-light windows and balustraded, machicolated balconies, staring morbidly, fascinated, at Vlad's hellish banquet far, far below. On the steep, receding steps to the main audience chamber/great hall, courtiers and soldiers-of-fortune alike gaped.

Vlad enjoyed the feast. His palate unhindered.

****

On sunny days, Vlad took Voica on high-spirited hunts. His finest, most obedient Lithuanian prancing ponies were chosen for he and his mistress's unhurried leisure. They hawked, watching Ţepeş' envy-inspiring peregrine falcons soaring high above the valley's pine forest. The master of Făgăras' impressive kennels accompanied him, Dachshunds, alaunts, greyhounds, bloodhounds, terriers, wolfdogs and mastiffs happy to be let out of their iron-barred cages. At times, Voica could forget that Vlad was a psychopathic mass-murderer. Even if his victims were mostly Muslims and devout Roman Catholics, she could never turn a blind eye to Vlad's horrendous atrocities. And yet, as the Carpathians' balmy, summer days grew shorter, she felt her inexplicable love for Vlad the Bad grow stronger as they galloped throughout the spruce-fir forests and leafy gullies. He taught her how to ride a warhorse like a man. The stags were plentiful, great, proud-antlered beasts silhouetted against moonlit crags. Vlad hunted even as evening drew forth, for he was a creature of the night, his lady at his side as they traversed the Transylvanian Alps and impressive foothills with Vlad's retainers guarding their voivode whilst wielding flaming torches. Never had he cause to raise a hand toward his submissive, faithful lover. On full-moon-lit nights, they might halt, share a passionate kiss or warm embrace among the dewy Făgăras foothills. The rushing, fish-scented Argeş twinkled under midnight, starlit moonlight, twisting and turning its way throughout the grassy mountains and scrubby open hinterlands of southern Transylvania like a true, German river route. Indeed, it was this watery passageway (along with the once-blue Danube) which allowed the Teutonic invaders to settle Romania and perch their lofty, forbidding, curtain-walled watchtowers or toll castles upon Transylvania's winter-darkened mountains. Like teenage lovers discovering the first bloom of springtime love, Vlad and Voica caressed and exchanged passionate French kisses, wildly making love beside the swift-flowing, reed-banked Argeş. Frolicking in the rushes, rolling, laughing, teasing ceaselessly, whispering sweet nothings in each other's ear. Their leather-clad guardsmen (stationed discreetly in the bushes) exchanged wry comments and bawdy jokes. But like all good things, even love must come to pass and perish like a wicker man's flames.

It was mid-week at the citadel when Vlad heard word of the renewed Turkish onslaught from neutral Bosnia-Herzegovina. The Sultan had crossed the Iron Gates (the great chain barring access to the Danube's upper courses), towing barges across the river-canyon and storming southwestern Wallachia. Within a fortnight, Vlad ordered his bondsmen to assemble at Brân and Hunedŏara castles for preliminary war exercises. Women and children, old and sick, were once more corralled on the overgrown, alpine trails toward the protective stockades of northern Transylvania, near Tîrgsor and Tîrgu Jiu, Hungarian suzerainty.

Monastery bells tolled from meadows, mountains, plains, leading the peasants forth like the Pied Piper leading rats. Again Vlad's envoys were sent to King Matthias' court at Buda-Pest, Hungary, again the strangely unmoved king hesitated to throw Hungary's formidable might against Mehmed's imperial army. The Ottomans' troops seemed limitless, their distinctive headdress (a tall cone with veil flowing down the back), bizarre-sounding horns, and gigantic bronze cannon the terror of Europe; not since the Mongols' Golden Horde had such an army, wave after wave, attempted to force its Mohammedan faith on its subjects-to-be.

The streets of towns and cities thronged with excited, horrified Romanians, Germans, Magyars, Szeklers, and Romany. Even the Gypsies had cause for alarm, thronging on the squalid streets with dirty, worried faces, begging passersby for news of the nation's peril. Mothers clutched threadbare-clothed, tattered, maimed, or crippled children to their bosoms, for now the merchants and *burgermeisters* would be more reticent than ever to offer alms to Gypsy beggars; thieves would be horsewhipped, or worse: they may be put in stocks, maimed, or blinded with red-hot pokers. Alas, Dracula's protection could no longer be counted upon, for the wealthy, *bourgeoise* merchants would turn to the German Palatines or perhaps Frederick III, Holy Roman Emperor seated at far-away Salzburg, Austria, safe inside Hohensalzburg castle.

And, unknown to Vlad, his support was rapidly falling away.

For the first time since Dracula's fledgling nine-month reign in 1449–1450, his mercenaries and common soldier/peasants were deserting in droves. The German and Italian moneylenders had pulled out of Romania immediately, as if abandoning a sinking, rat-infested ship. Peter Gareb de Waresmarth, Count of Rosia, and Peterman do Longo Compo, both prominent and powerful merchants, had fled Wallachia a month ago with Vlad unaware.

The streets of Tirgovişte and Bistritz were already aflame with riots. Anti-Dracula agitators had proclaimed Tîrgu Mureş an amnesty zone for repentant boyars formerly supporting Lord Dracula's six-year Reign of Terror. His traitorous half-brother, Vlad the Monk, residing in Bistritz had offered the downtrodden Saxon peasants of Transylvania new hope. Worst of all, the devastating news that Gypsies threatened to wrest the free *villeins*' permanent, hard-fought, conquerors' rights of land tenure away. The Saxon peasants rose up in force, murdering Vlad's bailiffs even as he assembled his massive, conscript army for an ambush campaign against the Turks.

For the turbulent, overcast remainder of July, Vlad Ţepeş resettled his court at mighty Hunedŏara castle for the upcoming fall and winter campaign. Freak snow shrouded the western Carpathians. Daylight would soon cease to frequent this high-altitude wasteland, perhaps the darkest, bleakest, coolest, midsummer remainder weeks within living memory (or folk memory, for that matter). Storms of frightening intensity, perverse rain squalls, alternated with sudden tempests of depressing, montane winds. Gone were the roasting days experienced less than two weeks ago, when Mehmed's army scorched underneath a merciless summer sun near Tirgovişte as they gaped up at the turbaned, richly-attired, human Forest of Stakes. Now, the moors blackened with the shadows of cumulonimbus clouds racing across the forbidding Carpathian wilderness, the heart of the Bihor mountains. Wolves howled hungrily, forlornly, at the late-night moon. No roads echoed with the racing wheels of coaches. The wealthy had already fled, sure of the final outcome this time, for Mehmed would not be defeated twice. Terms of surrender were at this moment being formulated by the Monk's supporters at Tîrgu Jiu. And worst of all, the imminent overthrow of Vlad Dracula: his brother Radu, stationed at Giurgiu, the Sultan's minion and proffered choice as alternative Prince of Wallachia. The fortified island-bastion was now the insidious agitator's base, drawing surrendering soldiers and boyars like a magnet. Only Sibiu, Vlad Dracula's favourite city, held strong for the Impaler, the great castle twice fending off sieges from pro-Monk boyars.

This betrayal hurt Vlad most. Radu had never been his enemy. Had he not defended Radu's honour as a prisoner in Sofia? Had he not almost forfeited his own life for his weakling brother? Bah! Rumours of Radu's shameful homosexual attachment to Ţepeş' mortal enemy stung Vlad's haughty family pride, seared his heart, shamed his soul.

Patiently, Voica stood at Dracula's side now, watching him fret, watching him pace the musty, cobwebbed, long-uninhabited master bedchamber, antechambers, and gothic-arched hallways of mighty Hunedŏara castle, ringing little brass bells for absent servants; half-expecting to meet Janós Hunyádi's angry ghost. The magnificent Renaissance castle with its strangely-slanting, diamond-checkered-masonry witch's hat turrets, exquisite, interlaced, gothic tracery and deep, dry moat (due to the drought) had been marvellously refurbished by the former viceroy of Hungary, but alas, upon Hunyádi's death, cartloads of fine furniture, glorious chintz materials, bright, allegoric tapestries, Persian rugs and carpets, expensive armour and silverware had been transferred to Hungary. Now the echoing, abbey-like castle was largely empty (only its glistening, coffered ceilings of oak remained), devoid of furnishings, for Vlad had little desire to inhabit or refurbish the great man's fortress in fear of coming across the ruddy-faced viceroy's shade. He did not sleep. Instead, Vlad paced till sunrise, then crawled into bed at first cock-crow, nestling beside his nubile mistress's warm, nude body. This insomnia was frighteningly unfamiliar; Vlad had only experienced it twice before: the eve of his overthrow in February of 1450, and for two months before and after Serena's assassination. It was not a good omen. Days went by like a nightmare. Vlad, haughty, headstrong voivode that he was, unaware of his country's abandonment of him. Yet his newly-formed Moldavian Gypsy army was strong; 10,000 strong. Even as his burghers, mercenaries, and merchants fled the realm, the great Dragon's brilliant, cunning, ruthless mind planned strategy after strategy to outwit his Turkish overlords. Cunning as a fox, wise as an owl, cruel as a wolverine, deadly as a snake, Vlad intended to go down in history with a *bang!*, not a fizz. He had no field ready cannon at his disposal. (The Sultan's captured cannon had been devoid of cannon shot, the Janissaries wise to flee with the powders and balls.) Instead, Vlad would choose marsh-traps and pits over bronze cannon, guerrilla tactics over chivalrous field contests, assassination over diplomacy. And woe betide the Turks' camp followers. The tactics which had won his first campaign must prevail, or all patriots die without fail.

Trebuchets and huge mangonels were ordered positioned along road verges. Whether major routes or grim mountain-passes, Vlad's intention was to bombard the Turkish frontlines with Greek Fire, rocks, and boulders. Terrible ballista were being constructed to combat Mehmed's cannon, just as the ancient Dacians had done against the invading Roman legions. Many a Turk would feel a six-foot arrow bolt pierce his body before Vlad allowed this human pestilence to conquer his country. No Pasha would walk this sacred soil unmolested and without fear while the dreaded *Kaziglu Bey* ruled from his demon-haunted citadel above the Argeș. (The Mohammedans could take their customary, *baksheesh* bribe payments and stick them where the sun never shone.) The rocky, cliff-flanking roads would prove the final grave of many a Turk. Green, tufted bluffs would hide waiting Romanian freedom-fighters, their fingers at one with the rocky, grassy outcrops overlooking foggy, mountain-pass roads. Transylvania's jagged peaks would prove the final fighting grounds.

****

30 July, 1462 AD

Northern Wallachia, Carpathian Mountains

Vlad peered out at the twilit meadow with eyes which seemed to virtually glow in the approaching darkness; wide, eerie green, twinkling lanterns almost bulging out of their sockets. He sat crouched in the high meadow grass like a predatory lion, cruel mouth stretched into a gruesome leer. His compatriots sat quietly all around him, crossbows and longbows cocked and ready, their swords, scimitars, battle-axes, halberds and shields clutched in leather-gauntleted hands. Fierce scowls of anticipated revenge marred their boyish, olive faces. Dark Latin eyes glinted with bloodlust. Most had lost siblings in the Holy war. Some were Catholic backsliders; others were Hussites; yet others were Orthodox. But most were Gypsies; Vlach and Rom alike. Vlad had demanded they substitute their tattered, colourful rags and plaid barbarians' kilt for dark, camouflaging linens. Many of his soldiers were beardless; dark, rough stubble covered their faces like dirt.

Matei Báthory crouched half on his side, half on his haunches. The damp, dewy meadow grass soaked into his brown, grey-cross-emblazoned, Crusader's tunic. Heavy earth smells of meadow Cattail and black soil circulated in the air, carried aloft by an uncertain west wind. Each man shivered, cold and miserable; missing their beds and wenches. Though the freak midsummer snow had melted, true summer had yet to return to this miserable, God-forsaken Carpathian region fifty-five miles southwest of Tîrgovişte. Beyond the forest, beyond Vlad and his silent watchers, treacherous pits and trenches had been cunningly dug, stakes positioned, lairs camouflaged. Only Vlad's soldiers knew how to circumvent them. A gibbous orange moon hung low in the sky, balancing on the deciduous trees encircling the large meadow. Jasmine and saxifrage, basil and mint scented the cool, late July breeze.

Beyond the tall grass, the full bulk of Mehmed's army, 65,000 strong, lay encamped within the musky meadow and surrounding environs, themselves entrenched behind their own fifteen-foot ditch. Their cowhide army tents extended into the forests ahead as far as the eye could see. Party-coloured pavilions dotted the landscape. It was the same one-night-stand, defensive technique which the Romans had utilised in these marshes 1400 years ago. The Turks were paranoid of attack, rightfully so, for the gritty Wallachians had been ambushing the Sultan's royal camp all year with shocking impunity, carrying away the Emir's unarmed, surprised ambassadors to adorn Vlad Dracula's macabre displays. Tonight, when the bloated, gourd-like moon sunk below the treetops, Vlad's new-model army, 23,000 strong, meant to ambush the Sultan's gargantuan horde though the odds be suicidal.

Sultan Mehmed's rejuvenated army at latest count was rumoured by Vlad's spy network to number around thirty, forty thousand. Perhaps fifty thousand. His own quickly-raised, elite host seemed like a pipsqueak by comparison. The collision of the two would seem like a battle between elephants and mice. But Vlad's tactics relied on hit-and-run ambushes. He would not be burdened by feeding prisoners, as they would.

Vlad leaned over, whispering to his thirteen-year-old squire, Demitri. Without a word, the gangly, dark-haired youth crawled away on his belly like a snake, slithering unnoticed towards the forest at his back, toward Vlad's main core of archers, infantry, and spearmen. Dracula had mostly javelin throwers, crossbowmen, longbow archers, lancers, and pikemen. A fine Dalmatian unit of pole-axe experts armed with formidable Viking battle-axes and wedge-shaped shields had thrice put fear into the hearts of Mehmed's previously invincible Janissaries: the Ottomans' elite infantry of fearsome renown.

The voivode had positioned his few, hand-picked commanders and boyars to crouch here and survey the movements with him. Vlad wisely chose a spot well away from the enemy camp's eyesight range, stealthily monitoring the lost contingent's actions. Knowledgeable insiders had informed Vlad of a terrible disease spreading throughout the Turkish ranks—the same insider/moles who had sabotaged their food supplies, poisoned their dogs which allowed Dracula's warriors to ambush the Turks' encampments at night like blind homing cattle. It was clear Çelebi (Man of God, in Turkish) had led his men astray. Again. Țepeș' men sat crouched, uncomfortable in the neck-high, rank grass, opposite to the wind to avoid having their musky, sweaty scent carried aloft toward the Ottomans' camp. The Sultan's royal tent sat well back within the trees, sheltered and protected by his frontline Janissaries.

Vlad's scouts had been spying for days now. They knew Mehmed's every thought, anticipated the Sultan's every action. A Turkish spy had been feeding Vlad information for weeks, a former Wallachian and kin who'd been forced into Janissary service at an early age, converted to Islam and subsequently risen to high office. He'd owed Vlad his life once for taking the rap for the friendly Muslim's thievery and subsequent guilt at Mured's fortress of Egrigöz.

At last, Vlad gave the signal to move out. One by one, in a rather undignified way, the soldiers crawled and slithered away into the opposite wilderness, undetected by the massive Turkish encampment sprawled in and beyond the muskeg-smelling meadow.

The plan was simple; and brilliant. The Devil himself would be hard put to devise a more cunning strategy. Come nightfall, complete darkness, Vlad's rehearsed youths would slither forward with boards on their shoulders, one at a time adding a long, wide, cumbersome plank over the embankment; by midnight, a broad, leather-strapped, heavily re-inforced bridge would be ready to cross. Clouds were moving in even now to obscure the full, orange moon. Come the blackest hour, Vlad's battle-frenzied men would sweep across the stake-infested embankment like a storm, unless Turkish sentries discovered the ruse and sounded the alarm. Each man must ride like all the furies of Hell were chasing him, as if *Waelcrigge* warrioresses from Valhalla were baying for his blood, slaughtering, burning, maiming all along the frontline without even slowing their horses.

The Turkish army had foolishly set themselves up for a disastrous ambush. Along a two-mile swath, their great Army of God clustered between forest and marsh, their pavilions, tents, pack mules, elephants, camels, baggage trains and royal harem squeezed together so tight they would hardly be able to re-arm and mount their beasts without bumping into one another. A speedily-executed lightning attack, a *blitzkrieg*, would create pandemonium. Romanian women and children were ordered to scramble down the embankments a mile or so down the camp and remove some of the stakes placed in the wide ditches while the Turks were engaged with Vlad's screaming *chevaliers*, providing an escape route out of the camp. Vlad Ţepeş' soldiers were instructed to hurl anything at hand at their bewildered targets. Foremost though was a truly diabolical plan to literally roast alive the crowded enemy—flinging oil-soaked torches at their dry leather tents and handfuls of poison-barbed javelins into their masses. The Dalmatians' task was to wade in full-tilt on horseback and attack the ghazis with their double-headed pole axes, lopping off as many heads as humanly possible before the Turks recovered their composure. Lastly, Vlad himself would storm the Sultan's gilded tent accompanied by his finest swordsmen and archers; he would be satisfied with nothing but the Sultan's head when he returned to base-camp. And return he would, dead or alive. He must not die. He would not die.

****

Like a midsummer storm the slumbering Turks heard Vlad Dracula's soldiers thunder across the bridged embankment. The ghazis, *bahouks* (lowly infantry), sipahis, Azabs, Janissaries, *yayas*, and disoriented, gem-fingered *nabobs* scrambled out of their tents in confusion when the first onslaught cut them down. Horses bolted.

Vlad Dracula himself led his screaming, baying, ululating men into the throng, racing like a Swedish berserker alongside the mile-long encampment, the *hospidar's* eyes afire with suicidal wrath as Dracula's great devil-horse flew toward the Sultan's heavily guarded pavilion. Many rolled out of bed and out of their rawhide tents, too late to defend themselves as they were slaughtered while they lay dazed upon the ground. Huge, yellow-silk-draped, jewel-glittering elephants protected the Sultan's tent. But they, too, fell when the second wave of mounted archers roared by.

The wounded elephants began to stampede, as well as the smaller, lumbering pack camels. Under a hammering cavalcade of mighty elephants and dromedary's feet the brave Turkish soldiers fell, brains squished out of their nostrils as the hysterical beasts thundered and faltered over them, the braying camels and wounded, trumpeting elephants lurching, collapsing with a horrific squeal atop the struggling human bodies. Skulls cracked like eggshells as the titanic, trumpeting, bellowing elephants rushed hither and thither throughout the besieged camp, finally breaking away from their shouting masters. The roar of elephants' trunks and thunderous feet deafened.

A third wave of Romanian madmen managed to set the entire camp alight, tents blazing now as the murder-crazed, Apocalyptic horsemen thundered down upon the as-yet unarmed ghazis. No moon nor stars lit the night to distinguish friend from foe, only the acrid flames of roasting tents, beasts, men or flaming torches flung at the pavilions and sacks of tar to engulf all. A flurry of Dalmatian pole-axes reaped Turkish heads by the hundreds, like *Samháin* run amok. Dracula's satanic, black warhorse vanquished, he leapt upon another, wresting the Arabian steed from its owner even as the Turk fell to the ground clutching Vlad's dragon-emblazoned dagger driven into his heart. Another and another, each warhorse expiring at the very portals of Mehmed's tent.

To every Turkish bodyguard's dismay, their Sultan had fled the mêlée.

Mehmed watched from the forest alongside a handful of Janissaries as Vlad Dracula's troops travestied Allah's war host. This was a midnight raid, totally breaking all the rules of war! Even Mehmed's enviable harem was being massacred. No time for rape or kidnappings, Dracula's soldiers butchered the veiled houris as they pleaded and wailed for mercy, therefore ending their disgrace. Halberds, shields, swords, daggers and metal armour flashed in firelight. Great clubs bearing iron, morning-star-spiked, ball-and-chain maces crashed through skulls, leaving bloody, spike-holed pulp in their wakes. Screams and shrieks and shouts of agony sprang up from the maimed, wounded, or dying.

Shouts and whoops of exultant triumph echoed from the attackers.

The *cai-aaying* of crazed soldiers set the rotund nabobs' short hairs on end (hundreds of miles from their native India); a primitive, otherworldly sound which drove the turbaned, Mogul demagogues to their heels: at once regretting having volunteered for an Islamic horde against Vlad Țepeș' Netherworld, here in benighted Transylvania.

As dawn came on Mehmed watched from the old-growth beech trees as his ghazis regained their composure and threw back their heavily outnumbered attackers. Fearsome 120-lb.-draw Mongolian hornbows created huge gaps in Vlad Dracula's cavalry, the dead piling up before the Ottomans' camp like a grisly wall of butchered flesh. Jubilant, the Sultan leapt from his hiding-place, clothed only in his colourfully-striped Turkish pyjamas. He rushed toward the smouldering, blackened camp, grabbing a battle-axe and joining the fray.

Dracula had failed to bring back Mehmed's head.

At last, with the grey, wraith-like mists shrouding the carnaged, blood-soaked meadow, Vlad ordered his infamous retreat. Sultan Mehmed's mounted troops chased Dracula's disintegrating, haggard, bedraggled cavalry into the forests, across the age-old, willow-veiled Ialomita river, plunging into the freezing-cold, rushing waters with the sun just barely clearing the nearby Carpathian foothills forty miles southeast of Tirgoviște. The slow and the weak were left behind to perish in the Ialomita's swollen, beaver-debris-clogged, flotsam banks. The Turks slaughtered Dracula's wounded retreaters stuck in the river's reeds.

Vlad halted among the rolling, verdant, Carpathian foothills, allowing his heaving, foaming warhorse to recover its breath. A small regiment of loyal soldiers and bodyguards accompanied him, glancing nervously over their shoulders as a brilliant sun peeped over the easterly mountain ranges. They had ridden perhaps ten miles. Forbidding grey/green moors held long morning shadows, the pastoral valleys hostile even in broad daylight. Trees here were scarce, no brilliant summer foliage in attendance, nor even the ubiquitous yellow gorse, primrose, broom, nor heather. Only close-cropped, sickly looking sedge grass and stunted, gnarled oaks stretching their knobbly, knotted, threateningly stark, leafless branches towards unsuspecting passersby. The early-morning sunlight filtering through ancient, dull grey, dying trees lent the verdant landscape a macabre air. Wych elms struggled to survive perched upon tall, grassy, rocky crags and higher altitudes.

Odd trails worn down by countless treads of Stone Age shepherds crisscrossed the moors. Parched, Vlad pointed in the distance toward a trickling, waterfall-like stream bounding over the uplands, then led the way. His troops were thirsty too, as were their horses, eager to taste the cool, refreshing, glacial water flowing sluggishly from the northern Transylvanian Alps. Vlad grumbled to himself, deeply disappointed at having failed to capture Sultan Mehmed's worthy head.

As Vlad's greatly diminished contingent crested a knoll, their horses reared back, bolting.

Before them, a large, well-armed troop of Turks faced them, suddenly alerted at the renegade band's appearance. Their splendid Arabian horses pranced about a moment, whinnying, unsettled; the white-draped ghazis suddenly let out a cry of jubilation, spurring their mounts forward in battle formation.

Vlad barked a command, ordering his small cavalry unit to stand their ground. But his troops were panicking, steeds retreating backwards in a vain attempt at escape. Each man knew there was no hope of outrunning the enemy, for their warhorses needed water and rest. Vlad cocked his head, listening with wolf's ears as Sultan Mehmed's resurgent auxiliary forces bayed down a distant ravine, tracking *Kaziglu Bey*. There were no means of escape, the only avenue blocked by Mehmed's gloating soldiers ahead.

"Stand your ground!!!" Vlad's bellow did no good. His soldiers' horses began to rear, fighting their reins as the ghazis pranced towards them in battle readiness, sabres raised, round shields positioned. Prince Vlad unsheathed his great broadsword, his remaining recruits reluctantly following suite. A galloping thunder of racing horses' hooves in the distance shattered the foothills' morning silence as Sultan Mehmed's regiments chased fleeing Wallach soldiers northwards, now, towards Tirgovişte. Suddenly the Ottoman commander gave a hair-raising battle cry, urging his compatriots forward with a stream of Turkish abuses meant for the enemies' ears.

Vlad's force met the first barrage without shattering. The next collision broke through his right flank, dropping his retainers under a flurry of Turkish sabres and long, Persian battle-axes. The mounted archers wreaked havoc on Vlad's battalion, the Turks renowned throughout Asia and the Mediterranean for their finesse at the composite short-bow, ideal for mounted, unarmoured horsemen. Their stirrups were also superior, allowing the Turks greater manoeuvrability on the battlefield.

Vlad's cavalry retreated down the hill. He screamed abuse at his soldiers, exhorting them to mount the steep, grassy, slippery knoll once more. They tried belatedly to carry out his orders, being forced down the incline each time, reforming battle formation. In a hedgehog pattern they fought, falling relentlessly as the Turks forced the renegades down the hill. Vlad's cavalry was thinning. And after hours of ceaseless fighting, their weapons had dulled or broken, arrows long-since exhausted. Their now-useless longbows, he felt, would have made short shrift of the Turks. None but Vlad had found time to sharpen their dulled blades whilst in the saddle, to re-hone their twin edges.

The Turks flung themselves on Vlad's overwhelmed force, the gravity of their downhill plunge sending his troops fleeing in disarray. Their Mongolian hornbows were decimating his ranks. Ottoman steeds trampled the fallen without remorse, grinding Prince Vlad's valiant but doomed Wallachian nobility asunder. His Satanic black cape, however, seemed to disorient his targets, like a matador outwitting charging bulls! (He soon flung it aside, engaging the Turks in earnest.) Only Vlad held his ground, recklessly goading his opponents, then sallying forth to smote his hated foes with a double-headed Viking battleaxe in one metal-gauntleted fist and a broadsword in another, charging the surprised Turks with a maniacal cry. His massive-thewed arms whirled among their masses like a deadly windmill, razor-sharp, steel blades meeting flesh and bone. He smiled gleefully, wickedly, eyes blazing in bloodlust. Crazed with battle frenzy, Dracula duelled with seasoned Arabs, Hindoos, and Persians simultaneously, any semblance of rationality long since departed his psychotic brain. Half an ounce of prime Turkish hashish had given Vlad the maniacal strength of ten men, desensitised now to his own butchery. He no longer felt the dead weight of battle-axe nor hand-and-a-half broadsword. Twice Vlad felt his padded jerkin and tunic severed, then his chain-link armour, watching the blood flow from his own wounds as if disassociated from it all. At ease now, he commended his spirit to the Sky.

Watching with horror, Vlad's comrades witnessed their berserk Prince sally forth on a grey Arabian gelding, only to be beaten back again and again. Against one hundred-fifty men he fought hand-to-hand, chopping, slashing, cutting like a perpetual-motion machine: whirling, spinning, ducking. Samurai-like, Vlad sought his milling enemies' flesh with a mad glint in his eye, venting his unholy rage against the untried Ottoman conscripts. Arrows stuck out incongruously from his destrier's ornate saddle, his embossed shield, penetrating Vlad's leather jerkin and dragon-emblazoned tabard though failing to pierce his chainmail shirt nor chain-link hauberk-skirt and leggings. The ghazis, renowned lovers of horses, chivalrously declined to bring down Vlad's spirited, pale grey steed. The majority watched from the sidelines, as if watching a jousting tournament.

Detached, Vlad barely felt his chain-links breaking. Foe after foe fell to his twin, cleaving, gleaming, crescent-shaped Dalmatian axe heads. Finally, a dozen arrows brought down his warhorse; but to every ghazi's surprise, Vlad clawed his way onto another, bodily throwing its rider to the ground before unleashing his unholy fury on the cavalry troop. He cleaved their commander in two, immediately dispiriting their contingent. Vlad ducked into a crouch; grinning evilly as he sought tender flesh. Prince Vlad's great, round, iron-studded shield hung suspended around his neck, absorbing much of the blows, a ploy never seen before. Dracula had received enough blows to vanquish fifty men. Still, he fought on.

After a time, the ghazis began to believe he was truly undead; undestroyable, Satan's minion, Lucifer's scourge upon the world.

Heartened, Dracula's valiant comrades surged forth from a nearby, stony bluff with suddenly renewed vigour, horses spanning a deep fissure and taking their opponents unaware. Most of the Turks had been prancing around in awe of this Vlachian madman, out of range of *Kaziglu Bey's* frenzied, twirling blades, so engrossed they hadn't a chance to check his allies' counter-attack. For Vlad's retainers now sighted a miraculous glimmer of hope. Țepeș had thinned out the centre of the Turks' cavalry; those foolish enough to challenge him in single combat soon collapsed, dismembered, onto the grass. The ghazis were now on the defensive, their commander having fallen under Dracula's merciless onslaught, leaving the battalion leaderless and rudderless. None had the seniority nor experience to usurp command. Instead, the hard-pressed Turkish soldiers now milled about in disarray, searching for a leader while Dracula's berserk war-wolves went on the attack with slavering, blood-flecked mouths and staring, hemp-maddened, bloodshot eyes. Vlad's troops jumped the backs of his enemies, abandoning conventional warfare tactics for wrestling, hand-to-hand combat. Shouts and cries from bewildered, bearded, moustachioed ghazis spooked their freshly broken warhorses, breaking the beleaguered contingent's morale. White turbans were wrested from their heads during the free-for-all, an unprecedented dishonour; the Turks suddenly felt they were grappling with octopus! Vlad and his regiment wore conical, iron-studded helmets with noseguards, the Viking-style war helms accounting for the Vlachs' continued survival despite repeated, brutal blows. By noon, Vlad's victorious cavalry remnant broke away.

****

When Vlad Țepeș' warriors broke away, not a single Turkish foe remained alive.

They had littered the mossy ground for half a mile, their horses having fallen with them, dismembered or gruesomely disembowelled. Staring, dark-brown eyes gazed sightlessly up at the azure-blue summer sky, heads tilted back in expressions of unimaginable horror. The defeated ghazis had foolishly pursued their rebellious prey; too close for escape when Vlad's soldiers suddenly turned on them like a catapult, slaughtering mercilessly, victoriously, then. Killing with glee. The foothills echoed with their butchered screams.

But Vlad had lost too much blood.

Disorganised, terrified, on the run, his remaining troops abandoned him on the battlefield at his stern orders. Dozens of bodies lay at Vlad's side, mostly Turks, his stolen warhorse standing cannon-shocked at his side. Even a doctor could see he would not survive the afternoon. His mortified squire, Demitri, cradled Vlad's head in his lap, ear close to hear Țepeș' rasping whisper. Blood trickled from the oddly-smiling voivode's bruised mouth, his eyes permanently glazed now. Tearful, the brave, young squire left Dracula to die a warrior's death on the moors, fighting his hereditary foes.

****

Sultan Mehmed's Janissaries chose to pursue Vlad's scattered cavalry remnants west through the gloomy Dimbovita forest. The disorganised partisans fled before them. The Wallachians no longer had any belly for battle. They ran on foot when their exhausted horses collapsed, not stopping till dusk. Transylvania's lofty, blue, Carpathian alps were their destination, the jagged, limestone mountain ranges shielding Țepeș' ingenious stockades from attack. The warriors jettisoned their heavy weapons and whatever armour they possessed, for it was now clear the ambush had been a terrible disaster. Some had been fortunate enough to enter the previous evening's melee with chainmail hauberks or even the latest Italian, pilfered, steel full-body armour. Others had had no protection whatsoever for their bare legs. If they had, they soon abandoned the heavy chainmail leggings or padded leather chaps, swimming frantically across the chilly Dimbovita at twilight.

When the stragglers of Vlad's vanquished contingent returned to their Prince's stockaded enclosure within the dark, treacherous oak forest of Calyna, near Sibiu, women and children, young and old gathered around the bloodied survivors only to hear their Prince had perished in the lower, Transylvanian foothills.

Some rejoiced secretly, certain the war was over. Others pulled their hair and gnashed their teeth. Each knew the resistance was over; the Ottomans could take Romania when they choose. Only Dracula, cruel tyrant though he was, had the forceful will to bend his countrymen to his bidding.

Even the younger, upstart scions of his marshals and lately-appointed boyar aristocracy knew the tide had ebbed; though many owed Vlad Țepeș, grovelingly, their prestige and high office, the strain of war with no chance at all of ultimate victory had forsaken *even them*.

Demoralisation immediately set in, with the horrid certainty of a nation's degradation and imminent enslavement. Any man accused of participating in or collaborating with Vlad's mad uprising would be impaled, at the Sultan's behest, or subjected to any number of horrific tortures until dying, screaming, begging for mercy!

The Gypsies now were outcasts within the darkening stockade as night descended. Dracula's promises were empty. There'd be no settlement now, for Vlad had left no heir, no ancestral House to settle the deceased ruler's affairs. No scrolls had been signed or exchanged, relying merely on the sacred blood-pact. Therefore the *Szgany's* land claims were terminated.

Few enough had survived the night's battle anyhow. Marooned in this superstitious forest in a mire of hate and jealousy, divided from the Romany who felt cheated of land they felt theirs by virtue of Attila's short-lived conquest, and by the Romanians' Aryan notions of Roman superiority over all others. Most of Dracula's conscripted Moldavians had yet to return, having been either run-down by Mehmed's marauding Janissaries or sheltered within stockades by Cirstian Mohác's reinforcements in Banat.

Seventeen abandoned families huddled near a large campfire as a pumpkin moon rose above the trees, eyes tearful and sad. Scared. Children wailed for absent fathers; mothers sobbed quietly over bereaved loved ones. The indigenous Vlachs occupied a lone corner of Vlad's encampment, shunned by the Romany like plague. The Romanian soldiers sharpened their swords with grim, smooth faces, eyeing the Wallach remainders with hateful, baleful glares. The Romany blamed Dracula, the *Szgany*, the Hungarians for having been dragged—*against their will!*—into this foolish, hopeless war *('Why not pay the Moslems their baksheesh, give them your excess daughters to stock Islamabad's venal harems?')*. Sultan Mehmed would annex Wallachia, would impale her citizens on a scale which would make Vlad's sadistic amusements pale in comparison.

Not that the *Romany* cared.

****

The *Szgany* awoke too late to save themselves.

Their fire burned low, the children and grandparents awakening to a hideous chorus of screams from their slumbering kin. The Wallachian soldiers were upon them now, hacking and pounding the unarmed

Vlachs into a bloodied pulp. The sickening crunch of tendons snapping and meat pounded like steaks filled the still, night air. The Romany would avenge themselves now, would purge Dracula's camp of these heathen viruses. The slain weren't Christian, therefore their Orthodox murderers would be exonerated for the senseless crime. Romanians and their uneasy, ungrateful allies, the Romany (!), made strange bedfellows as they butchered their hereditary enemy. The Goidel and Rom would triumph tonight (but only temporarily), chopping the *Cymbri* to bits, remembering Greece and all they'd lost, and would lose, recalling bitter, ancient loss when the Cimmerians had overthrown their Galatian conquerors. As torchlight flickered within the banked encampment, mothers watched their sons and daughters slain, and then, before their own butchery, were mercilessly, savagely gang-raped. None were spared from axe or sword, dagger nor mace.

When the travesty was over, the gloating, damned slayers returned to their tents for much-needed sleep as the dawn sun rose above the high Carpathian mountains like an orange candle flame.

****

Vlad woke in the morning believing he'd died and gone to Hell.

He lay paralysed on the hard, rocky ground, too weak to move. His eyes bleary. Blood caked the grass beneath him, his jerkin and tunic soiled and bloodied; ruined. He felt the broken chain links which had dug into his flesh as if for the first time, his legs and arms gored. The sun blazed in his eyes. He squinted at the eastern horizon, his mind rebelling at the unfairness of it all. Purgatory. Vlad left a pregnant mistress behind at Castle Dracula on the Argeş, a widow before she even bore his child. Was this the cruel Fate which life had in store for him? Doomed to wander the earth in limbo, a *wampyr* perhaps, seeking the warm blood of the living?

Vlad lay for hours. He remembered the previous night's battle, recalled his troops abandoning him on the battlefield. Left for dead. But was he? Had he become one of the undead? Or was this Vlad's purgatory. The sun felt gloriously warm, the Carpathian wind chilly to the bone. In the pastoral, surreal distance grazed a herd of wild bison, one of the few which hadn't been exterminated by the Saxons, Latins, and Hungarians for their thick, valuable hides. All around, high green quack-grass whispered in Vlad's ear. A turkey vulture screamed high above, soaring, circling the dead on the battlefield.

No Turkish soldiers had ventured into this windy, isolated valley. Mehmed's roving battalions had bypassed it. Ground squirrels scurried about on the earth, dashing down snug burrows as Vlad slowly raised his head. Painfully. All around, slaughtered ghazis lay where they had fallen, their clawed, stiffened hands turned palm-upwards.

As the sun neared midday, Vlad slowly felt the nerves returning to his joints.

First his fingers, then his hands. Then his arms, toes, legs. He could feel his fingertips tingling inside his sticky, hinged, mitten-lined steel gauntlets. Blood droplets impeded his eyesight. Vlad blinked painfully, tearfully. Overjoyed. He'd lost too much blood. Too much to be alive. The Great Goddess had spared him. The Turkish bodies lay in the line of Vlad's distorted vision, tempting...

Reluctantly, his body wracked with pain and convulsions, Vlad sluggishly inched forward. He slithered, half on his belly, half on his shoulder, legs refusing to cooperate. His mouth watered, so parched was he. Vlad's breath tasted terrible in his mouth. He knew he must soon die out here without water. Water! Vlad's mind screamed, propelling him toward a ghazi's corpse. At the same time, his Christian upbringing rebelled at what he must do. Abhorred it. The bodies were still fresh...their blood wet. Hopefully. Vlad prayed silently the blood hadn't coagulated. No canteens about to save him from this chore, this blasphemy.

He seized a Turkish body by the shoulder, rolling it over. Laboriously drew the ghazi's bone-handled dagger from its sheath, gashing the corpse's jugular vein. Sipping...

Vlad drank till he'd had his fill...warm blood, though soupy thick...salty, quenching human blood. Liquid had never tasted so good. As he drank, Vlad's mind recalled the gruesome taboos rumoured of the rituals of blood-drinking. For this blasphemy, men had devolved into vampires or werewolves...

The lapping, sucking noise filled Vlad's ears, listening guiltily, unavoidably to the smacking sounds his lips made against the cadaver's soiled neck, like a lamprey; fretting over what horrid disease he might contract from this stiff, horror-staring corpse.

Dracula lay back, mortally exhausted. Sated. He felt like a bloated leech. His stomach churned, queasy. Vlad felt suddenly elated, buoyant, floating in a dreamy, languid doze.

The sun began to set in the west. Howling wolves echoed eerily from the bleak, boulder-strewn Carpathian wilderness. Up above, a pale yellow moon hovered on the rough, mountainous horizon, casting silhouettes from spruce at nightfall. A deep purple sky met Vlad Dracula's glazed, bloodshot gaze, stars twinkling high above. Vlad kicked off his blood-filled steel boots with an effort, then instantly regretted it. He knew it was only a matter of hours before the wolves discovered his inert, live body, licking and chewing his flesh while he lay powerless; nibbling his toes. He began to wonder if the earth really were flat, or whether it be round, a truly heretical thought. For that alone the pompous Pontiff would burn him alive at the stake, like many before him. The purple, bowl-shaped sky, teeming with stars, seemed to spin miles above his gaze, dizzying. Vlad felt certain he would not survive the night.

"Keep away, Oh Children of the Night...for I and mine have left thy domains alone," implored Vlad in a hoarse, cracking whisper. He sincerely hoped the *llygans* heeded his entreaties.

Come midnight, he felt his strength returning with a painful adrenaline rush. Astounded, Vlad sat up slowly, like *nosferatu* rising from the battlefield, peering around in bewilderment. He glanced down mortified at the exsanguinated Turkish body lying at his side, the ghazi staring up at him with dark, glassy, accusing eyes. Țepeș had received dozens of superficial wounds; yet none had penetrated vital organs. Vlad wore chainmail stockings; his legs were at least intact, though sore; bruised and nicked. His entire body ached, however. Leather chaps beneath had saved his extremities from almost certain, bone-shearing lacerations, if not outright dismemberment. Blackened and bruised, bloodied, savaged in a dozen places, Vlad studied his wounds under faint moon/starlight. His chain-mailed arms were latticed with deep razor-cuts from broken chain links, bitterly painful; some of his tendons may have been severed. His muscles were practically unworkable.

Vlad's chest heaved for breath, lungs gasping for air like a marooned fish. His bruised ribs hurt. Some broken, others perhaps fractured. His handsome face had received several blows and minor cuts, though none fatal. He suspected his aristocratic, Slav nose had been broken. Vlad's still-bloodied lips were sore and puffy, as were his eyes.

Shaking, Vlad tentatively, wobbly, stood up.

Collapsed.

Determined, he got to his knees, shaking off his weighty, cumbersome iron gauntlets, then rose again.

And lo and behold, he could stand! His great broadsword lay a dozen feet away on the chilly ground. He lurched toward it, bending, snatching it up with a child's hand. Vlad grimaced, for he was not as young as he once was, and his lower back hurt. The heavy sword felt like a waterlogged tree in his quivering hands. A hundred-foot, green spruce-fir, branches, boughs and needles still attached. Vlad groaned aloud, stepping forward one iron boot (which he'd retrieved) at a time, awkwardly sheathing the bulky, Teutonic weapon. He glanced up at the twinkling stars, sighting Polaris, following his instincts as he trudged painfully forward, driven by some elemental will to survive.

He must reach the palisades. Warn the soldiers. Order the

evacuation of women and children, for the Turks would be regrouping soon. (Ottoman sources had already intimated to Vlad their Emir's eagerness to cross *Carpăti's* steep, jagged mountain ranges.) If they had discovered his four stockades in lower Transylvania, they may already have attacked. Vlad did not trust his own mercenaries, nor the hybrid Romany at large. The Gypsies may fall victim to the Romanian camp-followers who bore no love for *Szgany*. Without Vlad Țepeș' terrifying presence, who knew what the traitorous Latin half-breeds might do.

****

As if by miracle, Vlad reached his sub-alpine destination.

On the tenth day, he arrived; the advent of the sacred Sabbath Stones of Mamăglia, that venerable triad of triangular bluestones on the Black Sea's western shore where Druids once convened before the evil-incarnate *Lladins* carried them off to Rome; the holiest of holies whose pagan oracle provided the Wisdom of the Ages; the solstice tabernacle day of Sun Day which the Hebrews had stolen from their Sarmatian neighbours, the Samaritans of Galatia.

Vlad trudged until dawn. Day after day, like a corpse summoned through necromancy to some benighted wizard's montane stronghold. From sun-up to sundown, trekking towards some seemingly endless destination, his mind straying, the ancient, mist-bound Carpathians looming brutishly all around him. Falling, rising, stumbling. Relentlessly pushing onwards. He knew this mountainous, harsh but beautiful, flower-starred countryside well, had scouted the territory with his retainers during countless military expeditions. Vlad's eyesight was keen even in darkness, having spent many a night sleeping outdoors, hand on his sword.

The terrain was rough. Rocky. Great, rolling foothills, steep, eagle-haunted gullies, mystic lakes, threatening, alluvial ravines, bottomlands, the Transylvanian scrublands rife with wildflowers. Much of it was marshland, notorious, wolf-infested bog. The ungro-Transylvanian moors gradually escalated into *coombes*, mountainous valleys, and finally, into gargantuan mountain passes mantled in fir, pine, and spruce. Breathtaking in their bucolic, emerald-green beauty, the deep, leafy gorges, shadowy valleys, ravines and rivers studded with majestic oak, hemlock, fir and spruce along serpentine mountain passes. Rocky screes threatened unwary travellers with unpredictable rockslides. Countless times Vlad stumbled over rocks, cursing viciously; foundering in bogs, rising like a Phoenix. Bogwater brimmed his latticed, leather boots, insidiously seeping through their seams. Stiflingly hot afternoons were followed by cloudy, overcast days of sleet or thunder. Endless tracts of pine wilderness surrounded marshes so muddy one could drown as if in quicksand. Vlad was wily, however, avoided the overgrown, rolling, swamp mud. He fought through eye-high grasses and bulrushes, pushing aside Cattails; rank weeds glorious in his nostrils. For he was in his glory, despite the agonising, blood-seeping gashes to his skin compounded by tall grasses. The days-old battle wounds had begun to fester. He'd discarded his tell-tale chainmail shirt, hauberk, steel bootshells and chain-link leggings (having secured suitable apparel from some nameless, decomposing, Wallach soldier mired in a river's reeds), his sword as well, stashing the bundle in a familiar outcrop-niche near the sleepy village of Zărnesti; crawling along the moors in daylight for fear of capture. He'd rolled up his regal black cape, carrying it in a satchel, for, other than his father's signet-ring signifying the Order of the Dragon, this ultra-expensive badge of royalty was his only true identification among his folk. He shaved off his giveaway moustache. No Turkish units showed upon the horizon however, having chased their elusive prey south of Bucharest into Turkish suzerainty, like hyenas chasing prey into their lair. Vlad's mind began to wander, recalling long-ago days spent alone traversing such mushy, reedy marshes, swamps, and bogs, stamping gleefully over Carpathian mountain trails with his longbow while searching for game, through larch groves, and fording the rushing, almost winter-cold, alpine river streams in summertime.

 Vlad, too, recalled a time spent wandering with his father, sucking up these bitter-sweet glimpses from his cobwebbed memory. He remembered his smiling, placid, mustachioed *tată*, who unlike Vlad had had no belly to fight the Turks nor sustain a war against them. Until too late Prince Dracul (ironically, Vlad the Devil) had been forced into futile war. The Ottomans and their lackeys had crushed him like a bug. Dracul had brought him into these forests, the musky marshes, familiarising Vlad—his second eldest—with the plant-life and folklore of Romania. The superstitions, customs, and fables of local Orthodox peasants, reiterating to Vlad his deceased mother's Cimmerian fables which *Dŏmnul* (Lord) Dracul had only half-understood. Dracul had not spoken her mysterious language. Mirçea had been four years Vlad's senior, and was already gaining the famous reputation as a fearless, young warlord against the faltering Turks of Mured's reign. While beloved Mirçea was away at Janós Hunyádi's (*Ion de Hunedŏara* to Romanians) favourite, gigantic, Flamboyant-Gothic, Renaissance castle in western Transylvania, father Dracul was teaching Vlad the layout of the land. Together they would walk for days on end (Lord Dracul's security men close at hand), high up in the

Carpathian alps near Castle Brân, Braşov, studying the flora and naming wild game. 'Twas there, up in the high, snowbound, hoary altitudes that Prince Dracul had informed Vlad of his painful decision to send the twelve-year-old boy away to Turkey as ransom-due for the Wallachians' continued good behaviour. Promising to be brave, Vlad had not shed a tear.

And now he stumbled forward across the earthen ramparts of Calyna forest with tears in his eyes, bitter tears undiminished by the years. Serena's memory was equally painful and vivid, dancing rudely across Vlad's cold, crystal-clear brain as he approached the strangely-silent wilderness stockade. Forests pressed in gloomily on all sides. Careful, he avoided the cunningly concealed mantraps and their deadly wooden stakes, outwitted the various boobie-traps he himself had supervised while his soldiers rigged them: tree-rope trap nets. Only a trampled clearing and stout wooden walls built of seasoned pine logs betrayed the ingenious stockade's presence. Green overgrowth claimed the older, previous ramparts of Mirçea the Old's reign, crawling over the antiquated earth-and-wood palisade in riotous profusion. The plants, it seemed, were dying prematurely; indeed, most of the ivy vines were rust-spotted and dead.

Ominously, no forest sentries had detected Vlad's presence: it was their duty to intercept well-meaning but ignorant peasants and preventing them from impaling themselves in the dark forest.

No hails of warning or welcome sprang forth as Dracula drew near. Dusk grew nigh. Nightingale and swallow trilled in the underbrush; stirring their wings at Vlad's approach. For an uneasy moment, he wondered if the Turks had overrun the stockade, only miles north of Sibiu though it be, massacring those sheltering within inside timber longhouses and cowhide tents. Or perhaps the Turks occupied it even now, waiting to spring upon the hated *Kaziglu Bey*. (Impaler Prince.)

The palisades showed no sign of scorching or collapse. The crude, square-plan gatehouse's arched wooden gates were shut tight. Odd spiralling wisps of smoke drifted above the fifteen-foot-high log palisade. Vlad crossed the first earthen rampart, cautious, hailing the wall.

The sound of scrambling feet rose up from beyond the gates, the wall-walks. Terrified voices caused pandemonium within, the cries of women, girls, and babies wailing. Screeches of '*Ordog*' (Satan) and '*moroi*', '*nosferatu*', '*strigoi*', or '*poltergeist*'—Vlad's ghost—broke the noon silence borne aloft on a gentle breeze. Or *Dracul*—evil. *The bogeyman cometh.* Men's shouts roused the soldiers within, scrambling now to man the parapets. A white flag of truce immediately shot up to Vlad's consternation. His relief overwhelmed him however upon seeing the boyar Cirstian's coat-of-arms flapping above the ramparts on a tent-mounted flag mast; a great, cerulean boar's head on silver, silk cloth. Cirstian alone of all the old-guard boyars throughout Vlad's reign remained faithful. Nor would he betray him now. Cirstian's interests were Vlad's own. Vlad swore to have the traitorous boyar Rasalom Galeş' head on a pike for deliberately failing to attack the Sultan's rear flank ten nights ago.

The spectators within the fort barely recognised their sovereign—they recognised (along with his Order of the Dragon's ring) his ebon, blood-streaked cape, however. Vlad held it aloft like a flag, whipping it in the air frenziedly.

At once, with a woody creak and a timid avowal of fealty from the gatehouse guards, the great, arched, double doors were opened. A crowd of flabbergasted, motley-clothed, ragged spectators gaped as the awesome, ghost-pale *woiwod* strode forward. Vlad ignored the pain of pus-festering wounds, ignored the camp followers' surprised, horrified, disappointed stares, crossing the ramp and drawbridge.

There was fear in their eyes.

Immediately Vlad realised what had happened. The unspeakable, senseless horror of it all shocked even his jaded senses. Cirstian strode forth, dropping to one knee to reassert his oath of fealty; resplendent in a yellow, soiled tunic emblazoned with a purple Crusader's cross across his wide chest. But Vlad was not listening. He stared steely-eyed at the carnage within the camp, at the four impaled soldiers crowded in the inner courtyard on high stakes. At the blood-streaked, offal-smeared grass, the smell of death and decay tainting the calm air. And then he saw the bodies in a distant corner, some half-naked; brutally hacked to pieces and dismembered. All were Gypsies. Even the Romany, betrayed after aiding the Romanians in the raping and killing of their mortal enemies—fellow *Szgany*.

Vlad could hardly find his voice. He strode past the crowding onlookers as if in a trance, mouth grimly set. None of the seven hundred and thirty-eight Gypsies had been spared. The Romanians had finished off the Romany later that fateful morning while they slept. By the looks of the cluttered carnage within the camp, it seemed none of the Gypsies' menfolk had returned from the previous week's ambush. Indeed, it was a miracle the Turks hadn't ventured north to storm the camp.

Butchered bodies lay everywhere. Some had attempted to flee before being run-down and sexually assaulted. Body parts lay scattered about the camp; heads, arms, hands, legs. Old and young alike had been butchered like swine, their gaily coloured Szgany/Romany clothes blood-splattered and torn. Scarves had been utilised to strangle victims when knives or battle-axes weren't close at hand.

Vlad stared in astonishment. His spruce-green eyes sparkled with unholy wrath. Some corpses still maintained their gruesome, spread-eagled pose, their frilled skirts up, though bodies decapitated. Silken-haired, brunette heads of once-beautiful *Szgany* maidens lay strewn about the tents and longhouses, their coiled tresses matted and spattered with blood.

Spears stuck out from strangled matrons' orifices obscenely; maidens' breasts cut-off or mutilated.

Lord Cirstian followed at a respectable distance, occasionally tugging Vlad's cape as he attempted to explain the mysterious events occurred. Vlad barely listened; nodding distractedly all the while.

Cirstian intimated uncertainly that the four, impaled camp-guards had been the ringleaders. Multitudes of startled Romanians wore looks of guilt, however, having lied to save their own skins. Vlad could see this. The boyar Cirstian and his rounded-up, surviving soldiers had returned to the camp this morning finding it in a state of pandemonium. Among Mohác's men had been a division of Gypsy infantry. In fact, husbands and fathers or relatives of the slain. Utterly enraged, they had insisted the camp remainders be extirpated, as blood-guilt. It was all Cirstian could do to keep his soldiers from mutiny: the outraged Moldavians having to be restrained with pikes! His contingent had had to threaten the encampment with assault this morning unless they opened the stockade's gates. When they'd entered (with fanfare), the camp was in a shambles, campfires still smouldering with the charred bodies of Szgany/Romany. The guilty soldiers and civilians had immediately denied responsibility. But after a little judicious 'persuasion' Cirstian had elicited at least some of the awful truth.

Vlad would not be appeased.

The guilty camp followers wore looks of stricken anxiety. None had expected the heinous *voivode* to return alive. Men and women—aye, even children—had participated in the disgusting midnight massacre. Romany women had blasphemously, temporarily, watched—laughing with glee—their men assaulting the helpless *Szgany* maidens. Some of them of mixed Celtic/Indic ancestry, no less. When the Romanians had turned on them, knifing them in the back before dawn, their deaths were quick, bloody—and deserved. Pity was spared naught for young or old.

Forgetting his wounds, Vlad sternly, coldly eyed the guilty camp-followers. He halted in front of each, eyeballing the miscreants like a drill sergeant. None could meet his terrifying gaze. He wrenched a sword from one of his Vlachian bondsmen, wandering up and down the throng. *No,* Vlad thought to himself, *a sword would be...too merciful.* He walked among them slowly, gauging their guilt. Gauging the extent of their crimes, each and all. Saw in his mind's eye each single moment of that dreadful night, each man's participation; the depravity and avarice of their evil hearts. And even as he stared, wide-eyed, unblinking, Vlad formulated these douchebags' execution. Hm Hmmm. Slow, painful torture. Then impalement.

Some began to crack. They stammered, yammeringly protesting their innocence, pointing accusing fingers at friends, family, lovers. Their unity was disintegrating under Dracula's deathly gaze. The camp began to shout now at each other, hotly denying such damning accusations. They jostled violently; Cirstian's soldiers rushing forward to maintain order with their tasselled halberds. Wails of despair rose forth from the crowd, women and children who would die now with their men.

Țepeș coldly ordered his mercenaries to prepare fresh stakes. Screams and pitiful crying rose the hackles of his neck. Some were clearly mere accessories to the atrocity. With an unexpected show of mercy, Vlad ordered the children expelled from the camp. They would surely die of starvation or be mauled by wolves, or else captured by vengeful Turks.

The young wretches would not leave, clinging, screaming, to their mothers' skirts.

Instead, Vlad relented into expelling their mothers also, an act he would later, bitterly, regret.

****

Sultan Mehmed jabbered incessantly. He was no warrior; he preferred the lewd company of his minions. He knelt within his tattered command tent, praying fervently to Allah to strike these infidel Christians down. Upon attacking Wallachia, the misled Emir had failed to realise he was not attacking an ordinary feudal state (or such puny excuses for government as existed amongst these disorganised Slav nations), but a cohesive military force to be reckoned with. He had indeed been misinformed of Wallachia's military strength; unlike other European nations, the *Naši* (Prince) had the choice of calling upon the peasant-class as a fighting force, having no great army of his own save an elite core of mercenary horsemen: the dreaded *Armașii*; purveyors of doom. In *Kaziglu Bey's* realm, peasants were bondsmen, but essentially free, an idea which Mehmed had neither considered nor imagined. (Thus, a virtually limitless reserve of skilled fighting-men had been unleashed on the unsuspecting Asiatic horde.) Beside him knelt two holy men, repeatedly touching their spotlessly white, ruby-pinned, splendid turbans to the tent's clean linen floor, their egg-shaped heads pig-shaven, thin lips eclipsed under monstrous, black walrus-moustaches, curled up at the tips. They cried aloud in rapture towards their God, inflamed with the zeal of a holy war. These were members of the *Mujahedin*, Islam's premier, religious fighting-order. Yet the *Jihad* of 1461–62 had turned sour; much, much sourer than previous ones. For the first time, the Sultan's imperial forces had been shamed on the battlefield, albeit a midnight ambush perpetrated by that unscrupulous madman, Vlad Tsepesh, a war-wolf cunning enough to avoid confrontation by the light of day; when *Kaziglu Bey* did attack, it was usually dusk when the Turks were at supper. Not since the Khan Mongols of *Timur-Lenk* (Tamerlane) or Richard the Lionheart had Allah's Chosen Ones been defeated so utterly. Dracula's attrition campaign had been masterfully executed. None of the Sultan's generals had anticipated this madman's brilliance on the battlefield nor skullduggery in the forests.

The leonine crazy man on the Romanian throne had already staked over *80,000* of the Ottomans' finest, and showed no sign of slowing nor relenting; the Sultan's Pashas could almost hear the crazed Wallach's depraved laughter…

A winter campaign would stretch Mehmed's funds to the limit. Overnight, Vlad Dracula's elite fighting force of Gypsies, vagrants, peasants, and striplings had decimated the imperial army of God. Mehmed's mathematicians were already counting the dead, the wounded, the maimed caused by Țepeș' wholly unexpected counter-attack. To assault isolated parties was one thing, but not a few times had Vlad the Mad brazenly attacked Mehmed's main army at dawn or twilight, then disappearing into the mists like wraiths. (The Emir's vanguard had been devastated; the greatest fighting force of their time turned into a rabble of cringing, whining idiots!) Several mistakes in battle strategy had cost Mehmed a victory here in Wallachia; elephants which had unexpectedly stampeded his ghazis during the midnight ambush; failure to man the ditches with sentries or healthy guard dogs; inefficient spy networks to monitor Vlad's movements. Sultan Mehmed was certain there were under 10,000 soldiers remaining, the majority having either deserted come dawn or having been trampled or perished in flaming tents. The Holy Roman Emperor's moneylenders would be ill-inclined to add to Mehmed's depleted treasury. Pope Pius and Frederick III would no longer be willing to finance the imperial Ottoman war against Wallachia as long as the partisans kept scoring victory after victory. Thrice Mehmed had crossed the Danube into Wallachia, thrice he had been sent scampering (tail between his legs like the cowardly dog that he was), back to Bosnia-Herzegovina. In Transylvania's benighted alps, the holdouts might survive for years, harassing the Sultan's troops based on the *Cîmpia Româna*; those gruellingly hot plains south of Tîrgovişte. Emperor Frederick III had already hinted to Mehmed's ambassadors that their mutual alliance may be at an end. Frederick had implied that Austria might seek to annex Wallachia with the aid of staunch ally Hungary.

Even now, the Wallachian-born King Matthias of Hungary was starting to siphon Crusade funds from the Vatican to enrich his own coffers. His deception was said to be the talk of Europe, relieving the Pope of precious gold and silver. Instead of fuelling an anti-Turkish Crusade, Matthias schemed to annex Wallachia for himself. Mehmed could have Moldavia if he wanted it.

And Sultan Mehmed's secret alliance with Hungary still stood.

****

November 13th, 1462 AD
Castle Dracula, Argeş, Near Curtea de Argeş

Dracula paced the Renaissance bedchamber restlessly. Outside the bubble-paned gothic window, snow drifted down from glowering skies, speedily blanketing the frozen Transylvanian countryside. He glanced at the small, ornate fireplace, noting without pleasure his own, gilded armorial crest impressed into the plaster. The fireplace-hood tapered upward from several leering, jutting, ghoulish corbels; a relatively recent invention. The apartments were cold, despite the roaring, spitting hearth. Voica sat content inside the splayed-windowed recess, knitting to pass the time. There'd be no hunting today, no frolicking nor walks in the snow.

Vlad was deeply worried. King Matthias had promised his undying support against the infidel Turks four months ago. He had led an army toward Cluj from Buda-Pest, having arrived September 17. There the Hungarian king had halted, setting up his fine court at decrepit Cluj castle. He had lingered, lingered, reluctant to save Dracula's tyrannical regime. All the while Ţepeş had ravaged the Sultan's forces from Tîrgu Mureş to Giurgiu. Occasionally Turkish expeditions had wandered into Transylvania, searching out Prince Vlad's notorious Castle Dracula, but *Kaziglu Bey's* partisans had destroyed their legions without mercy, impaling the captured ghazis, Janissaries, Azabs and sipahis at Sibiu. (Prince Dracula had paraded his skewered meat-puppets at such choice venues as Raznov, Rupea, Feldiora, and

Ghimbav like he was operating a circus circuit!) Since Vlad's infamous 'Night Attack', Matthias had vainly expected the Wallachians to fall any day. But the ambush which had crippled Mehmed's forces had proved amazingly indestructive to Vlad's army, barely touching his archer, spear, lance, and infantry reserves. Despite Dracula's rapidly diminishing forces, he had dealt the astonished Turks defeat after humiliating defeat, ambushing then retreating; leaving chaos and horrible carnage in his wake. In the streets of cities across Wallachia, people openly jeered Vlad, no fear now of his Gypsy thugs who were often busy elsewhere with their grisly tasks. Every Wallachian knew Vlad's 'Reign of Terror' was at its end. They could take no more of his Draconian policies.

The Germans were petitioning King Matthias to overthrow Vlad Dracula, 'Scourge of the Saxons'. Sultan Mehmed had offered the Saxons Vlad's ineffectual brother Radu as the new puppet-Prince of Wallachia, which they'd already, secretly, accepted.

But Vlad had yet to be overthrown. He held Wallachia and Transylvania firm, from Sighişoara and Tirgovişte to Feldiora and Bistritz, having brutally crushed abortive uprisings. His policies excluded German peasants and *Burgermeisters* from authority and the general law of the land, reversing their own tyrannical policies on them. Though by far the numerically superior (in Transylvania, at least), the Saxons now took second-place to monoglot Romanians, Daco-Wallachians, Szekely, Magyar, Poles, ethnic Russian/Ukrainians, and *Szgany*. The majestic, impenetrable, limestone, Transylvanian mountain ranges were Vlad Dracula's natural stronghold.

Voica glanced up, noting Vlad's pinched expression. He paced back and forth between the immense, oval-shaped, silk draped four-poster bed and the *boudoir's* triangular-etched door of African mahogany, fingers tented under his chin. Ever since his return from that awful ambush, Vlad's pallor had been unnatural. Frightening. He looked like a walking dead-man. His face no longer dusky, but death white. And even more gaunt than before. Vlad had explained to her tersely of his near-fatal wounds upon his return. But somehow Voica felt he was holding something back.

Vlad's silken garments were immaculate as usual. He wore his favourite cape (which doubled as a cloak during inclement weather), the same cape which had accompanied him into so many battles, so long, that it trailed on the bedroom's Turkish-rug- covered floor. His face twitched. Vlad swung his arms jerkily, muttering under his breath, hissing. Voica peered out the glazed window with a melancholy sigh and gaze, watching snowflakes fall. Larch boughs draped in silvery hoar-frost presented a romantic Transylvanian vista. Christmas would soon be here. Fir and pine towered across the rocky gully like an angry, marching army. The great, wooden bridge was snow-packed in places. Work-gangs of grumbling men feverishly sought to keep the redoubt's route of access open with snow shovels and makeshift, burro-drawn ploughs; nervously awaiting long overdue rations. Ice sparkled on planks not yet smothered with snow, making the partially-cleared bridge glitter with treacherous, slippery stretches. Icicles clung to the girders underneath. There'd be no horses or coaches crossing the bridge today, for the drawbridge was up, and would stay up.

Great icicles clung to the raised drawbridge. This morning the chains had been coated with ice, temporarily making the sprawling, towering fortalice unapproachable. Then the drawbridge itself had stuck, ice-water bulging its wooden sides. Men had been dispatched to chop the ice away. The air was brisk and hellishly cold. Far, far below freezing. Along crow-stepped, multi-level ramparts, lookouts suffered even more.

Up in the watchtower's sole, upper-storey window, red noses surveyed the snowy Transylvanian countryside in intermittent shifts, watching for approaching Turkish contingents. Men with Russian-style fur caps and *tulwars* (Mongol swords) stamped their feet and cursed their misery to private gods. Inside the cloister-windowed, attached ladies' bower on the west side of the castle, ladies-in-waiting complained bitterly of the fortress's damnable heating system (the most sophisticated of its time). The vast, feminine apartments billowed with the soft, mesmerising swish of pink, yellow, or white silk drapes over man-size gothic windows embellished with interlacing, floriated designs, the women chafing their hands or exchanging perfume samples, cursing Vlad Dracula's name. A myriad of honeycomb passages, chapels, fighting-galleries and countless antechambers and rooms bound the fortalice's precincts to the great keep, attached to its core yet egress barred by a staggering number of thick, iron yetts. Cold drafts whooshed down large, cylindrical cistern-drains throughout the castle.

The entire fortress was cold. Voica shivered. Her heavy woollen shawls, crinoline bustles, stockings, scarves, and linen wimple failed to keep her warm. An unexplainable, bone-numbing chill afflicted her. The place was a sieve, a drafty, frigid, fairy-tale palace of ice. Voica sat uncomfortably on a hard, high backed, floral-traceried chair, her derrière sore. Cold. Her numb hands shook so much she could hardly knit, despite the spitting hearth-fire nearby. Last night's lovemaking with Vlad beneath heavy sable furs and motley-coloured Persian rugs had been her only respite from the chills. She'd had no exercise whatsoever for over a month, her knees aching, restless. She was four months pregnant, though it barely showed. Voica did not at all look forward to her long winter imprisonment inside Castle Dracula's gloomy vaults. She would be denied the pleasures of outdoor walks in deference to her foetus. Vlad had promised her otherwise, but Voica knew he had a war to wage. Her chambermaids would rule her.

The air was placid outside. Serried ranks of evergreens hovered below the keep, swathing the montane landscape with a ruthless permanency. Vlad moved to Voica's side, leaning over her shoulder as, together, they watched the goings-on outside the splayed lancet window. On the Argeş far below a smattering of adults and children frolicked on the ice, sliding, colliding, laughing. The river had partially frozen near Cimpŭlung, a truly rare phenomenon. The skaters (their bladed footwear a new fad, recently imported from Sweden) looked no bigger than ants, throwing themselves into the snowbanks with careless abandon; unaware of who was watching. Vlad could see their rosy cheeks from here, their shiny red noses. He and Voica glanced at each other a moment, returning their gaze to the idyllic, Transylvanian scenery below. The great donjon, Prince Dracula's impressive *'magna turris'*, overlooked the river on its sloping 1000-foot-high mountain spur, the village of Arĕfu downstream, the keep looming above on the mountainous precipice of a sheer four hundred foot drop. Laughter trickled upwards, as if borne aloft on wings of wind. Vlad reassuringly placed his hand on his consort/wife's shoulder.

"You want to go outside, don't you?" murmured Vlad.

Voica nodded, raising her wide, deep-blue, imploring eyes to his questing face.

"Alas, it is too cold for you, my delicate autumn rose. The castle bridge would be too treacherous, and I am in no mood for making snow angels. You do understand?"

Voica nodded reluctantly, hating this kid-glove treatment she often received now it was known she bore Vlad's child.

"Are you blue?" Vlad insisted.

"I am lonely and bored," Voica muttered.

"Lonely? Am I not here?"

"You are here, milord, but your brooding makes you a ghost."

Vlad laughed aloud, shaking her shoulder gently. "I am, indeed, pale of late!" he exclaimed. "Very well. I shall take you for a long walk, though my *teulu* shall resent you for rousting them from their hearthside dice-games down in the great hall."

"Your bodyguard is too lazy anyway," Voica retorted with a giggle.

Vlad whisked her up into his arms, striding briskly toward the door.

"Yes. You Gypsies are a lazy race."

Cautiously, Vlad carried her down the wide, spiral stairwell of ironstone and red brick. The soldiers in the great hall looked up in surprise. Courtiers crossed themselves, retreating back into the shadows like spiders; muttering. (He could've sworn he saw a couple of them disappear behind a Moorish tapestry.) Vlad's ashen face rarely showed such animation. Still, his was a somewhat sinister, stern expression, thick lines etched into his face after decades of strife. The massive yett was already swinging open for Dracula's departure, held open by a gaunt, respectful, giant of a butler. The lean, close-cropped, swarthy brute watched with impassive, lustreless eyes as Vlad swept out of the gloomy, candlelit, shadow-stalked hall with his comely young mistress in his arms. Numerous seven-branched bronze candelabra stood scattered about the hall. Immediately, the lord's personal bodyguard leapt up from their dice table, wisely following their liege-lord.

Vlad still felt weak. He'd felt so since that fateful ambush four months ago near Tirgoviște. Outside it was bitterly cold, snowdrifts deepening by the hour. Snowbanks were mounting steadily, gathering against the blood-streaked bailey's rough, limestone walls. Soon the mighty citadel would be snowbound, cut off from the outside world for weeks. (The thought of an Ottoman incursion into 'his' mountains at this time, vulnerable as he was, made Țepeș *cringe*.) Vlad had much difficulty carrying Voica's slim, buxom figure down the last few steps inside the grim, dark forebuilding. He stumbled once, righting himself. He crossed the tiny drawbridge over its dry, shallow pit giving access to the looming forty-foot-tall forebuilding of the monstrous keep.

He set Voica down, breathing hard yet smiling.

Taking her hand, he led her toward the twin-towered, colour-banded, polygonal, checkered-masonry gatehouse. Its triple portcullises rose with a slow, rusty, infuriating grate; immense, spiked, hulking dragon killers. Their chains squeaked and squealed noisily. Vlad's *Armașii* followed obediently, matching his stride, their long, brown, woollen capes streaming out behind them. Above the chevron-moulded arch, Vlad's acorn-shaped, intimidating armorial crest bore an ominously rearing, flame-spewing dragon carved in sandstone as his coat-of-arms. At once, the main drawbridge began to lower, reaching out to touch the outer bridgehead and connect with the girder bridge. The lengthy drawbridge hovered above a virtual abyss, the snow disguising murderous, jagged rocks far below. The bridge struts extended a hundred feet down to the chasm's rocky floor; a steep carriage ramp ascending to the top of the summit.

Vlad's bodyguards walked ahead, some behind, escorting their Prince across the long, slippery bridge. They had to plough through hard-crusted snow too soft to walk on, for, unlike the castle's cobblestone bailey, the stupendous bridge-way hadn't been cleared yet. The snow crust broke like eggshells, plunging their furred boots into crystalline snow. Soon Voica's feet began to freeze. Gallantly, Vlad swept her off her feet, finally reaching the end of the causeway. He paused; there were three paths he could follow. One led straight ahead into the towering, evergreen forest; Vlad and his comrades now stood on the opposite bluff to the castle. Another trail meandered to the right, along the edge of the mountain scarp, snow packed by innumerable tinker's boots.

The opposite trail meandered to their left, toward the Gypsy settlement hidden behind hoar-frosted furze bushes. It was this snowbound route Vlad chose, setting Voica down once more, entering the forest and immediate winter gloom. He whistled, off-tune, a wistful Magyar ditty. Fir trees loomed above, magnificent alpine specimens so near to Vlad's heart. He loved these coniferous brutes more than he loved his fellow men. Vlad reached up, snapping off a crisp, brown cone from an easily bendable fir bough, bowing regally, then handing it to Voica as an inexpensive gift though sparkling emeralds, amethyst, opal, topaz, and diamonds hung at her necklace's bat-winged pendant. She curtsied. Voica smiled in wonder, rouged lips tilting to one side becomingly, eyeing the scaly cone with deep blue, rapturous eyes.

The Gypsy camp was gone.

Vlad halted, faltering. Snow shrouded the tiny burdock and milfoil-infested clearing, beyond which lay the village cemetery further back in the bushes. The Gypsy tribe had vanished. No footprints nor wagon tracks marred the fresh, pristine white snow. The *Szgany* caravan had moved on to safer pastures.

Astonished (and not a little annoyed at their audacity for leaving without their *seigneur's* consent), Vlad and his companions turned back, muttering, searching out other trails. The lone path had ended there in the clearing, beside the giant, ash-trailing, cylindrical brick incinerator where Vlad and Voica had often stopped to converse with the Romanised, Christianized Gypsies.

Voica trudged along in bewilderment, her mind wandering. Something had happened. Something dreadful. Since Vlad's brazen assault on Sultan Mehmed's forces, Voica's Gypsy acquaintances who had often visited the castle for various nefarious tasks had stopped coming. The Romany had recently become sullen, untalkative, hurrying away before she could seek their company. (She had often sought their blatherings; chaperoned, of course, as was necessary for the voivode's premier bedside companion.) They had always received Vlad's favour, played jigs in the castle's spectacular, gothic audience-hall outside the great keep during social occasions and royal feasts. They had often been invited into the *donjon* as well, playing familiar strains for his often-bored courtiers. Had Dracula harmed them in some way? Vlad had appeared strangely secretive about the so-called 'treaty' he'd made with their hereditary foe, the *Szigany*. Whenever Voica questioned him about it, Vlad clammed up like a mollusc. Yet countless efforts to contact the Gypsy clans of Moldavia's lofty plateaus had proven fruitless. It seemed they had packed up their belongings and vanished.

Vlad knew why. (He couldn't blame them either.)

Often Voica had sought the Gypsies' company, listening with girlish rapture for hours to their exotic, romantic music and their lilting, Daco-Romanian musical accents. To their speedily-played fiddles, their reels, the strange Celto-Hungarian melodies. Their colourful, covered wagons especially fascinated her, bright, gaily-painted, thatched family wagons with protruding tin chimneys where the Rom/Szgany slept, ate, and told fortunes for profit under Vlad's protective umbrella. The women, though they wore comely silk kerchiefs had more personal freedom than any in mainland Europe. Many of their cronies were wise-women, judges on the elder council. Witches, one might say. Some were (secretly) worshippers of Wicca, the great Mother Goddess *Ma Gog*, whom Old Testament Jews had mistakenly referred to as the land of Magog—Cimmeria, land of the Sea People, the *Rus*. (Old Welsh; *gogledd*, 'north'; *Rus*, c.f. archaic *rhos*, 'steppe lands'.) Scythia, Dacia, Illyria, Galatia. However, the Latinization of their dialects and the insidious advent of Punjabi customs and Christianity were slowly melting such fair traditions away.

The forest echoed with the royal party's boots. Crunching snow burst with a spray of brilliant, diamondy crystals. Winter skylarks sung among the fir boughs. Voica held Vlad's icy hand, her feet cold, her brain in rapture. It was so lovely here, she reflected; so untamed: wild, uncontaminated, unconquered. Only these nature trips brightened her days, these long, exploratory walks warming her questing soul if not her flesh. Not a few injured or abandoned baby birds and animals had Voica found, taking them back to the castle and nurturing them as pets at Vlad's whim. (Once she'd even brought back a bear cub, to Vlad Țepeș' ire!) Thick clumps of snow flew up from the walkers' insulated, fur-lined leather boots like warhorses churning up snow. Even Voica wore the ubiquitous, cross-hatched, rawhide boots, the true sign of a barbarian's woman. She pondered Vlad's often gloomy, mysterious personality.

Fortunate she was not to share a household with a bevy of concubines. Or wives, as in the Mohammedan fashion. (Most of the hereditary lords of Transylvania, as well, had large seraglios of willing wenches.) Certainly Dracula was unique among European *mormaers* for his cool-headedness. He was no hot-blooded rake. (Though he was certainly hot-blooded!) In fact, Voica had heard those shameful, dishonourable, dishonest rumours so viciously spread by Vlad's detractors—Romanian or otherwise. She knew he was not impotent, nor sexually abnormal. Cruel lies were being spread of his dastardly impalements; worst of all were tales of anal fixation indulged through the vague method of impalement. This she knew was a lie, for Vlad utterly despised men who lie with men and sodomisers. If anything, Vlad was utterly intolerant of such blatant fornication (his spies ever-vigilant). It was these wretches Dracula perpetrated some of his most horrendous cruelties on. Voica knew from Vlad's own self-confessions that he had boiled alive lascivious, unnatural people, flayed their skin, roasted them alive, afterwards baking what he called 'people pies' and feeding them to his victims' relatives—and then telling them. She still battled with herself trying to come to grips with his darker personality.

Another path led Vlad's entourage deeper into the outcrop's pine-cone-littered woods. They trudged ahead, their pink hands numb and freezing. Each warrior held his curled-up hands inside his frock, silently cursing Vlad and his leman for drawing them out of the castle and into this snowbound, wintry, alpine, Transylvanian purgatory. Sporadic forests extended beyond Little Poenari, the castle proper, adjoining the nearest mountain ridge affixed to the citadel via its long, wooden girder-bridge. (A jagged fissure in the escarpment separated the two.) Snow flurries continued to flutter down from overcast skies. Frost clung doggedly to the bodyguards' long, black, walrus moustaches or from unruly sideburns. Most were beardless. Often, at times such as these, the men wished fervently that they had thick, bushy beards to combat the Carpathians' stinging cold. But it was not their custom; but that of the Scythians; the Saxon, Goidel, and Ossetian.

Vlad crested a low knoll, looking out across the Transylvanian Alps with obvious, patriarchal pride. It was as if he himself had created these breathtakingly beautiful, frozen, Teutonic peaks with his bare hands—moulding them, as a potter with a wheel—building this awesome Carpathian mountain-chain as a natural stronghold to keep marauding Saxon and Austrian invaders out. He wondered uneasily if the venerable *Cŭmric* of his youth would still be spoken here, hundreds of years from now. To the immediate western marches lay overlord Hungary; northwest of that, Austria, the Germanies. Vlad could see the Tyrolean Alps despite snow-flurries and heavy blankets of snow. Or at least he fancied he could. Austria, his greatest, most lethal enemy—or potential ally. The Holy Roman Emperor was secure for now in Salzburg at ancestral Hohensalzburgh castle: first

Wallachia, Bohemia, and Hungary must fall before Emperor Frederick III of the House of Habsburg felt his beloved Tyrolean and Styrian alps threatened by Islam.

The Kingdom of Poland, as well, ever a source of friction to the fledgeling Romanian principalities of Wallachia and Moldavia—often invading, or imposing crushing penalties of tribute.

Vlad stood motionless, biting, ice-cold wind bringing tears to his eyes. His long, black, greying hair billowed out in disarray, the small, red-velvet cap atop his head threatening to blow away. His grotesque, plaited moustache tugged at his skin.

Voica stood patiently below the knoll, watching with anxious eyes as Vlad surveyed his stormy realm. She sensed his reflective mood, allowing him his distance. His escort stood at her side, shivering, their toes froze.

Vlad felt a curious twinge in his heart. A nostalgic longing, *hiraeth*, as if he were surveying this windy mountain slope for the last time. He knew not why. In all the years, throughout strife and intrigue, except for his brief exile in Moldavia, this had been Vlad's bastion. His retreat, a lofty eagle's eyrie, Dacian *eryri*, a place to hunt, fish, wander for hours. Vlad loved fishing for pike, trout, or bass in the cold mountain tarns and winding rivers down in deep, rocky ravines almost as much as he loved to war. Nighttime placed no bonds here. Vlad was free to walk at night, a nocturnal beast, shaking off his escort. Many a time he walked till dawn, wandering afar. He would bypass the noisy portcullis gates, slipping underground beneath the keep toward the castle-well in the middle of the courtyard, torch in hand, descending below the family vaults and chapel and down into the mountain's subterranean passage emerging at the Argeş' riverbanks and adjacent, Orthodox chapel. The underground tunnel had been built by Vlad's boyar-slaves while he supervised, the wretches bracing the tunnel with beams and reinforcing it with mortared stone. He had often dressed as a peasant afterwards, travelling to villages and towns, his own spy. The villagers had revealed much to his keen ears, mostly secrets safe only within a Saxon town. Come daylight, the plotters would be astonished when Vlad's retainers came to escort them to the impaling grounds in the citadel high above. In the villages at night, in taverns, on streets, Vlad had overheard much, discovering who be traitors and who be ally, afterwards rewarding his surprised supporters with gold, his detractors with death. He had a keen judgment as to what extreme criticism constituted 'treason'. The faithful would be richly rewarded; with gold, land tenure, or high office. For sure, the Saxon drunkards had soon cautiously guarded their tongues while this mysterious, cloaked stranger was about. (Even had he threw back his cloak the peasants would've simpered and marvelled in awe, for none had the temerity to assault a Prince, a Divine ruler.) No one accosted nor suspected the dark, patch-eyed wretch, for Prince Vlad was utterly intolerant of the crime of common assault against the poor. (Or *any* unprovoked assault, be it against the elderly, strangers, the fairer sex, or the homeless.) Some may or may not have suspected he was a spy for cruel, dreadful Vlad Dracula, but dared not molest him for fear of the Impaler's diabolical wrath.

Vlad looked down the wintry bluff. Heavy snowdrifts were building up below, tree boughs half-buried and bent in snowy submission. A vicious gust of snowflakes swirled below in the misty Argeş valley, coming his way and smacking him full in the face with an icy flurry. Vlad struggled to catch his breath, the west wind seemingly departing with his inhalation.

At last, Vlad hopped down, suddenly scooping Voica up in his arms. He rushed toward the trees, eyes agleam with mischievous, wide-eyed glee before tossing her into a monstrously deep snowdrift. She screamed aloud, plunging deep into a snowbank, sputtering with indignation as Vlad laughed aloud, turning to his startled bodyguards. Voica's legs stuck out from the snowdrift indecently, crimson/blue, pleated skirts partly revealing her shapely, blue-stockinged, envy-inspiring legs. (A choice slice of thigh caught the men's rapturous attention, much to her master's ire.) The snow made her squeal with anger, icy, wet snowflakes hiding within her slips and down her bodice.

"There you are, laddies, you may bury her alive now!" jested Vlad, laughing uproariously once more. He clapped his scarlet-stockinged knees, watching with amusement as the eight young guardsmen exchanged confused, startled glances. Two of them began moving forward like Swiss wind-up curiosities while Voica struggled in the snow, as if to carry out Vlad's mad orders. They halted as he grasped Voica's pink, searching hand and hauled her up and out of the icy bank. She glared at him, patiently shaking the sticky snow out of her hair and muslin headscarf. Voica held her tongue, too shrewd to rebuke Vlad in public or otherwise. She began to shiver intolerably, her teeth chattering, cheeks red and flushed. Her nose glowed a shiny pink.

Vlad continued to chuckle, upbraiding his gullible, Wallachian soldiers with cruel humour. "You pitiful wretches," he cried, "you would bury her alive if I asked! You would throw yourselves off the cliff if I commanded it. Ha, ha! Go on. Take a running jump. Vault yourselves off the cliff. Do it now."

A couple of them began shuffling their feet nervously, casting appalled glances over the mountain ledge. The men's faces turned ashen, seriously considering the terrifying distance plummeting to the frozen Argeş' banks and weighing their chances for survival.

"Never mind, you Wallach cretins," Vlad muttered at last, still chuckling, swooping Voica off her feet once more. Her stomach lurched uneasily; accidentally bumping her forehead against his long, patrician nose. He ignored the pain, ignored Voica's grimace. She hated such bluff, casual treatment, expected to tolerate Vlad's rough—*childish*—games. "Back to the castell," cried Vlad, stomping determinedly toward his brooding mountain-fortress upon Little Poenari's outcrop. Across the valley, the larger hill of Poenari—Hill of Pain—towered over the glimmering Argeş river, its ruin-festooned mountaintop the site of many of Vlad's horrible impalements. Towering, unburdened stakes of cypress crowned its summit. Vlad was jolly today. Most days he brooded indefinitely; a gloomy, melancholy man, paranoid of intrigue and bad blood.

He stumbled along, carefree, ignoring Voica's pleas to set her down. Her moodiness puzzled him. Had he not spared his time, his fear-riddled thoughts to walk with her? And all these days she had accused him of crankiness!

Vlad began to scowl as he neared the castle. Voica watched with ill foreboding as Dracula's face clouded, his dark, emerald eyes glittering. She waited with resignation for the storm of vituperation from his protruding, blood-red lips once inside Vlad's private apartments. She knew not why, for he had never once rebuked her unnecessarily. Ţepeş' noble profile seemed unusually wan and emaciated now, his nostrils wide and arched, eyes glowering. His nose long, straight, and prominent, though curiously beaked at the tip (a peculiar trait of Dracul's bedevilled progeny). Voica began to shiver uncontrollably, trembling in trepidation as Vlad calmly crossed the lengthy castle bridge.

She felt heavy in his arms. Vlad's breath laboured, his heart drumming. Voica lay crouched across his bulging biceps, head lolling against his shoulder, her feeble, numbed hands placed timidly one inside the other. Her skirted legs stuck out from Vlad's arms, almost catching the left bridge struts with her pointed boots. Behind him, Vlad's protectors walked dutifully, and in silence. Their boots crunched hard, noon snow. Fir boughs waved back and forth under a heavy November wind across the gully, sheltered inside the castle bailey.

Voica's belly growled. She was famished. She looked forward to lunch, to ham, cheese, pastries. The arched drawbridge began to lumber downward on its chains as Vlad neared the dizzyingly terrifying, empty chasm. Three wooden beams exited their stone wall-slits like arms, lowering the chained drawbridge across Castle Dracula's horrifying gulch.

Vlad smiled complacently now, watching pleased at the fortress's smooth function, its intricate machinations exciting his calculating mind. *She*, this macabre fortalice, was Vlad's invention, the pride of all Wallachia. Vlad's monster. He could almost see the machinery working behind the machicolated, ironstone walls as it rolled, clanked, squealed. Wooden cogs caught like precision clockwork as the three huge, spiked, wood/iron portcullises rose, jerking free from their frozen ice patches beneath a cobbled entranceway. At last, Vlad strode forward across the drawbridge, passing beneath the sombre, arched, rainbow-machicolated gatehouse entrance. Suddenly, he nudged Voica's thigh, looking upwards.

"Murder-holes," murmured Vlad. As they entered, Voica noticed a menacing, arched slot as if for the first time, guarding the gatehouse's entrance from outside. The slots were designed for pouring boiling water or pitch, either to extinguish a burning gate or to scald unwary besiegers. Other round holes, however, inside the gatehouse passage would further discourage attackers, holes placed with checkerboard precision to scald the unwary. On either side of her, closed doors led into the gatehouse, whose vermiculated keystones accentuated the palatial fort's Byzantine grandeur, where the guards and Vlad's newly-appointed castellan, Morič Milösovich, had their lodgings.

Voica nodded. She was not interested in military technology. Yet her basic role in life now was to provide Vlad with sons, so she must acquaint herself with Ţepeş' peculiar, morbid interests. She knew her sole purpose according to strict, Romanian court etiquette was to be his mistress as well as child-bearer. Vlad had told her he loved her, that he considered her to be his wife. Voica did not believe him. She was his concubine, nothing more.

Up the keep's gloomy, ashlar-cornered forebuilding's stairs, into the banquet hall Vlad and his entourage dashed. He had set Voica down brusquely, allowing her to keep up or be left behind. The second story yett was already open upon his command. The sentries watched the cyclopean walls night and day, taking careful note of Vlad's departure and return to suit his pleasure.

(It was his penchant for showing up at the outer bailey's disused postern gate's portcullis at the wee hours of morning, demanding to be let in, which lent Vlad his ominous reputation as a *moroi*. Yet not once had any of the numerous sentries on patrol seen him depart the previous night.)

Vlad cultivated the illusion of *wampyr*, revelling in his subjects' abject, superstitious terror to his sadistic heart's delight.

The donjon's wainscoted, dim-lit, great hall was warm for a change. Antler trophies up high on whitewashed, ashlar walls testified to the drafty, echoing *Rittersaal's* vibrant court. The gargantuan, taper-hooded hearth crackled and spat merrily. Servants scrubbed the mixed stone/brick floor, oblivious of Vlad's dramatic, cape-winged entrance. (Despite the great size of *Draculeşti's* feast hall, he rarely used it; preferring the more grandiose one beyond the keep: the change of venue often lifting his sodden spirits.) A flaxen-haired minstrel wearing a green, feather-topped, three-cornered hat plucked at his lute near the garderobe stairs whilst another frowsty old-timer with grizzled, balding white hair blew Romanian folk tunes on wooden panpipes up on the dais beside him. Three ladies-in-waiting clapped along, humming to the infectious, Latin rhythms. Maidservants busied themselves at clearing away the morning's repast from several massive trestle tables. Dim, shadowy, guttering white candles poorly lit the cavernous, majestic Knights Hall from triple-columned brass candelabrum scattered throughout the hall. The surrounding minstrel-galleries high above were lost in spectral, vaporous shadows, colourful armorial flags fluttering softly in a draft.

"Wine," Vlad muttered to a nearby servant, watching, bemused, as a chambermaid dashed toward the steps leading to the wine cellars. "Walk, don't run!" he bellowed. "Stupid wench," muttering to himself.

Voica sat down wearily on a stool next to the hearth, warming her icy, wet hands. Snow melted from her luxurious brown hair, her clothes. Her teeth chattered, hands shaking. Vlad blithely joined her, standing with his back against the escutcheoned mantel. Voica eyed his black silk cape with a worried, sideways stare. She was sure the garment (absurdly long, a new style popular at court but, for most, useless in combat) was about to catch aflame.

"Did you enjoy our walk today, *domnişoară?*" inquired Vlad, automatically switching back to Romanian, his heavy-lidded eyes never leaving the brick, groin-vaulted ceiling.

Voica cleared her throat, choosing her words carefully. "Yes, my lord," she prudently lied.

"You are a very poor liar, milady," Vlad murmured, chuckling. He turned his eyes to her, sparkling with grim, black humour. "I don't tolerate liars in my Kingdom. Please reword that phrase."

Voica stared in astonishment.

"You are pouting, *domnişoară*," Vlad commented. "Admittedly, you have a very comely, very *sexy* pout…but I would rather you spoke your mind. You're a woman, not a mouse."

Voica looked away, embarrassed. Her cheeks and neck flushed with anger.

Vlad reached out, tilting her chin towards him. "Do I make myself clear?" She nodded.

"Good. Come."

****

Vlad wasted no time in rushing Voica up the keep's spiral stairwell. She clung to his clammy, cold hand fearfully, waiting for Dracula's rage once inside the privacy of his gothic bedchambers. (The last time she'd seen that glint in his eye he'd murdered a yeoman, personally, by nailing the sullen farmhand's *fez* to his head for spitting on Țepeș' boot!) At last, pushing open a small, arched door, Vlad swung Voica none too gently towards the purple, chintz-draped, four-poster bed. Voica gasped, her coiffure coming undone. She collapsed awkwardly onto the undulating, down-filled mattress, reclining against the yellow silk quilts and sable furs, almost against her will. Vlad slammed the door.

She expected an assault. Instead, Vlad calmly moved toward an opulently-carved dresser of walnut, pouring each a crystal glass of cordial. He swung the bureau's ornate, rotating, round mirror away with a relaxed hand, hating its omnipresent stare, the ghost in the mirror which was now him.

Voica tried in vain to sit up. The gravity seemed to weigh against her. It was as if a malignant spirit, a *poltergeist!* in Vlad's bedchamber, was holding her down. Her legs stuck out from the canopied bed, ruffled Gypsy skirts exposing her cold knees. She felt as if she were floating on a beanbag.

Vlad set the glasses down.

"I am very displeased with you!" he cried. The unnatural pallor of his skin plucked at Voica's heart strings, setting her nervous system a-jangle.

"My lord?"

"My best is never good enough!! I try to please you, but you only brood like a hen!" he accused. "You think I am a fool, that I don't realise what you *really* think of me? Now I am a monster to you! What hath happened to our play? Our love?"

She scrunched up her beautiful, half-moon eyes, stammering. "But-but-but my lord, I'm pregnant," she wailed.

"Pregnant! I KNOW you're pregnant. But this is Transylvania, not Saxony. You are four months pregnant. You have many months ere the foetus is endangered by rough play. Woica." Vlad stepped forward, seizing her wrist. "Look at me. I am an ageing man—"

"That's not true, master—"

"It is. Only enemies have I now. Are you to be my final nemesis?"

Voica stared back, helplessly commiserating with Vlad as she watched, day by day, his power base in Transylvania disintegrate, his subjects fleeing now by the thousands. Her wide, questing eyes became luminous, bright blue, brimming almonds, thin brows slanting; misty-eyed, though with scant comfort to give.

"I shall never forsake you," she whispered. She reached up, brushed a tender forefinger against Vlad's smooth, pale cheek. Tears welled up from her eyes. And it was then she realised that her and Vlad's love was at an end. Forcefully, miserably wrenched away from them. Deep inside, she knew she'd never see him again. Sobbing, she leaned forward, accepting Vlad's embrace with bitter, instinctive resignation. Responding to her passionate, urgent caresses, he pushed her backward, unlacing her bodice, making love to her on top of the rumpled bedsheets till nightfall.

Afterwards, they strolled down in the valley below till dawn, silent, Voica's head on Vlad's shoulder. At peace now.

****

2 December, 1462 AD

Transylvanian Alps

Vlad led his forces up the Argeş valley, glancing back disconsolately from his slowly trotting warhorse at Castle Dracula's long, jagged silhouette over the Făgăras foothills. His heart twinged with farewell foreboding, afraid to leave the bearer of his child with the castle's jackal servants. Yet he knew she could be nowhere safer, for this mission would be his riskiest yet. She had begged to come with him, to be free of the castle's oppressive, sepulchral atmosphere. Only days ago, a turncoat Turk in Vlad's pay had climbed Poenari mountain, opposite Vlad's citadel across the winding Argeş river, at night, firing an arrow from a Mongolian hornbow into the watchtower's narrow, lone, upper-story window. Voica had been alone inside the candlelit archive chamber wearing a fur-edged shift, helping sort important documents when the arrow thudded into a bureau, arcing high to climb through the air and eventually fluttering through the tower's embossed window-embrasure. Fearing an assassination attempt on Vlad's life, she had suddenly noticed a queer note pinned to the arrow's shuddering quiver. The shaft had slammed into a black candle, knocking it over and dousing it. Voica had shown the letter to Vlad; the Turk had warned that Mehmed and Radu were leading an army north, straight toward Cimpŭlung and only a day's march distance with a sizeable battalion of cherry-wood cannon. Vlad knew he must leave immediately, on the hour, calling for his castellan, knights, and squires. He feared he could not trust Matthias, deeply suspected an ambush in the Făgăras foothills by the Hungarians or some later betrayal. Castle Dracula was virtually unassailable; its reinforced south walls would easily absorb any cannon-shot Mehmed chose to pelt it with. The watchtower would signal approaching enemies.

He was leading his troops toward Teutonic Köenigstein castle, eastern Transylvania, where the turtlish King Matthias of Hungary's impressive war host awaited him. Starting from July, Matthias had taken five months to reach Cluj, stopping here, stopping there, bypassing Vlad's grim fortress and eventually arriving at Castle Brân, holding court at various Romanian castles as if he were the Holy Roman Emperor himself.

Vlad deeply mistrusted Matthias. Such snail-like progress could only be a bad omen. The Hungarian courtiers in their fine, frilly, colourful silk brocades and padded blouses had boasted much of their intention to crush Mehmed's invading forces entrenched at Giurgiu. But talk was cheap. King Ladislas III of Hungary had died on the battlefield of Varna leading a Crusading army against Islam many years ago, plunging that country into internal strife and civil war for years to come after the Magyar's army had been annihilated by Sultan Mured II. Only Janós Hunyádi's heroic defence of his Transylvanian homeland had saved Hungary from conquest and domination, denied Sultan Mured of such rich, exorbitant *baksheesh* payments. Such memories would surely be in the back of Matthias' knights' minds. Catholic Hungary could be as much Vlad's foe as Ottoman Turkey.

He rode astride a massive black destrier, his mind wandering as his convoy marched towards decrepit Köenigstein castle. Vlad prayed that Matthias' treaty with Turkey had collapsed as his informants claimed. Snow still crusted the ground, though not as much as before since last weekend's temporary thaw. The Wallachian foot soldiers, pikemen, lancers, chevaliers, and infantrymen were worn-out and bedraggled, their sheepskin vests dirty and caked with mud. Their long, dark, greasy hair lank. Vlad's royal baggage-train was meagre. At last count, his army had dwindled to less than four thousand.

The covered supply wagons crunched and squeaked, their wheels embedded in the hard snow. Horses neighed, whinnied, snorted; donkeys brayed, their protruding ribs a sure sign of severe malnutrition; military commanders and boyars shouted at lazy, straggling, kettle-helmeted soldiers. Buzzards hovered high under a pale blue winter sky, mewing, as if waiting for men to fall.

Slowly, Vlad's convoy rounded a bend in the valley, dreary Castle Dracula disappearing behind a mountain scarp. Forests ahead offered a sparkly, wintry welcome, the boughs pregnant with clumps of snow. A narrow trail wound its way through mixed fir, pine, and spruce towards some unguessable, seemingly unreachable destination. A trail to Hell. Dracula's regiment passed a crossroads: a few of his soldiers pausing to say prayers at venerable St Iuliu's; the roadside chapel with its fairy-tale frescoes and onion-dome one of many secular churches dotted across the land. The disgusted *woiwod* spat on its holy ground, snapping an order to move on, cursing one of the Orthodox lay brothers as he passed.

No less than half a dozen middle fingers were aimed at his back; the scowls of Swabian and Magyar, petty criminals, seeking sanctuary from Vlad the Stake's tyrannical regime.

The multitudes of horses, pack mules, donkeys, wagons and marching, halberd-bearing men entered the green-gloom forest, following a narrow wagon trail deep into the benighted wilderness. (Daunting Făgăras pass, often misty, cold, and uninviting, awaited with a days-long trek over unforgiving alpine terrain: No one in Vlad's rabble looked forward to its traversing.) Pine cones and needles littered the snowbanks, the trail rutted and flattened by countless feet, hooves, or wagon wheels. Mud and horse dung were trampled into piss-yellow snow. Peasants used this lonely forest trail for trade purposes, sending loads of furs on donkeys and carts toward distant Yugoslavia or Hungary, or perhaps Austria. Vienna was the goal of most wealthy merchants, the stronghold of Austria's awesome mercantile trade. From Styria and the Tyrol's alps, they would come, trading goods with Vlad Ţepeş' laughably-backward country. The Wallachians were goofs, too stupid to realise the Austrian merchants were notorious crooks; coin-clippers, slavers, and fraudulent adventurers. Normans were no better, gluttonous swine with a taste for adventure, an eye for gold and swine's morals. Vlad had long ago stopped being diplomatic; when merchants had been halted at various tollgates across the country for levying of tariffs, they had smuggled goods out of the country. (When confronted, they had, on occasion, killed Vlad's bailiffs and customs officers, unprovoked.) Tirgovişte was Prince Dracula's main checkpoint, with three different tollgates leading out of the Renaissance city. He now treated the merchants with iron gloves. Vlad impaled them instead.

By snowy midday, Vlad's morose partisan army entered the lofty eastern-Carpathian range, their feet frozen, their bellies growling. They had much to pine for. Late November, Mehmed's Turks had made a surprising counter-attack from Macedonia, reclaiming southern Wallachia without opposition; requisitioning the once-productive prairies, which were the bread basket of Romania. Mehmed's roving Janissaries seized the *Cîmpia Româna* and Getic plateau with nary a shot fired, freeing the region—with the public's applause—from *Kaziglu Bey's* mad regime. This time the Ottomans had been invited, welcomed by various boyar factions opposed to Vlad Dracula "Son of Satan's" Reign of Darkness. The Turks would have to wait for next year, however, to benefit from Romania's granaries; Vlad's partisans had scorched the entire southwestern quadrant of Wallachia, their terrible 'scorched earth' policy also poisoning wells and burning shacks where families had once lived. Only in northern Transylvania was the modest barley harvest reaped. However, in the east, near the Moldavian border and Russian hinterlands, peasants in the Dobruja district near Mamăglia had watched, dismayed, as the Turks reaped their cereal fields. Dracula had by that time retreated with his dwindling forces into lower Transylvania, setting up base at Braşov, Mediaş, Tîrnuveni, and outlying districts. It was clear by now that Ţepeş' army was deserting in droves, however, some abandoning their posts at night or plotting mass nocturnal desertions. Vlad could see it all now, his eyes clear for the first time in years. Despite his dogged determination, his reign was at an end.

The only question now was whether he die defending his country, be sent into exile, or assassinated by his own henchmen. Vlad saw this risky reconnaissance with King Matthias' army as a last-ditch effort to rescue his Principality. His only other option was voluntary exile (although many of Vlad's low-born boyars still marched with him, scores of others, easily seduced by the jaded life of pampered nobility, had long-since deserted to the enemy camp).

To be sure, as long as Dracula drew breath, Turks would never claim his country.

Vúc Brancovic's small Serbian army was even now reconnoitring with King Matthias' battalions for the upcoming strike against Sultan Mehmed's artillery corps, so sure that the Triple Entente meant to march against Mehmed's Janissaries with assured victory. At five thousand men, Vúc's army would make small impact against the titanic Ottoman legions, but combined with Vlad's seasoned troops they would make a formidable, and mobile, guerrilla force. According to Vlad's informants, the Serb guerrilla-fighters had rendezvoused with Matthias' viceroy two days ago at Hunedŏara.

Vlad's army set up camp at nightfall, campfires blazing now as the soldiers sat cross-legged around their hearths while waiting for the roasting, wild boar. Dried vegetables steaming in an iron pot supplemented their meagre diet, oatmeal and fried sourdough their morning breakfast. Chunks of *brînza* (sheep's milk cheese) were brusquely passed around to salivating mouths. It had stopped snowing.

They were sleepy; heads drooped, bleary eyes flickered. Some snored loudly, shamelessly, while others stood guard in the boreal forest till dawn. For once, Vlad did not protest. He was tired. Tired of war. Of countless years of nocturnal campfires, counter-massacre, rapine, pillage, Inquisition.

High up in the brooding, northwestern Bihor mountains, black clouds rolled in. Somewhere from the inky darkness, hungry wolves howled eerily; their hound-like, sporadic yelping and long, mournful, ululating, drawn-out howls raising the hackles on men's necks. Hawk owls hooted. Wind whispered high up in the pine trees and dead willows. Stealthy animals with glowing red or yellow firefly-eyes prowled the flaming camp's ditched perimeter. Predators literally crawled out of the woodwork, and from Vlad's overwrought imagination. Werewolves. Vampire bats. Spooks. Ghouls. Strigoi, *nosferatu*. The superstitious knowledge of Satan's school of necromancy and wizardry high up in the mountains nearby (the *Scholomance*) made the soldiers' blood run cold. Surprisingly, a castle-bell tolled the hours from a distance. A hand made of clouds occasionally closed around a fleeting, gibbous moon, plunging the snowbound night into starless, Stygian darkness. 'Twas the Hand of Doom.

Vlad was drunk. He'd emptied his wineskin hours ago, and his squire's as well. Then he had emptied Cirstian's (who had never been a dedicated drinker), Cirstian who sat snoring beside him, half-slumped over his sleeping squire.

Vlad's sword lay across his cloaked thighs, ready for battle, fingering the steel pommel nervously as he'd done for fourteen, nightmarish years. Beneath Vlad's cloak, pure white, sheepskin breeches (which Romanians as well as Britons hotly claimed to have invented) warmed his muscular legs. Vlad eyed the camp suspiciously; paranoid. Suspecting some miscreant might try to assassinate him. He began to doze, one eye open. Worried about tomorrow.

His small army would arrive at Köenigstein by noon. What then? Could Matthias be trusted? That turn-coat, snake-like midget. Vlad had never met King Matthias Corvinus-Hunyádi, but nasty court rumours depicted the son of Ion de Hunedŏara as a short, snub-nosed, indecisive pipsqueak. Vlad knew he could break the little tyrant with one hand. Țepeș smiled at the thought. He reached out his hand absent-mindedly, instinctively reaching for Voica's rump to pat. He remembered with a sleep-riddled shock that she was not there. He was alone. And infinitely lonely. He felt a bitter regret, suddenly, irrevocably certain that he would never see Voica's lopsidedly-smiling, blue-eyed, dimpled, mischievous face again. The son or daughter he might never gaze upon, whose fat chin Dracula might never tickle.

And Vlad knew. Vlad knew. The sky had fallen. And he felt himself drifting off into spiritual limbo, falling off the edge of the world.

****

December 4th, 1462 AD
Köenigstein Castle, Central Transylvania

Vlad's ragtag army was met by a less than exuberant Hungarian court nestled within modest Köenigstein castle, roosting high up on its 1000-foot crag. The mercenaries posted at the snowbound fortalice's half-timbered gatehouse balked at opening the gates to Vlad and his retainers. It was snowing again. Far below, Dracula's ant-like army huddled miserably in their portable rawhide tents, the disgusted men crowded around their campfires. Gusts of snow obscured the tall, triangular-peaked, Germanic gatehouse from view. Snowflakes the size of a man's fist drifted down lazily, suddenly borne aloft on a swirling wind. A whirlwind high up on the mountaintop. Bright snow made the eyes smart. The castle's hexagonal, onion-domed, Teutonic donjon loomed above the heavily-machicolated, flintstone walls, Austrian-style, conical lookout towers with narrow murder-holes below surveying the Yuletide landscape with hostile black apertures for eyes. Three glazed, unshuttered windows, two above the other, the recurrent gothic pattern. Like a ghostly, moaning face. Ancient masonry crumbled from the walls, toeholds for nocturnal creatures from Hell. Even Vlad had to admit, it was a truly ghastly, brutal fortress. A miniature tour-de-force. *Chemin-de-rondes* guarded the gatehouse arch.

Wooden hoardings (fighting-galleries) topped round stone towers in the Austrian fashion, convenient archer galleries perched below bluish grey, slate-topped witch's caps. There was no sun today. Only pale grey clouds. Low clouds. Misty. Along battlemented wall-walks, hostile Austrian mercenaries patrolled the multi-level, crow-stepped ramparts, leering and shouting German abuse at notorious, bloodthirsty Dracula. Vlad enjoyed his awesome reputation. The Impaler. (*Țepeș*, in Latin.) It suit him well. He smiled, grimly meeting their cowardly stares.

With a grating noise, the old, iron portcullis began to rise. Beyond the rusted, latticed bars Vlad and his retinue could see the snowbound, cobbled courtyard and the *seignior's* armorial crest high above the keep's seven-sided forebuilding. Far above, a murderous sentry gallery glowered down from a leaden, many-sided, green patinaed roof cap. Arrow loops peered out over the frozen wasteland of east-central Transylvania; the heavily machicolated, stone wall-walk bristling with gunports carved into the older arrow embrasures.

Vlad strode forward, aiming grimly for the oolite forebuilding. His bodyguards followed closely, ready to leap out in front lest an assassin appear. (He wore a steel breastplate beneath his tunic-blouse, in any case.) Vlad wanted to impress upon Matthias just who was in command here. Transylvania, though technically Hungarian—Austrian—domain was his by divine ancestral right. The Motherland of Wallachia, "Land Beyond the Forests". His Cimmerian ancestors had settled these dark, hostile mountains as Stone Age cave dwellers. They had traded greenstone ceremonial axes and called themselves *Prydein*. (Brythonic—Briton: Prydein, 'countrymen'—brethren—NOT referring to the later-coined British Isles.) To the Romans, *Pictae, Alemanni, Alanae, Gelonae, Belgae, Getae*…all the same folk; enemy of the Germanic *'Gaedheltschach'*. (Irish, Scottish *Germailtschach.*)

A tall, fair-haired, elderly man stood at the head of the forebuilding's stairs. Vlad halted momentarily, assessing this potential foe. The looming stranger wore crimson livery of the King of Hungary and a short, bum-freezing, navy blue cape. His waist-high stockings were a bright, iridescent, turquoise-blue. On his breast, the leopard insignia of the King of Hungary glittered with sapphires and gold. His hair was neither brown, nor flaxen—but dirty blond. A short, brown, forked beard and drooping, curled moustache graced the commandant's chin and upper lip. Wide, pale grey eyes surveyed Vlad with haughty disdain.

Slowly, the commandant descended the steps while Vlad Dracula climbed undaunted. Vlad lowered sinisterly at this imbecile field-general, eyes unyielding and overtly hostile as he neared the well dressed, long-haired rogue. The man had the look of a Pole or a Czech. Instinctively, Vlad fingered his dagger hilt.

"Welcome, Lord Dracula. Come freely. Go safely; and leave something of the happiness you bring." The stranger spoke Romanian, albeit not fluently. He had addressed Vlad in the standard Wallachian greeting. Vlad spat in disdain, halting belligerently below the commandant. The lone stranger smiled disarmingly, extending his left hand, gapped teeth rotted and chipped from countless tavern brawls.

"I bring no happiness where I go, only death," muttered Vlad in a dire tone. He clasped the commandant's rough hand, shaking it brusquely as he stared the stranger down.

"So I hear, Your Excellency," replied the tall, raw-boned, elderly man good-naturedly. "Indeed, your reputation as a fearless warlord precedes you, sire."

"Ah—Vlad the Great, you may call me. And you are?" It was not a question, but a demand.

"Ján Jiškra; supreme commandant of King Matthias' royal court and His Immaculate Majesty's armed forces."

"Where is Matthias?"

"He, ah, unfortunately could not relay his personage here from Braşov at such short notice, therefore I am here as representative of His Majesty's royal court."

"I see." Vlad shook his head in amused disgust. "King Matthias needs faster wheels than those he has. Are you to tell me, good sir," continued Vlad, "that after four months of continuous travel over the tremendous distance of three hundred forty-odd miles your illustrious King is unable to parley with us. Sacrilege! Your lies are as feeble as he!"

The commandant's eyes flashed. His face turned beet-red, pride lashed by Dracula's vicious tongue. Ján looked away temporarily, meeting Vlad's hypnotic gaze once more. The implication that his master was a feeble tyrant shook Jiškra's calm composure. A rage lurked beneath the surface of his uncanny eyes.

"I swear!" Jiškra threw up a flat left palm to his shoulder, his tone subservient, the stance and oath of a Roman stormtrooper. Vlad despised him immediately. The Pax Romana! Bah! The stink of Popish, decadent Romans permeated the castle.

"He is not here?"

"I swear!!" Again Jiškra responded with a gladiator's hail, thumping his heart speedily and raising his left palm to his shoulder. He reminded Vlad of an automaton. A stone-faced, glassy-eyed puppet.

Vlad inclined his head, his tantrums threatening to overwhelm his better judgment. It was clear now Matthias had no intention of leading the Hungarian army against the Turks. At best, Vlad could expect this strutting popinjay's leadership on the battlefield only. And then a sudden, dim memory jogged his brain. Ján Jiškra…Ján Jiškra…Christ! Why hadn't I recognised the notorious name earlier? Vlad scolded himself. Ján Jiškra, famous Hussite (Protestant) leader who'd defied Emperor Sigismund's Crusader army in Poland, fighting hand-to-hand from chained wagons; the same hero who'd halted the Crusaders in Lithuania. But what was the rogue doing in King Matthias' imperial— Catholic—army? Had he deserted the Hussites?

"*By Belinus!*" cried Vlad. "I know your name now. Infamous, glorious Hussite leader!" Vlad beamed, shaking his head. "But what do you be doing here? What of your Hussites?"

Jiškra shuffled his knuckles, his feet, for the first time looking infinitely uncomfortable. "I, ah, had a sudden—glorious—change of faith."

Vlad raised an eyebrow, uncomprehending.

"I serve the True Lord now—Rome and Pius, His Glorious, unquestionable Piety."

Vlad was flabbergasted. He sputtered indignantly. "How?! Why! Have you sold out to avoid your pyre?"

"Er, aye. A rosary is preferable to an *auto-de-fé*." Jiškra straightened up, his face twitching momentarily with shame. "Come. Your apartments are ready, Lord Dracula, as are the banquet feasts to cement our mutual alliance against Mehmed Çelebi."

Vlad followed, perplexed. He had been under the impression that his army would be joined immediately by King Matthias' superior forces. Knights, Crusaders, cannon, horses, armour. Plenty of armour. And baggage-trains of fine weapons to combat the infidel. King Matthias' own goodwill ambassador, Papal Legate Nicholas Modrussa, had ratified their pact, himself had signed the sacred parchment scroll bearing Vlad's signature in blood.

Vlad's retinue followed hot on his heels, their boots tapping noisily on the stone steps. Niches in the walls held Papist relics; a Black Virgin; holy thorns in tiny caskets; Christ on the Cross; relics of the True Cross; Christ's blood in phials. Immediately Vlad's men felt uncomfortable, lodged here almost against their will in a Teutonic stronghold held directly as a fief of the Austrian Holy Roman empire. Frederick III himself would pay a goodly sum for villainous Vlad Dracula's head for the ungodly atrocities and cruelties perpetrated against innocent Saxons and Catholic Transylvanians.

Voices echoed eerily in the great, hexagonal keep's multifaceted, septagonal forebuilding. The donjon was old, several centuries old, in fact. Its steps rose and rose, changing pitch at each flat level. Torches flickered on fancy brass cressets bracketed on smiling, freestone corbels. At the final threshold, a gaping abyss waited for a short drawbridge to lower. From various honeycombed chambers, curious mercenaries (two or three of them spitting in disdain) strolled forth, eyeing this cape-cloaked, Wallachian berserker with ill-disguised hostility. Passages and mural galleries branched off into multiple guardrooms. To Vlad's left, the castle's chapel door stood open. In the shadowy doorway, a chaplain blanched, spewing verbal abuse at Vlad as the great voivode glared back across the precipice.

"You will most certainly rot in Hell, Lord Dracula; you shall certainly burn forever you hated tyrant, woe betide your soul, you foul bloodsucking leech, yea, Woe for we on earth who see, for He is a human beast, His number, is six hundred and sixty-six..."

"You will most certainly die, good priest," Vlad retorted.

He had no authority here, however. No justifiable grounds to execute this haughty, black-robed Benedictine monk. The old friar seemed vaguely familiar, a pock-marked face Vlad had glimpsed before. The ugly monk's hair was snow-white, his scalp tonsured. A big, red, shiny nose made the monk look as if he had a permanent cold. Crater-face. Yes. That was what Vlad had nicknamed this insufferable little man one misty day long ago. He and his brigand soldiers had stopped the friar and several companions on a gravel trail near Tîrgsor, harassing the caravan of monks just for fun. Vlad had confiscated the monks' holy relics, laughing all the while as the fraudulent relics were snapped in his hands. He knew what they were: duck's blood, Islamic shrouds, "Mosaic" texts. This old monk had had the gall to lecture Vlad on the finer merits of Scripture. Indeed, the monk had escaped lucky by only having his Bible burnt.

Vlad smirked, shrugging the memory aside as he crossed the lowered drawbridge while the keep's small portcullis rattled upwards. The chaplain backed away into the shadows, as if expecting Vlad to come a-chasin' after him. Jiškra strode ahead, towering over Țepeș and his Wallach retainers. The great hall was surprisingly large; square. Musty. A few servants gathered to stare in awe at the dreaded Vlad Țepeș, this legendary 'Carpathian devil'. No respect shone in their heavy-lidded, hooded eyes. Only fear and hatred.

"Scoundrels! Set the trestles, pour the wine. Work serf, work serf!" Ján shouted, then laughed mercilessly. "Bah!" The giant raised his hands threateningly, advancing toward the scuttling servants. "Beelzebub is here! Ha, ha, ha, ha!"

Vlad was not amused. He exchanged rueful glances with his retainers, shaking his head. Was he meant to be amused? It seemed Jiškra was somewhat of a jester.

Vlad did not like jesters.

A stray black cat darted toward Dracula's boot, rubbing herself rapturously against his trousered leg. Hands shot up to cross hearts, to make the sign of the Evil Eye. A vampire was abroad. In broad daylight.

Vlad scowled.

Suddenly he hissed, snarling an oath, involuntarily reverting to his old phobias. A glinting, glass mirror hung on the limewashed wall to his right. A small, gilt-framed, Turkish mirror. He adroitly flipped it around to face the masonry, his actions missed by none. Vlad's features looked weathered, his green eyes feverish. He wore the look of a hunted man. His sparkling canines seemed unnaturally long and sharp in the glinting candlelight. His long, black, curly hair streaked with a hint of grey, his moustache also. Deep lines marred his noble, gaunt face. And his skin…pallid…ghostly. Țepeș' lips were blood-red. Strange…

A short, balding, grey-haired butler hobbled forward, mumbling, beckoning Vlad to his chambers. Vlad's dishevelled soldiers followed, looking bewildered as the stooped crony led them toward a zigzag, oaken staircase.

Jiškra had disappeared.

Jan Jiškra stood immobile in Vlad's richly-tapestried bedchamber when Vlad and his lagging bodyguard walked through the door.

"Ah, my good Prince, do be seated," drawled Jiškra, pouring Vlad a crystal glass of malmsey. The tall Pole's gravelly, imperfect Romanian speech infuriated Vlad, putting him on the defensive.

"Get out," Vlad growled.

"Ah—"

"Get out! Sleep first, talk later."

"Er, my dear Count Dracula, I am afraid I shan't do that. We must negotiate terms—"

"WHAT DID YOU CALL ME?!"

Vlad strode forward, his great broadsword already half drawn when three brawny sword-masters stepped forth from concealing shadows. He instantly halted, measuring his opponents with wolfish eyes, ready to strike them down. Behind him, the clink of multiple tulwars grating against their scabbards caught his attention.

Vlad's bodyguards tipped the scales. Jiškra snapped a command, disarming his swordsmen. Even he realised that Vlad never travelled without bodyguards, Gypsy thugs by the looks of them. Sighing, Ján spoke up, his voice belittling, buttery, low baritone.

"My mistake, my mistake, Prince, Dracula."

"What did you call me?" Vlad stepped forward threateningly, aiming his sword-tip at Jiškra's bulging Adam's apple. His voice was low, gruff, menacing. Jiškra gulped, looking down the end of Vlad's long, wide, battle-worn blade.

"Er, ah, pardon my inexcusable error, Your Highness," he murmured. "You are indeed Prince, not Count. Vlad the Great. My mistake. Memory lapse, you see."

Vlad nodded slowly. "You are clearly incompetent then—cannot have you leading an army. You are dismissed from your services."

Jiškra flushed, inclining his head. "As you wish, my Lord." He clicked his heels together once, bowing stiffly, submissively, at the waist.

Then stalked out of the chamber.

****

6 December, 1462 AD

Köenigstein Castle, Near Braşov, Transylvania

Vlad flew to the window in dismay. Jiškra's entire army, meagre as it was, sheltered below Köenigstein's tall crag, encamped below the mountain in a snowy valley. Snow and wind obscured Vlad's view of the Hungarian encampment. From the castle courtyard, smoke billowed from the peaked, half-timbered gatehouse. The sun had barely risen; the sky still purple with wintry, dawn darkness. Encamped below the mountain, during a blizzard, the Hungarian regiments scrambled to secure their accoutrements. Below Ţepeş' gothic window, men shouted in confusion as the short wooden bridge spanning a deep gorge blazed. Thick snow blanketed the entire castle; towers, covered sentry walks, barracks, courtyard. The air was well below ⁻ 10 ° C. Two massed squadrons, Vlad's own plus Vúc Brancovic's small Serbian detachment stood packed inside the oval bailey; most, however, were crowded on the mountain crag's perimeters abutting the castle walls. Immobilised. Someone had sabotaged the bridge. Crackling, spitting brushwood blackened the now-collapsing girder bridge. Before nightfall, Vlad had completed the transfer of his ragged army up to the castle precincts from the cold valley below, ensconced in the Dimbovita river's swampy basin. He could not trust the traitorous Hungarians, not even if they had sold him their souls (which souls Vlad doubted they had). Sheer, shalestone walls plunged to the valley floor. A cliff. The bloody castle stood on the cliff like a stranded goat.

Vlad cursed aloud, thumping his fist on the stone window-recess. He sat down, swearing, slumped in a cold, hard, splayed window seat. Jiškra. He was to blame. That ex-Hussite traitor!

Buckets of ice-cold well water were being vainly tossed onto the burning bridge. Ten-foot flames roared high. Where water met flame a tremendous hiss accompanied a billowing of pitch-black smoke. Men coughed, eyes stinging. From battlements, requisitioned servants' quarters, cellars, castle towers' soldiers watched with astonished shock as the bridge collapsed a couple hundred feet or more to the declivity's floor, echoing across the valley with the snapping crunch of wood in the gorge's craggy basin.

The bedroom door burst open. Lord Cirstian strode to Vlad's side as the voevode stood up. He knelt on one knee as Vlad laid a hand on his shoulder. "Speak."

"Someone has sabotaged the bridge, my Lord. Before dawn. Peasants, I think."

"Did anyone witness?"

"Aye, sire. Sentry guards. But by the time they scrambled down from the ramparts the gatehouse was aflame, as well as the bridge. The vandals spread lard and pitch all-about to ensure the job. Both Serbian and Wallachian captains report no soldiers having left their camps last night on the opposite side of the crag."

"This is madness!!" shouted Vlad. "Where is Jiškra? He will answer for this!"

"In the great hall, sire, questioning the garrison."

"Rise, lord Cirstian. Bring him to me immediately."

"Aye sire."

Vlad waited, impatient, his fingers drumming on the stepped windowsill as if with a will of their own. His dark green eyes flashed. Vlad hissed like a cat, cursing, pacing the bedchamber while crying, "Sacrilege!" loudly all the while. He swung his majestic, serrated-edged cape around the room, his arms jerking spasmodically.

Cirstian opened the door tentatively. "Baron von Jiškra, your Majesty."

Ushering in the Hungarian commandant, Cirstian bowed stiffly, disappearing once more; anticipating Vlad's vituperative tirade.

"You douchebag," growled Vlad. He pointed a poorly-manicured finger at the startled Jiškra. "You it was who sabotaged the bridge. Confess, malignant. You done NOTHING! to apprehend these vagrants, you mould spore."

"Sire," Jiškra stammered, "t-t-truly I say to you, my patrollers were not at fault. The night was cold, windy, the sentries had unfortunately gathered near the barrack's bonfire for warmth."

"You lie! Where were you last night? Your captain of the guard? Hm? Hmm?"

"Your lordship," barked Jiškra, hands behind his back, standing stiffly at attention now, "I have submitted myself to your mercy. Do as you will."

"So I shall! Guards!"

Four heavily-bundled Romanian soldiers in white sheepskins rushed into the room.

"Take this pompous traitor to the castle dungeons. Confine him indefinitely; feed him only bread and water. He can eat rats to supplement his diet. Do it now."

Saluting, the guards left with their astonished, sputtering prisoner. Vlad turned to stare out the oriel window, slowly letting out his breath. Outside, it had begun to snow again.

****

Reconstruction of the bridge was going poorly.

Continued snow-flurries severely hampered the rebuilding of the bridge. A shortage of lumber inside the castle caused a minor panic.

Jiškra's captain ordered some of the floors and half-timbering within the decrepit castle dismantled.

More worrying was the disturbing news of a Turkish contingent roaming deep into Transylvania. A large battalion was already besieging Castle Dracula-on-the-Argeş. Another was swiftly racing towards Köenigstein, according to this morning's scouting report; obviously an intelligence leak had alerted the Ottomans of Vlad's whereabouts and of the puny army mustered by King Matthias. Vlad lost sleep at night, roaming the parapets like a departed shade until daybreak. The old border castle was barely defensible; its food larders were low, there were no trebuchets, mangonels, nor cannon, its portcullises, sally-gates, and postern gates were derelict and badly corroded. The Turks could easily saw through the rusted bars. To be trapped here in hostile Saxon territory would be a living nightmare. An unprecedented national disaster. The Ottomans would relish Dracula's slow torture, not just the mild physical and psychological torture of his earlier, youthful imprisonment—savouring his death—impalement. His head would be sent to Constantinople—or rather, Islamic 'Istanbul'.

Grudgingly, Vlad ordered his soldiers and war equipment lowered down the 1000 ft. precipice. He had dreaded this. An operation such as this would be no easy task. Horses and wagons would need to be carefully lowered via pulleys and ropes and possibly large suspension cages made of wooden hoardings. And Köenigstein castle would have to be virtually shorn of timber. (And, needless to say, 1000 feet of rope would be no easy task to commandeer.) Daily, reconnaissance scouts were reporting Turkish regiments nearing the so-called "Valley of the Saxons", prime grain-growing area—one of the few in rocky, thin-soiled, gloomy-green Transylvania, a land of forbidding alpine forest and abrupt, rising peaks. The castle cliff may not want for water however. A two-hundred-foot well shaft sunk into the cellars centuries ago would suffice for all the garrison's needs, unless it were poisoned.

Throughout the week, Vlad oversaw the construction of cages and horse harnesses for the proposed evacuation. More disastrous news came on Woden's day *(Lludd of the White Hand)*; the stone ledge supporting the castle's former bridge-struts had collapsed with the burning bridge. The worn, granite slag had been an accident waiting to happen for years. A miracle no great tragedy had occurred from it.

Freya's day *(Dydd Gwen)*, a miserable, blizzard-blowing day, Vlad ordered the first evacuations from the summit.

****

The garrison had gathered outside in the courtyard and immediate vicinity at daybreak. Cocks crowed as the grumbling, tired, malnourished Serb/Wallach soldiers crowded beyond the gaping gatehouse, spilling over onto the snowbound, hoar-frosted, trampled incline abutting the limestone castle walls. Tents jammed shoulder-to-shoulder beyond the stronghold's ramparts had been folded up and packed in carts, the Serbs muttering in disgust to themselves as the mad voevod from Transylvania looked on. Nine-thousand-plus mixed soldiers loitered up on the lofty, spacious outcrop, shivering in their boots. The blizzard was in full progress by now, howling, lashing, assailing the heavily-bundled men like an army of demonic snowflakes from Hell. Their caps of ermine fur (in the Russian fashion) spared them from certain frostbite about the ears. Vlad stood like a *moroi* apart from the swearing, shivering warriors, great green eyes unblinking. His shiny, black, shimmering cape stood out easily in the blizzard, whipping in the wind. Scarlet rubies glittered on his long fingers. Vlad's fingernails were monstrously long now, unkept. He had once prided himself (erroneously) on his harp-playing. He would be incapable of plucking the strings, now.

The assembled Hungarian army below Köenigstein's towering crag was not nearly as large as Vlad had anticipated. Or needed. A rabble such as this, even with King Matthias' well-armed Magyar knights, their pennants flying, would be no match for Sultan Mehmed's hardened Janissaries. Vlad guessed there were no more than 12,000 soldiers below. The Sultan often went on showy hunting expeditions with more men (which Vlad knew from experience).

Admittedly, if he were to encounter Turkish troops Vlad would be assured of a stand-off, for his brilliant, strategic mind and prowess on the battlefield were legendary. But to be assailed up here inside Köenigstein castle would be suicide. Mehmed's army was rumoured to number 45,000 men—a very moderate estimate. No reinforcements nor supplies could be expected up here in this rocky eagle's nest.

The first cage-load of men lowered easily enough. As did the second. Nearby, the postern gate was open and sending down empty wagons. Cages wobbled and jostled, trembling on their uncertain downward descent.

Trussed-up, blindfolded horses whinnied and trembled while being lowered. Weapons and chests of gold, silver, armour, jewellery, firearms, wardrobes were all successfully being lowered. Culverins and cannon demanded an even trickier assortment/combination of latticed ropes, boards, and scraps of steel lest the weapons plummet from their wooden baskets into oblivion. Below the cliff, stagnant pools of water waited to catch some fallen prize. Tall, riverine weeds along the cliff's base would make search difficult.

And then luck ran out.

By midday, three quarters of the garrison, baggage-train, wardrobe, treasury and weapons had been safely lowered without serious loss. A few culverins and sabres had plunged from up high, falling unmissed, unhunted for among the reeds, left for future generations of Transylvanians to discover like ancient treasures.

But while Vlad animatedly surveyed the final operation, Johannes de Wermark, captain of the Hungarian guard and loyal vassal of Ján Jiškra rushed unmissed toward the unguarded dungeons beneath the keep.

Jiškra was free within fifteen minutes.

Other than Vlad's own personal bodyguard, the bulk of his army had been transported below. Each man, 4917 in all, including those huddled in unsanitary cells below the donjon and barracks had been laboriously-but-speedily conveyed by multiple guy-ropes and baskets. Fifty Hungarian mercenaries still remained in the deep, snow-drifted courtyard. The 4,600 Serbian forces had been the first to be transported down the mountain. Snowdrifts impeded men's progress as they rushed to and fro, gathering up the debris left behind; clothes, weapons, keepsakes.

When Jiškra exited the tower, the mercenaries' desertion of Vlad was quick, and decisive.

Foolishly, lord Cirstian and his loyal regiment had been allowed to descend with Vlad's last batch of soldiers. Țepeș' secretary-treasurer, Tudur Mihnea, and old friend Matei Bathóry, captain of the Hunnish king's royal guard, waved from their rocking, jerry-built conveyances as they were whisked to snowy, riparian freedom.

Dracula's bodyguard, twenty-four in total, formed a semi-circle around their Prince, ready for the final battle. Trapped, cornered against the looming, battlemented, ragstone bailey's wall, the defenders prepared to die.

Vlad had no experience of fighting on the defensive. Cornered by over fifty hardened mercenary veterans armed with crossbows and tasselled halberds, his prodigious, strategic skills were suddenly immobilised.

Crossbow bolts began to fly.

One by one the Gypsy defenders began to fall, butchered mercilessly from afar; taking an arrow to the head, stomach, heart, leg, or perhaps the eye. Their pitiful wails rent the snowy squall, falling in a heap of twisted arms and legs, dying like vampires. They ducked, dodged away from the whistling, cascading, whizzing iron bolts; blocking those they could with their big, round, iron-studded shields. Blood oozed into the snow, painting the snowdrifts a gaudy pink. And then the seasoned mercenaries began to advance.

Vlad fought like a man possessed. But his strength was not what it used to be. His eyes glowed with maniacal fury, his mouth stretched wide in a snarl, teeth clenched. He cleaved at his foes with his great two-hand broadsword, fending off their crossbows' arrows with his own heraldry-embossed shield. Now, a greying, gasping, middle-aged man fought desperately back-to-back with his chosen comrades. The comrades he'd betrayed.

Whirling, hacking, parrying, the Gypsy retainers exchanged blows with expert mercenary swordsmen; forced backwards with their empty quivers against the wall, sallying forth in vain. Vlad leapt upon his enemies, slitting their throats.

Jiškra's men captured Vlad before the last of his bodyguard were even vanquished. For half an hour, the battle raged on, the shouts of agony or elation springing up from the dying or from victors. Shrieks of rage uttered from Vlad's lips, hopelessly outnumbered and blinded by swirling snow. A bad wound, deep and bleeding, seared his left thigh, leaving him hopping about like a wounded wolf. Cornered. Jiškra was certainly Vlad's match, the ex-Hussite hero parrying him blow for blow, their broadswords hot now with each spark from their colliding, steel blades. Clangorous, two-hand broadswords created an awful din above the roar of wind and shrieking screams. Vlad's men had no pikes; no crossbows, longbows, maces, spears, halberds, nor battle-axes. All had been transported to the musky, frozen valley floor. They tried instead to jump their attackers and wrench their crossbows away, with varying degrees of success.

They batted at their foes with their wooden, iron-bossed bucklers engraved with Vlad the Impaler's tail-in-mouth dragon heraldry. Once the Wallachians' broadswords were wrenched from their grip, their traditional, ceremonial daggers were soon plucked from their hands.

Jiškra failed to defeat Vlad. A dozen, circling, hyena-like mercenaries suddenly tossed aside their weapons and overwhelmed the Dragon's Spawn while he screamed with impotent fury. Jiškra, on his knees, had been shielding himself with his own wedge-shaped shield and parrying Vlad's maniacal blows with waning vigour. Disarmed, held kicking and squirming now, Vlad could expect no mercy.

Instead, Jiškra, gallant to the last, spared the cruel tyrant's life. Flailing wildly and shouting obscenities, literally frothing at the mouth, Vlad Dracul III was bound hand and foot, his surviving Wallach bodyguards afforded the same treatment.

Chapter Twelve

Diary: 19 December, 1462 AD
Vizegrád Castle, City of Buda—Adjacent Pest; Danube River,
Hungary

Dear diary,

I am infinitely lonely today. I stare out of my solitary, splayed arrow-loop-for-a-window, watching little children playing on the Danube's frozen banks. Hungarian children. Little monsters. I feel no compassion. No love in mine heart. I would wring their necks, each and every one of them if I could. Day by day I feel my former vigour draining, my heart pining for One. For death. My mind, I feel, becomes unhinged even as I write; with quill pen and parchment which King Matthias has so graciously (Ha, ha) allowed me, slumped loosely shackled beneath this narrow arrow-slit which provides the only light. Demons crowd my sleep at night.

'Tis been days since Matthias betrayed me, transporting me in chains upriver to Buda-Pest, first to the royal court of Vác (after a short detour to Hunedŏara), thence to Vizegrád. Here reside I in a dungeon below Solomon's Tower, a grand, hexagonal, Byzantine tower on the riverside heights of Mam Danufye with the crenelated royal palace looming above.

I pine for the days of glory, the forest of stakes beyond Tirgovişte, the 50,000 impaled Turks which so cheered my heart. Even my memories of home are fond. I regret leaving Woica behind. I should have strangled her when I had the chance, as a mercy-killing. I know not what fate awaits my sweet Beloved. And the child. What of the child? Will young Mihnea (for I am sure it will be a son) be butchered at birth?

I am Dracula...I am Dracula...I am Dracula...I am Dracula...I am Dracula...I repeat thus so I'll not forget. Dracula, son of Dracul. Ap Draigh, fab o Ddraigh, Waelas Prif, Woiwod, Troika. Haûl. Dracula, son of Dracul, Prince of Wallachia, voivode, III. The Shining One.

For I am thy Saviour, foretold by prophets, who would free Wallachia from the Saxon/Magyar yoke...

The dark dungeon provides me with little food. Worms be surprisingly tasty. My leeches (doctors) once claim they bear much nutrition.

And I have befriended the bats. Four lonely little bats who share my cell, sleeping by day while hanging upside-down from the dripping stone ceiling, their leathery wings folded around their furry, cuddly rodent bodies. I would eat them, but they are my friends.

I have as of yet not met that traitor King Matthias Corvinus. By day, I plot his murder. By night, I await taunts from wicked little girls who have recently discovered my 'window to the world', a four-inch-wide arrow slit. They creep out at night it seems to shout abuses through the donjon's embrasure. I never see them. Many nasty things have they called me, these dirty-minded little wenches. Would that I could get them inside my cell, these lewd, lascivious little whores. What I could do with their plump little bodies.

How young they be I am not sure. Twelve? Fifteen? Eighteen? Whether they be serving-wenches or royal little bitches I know not. Nor do I care. Perhaps I would hang them up by the thumbs, these haughty, virgin Catholic girls. For my knowledge, they could be nuns. Oh, how I DO hate nuns.

For their taunts, I'll not forgive. Bastard-son, they call me. No disgrace. Devil. "Where's your horns, Vlad Dracula?" They hath remember thy terrible war host. Child-slayer and profaner of the Host. Aye. Aye, saith I to all charges. I am Satan himself. Beelzebub. My number they seek: 666. The Beast of Transylvania. "I am the Count, I've come to suck your bl-o-o-d!" cry I with glee to these wenches' shrieking dismay. And I laugh demonically. "Ha, Ha, Ha, Ha, Ha, Ha, Ha! Beelzebub come for you!"

And they run.

Foolish, misguided little virgins.

For what I fought for they could not possibly understand. To balance my mass-murders, the Wallachian folk whom I tried—and failed—to protect from marauding Saxon brigands, Turkish thugs. 'Twas these filthy Huns and Krauts who blasted my illustrious name for all eternity, the first Prince of the Church (ha, ha) in Europe's history to liquidate Germanic settlers. Spoilt Catholic girls—they would never understand, these half-breed Hungarians, never even COMPREHEND the injustices dealt to their less-fortunate sisters across the blue Danube, beyond the forests of Transylvania—Dacŵ Goeddeu. These little whores couldn't possibly comprehend what it be like to journey as a bought and sold slave-girl destined for Turkey or Egypt. No. But I have seen such. I shall 'remind' these little tarts of what they may expect for the future of Hungary. For I have seen their future (I the seventh son of a seventh son), the eradication of Hungarian chivalry at Mohács. Soon. Soon.

The jongleurs (minstrels) *and Meistersingers dub me a sorcerer, a black prophet, and I acquiesce. Mine crystal ball and Gypsies' tarot cards prove me so.*

****

7 February, 1464 AD

Vizegrád Castle, Buda-Pest, Hungary

The guards rushed Vlad, sore and exhausted, into Solomon's Tower's great, hexagonal hall. Or rather, they pushed and prodded him towards the stupendous, tapering hearth. Beside it, a short, dignified King stood with his right hand against the frieze-ornamented, plastered hood. King Matthias stood erect, looking aloof while staring down his nose at the dishevelled Impaler, his fine, silky brocades a wine-red; maroon and aquamarine silks a riot of satiny exquisiteness. Diamonds, rubies, emeralds adorned his stubby fingers, brooches, or blouse buttons. His shoulders were exaggerated beneath a fluffy maroon blouse with padded shoulders. His face was wide and flat, (Corvinus-Hunyádi's Mongol dog lineage). Matthias' eyes were hard reminding Vlad of one *very* ugly duckling, his nose snub beads of jet, unblinking.

"Ah, my good Dracula," Matthias started without preamble, "you do know the trouble you've caused me. Your cruelties I must confess surprises even I. You do understand that we are going to have to hold a jury to verify your heinous crimes." King Matthias stepped forward, eyeing Vlad with poorly concealed, disdainful amusement. Vlad was taller than he. The King circled around, clucking his tongue while shaking his black locks.

"So this is the wolf of Transylvania, the Beast beyond the forest. A Cruel and bloodthirsty tyrant."

Vlad struggled, baring his unnaturally-sharp eyeteeth as two muscular guards held his beefy, bare arms. He'd been denuded of his magnificent royal garments and proud cape of State; now wore only a homespun, sleeveless tunic.

"You do understand that if you are found guilty," Matthias continued, "the consequences shall be dire. It seems a certain Benedictine abbot has it in for you in a big way." Matthias chuckled. "You see, good sir, I too am on the hot seat, regarding a certain sum of gold borrowed this nation from poor Pope Pius' Vatican coffers."

Matthias laughed again, harsh, hoarse. His brows knit together in obvious disdain.

"You are a thief!" growled Vlad.

"Ye-es. I need the money. And I have you. I'm sure Pope Pius would forgive me this goodly sum if I were to hand you over for Vatican trial and the secular authorities."

"Sacrilege! You are a traitor, Corvinus. To Hungary, to Europe, to Wallachia. And Christianity. Believe you," murmured Vlad, leaning forward, "believe you that God will forgive your alliance with Turks?"

"Oh, please!" shouted Corvinus loudly. "Spare me the guilt-lecture, Wladislaus Dragwla. You are no man to speak of honour and good deeds. Was it not you who massacred Gypsies on St Bartholomew's Day? The poor citizens of Amlăs the year before that, impaling 26,000?" Matthias chuckled, moving toward a small mahogany table to pour himself a glass of cordial. The crystal decanter twinkled in firelight. Vlad's mouth watered, craving wine instead of stagnant, putrefying spruce-water. He licked his lips thirstily. His eyes still smarted from countless months within Vizegrád's dark dungeons. His arthritic joints ached from lack of exercise.

"On the other hand," Matthias interjected, "we could make a deal."

The hall fell silent. Eager ears perked up, servants, courtiers and one suspiciously-familiar minstrel seated unobtrusively on a window seat in a dark, distant corner. His name was…

Vlad could not remember. Eavesdroppers crept closer, ready to snatch some scandalous oral titbit.

"Back dogs!" Matthias shouted. The courtiers drew back, their eyes flashing.

Vlad could almost hear the Huns whispering; plotting.

"A deal." Vlad licked his lips, his brain working feverishly. "What sort of 'deal'?"

Matthias paced, his brows furrowed, chin propped on his fist. Paced back again, facing Vlad with a sudden, victorious smile. He, too, was Wallachian; son of *voivod* Ion de Hunedõara of Transylvania. Corvinus spoke Romanian fluently, conversing with Vlad in their native tongue.

"Why, a marriage alliance."

Vlad blanched. Such an offer, another time, would have been welcome indeed.

"Alas, tempting as your offer seems, I am already pledged to another."

A slight smile twitched Matthias' lips. He knew more than Vlad could have possibly suspected. He knew of the Hungarian wench left behind at Castle Dracula. *Kaziglu Bey's* 'consort'. Țepeș was in the dark—literally in the dark, after over two years' imprisonment.

Matthias knew of the wench's fate. Of the Valley of the Saxons and the *Riŭl* (river) *Domnișoară*. Of the combined Turkish and Saxon assault on the castle, and subsequently the girl's fate…

"But you are a shrewd man, Count Dracula," King Matthias said at last. "A shrewd man." He narrowed his eyes. "A wise man. I am sure, in time, you shall come around." King Matthias nodded slowly, smiling, knowing.

"Take him back to his cell."

****

18 July, 1464 AD
Vizegrád Castle, Hungary

Lord Cirstian, *voivod* (viceroy) of Transylvania, Protector of Wallachia, treasurer and seneschal to Wallachia's new Prince, Radu Dracula III, reported faithfully to King Matthias of Hungary at the mighty, royal palace of Vizegrád above the rushing green Danube on a sombre, grey day, downstream from Buda (opposite Pest).

Prince Radu, minion of Sultan Mehmed Çelebi II, Vlad Dracula II's own flesh-and-blood brother, was now safely enthroned at the stately royal palace of Tirgoviște on the crest of mass popular support. Riding a wave of public opinion against Vlad Dracula's tyrannical Reign of Terror, Radu 'The Handsome' (a Mohammedan catamite to the very bone) adroitly pacified the nation's citizens, soothing the Wallachians with honeyed words even as the Turkish imperial army entrenched itself in once-Wallachian fortresses 'for the security of all Romanians'. Castle Dracula had been taken in February of this year and slighted. (Dismantled.) It was bad news that the boyar Cirstian brought to his former master imprisoned beneath Vizegrád's hexagonal Solomon's Tower.

Cirstian was grey and stooped now. He hobbled toward Solomon's Tower wearing a permanent, bitter look on his face. Deep wrinkles lined his forehead, scarred his lips, cheeks, eyes. In just one year, he had witnessed Wallachia's proudest moment of independence shattered, the work of Vlad Dracula—right or wrong—as if it had never been. Too many cutthroats and shameless catamites among the populace's disenfranchised *bourgeoisie* had undermined the Impaler's virtually criminal-free (and free at last), autocratic state. Police state. Politically, not much at all had changed since the subordinate days of Vlad's father. The Wallachians still paid their ransoms and baksheesh-dues, still offered tribute to the Sultan of Turkey "Lord of the Universe". Cirstian had lost two sons in Dracula's holy war, killed by Turkish arrow. With a sorrowful pang in his heart, Cirstian had been forced to send four daughters and three sons to the Sultan's court at Istanbul, as ransom for the boyar's continued good behaviour. Mohács had been outraged when the Turkish *bey,* Alibaba, decreed all Romanian women now cover their heads. (Insidious communities of Turks were already being established in Wallachia's southern cantreds.) Soon afterwards, his wife Magda of forty years had died of grief. All those deaths, the thousands, traitors, partisans, innocent or guilty. ALL FOR NAUGHT. Cirstian felt sick and remorseful whenever he thought of it. Dracula. The name was like a taboo now. Vlad's "method to his madness" had brought no lasting joy to the people's hearts, only tears and endless burden. And the Gypsies...

The Gypsies were being *decimated.*

The Gypsies. Of all the bad tidings, it was this Cirstian dreaded most. Dracula's fickle, unstable allies were being massacred in every city right now, in every town, village, hamlet. Peasants were abandoning their implements in the fields to rape, pillage, massacre. The spring planting had been neglected, the Saxons organising night posses to find loot and destroy pestilential Gypsy bands.

Caravans were being ruthlessly waylaid on roads, the victims either massacred or sold into Turkish slavery, or stocking Romanian brothels, for *Szgany* were considered neither Christian nor human. They eked out a perilous existence (in a state of perpetual *fear*) without rights, least of all during anarchic times such as these. Their thatched wagons were burnt on roadsides, often with dwellers still inside. The butchery and cruelty exhibited by otherwise seemingly-decent Wallachians sickened even Cirstian, who had witnessed countless scores of malefactors put to death in various, gruesome ways in his day. But those wretches Vlad had impaled had often deserved no less. (His favourite phrase being *"I never killed a man who didn't need killing."*) The *Szgany* murders were senseless butcherings however; innocent, peaceful folk who had never attacked a nation within documented history. Now, *Romany* and *Szgany* alike suffered the same fate, the only thing in common their uprooted lifestyle, victims of the dominant Swabian, Magyar, Szekler, Ukrainian, Romanian, Saxon populations.

No. No. Cirstian could not bear to tell Vlad of the Romanians' shameful behaviour. Only two years ago they had fought against the Ottoman invaders with such gallant bravery. The news of Radu's inexplicable, unstoppable extirpation of Gypsies would break Vlad's heart, knowing the last of his fellow Dacians had suddenly vanished from the face of the earth. No. Cirstian would not be the man to slay Vlad Dracula, Dragon of Wallachia.

King Matthias' chamberlain wasted no time in installing his informant in a suite befitting a boyar's status. Cirstian gratefully climbed to his chambers, high up on the donjon's third storey. A large, hood-moulded, cloister-like gothic window overlooked the empty courtyard, incidentally, directly above Vlad Dracula's dungeon-slit far below.

Cirstian slumped down in a traceried, high-backed wooden chair, his lungs wheezing from the climb. No one had offered to accompany him up the steep, winding stairs. He was too proud and stubborn to ask for help. His retinue had disbanded once inside the bacchanalian luxury of the castle. Bordellos and taverns littered the begrimed Renaissance city, the once-blue Danube murky and polluted with the royal ironworks' effluent or raw sewage. Here the retainers could swill themselves into oblivion sampling the delicious forbidden wares of Pest's ghetto brothels. The Jews' women would provide ample, lawless sport, for no one (except Jews) would grieve for the unwilling prostitutes dumped murdered into the gutters of segregated Jewish ghettos. The men were already anticipating the night's debauched sport.

In Vlad's day, his soldiers had been castrated and impaled up the arse for such crimes.

Old Cirstian closed his eyes, pale blue eyes which had witnessed too much. His long hair was balding at the crest, hair which had once been as black as Vlad's and straight as a crow's feathers. Vlad had nicknamed him *Bran*—Dacian for "crow." At forty-five, Cirstian felt like Moses at 900. He was a mere sixteen years Vlad's senior. Yet his lungs were failing, useless, wheezing bellows within his chest. His heart was chronically weak. No longer would Cirstian earn sobriquets for fearlessness and reckless bravery on the battlefield. Nor had he anyone to fight for. Really, he had nobody else left to live for. His remaining children, legitimate or no, despised him for supporting Vlad Dracula's bloodthirsty Terror. Fourteen, intermittent years of blood-spattered horror. Unless familiar with Vlad's strange mentality, to an outsider his executions would appear to be entirely random, the hilltop of Tirgovişte rank for weeks with the stench of pierced kidneys or intestines, the palace bailey crowded with stakes. Cirstian's children had not understood Vlad's manic killings, his insistence on an orderly, Mother Earth-respecting society. Nor had anyone else, except for the dwindling Vlachs. (God knows Mohács had tried to persuade his unruly kindred; the result being shouting matches and dropped gloves of honour). All seventeen of Cirstian's offspring had grown up, married and gone. None had bothered to visit Cirstian at his Transylvanian border-castle of Hräd Spasky, admittedly a brutal, uncomfortable, multi-baileyed former Crusader fortress with square corner towers. These memories brought Cirstian no pride, only fear of what was to come, for his children and grandchildren, dreading the ramifications of their abominable Aryan notions of what life should be. Most of all, however, Cirstian dreaded facing Vlad one last time, dreaded seeing the proud, old warlord locked up in a dark *oubliette* (bottle dungeon) like an animal. Most of all, their shared memories of glory.

For Cirstian was dying.

He awaited the Chore ahead with sunken heart.

****

A long wooden ladder was being lowered down into the *oubliette*. (French, "place forgotten".) At first, Vlad, jerking awake with a snort, was perplexed by the eddying stream of light shining down from above. (It seemed to him as if the angels of Heaven were descending on a luminescent, celestial stairway.) A clang of heavy chains and a trapdoor slammed upon the ray of light.

A tiny pair of yellowish-blue lights bobbed down towards him. Twin candlelight. A candelabrum bobbing down a narrow flight of ladder steps. Soon a glimpse of silver twinkled high above, from an ornate, shapely, exquisite pair of torc-twisted candelabra. The soft, unsteady sound of footfalls and wheezy breathing echoed throughout the noisome, clammy dungeon. Vlad blinked his eyes, the candlelight harsh on his ageing retinas. He awaited his fate with stilled heart. The executioner cometh…

"Vlad? 'Tis I, Cirstian, your humble servant," Cirstian said aloud, his voice cracking, shaking.

"You have come for death," Vlad echoed cryptically.

Cirstian jumped, his boots on solid ground now, candles momentarily wavering in the draught.

"Master, I bring news of your country. Still your faithful servant, I am. I bring news of your child!"

Vlad sat bolt-upright, his wrists still shackled.

"Yes, yes, sire, news of your child," Cirstian cried, his voice excited now. Even so, his hoarse voice was no more than a loud whisper. "A baby boy, Your Excellency, safe with me at Hräd Spasky even as we speak. Prince Radu does not yet know of the boy's existence."

Vlad grabbed the old man's grey, rabbit's fur collar. "How. When? And…Voica?"

Cirstian took a deep breath, deeper than any he'd ever taken, until his lungs felt ready to burst. He felt as if he were drowning. He momentarily choked, angrily wiping tears from his eyes with the wrinkled palm of his hand.

"This news I swear has never pained me more, sire, for truly I have felt closer to you than even my own wife, Magda. Voica…the Saxons and Hungarians of Arefŭ besieged your impregnable castle, my lord, besieged it for two hundred eighty-eight days alongside the Turks, these filthy Krauts, until the food-stores were emptied or were poisoned and your garrison down to eating rats."

Vlad waited, for the first time patient and cold as Siberia. Strangely calm now. Surely Cirstian could say nothing more so devastating as to break his iron will.

"The girl, sire," Cirstian continued, sobbing shamelessly now, "she fought like a warrior when the Saxon scum stormed and captured the ladies' bower. On the seventy-fifth day, her child born and healthy, *Doamnă* Voica—after a prearranged nocturnal rendezvous - lowered your child down the mountain into one of my wet-nurse's waiting arms, saving the House of Dracula. However, the Turks encamped in the valley sounded the alarm before she, herself, could descend. They chased my retainers off before her rescue could be carried out."

Vlad lowered his head to his chest, defeated. So, the end had come at last. He prayed Voica had died with honour.

"The Saxons, sire," hissed Cirstian, his old voice virtually shaking with rage, "they dis-disarmed your beloved after storming the fortress while the Turks bombarded the castle into submission; then repeatedly, cruelly, systematically raped and tortured her! For days the bastards abused her, each taking his turn while Radu did nothing. Finally, the end came on All Hallow's eve. I am not sure which rumour be true: either she was thrown from the ramparts, or she jumped. Peasants discovered her body clad in a shift below the crag, horrible, unrecognisable almost. But she was wearing your Dragon ring, the ring thrown to your father many years ago by some damsel while he was a guest of Emperor Sigismund's court at Nuremberg. A ring only a male member of the Order of the Dragon is allowed to wear by virtue of chivalry."

Cirstian withdrew a large ruby ring from his tunic, pressing it into Vlad's ice-cold palm. "Sire…" Cirstian choked on his rage, sobbing unabashedly now. "The monks—Orthodox and Catholic. Have refused to allow Voica hallowed burial. She was buried at Arefŭ crossroads."

"Suicide?"

Cirstian nodded, worn out, mortally ashamed of his countrymen. And for the first time in eight years Vlad cried. Racking, injured sobs of painful, frustrated impotency. Cirstian wanted nothing more than to close his eyes and sleep forever. Patting the Impaler's quaking shoulder,

Cirstian stood up, vainly offering his condolences, but unable to reach Vlad's ears. He had fulfilled life's hardest task, would see Vlad no more.

Turning away, the sobbing, weeping boyar hobbled towards the *oubliette's* ladder.

Chapter Thirteen
The Retribution

1 December, 1465 AD

Vizegrád Castle, Hungary

For dark days, Vlad had stared into space. Unblinking. Days flashed by like lightning, unnoticed. No solace could be found from bats, mice, spiders, beetles, or ants. By October of last season, rains had poured down from merciless, Hungarian skies, flooding the Danube below Vizegrád palace. The dirt under Vlad's body turned into slimy muck. And then one day when Matthias' soldiers came to summon him, Vlad had not moved or even blinked. Awkwardly, they had hauled him up the rough ladder, dragging his inert body towards the king's solar on the third floor of the keep. They had dropped him at their monarch's feet; astonished, King Matthias stared at the listless Devil. The court physician immediately declared that Vlad Dracula suffered from maudlin, melancholy depression. And Matthias had laughed. "How in Hades could this serpent be maudlin! *Ha, Ha, Ha, Ha!* Lovesick, you say, old boy! Lovesick for what? His impaling stakes? *Ha, Ha, Ha, Ha, Ha!*"

He had not been laughing for long.

For Vlad was like a wild timber-wolf then, his awakened rage suddenly terrifying the speedily-evacuating, royal Hungarian court, leaping up and clawing vainly at King Matthias, snarling while five husky soldiers fought to contain this werewolf specimen. He had thrown them about like sticks. Never had Vlad succumbed to defeat. Not even then, in his darkest hour. Experience truly hardened the heart. And now he was a wildman, a dangerous, wicked madman.

For days, Vlad would demonstrate his morbid impalement techniques on hapless insects. The courtiers humoured his eccentricities. The impalements were for their pleasure, however, their wintry entertainment. They it was who were heartless. Vlad took no pleasure in sacrificing insects. Instead, unbeknown to the haughty, frivolous, spoilt courtiers, Vlad imagined their squirming bodies on the pins, imagined their horror-stricken faces as they writhed with bloody agony. Like thousands before them. Unholily eyeing these 'aristocrats' who took pleasure only from richly-woven, beautiful, wall-to-wall tapestries, from hunts, executions, auto-de-fé's. And they said he was mad.

And King Matthias of Hungary, after countless months of dark confinement, finally relented to allowing Vlad Dracul III out of the tower's dungeon, installing the former *Naši* in comfortable chambers on the fourth floor of the keep—albeit heavily-guarded.

Many times since then, royal visitors from abroad or otherwise had sojourned to Buda-Pest to see the Wildman of Transylvania, as if he was some sort of circus freak. Russian ambassadors, chetniks (outlaws), Papal Legates, dukes, barons, minstrels had all oohed and aahed from a safe distance while Vlad tapped his hairy fingers nervously. Yet totally sane.

Now sat Vlad in a plain wooden chair, eyes unfocused, remembering better days as the courtiers in the donjon's hexagonal great hall gathered around a somnolent chess game at a separate table. Haughty courtiers cast amused, disdainful glances in Vlad Dracula's direction. Outside, it was snowing again.

A knot of spoilt castle women and ladies-in-waiting whispered scandalously amongst each other, eyeing Vlad with horrified—yet fascinated—dark, Magyar eyes. The same tarts who had often mocked him in his dungeon, free from Țepeș' groping, vainly-stretching claws. Clustered near the chess combatants' pristine, white marble table, they leaned forward, watching him despite themselves. Dominant streaks of black still ruled Dracula's long locks and drooping, uncared for, *condittiere's* moustache. His green eyes wore a glazed, far-away expression.

Vlad sat slumped backward, hands limp on his orange silk stockings.

Three years it would be since King Matthias had so treacherously betrayed him. Vlad's heart felt heavy day by day. No aspiration had he. No hope. No life. Winter seemed omnipresent. Permanent. Summers he had not experienced since his imprisonment. This autumn King Matthias had freed Vlad from his fetters, allowing the former *Cnéaz* restricted access to the palace's courtyard to regain his strength. Guarded, Vlad had vainly, surreptitiously, searched for a way to escape. And found none. The little wenches (and older wenches too!) now ran away from him as he would approach. Their boldness, evidently, had vanished.

Only a year ago they had cracked Vlad's hairy knuckles with sticks.

The palace yards were tight. No escape would be forthcoming unless sheets could be requisitioned for Vlad to shimmy out a window and down the tower's walls. The garrison had foreseen such a rash attempt, hiding most of the sheets in those rooms not denied access to him.

Vlad, after all, was a high-security prisoner. His head would soon be worth *many times* its weight in gold.

As if from a dream, Țepeș slowly glided back to reality. He glanced up, chin on his chest, unmoving. A dark, youngish (15–25?), attractive wench was staring at him with wide grey eyes. Ah yes, the King's sequestered elder sister, Caltuna. Lovely girl. For a whore. Vlad could almost feel the searing hatred rolling in waves from the little bitch's queer, black-pupiled, storm-grey eyes. She squinted bitchily at him, grimacing.

Vlad felt like laughing. This tart was King Matthias' proposed Dracula-Corvinus betrothal. With one hitch. Vlad would have to renounce his Orthodox faith and embrace Pope Pius II. Popery. Embrace his bitterest enemies. All the devils of Hell couldn't force Vlad to adopt the Babylon faith. This woman was no comparison to his beloved, deceased Voica. Her face seemed too…too round. Her perky, toffee-nose too high. Eyes too big. Cruel, capricious grey eyes, always squinting. *Uigr's* eyes. The eyes of a succubus. Pronounced chin. High, Asiatic cheekbones. On the plus side, she had long, black eyelashes which were most becoming, lips full and sensuous, plastered with the latest, gaudy, scarlet Egyptian lipstick. Best of all however was her figure, a Greek goddess's voluptuous, white-swathed, hourglass figure. An evil Venus. Though not very tall: even by these diminutive Magyars' debased standards.

With a determined jut of her chin, the wench moved towards him, passing Vlad with her head held high, her nose in the air—watching surreptitiously with secretive, slanted eyes. Vlad followed her with his cryptical, green gaze, face stern. She avoided his hostile stare.

Caltuna calmly poured herself a silver goblet of claret from a crowded trestle table, casting oblique glances at her despicable, proposed fiancé. Thank God he had turned Matthias' foolish offer down! The man disgusted her. How dare Matthias propose such an alliance! Caltuna would be loath to lie with such a monster in holy matrimony. Orthodox. *Ugh!*

She stood behind him some distance away, carelessly downing her claret. Caltuna felt giddy of a sudden, the smooth liquor warming her icy blood. The keep was, well…an iceberg. A frigging Hungarian stone prison meant for innocent guests. A treasure-house, and treasured State prison.

On a hill above the scenic Danube bend, the royal palace received winter's iciest gales.

Vlad stood up, sauntering towards her. He passed without a glance, staring out the glazed, diamond-latticed window into snowy Christmas scenery. Frost ringed the lead-framed windowpane. Beyond the Danube, beyond the city of Pest across the river, great, frozen expanses of old-growth timber and man-made tributaries (awash with the woody debris from riverine bottomlands) stretched to the dusk horizon. Newly dug canals reminded Vlad of Venice, a glorious water-bound city he'd once seen as a toddler. Fluttering snow drifted from ashen skies, obliterating everything in sight, roofs neatly covered with a cake-icing layer of hard snow.

High peaked, shingled roofs rose up from narrow, cobbled streets. Triangular, timber-framed, mudbrick, overhanging medieval townhouses, German in style and design, some already three hundred years old prettified Pest's picturesque, twilit skyline. Spiral-patterned brick chimneys belched smoke into the sky. Garlands, mistletoe, holly and heather adorned the festive, Plantagenet-era houses, two-storey, *bourgeois* homes for the most part. Anticipating Yuletide, the teetering, Hungarian townhouses slumbered under approaching twilight, residents only half-aware of the bloody Celtic significance of the holly and mistletoe over their doors.

Down a grungy, cobbled street ambled a squat, overweight Christmas-tree pedlar bearing a large spruce on his shoulders. He laboured toward a prominent townhouse in a half-crouch, festive clothes flapping in the wind. A short, green, saw-tooth-fringed cape hung from his shoulders, its characteristic, serrated border around his collar as well—a pseudo-shawl. German's clothing. Pointy, curled-up shoes covered his feet; each terminating with an odd, red, fluff-ball at the toes. On his head, a jolly orange toque copied the same fashion. His hair was white, stringy; a ludicrously long, snow-white beard and handlebar moustache obscured the lumberjack's weathered face, his cheeks and bulbous nose flushed and rosy. He had a bulging, grotesque beer belly. He reminded Vlad of the innkeeper Radu whom he had richly rewarded in gold all those years ago.

The distant, old codger knocked awkwardly on a big, stout, arched door, waiting. Snow flurries continued to assault the majestic, Renaissance city. Torches fluttered in iron-protected brackets set on the townhouse's important, red-brick walls. No one else braved Buda-Pest's ploughed streets. Above the Christmas-tree pedlar, a glazed window swung open, high above the slouched figure from a crazily-leaning, oversailing, heavy beamed, peaked section of the house. An oriel window, frieze-plastered, of the finest quality. A nobleman's townhouse.

Candlelight twinkled somnolently beyond mullioned, glazed windows, Yuletide trees ablaze with trimmings, miniature candles, wax figurines, wooden ornaments. Shutters hid most of the townsfolk from view. Darkness descended upon the city as an inky, purple dimness. Most of Buda-Pest's steep, shingled roofs were blanketed with snow. Spiralling pinnacles rose up from fancy gothic gables and dovecotes, as if competing with St Malachy's Romanesque cathedral towers in the hazy distance; gargoyles, belfries, open bell-turrets, campaniles and allegorical religious sculptures of Catholic Hungarian piety.

Vlad stood mesmerised by the sheer beauty of it all. His eyes wore a far-away look, his mind wandering to happier days, days of rambunctious winter hunts, Yule logs, Transylvanian sleigh rides. His father celebrating Yuletide at old Castle Brân with typical, open-handed generosity, plenty of wild roast boar, wine, *slivǒvitz*, sweetmeats, *mămăliga* (cornmeal porridge), and the finest minnesingers plucking their lyres and blowing happy whistling tunes on flutes.

Caltuna watched with morbid fascination all the while, eyes settled obliquely on Vlad Dracula's broad back. The ex-Prince stood motionless, unaware of scrutiny, standing till his feet hurt and the sky darkening. '*Yes, he* is *a strange creature*,' Caltuna thought to herself, peering out the window as if he longed for home. A weird, sick creature. Perhaps he was studying the layout of the city, scrutinising its citizens for future impalement victims.

Bravely, with cruel intent, Caltuna slinked towards him, at once relishing what she might say, yet dreading Vlad Dracula's unpredictable wrath. She moved with the grace of a cat, unnoticed by the courtiers, sidling up behind him. She was most practiced at court snobbery and etiquette, knew just how to deflect such a woman-hater's bullying aggression, the uncivilised behaviour that was a trademark of a bloodthirsty tyrant—a barbarian. Vlad Dracula's name stunk already throughout Europe.

Caltuna felt little fear. She knew sentries inside the hall were nearby, guarding the gaily-tapestried entranceway lest Vlad turn on her. Or anyone else for that matter. He had no dagger or any other such weapons on his person. (Though Matthias had given Vlad back his sword.) And her only weapon was her innocent tongue, which she had used many times on younger girls or jealous paramours whom she kept a close secret from brother Matthias' ears. Caltuna's searing wit was like a cat's claws unsheathed.

She stood slightly behind him, to his right.

"You do wish for freedom, do you not sire," Caltuna hinted

innocently, thin brows raised in jest. "You wish to flap your leathery wings and roam the night." She kept her voice low, lest her fellow courtiers overhear or perhaps mistake her acid conversation for scandal. Caltuna licked her lips, glancing sideways over her shoulder to note if anyone be watching. Wind rattled the windowpanes, heavy shutters creaking forward outside the icy-cold glass, threatening to slam against the three-light, tri-lobed window frame.

Vlad slanted his eyes sideways, turning around slowly, imperious as Lucifer himself. He wore his splendid black cape once more; its vibrant, silken fabric seeming to shimmer and glisten with a reflective gloss. A gem-encrusted band of gold encircled Țepeș' high forehead. His emaciated face was waxen, body clad in ebon silk from head to toe. A crimson bow-tie, alone, broke the starkness of his dark visage. Caltuna avoided Vlad's contemptuous gaze, staring out the window into the snowy night. She especially ignored the imperious, appreciative once-over down the length of her body, taking in Caltuna's clinging, cream-white evening gown with a leisurely, chauvinistic glance; her breasts high, pointy, and inviting; her waist enviously narrow, would fit his handspan easily, hips wide and comely; her neck that of a pale white swan's. Vlad guessed Caltuna never stayed outdoors longer than two hours at a time, the lazy flaunt.

Dracula held his head high with the pride of his blood: despising Hungarians in general, but this *doamnă* in particular.

A loose, brown, transparent silk kerchief immodestly concealed Caltuna's lustrous, coal-black tresses, straight hair except for the occasional strand of curly, gossamer tendrils. She washed her hair every day in lavender water. Thick braids hung brazenly down her breasts, drawing men's stares. Her eyes, if they would abandon their insufferable haughtiness, could be considered sensitive and passionate, as Caltuna's various paramours who had experienced her favours might surely attest. Huge, grey, slightly slanted almond-eyes with long, black, upswept eyelashes which in Hungarian court whispers, termed: eyes to die for. The young men (or otherwise) of King Matthias' royal court at either Vác or Vizegrád had often been privy to her pleading, soft, dog-like eyes while in the throes of lovemaking.

"Like the wolf, *domnişoară*, I seek the wilderness of my homeland." Vlad's gravelly voice was low; deep, menacing. Virile. His strange, Wallachian accent seemed to skip, his *ll's* trilling oddly. He spoke in Romanian.

Caltuna laughed cruelly, acidly, throwing back her head. Courtiers turned their heads, eyeing the two conversing war-wolfs with curious eyes.

"You would long for the backwardness of Romania, that

bog-infested posterior of the world?" Caltuna snickered. "Perhaps it is human victims you do miss, sire?" She stared coldly.

Vlad narrowed his eyes. "You, *domnişoară*, are Romanian, too. Or have you forgotten that?"

Caltuna flushed. Her cheeks felt aflame. Her grey eyes no longer held that aura of imperturbable certainty. She wavered. Her lips momentarily puckered, despite herself, self-consciously sizing up her opponent. Being Romanian by blood as well as by birth was one of her most shameful secrets; those who dared bare her soul must risk having their eyes clawed out. Caltuna stuttered, a truly remarkable collapse of her defences.

"A-A-Am not..."

Vlad chuckled, his tone condescending and cold. "You, milady, are Wallachian. And there's nothing you can do about it." He laughed cynically.

"'Tis Hungarian you are ashamed of, *domnişoară*," Vlad continued. Caltuna stared with hostile wide eyes, her cheeks rosy, unable to believe her ears. This, this TYRANT dared offend a royal sibling. King Matthias would make him pay for this; the mad tyrant (Vlad) would lose his head.

Caltuna had lost her incentive for attack. She faltered, hastily searching her brain for a fresh verbal assault.

"Perhaps you miss Wallachia," Vlad remarked. "You miss our freedom, our patriotic righteousness. Am I right?"

Caltuna narrowed her eyes. She had finally met her match, overstepped her bounds of authority and superiority. Here was a *voevod*; not a servant, not a mere, court dandy. But a Prince of Wallachia, a warrior-Prince, and one of the most ruthless, authoritarian, despot rulers of all Europe. *Kaziglu Bey.* The very name put fear into the hearts of mortals; the only man alive to absolutely crush Sultan Mehmed II "The Conqueror" on the battlefield, to send the Turks rushing back to Constantinople as they had, just before Matthias so oddly betrayed the Impaler.

"Wallachia, my lord, is a poor land of tinkers and fools. Uncivilised barbarians. Such as you!"

Caltuna swung away, absolutely expecting the Impaler to grab her arm and twist until an apology was forthcoming. Surprisingly, he did not. Instead, the king's flustered sibling strode toward the exit, sweeping angrily through the lively, colourful, gold-spun tapestry after shoving aside a Hungarian sentry wielding a heavy, crescent-headed poleaxe. A more astonished guardsman could scarcely be imagined, a king's livery soldier and one of Caltuna's many former lovers.

While Vlad laughed; his deep, mocking, maniacal laughter filling the great hall.
****

23 December, 1465 AD

Vizegrád, Hungary

The Turkish ambassadors stared with hostile fear at Vlad Țepeș seated regally on his diminutive throne. King Matthias' own, royal, gilded throne loomed above his; draped with purple velvet, laced with gold along its fringed, satin edges. The monarch's armorial crest, too, was stitched with gold, deep inside the throne's high canopy; the royal lion-standard of Hungary. Vlad's polished, teakwood throne of State (the ancestral *ystedd*), blood red, flouted the Wallachian royal eagles carved into its armrests. Guests mingled among the great hall, exchanging gossip and lascivious whispers. Shapely, stockinged legs and fine, clinging, open-bust ballgowns—silk—colourful, Damask, ladies' finery—crowded the hall. The men were fine, colourful strutting roosters courting equally fine, female felines cloaked in furs and velvets.

"Your Royal Highness, the illustrious Pasha of Egrigöz, Abdul Hammurabi Fazal," cried Matthias' young, royal standard-bearer, deafened by a sudden trumpet score, a blast of three, shrill, loud notes. "Ambassador to His Immaculate Imperial Emir and Sultan of Turkey, Lord of the World, Mehmet-Ali Abdul Çelebi."

Vlad scowled menacingly.

He knew the Pasha of Egrigöz—personally. He had been tortured by Fazal.

Vlad tapped his fingers impatiently.

Silence gripped the hall. The odd cough came from nervous spectators, anticipating the forthcoming war of words, for Sultan Mehmed had recently broken the truce between Austria/Hungary and the Tripartite Alliance. Turkey, Egypt, and Persia; lords of Asia Minor and the Middle East. The Ottomans, as of November 27, had moved against western Transylvania. They had had no opposition from the Saxons, Magyars, or Szeklers. The true protectors of Wallachia, the indigenous Vlachs, were on extended—permanent—vacation. Prince Radu of Wallachia had effectively blinded the citizens of Bistritz and Tirgoviște of the Turkish designs on Hungary, and eventually, Austria itself—the Fatherland.

Transylvania, heavily forested, underpopulated, would provide either Imperial army with the means to conquer eastern Europe; Turkey wished to subjugate the Balkans, while Austria schemed to enforce its authority over western Europe as Holy Roman Empire now that Byzantium had ceased to exist. France would still be a major force to contend with, as would Castile, Portugal, and Aragon. (Spain did not yet exist as a unified, sovereign state.) Transylvania's expansive fir, spruce, and pine forests would provide either the means to pacify Europe, securing timber for catapults, war-wagons, and would also fuel the forges necessary to mould the gigantic iron (or bronze) cannon to be used against Europe beyond the snaking, stupendous Danube and Volga rivers. (The Russian fiefdom of Novgorod, to the north, and ever growing in power, was now well within range of holy Islam's pincers.)

The ex-*voevode* leaned forward from his mock throne threateningly, coldly looking the Turkish ambassador in the eye; murmuring in Turkish to the startled Pasha: *"I want to kill you, Fazal."*

Vlad sat in utter boredom as the tedious negotiations droned on through the night. He kept his ears open, however; Vlad still cherished devious designs of his own, concerning the regaining of the Wallachian ancestral throne, a title his family (ironically, formerly Basarab) had claimed intermittently since Mirçea the Old had crossed the Carpathians from Moldavia to carve out a country of his own, wresting the south from Hungary. Radu was a usurper, a Turkish puppet—Vlad would never recognise Radu's legitimacy.

He searched the hall for familiar faces; found none worth recognising. Caltuna, the slut, sat prim and proper in a distant corner of the high dais; nursing a wine goblet behind a bulky trestle table. Her face was pink and flushed, lips forming a coquettish smile for one of the court's newest go-boys. The flaxen-haired, Bavarian youth smiled back, blushing. He hadn't even a beard or moustache yet. Vlad found it immensely amusing to study this royal tart at discreet times such as this, noting her flirtations for at least half a dozen virile males of high-parentage. Dukes, earls, knights, barons. Even a particularly handsome and debonair minnesinger named Michael Beheim, a middle-aged, effete harp player with twinkling blue eyes and curly, rust-coloured, shoulder length hair.

The feast was but a carnival, a mock cover-up for some very heated discussions going on at the rear of the hall between Matthias and his Turkish guests (the delegation having since ordered Matthias' sumptuous throne moved to the other side of the great hall for more privacy). Fiddles, mandolins, pan-pipes, banjos and flutes were being played with a frenzy up on the king's exclusive, raised dais by a wild-haired troop of vagabond Romany along with a quartet of jesters and jugglers hired by the sovereign's bailiffs for the night's festivities.

Vlad, however, was the prime display; a straight-moustachioed, dark visaged, macabre *bandito* with curls at the tip of his long, greying moustache. A freak enthroned on his own, high dais. Vlad, the Death Lord, was whom everyone in the great hall had really come to ogle.

Vlad remembered suddenly with a cold-water shock where he'd seen the minstrel. December 25, 1456, the night of Vlad's coronation as Prince of Wallachia. For some strange, irrational reason, Vlad hated this German minnesinger with an unholy furor. He knew not why. The minnesinger had done nothing to incite Dracula's hatred. Yet Vlad felt something, something…call it intuition. And it had to do with Serena somehow, the suspicious circumstances of her wicked death and the ensuing plummet into madness Vlad had endured. Something unholy.

The minnesinger (mincing hither and thither, hand on his hip) too, was in the hall. He sat at the head of one of the massive banquet tables below, occasionally casting covetous glances toward King Matthias' sinful sister seated regally up on Țepeș' dais, the sexy bitch who even now tempted every dog in the throne hall. The men virtually salivated over her hot, yearning stare. All except Vlad. Cool, cruel Dracula (Son of the Un-nameable One), who had loved and grieved thrice, thrice the magical Druidic number of Mawrth, God of War (son of Duw). (Consort of Mardd, goddess of Death.)

Caltuna, in turn, found it infuriating that Vlad *The Impaler* (snicker, snicker) refused to meet her gaze. She meant to scorch him with her hate, for Vlad was a worm. He truly disgusted her. A wolf. A snarling, cunning wolf. Werewolf perhaps?

She wondered whether to inform brother Matthias of Vlad's suspected lycanthropic nature; to push for Vlad's execution for heresy would please Caltuna immensely. She would love to see him burn. He sat there on his mock throne, as if he were the King and everyone below his vassals. Țepeș sat across the table from Caltuna and her numerous paramours, high up on the dais across the hall from King Matthias' own busy, bustling platform. Marvellous tapestries of Christian piety shielded part of Vlad's allotted half of the throne hall (on two sides), a whispering-gallery for discreet lovers hidden behind the curtains.

By midnight, Caltuna was thoroughly drunk. She laughed like a stupid teenage girl tasting her first illicit alcohol, leaning coquettishly against men literally twice Vlad's senior. Yet she was clearly well past her early twenties, he surmised. He wondered why the slut hadn't been married off years ago. Or sent to a nunnery (*brothel* would be more her station). Vlad had turned 36 on December 14, but tonight he felt ridiculously like a crony. He was not in power here, only a prisoner/guest. He despised everyone. *These Hungarians, these Hungarians must die,* Vlad thought to himself with a cruel, private smile. *If only I could wrest the swords from their stacked scabbards,* mused Vlad; *behead them all, men and women.* He thought about dashing upstairs and fetching his gilded sword of State, but knew it would be a suicidal gesture.

By one a.m., by the waning light in the great hall cast by wax-lump candles and the emptying of the huge, ornamental, brass hourglass standing regally in the middle of Vlad's banquet table, most of the guests and associated free-loaders were yawning unabashedly, drifting away to their respective chambers like moths. Vlad dozed. He sat slumped in his solitary, red-silk-draped, mocking throne, snoring, dimly aware of a cunning tread of feminine footfall. Slippers. Even in his semi-conscious state, Vlad could inexplicably recognise the shuffling tread as that of a stealthy, slippered female. His psychic faculties were honed to a razor's edge. Even knew what those slippers would look like: red silk; plush, grey, rabbit's fur trimmings; green-velvet-stitched ladies' slippers. Royalty.

A hand reached out to shake his shoulder suddenly, and then, to Vlad Dracula's utter astonishment, followed a cold, sticky liquid splashing into his face. And then into his crotch. And wicked feminine laughter. Cold wine.

Vlad jerked awake, sputtering, lurching forward toward his attacker. Caltuna shrieked playfully. She dropped her crystal goblet in a panic, meaning to make a quick getaway; her goblet hitting the hardwood floor with a smashing tinkle of shards shattering into a thousand pieces. Caltuna was clearly pissed out of her skull. No longer in her senses at all. All night, brave men had copped a feel, their actions unnoticed by inebriated King Matthias. Not even his usually eagle-eyed, stiff-necked, frigid Hungarian Queen, Esmeralda, had noticed.

Vlad seized her arm roughly, dashing Caltuna against the wall. Her eyes widened, stunned, unable to move when Dracula strode forward in one, swift motion and struck her hard across the face.

The sting felt good on the back of Vlad's hairy hand. It had been so long since he had exercised such brutal authority. It felt good. He raised his left hand again, preparing another vicious backhand.

Caltuna virtually cowered, sobbing with fear. Never, never had she been struck across the face. A spoilt little girl in a woman's body, she was.

Her translucent, dark-silk head veil slewed crookedly from her hair. Ludicrously, no guards were in sight, just she and Vlad alone in the echoing throne hall. 'Twas conceivable the sentries might not even hear her cries. Vlad could murder her swiftly, unnoticed, with a single twist of Caltuna's slender neck with his bare hands. Huge, hairy hands. Or—God forbid—he might have his way with her here in King Matthias' curtained audience chamber. *Jesu!*

Vlad stood poised to strike. His queer, dark green eyes glowed with unholy furor; his teeth bared. Monstrously long, vampire's teeth, one on each side. Or so it seemed in the dim candlelight. They were merely severely worn. Caltuna sobbed, hesitating to scream. Now, she was at the point of no return. Perhaps, just perhaps he might show mercy, a trait Vlad was not known for. Caltuna whimpered, her cheek aflame and stinging. Her lip was bleeding at one corner. A nasty lump would show come morning, ruining her overestimated good looks. Surely, THAT was punishment enough!

Vlad breathed hard. He wanted to strike her hard, repeatedly. To beat her black and blue. But the little bitch was King Matthias' sister. A serious blow could cost Vlad his head. He had so much yet to do, a country to reclaim, a world perhaps. His hand shook, eager to chastise this royal harlot. Caltuna pouted, unintentionally sexy, her grey eyes begging for mercy. And for something more.

Her cheeks were waxen and rosy. Vlad made as if to strike, wondering at this woman's unfathomable cowardice and lack of shame.

Caltuna shrank back against the harsh, stone wall.

Vlad began to lower his hand. "Yes, I can see you are Wallachian—*Romanian*. Your cowardice tells me all I need to know. Your mother, like you, was a whore. Your father a Saxon slave-trader. And you a lovechild. You, *domnişoară*, are the lowest of the low, a Harlot of Babylon. If you were in my court, in my country, I would have you…impaled." Vlad inclined his head regally, eyes closed.

Caltuna blanched, grimacing, her cheeks draining of colour. She looked up with worried eyes.

Vlad smiled coldly.

"Tyrant! I will tell—"

Vlad seized Caltuna's chin with his right hand, cocking her head to meet his stern gaze. He raised his left palm, threatening.

"Do you think I couldn't wring your neck like a turkey, madame?" Vlad glanced cunningly toward the tapestry billowing at the hall's entrance. The great hall was dark. After a moment, satisfied no one was near, he turned his triumphant, merciless eyes toward her. Killer's eyes.

Caltuna, to her weakness and horror, felt a familiar, fatal lust claiming her senses. She immediately despised herself for wanting this hated tyrant in her bed, her *boudoir*. Lust. Carnal knowledge, what priests, cardinals, and bishops had drummed into her impressionable young mind from childhood as a consequence of her weaker sex. Those who themselves hadn't succumbed to her ample charms since the tender age of nine. A little girl.

Vlad sensed it. He felt nothing for this whore. Only disgust. Any lust was all on her part. He lacked even the desire to screw her as a badge of violent conquest. Vlad's control of his sexuality was a mystery even unto himself. And others.

"Let me go." Caltuna's voice firmed, her resolve returning. She straightened up carefully, maintaining eye contact with Vlad's uncanny, hypnotic, forested gaze, all too aware of Țepeș' hot breath smelling of *țuica*, his male closeness. All too conscious of the feel of his rough hand against her chin. She was NOT going to allow herself to be conquered by this male beast. "Let me go. I am warning you, Count. Matthias will torture you horribly if you touch me." She met his unyielding stare.

Suddenly Vlad's eyes flashed.

He snatched her arm, twisting until she was on her knees, begging, sobbing, crying out.

"What did you call me?! What is my royal title?"

"Prince, Prince!" cried Caltuna, her arm threatening to break at the elbow. Her eyes clung to Vlad's own, beseeching. For an agonising moment, she felt sure he meant to break her arm.

Suddenly, like a storm abating, Vlad's iron grip relaxed. He bent down, murmuring.

"Now you belong to me. You are my slave. Any chore I ask of you, you shall do. Is that clear? Disobey me, and you shall certainly die. Believe me, missy; I can bring you much grief and sorrow; much agony. Value my words, wench. I can break your bones, bruise your skin. You'll not escape my wrath. And I have news for you. King—Matthias—will—not—help. He is in my power. He plans to release me upon the world, to reclaim Wallachia. Understand? Nod. Nod or die."

No help was forthcoming. Wincing, Caltuna nodded, knowing Vlad would wring her slender neck should she scream or cry out for help. (Apparently he hadn't forgiven her after all for fracturing his knuckles with her stick.) He had saw her face that day, long ago. Vlad grinned savagely, dismissing her with a contemptuous wave of his hand.

"I shall seek you out again," reminded Vlad, brusquely hauling Caltuna to her feet. "Begone now, wench, I tire of your inferior presence."

Infuriated, frustrated with her helplessness, Caltuna angrily strode away into the darkness; cursing Vlad's name once out of earshot.

Chapter Fourteen

19 August, 1467 AD

Vizegrád, Hungary

Once again King Matthias Corvinus (aka Hunyádi) offered Vlad the outrageous offer of betrothal with the king's Catholic sister, much to Vlad's hostility and Caltuna's private embarrassment. Winter had come. Had gone. Spring splashed forth from the depths of trans-alpine Hungarian winter, one of the muddiest, warmest, wettest, freshest-scented springs by paradox. Forests sang with mating birdlife, the Hungarian steppe-lands lush with grass; the rivers, creeks, and streams gurgling with spring joy. Bullfrogs croaked as if in an endless contest to raise one's voice above thy neighbour. Flowers abound. Heather, cowslip, primrose, tulip, saxifrage, clover, thistle, coltsfoot, giant lily claimed the sovereign nation of Hungary. Three hundred miles to the southeast, down the meandering, blue Danube, annexed Wallachia fared not so well. Ill-planned, half-hearted insurrections against Radu's entrenched Turks had failed miserably. Men were once again being sawn in half at Pitești, Tirgoviște, Tîrgu Mureș (ironically, within the very walls of one of Vlad's newest, and most sumptuous, monastic edifices, recently endowed), and Bucharest, impaled or burnt alive at various other burghs across Wallachia. The Gypsies were being exterminated.

The Wallachian rebels had withdrawn beyond Bistritz, into the Apŭseni mountain range, effectively abandoning Transylvania's mountainous heartland, the southern steppes, to Mehmed II. Prince Radu, by offering pardons to disaffected Wallachians (mainly, the boyars), had successfully stemmed all opposition. By royal decree, the Turks were formally empowered with the bountiful castles and mountain-pass watchtowers scattered across Wallachia/Transylvania.

More scandalously, Prince Radu had usurped control of Hungarian Transylvania. The Ottomans now held Bulgaria, Greece, Cyprus, Sicily, Wallachia, southern Moldavia, Bosnia, and Albania with an iron hand. Mass subversion to Islam was underway. Local *hetmen*, lured by the prospects of prestige and privilege—and no doubt by the legality of owning numerous wives (forbidden by Church canon)—flocked to the Mohammedans' *imams* like migrating geese. Across Romania, loyal Orthodox adherents were being burnt at the stake by allied Catholic and Turkish authorities. Entire populations were being expelled to make way for reliable, Turkish settlers. Bedlam reigned. Greece, Genoa, and Venice were virtually vassals now of Sultan Mehmed Çelebi II, Caliph of all the Known World. Austria and Hungary now lay within striking distance of Mehmed's forces based in northwest Transylvania.

And meanwhile, King Matthias Corvinus and his royal judiciary council had studied Prince Vladislaus Dracula III's so-called "Reign of Terror".

They found the evidence needed to condemn Dracula puzzlingly wanting. Numbers tallied failed to correspond with facts. Witnesses' testimony proved contradictory. Matthias, at the behest of Rome (and his own sister!), had been prodded to ply for Vlad's execution for alleged crimes against humanity, and suspected sorcery. The Vatican pressed for a heresy-burning.

The hearsay information, however, was shaky at best. Most suspicious. Vlad was rumoured to have changed into a wolf (!) on numerous occasions. Vlad was supposed to have turned himself into a bat. (The scuttlebutt on Dracula's alleged midnight blasphemies would have given an alchemist pause for reflection, roared one disgusted member in the Hungarian Diet!) Only Saxons and Magyars had come forward in any great numbers, their volunteered information tainted because of second-hand witness testimony. And King Matthias found their motives highly suspect. Some Gypsies, Jews, Szeklers had come forward. Though damning evidence was obviously in abundance, the details conflicted with each other. Execution of rapists and other nefarious criminals (Mosaic law; i.e., patriarchal position of men) could not be allowed, much as King Matthias sympathised, as evidence of "crimes against humanity". Vlad's laws were his own jurisdiction. Granted, Dracula's atrocities were truly atrocious; none more so than his horrific impalements of porn-ring leaders (their lewd art the disgrace of all Little Saxony), the Madams, Church official go-betweens, middlemen, and accessories to the now defunct child prostitution gamut in Ottoman-occupied Wallachia—skewering men, women and children (if one could believe such stories) through whatever orifice he deemed suitable to their misdeeds. It seemed the word "mercy" was not in Vlad's vocabulary. But the non-Wallach, non-aboriginal settlers harboured motives even Matthias could not fathom. He, too, hated Germans with a passion, sharing with Vlad an almost fanatical hatred of foreign settlers on his soil (though such were necessary for the commerce of his realm). And yet Vlad, gruesome as his regime had been, *despite* Ţepeş' many detractors, had still managed to cobble together a small but die-hard peasantry for his nation's defence. Vlad's unofficial claim of Dacian descent among minority Transylvanian "natives", however, was dismissed as "preposterous rubbish" by Vatican officials. They'd heard him speak the archaic Daco-Wallachian language for their benefit, afterwards calling it "speaking in tongues"—a Church offence. The babblings of a minion of Satan; warlock, leader of a continental-wide witches' coven stretching from Ireland to Hungary, from Anatolia to Russia.

As for the marriage proposal, Vlad had thrice balked. Caltuna was not his wineskin of *ţuica*. Besides, she was his private—though unwilling—slave.

How Caltuna hated this Wallachian Dragon. The Tyrant of tyrants. Tyrannosaurus Rex. Often she would be forced to commit the most humiliating of tasks; wash floors, sweep, empty latrines, wash Ţepeş' fine, imported, silk clothing. Abominable. She was being treated like a common slattern. (She had to empty chamber pots several times a day.) At least one thing: he was clearly celibate and perhaps impotent. Too old to function as a man, possibly. Though Caltuna didn't think so; Vlad seemed much younger and more virile than most younger courtiers. (Certainly the bulge in his tights was impressive.) Vlad had never requested her various other 'services'. Caltuna still found time for the various lewd men of the palace. Barely.

Many times she was forced into inventing fantastic excuses to vacate Matthias' banquets, council sessions, juries, and witchcraft trials. Just to serve her new—demanding—Master. Caltuna had been 'Prince' Vlad's personal maid for over a year now. Nasty rumours about her and Vlad's 'hot' and 'torrid' relationship had been circulating about the palace for some time now. She had never done servants' work, now understood only too well what wretched lives they led. Vlad was merciless in his wicked black humour. His tongue lashed Caltuna's pride like a nail-studded bullwhip. Ţepeş had no reason to beat her. His reputation alone terrified her. Terrified everyone, except King Matthias, who was too stupid to be afraid. Vlad never once punched with his fists, kicked her with his wooden-soled, leathern clogs. His eyes were all he needed to force Caltuna to do his bidding. Huge, half-moon eyes. Dark green, like alpine fir at twilight. (Yet iridescently aglow with an evil glimmer.) Like stagnant pools of bracken-infested water. Wishing wells. Cursing wells. Sensitive; handsome, yet forbiddingly mysterious, the eyes of the Ages.

Winter, needless to say had been a living Hell. Vlad had pestered constantly. (Nothing was ever good enough. Nothing!) "Do this," he would demand. "Jump! Bark! Roll around on the floor."

And do this she would, reluctant, humiliated; yet unable to resist deep inside her soul. Unable to resist Vlad's mysterious, hypnotic eyes, *Waelas* eyes which held Caltuna in thrall. She feared the immense pain he could inflict on her; the horror stories of flayings, burnings, boilings, impalements. She was spellbound. Caltuna feared Vlad like no mortal. 'Twas as if he were a God, miles above her intellect. The Dragon God of prehistory. So merciless, yet commanding unforced obedience.

The reason was simpler. Caltuna was fleshly weak; fatally attracted to charismatic men. Vlad virtually oozed personality; yet it was none the eye could see, for he was a loner by nature, naturally shunning all company save for his warband.

Caltuna hesitated to say she was in love. It was more a love/hate relationship. Perhaps the misguided, irrational love was all on her part. Sometimes she enjoyed making a buffoon of herself in Vlad's presence, unbeknown to him.

For Vlad utterly despised her. Her tainted Hungarian heritage, her 'civilised, lady-like behaviour'. Oh, how he rubbed it in, like salt in a wound, belittling Caltuna for her etiquette. This flustered her most, for she couldn't understand Ţepeş' uncouth demeanour. Vlad could see right through her. Caltuna had needed someone to put her in her place long ago. And lately, she began to re-evaluate her own personality, her sluttish nature, her immorality.

And strangely enough, had begun to despise herself as an extension of her implacable hatred toward Vlad Dracula.

Caltuna swished past one of the maids inside Vizegrád's great hall as she rushed toward the stair, casting a nervous glance over her bare shoulder as she ascended the spiral stairwell. No one following. Good. She was late. The sands in the banquet hall's silver hourglass had slipped past her allotted slave-labour hour. Dracula would be awaiting her. *Moroi.*

And he would be angry.

He wouldn't say anything; his actions spoke more than words.

Cold, disdainful green eyes. He might toss her a broom. Suggest she fly, or sweep. Cloaked in spiders' shadows in a corner of his bare, empty chambers, Vlad would laugh mockingly, eyes glinting beneath smoky candlelight. He might grin, a vulpine, evil smirk, self-satisfied.

Caltuna feared Vlad too much to confide in anyone of his unfair usage of her as his 'servant'. None of the unwed ladies-in-waiting liked her particularly. (Actually, they loathed her.) King Matthias would laugh and applaud Vlad's apparent enamourance of her, preparing for their marriage banns.

Except Vlad was not enamoured of her in the slightest. Never would be. Caltuna entered Vlad's private apartments, the wind rising outside the drafty, fourth floor of Solomon's Tower built by King Bela IV, 1263. Her heart beat a terrified tattoo. What might he do today? What sordid innuendos might he utter to crush her sodden spirits? Would he beat her? Sexually violate her *(Surely it was* inevitable, *given the irresistibility of mine royal personage*, thought Caltuna sagely*)*? Throw her out the window like a sack of barley to explode on the cobbles eighty feet below? Just for fun he would do it, she was sure. Even after more than a year in Vlad's 'service', Caltuna never ceased to be amazed at the former voivode's gall.

"You are late."

Caltuna shrieked, startled. Too absorbed in self-pity, she had allowed the mesmerising silence of the tower to lull her senses. Vlad stood hidden in a corner, a faint smile on his still-handsome lips. He often waited for her in the shadows. Arms crossed within that dreadful, black silk cape, his legs braced apart. Bare, hairy, muscular legs.

"Quiet wench. Dare you speak in my presence?" Vlad's eerie, lilting voice echoed off the masonry, the room mostly devoid of furnishings; a crude, hollow shell. Only a lone footstool, antiquated dresser, wardrobe hanger, single bed, and bone lantern atop an Ottoman enlivened the Spartan chamber. No tapestries hung about to liven Țepeș' lime-washed quarters. Caltuna shrunk back against the cool wall's masonry, dreadfully nervous, limbs already frozen with fear. Vlad held out a broom, smiling. Gloating. "Sweep, wench. Be quick. Be clean. If you are proficient, I may—give you a bone." He laughed harshly, sinisterly. *"On your knees, hussy; serve thy Master!"* How she HATED him.

"Yes, Your Eminence." Caltuna curtsied gracefully, dropping to her knees, utterly wretched. Unsmiling. Her large, grey, liquid eyes sad, watery, pitiful.

Like a dog's.

It was at this moment that Vlad felt a first flickering of mercy for this foolish wench. How she feared him! How docile she was, how spiritless. (He liked her better before.) As Caltuna curtsied, her pinafores and petticoats brushing the floor, he felt a new emotion called lust. For the first time in five nightmarish, blurry, easily forgettable years Vlad felt desire for a woman, an attractive, voluptuous—willing—woman. Not a young lass, not a girl a quarter of his age. A fashionable court harlot and amateur astrologer and fortune-teller, though no match for Vlad's uncanny, arcane knowledge. Admittedly, she would never be Voica; nor Serena (Vlad shuddered); her small nose was too high, her lips too, too heart-shaped. What a tantalising cupid, though.

Vlad knew Caltuna had many lovers. He suddenly hated himself immensely for even considering bedding this experience-beyond-her-years woman. Worldly as Jezebel. Gaudy rings adorned her slender, pink fingers; gold, diamonds, rubies, emeralds. Her immaculately clean hoop-dress was ruffled below the waist, the length of her legs, repeating the pattern in alternate bands; wires beneath supporting the rich, pink, shiny, silken material. A truly daring style terminated the strapless ballgown below Caltuna's narrow shoulders, highlighting her pink, bare shoulders and envious bosom. Such a fashion would bring a beating in more conservative Catholic or Turkish courts. Vlad knew she wore a tight whale-bone girdle underneath.

She caught his fascinated gaze. Somehow, she felt none of the usual pleasure of a man's interest in her. Instead, Caltuna's steely eyes turned mildly condescending. Each day was a challenge to deliberately dress herself to draw Vlad's aloof gaze.

"I understand Stephen Bathóry filled his cup with your charms last night," Vlad remarked. "I heard you both,...had followed you to his room, in truth."

Caltuna froze, shock flooding her veins with ice. *(The hangman danced upon her grave!)* She glanced up, her grey eyes betraying her unease. She knelt on her knees like a common strumpet, scraping grime from the floor and sweeping dust into a crude, tin dustpan.

"I—I-I do not know what you mean," stammered Caltuna guiltily.

"I followed you, missy."

This was no lie.

"You—You did not!"

"Did."

Caltuna could not meet his gaze. Her face flushed red. Fears of brother Matthias' wrath flooded her brain. Stephen was only one of dozens, met the previous night during a wild, bacchanalian banquet feast. He had appealed to her; blonde hair, moustache and beard (though streaked with brown), and plenty of virile charisma. Once inside his bedchamber, however, Stephen had raped her. Repeatedly. Violently. Degradingly, in ways not to be spoken of. With black leather gloves he had beat her, careful not to bruise her face too much; spanking, lashing, sodomising. Slapping her cruelly. He had gagged her, stifling her screams or cries for help, tying her to his bedposts so tight her wrists still bore the welts of raw rope. Caltuna could still feel the bloody lashes from his crop on her lower back beneath her uncomfortably tight gown. Her shoulders and backside were beginning to purple from the bruises; her hair still smarted from being nigh yanked out of its roots; what should have been a gentle and mutually fulfilling tryst had turned into a savage attack on her person. Never had she been treated so. The man was an animal! Most paramours had been paragons of love.

Vlad only smiled. He held the trump card, able to blackmail Caltuna into the most humiliating slavery.

"I don't know what you are talking about," mumbled Caltuna. She kneaded her dress pleats, her eyes watery with fear and shame. She gazed downwards, avoiding Vlad's searing stare.

"You think I am a fool, girl? Think you I be a gullible gaji-boy? A simple, Wallachian peasant?" Vlad suddenly grabbed her arms, shaking her hard. Caltuna's tresses tumbled forth from their restricting, translucent, purple veil with the force of the disturbance. She knelt on the floor, on her knees, unable to defend herself. Vlad's fingers dug into her bare arms. Caltuna grimaced, biting her lip.

Suddenly Vlad released her, grimacing as he turned away. He swung his arms jerkily, his black cape fluttering with each movement. Breathed deep, struggling to control his anger. She was HIS slave. Vlad knew he could wring the girl's neck easily enough. IF he were prepared to die. In truth, the wench was not his concern. Her moral ineptitudes were her own affairs. At last, Vlad spoke.

"God's truth, *domnişoară*, I don't care who you lay with, in all sincerity. Care not whom you spread your legs for, for it is known here what you are. A *houri*. Harlot. But let me say this." Vlad swivelled on his heel, standing authoritatively over her now. "Should 'good' King Matthias find out of your indiscretions, your head will surely roll. Perhaps I shall tell him. Perhaps not."

Caltuna's head jerked up, mouth open in dismay. She trembled on her knees like a mouse.

"You—you wouldn't," she murmured. "Would you?" Her eyes scanning back and forth, as if trying to probe Vlad's unreadable mind through his mad gaze.

"I might."

Caltuna's whole world seemed to be collapsing all around her. All her worldly finery, her rich wardrobe, her exquisite jewellery. Her head. King Matthias would be FURIOUS. At best, she could expect lifelong solitary confinement or a nunnery for scandalising his court.

For dear, brother Matthias held a very dim view on adultery (as did nearly all contemporary monarchs—the standard punishment for a sullied maiden—death). "Oh please, sire," she begged, her voice cracking, frantic now; mindlessly clutching the end of Vlad's floor-trailing cape. "Please. Anything! Anything you ask, I shall grant—only do not tell Matthias!"

Vlad smirked. "Hmmm. Perhaps. Let me guess—you offer me your services."

Caltuna's heart skipped a beat, threatening to stop. Her worst nightmare had indeed come true. Last night was only a horrible prelude.

Speechless, she nodded. "I—I do, sire. I offer myself."

For a long, terrible, heart-stopping moment, Vlad glowered. His eyes widened. Then narrowed. Cold, hellish portals to Hell.

Vlad reached down, snatching Caltuna by the left arm. He hauled her savagely to her feet. Without a word, he strode toward the door, opened it, hurling her by the wrist out into the brick, herringbone passageway. Stunned, she slammed into the wall, sinking remorsefully to her knees; crying openly now.

"Get out. Never frequent my part of the castle again, lest I decapitate your head with a smote of my sword. Begone, wench!"

She ran.

Chapter Fifteen

7 October, 1469 AD

Townhouse, Buda-Pest, Hungary

Vlad stared across the Danube's muddy banks. For weeks, rain had been turning the foaming shores into a quagmire. Brushwood, driftwood, and various refuse from the city's abattoirs and royal iron-foundries clogged the riverbanks. Children played near the perilously-steep embankments unchaperoned. Tinkers' trails meandered along the swollen river, the mightiest, longest, most-travelled river-route in all of western Europe.

Vlad was free. Or semi-free. King Matthias, upon adjourning Vlad's trial for treason, heresy, and crimes against humanity, had once again offered a Wallachian/Hungarian marriage alliance. Again Vlad had politely refused. The Turks had been making dangerous encroachments on Hungarian suzerainty in Transylvania. It was clear, seven long years after Vlad's capture at Köenigstein, that King Matthias was not going to find an ally in the form of Prince Radu "The Handsome". Or any other worthy contender still residing in Wallachia, for that matter. Other methods to dislodge the back-stabbing Turks would have to be considered. One option was the increasing animosity between Prince Stephen Cĕl Mare (The Great) of Moldavia versus Radu Dracula of Wallachia. Most alluring, or, most distasteful, was the idea of reinstalling Vlad Dracula on the rightful, ancestral throne of Wallachia.

Though nominally under house arrest, the King's bailiffs rarely encroached on the ex-voivode's sacrosanct space. (And for good reason, for they still relished having a head on their shoulders.)

For nine months now, Vlad had been free. His servants were polite, punctual, obedient. Terrified. That harlot Caltuna Corvinus no longer troubled his thoughts, no longer brought out Vlad's rages. What a fool she was! He hated her not as much as he pitied her. Risking pregnancy (and disgrace!) for brief, illicit flings with married court dandies. Had she no shame? No brain? 'Twas once said in the Old Country that perfectly fertile women could prevent conception through continuous use of potentially-deadly herbal remedies or potions. But perhaps the brazen wench and her partners relied on a more prosaic birth-control method—*coitus interruptus,* a perfectly respectable, natural method preferred by most Cimmerians (proto-Hittites) in the Olden Times to prevent overpopulation within a *cllwth*, or clan, before the dawn of Christianity. Unfortunately, the terrible side-effect (Vlad shuddered) was a population too small to resist Greek invasion, Roman invasion, Gaulish, Thracian, Saxon, Scythian, Parthian, Viking, Magyar, Slav, Mongol, Ottoman invasion over a 2000-year span right through into murky prehistory.

What remnants the dreaded plagues hadn't wiped out, were easily assimilated or extirpated by the intrusive hordes.

The city of Pest was busy today. Beggars, merchants, smiths all vied for the population's trade. Begrimed children ran carelessly along the street, their mothers and fathers preoccupied with manning the market stalls. The cobbles were worn or loose, the wheels of wagons dislodging the small, ironstone blocks as farm carts and merchants' caravans trundled down the squalid thoroughfare. The stink of cow or horse dung tainted the air. At the head of the main street stood Vlad Dracula's modest townhouse; his mini-court and subversion base. Any man fool enough to risk venturing, uninvited, into *Kaziglu Bey's* manor, be it for thievery or apprehension of common criminals seeking sanctuary must risk Lord Dracula's merciless wrath (as one hapless sergeant had found out to his mortal cost, after having had his head smote off by Vlad's sword whilst pursuing a runaway slave).

Ale signs swung over cobbled alleys and broad avenues, rusty chains creaking noisily overhead as Vlad and his watchful contingent passed underneath. Irate traders spouted profanities in half a dozen different languages, raising their voices to indifferent customers. Beet-red faces showed signs of displeasure and frustration as the various nationalities of peasants and street merchants haggled. Rednecks. The cattle aristocracy, spreading their heinous doctrine of beef and gold across the world like a virus. (They were the new elite, Swabians, mostly, whose ranches continued to expand at the expense of the free peasants and local gentry.) Some shook hands after spitting in their palms to finalise a particularly lucrative livestock deal. In Pest's central market-place near the market cross, men settled deals by placing coins in a shallow basin.

Vlad glared at them, toying with a Druidic medallion; talking to his lackeys from the side of his mouth, as if sizing up potential victims.

Florid faces followed curiously, aggressively, as Vlad's armed quintet passed by, the numerous peasants or Italian traders no doubt curious as to the nature of this short, dark, imperious, caped nobleman's identity. Scandalised whispers arose all around him, the folk gaping in awe and superstitious fear. Some crossed their breast, others holding up two fingers to ward off the Evil Eye. No doubt this royal prisoner was a long way from home.

Dracula avoided their stares as his henchmen cleared a way amongst the mingling bystanders. Head held high, Ţepeş craftily eyed the cowering, low-caste citizens of this wretched Hungarian metropolis. He gripped his sword-hilt lightly with one hand. It was not that he completely mistrusted his guards. Rather, Vlad had always looked after himself, on the battlefield or otherwise. Not a few times had he killed would-be assassins with his bare hands. Like a wolf, he eyed the spectators haughtily now, aloof eyes noting their fear, hatred, or perhaps even admiration. He walked with a curious, stilted gait, his shiny, black satin cape (crimson on the inside), enveloping his figure almost entirely. Only the silk leggings of his navy-blue jodhpurs showed as he strode ahead of his jewel-clasped, leathery-like, scintillant cape. Vlad wore furs as well, for the weather was chilly. He was, indeed, conspicuous as the only man on Buda-Pest's broad, main street without beard nor sideburns.

Up ahead, the townhouse beckoned.

Vlad loathed the hostile stares of these strangers. Mixed among them were black-robed Benedictines, Augustinians, white-robed Dominicans, or grey Franciscan monks with baldish tonsures, beady, glaring eyes piercing his soul, searching for dirt. He smiled cunningly when meeting their gaze, nodding. Plenty of dirt had Vlad. Mass atrocities against Catholic or Orthodox enclaves in Transylvania, where he had systematically tortured, slaughtered or dispossessed the holy brothers of Christ. Dominicans had soon learnt to avoid Romania, the most fanatically anti-heresy branch of the Church. There was a method to Vlad's madness, foremost the successful curbing of Church power concerning temporal or spiritual matters. Vlad turned swiftly, striding back to the heart of the city. His face set like stone. Half a dozen loyal Wallach escorts followed obediently (grudgingly joined by a jocular captain from a nearby tavern), ready to jump out in front lest an assassin appear from one of the many gloomy, fetid alleys. And many there might be, too, of several nationalities.

Vlad had plans to formulate. A nation to reconquer. For this, he must study his diagrams, his charts, his secret scrolls. Granted, he was no spring chicken, but Vlad was no old man either, still had fire in his veins. A dragon's heart beat in his chest, the Dragon heart of Wallachia. Indeed, Vlad felt younger now than he had seven years ago whilst a prisoner in a dungeon beneath Solomon's Tower. As long as the last dwindling *Combrŏgos* (Old Greek; "Koine") still drew breath, Dracula would fight, push the Muslims back into the Black Sea. He would reclaim Serbia. Montenegro. Transylvania.

But time was running out. The old tongue was even now in its death throes. Unchronicled, unmentioned in foreign folklore (except for vague references to the "Old Ones"), the disappearing, illiterate language of the ancients may perish within Vlad's lifetime should by some cruel twist of Fate he be unable to reclaim his birthright, rescue his people before the darkness descends forever and the scorn of 'non-written conjecture'. And then the multilingual nation of Wallachia would be swallowed up by a bland uniformity—of Latin, German, or Mongol.

Romanian.

Ordinarily, Vlad would've ridden in his royal, crest-emblazoned black coach, rather than walk like commoners. But the Danube's mudflats were nearby, excellent for a leisurely stroll, and he was more determined than ever to get his body back into shape. Five years in the dark, damp, solitary, musty dungeons had done his ageing eyes and joints no good. Two years of minimum-security incarceration in Vizegrád palace's Solomon's Tower had not allowed him to exercise strenuously on a regular basis, nor had he been privy to the royal court's numerous stag-hunts as the courtiers sallied forth from the postern-gate overlooking the growing, divided towns of Buda and Pest intersected by the wide Danube river. If he meant to truly reclaim the throne, Vlad knew he must be ready to fight. Now his muscles were weak, almost flabby, no longer the proud iron of his Wallachian youth. Every day Vlad practiced his sword-drills at his private quintain, reclaiming old secrets.

A coach sat in Vlad's stone-walled courtyard. As he neared the Renaissance, traceried, scroll-worked iron gate barring entrance to his townhouse, Vlad began to recognise the orange/gold armorial crest of the Hungarian Crown painted on the high *caléche's* passenger door. A shiny, luxurious, midnight-black coach headed by two big, beautiful, dappled white Percherons wearing blinkers. There was no driver up on the cab. The horses snorted and stamped impatiently, waiting for the royal visitor to return. Vlad's own, royal Dragon crest had been recently impressed into the manor's opulent, frieze-plastered, ochre, arched gateway; an escutcheon famed yet vilified throughout Hungary/Transylvania.

No one sat inside the buggy's red-velvet interior.

Two guards unlocked the flamboyant, cast-iron gate, allowing Vlad and his seven cohorts into the demesne's rough-hewn, ragstone walls. Crisp, motley-coloured, autumn leaves littered the derelict manor's cobbled precincts. The two sentries bowed stiffly, regally at the waist as Vlad and his bodyguards entered, leading him towards a half-timbered, three-storey, brick/stone, haphazardly-leaning, overhanging townhouse. Overhead, red-brick, spiralling chimneys belched smoke into the bleak Hungarian skies. Splendid, heraldry-patterned, stained-glass windows embellished the upper storey. Thick, oaken beams vaguely resembling machicolations or corbels supported the upper floor's jutting superstructure. Oversailing half-timbering made up the upper storey. Flickering torches bracketed in grim, black, iron cressets on red-brick walls betrayed a gust of west wind as the Prince of Darkness strode toward his decrepit manse's long, steep, curved stairway. The townhouse was only one of many pseudo-identical manors dotted throughout the city, the privileged abodes of Hungarian and foreign nobility.

The old townhouse was shabby and dilapidated. Nobody had swept the dusty, grimy, cobweb-frocked wooden steps for many years. Vlad's 'servants' consisted of one mad butler and four chambermaids. The Hungarian sentries— all nine—would find it below their station to sweep steps. Vlad needed his Wallach bodyguards to help practice with his weapon drills.

Vlad did not mind a whit. He rather cherished the run-down atmosphere of the place. (It reminded him of his favourite, pagan, Holy day—*All Hallow's Eve!*) The years of confinement had dulled his sense of pampered refinement. Dust was not his enemy, nor cobwebs, nor grime nor vermin (cockroaches, spiders). Black plague-rats were Vlad's greatest (and only) fear. The city was experiencing a brief respite from the dreaded bubonic spores. Spiders, mice, beetles, cockroaches barely caught Vlad's attention. Years in a foul, dark dungeon had calmed his mind. If anywhere one were to catch the Black Death from rats and their fleas, a dungeon was surely a likely candidate! But perhaps the lack of human contact had a bigger bearing.

The major-domo of the residence opened the heavy, creaking, walnut door slowly, peering myopically out into the empty, encroaching twilight. Vlad's impatient, hammering knock had resounded throughout the empty cul-de-sac of the dying street. Curious spectators returning to their homes cast forbidden glances through the locked gates. Some dared peek over the low stone wall, no doubt hoping to catch a glimpse of Vladislaus transforming himself into a bat, or perhaps a grey timber-wolf, come sundown. Bats flapped over the twin-gabled double attic, slipping from dovecotes, hiding themselves in the dusky grey mist of the city. Fruit bats, the largest of European bats. Harmless. To the superstitious, however, *moroi*, *nosferatu*. Or female *strigoi*, sent from Hell to claim men's souls and privy members.

"A visitor to see you, sir," drawled the major-domo/butler, his Hungarian voice gravelly and slow, aged. "A miss Caltuna Corvinus-Hunyádi, sister of our Illustrious King of Hungary. She has been waiting for about one hour, refuses to leave. Shall I expel the missus, sir?" Gracchus waited expectantly, his pale grey eyes feverish. He was dim-witted, balding; tall, bulky, and stooped.

"Caltuna?" Vlad frowned, casting quick, furtive glances to either side where his sentries stood stiffly at attention, awaiting dismissal. They shared accommodations in the ancient, echoing, partitioned house; warm, fireplace-graced rooms.

Vlad had been expecting Matthias' courier with his elusive pardon. It seemed the Hungarian Diet was using it against him, withholding it as a bargaining tool. The king's council had already decided in Vlad's favour regarding his trial for treason. As for the Hunnish nobility whom Vlad had liquidated during his extirpation of the boyar-class of Transylvania back in '49, Matthias had forgiven him that too—the boyars had evidently been as much a thorn in the Hungarians' side as they had been to Vlad!

"Caltuna?" Vlad paused, surprisingly speechless. She had not crossed his path for over seven months. Vlad had been enjoying his freedom. "Very well. Where is she?"

"In the solar, sir, upstairs—warming her delicate self near the hearth."

"I see. You are dismissed, Gracchus."

The former *hospidar* jerked his thumb toward the pantry, excusing his Wallachian sentries.

Vlad bounded up the wooden stairs, oddly disturbed. The king's insufferable sister was the last person he wished to see.

At first, he thought the dusty solar empty. Slowly, Vlad drew his dirk.

From a shadowy corner, a dark, slender figure detached itself from the manor's cold, stone wall. She curtsied, then pushed back the black veil and snow-white wimple from her head, her body cloaked demurely from head to foot.

"Hello, Vlad."

****

Vlad was unable to decide whether to shout or simply throw her down the staircase. He had, after all, warned Caltuna never to seek his presence again on pain of death. And she had faithfully avoided Vlad's presence afterwards, exiting rooms whenever he arrived. For this breach, however, she must die. He could seize her by the throat and dash Caltuna out the glazed, tri-lobed window to the cobbled courtyard forty feet below to splatter on the stones like a sack of offal.

For a long moment, neither spoke. Caltuna stared expectantly, her face ashen. She'd removed her wimple, shaking out her long, black hair, discarding her image as a prim and proper, nun-like lady of the court. Vlad's eyes were cold, his countenance stern. Caltuna felt frozen to the flagstone floor, vaguely aware of the dusk light filtering through the lone window at her back. Dust spores danced in the fading light.

The chamber was darkening. Forbidding. To her right, a small, wooden door led to an equally empty chamber. The door was shut.

"What do you want, wench?"

Caltuna stammered haltingly, clamping her mouth shut. "I should not have come," she said at last.

"Do you know you risk your reputation as well as mine by coming here?" Vlad remarked. "We both know you've no chastity to lose. But others do not!"

She jumped, taken aback by Vlad's enduring grudge. He never had forgiven her for so cruelly teasing him in his dungeon, all those years ago. Caltuna closed her eyes a moment, regaining her breath.

She strode forward, hitching up her skirts.

"Good sir," begged Caltuna, "please hear me out. I have much to say. Would that you would listen."

Vlad stared up at the oak-beamed ceiling. "Very well. Speak. Be forewarned; I shall not tolerate disrespect." He glanced at her, warning with his eyes.

"As you know, sire," she began, "as only you and I know, I am not chaste. I freely admit it. I have sinned, but these past five months have received Redemption through holy confessional. Only the chaplain of Vizegrád and my former lovers know my shameful secret.

As you well know, sire, King Matthias has offered me as a betrothal. I would be your plight troth; in return, I feel my brother would relent to set you free to reclaim your throne."

Vlad pondered this a moment. Thrice he had rejected such a ludicrously absurd offer. But now…now he was not so sure. He would be celebrating his 37th birthday this December. The sands of time were running low. He had no heir. Could not be sure whether the son he'd sired on his beloved, deceased Voica be living or dead. He'd heard nothing from Cirstian for well over four, lonely years. Had young Mihnea been butchered?

He also knew, however, that Caltuna sought a Queenly throne—a Wallachian throne. Vlad knew instinctively that she loathed him with all her worldly being.

"What you say makes sense; alas, I cannot comply."

Caltuna blinked, flushing with anger. Astounded. Never had she been turned down before. For anything. Any man would jump at such an opportunity. She changed her tactics, stuttering, desperate now.

"I-I-If it be your conversion to the Catholic faith, I am sure a compromise could be worked out," Caltuna pleaded, her voice whining now, cracking with emotion.

Vlad laughed. It was the most defeating, mocking, ruthless laughter Caltuna had ever encountered. A madman's laughter.

"What you say is utterly impossible, my child!" cried Vlad. "I am no more prone to adopt your Romish faith than to fly to the moon. You would of a certainty need many more feminine charms to induce me so. Nefertiti, Cleopatra, Venus herself could not induce me to kissing your Pope's arse."

Caltuna's eyes flashed, a lightning storm over a stormy, slate-grey sea. She was left speechless.

"You forget also," continued Vlad, warming up to his diatribe, "you are a proven harlot. In my country, harlots are buried alive. Rightly or wrongly. Granted, I have no particular aversion to non-virgins. But you, you have no chastity to speak of, you who lay with men for baubles—you would copulate with a dog."

Caltuna's mouth dropped open.

She strode forward, striking Vlad full across the face. The force of the blow rocked his head sideways, Caltuna's palm stinging as well as Vlad's cheek. A red handprint glowed on his ashen face.

"You are a tyrant!!" she screamed, no longer fearing death. *"How dare you speak to me thus!"* Caltuna raised her right hand to strike again, her grey eyes blazing, tongue poking out from glistening, ruby-red lips.

She almost believed the blow would connect. But only inches away from his face Vlad seized Caltuna's hand.

She grimaced with a shock of pain as Vlad's metallic grip squeezed her wrist. It was as if her wrist-bone threatened to break in his taloned grasp. Crying out, Caltuna slowly sunk to her knees, helpless.

Vlad could have killed her then. He had the right. He had the strength. But not the will. He preferred to kill in combat, when the foolish—maidens. (It was the taste of *sweet revenge!*, Vlad Death blood was flowing, or in execution; not guileless—though craved, like a narcotics addiction.) The wench was unrepentant, even now. Her great eyes blazed defiance, lips stretched back from perfect ivory teeth. Dimples showed on both cheeks, one side accentuated by a tiny, black, artificial beauty mark. Caltuna cried out in pain, her voice ascending into a crescendo wail.

Vlad released her in disgust. She dropped to her knees, collapsing in a heap onto the flagstone floor, rumpled, ashen, slumped on her side. Tears streaked her cheeks.

"Kill me," she crooned. "K-K-Kill me and release my suffering," Caltuna whimpered, "for I love you, milord, with all of mine heart."

Vlad remained expressionless. "You lie!"

She began to sob. "I love you, and I hate myself for it!" Caltuna glanced up, teary-eyed. "F-F-For months I have waited for your forgiveness. I have tried hair shirts, fasting, flagellation; confession. Now I wear an iron chastity belt as a vow to myself."

Scrambling to her feet, Caltuna brazenly raised her rumpled, scarlet skirts, her slip, exposing her iron-bound thighs. Pure-white skin reflected strangely next to cold, grey iron. A small metal lock hung tight on its clasp.

Vlad was utterly shocked. What a confounded, wretched mystery this woman was! She dared confess her hate yet undying love for him. Pitiful, confused wretch. Still the thought crossed his mind to dash her out the window.

Bemused, Vlad shook his head. Never in one hundred years would he be able to understand the female species. Totally, absolutely irrational.

"Get up, you trembling dog," Vlad ordered. Caltuna had once more sunk to her knees, beseeching him with red-rimmed, tearful, grey eyes.

"I have told you that marriage is out of the question," continued Vlad. "I'll not take you as a mistress, and I'll not embrace the Papist faith."

Caltuna stood trembling in the faint dusk light now, her face waxen and tear-streaked. She rubbed her bare arms beneath her shawl self-consciously, ashamed of her begging. Only Breton women (western France) asked for their husband's hand in marriage, pagan, barbarian sluts that they were! Caltuna's hair was once more bound chastely beneath a muslin headscarf, her wimple cast to the floor. She had noticed Vlad's scowl of disapproval at her loose-flowing tresses earlier, had concealed her glossy hair to forestall his wrath. A thin, deep purple, woollen shawl hung demurely over her shoulders. Defeated, she wiped her tears away, her right wrist still aching. It felt as if it were sprained. At last, she regained her voice.

"Then you'll not regain your throne, milord, for brother Matthias would rather see you rot in Hades rather than tolerate an Orthodox

Princeling such as yourself ruling Wallachia once more. I am sorry. I should not have come. By now I should have realised that there are some things I cannot have." Gathering up her bulky Damask skirts, Caltuna, head held high, marched past Vlad toward the solar's exit.

"What you say is true."

She stopped, rigid, her hand frozen on the metal door-latch. She'd snatched up her fallen men's cloak from the floor.

Vlad turned to face her, his deep voice suddenly conciliatory. "'Tis not that you are undesirable," he conceded reluctantly, "but your honour is dubious. I demand a wife who is obedient, and as faithful as myself. Not a harlot. I would give up my non-faith no more than you would give up your own misguided Christian heritage."

Caltuna stared, wide-eyed. "Have you no faith in Jesus Christ, Our Lord Redeemer?"

Vlad laughed cynically. "*Domnişoară*," he replied, "I jettisoned faith in Christ the night of my official coronation in 1456. Perhaps someday I'll tell you about it."

She could hardly believe it. An atheist at court, a true heretic! Suddenly Caltuna regretted plying brother Matthias for Vlad's execution for heresy, failed though the charges were. It boggled Caltuna's mind that Matthias hadn't been able to indict Vlad on that alone. Now Vlad Dracula's atrocities took on a different perspective.

"Are you a..." Caltuna flashed a furtive glance about the empty solar, to be sure no one eavesdropped. "Are you—*drui?*" She had switched to Romanian, lest big ears eavesdrop from beyond the slim, oak door. Vlad's Hungarian was atrocious, but Caltuna steadfastly refused to speak in her hated, native Romanian unless strictly prompted.

Vlad chuckled, suddenly at ease, his deep, throaty laughter echoing among the cruck-framed rafters. "No," he answered—"not officially. But I *am* Cimmerian—of *Getae* descent: or Dacian as you would know it."

Caltuna's eyes were like grey orbs with black pools at their centre. Here Vlad was, a voivode—admitting to witchcraft, heresy! She had heard of such mysterious men of wisdom, the *Keltoi* druidic ancients, among whom some had adopted bloodthirsty sacrificial rites and various nefarious customs when the Aryan tribes had unwittingly wandered into India, Ceylon, and Mongolia, in search of loot (or so saith the bishops and wisemen of her time, the all-knowing minions of disinformation). 'Twas there they had adopted horse sacrifice and the barbarous practice of *suttee*—wife sacrifice (still practiced on the modern-day funeral pyres of India). All this was but a mere trace memory however, unwritten folk-memory legend assigned two thousand years before the birth of Christ. Even Caltuna, herself half-Romanian, was only dimly aware of such murky, prehistoric folklore of sinister Fairy Folk—the Cimmerians and later Scythian and Galatian slave-states of Turkey and Dalmatia (whose horrifying hordes had upset the great empires of Phrygia and Hattusa).

"If your faith is weak—why not marry for a crown," Caltuna hinted with a mischievous smile and a glint in her eye which intrigued Vlad immensely. "Be a backslider…sire, if it be *my* faith you worry about, I, too, have a confession…my faith in the Trinity is only skin deep."

Vlad slanted his head slightly, face impassive. His bushy, black eyebrow rose however; a part of him was scandalised; another part of Vlad's soul was fascinated. He had not suspected the King's sister of heresy. Indeed, this was a new and startling revelation. A foothold perhaps…

He strode forward, chastely kissing Caltuna's surprised, blushing cheek, clutching her arms. "Go. Go safely. Come freely; and leave something of the happiness you bring. In the meantime, I wish to evaluate my strategies. Tomorrow, then come. I shall have a decision for you."

Taking her by the arm, Vlad opened the door, ushering her out of the solar before shutting it once more.

Chapter Sixteen

1469 AD
Vizegrád Castle, Buda-Pest

The great hall of Solomon's Tower was teeming with royal guests. Crimson swirls of Damask-silk ladies' gowns filled Dracula's vision, the smell of perfume, roast beef, jasmine and incense overwhelming his arched nostrils. Vlad's entrance put a dent in the garrulous talk and women's gossip pervading the sumptuous, tapestried *Rittersaal*. Two long, heavy banquet tables had been arranged in a T, preparing for the Feast of All Souls' Day.

He was here to present his decision. To petition the King for the right of Matthias' sinful sister. For long days, Vlad had tortured his immortal soul over this most contentious subject. To abjure one's faith would be tantamount to treason amongst his fellow Orthodox comrades-in-arms ruling Wallachia (or otherwise). Vlad wasn't sure he could succeed in subjugating the Orthodox establishment a second time, for one could only pull the lion's tail so many times. To reclaim the throne of Wallachia as a Roman Catholic would be suicidal, however.

His own henchmen might even assassinate him, for they would surely remember the scores of Gypsies and fellow *Combrŏgos* which the Holy Church had persecuted by the thousands. A Wallach's memory was as long as an elephant's.

Vlad had no relish for his future marriage with a proven whore. Indeed, he was amazed King Matthias hadn't already known of Caltuna's scandalous behaviour at court. (She was his eldest sister, however, four years Matthias' senior; offspring of John Hunyadi's short-lived marriage to the Princess of Franconia, annulled in 1443.) But a throne was a throne, and Vlad was iron-determined to curb Caltuna's whorish ways. One indiscretion, one adulterous act of treason would forfeit her head. At the very least, her marriage.

Another veritable cow of Magyar nobility was present, Vlad saw, a gross and ungainly, hideously ugly woman of fat and more facial hair than some men in the hall, whom Corvinus had offered as an alternative to his sister; one Ilona Szilágy, daughter of Mihály (oh, poor man!), whom Dracula, son of Dracul, had most ungraciously *declined*.

King Matthias stood at the rear of the crowded, hexagonal hall, soaking up praise like a daisy soaking up water. Even this month's disastrous fire in Matthias' palace up on its hill, destroying the banquet hall, dormitory, chapel, and jealously guarded Treasure Tower (including important state documents) could not dampen his spirits. He beamed incessantly, long horse-face flushed and shiny from too many brandies. Other men and even women towered over the Little Caesar, subservient and simpering to Matthias' every word. His clothes were of the finest, royal purple brocades, gold buckles on his pointy, curly, absurd green shoes. A fabulous, bejewelled, velvet/gold, orange crown sat his dark head coiffed in the latest fashion, hair curled up around his ears like a woman's. Bright saffron tights embellished his stumpy legs. His Imperial Majesty's doublet glittered of goldspun embroidery upon a deep-purple background. A satiny, purple cape/cloak hung clasped from his broad shoulders, as if imitating the usurped Purple Royal of the Holy Roman Emperor, Frederick Habsburg III of Austria. The king's teeth were bright white, buck-teeth tombstones.

Dracula despised the little tyrant. He swore that someday he would plunge his dagger into Matthias' black heart for the traitorous douchebag's unlawful capture of a voivode, a royal, sovereign Prince of Wallachia.

But to ask for this little man's filthy, unashamed sister…

Vlad searched the hall, his eyes not as sharp as they once were. His muscles were sore and stiff after last eve's strenuous exercise/torture. He would get in shape. Even if it killed him. Already Vlad's muscles had regained their suppleness, were nearing their rock-hard former pride. He used dumbbells, a new and marvellous invention; round iron plates stacked and bolted onto either end of a thick, steel rod.

Caltuna, too (drink in hand), was also present inside the hall. Various men flocked around her like moths to candlelight. She was not smiling, nor enjoying herself fending off their discreet, awkward advances. She held a crystal goblet of hippocras, nursing it slowly, bored. Occasionally she would dismiss some nagging male admirer, tacitly avoiding their searching stares. Caltuna was in no mood for festivities, was now in her menses, virtually glaring at chauvinistic males.

Caltuna wanted nothing more than to flee the hall and retreat to the lavatory, hide away in a latrine chute. Embarrassed. Frustrated. Confused. As she had been ever since her first period twelve years ago when she was thirteen and a priest-molested, sodomised virgin before the castellan Hzingemäirickski had raped her in her bed one night after a boisterous, drunken revelry.

Fortunately Klaus had spilled his seed outside Caltuna's womb, aged and inebriated as he was. Seventy-two years, to be exact.

She, too, did not relish an aged husband. But Vlad Dracula, though a touch of grey now streaked his black hair and stern wrinkles made his face harsh, would perhaps make a tolerable husband. All she could hope for. He was not elderly, only a dozen years her senior, in fact. True, Vlad's face was death warmed over, as if he'd been in the dungeons too long, and his reputation unsavoury to say the least. But he was no Christian. It was that which had attracted Caltuna to him, for she had suspected it all along. She had heard of his so-called 'Devil's language', leaked laughingly out of the Vatican officials. Matthias had puzzled for months over Vlad's "Reign of Terror", sharing with Caltuna his suspicions of a Romanian conspiracy, a scapegoat theory which had harpooned Vlad as a bloodthirsty, psychopathic monster, an undead fiend. Certainly Vlad's law tracts written on rare parchment scrolls were the strangest, yet most sensible, laws which either Matthias or Caltuna had ever encountered, yet the most bewildering. (Much of Vlad the Devil's codicils were inscribed on perishable rabbit skin— the 'Impaler Prince' having used a most unorthodox lexicon for his codices.)

Most maidens and women would've shuddered at the thought of laying down with such an inhuman monster. Indeed, if the rumours be true, Dracula was *moroi*, one of the bloodsucking, grave-inhabiting, garlic-breath-infested undead.

Vlad finally caught Caltuna's eye. Her grey, storm-witch eyes widened with shock and surprise. She felt a guilty pang for thinking of her possible, future master in such a sacrilegious manner. Vlad nodded slowly, answering her unspoken, telepathic question, an answer he had put off for days. (He had even sent a courier postponing Caltuna's return visit.) Yes. He had decided. He would take her as his plight troth.

Several Wallach guards trailed Vlad into the tightly-packed crowd, for, even here assassins might lurk. They brusquely pushed aside astonished dukes and inebriated boyars, marquises and Pashas, raising their loud, accented voices above the din to call attention to Dracula's heralded entrance. *Vlad Țepeș*, great and feared Dragon of Wallachia. The unholy firebreather himself.

Surprised courtiers could almost smell the fire and brimstone in the great hall now. Voices raised to rebuke this haughty, brawny little stranger halted half-formed on their lips. Even those with much unexpiated blood on their hands had to concede defeat, Prince Palatines of Germany, Archbishops, Grand Inquisitors and Papal Nuncios responsible for the torture and burnings of thousands, dukes, earls, barons, all had been outdone by *Kaziglu Bey*. His very name invoked superstitious fear.

Not a few signs of the Evil Eye were indiscreetly raised, three fingers up, Hungarian courtiers wearing ludicrous, velvet, serrated round collars, crossing their hearts now and toying with their rosary beads as Black Lucifer stalked toward the high dais, as if to claim his throne over the earth.

Vlad Tsepesh (*a.k.a.* Dracula, the *Impaler*, son of Baal) wore a red velvet cap sprinkled with precious stones, gaudy peacock feathers sticking out of its headband; enormous gems graced rings on every finger. (Those coming into contact with his silken raiments brushed their hands on their doublets with disgust.)

Vlad held his sword out to King Matthias, submitting himself while on his mauve-stockinged knees. Gritting his teeth. Even the Sultan of Turkey had never received such fealty from him. The King accepted the long-hilted sword with bemusement, hoisting Vlad's heavy broadsword high in the air to a chorus of feigned applause. *"Behold, a True Knight of the Order of the Dragon!"* cried Matthias, beaming at his pale, brittlely-smiling guests. (Their clapping was noticeably lacking in enthusiasm.) The king formally welcomed Vlad (*Vlad Death!* whispered detractors about the hall) to his court, giving *Țepeș* the customary kiss of peace on his unnaturally pale cheeks. Grimacing, Dracula imitated Matthias' actions. "Welcome, brother. Come safely. Go freely; and leave something of the happiness you bring," Matthias murmured.

Snickers arose from the great hall. Happiness? Highly unlikely. Misery and disgust, surely.

Vlad avoided Matthias' searching, watery-brown eyes. How he hated this usurper, how he longed to clench his fingers around Matthias' scrawny neck.

Caltuna watched anxiously. She admired *Țepeș* for his bravery, his twisted sense of honour. Of all men, it was he she could attest to having respected her womanly inferiority, having foregone the customary and perfectly exemplary right to beat a foolish female or have sexual relations with her, even against her will. Even a king's sibling, for Vlad was *voevod*, *Cnéaz*, not a mere peasant to be spat on. Or to have brandy poured onto his private parts!

The hall's mezzanine, thronging with human swine, was abuzz with gossip and innuendo.

Caltuna suddenly realised with a brief shock that Prince Vlad, despite his ghastly pallor, was still the most handsome, debonair, yet ominous man in the hall. She had experienced the same illicit thrill yet disappointment the day Vlad was first released from his solitary, bottleneck-dungeon several years ago. He had glared at her with his big, green, hypnotising eyes while the sentries prodded Vlad down the corridor, murmuring dire Romanian threats: Caltuna had uttered a particularly unladylike four-letter word. (He was a veritable beast of a man, she'd marvelled: his masculinity had frightened yet aroused her.) She had expected an old, greying, goatish caricature of a man, had almost felt guilty for cracking his hairy knuckles so often when he would reach for her blindly through the narrow arrow-slit to seize his accusers.

Vlad resisted the impulse to ask for Caltuna's semen-stained hand in marriage in front of all these irrelevant strangers. This task he must do in private. To abjure one's faith in public for a lowly wench was no way to restart a warlord's career—no way to reclaim a throne, certainly.

The feast was but a repetitive, mundane affair. Too many banquets had Vlad witnessed over the years. The scheming plotters at Tirgovişte's ducal palace's banquet hall had quickly weaned Dracula of his fondness for such merriments. His holidays were no longer festive seasons of childish joy. He preferred hawking and hunting to gluttony and wenching, which this sordid affair obviously was designed for in its secretive, hand-signalish way. Not even delectable *fois grás*, butter-basted turkey (a delightful, imported delicacy), marinated pheasant, roast lamb, T-bone and sirloin steak, roasted, suckling pig, Russian vodka, red wine, claret, sparkling white champagne, *slĭvovitz*, stuffing, cream tarts, apple pie and toffee with whipped cream on top could raise Vlad's spirits.

By midnight, the more absurd dashed their fingers down their throats, inducing vomit so as to continue their gluttony. This peculiar trend Vlad found most ridiculous, for it was indeed acceptable, trendy behaviour to stuff oneself beyond reason with blessed, royal duckling, *fois grás*, patisserie, young roast boar, etc. In his day, he had banned it from his court. The matrons looked on in amusement as fellow—corpulent—females vomited in discreet wooden buckets beneath the two, thick, obscuring trestle tables.

Caltuna was disgusted. As she always was now at these ludicrous feasts of debauchery, gluttony and drunken tomfoolery. These Hungarian courtiers, noblemen and ladies alike, were not human. They were animals. Kings and bishops, their brains spongiform, riddled with holes, full of nonsense. Faces shone, red and sweating, some smiling a sickly grin. For the first time since her virginity and childhood-innocence were so cruelly wrenched from her, she felt ashamed to be Hungarian. And it was rare moments such as these that Caltuna Corvinus/Hunyádi longed for mysterious, misty, mountainous Romania.

Vlad avoided her gaze. Twice, when all eyes had been turned to King Matthias, a figurative, wisecracking ass with donkey's ears wearing a king's crown at the head of the banquet table, Caltuna naughtily sought Vlad's fingers across the trestle table while Matthias told one of his numerous, tasteless jokes denigrating women.

Vlad snatched his hand away each time. He stared morosely into his gold goblet, savouring his apple brandy while these imbeciles roared with laughter at jokes he would not have even tolerated at his own royal feasts. The king and his stuffy cohorts laughed over tales of gang-rape, dismemberment, castration, Jews, Gypsies and what good crusader Catholics might do to their women. Vlad flushed red, clenching his fist white underneath the table to suppress his anger. Among the numerous tales, was that of St. Louis IX of France, whom when replying to enquiries discerning Jews from Arabs in the Middle East had said: *"Put a sword through all! Ask questions later!"* 'St.' Louis had uttered the same regarding innocent Catholics put to death in southern France during the Albigensian Heresy.

To Vlad at the moment marriage with Caltuna seemed akin to incest or bestiality. A Hungarian quasi-human.

The second time Caltuna sought his fingers, smiling impishly, coyly, Vlad spilled his delicious brandy on his sleeve. He scowled.

****

A hand shook Vlad's shoulder. He snored unabashedly, the hall dark now and quickly emptying of human company. Several snarling, mongrel dogs prowled beneath the trestles, searching for bones or clumps of fat dropped by the revellers. Beer, ale, wine, whiskey slopped the twin, dislodged tables with an alcoholic lake. Puddles showed where every drunken fool had sat, staining the silken, cream-white tablecloth yellow or red. Only servants buzzed about now, dousing candles on the walls with long, iron candle-snuffers.

When Vlad looked up, his awaker had respectfully vanished, as if expecting *'Dracul'* to cast a spell upon him.

Vlad was drunk. Very, very drunk. From the ceiling, oil lamps hung smoking from chains, corrupting the hall's very atmosphere with their awful, yet all too familiar, reek. His faithful bodyguard sat nearby with their feet up on the trestle table, laughing as they finished the courtiers' half-emptied goblets. After what Vlad had done, a thorough smash be in order. Around midnight, fortified with drink (desperately needing a piss), Vlad, following Matthias' retinue to the latrine's buttress tower, had formally accepted Matthias' sister as plight troth. The actual submission had not been that difficult. The king (plus retainers) had graciously insisted they discuss the matter in private inside a gothic-arched, empty, early Renaissance drawing room, arranging Caltuna's dowry price. With only his retainers plus Matthias' own to hear, Vlad had knelt for the king's sister's hand.

Afterwards he'd felt anger and injustice.

Vlad glanced around now, realising with a flood of relief that, except for his companiable, Cumbrian retainers (at least nine having fled that war-torn realm during the Yorkist/Lancastrian troubles, securing employ with Vlad Ţepeş' grisly regime), the *Rittersaal* was quite empty. The enormous hearth, with its twin, tri-lobed pillars, glowed only with tiny orange/blue/red embers now. October, the night was cold. The hexagonal, Oriental-tapestried hall colder than an alpine shepherd's hut. Vlad shivered, rubbing his crimson blouse sleeves, blowing warm air into his hands. His black, silk cloak lay draped across his stockinged knees. Outside, the air was still and winter-cold with a thin layer of hard autumn snow on the ground. Vlad looked around, wiping beer froth from his rakish moustache, at once glad these non-human courtiers (royal fops!) had vanished, for he was a loner at heart. He pined for spring, however; pined for the day he might hunt on his native, Transylvanian soil once more, watch majestic, elk stag attempt to outwit his arrows, or merely to listen to the lovely, somnolent gurgle of melted, spring snow-water flowing in streams down deep, green, rocky ravines and towering mountain gorges. To hear ice crack as frozen sloughs melted, bullfrogs croaking, buttercups and primrose opening with the first youthful, joyful, warming, life-giving sunrays. *Haûl.* (Sol, the sun.)

Freedom.

The great hall swam in his vision. Elated, giddy, Vlad stood up, tottered across the empty banquet hall, mounting the spiral stairs carefully. His bodyguards followed with bemused, respectful silence. Also quite drunk.

Once inside his wainscoted bedchambers, Vlad smiled the languid, dreamy, silly smile of a drunk. His retinue had dispersed to their own rooms outside his corridor, gratified to settle their exhausted bones on heather-stuffed pallets rather than cold, winter ground, as was once Vlad's wont.

Vlad had only one thing left to do. He must formally notify Caltuna of their betrothal. He wouldn't do it personally, of course; rather, he must ask a chatelaine or some chambermaid suitable in office to pass the information along, for he would not lower himself to draw another unnecessary breath in this accursed fortress/palace cum-royal-prison, come daybreak. There were too many sour memories here. Of endless, chilly nights in the tower's rat-swarming, bottleneck dungeon. Nights of freezing cold, huddled beneath a blanket in front of a bonfire (which his gaolers had grudgingly lit). Or when Cirstian had brought The News...No. It was a matter of honour and courage to notify this spoilt wench himself rather than have her own, majestic brother notify her, as if it were an arranged marriage and he the shy, lovesick junior.

Vlad stumbled toward a bureau, cursing, rasping in Dacian of his yearning desire to feed all Magyars to the sharks. He splashed ice-cold water from an iron laver bowl onto his face, gasping, the cobwebs of drink dissipated by the nasty shock of cold water. An inglenook fireplace spat lethargically in a corner. Goldspun tapestry, depicting Christ's Passion, fluttered on all four walls.

He crept silently out of the smoky, candlelit room, every sense alert. Then down the cloister-like passageway. He knew where Caltuna's bedroom was, her *boudoir*. Vlad had stalked her many times, intending to rape the royal bitch but unable to bring himself to do what Teutons and Latins did every day as a matter of course during their Crusades in Estonia and Lithuania. (Of the many cruel deeds he'd done—murder, larceny, torment, and mayhem—rape was not amongst them.) Vlad now carried a dagger, just in case...Can't have his bodyguard along for this. He padded clumsily down the dark, crypt-like, narrow hall, his feet cold even with boots on. Stealth was difficult in his inebriated state. Occasionally, Vlad's broad shoulders or sword's hilt would bump and scrape along the crumbling corridor. His breath came forth in harsh, ragged gasps. Unnaturally loud in that entombed, masonry silence. Down a twisting, spiral stairwell he crept, blindly groping for the rail rope. His wooden soles clicked naggingly, like chattering teeth, on the worn, limestone steps. He carried no candle, lest an enemy or eavesdropper note his stealthy passage. Vlad inched downwards slowly, one foot at a time, slightly disoriented; therefore knowing his limits.

On the third-floor landing, a lone candlelight bobbed towards him.

Vlad hid behind a door, waiting for the nightwalker to pass. He watched, peeping around a corner, thrilled; heart pounding with delicious, forbidden anticipation. Waiting for this lost soul to pass so he could continue on his way.

The light neared. A soft tread—servant. Slippered feet. Chambermaid, most likely.

Candlelight illumined the wainscoted corridor now; its wan glow eerily tracing the pinched profiles of long-dead denizens on superb, rosewood-framed paintings. Vlad could see a hand, a silver, twin-columned candelabrum, a—face. An angel's face, unblemished by the years. Caltuna Corvinus/Hunyádi herself, out to visit the latrine closet. A surprising, unexpected bonus.

Vlad leapt out. Seized her face from behind with one slab hand, gripping her left with another. Her candlestick she could not use, her left hand clutching it—wrist seized by Vlad. Caltuna struggled violently, surprised momentarily until Vlad spoke. He whispered in her ear lest she cause a commotion. "Shh! Calm yourself, *domnişoară*. 'Tis I, Wladislaus Dragwla. Cease your struggling, wench. I bring joyful news, for you at least."

Caltuna ceased her struggles, awaiting Vlad's momentous declaration. Anticipation, dread, fear, disgust all flooded her being. Or joy.

"You'll not scream? I've come to my decision. I'm going to release my hand."

She remained silent. Vlad pulled his hand away from her soft, pillowy lips, somehow regretting doing so. Caltuna half turned toward him, huddling against his breast, looking expectantly into his aloof, mysterious eyes, waiting.

Her curvaceous beauty jolted Vlad. Only a pink shift she wore. Her shapely legs and full bosom shamelessly bare, porcelain skin dotted with goosebumps. Pure, pink, virginal skin—visual lies. Straight, lustrous black hair cascaded luxuriously down her shoulders in careless abandon, free of ribbons, veil, and wimple. Her eyes bore a slight expression of reproach. She measured Vlad's burgeoning desire by the way he took in her heaving bustline with a look of almost virgin shock. Hilly mounds of pleasure denied him for seven, dark, hellish years. Vlad glanced momentarily down at his fingers, mentally counting the years...a thin strap of silk dislodged itself from Caltuna's bony shoulder, shift mercifully not baring her large, conical, left breast.

"I have decided to take you as my wife—to abjure my faith for the throne which be rightfully mine. You'll help me won't you? I have—I have never abandoned a faith before." Vlad chuckled sardonically, gently cradling Caltuna's pretty face in a hand which had once cut men in half with a single smote of sword or battle-axe or ball-and-chain mace.

"I—I shall help you in all things, Master. Whatsoever you desire." Suddenly Vlad's grip tightened.

"Tonight, woman," Vlad hissed, "tonight your brazen actions almost humiliated me in front of my hereditary enemies. Do not do it again! I have a blood-feud against your folk."

Terrified, Caltuna nodded.

And then Vlad's left hand softly cupped Caltuna's breast.

It was like a sudden, involuntary reflex action, that of a boy with his first woman. But the feeling was incredible. A tidal wave of unbridled, delicious lust swept over Vlad "The Iceberg" as he gently squeezed Caltuna's heaving, goose-pimpled breast. And she did not protest. Only assenting with her eyes. Their breaths grew heavy, his own against her neck.

"By Belin, I think I shall take you tonight—"

Caltuna cut his words off, throwing herself wantonly into Vlad's surprised arms, kissing his lips now with more womanly ferociousness than he'd yet encountered. A blazing desire burnt inside her like a forge, arms wrapped tight around his muscular neck. One hand seized Vlad's long, barbarian hair in the throes of passion, while another caressed his upper back hard, fingers digging into his blouse. He reciprocated the favour, gripping Caltuna's long, unruly black hair in one great handful, the other crushing her waist, his hand in the small of her back. Deftly, Vlad slid his knee between her thighs, making her groan in exquisite pleasure.

He hoisted her up into his strong arms, striding toward Caltuna's bedchamber.

"Oh God, Vlad, screw me till I die," begged Caltuna, laughing coquettishly, her wet tongue on his ear now as he headed uncertainly for her *boudoir*, following Caltuna's aloof directions.

He took her again and again. Caltuna's body was slick with sweat, glistening, naked now under his bouncing body; and then on top, breaking the Church's holy commandment sinfully. Vlad quickly forgot the difficulty he'd had locating Caltuna's bedchambers, her boudoir. Sheets covered their interlocked bodies, on now, off again—scarcely needed.

And, in a sense, they were already married.

Chapter Seventeen

4 July, 1473 AD
Timişoara, Transylvania

At the chapel of St Mary the Virgin, Székesfehérvár cathedral, Buda-Pest, Hungary, Vlad 'the Impaler' and Princess Caltuna Corvinus-Hunyádi said their marriage vows under the cold, hostile disapproval of the Irish Archbishop Finnio who conducted the betrothal ceremony. The Papal Nuncio, Nicholas Modrussa, too, was also present. He it was who had witnessed Vlad's peculiar habits whilst still a prisoner in 1465, had noted the Antichrist's oddly pale features, his long teeth, his atheistic tendencies. Nicholas had spoken to Vlad himself, spent many cold winter nights discussing philosophical issues with Vlad Dracula (who kept his real views well hidden) over games of chess. It was his duty to report back to the Vatican of Vlad Dracula's religious intentions, whether this former Orthodox sinner had truthfully embraced Christ or had backslid into shameless heathen immorality. Nicholas had his doubts.

Dracula had attended Mass faithfully every day, listened to the bishop's sermon at Sunday Mass inside Solomon's Tower's donjon chapel. Caltuna, it soon became apparent, had conceived quickly. The wedding feast had been a surprisingly low-key affair, for Dracula was no Prince, only a dethroned has-been marrying a king's irreverent, inconstant elder sister whom Matthias had always swore belonged in a nunnery, not at court. (His father János had been partial to her, however.) There was very little public show of affection. As the months flew by and Caltuna's womb quickened, the kicking babe inside her belly growing monstrously large entered its seventh month.

The birth had come prematurely in November, 1470; a sickly, small child whom Vlad quickly christened Mihnea. Caltuna had barely survived the birth.

She had lain in bed for weeks, too sick to stand. For four perilous months previously, she had teetered on the comatose brink of death, her skin pallid and sallow, her pulse slow. Rumour circulated about the city like flies; Caltuna had yellow fever, sleeping sickness, plague—or conversely, the victim of an unspeakable *nosferatu*—who happened to be her husband, one Vlad Dracula, Count of Bucovina. (Officially.)

Vlad had waited at her side as if at a wake, watching miserable, March blizzards build horrendous mountains of snow outside Caltuna's glazed, third-storey, Perpendicular Gothic window of crenelated Vizegrád palace up on its hill, overlooking Solomon's Tower below the sumptuous royal palace's inner bailey's arcaded walls. Vlad sat listlessly through the drafty, cold nights, candles flickering in their bronze candelabrum. Servants had changed Caltuna's bedsheets, her bedpan, shaking their heads. How could this poor girl recover with this blood-bloated leech crouching at her bedside, draining the life from her jugular late at night while mortals slept. The bride had, indeed, lost plenty of blood during childbirth.

Whatever fever gripped her, it had proven undiagnosable to King Matthias' royal physicians. The monks had even tried bloodletting.

Vlad, in turn, failed to endear himself with the castle's attendants, his words terse or downright threatening when chambermaids insisted on showing him to his bedchambers. He was sure their offers of nightwatch lest the new mother awaken during the night asking for a glass of water were mere pretences. For he was sure the moment he closed the door the wicked maidservants would be asleep within minutes. As it was, Caltuna had not awoken, day or night.

But spring had come, and Caltuna's eyes had fluttered open, her colour returning to normal. The castle chaplain had sprinkled holy water on her bed one night while Vlad slept, had scattered garlic flowers and cloves about her *boudoir*. (No longer had the ex-voivode allowed them to use their leeches or monstrous bloodletting tubes and bowls on his beloved.) Vlad had awoken one morning, enraged, to discover crucifix, bible, pagan Magyar talismans on Caltuna's four-poster bed. These he'd thrown out the window. Dracula, taciturn even when relieved, held Caltuna's hand tight when the royal nursemaid brought forth their son for Caltuna's joyous, surprised inspection, cradling baby Mihnea in her arms with rosy cheeks and a motherly smile. She hadn't even been aware these past sixteen weeks whether her child had lived or died, whether boy or girl. A son. A future Prince of Wallachia, to follow in the huge footsteps of his illustrious, notorious father. Vlad's second son. However, due to the often strenuous Wallachian custom of non-primogeniture (fast dying), young Mihnea would also have a bastard elder brother contending for the throne; in Wallachia, amongst the native *Wallachs*, illegitimacy was unheard of. A child, begotten by lawful Church marriage or no, was the moral responsibility of its hereditary sire and therefore heir to a share of all he'd owned, regardless of the mother's present husband. (Polygyny was strictly forbidden, punishable by death—death by *torture*.) Hence, the use of a *nain*, or grandmother, to raise a child whom otherwise would be a bone of contention in a household. (Women, needless to say, generally did not inherit land unless bequeathed to an only child, although inheriting that of a spinster and half of her ex-spouse's belongings.) The bastard offspring, goods divided amongst all as well as legitimates were, unfortunately, the insidious cause of endemic, internecine warfare. (Albeit inhibited men's wanderings!) Dogs tearing at a Kingdom; fair for offspring, but, in historical times, disastrous for a Crown. And only one rule of law be universal: Survival of the fittest.

Caltuna stood at Vlad's side now, looking apprehensively across the unfamiliar, yellow plains of Banat, at the blue, red, and yellow patchwork of opium plantations (property of the boyars, and their Turkish overlords) and sharecropper allotments, western Transylvania's craggy, snow-capped Bihor mountains looming hazily, bluishly, in the east. Summer now. The last strongholds of snow were the various, independent Carpathian mountain ranges. The city of Timișoara had grown considerably since Vlad's first premature visit and subsequent claim to the Wallachian throne over twenty years ago. During his long, intermittent reign (reign of terror) he had bestowed many charters to this traitorous burgh. A warm, southern *foehn* (wind) blew from Bulgaria's steppes to the irritancy of bondsman and mercenary alike. Barley fields billowed in the distance; beyond the modest burgh's walled outskirts, radiant sunflower fields waved yellow, daisy-like heads under a scorchingly hot, July sun.

Caltuna held little Mihnea in her arms. The boy was almost three years old already, and heavy. Only recently had her wetnurse weaned the boy from her breast. To Caltuna's dismay, Țepeș had insisted that, in the future, she suckle her children herself rather than designate a wetnurse as was customary in most royal households.

Vlad was here on a reconnaissance mission.

A small mercenary army had accompanied Vlad across the Hungarian border (near Oradia) toward Timișoara to gauge the countryside's loyalty to Prince Radu. Turkish garrisons were entrenched at Ceteștani-București, Tîrgsor, Craiova, Rimniu Vilcea, and Risnof (two of Vlad's favourite cities), as well as Ploești, Constanta, and Giurgiu. Yet all was not as it seemed. The natives were restless. Three years ago, 1470, Radu had rashly attacked Moldavia over a petty squabble. He had greatly misjudged Prince Stephen's power, Radu's own cousin. (That minor border dispute had quickly become a fiasco.) Since then, Moldavian troops had occupied Sighișoara, Bistritz and București (recently expelled), steadily advancing, pushing Radu's disloyal mercenary forces into the western quadrants of Wallachia. Towards Vlad's wholly-unexpected lair. By April of this year, King Matthias of Hungary had reclaimed suzerainty over Transylvania in the sake of 'national interests'. He had finally realised his mistake, releasing Vlad upon the world.

By June, Stephen 'The Great' (*Yr Mawr*, of the notorious House of Bathóry/Musats) was within striking distance of Tirgoviște, Wallachia's former capital. The precious prairie fields of eastern Transylvania had been confiscated by Prince Stephen's marauding forces. Turkish garrisons had finally, belatedly, joined the fray. At first, they had scattered the Moldavians' home-grown army.

But Stephen had soon resorted to Dracula's guerrilla tactics which had proved so effective against Sultan Mehmed eleven years ago, an era now looked back on as glorious by most Romanians.

Stephen, too, had become a famed Impaler.

Now Dracula himself was back in Transylvania, surveying the mountainous countryside like an outlawed wolf which had snuck back from the forbidding, transalpine forests of Hungary's uneasy border. Here to terrorise the villagers and city folk once more, to drag the Wallachians down from their walls into war against the heretical Turks with grappling irons, if need be. As long as Vlad threatened to rule, cowardice would be an unpardonable crime. For in his day, power could not save a man from Vlad's justice, nor could *baksheesh* money save a boyar's skin.

Little Mihnea began to whimper crabbily in Caltuna's arms. She scowled, her temper short. Few nursemaids had she, those present already overloaded with luggage; nor had she the usual slaves customary of the Hungarian court. Vlad had shockingly cut their shackles, inducting them into his own personal bodyguard. Caltuna hadn't even a perambulator handy to push the boy. Today Vlad and his mission seemed like an insane obsession to Caltuna. Here they were, the three of them, their servants and a small, hand-picked mercenary army, marooned in this hostile Transylvanian border town. (Most of the townsfolk hadn't even been able to speak Magyar!) Caltuna felt homesick already. As did Vlad's Hungarian soldiers.

Relentless, steppe-land winds howled across the Tisa plain, hot and dry, so very unlike Transylvania's misty mountain ranges to the northeast, the arid lowlands withering under months' long, annual droughts.

Slowly, deliberately, Vlad began to retrace his steps back to Timişoara's cobbled streets. The rectangular, widely-machicolated, Italianate clocktower tolled 4:00 o'clock. Caltuna followed, rolling her eyes as her master strode toward the burgh's red, sandstone walls. She glanced up, noting the menacing, moss-dotted battlements and ancient clocktower's pitch-black onion spire rising majestically behind crenelated walls. Outside the ramparts and earthworks, Vlad's Hungarian army bore the royal lions on the command tent's flag mast, gold and red lions against a dark blue, silk background, fluttering in the wind. Vlad's loyal *Szgany* bodyguards walked on ahead, studying the streets with provincial curiosity. Caltuna could not for the life of her understand why Vlad tolerated these human dross's presence, one of his most disgusting eccentricities. *Gypsies!* They spoke a maddening, foreign tongue; these particular *Suevii* always accompanied Vlad's retinue, for they were utterly unlike the mainstream Gypsy caravans now roaming Europe (who called themselves *Romany*—in fact an Indic/Romano-Celt pidgin language). Indeed, their names, their very customs were different; pagan marriages were often conducted thus: betrothed couples would leap over a willow branch, thereby formalising their marriage vows under the watchful eye of the caravan's parental godfather, a clan leader or head of the *teulu*, or family, often accompanied by the clan witch. Most (if not all) Gypsy caravans, nowadays, were of Romany ancestry; that is, of Latinized, East Indian origin. (They'd left their Indian sub-continent so long ago that their pagan superstitions actually *pre-dated* Hindu beliefs.) Many were polygynous. Others were not native Indo-Europeans at all; rather, Egyptians (the original *Gypsy*, having eschewed Arabic/Islamic overlordship), Bedouins, or Nubians who'd wandered north from Africa, having crossed the arid Anatolian plains and difficult Caucasus massifs into southern Russia. These often wore rings in their noses! Caltuna shuddered at the thought. She had no love for Gypsies, indigenous or otherwise. But mulatto Africans—certainly not!

Some of the names of Vlad's taciturn, blood-kin bodyguard had roused Caltuna's curiosity: all were Latin corruptions of some bewildering, unpronounceable dialect previously prevalent throughout Romania, the Germanies, Hungary, Albania, Czechoslovakia, and southern Russia—all of continental Europe and western Asia for that matter—a proto-Celtic language of the now extinct Cimmerians, Dacians, Thracians, Illyrians, Getae, and Sarmatians: Caractacus—*Caradóg*; Cartimandusii—*Garethwëndis*; Venedotii—*Venedda*; Vleidisluisii—*Bleiddig*; Dinocasii—*Dinogad*;

or Marclewi—*Marchlew*.

Swaying inn signs creaked annoyingly as Vlad's cohorts approached one of Timişoara's many taverns frequented by nefarious German or Hungarian tradesmen and peasants. Vlad's retainers buzzed among themselves in their strange, incomprehensible gibberish till he snapped a command in Romanian. The unruly louts grumbled quietly, then lapsed into silence, their boots tapping noisily on the cobbled street as they passed an open tavern door with dark, longing eyes. Caltuna tagged along, struggling to keep up with Vlad's brisk stride, cursing the retainers roundly as she brushed past. *Clack—clack—clack*. Even the sound of their primitive wooden clogs on cobblestone irritated her, as did the exasperating clink of sword hilt and wooden crossbow-butts against steel belt buckles. Scores of Vlad's moustachioed guardsmen brandished obsolete longbows slung over their shoulders, long, bulky defensive weapons now outdated but surprisingly making waves in the West after the English usurpers had won the decisive battles of Crécy and Agincourt in France, decimating the *Fleur de Lys'* chivalric nobility—terrible carnage for such 'obsolete' weapons. (Incidentally wielded by Welsh bowmen recruited into Edward III's and Henry V's armies from South Wales.) Bows which had tipped the balance of power in England's favour overnight. Even Aragon, Castile, and the Holy Roman Empire of Austria had taken notice with morbid foreboding. Competition they did NOT need.

And soon the Catholic axis powers would have another slippery contender to deal with. A fire-breathing, smoke-and-brimstone *Tyrannus Rex* by the name of Vlad Dracul III, Dragon Prince of Wallachia.

The autumn of 1475 would bring fire and slaughter to Wallachia/Transylvania.

****

1475 AD
Craiova, Southern Wallachia

ARMAGEDDON.

Fireballs plummeted from the midnight skies.

A wintry, starry night belied the previous arrival of spring. Somewhere in the hostile Transylvanian wilderness a "Great and bloodthirsty war-wolf" plundered and massacred by torchlight entire

German villages with a savage, unrelenting ferocity which could be the work of only one madman, the cruel, coldly-calculating berserker Vlad Dracula "Son of Satan". Entire communities fled by torchlight at the merest, wild rumour of Dracula's dreaded approach; only to be slaughtered and raped by newly appointed Prince Basarab Laiota's gluttonous Turkish forces roaming the nocturnal wilderness bogs and highland roads of Wallachia. Mountain passes had become the abode of criminals once more. Some "fortunates" might be shackled and shipped away into Turkish slavery.

Vlad's homosexual brother Radu, after goading Prince Stephen Cĕl Mare (of the House of Muşats) into open war, fled Bucharest only days before his new capital of ungro-Wallachia fell once more to Vlad Ţepeş' most ardent supporter. The incident of 1462, when Stephen had treacherously besieged the Black Sea fortress of Chilia (though failing in the attempt) had been—conveniently—forgotten. Almost two months now already Prince Radu had been in his grave. November 23, 1473, Vlad Dracula's own, Chîndia watchtower at Tirgovişte's ducal palace had been successfully stormed by Prince Stephen's Moldavian infantry whilst Bucharest, too, surrendered, smoking and in ruins, to *Cĕl Mare* in person.

The two Transylvanian voivodes had made a terrifying pact.

In January, 1475, Prince Radu had perished at Sighişoara citadel after a long bout with syphilis, coinciding with Sultan Mehmed's official declaration of annexation at the small, fortified enclave of Reşiţa (Radu's rulership was no longer needed). Here, in the grain-belt of Wallachia, Mehmed held the Principality with an iron hand, surveying the conquered prairie fields with a pleased eye. Truly, the lowland bread-basket of Romania. Here Mehmed was ruthlessly invincible.

He couldn't have been more wrong.

At the stupendous, concentric island-fortress of Giurgiu Basarab Laiota 'The Elder', former Turkish spy and, indirectly, assassin, formally pledged his allegiance to Sultan Mehmed and the Emir of Iran's Pasha council, kneeling and kissing the Sultan's hem. Basarab, now completely in the yoke of Arabs, also acted as puppet-ruler on behalf of the Ottoman Empire, having kissed the Emir's foot.

Basarab Laiota, Dracula's sworn blood-feud, arch enemy, murderer of the former voivode's first love. Twenty years after Laiota's heartless act of attrition, only he among thousands had escaped Vlad's wrath. All others, including Vintilă, Dobăca, Gales, Kai, and Dorgoi had been impaled.

The Ottomans' lackey and his namesake heir to numerous Hungarian estates had celebrated All Souls' in fine style; surrounded by Laiota's multitudinous brood and his Turkish overlords, they had feasted (at Rașnov's square keep) in a way not seen since Dracul's extravagant days.

Meanwhile, Vlad terribly tortured Laiota's hired killer Béla Blásko at the island-prison of Snagov; first he tied Béla by the thumbs to the monastery's ceiling; next he applied pincers; red-hot tongs to the tongue; then he pulled his fingernails out; finally, most gruesome of all, Vlad had the assassin enthroned upon a white-hot metal throne until Blásko's skin peeled from the chair, Vlad laughing all the while. And then he had Blásko broken on the wheel in the monastery courtyard before slowly impaling the wretch, gathering the monks for all to witness.

The spring of 1474, forests burned, the two opposing armies clashing with the implacable hatred and din of two dragons thrashing in the Transylvanian wilderness, their molten breath turning the land to cinders. For days, the sky roiled black with the rolling smoke of torched forest, lowland towns, or mountain-pass villages. Thunder rumbled over the Carpathians as perpetual, spring darkness plagued the gorges and swollen river streams. No man dared venture forth. Only mountain goats wandered the misty mountain passes, now.

By March, Dracula had inflicted the first decisive defeat on Basarab's Turkish forces, a pre-emptive strike which would eventually prove fatal; cutting off Basarab's access to neutral Transylvania, Vlad then moved with ruthless, lightning-speed to force the cowed citizens of Bistritz and Sighișoara to submit to his authority, pulling the folk from the Carpathians it was said with grappling irons into war against Turkish-held southern Wallachia.

By June, Mehmed's Janissaries were deserting in droves. Starvation and disease decimated his already impoverished armies; yellow fever and malaria obliterating its ranks. They'd been reduced to eating their dogs, cats, and horses. Soldiers, mistakenly buried alive, desperately clawed their way to the surface before the last breath of air eluded them, therefore giving new impetus to ancient superstitions. 1462 had witnessed the chastised Sultan's return with his tattered army-remnants to Turkish Constantinople—or *Istanbul* as they now called it—an equally humiliated army devoid of cannon, food, and weapons, forced to enter the great city's walls by torchlight to avoid scandal or suspicions of defeat. The next morn decrees had been issued praising "Mehmed's rousing success."

Thirteen years later the only difference now, was that Mehmed had no route to herd his depleted, pummelled army back to Istanbul. Trapped within southwestern Wallachia's treacherous marshes, Mehmed watched, helpless, as day by day Wallachian patriots brazenly ambushed his haggard soldiers. Vlad Dracula's headquarters lay nearby, but Mehmed knew not where. But too close for comfort.

Sultan Mured II had once warned his precocious son Mehmed that Dracula, whilst still a prisoner, might someday turn out to be a formidable warlord, for he had proven after a time fearless and impervious to the Turks' physical and psychological tortures.

This time Vlad's campaign was smoother, less, less 'showy'. His soldiers left the impaled ghazis on stakes within their smouldering camps. Just so Mehmed would know he'd been there.

At night, marsh gases lit up the countryside, phosphorus Will-'o'-wisps which the superstitious mistook for the spirits of the dead. *Bogeys, pucas, bwgans*, returned from the Netherworld to defend buried treasure hidden by Dracula's retreating forces in 1462. Dismantled Castle Dracula, especially, had become off-limits to peasants. The Turks dared not venture out at dawn or dusk to patrol their fog-bound, fortified encampments. Dared not venture into the bogs, or traverse the horror-inducing mountain passes such as the eerily sinister Dinŭ pass, central Transylvania (where scores of skewered Moslems remained from Vlad Death's last grisly campaign), where black castle/watchtowers guarded the lonely, empty valleys. Here the burnt-out, once-thatched villages were abandoned. Mist swallowed up the landscape; cold, moon-washed scenery with only forbidding, eerie, spruce-fir forests to greet weary eyes. Rough-masonry fortresses threatened Turkish scouting expeditions, black, gaping lancet-windows seeming to stare out across the ravines like hollow, skeletal eyes, as if watching the trespassers' march toward Transylvania. Wolves howled spine-chillingly at the full moon in packs, waiting for exhausted ghazis to fall. Ancient, drystone Celtic encampments, their ramparts still high and intact loomed above the lofty mountain passes—vengeful refuges for the dead who still manned the concentric, unmortared, masonry ramparts.

Lammas Night neared.

****

Basarab screamed in agony as Vlad tightened the screws. The captured imposter/Prince hung by his head in Hunedŏara castle's subterranean dungeons. Diabolical wire threads ground their way into Laiota's skull, bulging the traitor's bloodied eyeballs from his gouged forehead. Blood trickled down Basarab's temples, staining his royal purple, silk robe. Fifteen feet in the air and still kicking, dangling wildly, the tightening wires winding their way into Basarab's brain.

Vlad beamed with unholy satisfaction, watching his worst enemy die slowly from this horrendous torture instrument. At once deeply satisfied with himself. (The knowledge that the old traitor had been handed over to him by Basarab's own *kinsmen* made Dracula positively glow.) He cranked the windlass's rotor gleefully, the gears up high tightening the wire on Basarab's cranium until, suddenly, grey brain-matter oozed out as Laiota's skull imploded, his twitching body crashing to the wooden trestle table below.

"It is done." Vlad's voice echoed hollowly inside the earthen chamber, his strange, lilting dialect eerie in the chilly dungeon. He spoke in Dacian, the tongue of his fathers, utterly alien to Caltuna's ears. She sat on a bench, horrified, eyes clamped shut. Young Mihnea sat in her lap, wide-eyed, staring, as if fascinated. Vlad had forced Caltuna and her son to watch, threatening death if she refused. Even after he'd explained about Basarab's horrible crime all those years ago, Caltuna could not—would not—justify Vlad's horrible contempt for human life—even a putrid douchebag such as Laiota. All other contenders for Vlad's throne had wisely fled the country, waiting for better days.

And now the Crown was his.

Dracula bent over the table, brandishing the ancient crown and sceptre high, reverent, eyes sparkling as he slowly set the pair down on the table once more and removed the rubrous, emerald-adorned, velvet cap garnished with peacock feathers from his greying locks.

The grisly Prince placed the squat, heart-shaped crown on his head, smiling macabrely now. The ancient crown consisted of a gold, gem-studded diadem; orange, velvety material with simulated leopard spots, and a majestic bronze ring of unfathomable antiquity inscribed with undecipherable, Pictish ogham-script, the meaning of the headband's dots, dashes, and squiggles long since forgotten. Caltuna stared tearfully at the tarnished, weather-beaten, bejewelled crown. Emeralds, rubies, diamonds, amethyst, jade, sapphire, and onyx glittered brilliantly in bluish-yellow candlelight shed from two bulky, ornate, torc-twisted, silver candelabra reposing unshaken on the massive trestle table. For centuries after Vlad's reign men would search for this elusive, mystical crown of ancient Dacia. Its slender, original, gold/metal ringlets were aeons old. Older than Athens, and Rome. King Decibal had taken poison while wearing this very diadem after Trajan's legions had conquered Dacia in 106 AD. It would be in the future Romania's own Holy Grail, searched for but not found, buried with Vlad's treasure here in Hunedŏara's collapsed subterranean dungeon forever.

Caltuna shuddered, shivering.

A cold, damp draught flickered the twin, black, beeswax candles in their silver candlesticks. Caltuna stared, mesmerised, at the white-haired, purple-robed, gory ex-Prince of Wallachia, half expecting Basarab's reanimated corpse to slowly rise from the frigid clay floor. The 'thing's' head was now but a shattered remnant of crimson blood, white bone, and intestine-like grey brains. Like a crushed, living eggshell. Caltuna's gut wrenched.

"I think I'm going to be sick," she moaned.

"Go. Lest my exalted mood flees and I ascertain that you pity a traitor."

Caltuna lurched to her feet and ran from the dungeon.

Little Mihnea stayed behind, smiling in his father's arms now at the twisted, stiffening corpse of Prince Basarab Laiota I of Wallachia.

****

7 November, 1475 AD
Bosnia-Herzegovina, Yugoslavia

Vlad was not satisfied merely to be reinstated as Prince of Wallachia and voivode of Transylvania that hot, sultry day of August, 1475. From the red-brick, cylindrical, battlemented Oriental-style Chîndia watchtower/donjon of the fortified former capital Vlad had planned his final campaign. None other than the subjugation and occupation of Yugoslavia, master-minding a Crusade to drive the Turks from Bosnia (themselves preoccupied with the final push into Greece), and then Bulgaria, liberating eastern Europe the sure symptom of his madness. For Vlad was a megalomaniac, born and bred to fight and die at war, carrying a vendetta from cradle to grave. By summer of '75, the inhabitants of linguistically divided Wallachia could take no more. Constant civil war during that year from spring to bitter winter had scorched crops, crofts, noblemen's demesnes, churches, towns, villages, cities. Wells were poisoned. Blood filled rivers.

The Saxons of Transylvania planned his final downfall.

Tens of thousands of able-bodied men were called to arms by Vlad's mortified boyar council at Bucureşti, however, to march into Bosnia.

March they did.

For fourteen, nightmarish months Vlad's occupying forces (coordinating their efforts with Stephen Cĕl Mare of Moldavia, after his astounding victory over Sultan Mehmed at Vaslui) terrorised the Turkish garrisons billeted in Macedonia, then Bosnia, then Herzegovina and Serbia itself. (Defenceless, starving, the peasantry of those war-torn principalities submitted to Vlad Ţepeş' arbitrary authority with much trepidation: With Mehmed's jubilant Janissary forces celebrating the surrender of the Greek fortress of Monemvasia, His Majesty's newly-won Romano-Slav territories had been unwittingly undermanned during the Ottoman conquest of the Byzantine despots.) Converted Bosnians (former Bogomils, whose outlawed faith closely approximated that of Islam) were mercilessly butchered. Croatia was utterly devastated for its alliance with the Muslim forces stationed at Sarajevo. Cities and towns burnt, the line of ally or enemy no longer drawn, for there could be no neutrality; townsfolk expelled from their homes, evacuating the Serbo-Croat, Renaissance cities as news of Dracula's rampaging armies from the northeast reached the Bosnians' ears over the mournful tolling of monastery bells. Like Braşov's Black Church which Vlad had ruthlessly sacked sixteen years earlier, chapels (their sanctuaries defiled) and bell-towers were burnt. Dracula's enormous Dragon standard had carried the field, scattering his enemies before him with an allied Christian host numbering a quarter of a million recruits from various countries—one of history's quickest and *easiest-forgotten* episodes. The leviathan might of the Ottomans' war host had finally been matched, then overshadowed. Rapine followed plunder. Vast wagon-trains of fleeing refugees had been driven south by *Kaziglu Bey's* diabolical horde. Serbs from the hills flooded the valleys, so eager to join Prince Dracula's liberating, multinational army to 'cleanse' Serbia of Croatians and Muslims. They sung 'Te Dieum' and 'Hallelujah' in glorious bass voices all the way from Belgrade to Bitoli; the mountains shuddering with the voices of ten thousand Macedonians. The Turks fled at the awful sound.

Catholic monasteries were razed to the ground, monks slaughtered like pigs even as they knelt at Vlad Dracula's boots begging for mercy. The Sisters of Mercy fared worse.

And, indeed, what goes around comes around.

Across Europe, the news of Vlad's unprovoked transgressions against Turkish Bosnia, Bulgaria, and Albania reached scheming ears. Already halfway to Sofia, Lord Vlad's Serbo-Hungarian third division prepared for the siege of the Sultan's premier capital in Europe; carting plenty of iron/bronze cannon, trebuchets, ballista and ammunition to bombard the illustrious city's stout, reinforced, sandstone walls. George Podebrády IV 'the Younger' of Bohemia, that wicked schemer, contemplated with glee a *coup d'état* in Wallachia, with himself as possible claimant to an empty throne. Vlad had, after all, broken the truce with Islam. It would only take a large army…

Matthias listened uneasily as daily reports of Vlad's atrocities shocked the courts of Europe. Pope Sixtus IV rejoiced at Dracula's horrific punishments meted out against Turkish garrisons who'd begged for mercy in Sarajevo, after defeat. Even though Vlad's Crusade was essentially an Orthodox one, with little encouragement from Rome. The Vatican's newest champion was also Her biggest embarrassment. Vlad Țepeș, *a.k.a* Dracula (the Devil's Spawn), had cast aside his new faith—scorning Papists or putting them to the sword. He was now the most wanted man in Europe—dead or alive, depending on the warlord's religious sympathies...

Vlad's first victory, February 8, 1475, culminated in a mass stake-burning of the Turkish contingent at the city of Šabac after Serb partisans had opened the portcullises leading into the metropolis' precincts. Hence, Vlad the Impaler had pillaged, massacred, impaled, burnt, blasphemed the entire region of Yugoslavia plus much of northern Bulgaria, razing monasteries and mosques like a man with a mission from Lucifer. For over a year, wantonly spreading mass destruction from district to district (his Catalan Free Companies—mercenary corps—especially ruthless), spending a few months here, a few months there, leisurely murdering those who displeased him most, those who could not answer to Vlad's satisfaction his Four Questions.

Sultan Mehmed II 'The Conqueror' had retreated to Constantinople until the heat wore off.

Srébreniča, too, had been taken, where guerrilla fighters cheered and jeered by torchlight while witnessing one of Dracula's infamous, numerous mass impalements in the citadel's cobbled marketplace.

(Meanwhile, Prince Stephen's forces, unimpeded, had raided deep into Albania [much of which encompassed Old Wallachia], causing havoc for the satraps controlling that beleaguered country.)

Kuslat and Zwornik, too, suffered the funeral pyres of Dracula's merciless onslaught, as well as Šabac, Zagreb, and Novi Sad, his last act of victory on this earth before fading away into the dark, vaulted realms of historic folklore.

****

6 April, 1477 AD

Snagov Monastery, Southern Wallachia

The good brothers of Snagov monastery welcomed Vlad's family and retinue into the sacred precincts of the island-fortress at the misty onset of dusk. Torchlight illuminated the dusty, dirt courtyard as Vlad's royal *caléche* rumbled into the oval bailey, driven by a lone driver high up on the front seat of the cab. The *voivode* and his menagerie had been rowed across the treacherous lake of Snagov, landing ashore at the monastery's stout walls where Lord Dracula's crest-emblazoned coach with its team of four-in-hand, white horses awaited. The royal conveyance, as well, was illumined with wildly-flickering torches in glass lanterns as it rolled through the portcullis gates and halted in the yard.

Several times, monks had fled the monastery upon the news of Vlad's impending arrival.

Vlad stepped down from the carriage, sweeping his cumbersome, silk cape about his shoulders as one of the subservient monks opened the door. He bowed majestically at the waist, crooking his arm in high-court fashion.

Caltuna accepted Vlad's hand as she, too, alighted from the benighted coach, attractive features humbly veiled so as not to offend the good brothers. Her slender hands draped inside white, silken gloves, identical to Vlad's own. Four-year-old Mihnea crawled out next, his short, knickered legs barely reaching the coach's retractable iron step. The boy looked around with excited, dark green eyes—the eyes of his father, his hero. Vlad gazed down upon his second-born with fatherly pride, turning his eyes to the lay brothers gathering around his carriage; a haughty, aloof stare, his pale, shaven chin held high. Upon the ground, Vlad's sharp-nosed profile loomed long in a monstrous, bat-winged shadow. Next, Vlad's first-born, Vladislav, Caltuna's alien stepson, alighted from the ebony carriage, uncertain and intimidated by his terse, larger-than-life father whom ten days ago he'd never met, only heard wild tales of bravery, high intrigue, and bloody deeds done dirt cheap.

Young Vladislav was thirteen years old already, eager to take up his father's mantle and begin the hard grind of weapons' training and the art of chivalric warfare. He was a virtual look-alike of his father's own youth. Murky, green eyes, unruly black locks tumbling over his broad shoulders. A handsome (if somewhat *docile*) boy. Vladislav had learned the basics of swordsmanship at Castle Brân, but knew he had much more to learn; jousting at the quintain, axemanship, armoured cavalry charges. Vlad was indeed eager.

As was Mihnea.

Neither would learn the art of chivalry and fair-play honour they both expected from their father, the Devil. Neither were fully aware of Vlad Dracula's numerous excommunications for horrific deeds.

Neither were aware they'd soon have no throne to fight for.

And no father.

Young Vladislav was now as tall as Vlad. Would soon be taller than his father had ever been, the blood of Voica's mixed Hungarian ancestry coursing through his young veins. Vlad junior was the only reminder Dracula had of his once beloved, long-deceased, unlawfully-wedded wife. It was not a reminder that brought joy to Vlad's old heart. Even though he now possessed another woman's heart, her sworn allegiance. Vlad still felt a deep, melancholy emptiness inside his soul, as if an enemy had ripped away three quarters of his life, for he had felt naught but pain, anger, and sorrow throughout his forty-five, stormy years. And, strangely, he now felt as if a lance had pierced his heart, looking across at this young stranger who was his son, flesh of his flesh. Vlad felt resentment, paternal protectiveness, sorrow all at once. As with Serena, he had not been able to tell Voica how much he'd loved her, nor even goodbye. What a fool! He'd had no idea he'd not be coming back, no idea King Matthias The Traitor meant to capture Vlad the Devil. Had the boy missed his mother? Had Vladislav pined for one at Castle Brân? Could one really forget deceased lovers, brooded Vlad; especially Gypsy ones? Young Vlad had Voica's finely proportioned facial features. His father felt no joy looking at him, did not feel he could reclaim the woman he'd lost through the boy.

Vlad was suddenly immensely grateful that Serena had been barren. He couldn't stand the thought of being reminded of that terrible night every time he gazed at her son. But even more, Vlad was thankful there was no sweet, young daughter to remind him of what he'd lost. In that, that alone God had been merciful.

Hand in hand, the quartet walked toward the chapterhouse, for it was their duty to say a few, token prayers in the empty chapel before being served supper.

Vlad had no intention of offering up prayers to the Christians' heathen god. He had served Him long enough.

From now on and evermore, he would offer his devotions to *Crom*; Lord of wind, fire, and steel...

Caltuna, seven months pregnant, wondered how and why she had gotten into this predicament: a Catholic monarch's sister, abandoning her faith for Orthodoxy to follow her man into destruction. Vlad was the one who had vowed to abandon the Orthodox establishment; yet it was she who now followed her husband into this dreary Orthodox monastery. She guessed she loved him.

Vlad felt acutely aware of the monks' hostile stares as he and his small family entered the reredorter passage, their boots tapping noisily on flagstone. The voivode let out a discreet sigh of relief as the great, oak door slammed shut, cutting him off from the resentful stares of the brown-cassocked monks huddled together in the courtyard beneath dwarfing, all-encompassing, mauve twilight, the limestone Carpathians looming majestically, snow-capped, in the distant northern quadrant of Wallachia. A full moon shone down upon the walled island, yellow cheese-face shimmering in the rippled, grey-green waters of Lác

Snagov near the marshes of Bucureşti.

Vlad was here to inspect the royal treasury, greatly depleted after Basarab's payment of Vlad's allegiance-dues owed to the Turkish Sultan. Laiota had shipped most of the crown jewels to Istanbul. Vlad's traitorous brother Radu had depleted the treasury and exhausted Ţepeş' new, state mint during his abortive wars against Moldavia. Vlad was undecided whether, were he to have met his long-lost younger brother before Radu died, whether he would have hugged the man or strangled him. He still felt guilty, all these years, for abandoning Radu to Sultan Mured's clutches and his son Mehmed's homosexual advances.

But Dracula was here for more important—and private—matters. A small Turkish contingent—about 1500—had swept into Wallachia unopposed two nights previous, crossing the Serbian border under cloak of night. Swift Ottoman cavalry and light infantry had taken his border guards unawares. Two of Vlad's largest divisions were stationed in Kosovo, Yugoslavia; another besieging Sofia in Bulgaria. Unencumbered by baggage-trains, camels, or war elephants, the Turkish commander had raced with lightning-swiftness toward Bucharest, taking Vlad's reserve home-army by surprise. He'd had no choice but to retreat, not daring to risk all in a single, pitched battle against cocky Janissaries when his own soldiers be so exhausted and decimated by disease after a year and more of destructive civil war, of ambushes and counter-sieges. Although his campaigns in Bosnia, Serbia, Croatia, Albania, Macedonia, and Bulgaria had been a rousing success so far, the expense of manning these former Turkish garrisons was a heavy burden. The Vatican and various other Kingdoms and moneylenders had proven surprisingly tight-fisted.

Even a gigantic bagful of Islamicized Bulgars' ears lopped from men, women, and children, sent to King Matthias Corvinus at his royal palace of Vác, near Buda-Pest, had failed to move the stingy Hungarian monarch to provide further funds.

Across the treacherous marshes Vlad had marched his meagre, tattered, reserve army, men so hungry they made Gypsies seem well fed. Another severe drought that summer had devastated Romania's harvest. Many men had deserted after Ţepeş' final, rousing victory seven months previous, having chased Vlad the Monk—temporarily—from the country once more. The peasants had returned to their styes and fields, blithely assuming that peace and stability had been achieved at last. Vlad had received more recruits from Bulgarian, Serb, Albanian, Hungarian, and even Russian volunteers now stationed in occupied Serbia, than had procured conscriptions from Romanians. It seemed they were plotting his overthrow. Vlad's Gypsy recruits no longer marched with his armies, not since his treacherous dealing in '62. Not since he abandoned them to an Inquisition during Radu's foolish reign, decimating their over-exaggerated population.

But Vlad was also here to ensure his final resting place, a glorious, gold-gilt tomb emblazoned with the ancestral coat-of-arms of the House of Dracula, for all to see.

For all eternity.

For, instinctively, he knew it was the end of an old, long song.

Caltuna was seven months pregnant and bulging. She had tremendous difficulty moving, walking, her bloated belly demanding the most outlandish food-cravings. Previously, he'd had her on a rigorous exercise programme to make her strong, to prepare for childbirth. Her days of lazy, hazy days inside a palace cloister were long-since over. Caltuna would want a husband to rear her children. But Vlad knew he would not be there. He could feel it in his tired bones, even now as he looked out a cruciform, traceried, quatre-lobed window into the oncoming night. Cold stars twinkled high above the northerly horizon. The great lake froze his blood just looking at it, a dark, grey, shimmering body of water rimmed with tall reeds, bulrushes and monstrous Cattails on its distant shores. *Brrrr! What a cold, forbidding deathtrap this lake be!* Vlad thought to himself. Many a peasant had died crossing its frozen icefield during the throes of winter. Many a winter snowstorm had buried the great monastic house: occasionally, entire scouting expeditions had crashed through the ice. Vlad couldn't swim, shivered at the thought of that icy water enveloping him as he thrashed about in vain in its fathomless, murderous tides. He could easily imagine underwater kelp reaching up through the murky, peaty water to drag him down. Or a kelpie, a waterhorse, a maned, half-dragon, half-horse, serpentine beastie swallowing him in one gulp.

Caltuna watched with resentment as Vlad stood at the thickset, unshuttered dormitory window, his grey-haired profile stark under wan candlelight reflected from bracketed, iron wall-sconces. Iron chandeliers the shape of thorny crowns dangled haphazardly from the chamber's ceiling; empty, and unlit. Dracula's hair was still boyishly long, streaming out from the sides and full of greyish locks. His white moustache still plaited and straight—and gruesome. (It gave him the look of a leering devil at times when a certain light glinted in his eye.) 'Twas the style of his ancestors; designed to invoke fear into the hearts of enemies. His sallow, grotesque, pinched face was that of a deadman. His patrician nose (having once been broken in times of valour), vaguely resembled a hawk's beak in the chamber's dim, shadow-thrown candlelight, inexplicably adding a dimension of virile, rugged charm though he lacked the classic, wide jaw of the typical 'redneck'. Yet his nose was almost as straight as in his youth; his narrow, arched nostrils adding to the illusion. Vlad's eyes were not what they'd once been, yet far from short-sighted. At forty-five, he was still a handsome man, with a debonair air of mystery which no woman who'd come to know him could resist for long.

Caltuna scolded little Mihnea for attempting to climb up into her lap, slapping his dark head as he scuttled away. He was walking now, finally. She already had a growing babe in her bulging womb, did not need another tyke—a four-year-old at that—digging his knees or his bony rump into Caltuna's lap. Mihnea was long-since desensitised to his mother's occasional, grouchy moods.Like his *tată*, Mihnea was fearless; bold and irascible.

Except toward his father, of course.

Vlad the Younger watched his small stepbrother rollicking on the flagstones, chasing shadowy, sneaky mice with glee as they sped across the room amid dark shadows. Vlad had no particular love for the boy, nor rancour, only knowing that should young Mihnea someday stand in his way when Vlad eventually claimed his esteemed sire's throne, he'd not hesitate to murder the boy or perhaps merely blind him. However, Vladislav would have no qualms about joint rulership should Mihnea be like-minded. During his upbringing at Count Cirstian's court at Hunedŏara castle, Vlad had soon learned the rights he could expect as Vlad Dracula's first-born heir, even as a bastard. For now, the Prince's consort's son was no threat to him.

Even still, his eyes were wary.

"Supper will be served shortly," announced Vlad suddenly, glancing across at the unlaid trestle. "Tondhere!" he shouted, his threatening roar echoing throughout the adjoining chapterhouse and reredorter. "Supper! Immediately!"

A flurry of tapping sandals accompanied Vlad's summons, the brown-cassocked monks rushing toward the monastic kitchens to inquire if the lord's supper be ready.

Bats flitted from the red brick, barrel-vaulted ceiling, delighting young Mihnea as the winged creatures squeaked and flapped their leathery wings. Vlad junior waved his arms to ward off the dive-bombing rodents from raiding his hair. They were not large bats. If fruit bats, then only young ones. Caltuna grimaced, ducking and shrieking as one of the furry fiends flew towards her. One glance at Vlad Dracula's wide-eyed, disapproving stare stifled any further outbursts on her part. Vlad junior was merely curious. Mihnea was ecstatic. He loved bats. His first pet had been a tamed bat given him by his father. Unfortunately it had fluttered away out a window at Castle Brân one night, never to return; perhaps the victim of some superstitious peasant. Poor, sad Mihnea had been heartbroken for days. His father had given him another however, for Vlad had an entire menagerie of tamed bats for his leisure. Dracula continued to stare haughtily down his nose at Caltuna, not quite forgiving her for scolding his furry little friends.

"You don't like my bats?" Vlad's oddly-lilting, Daco-Romanian accent snapped Caltuna to attention, her straight, black, glossy hair unveiled now and flowing gloriously loose down her back.

"'Tis not that I do not like them," Caltuna murmured, grimacing. "But they might carry disease; rabies, plague fleas."

Vlad pondered this a moment, brushing his chin with a thoughtful, curled finger. "So might you. Or Mihnea. Or *Wlad.*"

Vlad snapped a command, ordering young Mihnea to stand up, stop tugging his fluttery, satin cape. (He switched cloaks frequently; undecided whether preferring satin or silk.) He spoke in Dacian, as natural as he spoke Romanian, Serbian, German, Turkish, Hungarian. The boy frowned, for he was not yet familiar with his father's strange, secret language. Both Mihnea and Vlad junior were confused by their father's native tongue. As was Caltuna. Why did he speak it? Why didn't anyone else speak it? And if not, why speak it? Mihnea answered back haltingly, his tongue seeming to trip over the strange conglomeration of *ll's* and archaic *w's* while Vlad frowned. The boy was not yet mastering the archaic dialect, but he was trying. Vlad junior, Dracula felt, would not be ready to learn the language. He would need a few months to get to know his father, this shy, reserved teenager.

Caltuna brooded over Dracula's morbid eccentricities while the monks brought supper, setting it softly on the trestle table and obeising to their liege-lord before bowing out of the guesthouse.

The bats, for instance. Surely Vlad's most disgusting trait: befriending bats; bats of all kinds, all sizes. Though Vlad owned many various types of hunting dogs, whether they be Alsatians, bloodhounds, Great Danes, terriers, or tamed wolves, it was the bats which accompanied him everywhere. And one black cat.

Vlad's familiar, Greedygut.

The bats seemed like some strange oracle, answering Vlad's questions with prophetic squeaks.

And then there was that weird, archaic, totally incomprehensible gobbledygook language he spoke amongst his even weirder retinue. They used white horses as oracles! Once, while she and Vlad had been making love at eerie, restored Castle Dracula, Vlad had spoken a few choice phrases for her. Caltuna had been able to master a few simple words: *caru*—love; *cariad*—dear; *ci*—dog; *mawr*—great; *mor*—sea; *merch*—daughter; *mab*—son; *mam*—mother; *tad*— father; *ap*, or *baban*—son, offspring; *plant*—children; *geneth*—girl. How those devilish consonants would mutate, exasperating her to the point of anger. Aspirate mutations. Soft mutations. Nasal mutations (all utterly unknown in her native Magyar/Romanian tongue). C mutating to G after a noun (of feminine gender), M to F, T to dd, B to F. Vlad had assured her with some pride that his was the original, prehistoric language of Europe, what Adam and Eve had babbled in Eden, with more declensions than any extant language. Needless to say, she had avoided Vlad's insistence to learn it like plague, evermore. Caltuna did not understand why he clung to the old tongue. No one but a smattering of mountain-dwelling Vlachs spoke it. Even they were beginning to adopt Romany, the international lingo of the Gypsy; part Latin, but mostly, Indic. Once, Caltuna had inquired at the Hungarian court at Vác. No one had heard of it. Apparently 'it' had vanished from Hungary in the wake of Attila's invasion in the fourth century AD. Its sister-language, still extant in Ireland, had theoretically evolved from Celto-Germanic (Hittite) and Indo-Iranian, then into Latin, Greek, and Armenian—finally metamorphosising into numerous unrelated tongues. While the Devil's language itself had become abruptly extinct, except, perhaps, in Transylvania. The Romans, Caltuna had learned, had dubbed these mysterious folk many names: Vulcae, Polak, Gaul, Galatian, Getae, Caledonae, Goidel, Scythian, Scotti, Suevii, Cimmerian, Cimbri, Sarmatian, Parthian, Briton, Cornovae, Pictae, Alanae, Gelonae, Allemanae. Pict, it seemed, was correct; people who had once painted their bodies blue and wore animal tattoos, a race named after their pictoglyphic, carved, indecipherable ogham script (ancestor of Sumerian), a recurrent tribal name ranging from southern Russia to the British Isles, and, earlier, Scandinavia. Gomer, Cimmeria, Chaldea. Caltuna shook her head now, confused. She had long believed that Basque, or *Euskara*, another obscure language of Europe, in the Pyrenees of Spain, was the most ancient: but Vlad had assured her that theirs was a Moorish hybrid (with elements of Turkic), a usurper, for after seven hundred years the Moors still held Spain in thrall—in fact an obtrusive, non-Caucasoid, non-Indo-European language unrelated to Sanskrit (a language 5000 years old already in 1476).

At last, Vlad sat down for supper. His family waited with respectful, subdued silence for the lord and master to inspect the food.

Three laybrothers entered the dormitory's guest cell, bowing graciously as they set the 'Tyrant King's' repast on the table for his perusal and possible praise or rebuke. Or reward.

At a clap of Vlad's hands, a royal food-taster stepped forward, having been skulking in the shadows after the monks' departure. The dark, gangly Romanian youth meekly tasted each vegetable entrée, each meat pasty, each bread slice. Mihnea giggled, his mother scolding him half-heartedly while squeezing Vlad junior's hand reassuringly, for such measures still seemed odd for the thirty-two-year-old mother and her four-year-old son. Vlad ignored their foolishness. Vladislav watched with bewilderment, his big, green eyes wide.

"Let us see what we have here," Vlad echoed, lifting each bowl-shaped, silver lid from its matching platter. "Stuffed turkey. Hmm. Turnips. Peas. Carrots. Garlic—Garlic!"

Vlad leapt up from the table, his big eyes blazing, bloodshot. *"Sacrilege!"*

He seized the handful of garlic. Strode toward the window, flinging them out over the machicolated parapet of the monastery walls surrounding the rocky, brambly island. Flung with all his might the uncooked garlic cloves into the black, starlit lake, the heady odour of fish, reeds, and algae wafting on the night air; a cold, brisk, Carpathian wind.

The monks knew Vlad the Vampire loathed garlic.

His family exchanged bewildered glances.

Over the years, since Voica's terrible accusations, Vlad had gradually shunned garlic. Gone were the days of such garlic snacks. Knowing what the natives thought of him, he had developed an irrational phobia toward garlic, toward mirrors, running water, the Christian cross. Making Vlad's life VERY difficult. Matins and Mass had been a living Hell, never knowing what religious-fanatic fiend might be lurking behind him in the shadows, waiting to hammer a wooden stake into Vlad's heart. Nightmares had unearthed similar fears from his subconscious mind. Every man was a potential enemy. These last few months of consolidated royal power and freedom from the Church's corrupting influence, Dracula had forbade the wearing of crosses at mealtime, from inside his numerous, private castles, even banning or vandalising the Christ-on-the-Cross in holy chapels sited on roadsides wherever he passed. He was truly possessed, men said. Satan's Spawn. Wondering what dastardly, magic rites Vlad had performed inside the tallest watchtower of partially-reconstructed Castle Dracula to ensure his undead existence.

Caltuna found this particularly alarming. Though no paragon of faith, she was not pleased to have her Catholic faith denied her, denuded of her confessor, her retinue of holy monks. Vlad had considered her clinging religion as unnecessary frivolity, the sign of a weak mind. He'd banished her priests to Hungary, where they could squawk and grumble to King Matthias until Hell freezes over.

Now Vlad ate with gusto, eyeing his two sons furtively. Vlad junior wolfed down his food. Mihnea picked at his trencher. As did Caltuna. She was not feeling well. The babe was kicking again. The first thing she wanted to do when he/she was born is spank the baby's smooth bottom for kicking her stomach so. Mihnea whined, wanting to be excused so he could chase the mice (and rats!). Caltuna, pursing her lips, grabbed his neck, pulling him into a motherly headlock against her breast. "Eat, Mihnea, or your *tată* will strap you till you're blue!"

"Eat, Mihnea," Vlad ordered, his voice booming. "Or you'll grow up looking like a scrawny girl, not a warrior. A skinny, weak girl. Like your mother." Vlad laughed aloud, uproariously, raising his dagger. "No slight intended, *breila* (primrose). For you, that is a compliment. I'd rather not have a butch, German *fräulein* as my wife." He roared again, spasmodically, as Caltuna raised her brows in quiet displeasure. Vlad wagged his finger threateningly. "Don't sulk, Serena."

Caltuna raised her eyes, stunned. "What did you call me…Master?"

Vlad opened his mouth as if to defend himself. Then clamped it shut. "Never mind. She was—"

"Vlad?"

"A woman I once knew. A dear, sweet girl. God bless her departed soul."

Vlad lapsed into a morose silence, slamming his dagger point-down into the table, its plain, brown hilt quivering wildly. Vlad scowled, glaring at his Dragon ring. Remembering…

Chapter Eighteen

Apocalypse

The battle came without warning, scattering Vlad's soldiers into the marshes after the first Turkish cavalry charge/ambush. Must regroup. Must counter-attack. Vlad's roan warhorse stood motionless in a marsh surrounded by about fifty assorted bodyguards, knights, generals, and mercenaries. Among them, Matei Bathóry, once a close friend, now married and with a large family of his own, the only ties to Vlad Țepeș his sworn allegiance. Matei's older brother, Stephen Bathóry, chief commander of Dracula's mercenary corps from Hungary, a brilliant strategist and brave warrior, fine horseman, expert sword-master. Dracula trusted Stephen as far as he could throw him, but Bathóry was an envoy and commandant of King Matthias himself, Matthias' finest field-commander entrusted with the uneasy Hungarian border. Țepeș had yet to have him impaled: but Vlad felt Stephen's usefulness was nearing an end *(and nothing, nothing was sweeter than revenge!)*. A gift of five thousand pikemen, archers, and mounted lancers had accompanied Vlad from Buda-Pest in '74. Vlad at least owed Matthias the honour of surveying the war theatre in Wallachia through Stephen's eyes.

It was a foggy, cold dawn morning, April 16, 1477. The soldiers became soaked each time they moved through the wet bushes, tall grasses. The sun had not yet risen, or if it had the air anyway was soup-thick with grey fog. Men could see one's own hand, only, approximately two feet ahead.

The group had gathered here in a meadow to retrace their battle plan. Vlad had unrolled a pigskin parchment scroll, pointing a hairy finger at the black-scribbled diagram set in an arc on the parchment. His hinged, iron gauntlets were off, tucked under his left arm. Vlad's broadsword-hilt nudged his shining metal breastplate emblazoned with a red, heraldic coat-of-arms, the Dragon crest of Transylvania. The sword and her plain wooden hilt had been with Vlad from the start, like a good woman. He would die with her if need be. 'Twas a good luck talisman, recovered from the sub-Carpathian mountains near Călimănesti after an exhaustive search in autumn of '62. Vlad's red-silk-caparisoned charger pranced impatiently. A long, black, scintillant cape with purple lining hung draped from his shoulders and over his horse's rump, its stiff collar poking up and outwards over his thick, professional-wrestler's neck. On his brawny arms and legs, chainmail provided flexibility and protection over a padded leather gambeson designed to absorb the bone-rattling shock of metal-on-metal. His black, flat-topped great helm provided air holes in its movable visor. Visibility was always poor, but sufficient for hand-to-hand killing, knight-style. A huge, round, iron buckler protected Vlad's left arm, strapped to his elbow. The helmet hung on his saddle pommel.

Matei and Stephen Bathóry exchanged glances over Vlad's bent grey head. Stephen nodded slowly as Dracula studied the map with harsh, green eyes, beaked nose dripping into his frosted, white moustache. The cold April morning made his sinuses run, his old joints (well, not so old) arthritic and numb. His hands numb. Vlad, for the first time, felt uncertain whether he could grip his heavy sword.

As it was, his fate had already been decided for him. Vlad, at least, would be spared the battle.

From the distance, a rolling, sudden roar of cannon and clash of swords rent the cold foggy dawn, for today the cocky Turkish commander was in for a nasty surprise. Unbeknown to him and his brazen sipahis and Janissaries, a fatal and wholly unexpected deathtrap lay encamped only four leagues away in the Bucégi mountains, responding to Vlad's battle-horns and scouts like evil demons. Prince Stephen of Moldavia, marching westwards with a fresh battalion of 15,000 men destined for Serbia and newly-forged cannon from Suceava now engaged the hopelessly outnumbered ghazis, massacring them to a man. Vlad smiled as he listened to the ghazis' distant cries and bloodcurdling screams.

Vindication creased his eyes, much pleased at the results of this, Prince Vlad's latest ruse (but used many times in the past)—having lured the Ottoman desperados into ambush by (he barely suppressed laughter) *sending a decoy, or masquerading as a Turkish scout himself!, hoodwinking one of the Sultan's own into believing in Dracula's 'incontestable' betrayal, capture, and beheading!*

Matei raised his finger to his nose, tapping its side, signalling to brother Stephen. Another scheming renegade, a minnesinger-rogue and former soldier of fortune Michael Beheim, pranced forward on his dappled grey warhorse to Matei's side. Helmeted, disguised, the German minstrel tapped another rogue's white flank with his iron boot. All had been well rehearsed. For twenty-odd years, assassins and malcontents had calculated equally rash coups against Vlad Dracula, paying with their wretched lives.

But none had been masterminded by field-marshal Stephen Báthory.

Vlad felt a sharp sword-point at his throat as the first of his bodyguards had their throats slit from behind. Then another and another, screaming aloud as daggers were carelessly plunged into their backs. Twenty in all, their throats cut from ear to ear.

The screams stopped. Vlad slanted his cold, green monster-eyes to his right, where his best friend held a sword to his throat. Matei held his gaze for a moment, haughty, self-satisfied. Then looked away in shame, remembering their childhood years together.

"You shall die horribly, my cherished friend," Vlad murmured. "And if not, may you and kind suffer a thousand sleepless nights, bowel infection, infirmity, your loved ones terrible suffering. May your name stink in the mouths of men, your family cursed with hereditary insanity. And oblivion…"

Stephen Báthory trotted slowly forward, chuckling at Dracula's horrid curse, unheeding. "Come, my friend, you did not really think we could allow you to abandon your chosen faith like a man discarding a barren woman?" Stephen laughed heartily. "All those good fellows you butchered, sire, fellow Catholics like yourself. Did you never heed the Vatican's long arm of the law? The exquisite Brothers do have their methods, you know, even as soldier/monks." Báthory nodded, smiling, eyes twinkling as three armed knights removed their conical, pointed-snout, rounded great helms. "Lord Dracula, meet the three men responsible for your death—brother Blasius, brother Jacob, brother Hans, courtesy of St Gall monastery Switzerland."

"Have you any last words, Your Highness, before we send you to God—"

"To Hell, you mean," grumbled the balding, brother Blasius.

"Er, yes," brother Hans continued. "To God—then Hell."

"I have no words," Vlad said tersely. "If this is death, then let it be. I have waited long enough."

The three monks exchanged amused glances. "Very well. Shall we?" Hans held out a hand, gesturing. "Come, my son. Your Master awaits your judgement."

Stephen drew Vlad's broadsword from its scabbard, motioning the voivode to dismount.

"I'll see you in Hell, 'good' brothers," Vlad hissed as Stephen and another soldier led him from the crowd. "You'll know me by sight, good brothers!" Vlad shouted over his shoulder. "In a black satin cape I'll be, Satan himself, dangling your roasting souls into the lake of fire. You may kill me today, friends," Vlad continued, laughing now, "but I'll walk the earth for all eternity. No matter where you hide, no matter where you run, I'll drain the life from you, each and all, for I am *moroi*, Lucifer himself. I'll plague the world with an undead army!!!"

Vlad saw his chance. He broke away from Stephen's startled grip, seizing his brother Matei by the neck before anyone could intervene.

A wild mêlée ensued, as Dracula forced Matei Bathóry to his knees, slowly strangling the life out of him as a dozen men jumped on his back, tossed aside like sticks as Vlad throttled Matei with one iron hand, then two. Matei's eyes bulged out of his head now, tongue lolling from his lips, his face turning blue. Vlad shook his nemesis hard, feeling with delight his long, talon-like fingernails piercing his old friend's throat, tearing his Adam's apple. Piercing Matei's jugular vein…

Matei was on his last breath when five powerful knights pried Vlad, hissing now, head switching back and forth, off the strangled man. The fog had lifted. In the distance, the tremendous clash of arms, blaring bugles, signalled the renewed offensive of *Ţepeş*' own soldiers, putting the doomed Turks to flight. The sound of crashing hooves tramping through the meadow urged the assassins to Godspeed. A mournful, grey morning sky met the awed eyes of bewildered bystanders. On a mountain-spur, a lone shepherd watched, enthralled…

Victorious, the *ritters* dragged Vlad kicking and screaming from the meadow, up a barren, rocky, windswept, green-turf bluff. A lone wych-elm would serve as Dracula's gallows.

A hangman drew forth a rope from his belt, throwing it over a gnarled, knobbly branch while another formed a hangman's noose and slipped it around Vlad's jerking grey head. Vlad bit Stephen Bathóry's right hand, spreading the disease…

And it was there they hung the Dragon of Wallachia (the blood-soaked demon whose crimes would span centuries), hauling Dracula up kicking and screeching, even as he dangled ten feet above. Clouds claimed the sun as their own.

THE END

Epilogue

Young Mihnea looked out the tower window of Vác. He was curious about his new home. Down below, Hungarian children played on the cobbles, tossing a wooden ball back and forth. Mihnea wished he could play too. He seemed to be some sort of prisoner though. His elder brother paced the bedchamber uneasily, restless. With Prince Vlad the Monk having triumphantly returned from Turkish exile, they were fortunate to have escaped Wallachia alive. Mihnea's mother sat sobbing in a corner, her hands held by one of the bower-women.

Mihnea missed his father.

The court believed he did not understand Vlad was never coming back. "When's he coming, when's he coming?" Mihnea would ask excitedly. Even now, two months after Vlad Țepeș' betrayal, Mihnea still imagined his father's profile amid the shadows. Seen the fluttery, bat-like cape Dracula had worn so often.

Young Vladislav had at first refused to believe Țepeș was dead.

Mihnea was smarter than the adults gave him credit for. He knew in some sad, empty way that papa had died. The boy's heart felt empty, as if the Sand Man had punched a great hole in it. And yet it felt heavy too, dragging Mihnea into unhealthy, fanciful delusions and manic depressions, even now. Dracula, his mentor, gone to Heaven someone had said.

But Mihnea didn't understand where Heaven was. He wanted to go after his father, search Dracula out and perhaps bring him back? Someone had pointed to the sky. But another selfish child had pointed to the earth.

Caltuna continued to sob in a corner. The German lady-in-waiting desperately chafed her hands, cooing, trying to raise Caltuna's spirits. The baby would be born any day now; in such a terrible state, it might be stillborn because of its mother's weeping.

"Come now, *Fräu*, please stop crying, the babe is due!" begged the bower-woman, veil slipping from yellow hair. "Why do you pine for the master? Dracula is dead! Dead and buried!"

"D-don't you understand?" sobbed Caltuna, eyes swollen and red. "He's not! He's not! I'll wait for my love! I-I cannot live without him! I-I…"

"Shh. Shh, lass. You'll be an Abbess soon, mustn't speak this way."

"Don't you understand? Even monsters need love!"

Caltuna wept in her hands, ignoring her two sons in the opposite corner.

"Vlad, look." Mihnea held a brown, white-polka-dotted butterfly in his fingers. Vladislav watched with a puzzled expression.

Until young Mihnea stuck a silver pin in the butterfly's wriggling body, impaling the insect.

"I saw Daddy do this once," Mihnea remarked.

Vlad junior smiled slowly, appreciatively, clapping the boy's back, nodding…

****

1479 AD
Sibiu, Western Transylvania

Snowflakes howled outside the snowbound inn as the three travellers sat nursing their *ţuica* tins, their faces florid, heads hanging low. Drunk. The small, dark, wiry innkeeper peered uneasily out the frosted window, rubbing the hoar-frost away with a weathered fist. He pressed his eye to the icy glass, backing away with a volley of uneasy Romanian curses. Charms and talismans decorated the rustic, log-built inn, the tavern empty of visitors except for these three, royal guests. Sawdust shavings provided a shibeen-type floor. Applewood crackled comfortingly in the tiny, inglenook hearth. Only madmen would traverse the harsh, sub-Carpathian, Transylvanian foothills this night.

Or *nosferatu*.

The innkeeper exchanged nervous whispers with his chubby, wrinkly wife as she dried the cups, murmuring of *Ordog's* (Satan's) nefarious presence, the stench of wolf in the air tonight. Howling shattered the night silence, occasionally causing the innkeeper or his wife to drop a pewter plate to the wooden bar-counter, or perhaps an earthenware vessel, smashing into a dozen pieces. The royal guests grumbled, subsiding into silence again.

Stephen and Matei exchanged startled glances as the mournful howling began anew, Children of the Night calling for their brethren to join the hunt.

Matei gave a nervous cough. The three men eyed the flimsy door uneasily, half-expecting Vlad's *'Children of the Grave'* to burst into the dim-lit, smoky tavern. Vlad Dracula had dangled at their hands, they had witnessed his slow demise on the tree. When he had finally stopped his kicking, the soldiers had cut Vlad down. And they had cut off his head, Stephen keeping it as a family heirloom.

Wind beat at the glass window like fists.

Michael Beheim continued to stare at the window, his mouth ajar in fear. Recently, gruesome, impossible tales too ludicrous to believe had percolated from the island of Snagov regarding certain 'irregularities' with Vlad's tomb.

His body was missing.

Beheim continued to stare, even as the door burst open…

****

October 4, 1509, Romania, Moldavian Carpathians.

As the legend of the undead Vlad Dracula grew, so too did the most absurd tales of his bloodcurdling lifetime blossom into romance. Yet on the goat-traversed, weathered trails leading up into Moldavia's Carpathians, the famished bodies of Gypsies littered the green, pastoral panorama for miles. 'Twas there they fled, the last blood of their forefathers, languishing for a time away from the populous Transylvanian cities. But within fifty years, not a single Dacian Gypsy remained alive. In Krakow, in Warsaw, Paris, Nürnberg, Vienna, Moscow, mass-burnings devastated the Gypsy populations of Europe. Ten shillings for every head, salvation for every follower of Christ who takes a Gypsy life, "The pestilence of Europe, 'tis a mercy for them to die."

Entire caravans were rounded up to be incarcerated in concentration camps until a 'solution' could be conjured. The Inquisition was in full swing, burning hundreds of thousands, possibly millions, of heretics, Jews, witches and Gypsies in major cities be they Norman, Venetian, German or Polish. In future times, imitators would copy such methods with high-tech machines…

March 10, 1510, one of the worst tyrants in Romanian history was assassinated outside the ancient Roman Catholic cathedral of Sibiu, thus ending the promising one-year reign of Mihnea Dracula, better known as 'Mihnea the Bad'. The Little Impaler's horrific deeds would have matched his father's had Mihnea lived to carry out his papa's grand master-plan…

Afterword

Neither Transylvania nor Wallachia today exist as sovereign states, although both once enjoyed such status. Wallachia, Transylvania, and Moldavia merged together in 1859 as the Orthodox Kingdom of Romania. Wales, also, no longer exists as a sovereign Principality, one of only three regions in Europe (Wallonia, Wallachia, Wales) which had been patronizingly dubbed *'strangers'* in German. I, like many others, first became acquainted with the historical Vlad Țepeș in my childhood, the proto-type of Bram Stoker's vampire "Dracula". (As a youth, I had read every ghost, monster, vampire book I could get my hands on!) Later, I became appalled by the chronicled accounts of Vlad Țepeș' ghastly, seemingly random executions of clearly innocent people. Still later, as an amateur historian and linguist, I began to learn the nasty realities of medieval Europe: A time when Church law stipulated that women must submit to men in all things (as in Islamic law). What we consider here in the West a criminal offence today—paedophilia—was a legitimate betrothal in Old World society, as is still the custom in most Muslim and Third World countries. The ancient Greeks and Romans practiced homosexual pederasty as an accepted (and, to them, exemplary) way of life. The Gaulish priesthood and warrior-caste, the *vergobrétes*, did also. (Gaelic, 'men of law'.)

(As an aside, the Gauls of France were not one people; but a variety of ethnically unrelated tribes: Basques [Euskara]; Goidels [origin of the name]; Franks [Germans]; Britons [Pictones]; and the eponymous Gauls, what one might describe as a hybrid language comprised of P-Celtic [Brythonic] and Q-Celtic [Gallic], much as English is a composite of Saxon and French. [A substantial sub-stratum of Iranian is also probable.].)

Surprisingly, during my many years of research, I first became interested in British history, Welsh history in particular. I had read the David & Charles' Book of Castles by P. Somerset Fry seven times. It was during youth that I first discovered certain uncanny similarities between Wales and Wallachia—both formerly independent Principalities. In Welsh legend, Prince Llywelyn ap Gruffydd (Llewellyn ap Griffith), last ruler of an independent Wales, turned his horse's horseshoes backwards to outwit his English trackers in 1282. During Vlad Dracula's official reign (1456–1462), the warlord was said to have done the same when chased by Turks—a seemingly impossible feat.

The essential popularity today of Dracula's persona is part of the mystery: other world leaders have persecuted people by the thousands, even millions, but Idi Amin, Josef Stalin, and Adolf Hitler don't figure into modern fiction or Hollywood horror movies (let alone Hallowe'en costumes!) as Vlad the Impaler does. Vlad Țepeș' reign counts as one of history's greatest, unsolved mysteries: in a region predominantly of Magyar, Saxon, Albanian, Slav, and Romanian nationalities, Vlad's persecutions during the 15th-century seem entirely random, murdering people of all ethnicities, all religious creeds. Which is the crux of the mystery: <u>*There is no known motive.*</u>

Certain names correspond between the two regions: Welsh *Tudur*, Romanian *Tudur*, Welsh *Wladwaladyr*, Slavic *Vladimer*, Welsh *Mihangel*, Romanian *Mihail*, Welsh *Ifan*, Slavic *Ivan*, Welsh *Ion*, Romanian *Ion*, Welsh *Matheu*, Greek *Matthew*, Welsh *Gwylim*, French *Guillaume*, Welsh *Gareth*, German *Gerhardt*.

It may seem that my portrayal of Dracula as a Dacian hero, champion of the peasants, is a travesty of the truth; but the identity of the Dacians themselves and their language (often described as *Thracian:* What the hell language is that?) remains unsolved. Certainly, Vlad's extirpation of the boyar-class has no parallel in recent history (with the possible exception of Ivan the Great's reign), and no explanation when one considers that the aristocracy—during the Middle Ages—perceived themselves as superior, in a true caste-sense, to the landless majority. Either Romanians were the world's cruellest, most gullible citizenry for idolising Țepeș' vicious eradication of women, children, Gypsies, and the elderly, or scholars have been grossly distorting the truth.

In 15th-century Wallachia, among the Wallachs, illegitimacy was unheard of. Whether women had equal (or any) rights in Old Wallachia is difficult to determine, since most historians hare-brainly interpret non-primogeniture as polygyny. However, in Islam, Hindu, Judaic, and numerous pagan cultures around the world there was (and still is) the crime of illegitimacy, even in Roman and Greek law: the penalty for infidelity in modern-day Saudi Arabia for women is death by stoning. For men, generally no penalty, even for rape or gang-rape, unless witnessed by another. (In which case, death be the penalty—for offending the family!) Koran law stipulates that a man's testimony is worth that of two women's. In 12th-century Wales, daughters had the enviable position as being the only women in Europe with the right to divorce her husband: for bad breath, infidelity, rough treatment, or lack of sexual relations! (*Cyfraith Hywel* [King Howell ap Cadell] law-code, 10th-century Wales.) If, indeed, non-primogeniture entailed such rights, Wallachia must have been the envy of mainland Europe. (In any case, it is well known that Latin matrons had scarcely more independence than their Greek counterparts.) Ironically, Vlad Dracula is remembered as a woman-hater, a psychopathic monster who slit open the belly of his first mistress for faking pregnancy, impaled others through the vagina, flayed women alive for not sewing their spouses' garments. (There may be some truth to these tales; due to Țepeș' puritanical nature, he may have impaled brothel owners.)

The excellent biography *"Dracula, Prince of Many Faces: His Life and His Times"* by Radu Florescu and Raymond T. McNally (without which, I could never have written this bizarre tale), the world's premier biographers of Dracula's historical reign and vampire-lore bear out much of Vlad's heinous crimes.

Unfortunately, the legends McNally and Florescu gathered while travelling in Romania—i.e., Magyar, Romanian, Szekely, and Saxon folklore—like obscure Third World tribal legends, though clearly holding a grain of truth—cannot stand up to scientific scrutiny since Vlad's motives remain unknown. Almost all accounts of his time are of second-hand nature. Obviously, a pogrom such as that perpetrated in 1460 cannot be explained by conventional theories, because, surely, a Prince of the Church, after having committed genocide against Gypsies and Jews, should have been venerated by the established Orthodox and Catholic churches—yet, exactly the opposite occurred. Vlad Țepeș was ignobly reinterred in a pit beneath the steps of Snagov chapel, his tombstone defaced, and all traces of his earlier sepulchre erased in disgrace.

Roman texts from the time of Strabo tentatively identify the people of what is now Romania as Dacians: Celts who painted their bodies with blue woad tattoos (generally, of animals). Earlier Greek legends concern a mythical tribe of warrior-women called Amazons, whom modern scholars have identified as Scythians. However, the Scythians' burial mounds, or *kurgans*, recently excavated in Russia held male skeletons of nomadic warriors whom had practiced *suttee*—the Indian custom of wife sacrifice to provide the superior male with a humble servant. Discovered within these huge, earthen burial mounds were dozens of sacrificed horses, slaves, and concubines—hardly indicative of a matriarchal society! Few scholars acknowledge that the Scythians' bloodthirsty, patriarchal practices which the Greek historian Herodotus described are *exactly the same* as the Hallstatt-era Celts of Czechoslovakia, later portrayed in Roman times as 'La Tène' culture (whom, incidentally, described the customs of 'Celts' in western Europe as that of a semi-matriarchal branch of their hereditary enemy/neighbours, the Gauls, or Goidels).

Oddly enough, the word 'Gaul' in Romance languages means specifically *Welsh*, not Gaelic, not German, not Slav, although, irony of ironies, the people of Wales have always called themselves *Cymry* ('countryman'), or *Prydeini* ("related"). The word 'Gaul' has its origins in the tribal name 'Gael' (c.f. *"Gaédheltchach"*), although the French recognise only the 'Gaulois', or Welsh, as their ancestors (Pays de Gaulle, Wales)! Confusing?

Somehow the legend of warrior-women with one breast cut off, terrifying the Greeks in 800 BC, does not identify at all with the Scythians! The Greek myth is hopelessly confused: common sense and modern Olympics prove that women didn't need to cut off their breasts to become equestrian archers. Probably these were Gaulish slave women captured, branded, and sold to the Greeks by Scythian slave-traders, as reported by Hippocrates. (Alternatively, the Romans referred to the nations of the east as *Celto-Scythians*.) Coincidentally, two Celtic tribes coexisting with the Scythians, the Cimmerians and Gelonae (Galatians?)—as well as the later Sarmatians—were noted for their hard-riding warrioresses. (The Sarmatians eventually conquered these ultra-warlike Scythians!)

I wonder…? have any of our esteemed scholars even considered the Cimmerians to have been the real-life Amazons of antiquity. (I doubt it, that would require some independent thinking…)

The Romans remarked of their own soldiers' fear when invading the Isle of Môn off the coast of Wales, confronted with male and female Druids prepared to fight and die, which the Romans considered very strange indeed! Conversely, Hellenic accounts describe 'Keltoi' in nearby districts and off the coast of France as notoriously homosexual: the sons of Milésios which crop up in the Irish mythological cycle, the *Gabala Labal Eirinn* (Book of the Taking of Ireland), can be traced to the island of Milós, off the coast of Greece.

On the other hand, 'Celts' whom the Romans encountered in Iberia and western France were recorded as having been remarkably monogamous (which is definitely not in accord with Irish legal texts, but does have an exact match with Welsh law tracts); the Gauls having made an agreement with invading Carthaginians to try wrongdoers in each other's courts: Phoenicians would convict Gauls, and Gallic women would convict Carthaginians. (Curiously, the real name which the Sarmatians called themselves was 'Alanni' [Gelonae?], Alans, according to Roman sources; the Greeks call themselves 'Hellenes', and, linguistically, have more in common with the Welsh [helios/haûl, hydro/dŵr, choir/chawr, polis/plas, pou/pwy] than with either Gaelic or Latin, and are likely descended from their hereditary, Amazon foes.)

Ultimately, one cannot shake the suspicion that neither modern linguists nor Greco-Roman chroniclers could tell the difference between Gauls, Germans, Britons, and New Guineans!

Most European nationalities cherish a mythical folklore recalling matriarchal, Neolithic tribal peoples who worshipped a Mother Goddess. Romanian, Lithuanian, Russian, Ukrainian, Greek, Roman, Polish, Albanian, Austrian, Norse, Basque, Finnish, Estonian, Irish, Breton, Welsh, etc., all dedicate a mythology to such mysterious—yet warlike—ancestors. Irish Brehon laws and the law code of Hywel Dda (Hywel the Good) are both unique as being the most lenient legal texts of medieval Christian Europe. Ireland, however, caught in the throes of constant warfare between rival religious houses and often under the rule of bishop-kings suffered greatly as a consequence. Though generally not inheriting land, a woman was eligible for half (one-third in Ireland) of her husband's belongings upon divorce, a custom which we in the West have unconsciously borrowed. And, if one can believe the garbled Roman accounts of Scotland, it seems women inherited Kingdoms and had numerous lovers in Pictish society! Incidentally, the Welsh word for Pict (the *Cornovae*, at the northernmost tip of Scotland) is '*Brythad*'.

Among historians, linguists, and laymen alike the word 'Celt' has been very liberally spread. It would seem that a people should be known for what they call themselves (try, for comparison, calling an Amerindian a *Hindi*). Due to a Greco-Roman misunderstanding, the generally wooded region of northern Europe, Scotland, and Greece which was called 'Celyddon', Caledonia, just as the Germans called their homeland 'Wald' (world, in English) was also applied to a royal Scythian tribe called 'Gelonae' in Russia (or *Scythoi*), a red-haired people who scalped their enemies, practiced human sacrifice, concubinage and incest, while introducing the hereditary, patriarchal surname. It is little known, much less acknowledged, that the early

Celts of Ireland and Wales (more properly known as *Picts* or *Cruitheni*), were the only people in western Europe—with the sole exception of the Spanish—definitely known to have named their children after both the mother and father's first name (Tŵm Sion Catti, famous sixteenth-century Welsh brigand, son of Sir John Wynn and Cathryn Jones, a custom carried on until the late 1700s when the English magistrates forced the change to patronymics).

Dacian and Illyrian root-words seem to have vanished, for the most part, from eastern Europe (largely because its Celtic sister-language, namely Gaelic, loaned copious amounts of Irish vocabulary into the major Indo-European languages, who were obvious allies and trading partners). Therefore, far more Goidelic words (of Turkic, Semitic, or Dravidian origin, one could argue) are found in Italic, Teutonic, Baltic, Armenian, Hellenic, and Slavonic than Welsh words. (There are exceptions, however, namely the word for red [coch] in Albanian/Greek, and the more common universal baby talk of *Mummy* or *Daddy*.) But for scholars to refer to Dacians, Illyrians, and Getae as Albanians is unfathomable: is this to suggest the Greeks and Romans (or their translators) didn't know the difference between Celtic and Thracian? Admittedly, neither Romans nor Greeks seem to have realised that the two continental-wide, Celtic languages were separate entities, but these chroniclers, unlike modern historians, did live at that time. They had competent, if misinformed, interpreters who knew which side of their bread was buttered.

Of all the intrusive cultures in eastern Europe, perhaps the Vlachs of Moldova, pagan, Romanian incomers of uncertain ancestry, are the closest descendants of the extinct Illyrians. After all, the Saxons who dubbed these people *Wallachs*, unlike what many historians claim, did not use a blanket term *Waelas* for all non-Germans encountered; Slav, Latin, Celt, Wallach were all specific designations for various ethnicities. The Germanic tribes were not the uncivilised barbarians Latin scholars would have us believe.

Only someone truly ignorant of the German language could be unaware that the usual term for an outsider, or foreigner, is *auslander*. Wallach = Welsh. (And, all too often, historians have shown themselves, whether they be writing of Stalin, or of ancient Rome, to be either uninformed or deliberately misleading.)

Old Testament Jews were constantly worried about their women falling into the grasp of pagan, Mother Goddess-worshipping religions and their 'temple prostitutes'. Israelites, also, stoned women to death for adultery. They may have also circumcised young girls (please remember that the Koran does not mention or condone this practice either). Since we don't hear of such rites today nor in medieval times, one must assume that the Jews abandoned their old, Mosaic law long ago when the Arabs dispossessed them from Israel. Christ may have been responsible, but then He, too, was against divorce. His disciples demanded veiling for women and for them not to speak in church, because even in the New Testament women were considered inferior because of Eve's transgression. At no time does Christ advocate women's equality in the Bible. He did recommend that husbands treat them fairly. But so did Mohammed. He had four wives! If Christ's disciples were misleading His followers, why did He associate with them or not set them straight? Incidentally, the nearest Celtic nation to Israel was Galatia, modern-day Turkey, only five hundred miles to the north.

Celts have gained a somewhat unsavoury reputation down the centuries for human sacrifice. I do not deny that the Gauls practiced human sacrifice, nor even on a massive scale. The Scythians' burial mounds conclusively prove Herodotus' first-hand, eyewitness accounts to be true. No doubt one of these ethnic groups did immolate and sacrifice their enemies, even innocent people, on a large scale. Such widespread, Bronze Age cults would surely infiltrate neighbouring states, culminating in the later *La Tène* culture (having its origin in central Europe), where in Scandinavia the bog-bodies are evidence of their bloodthirsty nature. However, few people, scholars included, seem to realise that Goidelic and Brythonic are totally, mutually unintelligible (not just distant dialects) and that they've been bitter enemies for centuries. (After having committed genocide against the Picts [*Cruithin, Prydein*] simultaneously in Ireland and in Scotland, the Irish have the audacity to accuse the English of the same!) Their rivalry is what caused the Celts' downfall when the Anglo-Normans invaded Ireland and Wales. Gaels—like the Hindi—sacrificed horses, whereas Britons worshipped them (the engraved images on hills, peculiar to England). And both Irish and Scots pride themselves for their red hair—a Nordic—and, possibly—selective-breeding, trait.

They (British and Irish) are, in fact, the most distantly related languages on the Indo-European family tree, sharing only *30 percent* of cognate words.

(That's less than the difference between Hittite and Indo-Iranian, which is 65% cognate words!)

Along the lines of the so-called Q and P Celtic languages, historians suggested that because Irish Gaelic lacks a P for most Indo-European root-words, and Welsh C mutates to G, then Goidelic must be Bronze Age Celtic pushed aside by Prydainic invaders. *What nonsense!* High German consonants NEVER mutate at the beginning of a word, and never in written form, as in Welsh. But Gaelic, like German, at the end of a word sometimes does mutate (the ubiquitous second-sound shift peculiar to Celtic languages), in spoken form only. And to suggest Gaelic lacked a P in prehistoric times leaves one wondering what accounts for the words *píob*, *puínnsean*, *píuthar*, *pampootie*, *pobull*, *spadádh*, etc. (For the past 100 years, linguists have been incapable of realising that the lack of initial 'P' in Erse is likely due to a permanent sound-shift of labial consonants [b, m, f, etc.,]. Compounds, quite probably, also had a role to play.) Of all the world's languages, only Welsh undergoes Radical, Soft, Aspirate, and Nasal Mutation, or consonantal sound-shift (C to G, B to F, M to F, P to M, T to D, B to M, N to M, G to W, C to NGH, etc.), which follow well-defined grammatical rules (as opposed to the accidental declensions throughout history effecting all languages, the so-called 'Grimm's law'). Celtic scholars such as Anne Ross, Barry Cunliffe, Miranda Green, John T. Koch, etc. have been unwittingly falsifying information for years to gloss their own Gaelic heritage, for surely it is a strange coincidence that no teacher of German has pointed out these well-known grammatical facts (German, one of the world's most spoken languages). Anyone who has studied foreign languages, be it through learning institutions, a tutor, books, or audiocassette, can soon verify this for him/herself. (Although no linguist, I have studied dozens of Indo-European and non-Aryan languages—Spanish, Latin, Italian, French, Portuguese, Romanian; Lithuanian, Latvian; German, Norse, Swedish, Danish, Dutch, English, Old English; Greek; Albanian; Russian, Serbo-Croat, Bulgarian, Slovak, Czech, Polish, Ukrainian; Sanskrit, Iranian, Hindi; Basque; Turkish, Finnish, Hungarian; Na-Dené, Okanagan; Malaysian; Mandarin; Korean; Tai; Japanese; Hebrew, Arabic; Swahili; Gaelic, and Welsh: having found Spanish, Italian, German, Japanese, Swahili, Iranian, Hindi, and Arabic the easiest to learn [to pronounce, at least—but depending on the guide book's ease of study], while French, Gaelic, Taiwanese, Welsh, Chinese, and Korean the hardest. [I reiterate, am no linguist, having just scratched the surface.].)

Two cultures, Hallstatt and La Tène, make up the earliest known prehistoric eras of Europe whose ancestry can be known; Hallstatt: short, dark, relatively peaceful, semi-nomadic farmers; La Tène: bloodthirsty, tall, and blonde, whose Irish vocabulary figures almost exclusively in the few Roman accounts of the Gauls' druidic religion (*Grannios*, Gaelic sun god, *Samháin,* All Hallow's eve, *Lughnasa*, Celtic festival). As of yet, no rational explanation through comparative linguistics can account for the existence of such radical sound-shifts in Brythonic speech through comparisons with Indo-Germanic (or any other) languages; a definite downgrading of consonantal values can be distinguished through Sanskrit and Irish Gaelic, to its gradual disappearance in Hellenic, Gothic, Latin, Slavic, etc. Also, scholars have erroneously surmised that because Roman and Saxon settlers occupied Britain, then Welsh, or *Cymric*, must be a German or Latin hybrid. NOT TRUE. The indisputable fact is, is that there are *hundreds* more Latin and Germanic word-cognates (of Indo-Iranian origin) to be found in Gaelic, words which, etymologically, have root compounds that are easily demonstrated to be of Gaelic origin. Yet such basic words (many beginning with the *q* sound) cannot be found in Welsh, thereby destroying this sanctimonious theory, because neither Romans nor Saxons **ever set foot in Ireland before the Viking era.** Radical mutation alone should qualify Brittonic as a proto- or pre-Indo-European language; conceivably, any parent language of either Tocharian, Hittite, Classical Greek, Sanskrit, or Persian must have enough similarities yet dissimilarities to be perceived as such. I don't believe I'm being overly patriotic (I'm not even Welsh), nor proposing a new idea. Several Celticists and etymologists have baldly stated that Brythonic was the Pictish language of Scotland before the Gaels' arrival, and the ancestor of Common Celtic. Goidelic has hundreds of words corresponding closely with Latin, Greek, Germanic, Sanskrit, and Slavonic. Close parallels can also be found in Turkic, Semitic, and Amerindian. (Linguists don't like this fact, the solution? Ignore it.) Latin for four is *quatre;* Gaelic, the same. German for knight is *ritter;* Gaelic, the same. Sanskrit for earth is *talamh;* Gaelic, the same. Hungarian for chicken is *circ;* Gaelic, the same. What is true is that the Romans and allied Goidelic, Saxon, and other Indo-European settlers exterminated Old Welsh from mainland Europe, from Ireland, England, and Scotland (note the dozens of Gaelic words inexplicably present in English, such as *whiskey, ken, tongue, slogan, hound,* etc.): right up until the late 18th-century, Welsh, or Cornish, was spoken in Cornwall; in Strathclyde and Cumbria until the twelfth century. Yet the word 'Gaulois' also means 'stranger' in Latin; translating as 'Waelas' in German; Gaulae, or Keltoi, in Greek; *Gaídhealtachd,* or Gall, in Irish. Its root-word could mean hero, thief, enemy, disease.

But not a single person on earth knows what it originally meant.

(Perhaps it meant '*hidden*', alluding to the ancients' frequent and wide-spread use of underground passages during times of war, who knows?)

Linguistics' experts have supposedly reconstructed the proto-Indo-European language of eastern and western Europe. Question: how do you reconstruct a language which has never been written and extinct before the coming of the Romans? (Though ground-breaking detective work has admirably elucidated the P-I-E proto-language debate, does anyone really believe that by snitching various words from numerous distantly-related languages one can reconstruct an ethnic group from such a hodgepodge?) Scholars and professors must think that everyone is stupid, that their master's degrees and Ph. D's allow these fellows with apes' I.Q.s to hoodwink us laymen.

The very reason for the novel '*Vlad Dracula: the Impaler*' was to determine the reasons for the Middle Ages' Inquisition. I, for one, believe I may have found it. Although Vlad Țepeș was almost certainly no Dacian Celt (but who can say?), he provides a classic example of a ruler gone off the proverbial railroad track, and a possible motive for his senseless murder sprees. The 'witch hunts' were perhaps aimed at pagan followers of the Greek goddess *Artemis*, *Diana* to the Romans (Gaelic 'Danu', Welsh 'Donau') and the proto-Celtic Mother Goddess Wicca, or Ma Gog. The major Indo-European cultures of Europe were responsible for all such atrocities against various peoples, responsible for the extinction of many flora, birds, and animals, not only in the New World but in Europe itself. In England, beavers, bears, wolves are all extinct—since the coming of we, the English. There is no doubt in my mind that the indigenous people of Europe (*Prydein* in Welsh means 'native, countryman', as does *'Cymmrodorion'*) were exterminated *en masse*. It is a credit to their tenacity and might that it took *over a dozen* nationalities to annihilate them. Vlad Dracula is unique in world history for having liquidated the Saxon Catholic majority in Transylvania. This scenic, montane region is dotted with the ruins of abandoned villages and towns—Amlăs amongst them. Never in the history of the world had a German people experienced the very extermination which they had advocated against others— i.e., the Third Reich. Whether Old Welsh was the pre-Celtic language of the Inquisition's victims cannot be proven; however, no other culture fits the archaeological evidence of a peaceful, semi-matriarchal society (there never has been nor will be such a thing as true matriarchy), and none had so deeply influenced an Empire concerning gender equality, especially now with the fall of Communism and plummeting women's rights in eastern Europe. No existing European society fits this cultural pattern. Basque, Latin, Irish, Germanic, Slav, Albanian, Greek, Ugric cultures all adhere to a religion, whether Orthodox, Catholic, Protestant, or Islam, which promotes Old Testament hatred of women.

The constant internecine warfare amongst continental Celts during the Roman conquest mirrors that of Welsh and Irish battles in the Dark Ages. Gallic tribesmen (i.e., Gaelic, erstwhile allies of the Gauls) marched with the Roman legions against their mortal enemies in Gaul. A permanent state of cultural non-intercourse must have existed between the Belgic Celts and the Romans. How can I prove this?

Simply by noting the bulk of ceremonial Gaelic words recorded by the Romans; the Italic, Germanic, and Slav languages' close resemblance to Old Irish; and the preponderance of Cymric place-names in Europe (*Bratislava,* Czechoslovakia; *Cambrai,* France; *Trier,* Germany; *Kaledonia,* Greece; and, of course, *Alban,* the highlands of Albania). (Albania's speech, to the natives, is not known as Albanian, but *Sqiperi.* It is also the name of that country.) The Irish invaded Scotland in 500 AD, exterminating the Picts. (Ironically, it was only after the Caledonians' conversion to Christianity that they lost the battle to the Gael; previously, the Pictish kingdom had proven itself more than a match for the Romans, Anglo-Saxons, and Irish.) Ireland, historically, was bilingual (T.F. O'Rahilly, Oxford History of Ireland), of Goidelic and Brythonic parentage. The folk who built the magnificent cromlechs, dolmens, henges, and stone circles were basically peaceful. Why would Gallic tribes massacre their own in petty wars? Aztecs generally did not sacrifice their own, but rather their enemies. The fairness of the Brehon laws (*Bréitheimh),* one should imagine, ought to have kept the peace in Ireland. Cattle raiders, abductions, mass burnings...bilingualism is an established fact of mutual cooperation. Even Hungarians, Szeklers, ethnic Russians, Saxons, and Romanians (much of whose vocabulary is derived from Slavic), despite hundreds of years of animosity, have managed to co-exist. Is it only coincidence that the great, drystone ramparts of Ireland are in the far-west 'Gall'-way, the land of the 'Don' gall (Dark Strangers) where, literally pushed into the Atlantic ocean at Inishmore ceased to exist? Or that the world's greatest concentration of prehistoric dolmens and standing stones are in Brittany? These *menhirs* are also amongst the oldest, predating Egypt's pyramids by over two thousand years. Southeast Ireland, as in England, has far fewer impressive hillforts than the west, indicating a total unpreparedness by the 'Tuatha de Danaan' to resist Goidelic invasion.

Evidence that the Cimmerians of south-central Russia, mentioned in antiquity (800 BC) were Celts is, linguistically, indisputable: yet not a single world-class scholar has forwarded this idea with any vigour, confusing the Cimmerian homeland with the later, and intrusive, Ossetian language—Scythia's Parthians (in much the same way, the English often call themselves 'Britons'—an obvious anachronism).

The Persians, evidently, took the name *Parthians* from their conquered neighbours.

In Biblical times, the tribes of Rosh, Tubal, and Gomer were the instigators of a war against Israel, led by a king named Gog from Magog. Etymologically, the word 'Rosh' in Aramaic makes no sense, because, in Hebrew, it means 'head'. People of the Head? However, if one assumes that it means 'people of the north' (Gog, in Hebrew—as in Old Brythonic (*gogledd*)—also means 'north') then it could translate as 'the people of Russia'. ('Ma[n] Gog', northland.) Linguistically, this is apt, because the Old Welsh word for moors, grasslands, steppes is *rhos*, the name for their language *Cymry*, and the word for burial mound is *crug* (compare with Russian 'kurgan'). 'Tis a sobering thought that it would take an amateur such as myself to discover what professionals could not or would not see for themselves.

In Dark Ages Europe, the Visigoths, conquerors of invincible Rome, were vanquished by allied Huns and Ostrogoths (Austrians); to this day, nobody can be quite sure what language these Gothic 'Germans' spoke. (The warlord in the forefront of these Vandals had the distinctly un-German name of *Fritigern* [First Among Kings]—I dare you to find the word *Tigern* in any Teutonic lexicon!) One suggestion which has not been forwarded is that the western Goths were actually Celts and Scandinavians, which have always shared a close bond, for in both Ireland and Wales the Vikings readily found staunch supporters; perhaps the reason Wales was alone amongst European nations in resisting conquest by the Danes was a mutual hatred of Saxons, Gaels, and Latins.

Currently, there are twelve Germanic dialects, each tolerating the other, including German/Hebrew Yiddish—yet not extending this olive-branch to the extinct Visigoths, vanished before the literate era. The intolerance of another causes a language's extinction.

Were the Gaels 'Scythians'? Well, yes, and no. These steppe nomads were of no one racial group, encompassing Uigers, Huns, Georgians (and god knows how many others) and ranged about Russia and eastern Europe, called themselves *Scolots* (Scots?), were not Iranians (well, not exactly) but Mongoloids and Caucasoids who depicted themselves admirably on silverware and gold. Lumped into these steppe-raiders by the Greeks and Romans for convenience sake were indeed Persian fire-worshippers east of the Caspian Sea (Parthians, or *Farsi*), but also Huns in the Altaic mountains of Siberia, Gauls in Hungary and Turkey (Galatia), Cimmerians, Alans, and Sarmatians between the Black and Azov seas, scattered all over continental Europe and even in Jutland, off the coast of Denmark (a tribe then known as *Cimbri*). All these peoples were disunited and fractious. And in 300 BC, the Scythians were overthrown in eastern Europe by the Sarmatians (Sarmizegethusa, capital of Dacia?); ironically, when the Romans encountered barbarians in Yugoslavia, Albania, Russia, Hungary and Romania, this vast empire had been called Dacia. How can this be when the Sarmatians conquered the entire region?

The answer is simple: the Sarmatians and Dacians were the same people.

The Turkish invaders of eastern Europe, 1453, brought to an

essentially pagan, Slavic Europe the concept of hate towards women, as had earlier Hellenic, Baltic, Romance, Teutonic, Gaelic, and Oriental newcomers. In 10th-century eastern Europe, there were no large cities (save for Byzantium), no widespread Christian missions spreading their chauvinistic gospel of Christ.

Even when the Orthodox monks had finally arrived in large numbers, the peasants had been forbidden entry to monasteries or to read the 'holy' Bible. The term 'Slav' comes from Latin and Norse—convenient 'slaves'. (C.f., Gaelic *"sliabhe,"* "in chains".) These people were originally known as Wends or Venedi (presumable ancestors of the Venetians)—a former Celtic tribe! (Venedda, southern Scotland; Gwynedd, Wales.)

In Islam, humiliating and painful circumcision is still performed on young girls to prevent their experiencing sexual pleasure after marriage. (As in Africa, and large parts of southeast Asia.) One can hardly wonder at the implacable wrath of Vlad the Impaler, whom in his brief but unforgettable reign executed at least 100,000 people, over half of whom were Turks. Germans utilised propaganda during World War II to blacken Jews' reputations, manufacturing absurd stories of Rabbis sacrificing babies, much the same way as the Spanish Inquisition invented tales about witches, Gypsies, and other heretics. Emersed in a war of extirpation during the 15th-century, no doubt patriotic Saxons would stoop to spreading ridiculous tall-tales, especially if on the losing side. Romanians and Magyars, likewise, for they, too, hated Gypsies, a people whose language is perhaps closer to Celtic than scholars have surmised. Why, indeed, would a Sanskrit-speaking (Romany) or Hindustani people have become nomads, unless expelled from India?

French, like Walloon, Celtic, and Romanian, has not inherited the general subject-verb order typical of Indo-Germanic (in Latin, predicate comes before subject, adjective after noun), totally unlike German, Finnish, or even the Hellenic, Slav, Hindu, or Mongol languages. Although both Romans and Franks conquered Gaul, the Franks, in particular, seem not to have settled that country in sufficient numbers to force their syntax onto the indigenous Gaulish dialects. The origin of Gaelic (and possibly all languages) can be tentatively linked with England and France's example, for all tongues must be descended from a mutating, common ancestor and are, in fact, *pseudo-pidgin* languages. (Most people would be shocked to learn that much of the world's languages' vocabulary stems from *pre-human* hominids!) Herein lies my argument: no known language family even comes close to modern Welsh concerning active sound-shifts, a candidate for the world's oldest language, or perhaps even a satellite language (also not a new idea), for dozens of words of seemingly common origin can be found in Amerindian dialects, Negroid languages, Asian, Australasian, etc. (Out of Africa theorists would have us believe that early hominids *were incapable of speech—which belies the question: How did five thousand languages evolve in a mere 100,000 years (100,000 divide by 5000 = a rate of 1 every 20 years*—mathematically impossible!) Since it was the Phoenicians, Greeks, and Romans who invented our alphabet, why do certain nationalities abrogate their rules? Or could it be that it was their ancestors who created our alphabet? A presently unidentified, linguistic strain called Cretan, Etruscan, or Lydian, long extinct. Since no real, comprehensive study of Basque has been undertaken (one prominent linguist has already shaken to its foundations the long-held theory that Basque, or *Euskara*, was the language of ancient Scotland, and several have already connected Euskara with North African dialects), one must assume an attitude of scepticism until further studies. (The most recent and groundbreaking discovery is the obvious kinship between Basque and Sino-Tibetan languages.) Consider this, however: the people of Spain, Basques in particular, are still strongly Catholic, and had no great effect upon the Spanish Empire regarding women's rights, a defunct empire in Latin America with one of the world's worst human rights' records. And if the Basques are descendants of Europe's Neolithic culture, how is it that it is the *Celts* of Europe who are extinct, both branches (Breton in northwestern France is a reintroduction), although numerous mountain chains in Europe or Asia could have sustained aboriginal populations indefinitely, while *Euskara* has been given official status in Spain; and why can't Basque speakers elucidate the purpose of megalithic monuments or decipher the ogham script of Pictish Scotland, say, or the Linear A and C tablets of Crete? It would seem the extinction of religious leaders such as the Druids of Britain and the priestesses of ancient Greece eliminates any possibility of deciphering these riddles. Unlike the Irish *filídhs*, the Rabbis of Israel, or the gurus of India, such religious leaders were ruthlessly, utterly exterminated for what other Druidic sects may or may not have done.

Albert A. Ernst
Glaslyn, Saskatchewan, Canada, 14 March, 2025.

About the Author

Albert A. Ernst, fifty seven, hails from Glaslyn, Saskatchewan, Canada, and has studied, as a hobby, over thirty Indo-European and non-Aryan languages as diverse as Mandarin, Japanese, Hungarian, Gaelic, French, German, Romanian, and Welsh. He has also lived on Vancouver Island, off-grid, for sixteen years. Mr. Ernst spent the summer of '92 touring various ancient sites in England, from medieval castle ruins to stately homes, hillforts, and megalithic monuments. Formerly employed with L&M Wood Products (now Northwinds Wood Products), Sask., as a trim-saw operator (14 years), he is now semi-retired to work on further writing projects. Operating a hybrid 1.1 kw solar/wind array, producing his own power, Albert's hobbies include gardening, playing guitar, reading, writing, exploring abandoned farmhouses on motorcycle, and listening to heavy metal music! (Up the Irons!)

His latest foray into the publishing world, *"THE FARM... Hell Hath*

No Bounds... (The Ranger Poltergeist)" is available now at major retailers including Amazon, Barnes and Noble, Google Play, Kobo, and other global booksellers. Go Check it Out!!!!!!

Please leave a rating or review on Amazon, or any other bookseller, as it greatly increases my visibility. Thanks for reading this book, your support is most appreciated!

www.ingramcontent.com/pod-product-compliance
Lightning Source LLC
Chambersburg PA
CBHW070523010526
44118CB00012B/1060